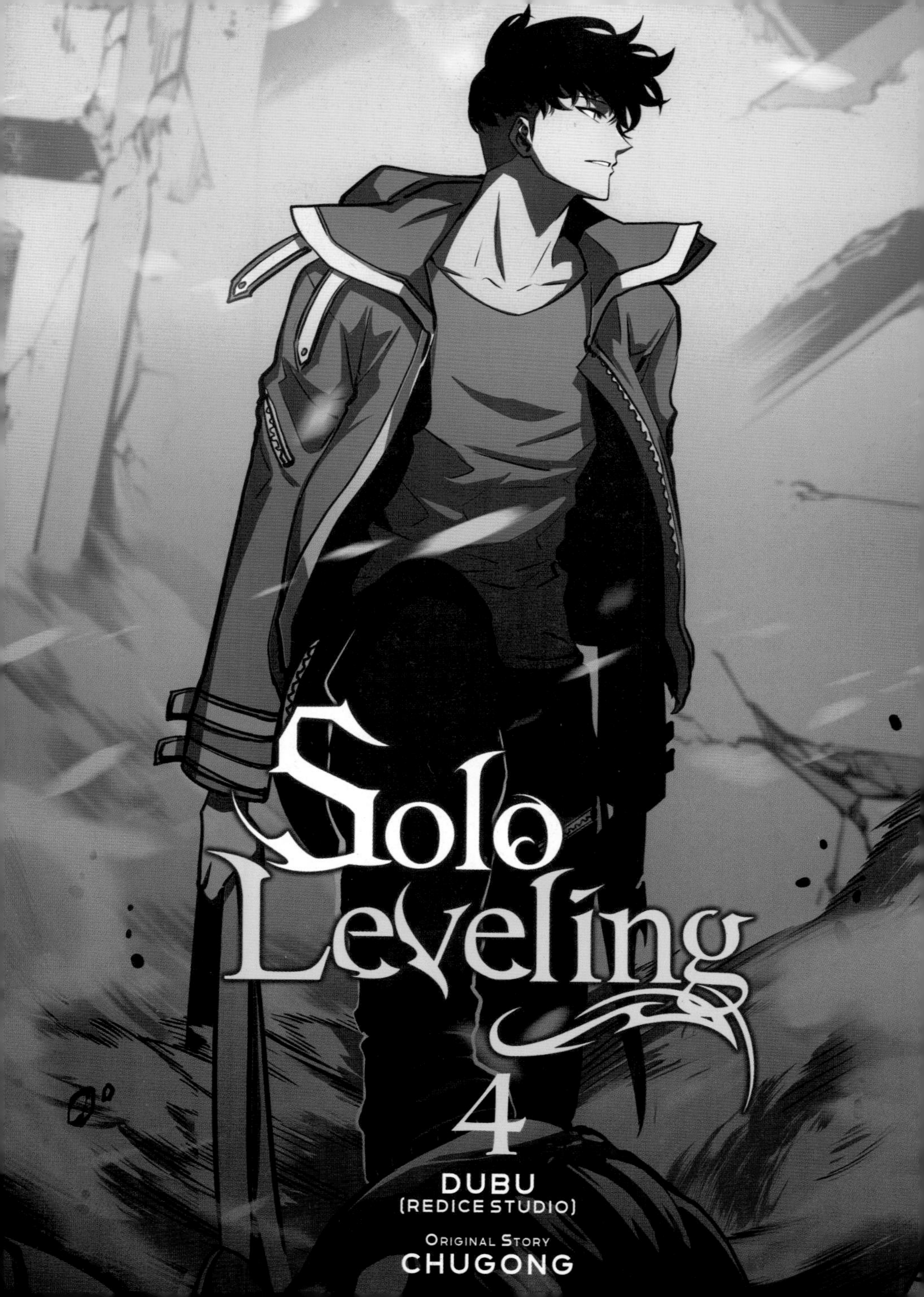
Solo Leveling
4
DUBU
(REDICE STUDIO)
ORIGINAL STORY
CHUGONG

# CHARACTERS

### Jinwoo Sung

E-rank Hunter

### Yoonho Baek

S-rank Hunter, Guild Master
of the White Tiger Guild

### Dongsoo Hwang

S-rank Hunter,
Scavenger Guild

### Jinchul Woo

A-rank Hunter, Hunter's
Association of Korea

### Chul Kim

A-rank Hunter,
White Tiger Guild

### Heejin Park

B-rank Hunter,
White Tiger Guild

# CONTENTS

Solo Leveling

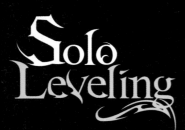

# CHAPTER 9

# The Red Gate

Solo Leveling

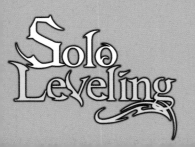

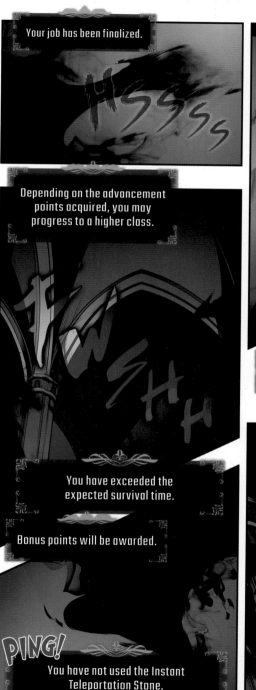

Your job has been finalized.

Depending on the advancement points acquired, you may progress to a higher class.

You have exceeded the expected survival time.

Bonus points will be awarded.

PING!

You have not used the Instant Teleportation Stone.

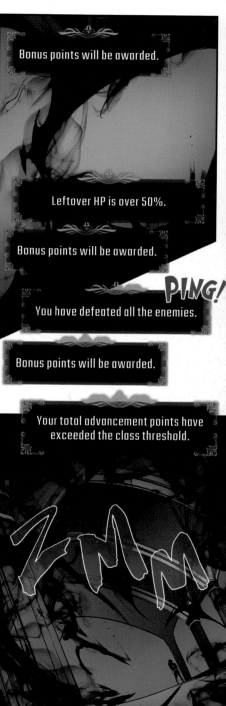

Bonus points will be awarded.

Leftover HP is over 50%.

Bonus points will be awarded.

PING!

You have defeated all the enemies.

Bonus points will be awarded.

Your total advancement points have exceeded the class threshold.

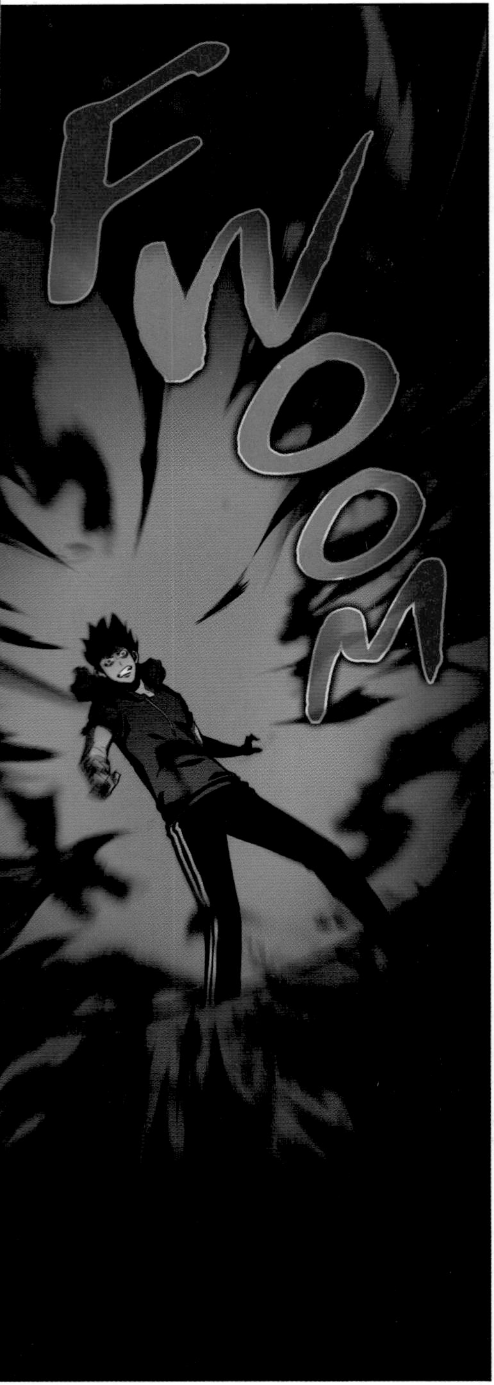
FWOOOM

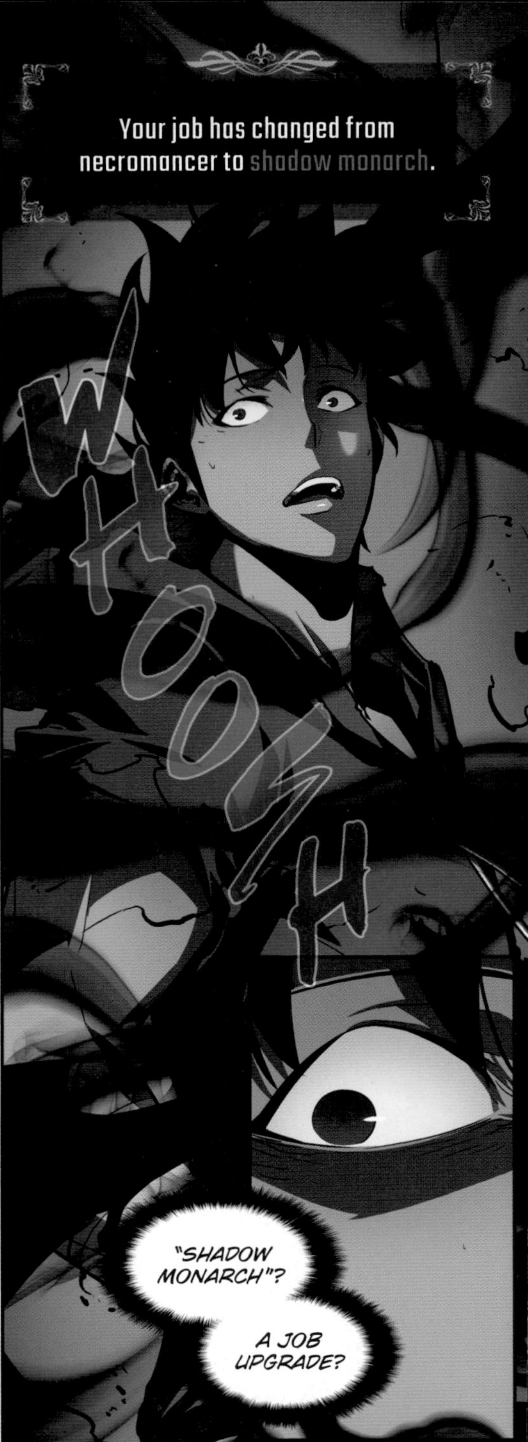
Your job has changed from necromancer to shadow monarch.
WHOOOSH
"SHADOW MONARCH"?
A JOB UPGRADE?

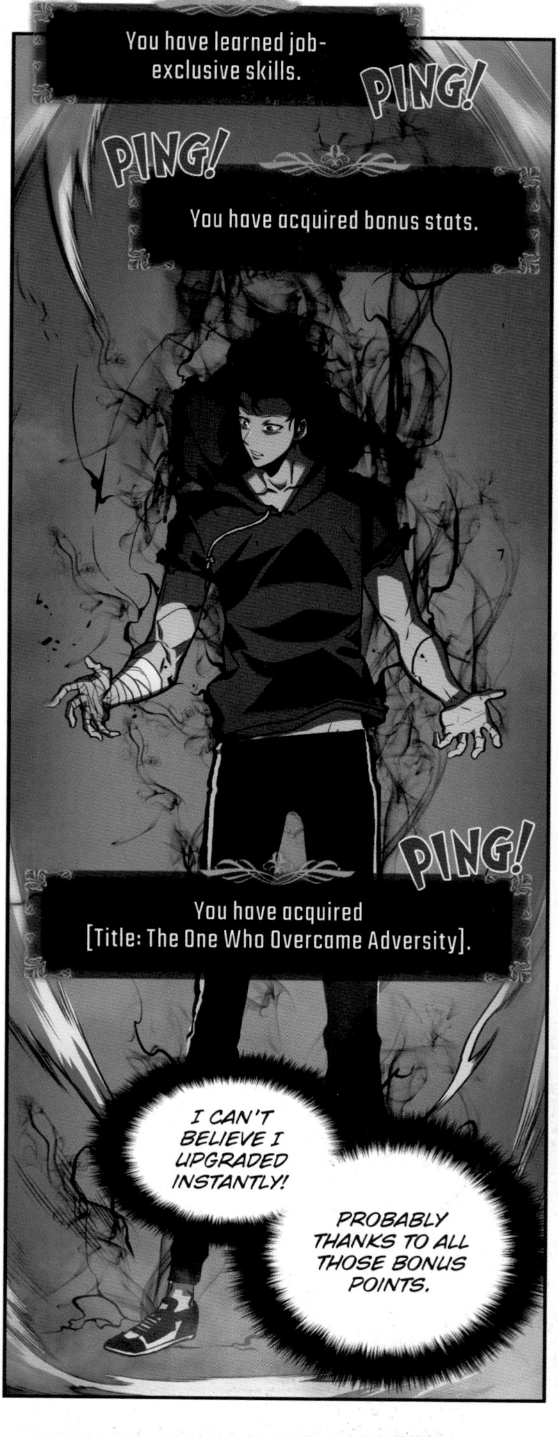
You have learned job-exclusive skills.
PING!
PING!
You have acquired bonus stats.
PING!
You have acquired [Title: The One Who Overcame Adversity].
I CAN'T BELIEVE I UPGRADED INSTANTLY!
PROBABLY THANKS TO ALL THOSE BONUS POINTS.
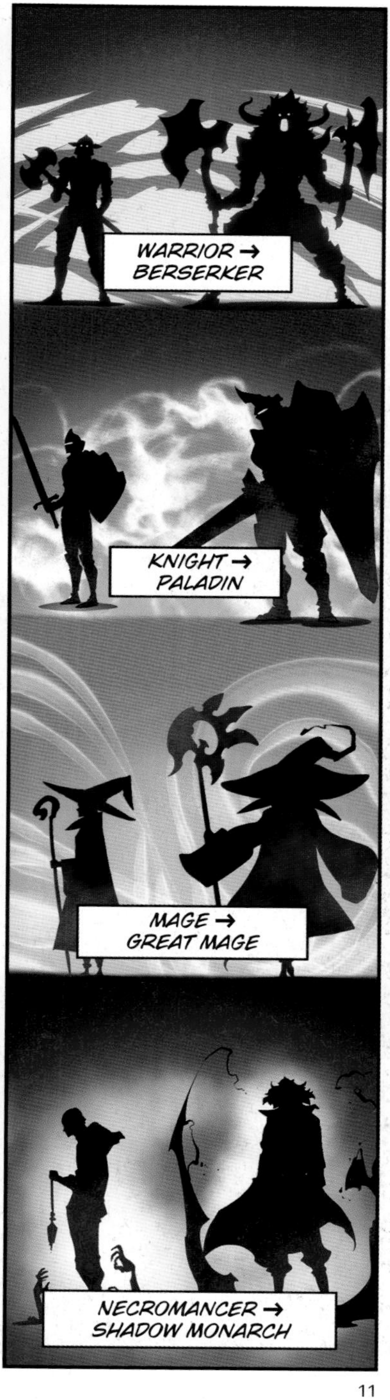
WARRIOR → BERSERKER
KNIGHT → PALADIN
MAGE → GREAT MAGE
NECROMANCER → SHADOW MONARCH

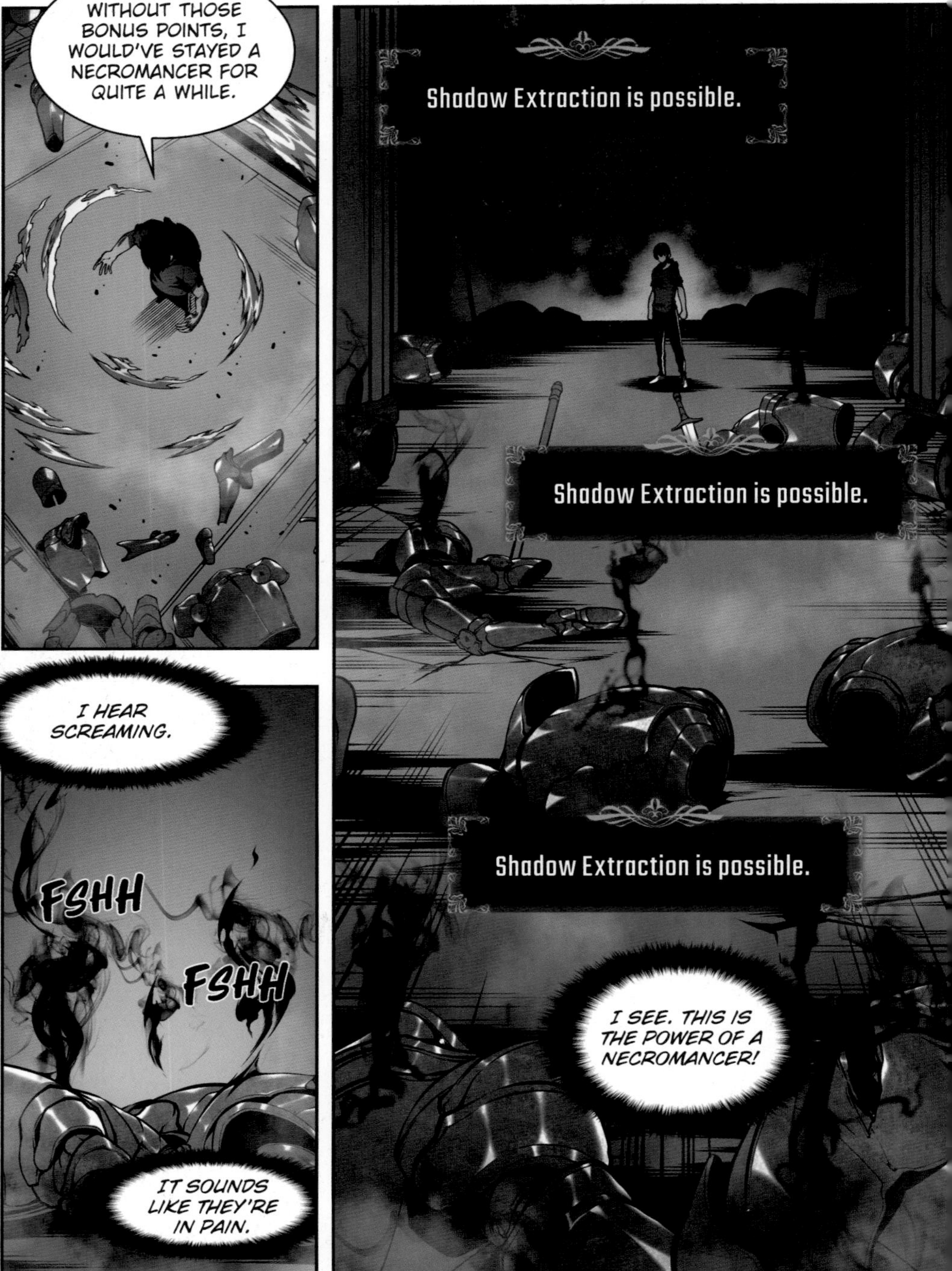
WITHOUT THOSE BONUS POINTS, I WOULD'VE STAYED A NECROMANCER FOR QUITE A WHILE.
I HEAR SCREAMING.
FSHH
FSHH
IT SOUNDS LIKE THEY'RE IN PAIN.
Shadow Extraction is possible.
Shadow Extraction is possible.
Shadow Extraction is possible.
I SEE. THIS IS THE POWER OF A NECROMANCER!

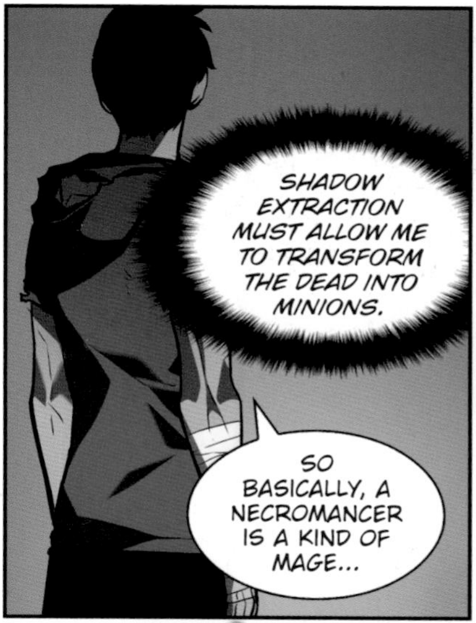
SHADOW EXTRACTION MUST ALLOW ME TO TRANSFORM THE DEAD INTO MINIONS.
SO BASICALLY, A NECROMANCER IS A KIND OF MAGE...

Please designate a command word for [Skill: Shadow Extraction].

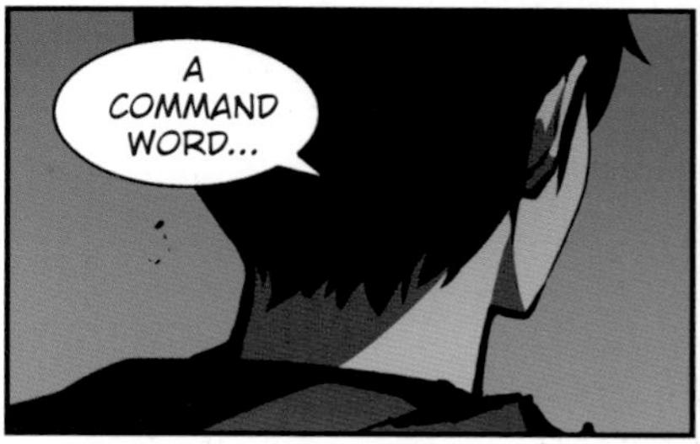
A COMMAND WORD...

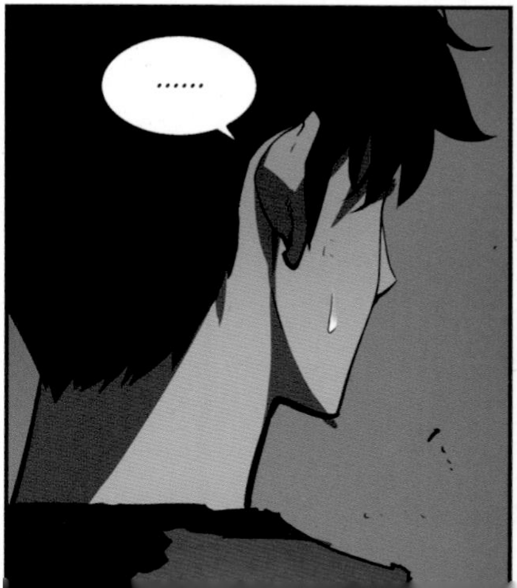
......

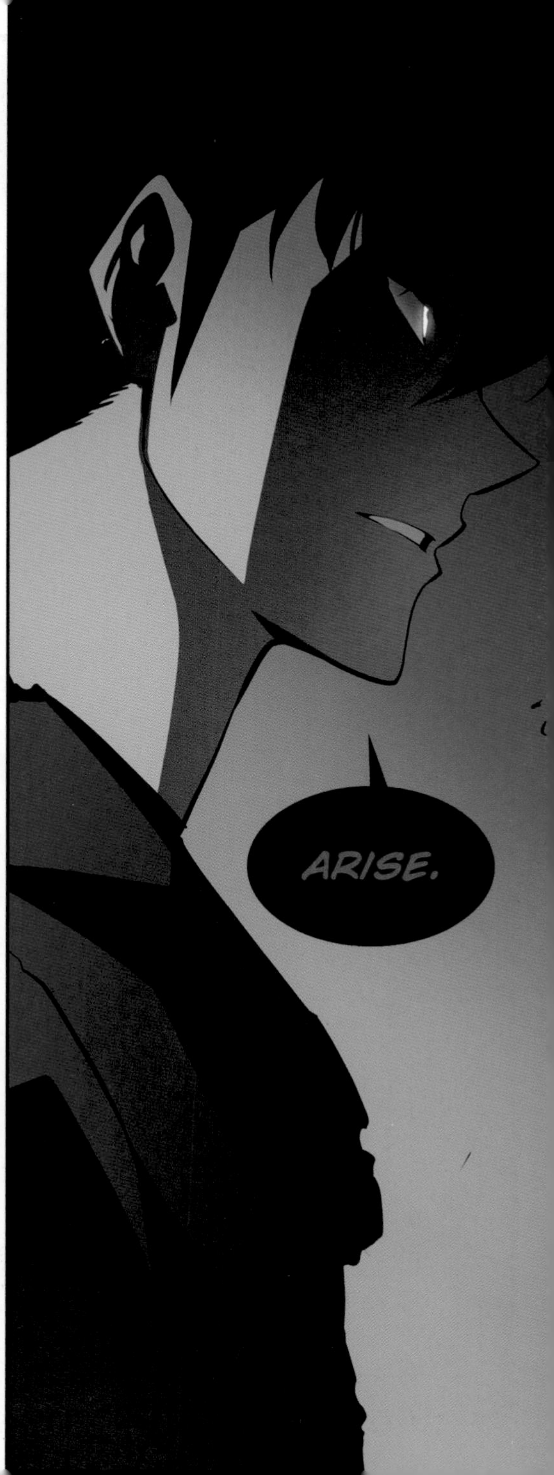
ARISE.

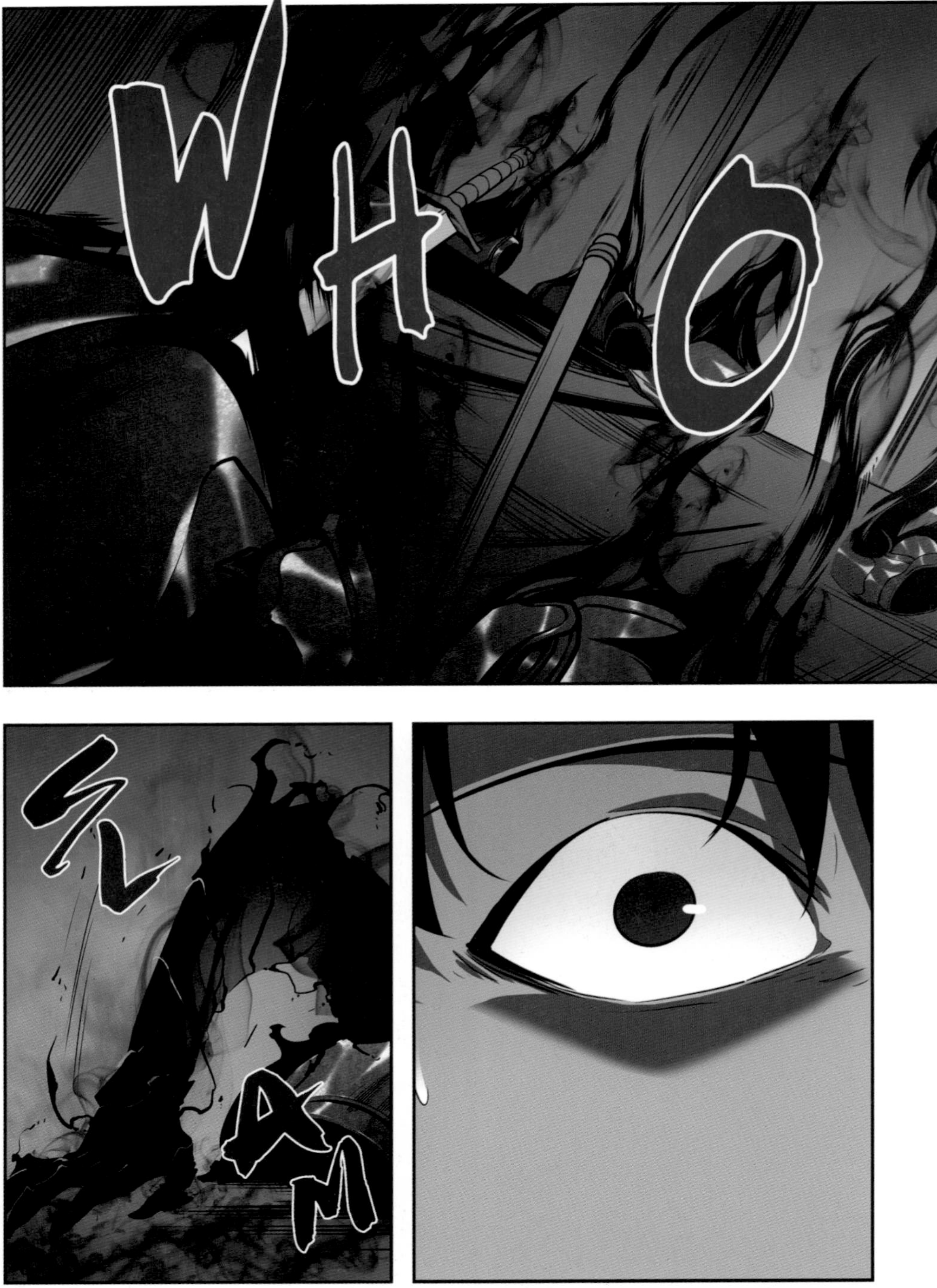
WHOO
SLAM

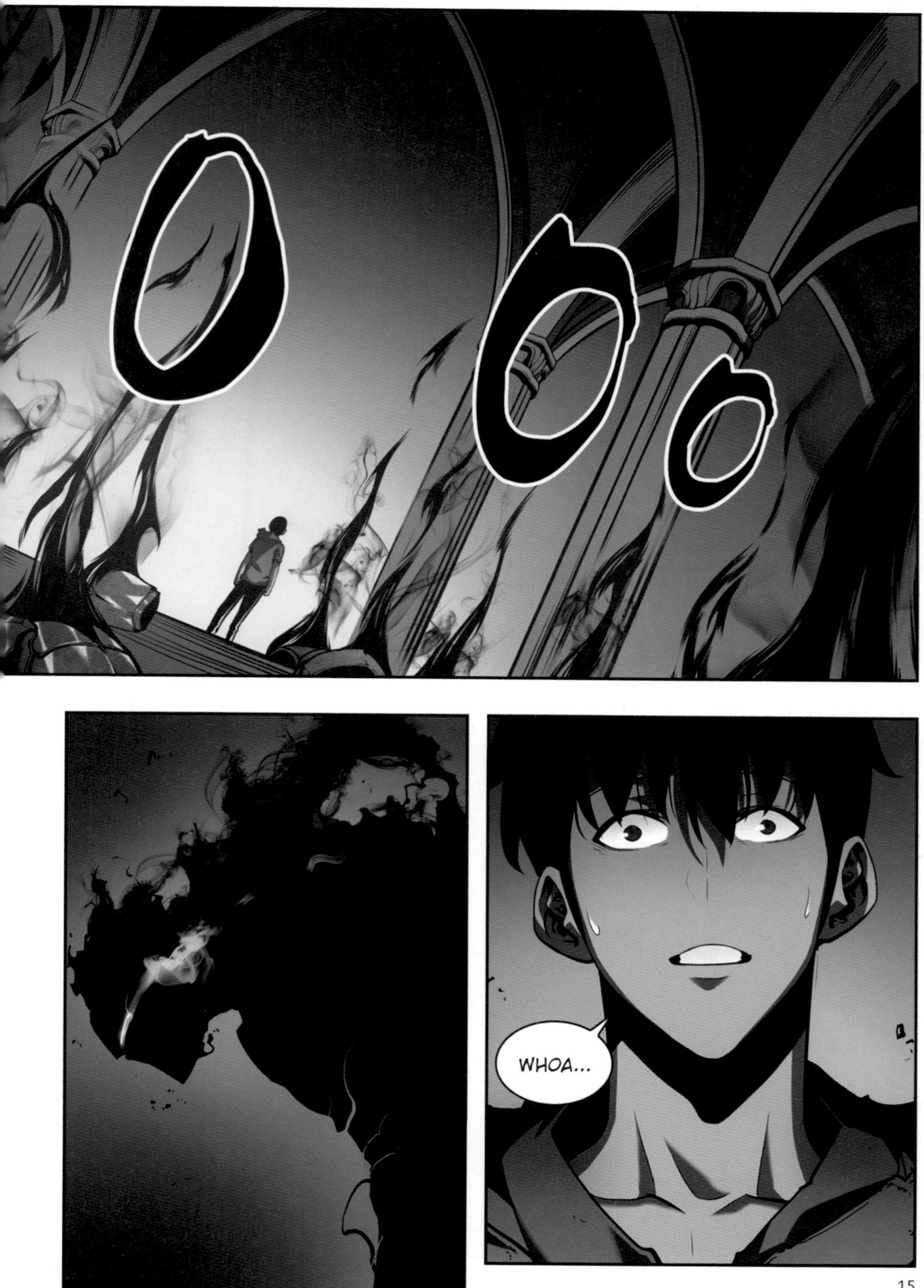
OOo
WHOA...

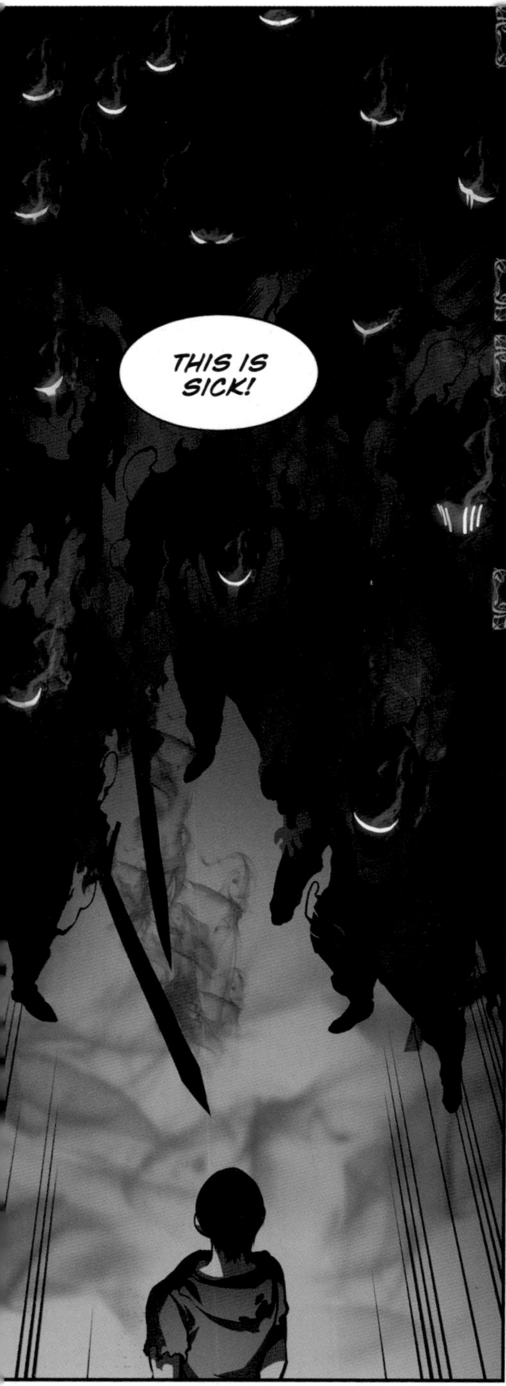
THIS IS SICK!

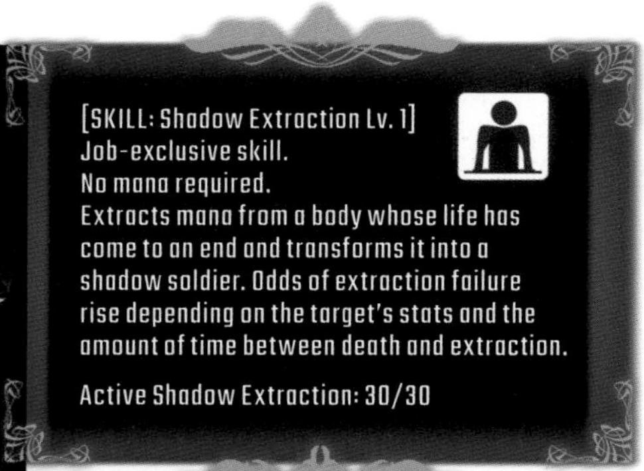
[SKILL: Shadow Extraction Lv. 1]
Job-exclusive skill.
No mana required.
Extracts mana from a body whose life has come to an end and transforms it into a shadow soldier. Odds of extraction failure rise depending on the target's stats and the amount of time between death and extraction.
Active Shadow Extraction: 30/30

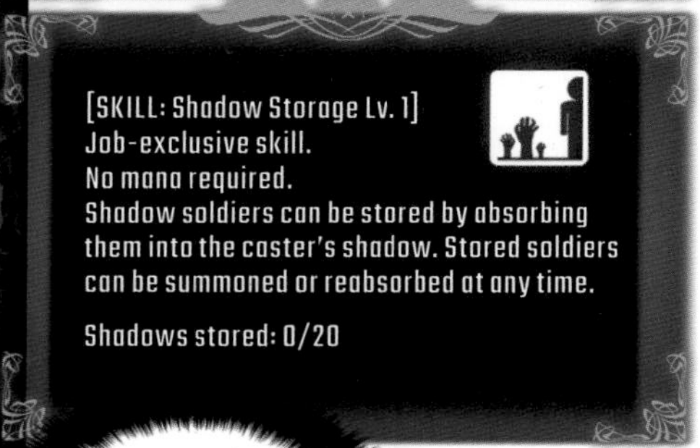
[SKILL: Shadow Storage Lv. 1]
Job-exclusive skill.
No mana required.
Shadow soldiers can be stored by absorbing them into the caster's shadow. Stored soldiers can be summoned or reabsorbed at any time.
Shadows stored: 0/20

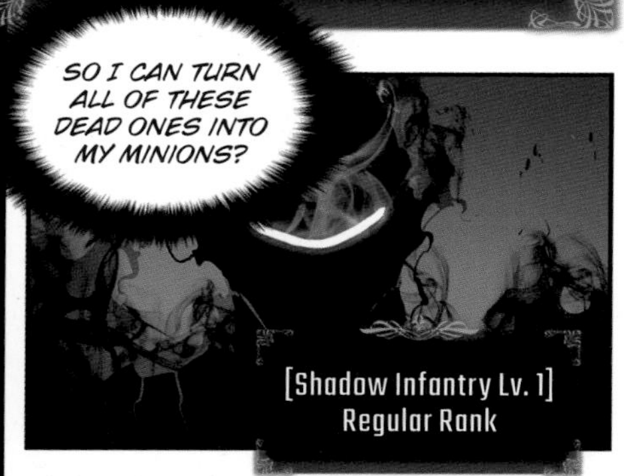
SO I CAN TURN ALL OF THESE DEAD ONES INTO MY MINIONS?
[Shadow Infantry Lv. 1]
Regular Rank

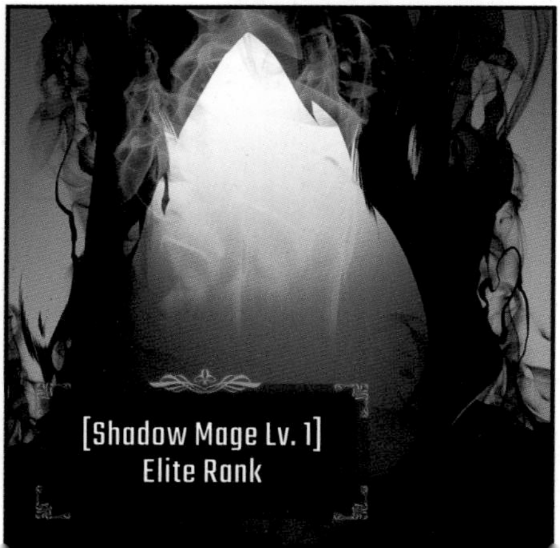
[Shadow Mage Lv. 1]
Elite Rank

TWENTY-SEVEN INFANTRY AND THREE MAGES.

I CAN CREATE THIRTY SHADOW SOLDIERS, BUT THE STORAGE LIMIT IS ONLY TWENTY.

You have exceeded the number of shadows you may extract.

[Active Shadow Extraction: 30/30]

[Shadows stored: 0/20]

WHAT IF I CAN EXTRACT AN A- OR S-RANK'S SHADOW?

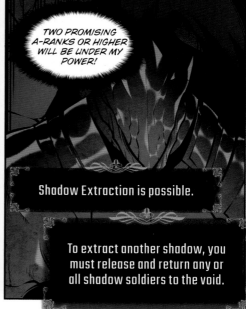

TWO PROMISING A-RANKS OR HIGHER WILL BE UNDER MY POWER!

Shadow Extraction is possible.

To extract another shadow, you must release and return any or all shadow soldiers to the void.

I SHOULD RELEASE ELEVEN OF THE COMMON ONES.

TAP

I SUMMONED YOU, BUT... SORRY.

RELEASE ELEVEN INFANTRY.

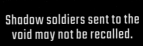

Shadow soldiers sent to the void may not be recalled.

VRMM

KNIGHT COMMANDER IGRIS THE BLOODRED...

IF I CAN MAKE THIS GUY MY SOLDIER...

ARISE.

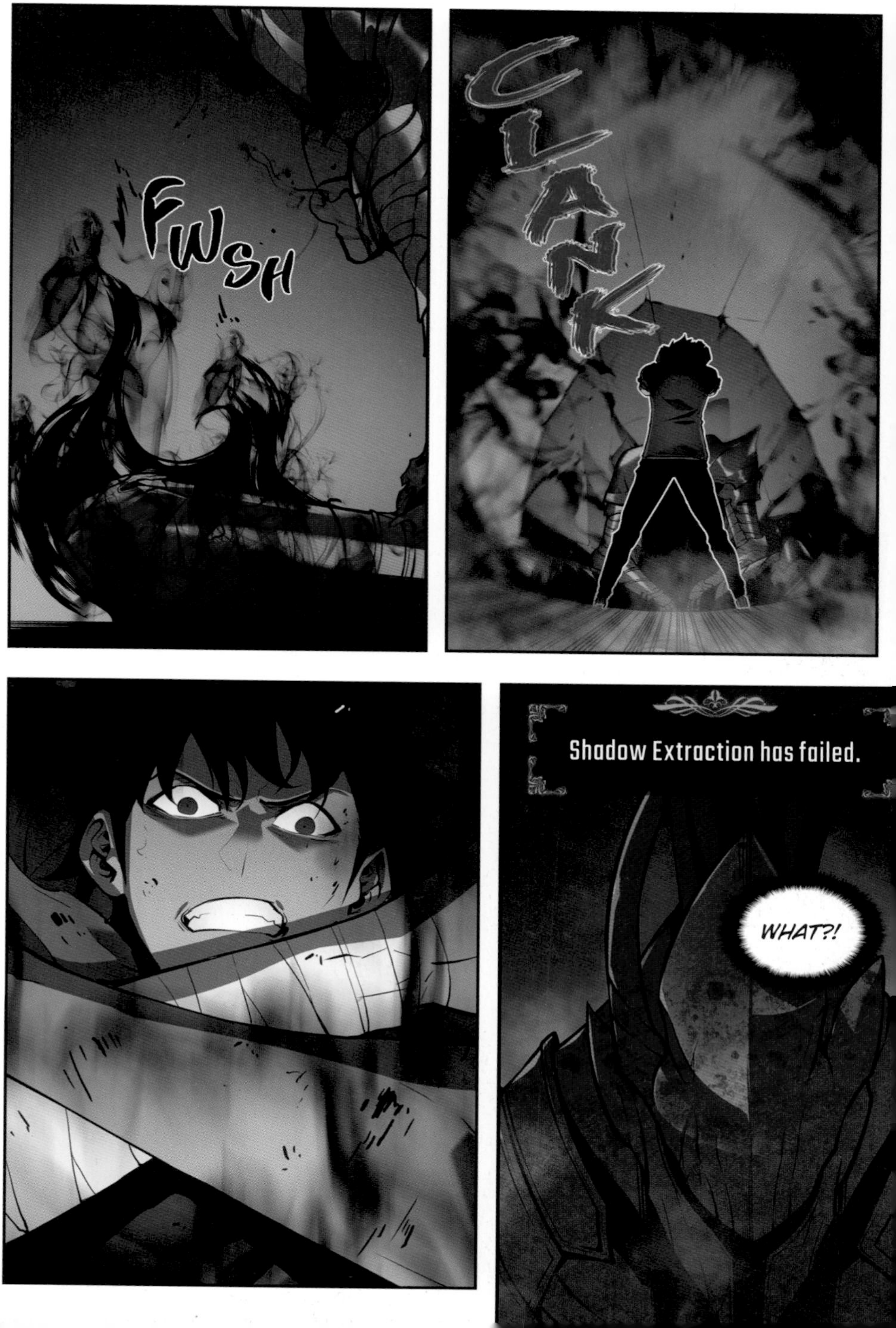
FWSH
CLANK
Shadow Extraction has failed.
WHAT?!

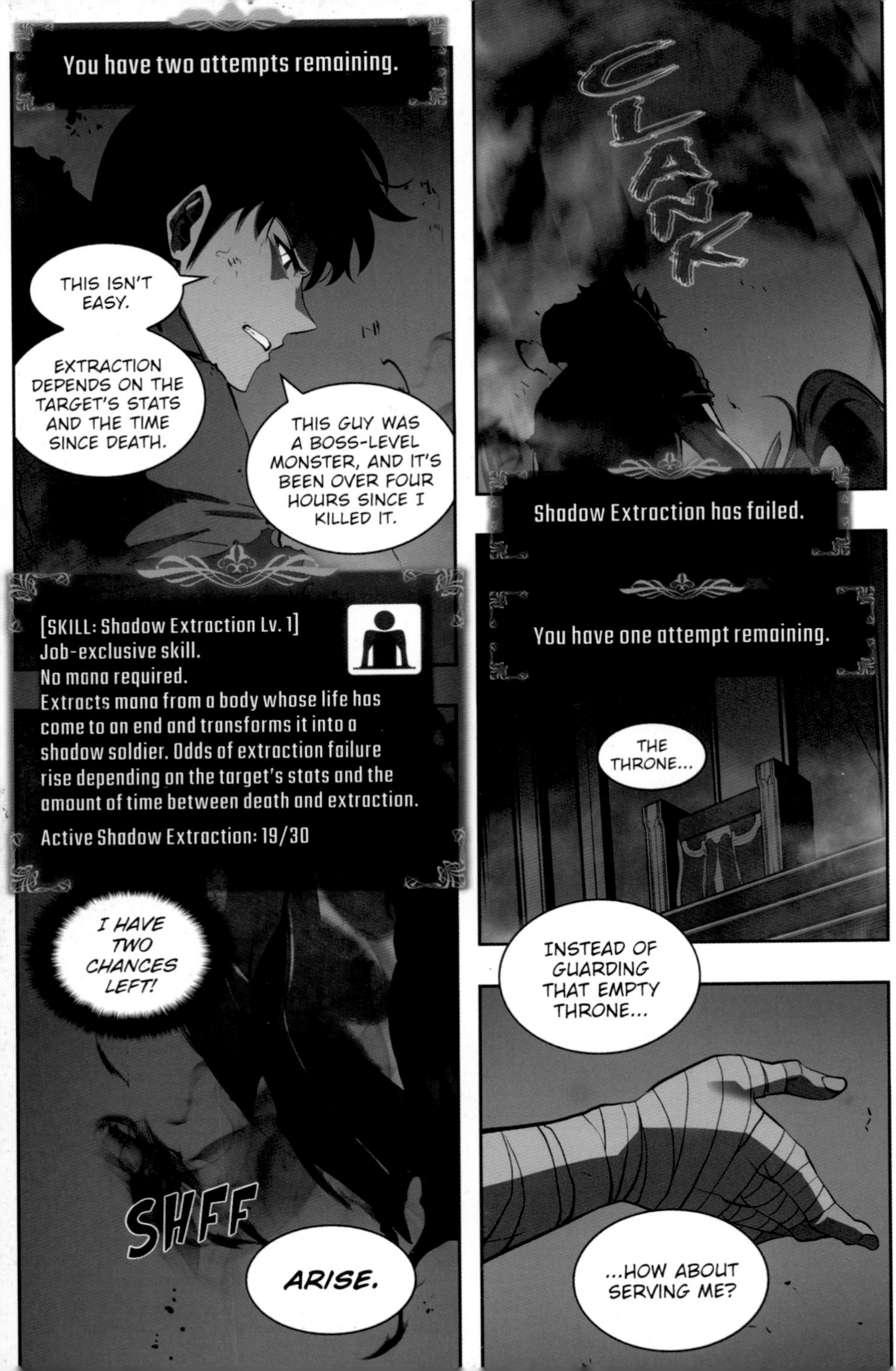
You have two attempts remaining.
THIS ISN'T EASY.
EXTRACTION DEPENDS ON THE TARGET'S STATS AND THE TIME SINCE DEATH.
THIS GUY WAS A BOSS-LEVEL MONSTER, AND IT'S BEEN OVER FOUR HOURS SINCE I KILLED IT.
[SKILL: Shadow Extraction Lv. 1]
Job-exclusive skill.
No mana required.
Extracts mana from a body whose life has come to an end and transforms it into a shadow soldier. Odds of extraction failure rise depending on the target's stats and the amount of time between death and extraction.
Active Shadow Extraction: 19/30
I HAVE TWO CHANCES LEFT!
SHFF
ARISE.
CLANK
Shadow Extraction has failed.
You have one attempt remaining.
THE THRONE...
INSTEAD OF GUARDING THAT EMPTY THRONE...
...HOW ABOUT SERVING ME?

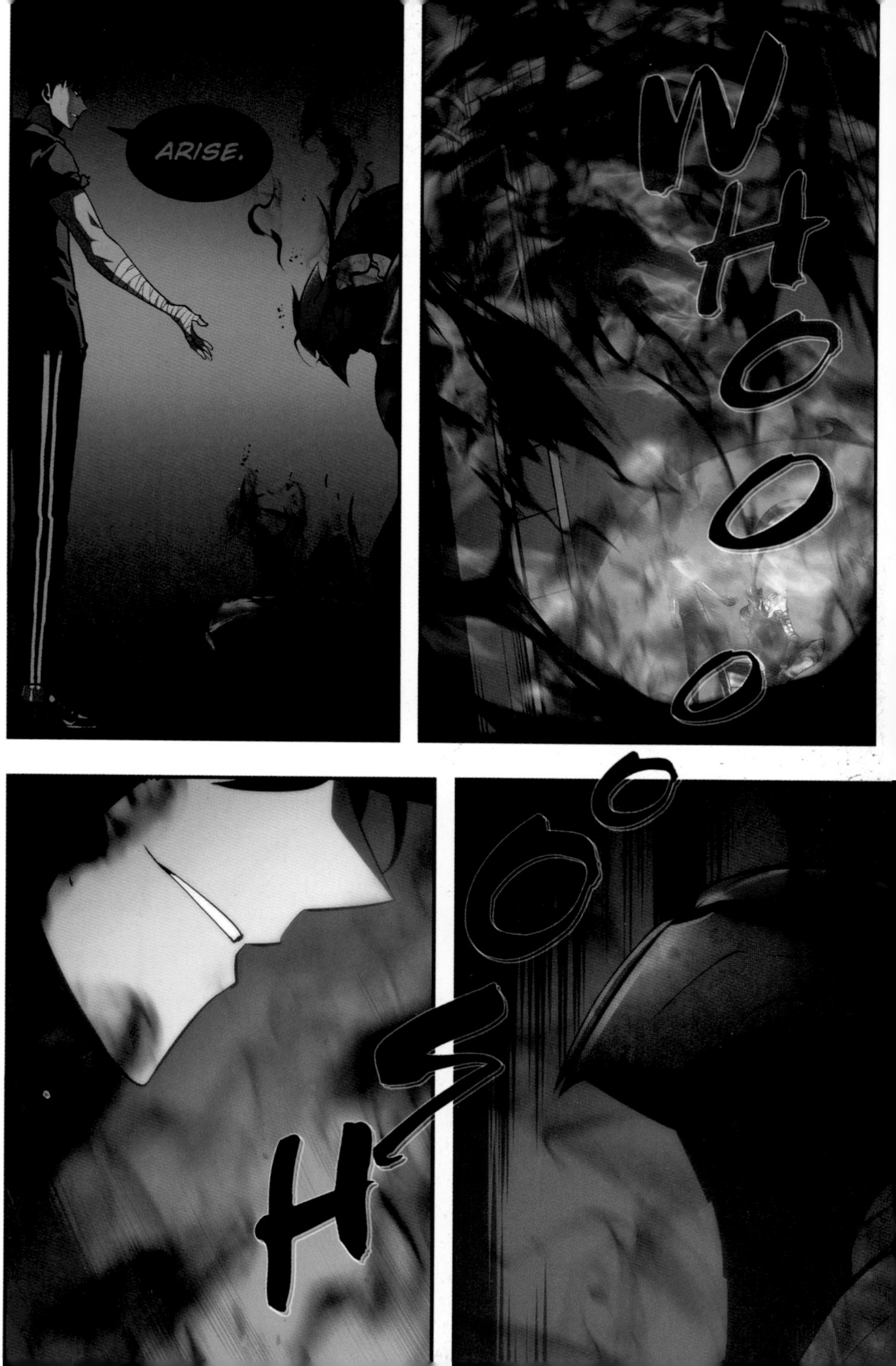
ARISE.
WHOOOOOSH

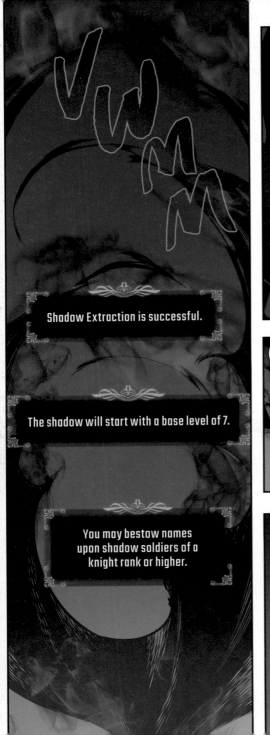

VWMM

Shadow Extraction is successful.

The shadow will start with a base level of 7.

You may bestow names upon shadow soldiers of a knight rank or higher.

IGRIS THE BLOO—

NO, TOO CHEESY...

KEEP IT SIMPLE.

IGRIS.

FROM NOW ON...

Shadow Extraction is complete.

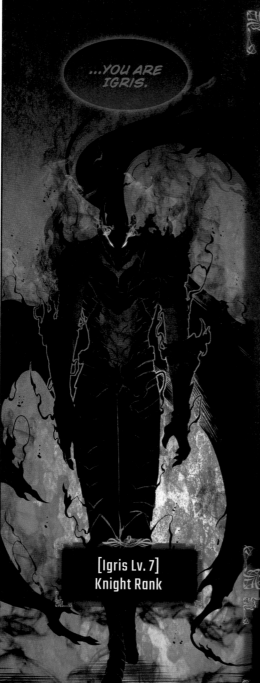

...YOU ARE IGRIS.

[Igris Lv. 7]
Knight Rank

# STATUS

NAME: Jinwoo Sung     LEVEL:    51
JOB: Shadow Monarch    FATIGUE:   0
TITLE: Wolf Assassin (and 1 other)

HP: 11035

MP: 1022

◆

STRENGTH:    132 ▣    STAMINA:    91 ▣
AGILITY:       111 ▣    INTELLECT:   70 ▣
PERCEPTION:   93 ▣

                                   ◆

Physical Damage Decrease: 46%    Activated
Available points: 10

[SKILLS]
[Passive Skill]
(Unknown) Lv. MAX, Willpower Lv. 1,
Advanced Dagger Wielding Lv. 1
[Active Skill]
Dash Lv. 2, Murderous Intent Lv. 1, Fatal Strike Lv. 2
Dagger Throw Lv. 1, Stealth Lv. 1, Ruler's Hand Lv. 1

[JOB-EXCLUSIVE SKILLS]
Active skill: Shadow Extraction Lv. 1,
Shadow Storage Lv. 1

[ITEMS EQUIPPED]
Crimson Knight's Helmet (S), Warden's Collar (A),
High-Rank Knight's Chestplate (B), High-Rank
Knight's Gauntlets (B), High-Rank Mage's Ring (B),
Mid-Rank Assassin's Boots (B)

[Title: The One Who Overcame Adversity]
A title given to those who have
gloriously overcome adversity.
Stat values will increase proportionally
as HP is lost (1% increase per 1% loss).

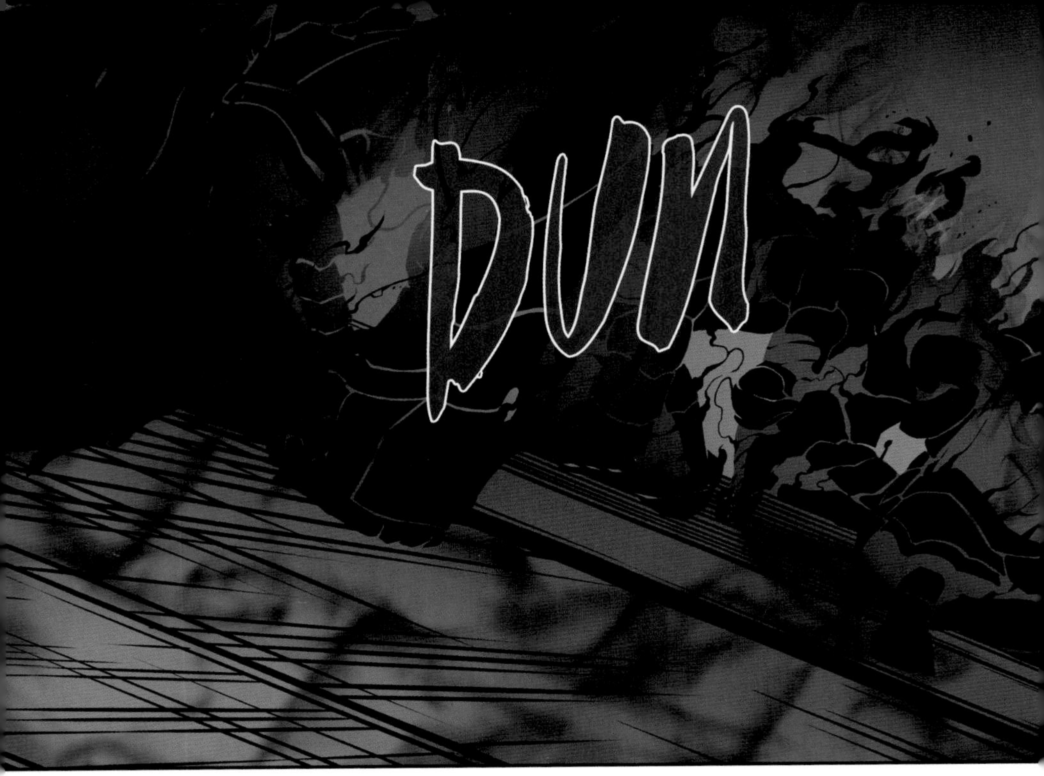
DUN
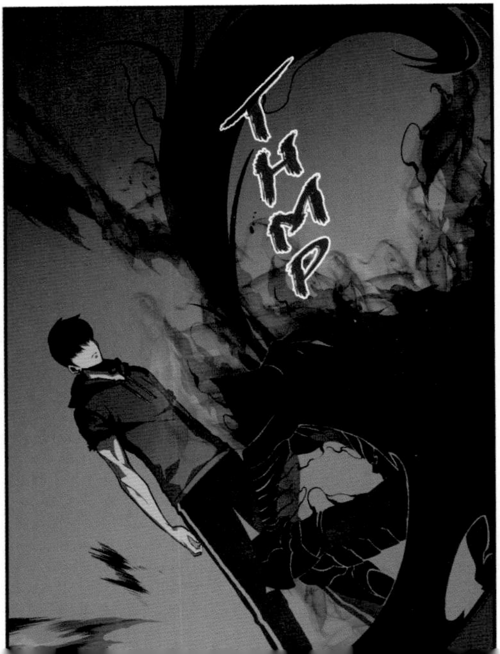
THMP
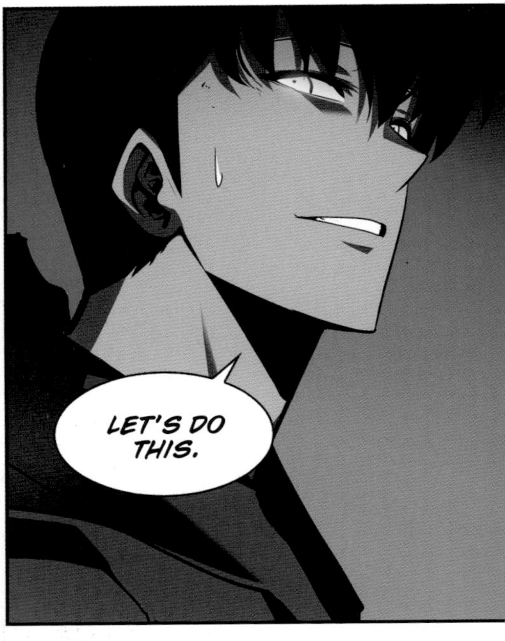
LET'S DO THIS.

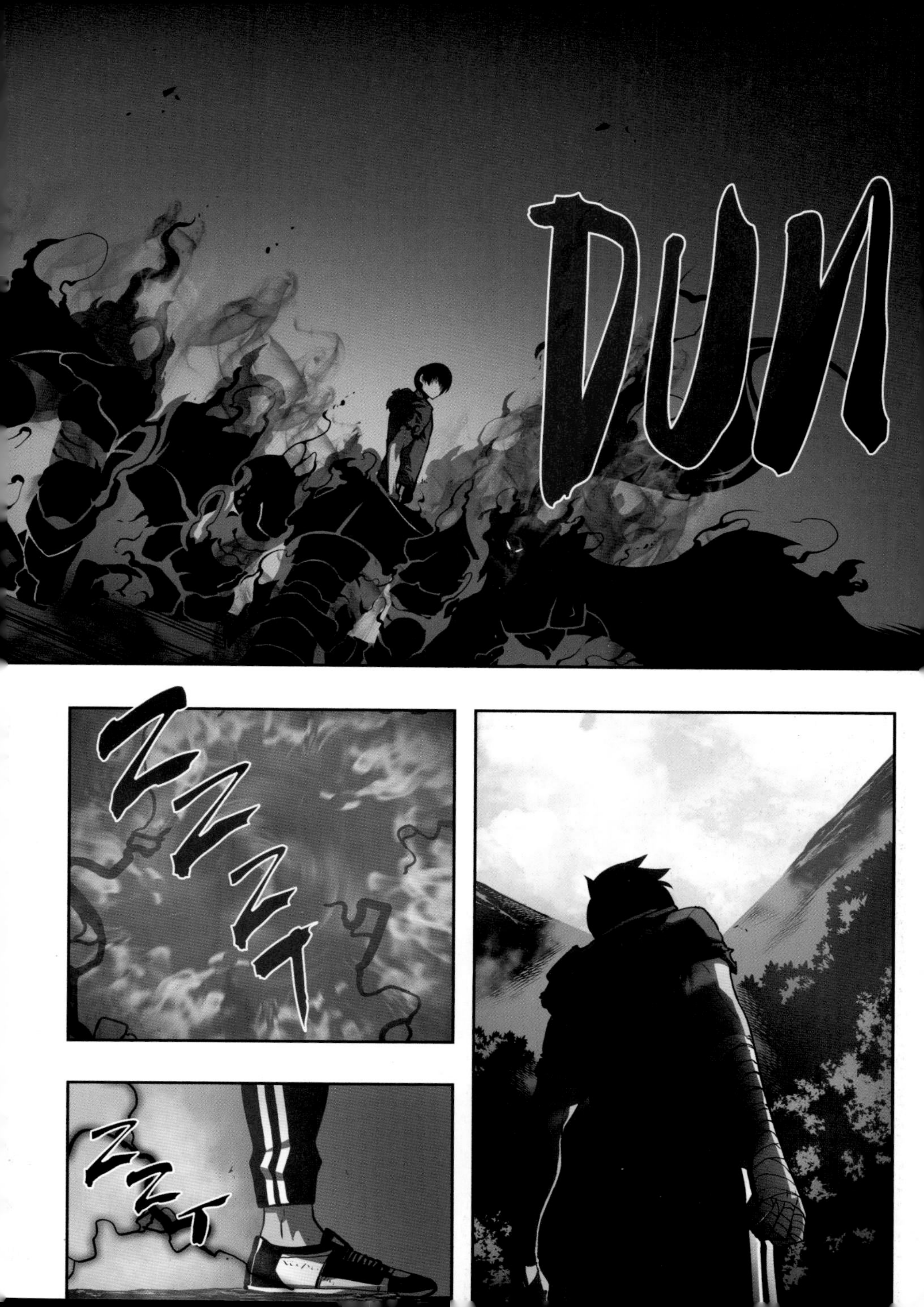
DUN
ZZZZT
ZZZT

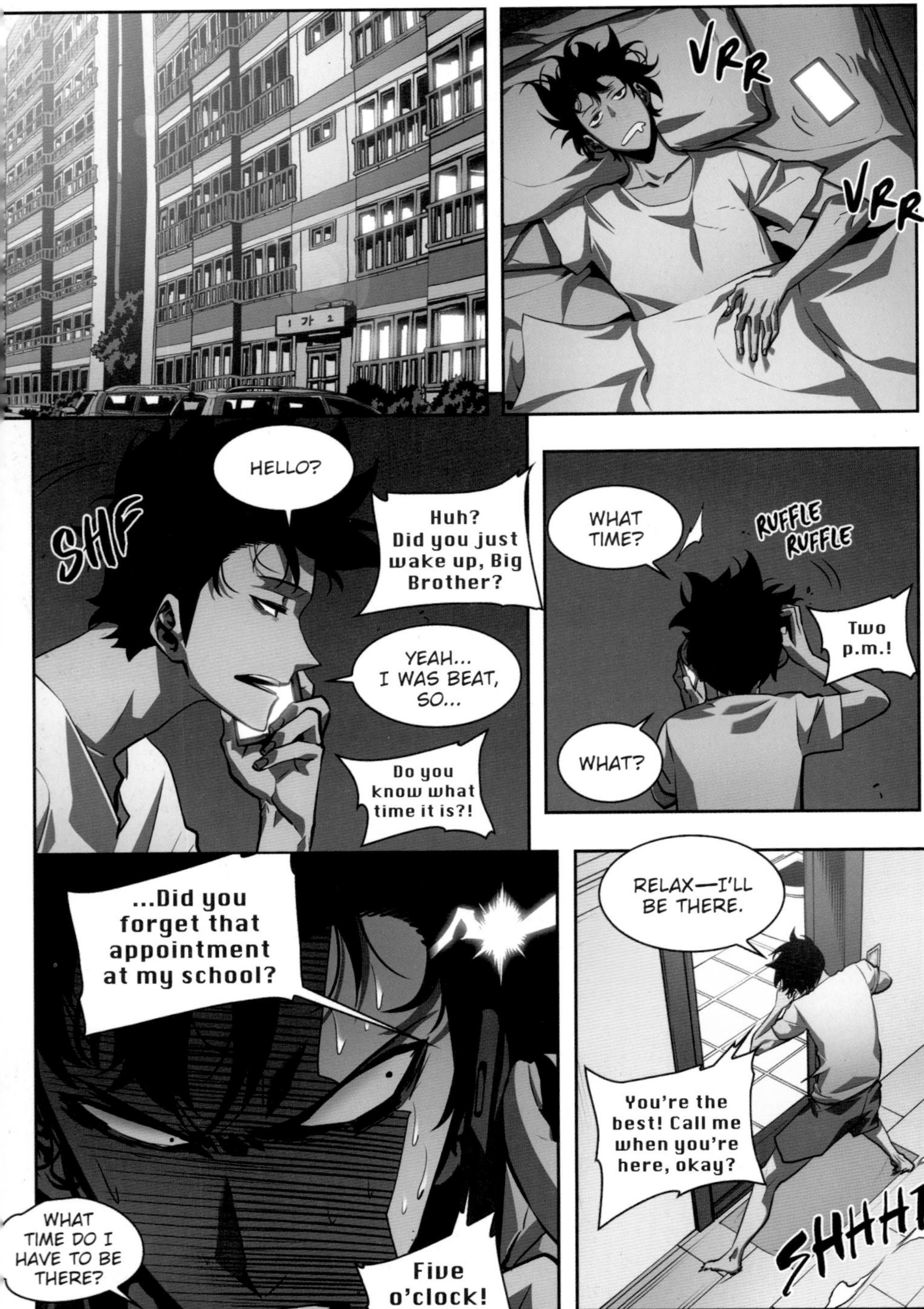
VRR
VRR
HELLO?
SHF
Huh? Did you just wake up, Big Brother?
YEAH... I WAS BEAT, SO...
Do you know what time it is?!
WHAT TIME?
RUFFLE RUFFLE
Two p.m.!
WHAT?
...Did you forget that appointment at my school?
WHAT TIME DO I HAVE TO BE THERE?
Five o'clock!
RELAX—I'LL BE THERE.
You're the best! Call me when you're here, okay?
SHHHP

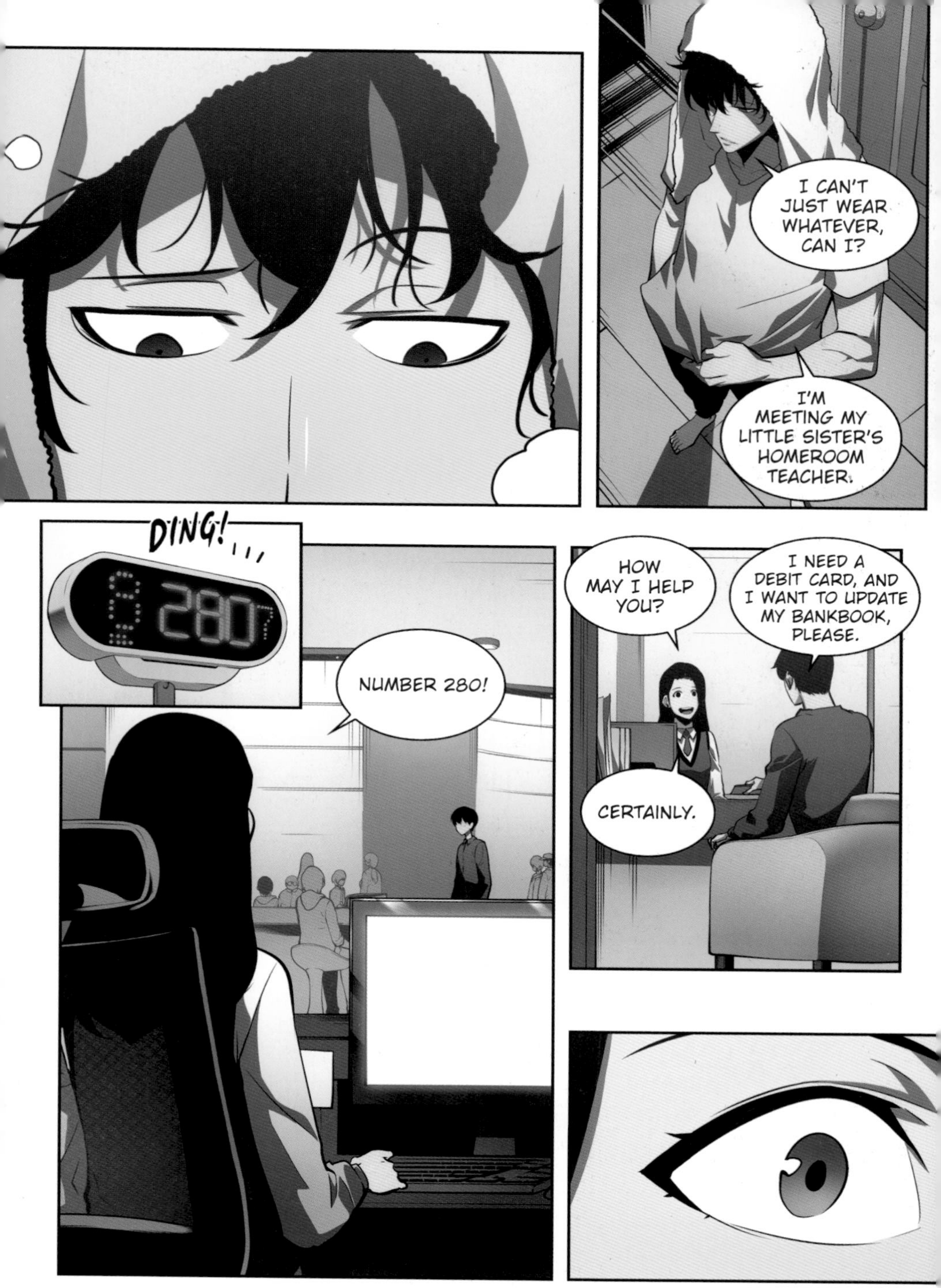
I CAN'T JUST WEAR WHATEVER, CAN I?
I'M MEETING MY LITTLE SISTER'S HOMEROOM TEACHER.
DING!
280
NUMBER 280!
HOW MAY I HELP YOU?
I NEED A DEBIT CARD, AND I WANT TO UPDATE MY BANKBOOK, PLEASE.
CERTAINLY.

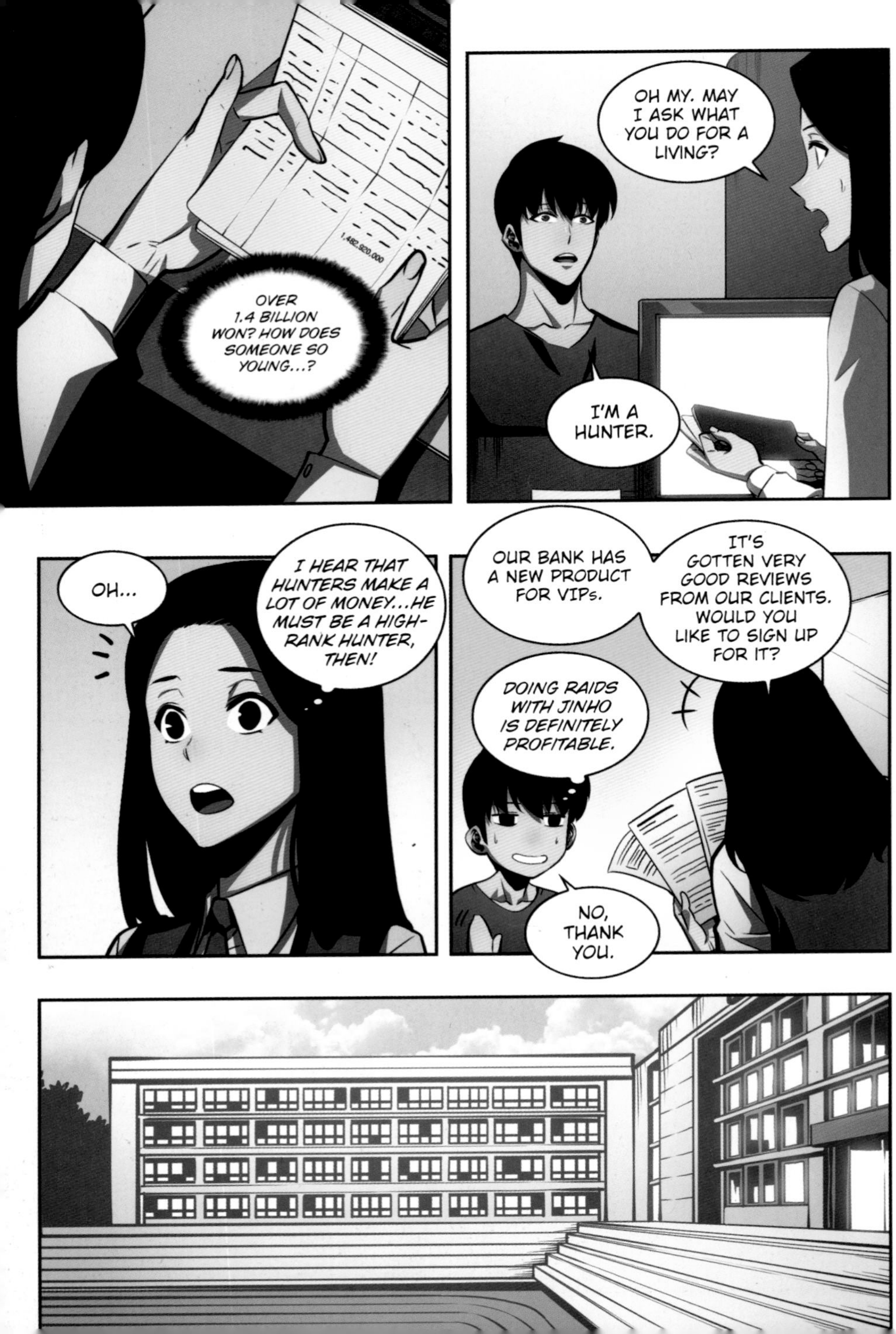
1,482,920,000
OVER 1.4 BILLION WON? HOW DOES SOMEONE SO YOUNG...?
OH MY. MAY I ASK WHAT YOU DO FOR A LIVING?
I'M A HUNTER.
OH...
I HEAR THAT HUNTERS MAKE A LOT OF MONEY...HE MUST BE A HIGH-RANK HUNTER, THEN!
OUR BANK HAS A NEW PRODUCT FOR VIPs.
IT'S GOTTEN VERY GOOD REVIEWS FROM OUR CLIENTS. WOULD YOU LIKE TO SIGN UP FOR IT?
DOING RAIDS WITH JINHO IS DEFINITELY PROFITABLE.
NO, THANK YOU.

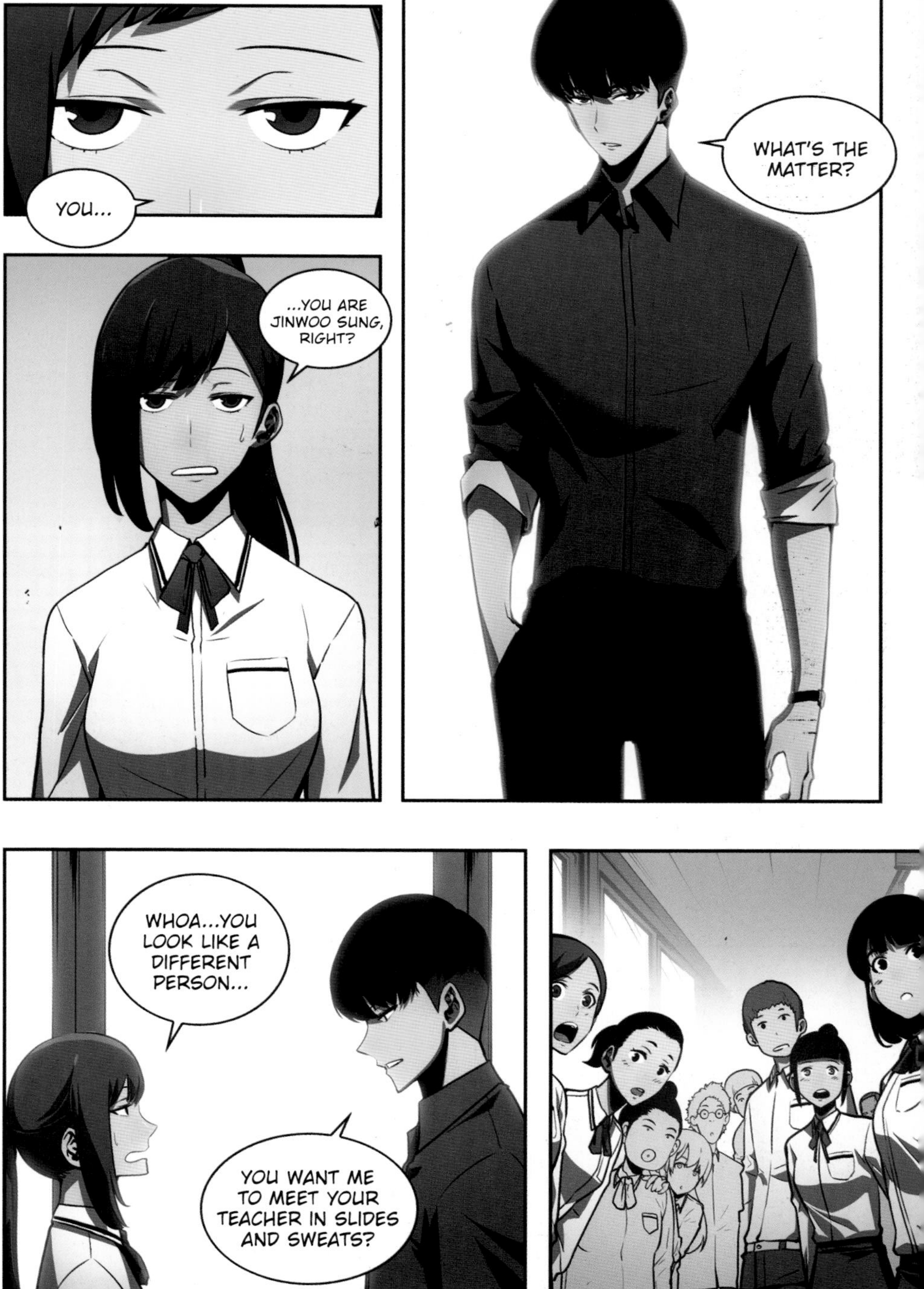
YOU...
...YOU ARE JINWOO SUNG, RIGHT?
WHAT'S THE MATTER?
WHOA...YOU LOOK LIKE A DIFFERENT PERSON...
YOU WANT ME TO MEET YOUR TEACHER IN SLIDES AND SWEATS?

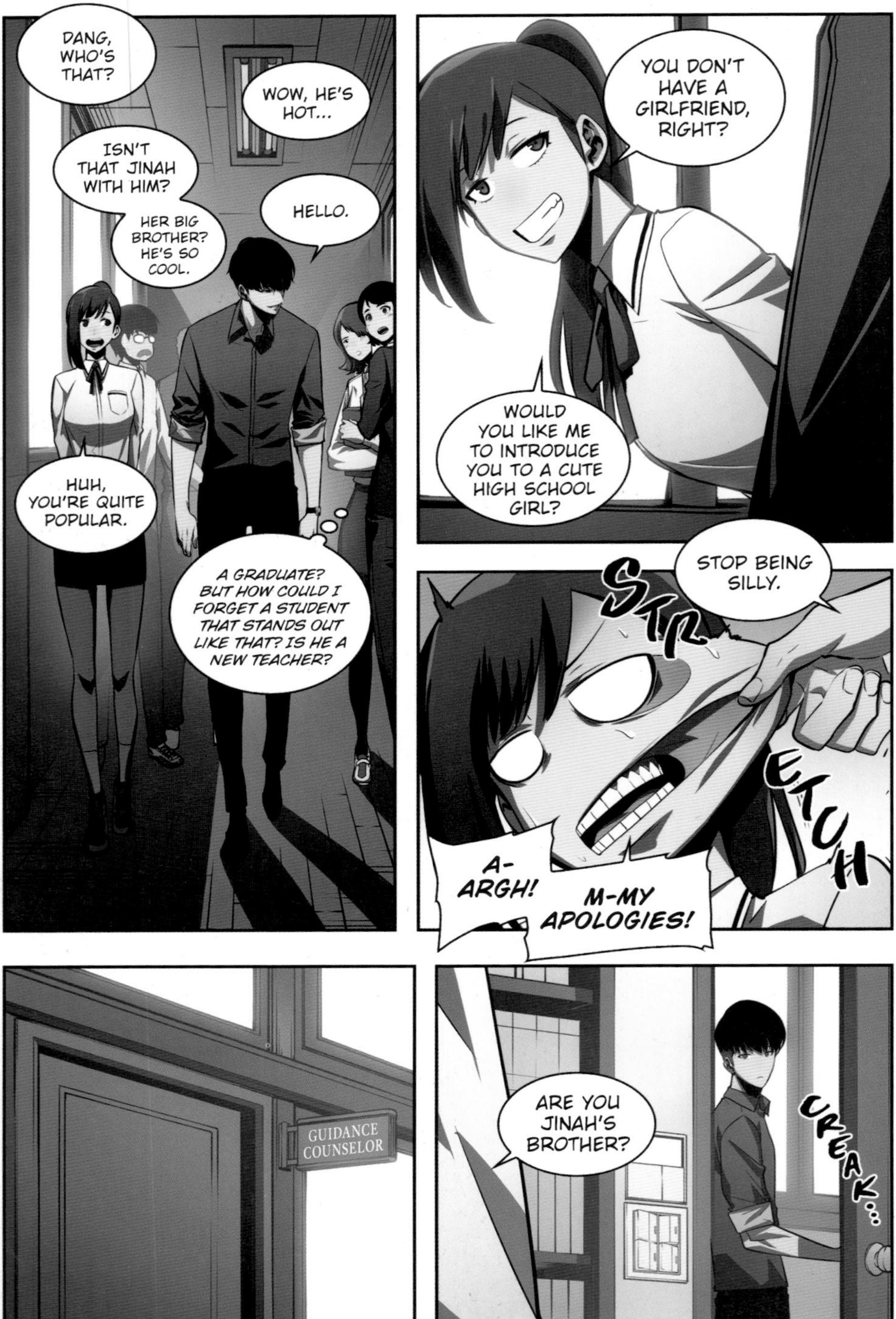
DANG, WHO'S THAT?
WOW, HE'S HOT...
ISN'T THAT JINAH WITH HIM?
HER BIG BROTHER? HE'S SO COOL.
HELLO.
HUH, YOU'RE QUITE POPULAR.
A GRADUATE? BUT HOW COULD I FORGET A STUDENT THAT STANDS OUT LIKE THAT? IS HE A NEW TEACHER?
YOU DON'T HAVE A GIRLFRIEND, RIGHT?
WOULD YOU LIKE ME TO INTRODUCE YOU TO A CUTE HIGH SCHOOL GIRL?
STR
STOP BEING SILLY.
ETCH
A- ARGH!
M-MY APOLOGIES!
GUIDANCE COUNSELOR
ARE YOU JINAH'S BROTHER?
CREAK...

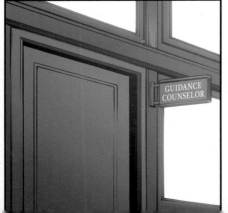

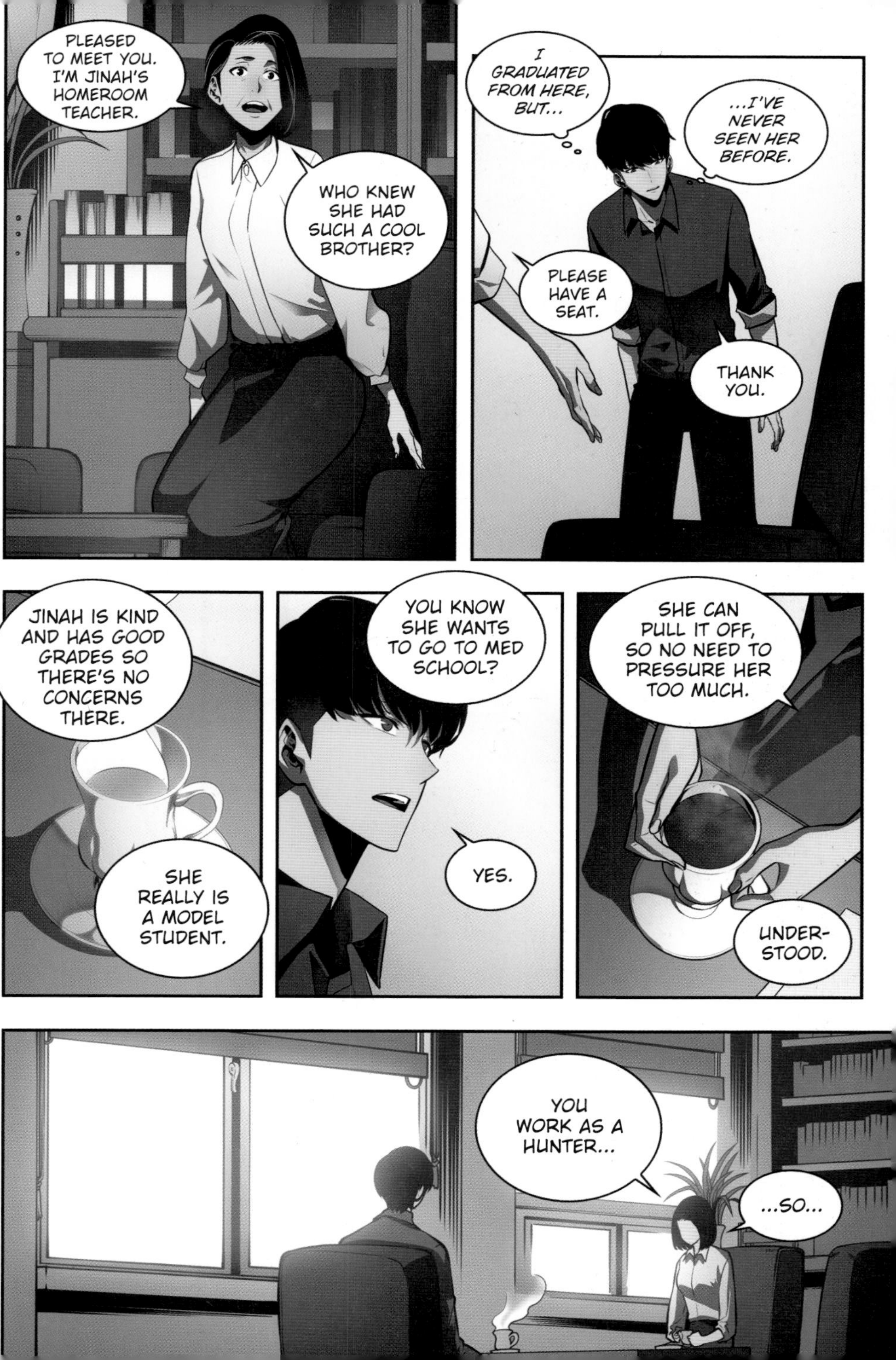
PLEASED TO MEET YOU. I'M JINAH'S HOMEROOM TEACHER.
WHO KNEW SHE HAD SUCH A COOL BROTHER?
I GRADUATED FROM HERE, BUT...
...I'VE NEVER SEEN HER BEFORE.
PLEASE HAVE A SEAT.
THANK YOU.
JINAH IS KIND AND HAS GOOD GRADES SO THERE'S NO CONCERNS THERE.
SHE REALLY IS A MODEL STUDENT.
YOU KNOW SHE WANTS TO GO TO MED SCHOOL?
YES.
SHE CAN PULL IT OFF, SO NO NEED TO PRESSURE HER TOO MUCH.
UNDER-STOOD.
YOU WORK AS A HUNTER...
...SO...

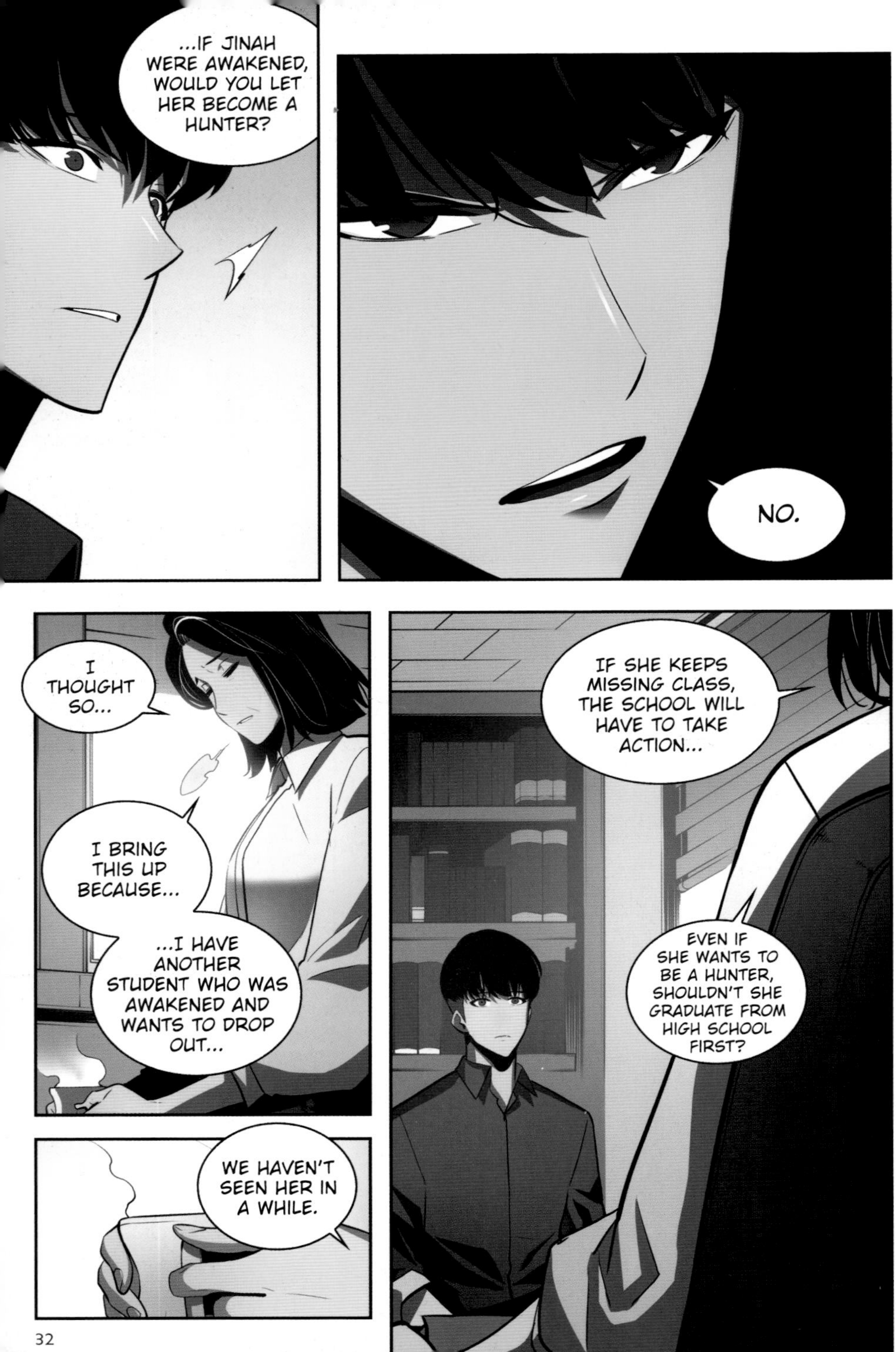
...IF JINAH WERE AWAKENED, WOULD YOU LET HER BECOME A HUNTER?
NO.
I THOUGHT SO...
I BRING THIS UP BECAUSE...
...I HAVE ANOTHER STUDENT WHO WAS AWAKENED AND WANTS TO DROP OUT...
WE HAVEN'T SEEN HER IN A WHILE.
IF SHE KEEPS MISSING CLASS, THE SCHOOL WILL HAVE TO TAKE ACTION...
EVEN IF SHE WANTS TO BE A HUNTER, SHOULDN'T SHE GRADUATE FROM HIGH SCHOOL FIRST?

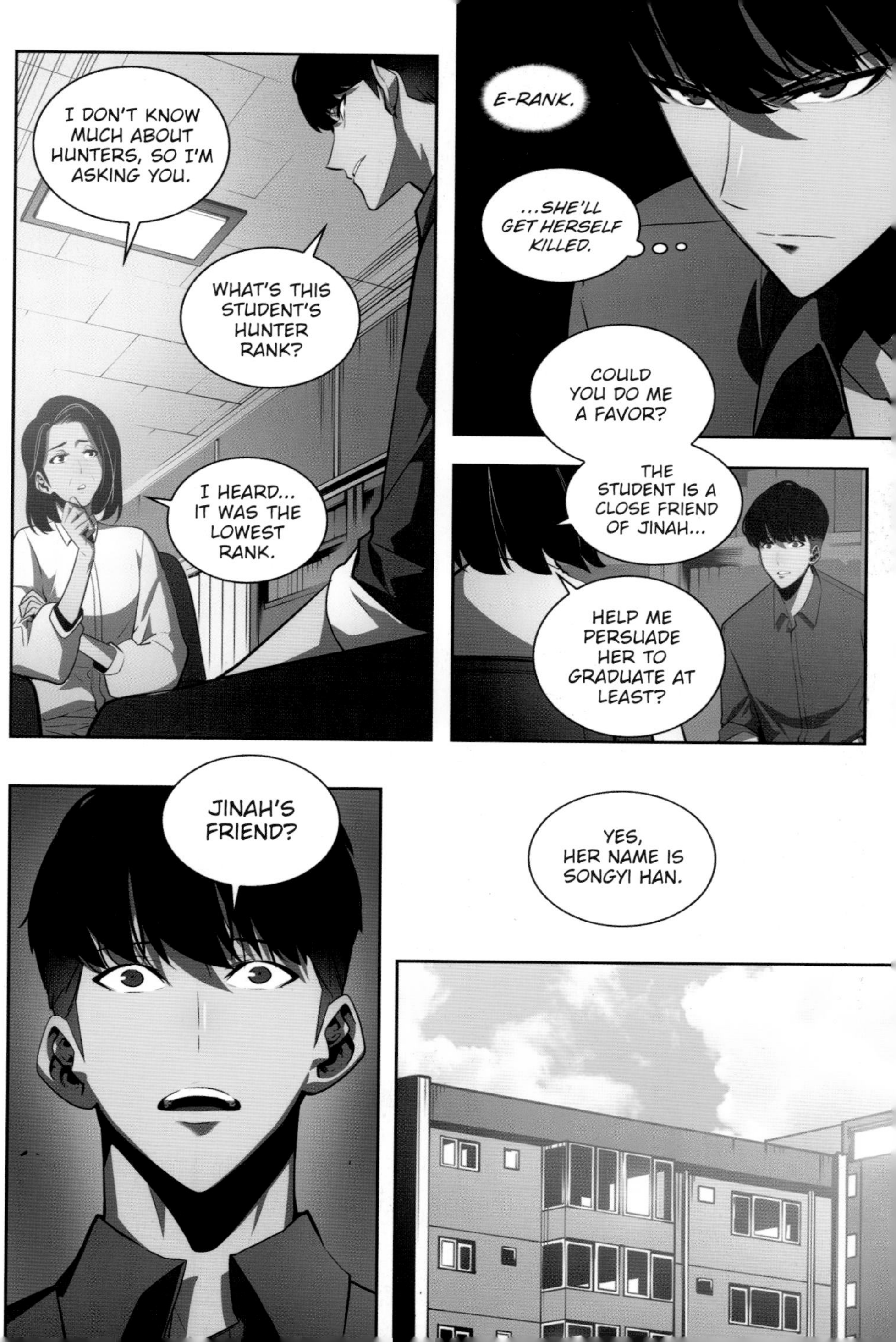
I DON'T KNOW MUCH ABOUT HUNTERS, SO I'M ASKING YOU.
WHAT'S THIS STUDENT'S HUNTER RANK?
I HEARD... IT WAS THE LOWEST RANK.
E-RANK.
...SHE'LL GET HERSELF KILLED.
COULD YOU DO ME A FAVOR?
THE STUDENT IS A CLOSE FRIEND OF JINAH...
HELP ME PERSUADE HER TO GRADUATE AT LEAST?
JINAH'S FRIEND?
YES, HER NAME IS SONGYI HAN.

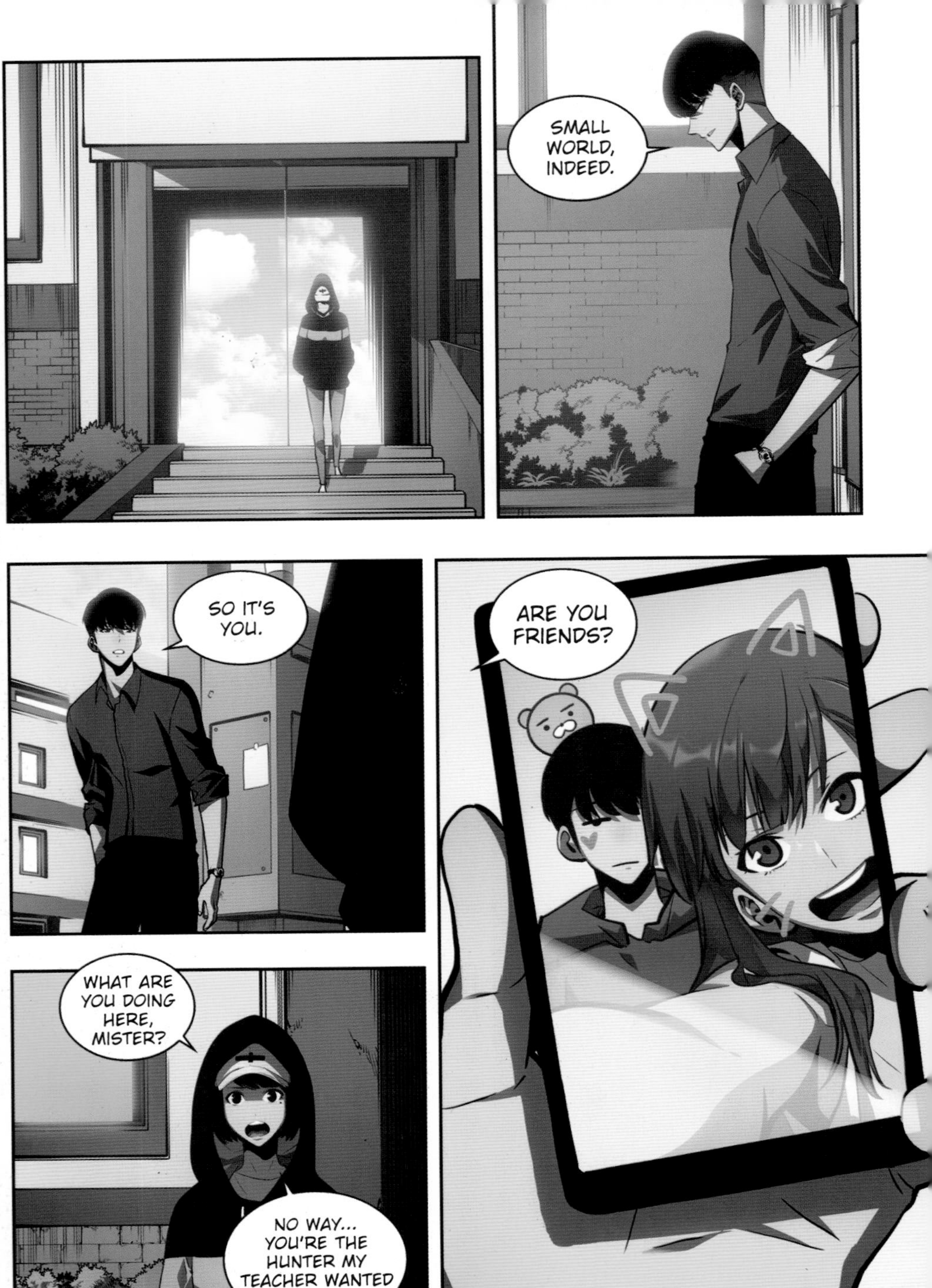
SMALL WORLD, INDEED.
SO IT'S YOU.
WHAT ARE YOU DOING HERE, MISTER?
NO WAY... YOU'RE THE HUNTER MY TEACHER WANTED ME TO MEET?
ARE YOU FRIENDS?

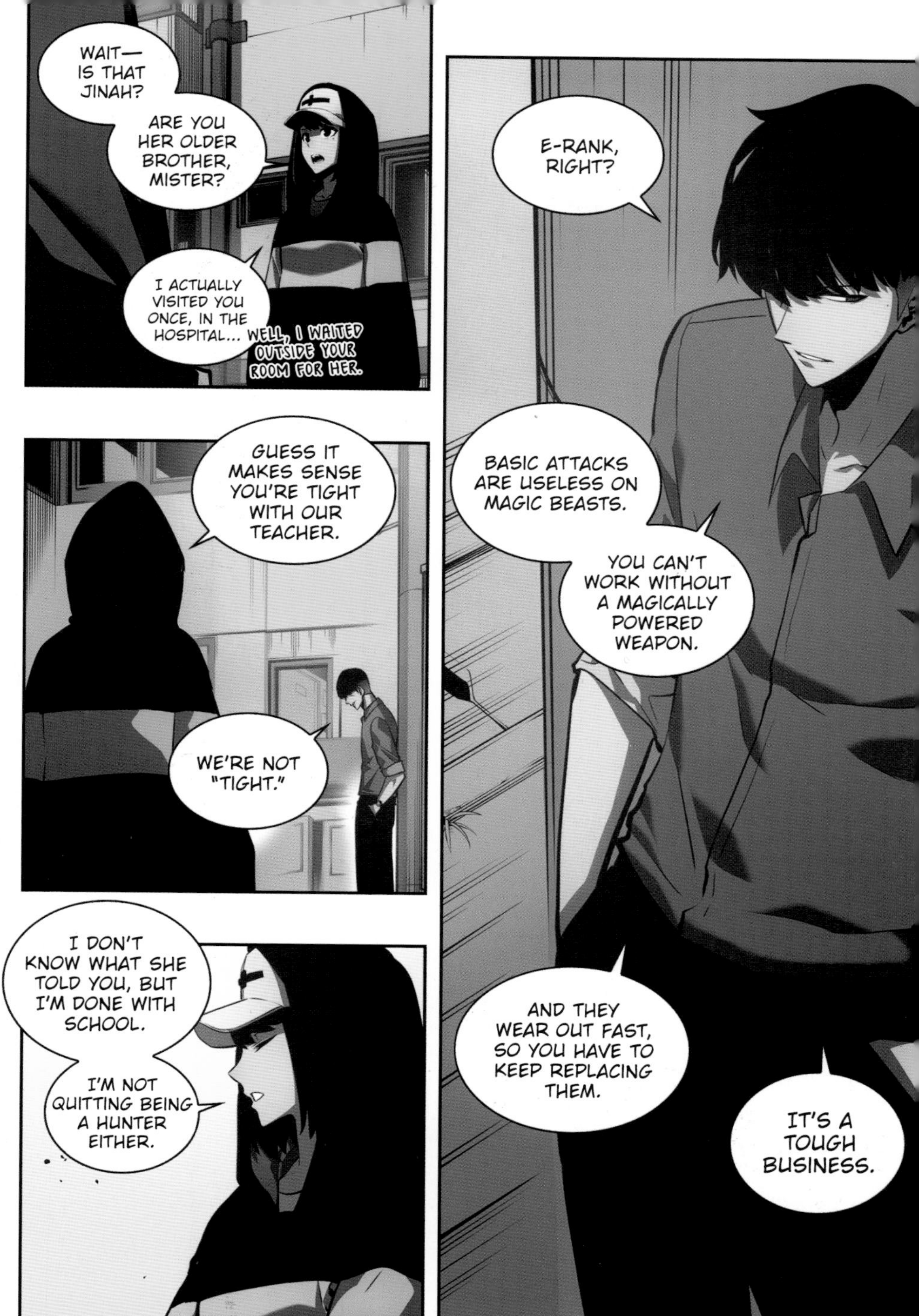
WAIT— IS THAT JINAH?
ARE YOU HER OLDER BROTHER, MISTER?
I ACTUALLY VISITED YOU ONCE, IN THE HOSPITAL...
WELL, I WAITED OUTSIDE YOUR ROOM FOR HER.
GUESS IT MAKES SENSE YOU'RE TIGHT WITH OUR TEACHER.
WE'RE NOT "TIGHT."
I DON'T KNOW WHAT SHE TOLD YOU, BUT I'M DONE WITH SCHOOL.
I'M NOT QUITTING BEING A HUNTER EITHER.
E-RANK, RIGHT?
BASIC ATTACKS ARE USELESS ON MAGIC BEASTS.
YOU CAN'T WORK WITHOUT A MAGICALLY POWERED WEAPON.
AND THEY WEAR OUT FAST, SO YOU HAVE TO KEEP REPLACING THEM.
IT'S A TOUGH BUSINESS.

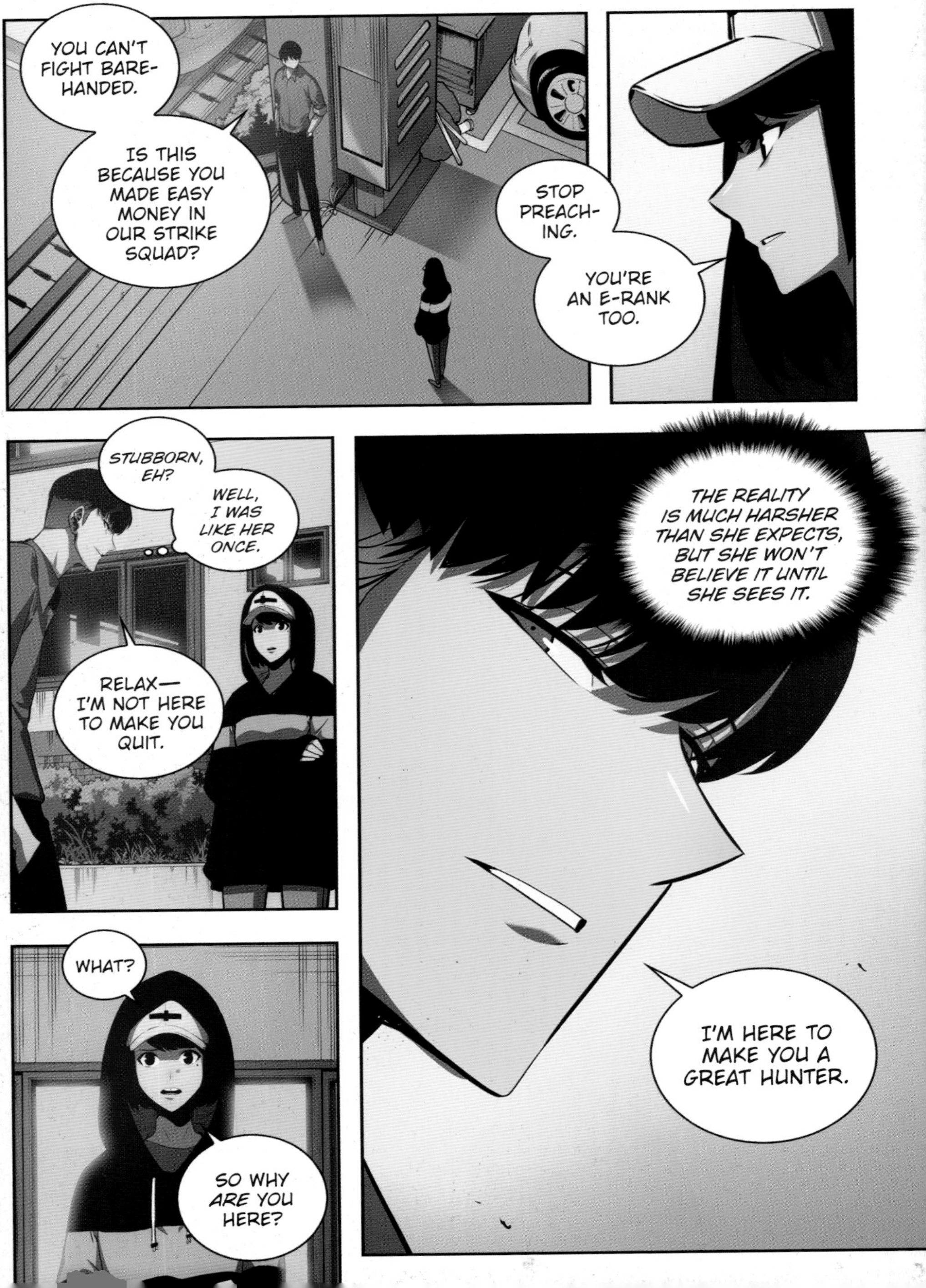
YOU CAN'T FIGHT BARE-HANDED.
IS THIS BECAUSE YOU MADE EASY MONEY IN OUR STRIKE SQUAD?
STOP PREACH-ING.
YOU'RE AN E-RANK TOO.
STUBBORN, EH?
WELL, I WAS LIKE HER ONCE.
RELAX— I'M NOT HERE TO MAKE YOU QUIT.
WHAT?
SO WHY ARE YOU HERE?
THE REALITY IS MUCH HARSHER THAN SHE EXPECTS, BUT SHE WON'T BELIEVE IT UNTIL SHE SEES IT.
I'M HERE TO MAKE YOU A GREAT HUNTER.

Solo Leveling

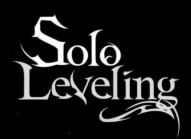

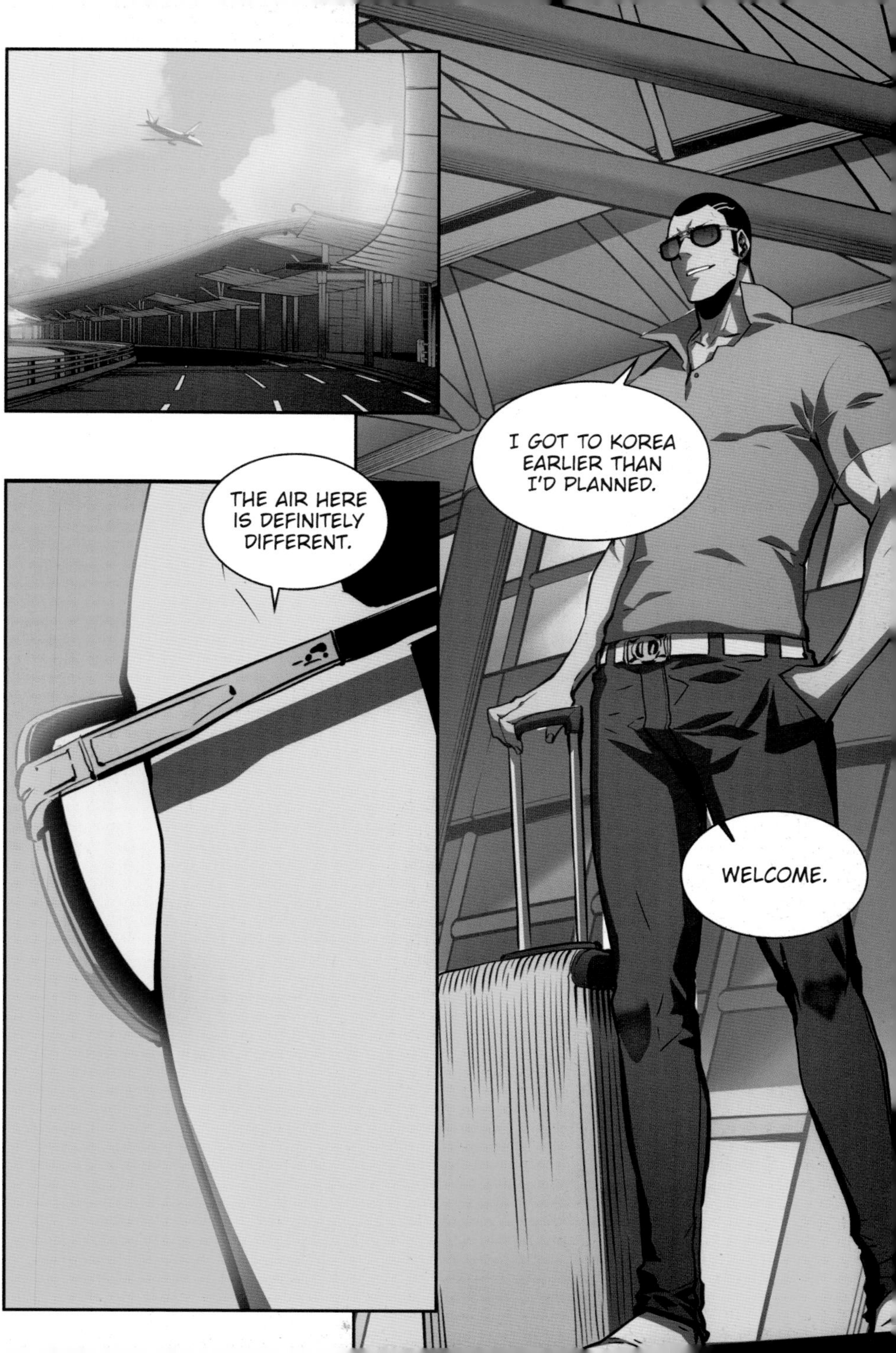
THE AIR HERE IS DEFINITELY DIFFERENT.
I GOT TO KOREA EARLIER THAN I'D PLANNED.
WELCOME.

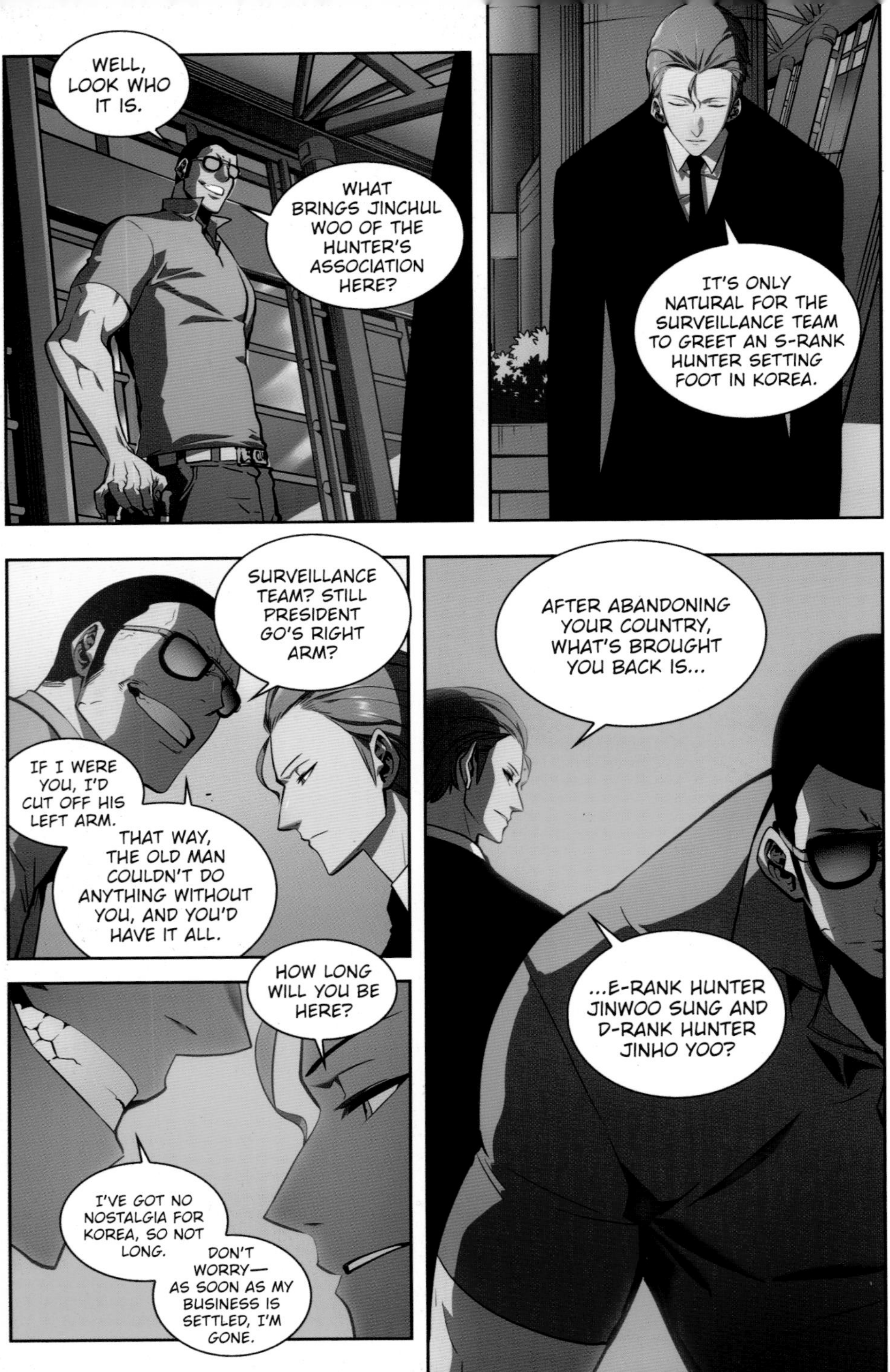
WELL, LOOK WHO IT IS.
WHAT BRINGS JINCHUL WOO OF THE HUNTER'S ASSOCIATION HERE?
IT'S ONLY NATURAL FOR THE SURVEILLANCE TEAM TO GREET AN S-RANK HUNTER SETTING FOOT IN KOREA.
SURVEILLANCE TEAM? STILL PRESIDENT GO'S RIGHT ARM?
IF I WERE YOU, I'D CUT OFF HIS LEFT ARM.
THAT WAY, THE OLD MAN COULDN'T DO ANYTHING WITHOUT YOU, AND YOU'D HAVE IT ALL.
HOW LONG WILL YOU BE HERE?
I'VE GOT NO NOSTALGIA FOR KOREA, SO NOT LONG.
DON'T WORRY— AS SOON AS MY BUSINESS IS SETTLED, I'M GONE.
AFTER ABANDONING YOUR COUNTRY, WHAT'S BROUGHT YOU BACK IS...
...E-RANK HUNTER JINWOO SUNG AND D-RANK HUNTER JINHO YOO?

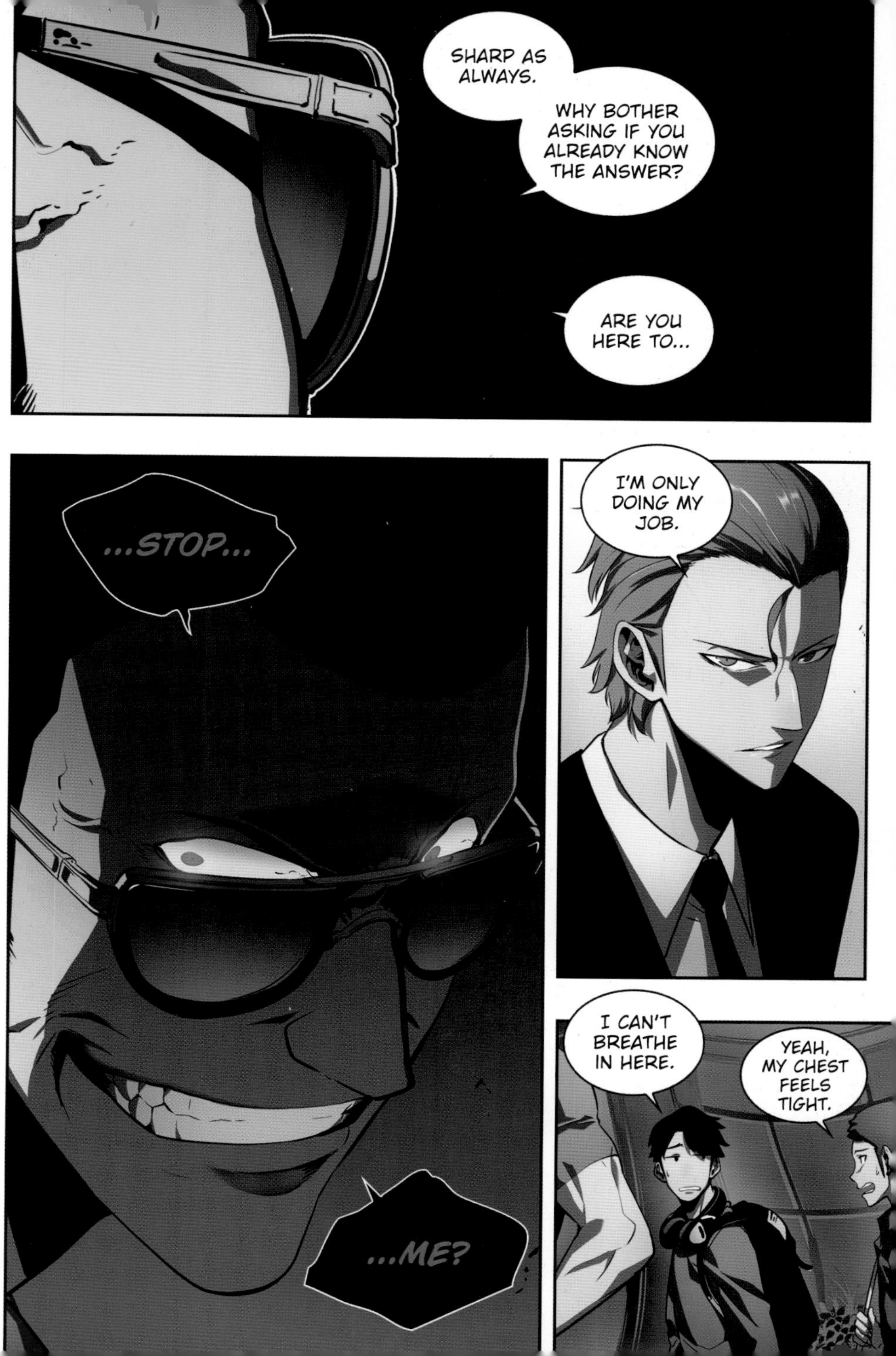
SHARP AS ALWAYS.
WHY BOTHER ASKING IF YOU ALREADY KNOW THE ANSWER?
ARE YOU HERE TO...
...STOP...
...ME?
I'M ONLY DOING MY JOB.
I CAN'T BREATHE IN HERE.
YEAH, MY CHEST FEELS TIGHT.

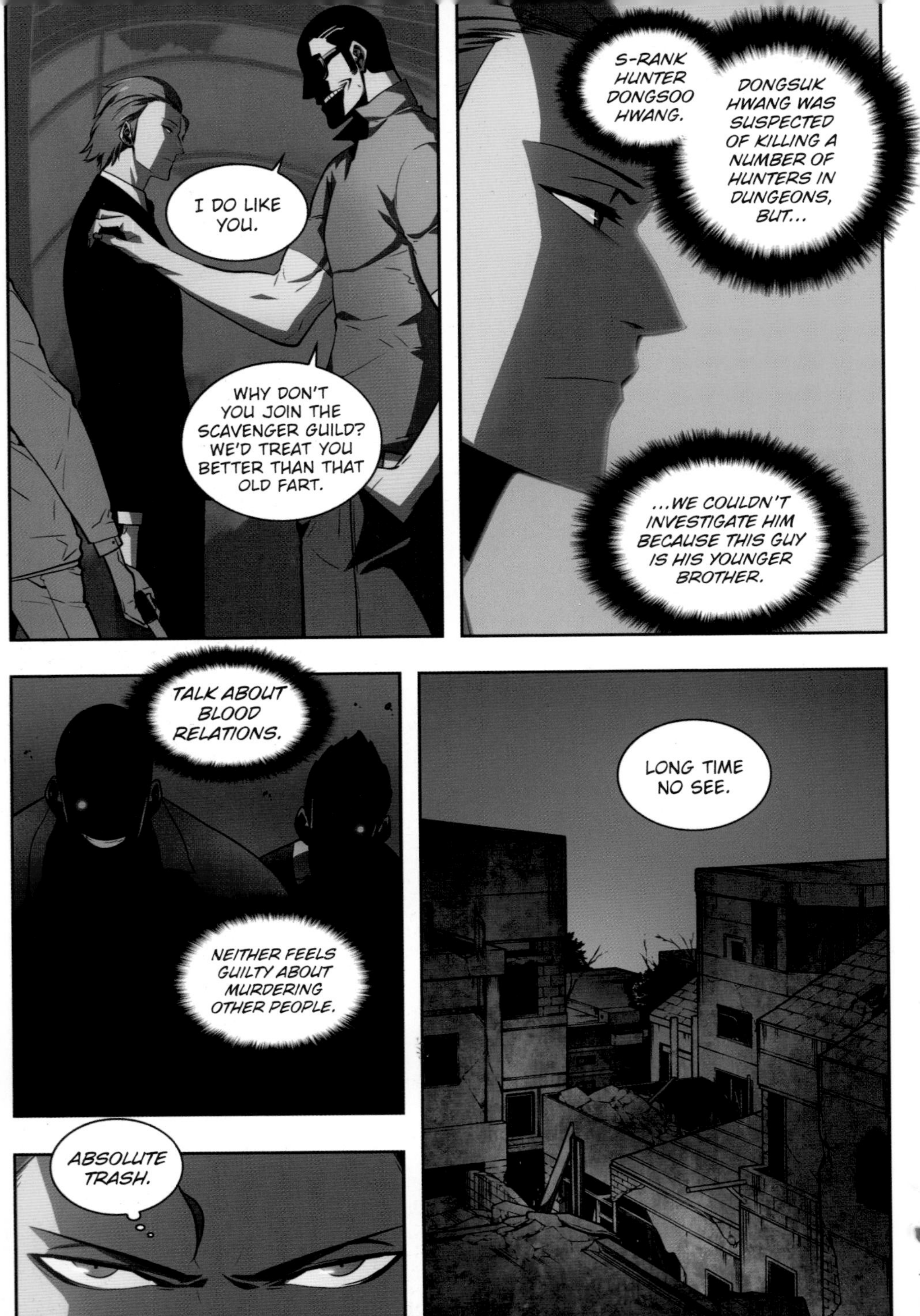
I DO LIKE YOU.
WHY DON'T YOU JOIN THE SCAVENGER GUILD? WE'D TREAT YOU BETTER THAN THAT OLD FART.
S-RANK HUNTER DONGSOO HWANG.
DONGSUK HWANG WAS SUSPECTED OF KILLING A NUMBER OF HUNTERS IN DUNGEONS, BUT...
...WE COULDN'T INVESTIGATE HIM BECAUSE THIS GUY IS HIS YOUNGER BROTHER.
TALK ABOUT BLOOD RELATIONS.
NEITHER FEELS GUILTY ABOUT MURDERING OTHER PEOPLE.
ABSOLUTE TRASH.
LONG TIME NO SEE.

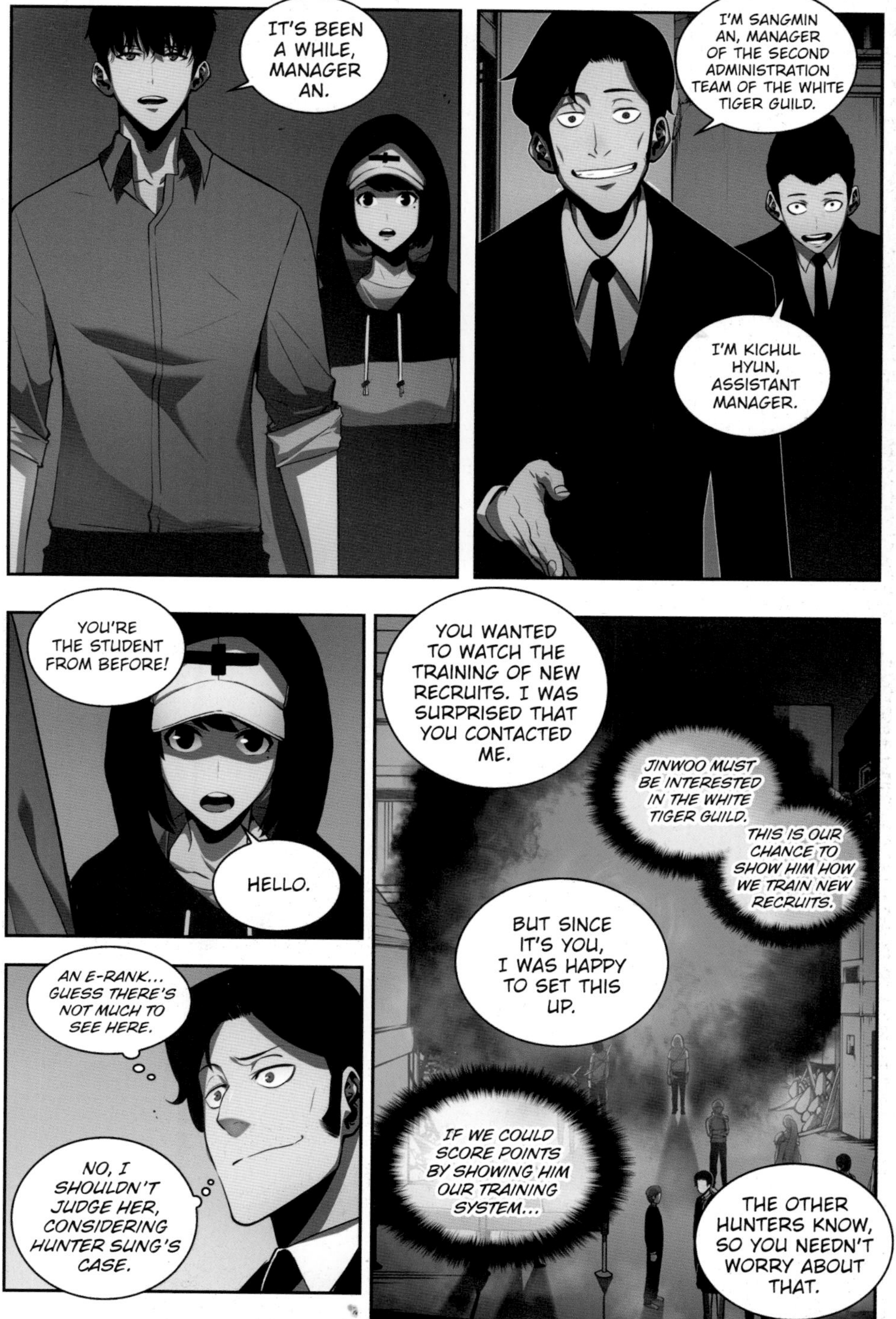
IT'S BEEN A WHILE, MANAGER AN.
I'M SANGMIN AN, MANAGER OF THE SECOND ADMINISTRATION TEAM OF THE WHITE TIGER GUILD.
I'M KICHUL HYUN, ASSISTANT MANAGER.
YOU'RE THE STUDENT FROM BEFORE!
HELLO.
AN E-RANK... GUESS THERE'S NOT MUCH TO SEE HERE.
NO, I SHOULDN'T JUDGE HER, CONSIDERING HUNTER SUNG'S CASE.
YOU WANTED TO WATCH THE TRAINING OF NEW RECRUITS. I WAS SURPRISED THAT YOU CONTACTED ME.
JINWOO MUST BE INTERESTED IN THE WHITE TIGER GUILD.
THIS IS OUR CHANCE TO SHOW HIM HOW WE TRAIN NEW RECRUITS.
BUT SINCE IT'S YOU, I WAS HAPPY TO SET THIS UP.
IF WE COULD SCORE POINTS BY SHOWING HIM OUR TRAINING SYSTEM...
THE OTHER HUNTERS KNOW, SO YOU NEEDN'T WORRY ABOUT THAT.

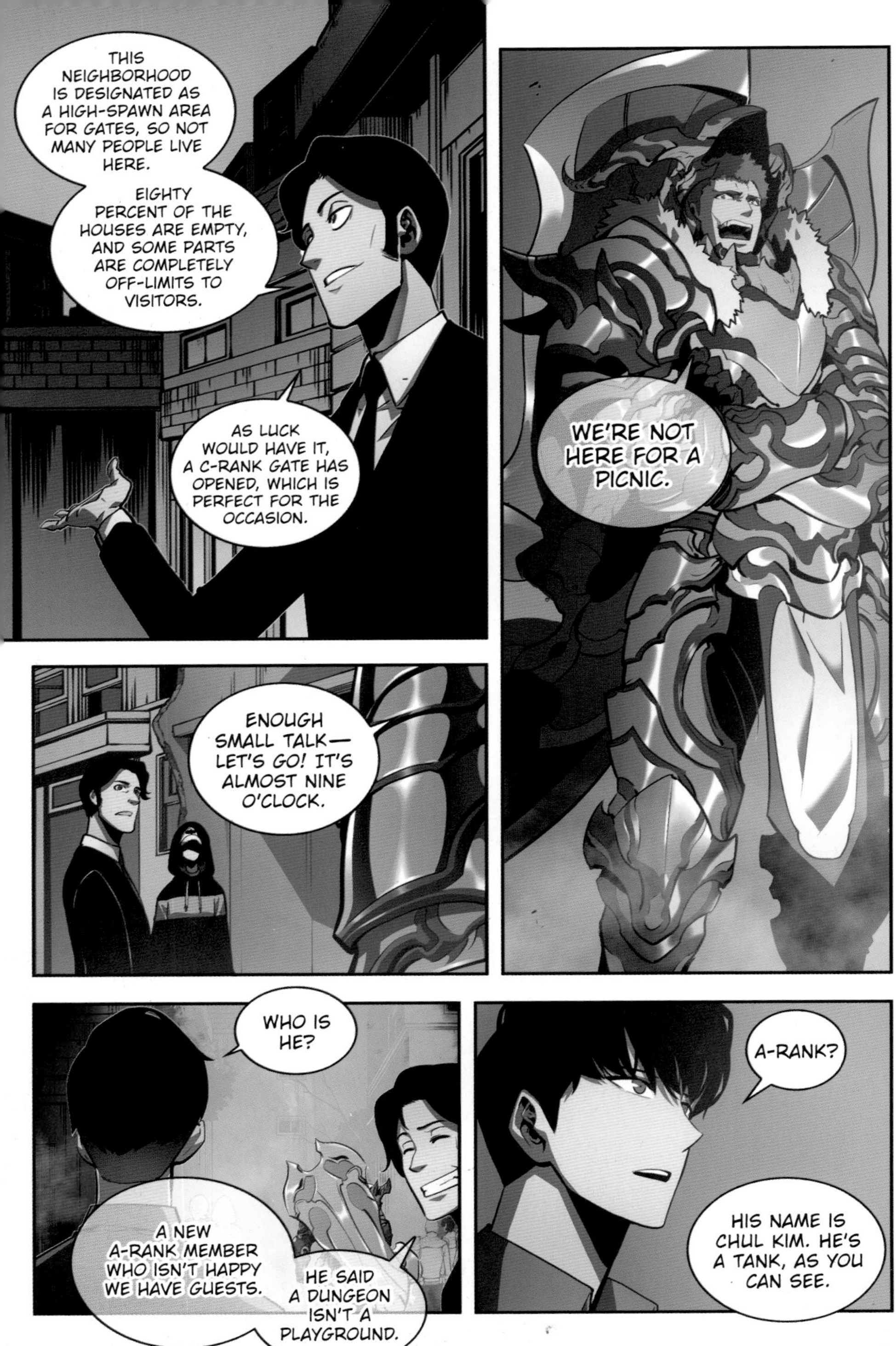
THIS NEIGHBORHOOD IS DESIGNATED AS A HIGH-SPAWN AREA FOR GATES, SO NOT MANY PEOPLE LIVE HERE.
EIGHTY PERCENT OF THE HOUSES ARE EMPTY, AND SOME PARTS ARE COMPLETELY OFF-LIMITS TO VISITORS.
AS LUCK WOULD HAVE IT, A C-RANK GATE HAS OPENED, WHICH IS PERFECT FOR THE OCCASION.
ENOUGH SMALL TALK—LET'S GO! IT'S ALMOST NINE O'CLOCK.
WE'RE NOT HERE FOR A PICNIC.
WHO IS HE?
A NEW A-RANK MEMBER WHO ISN'T HAPPY WE HAVE GUESTS.
HE SAID A DUNGEON ISN'T A PLAYGROUND.
A-RANK?
HIS NAME IS CHUL KIM. HE'S A TANK, AS YOU CAN SEE.

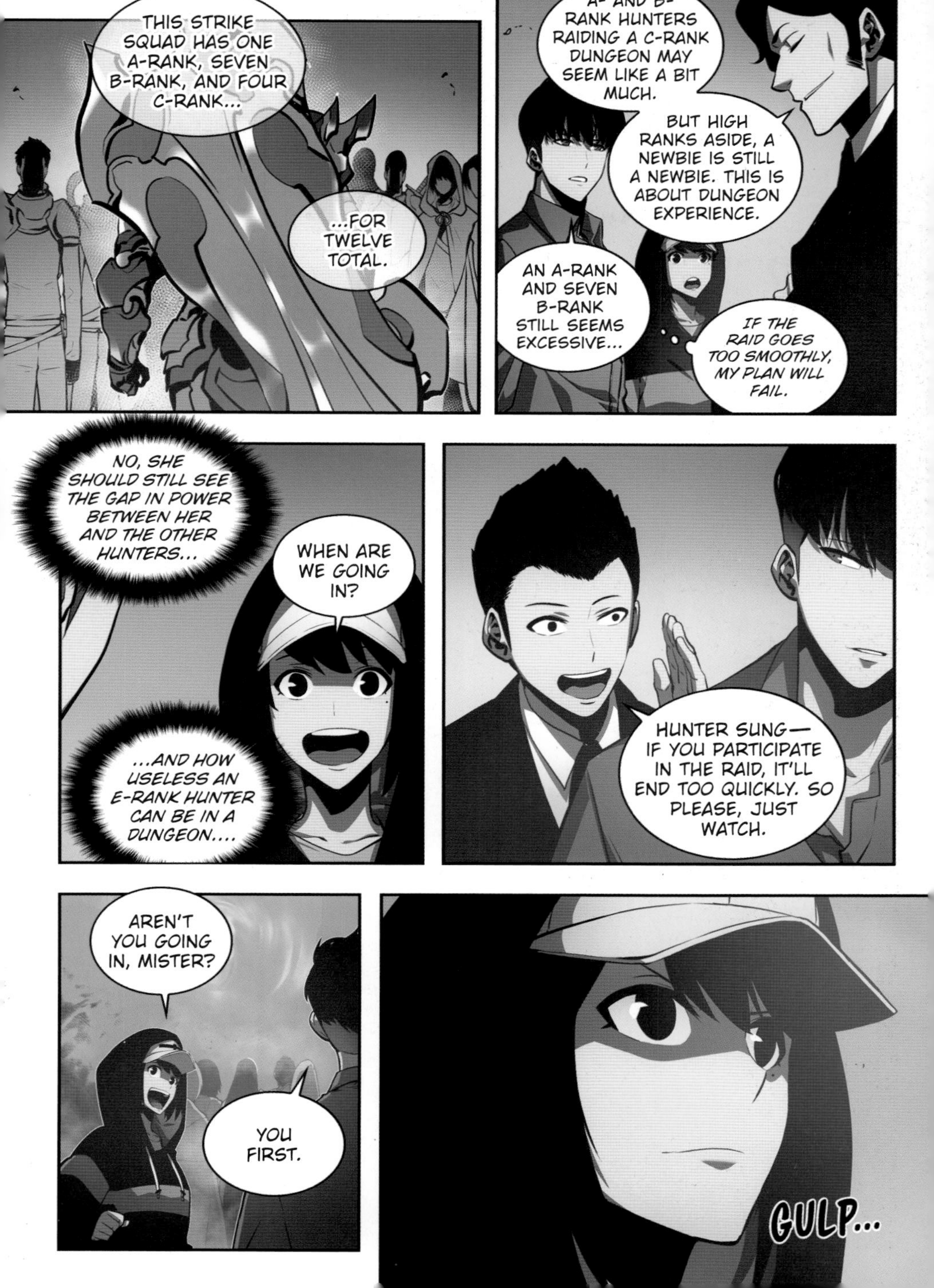
THIS STRIKE SQUAD HAS ONE A-RANK, SEVEN B-RANK, AND FOUR C-RANK...
...FOR TWELVE TOTAL.
A- AND B-RANK HUNTERS RAIDING A C-RANK DUNGEON MAY SEEM LIKE A BIT MUCH.
BUT HIGH RANKS ASIDE, A NEWBIE IS STILL A NEWBIE. THIS IS ABOUT DUNGEON EXPERIENCE.
AN A-RANK AND SEVEN B-RANK STILL SEEMS EXCESSIVE...
IF THE RAID GOES TOO SMOOTHLY, MY PLAN WILL FAIL.
NO, SHE SHOULD STILL SEE THE GAP IN POWER BETWEEN HER AND THE OTHER HUNTERS...
WHEN ARE WE GOING IN?
...AND HOW USELESS AN E-RANK HUNTER CAN BE IN A DUNGEON....
HUNTER SUNG—IF YOU PARTICIPATE IN THE RAID, IT'LL END TOO QUICKLY. SO PLEASE, JUST WATCH.
AREN'T YOU GOING IN, MISTER?
YOU FIRST.
GULP...

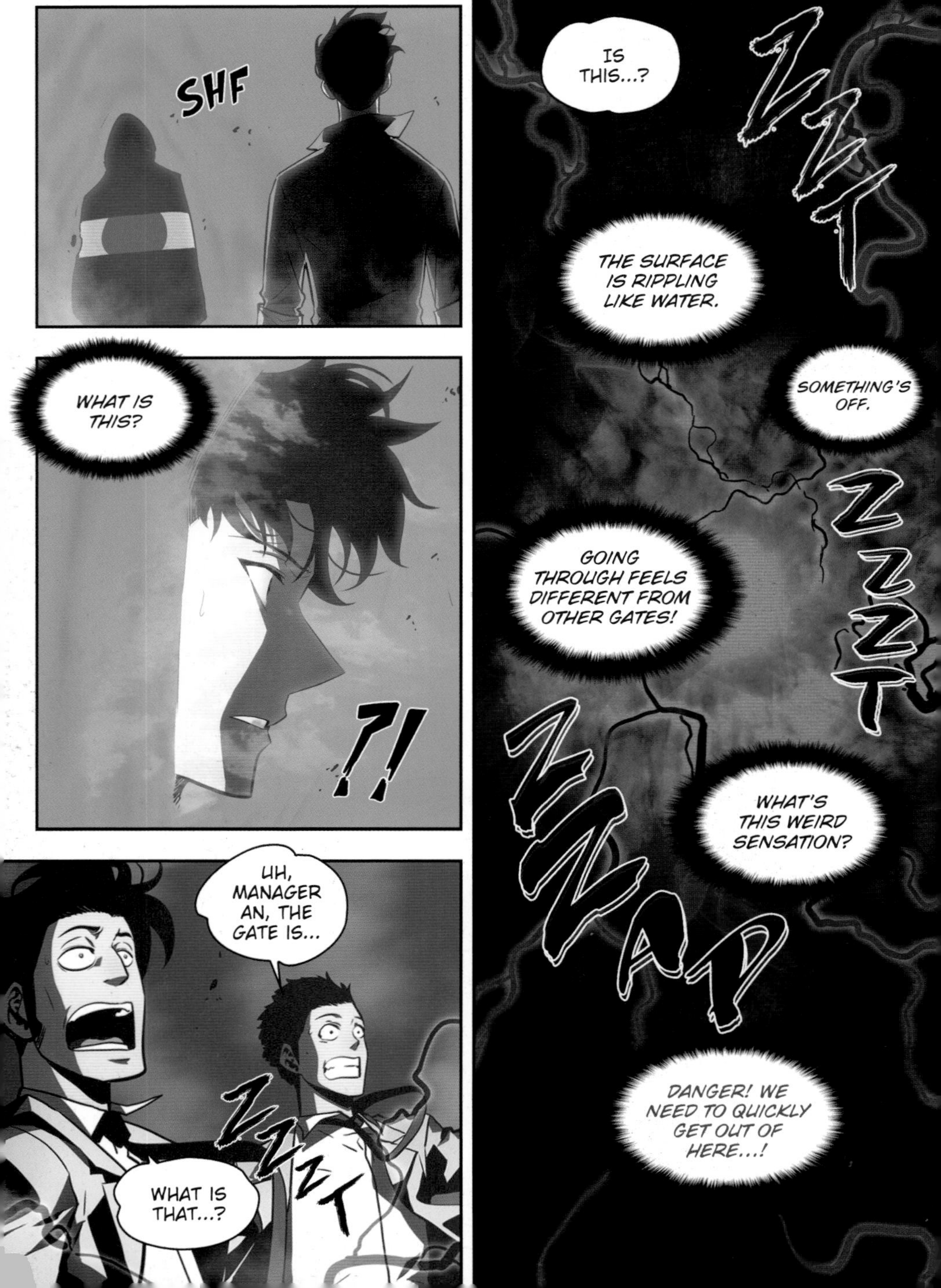
SHF
WHAT IS THIS?
?!
UH, MANAGER AN, THE GATE IS...
WHAT IS THAT...?
ZZZT
IS THIS...?
ZZZT
THE SURFACE IS RIPPLING LIKE WATER.
SOMETHING'S OFF.
ZZZT
GOING THROUGH FEELS DIFFERENT FROM OTHER GATES!
ZZZAP
WHAT'S THIS WEIRD SENSATION?
DANGER! WE NEED TO QUICKLY GET OUT OF HERE...!

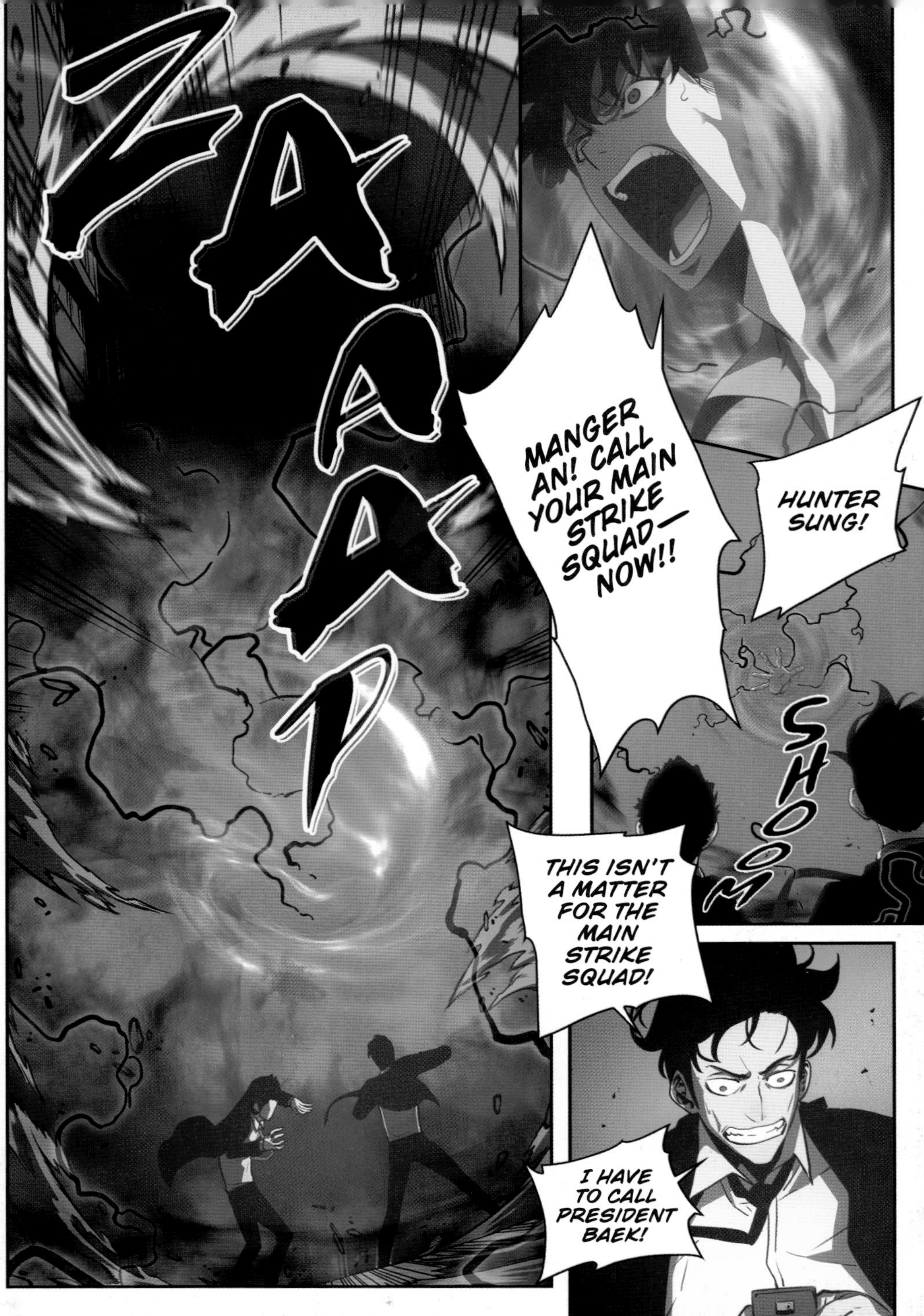
ZAAAP
MANGER AN! CALL YOUR MAIN STRIKE SQUAD—NOW!!
HUNTER SUNG!
SHOOOM
THIS ISN'T A MATTER FOR THE MAIN STRIKE SQUAD!
I HAVE TO CALL PRESIDENT BAEK!

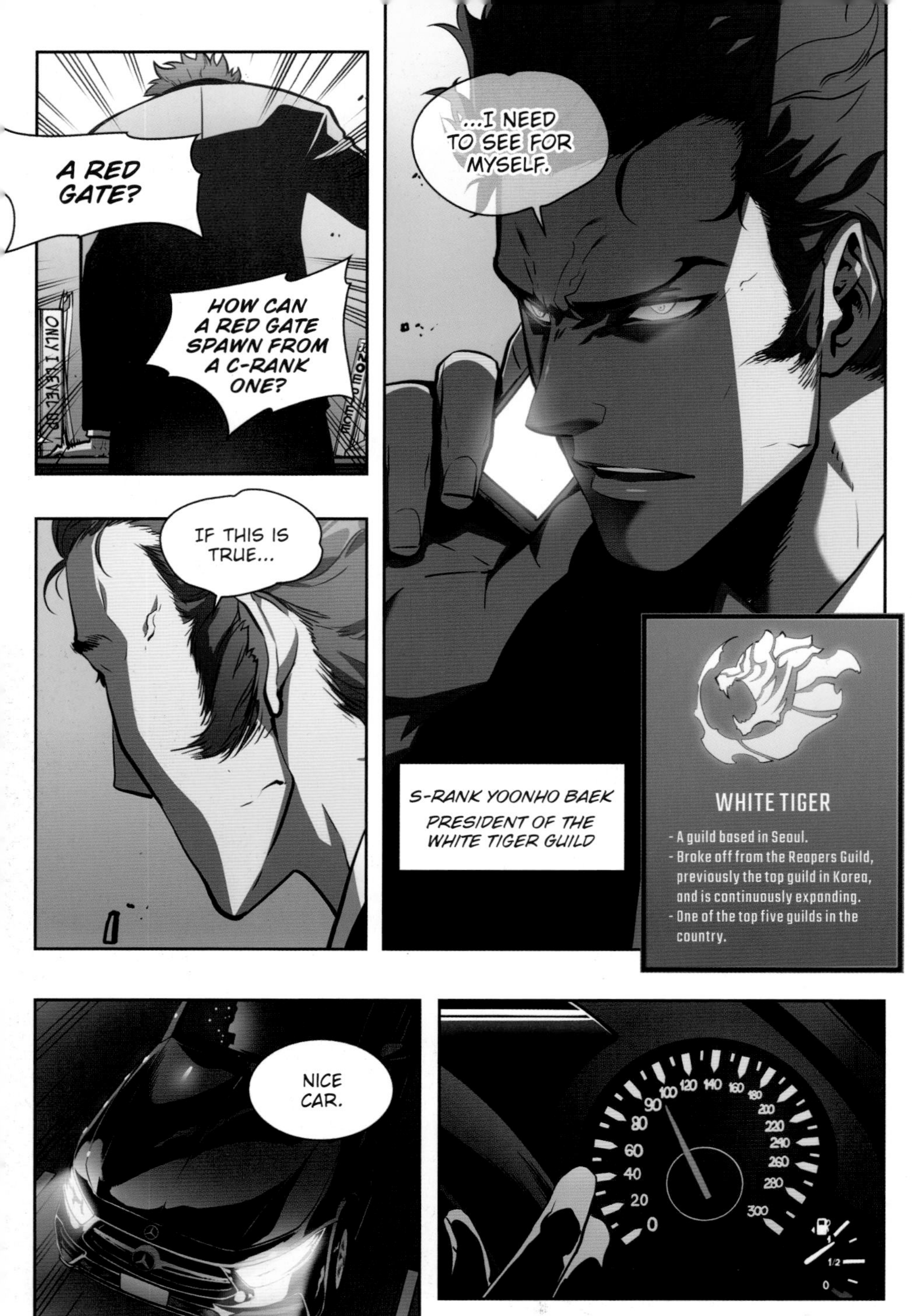
A RED GATE?
HOW CAN A RED GATE SPAWN FROM A C-RANK ONE?
IF THIS IS TRUE...
...I NEED TO SEE FOR MYSELF.
S-RANK YOONHO BAEK PRESIDENT OF THE WHITE TIGER GUILD
WHITE TIGER
- A guild based in Seoul.
- Broke off from the Reapers Guild, previously the top guild in Korea, and is continuously expanding.
- One of the top five guilds in the country.
NICE CAR.

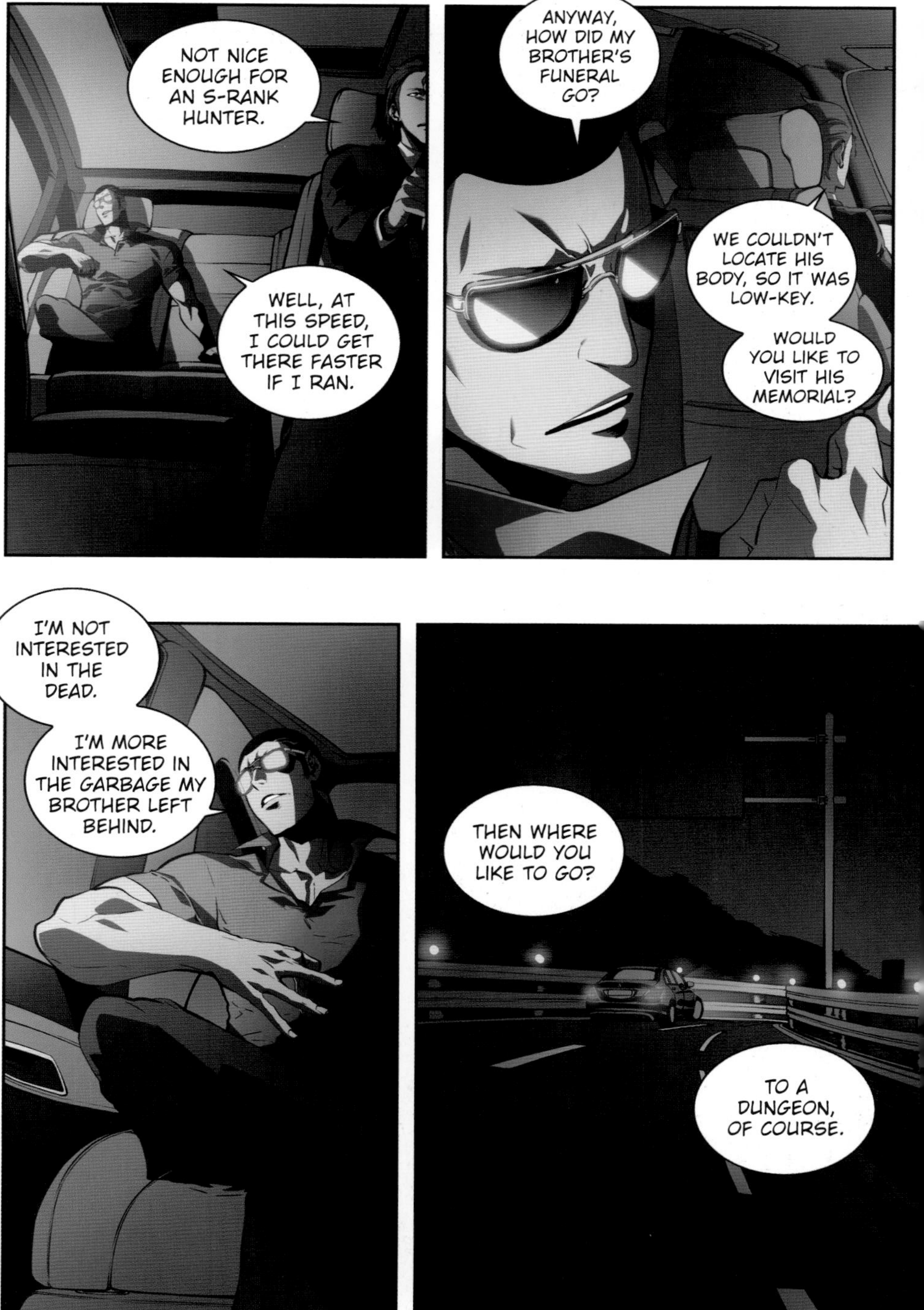
NOT NICE ENOUGH FOR AN S-RANK HUNTER.
WELL, AT THIS SPEED, I COULD GET THERE FASTER IF I RAN.
ANYWAY, HOW DID MY BROTHER'S FUNERAL GO?
WE COULDN'T LOCATE HIS BODY, SO IT WAS LOW-KEY.
WOULD YOU LIKE TO VISIT HIS MEMORIAL?
I'M NOT INTERESTED IN THE DEAD.
I'M MORE INTERESTED IN THE GARBAGE MY BROTHER LEFT BEHIND.
THEN WHERE WOULD YOU LIKE TO GO?
TO A DUNGEON, OF COURSE.

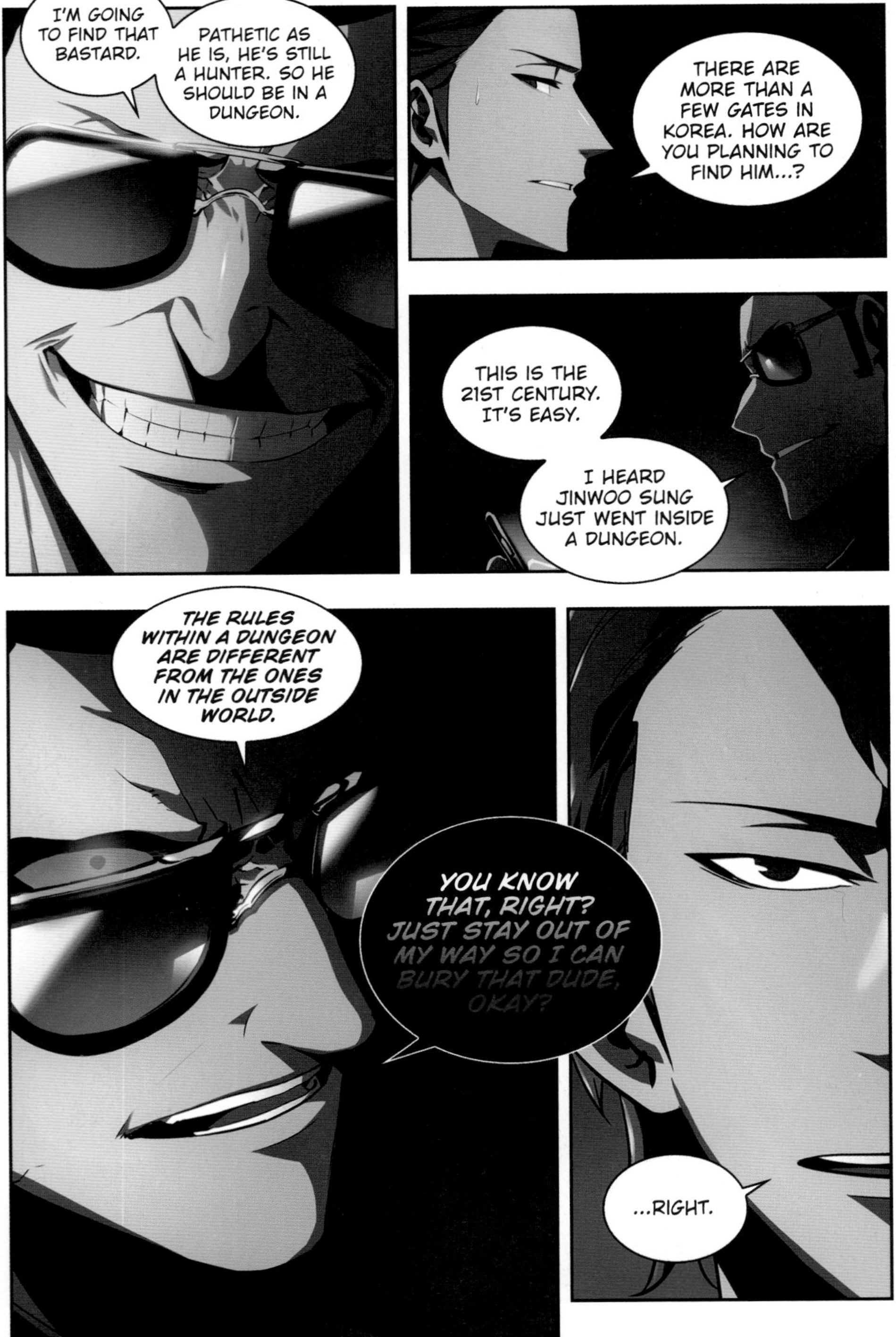
I'M GOING TO FIND THAT BASTARD.
PATHETIC AS HE IS, HE'S STILL A HUNTER. SO HE SHOULD BE IN A DUNGEON.
THERE ARE MORE THAN A FEW GATES IN KOREA. HOW ARE YOU PLANNING TO FIND HIM...?
THIS IS THE 21ST CENTURY. IT'S EASY.
I HEARD JINWOO SUNG JUST WENT INSIDE A DUNGEON.
THE RULES WITHIN A DUNGEON ARE DIFFERENT FROM THE ONES IN THE OUTSIDE WORLD.
YOU KNOW THAT, RIGHT? JUST STAY OUT OF MY WAY SO I CAN BURY THAT DUDE, OKAY?
...RIGHT.

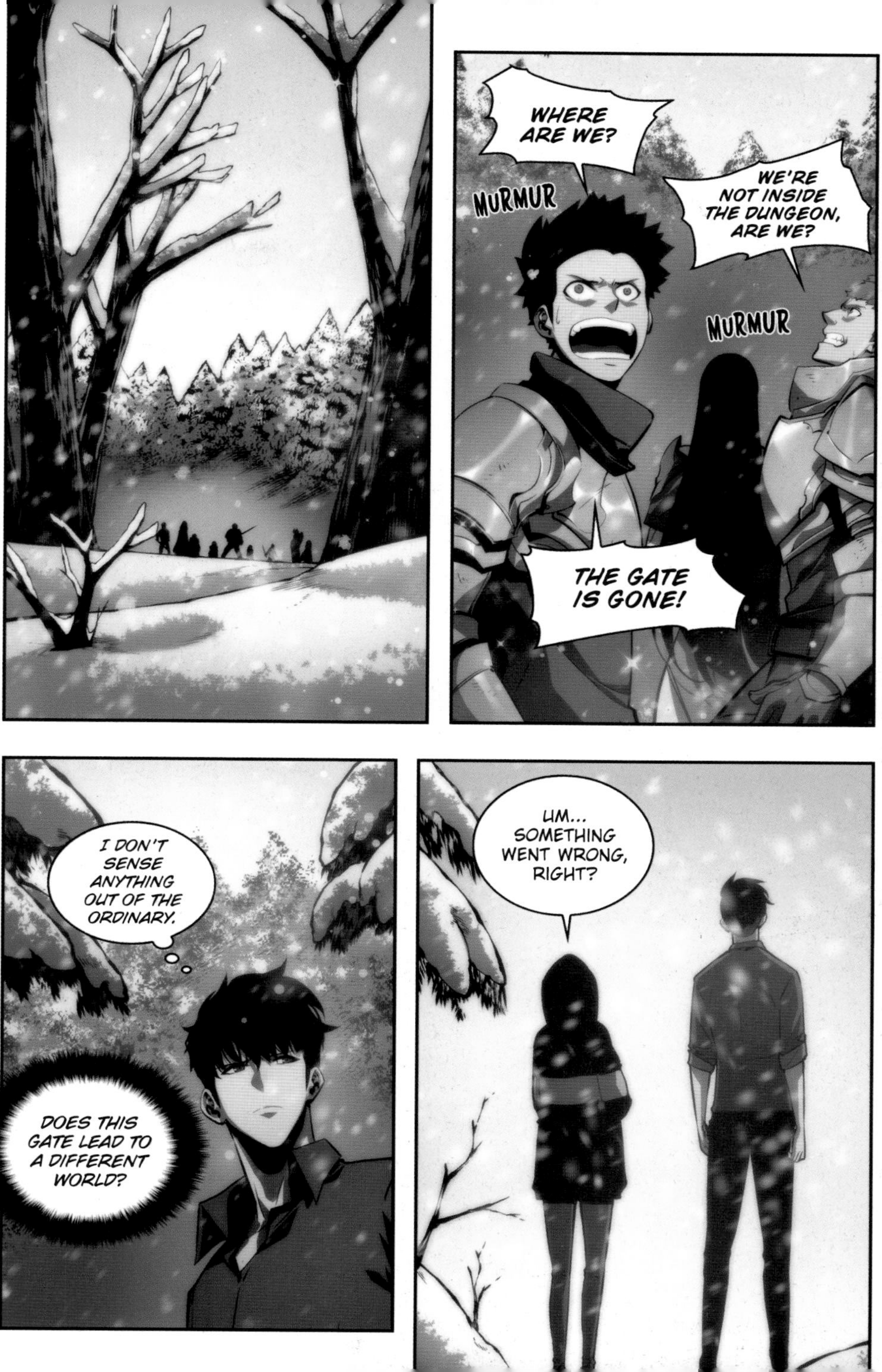
WHERE ARE WE?
MURMUR
WE'RE NOT INSIDE THE DUNGEON, ARE WE?
MURMUR
THE GATE IS GONE!
I DON'T SENSE ANYTHING OUT OF THE ORDINARY.
DOES THIS GATE LEAD TO A DIFFERENT WORLD?
UM... SOMETHING WENT WRONG, RIGHT?

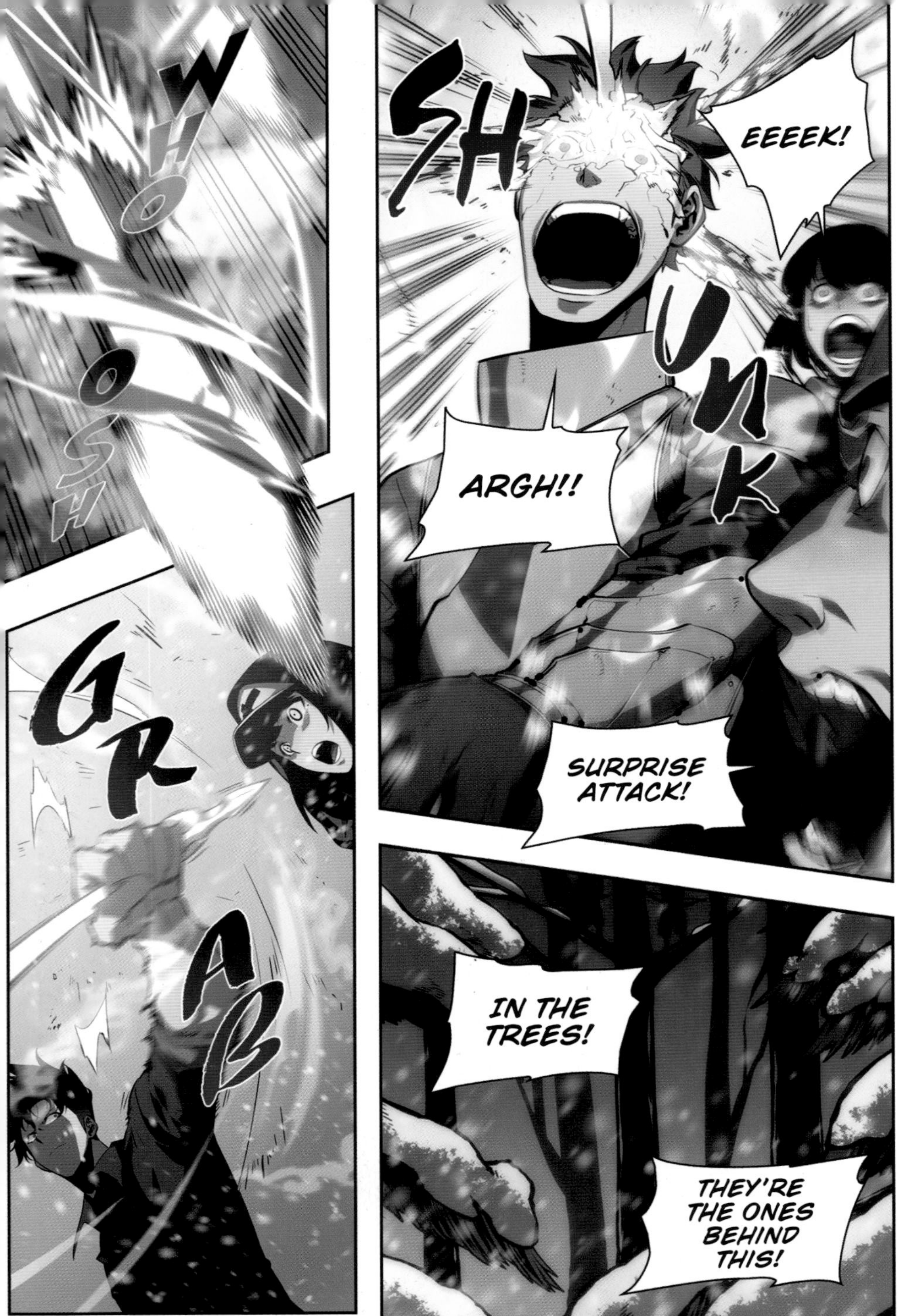
WHOOSH
SHUNK
EEEEK!
ARGH!!
SURPRISE ATTACK!
GRAB
IN THE TREES!
THEY'RE THE ONES BEHIND THIS!

ICE ELVES?!

ICE ELVES...
THAT'S WHY
WE COULDN'T
SENSE THEIR
PRESENCE.

ICE ELVES—

HUNTERS WHO
HAVE FOUGHT
THEM CALL THEM
BY A DIFFERENT
NAME.

IT'S COMPLETELY DIFFERENT
FROM A PRETTY WORD LIKE
"ELF," BUT IT'S ONE THEY
EARNED FROM THEIR BRUTAL
ATTACKS ON HUNTERS—

SMIRK

ICE
SLAYERS.

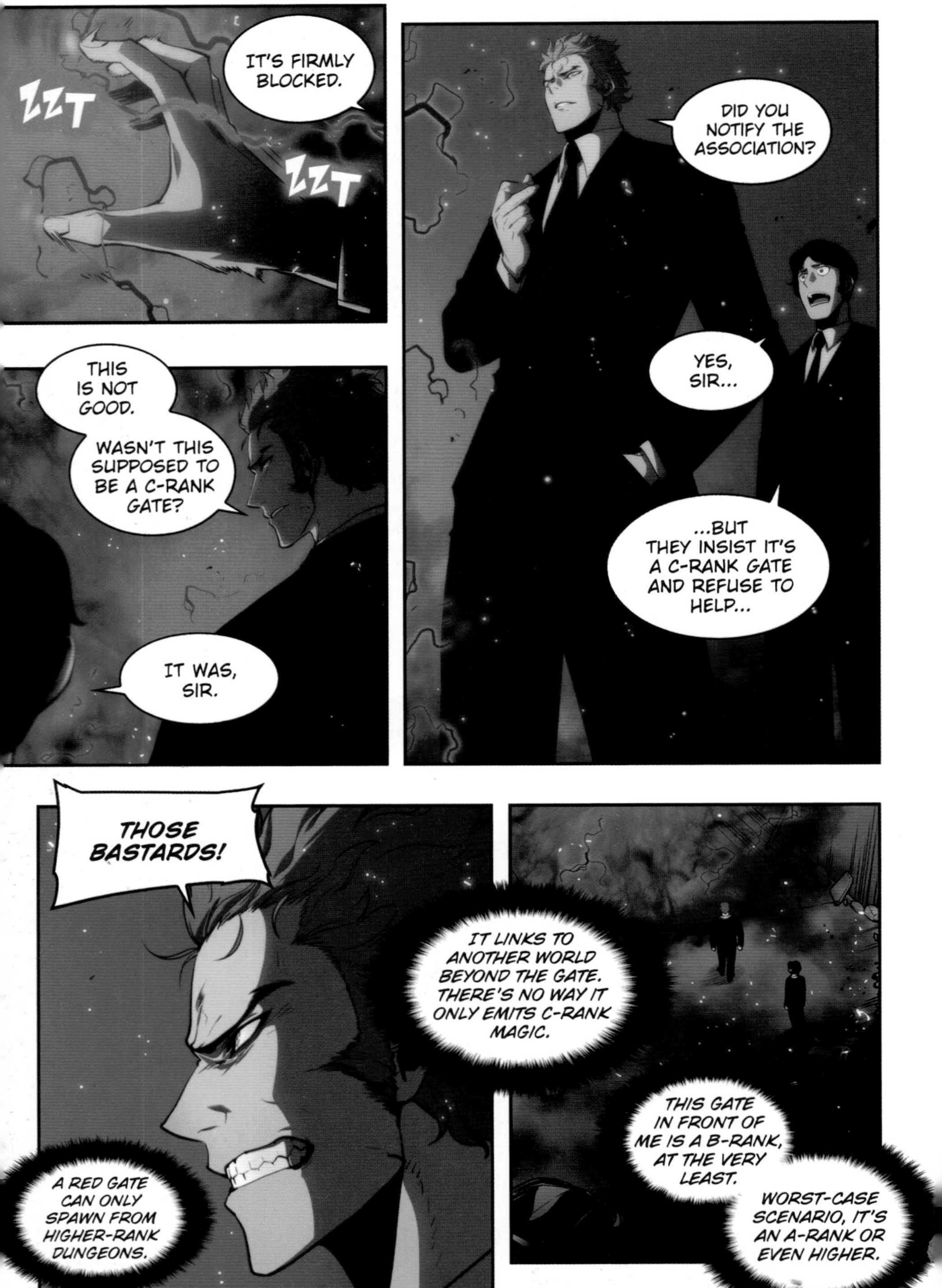
IT'S FIRMLY BLOCKED.
ZZT
ZZT
THIS IS NOT GOOD.
WASN'T THIS SUPPOSED TO BE A C-RANK GATE?
IT WAS, SIR.
DID YOU NOTIFY THE ASSOCIATION?
YES, SIR...
...BUT THEY INSIST IT'S A C-RANK GATE AND REFUSE TO HELP...
THOSE BASTARDS!
IT LINKS TO ANOTHER WORLD BEYOND THE GATE. THERE'S NO WAY IT ONLY EMITS C-RANK MAGIC.
A RED GATE CAN ONLY SPAWN FROM HIGHER-RANK DUNGEONS.
THIS GATE IN FRONT OF ME IS A B-RANK, AT THE VERY LEAST.
WORST-CASE SCENARIO, IT'S AN A-RANK OR EVEN HIGHER.

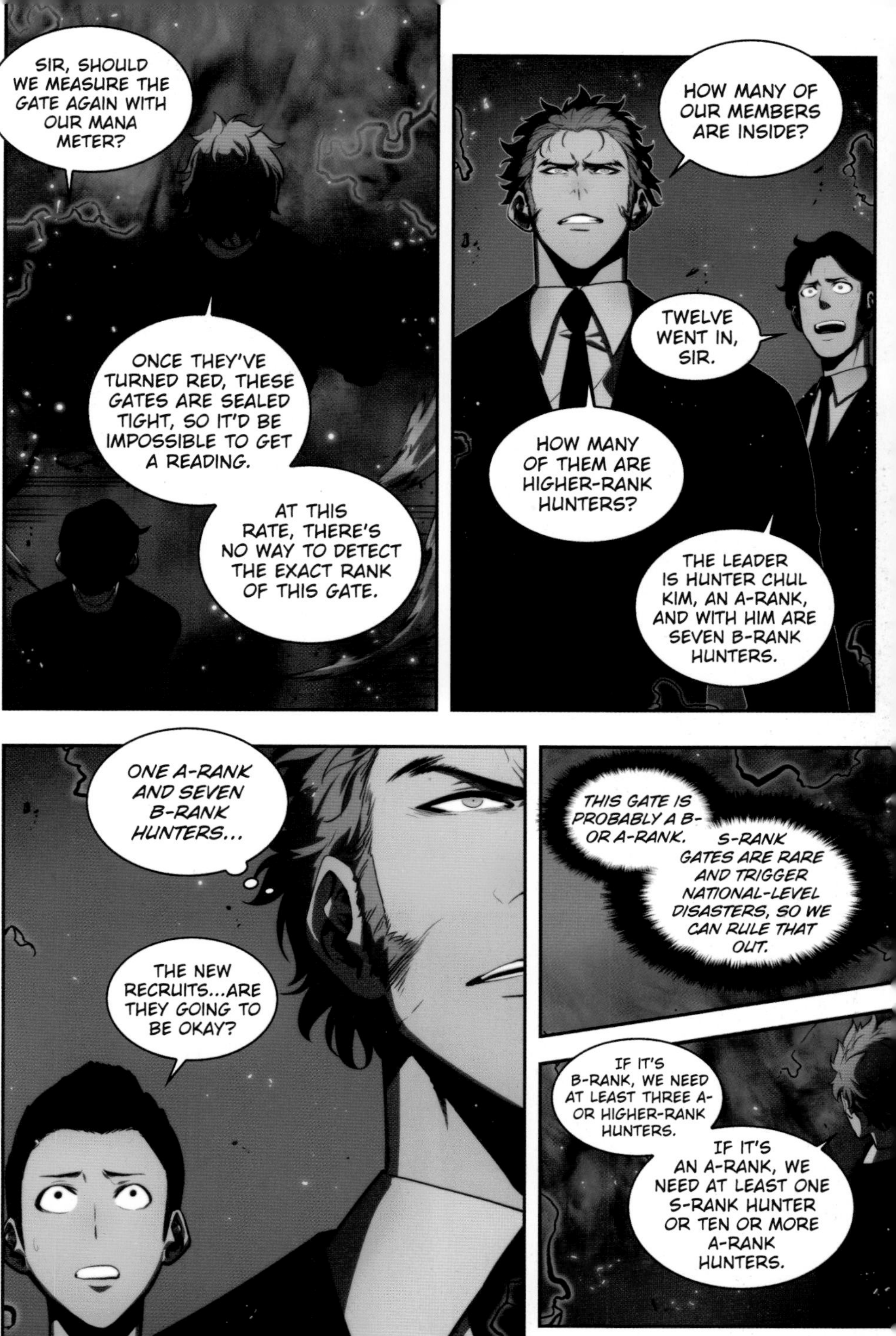
SIR, SHOULD WE MEASURE THE GATE AGAIN WITH OUR MANA METER?
ONCE THEY'VE TURNED RED, THESE GATES ARE SEALED TIGHT, SO IT'D BE IMPOSSIBLE TO GET A READING.
AT THIS RATE, THERE'S NO WAY TO DETECT THE EXACT RANK OF THIS GATE.
HOW MANY OF OUR MEMBERS ARE INSIDE?
TWELVE WENT IN, SIR.
HOW MANY OF THEM ARE HIGHER-RANK HUNTERS?
THE LEADER IS HUNTER CHUL KIM, AN A-RANK, AND WITH HIM ARE SEVEN B-RANK HUNTERS.
ONE A-RANK AND SEVEN B-RANK HUNTERS...
THE NEW RECRUITS...ARE THEY GOING TO BE OKAY?
THIS GATE IS PROBABLY A B- OR A-RANK.
S-RANK GATES ARE RARE AND TRIGGER NATIONAL-LEVEL DISASTERS, SO WE CAN RULE THAT OUT.
IF IT'S B-RANK, WE NEED AT LEAST THREE A- OR HIGHER-RANK HUNTERS.
IF IT'S AN A-RANK, WE NEED AT LEAST ONE S-RANK HUNTER OR TEN OR MORE A-RANK HUNTERS.

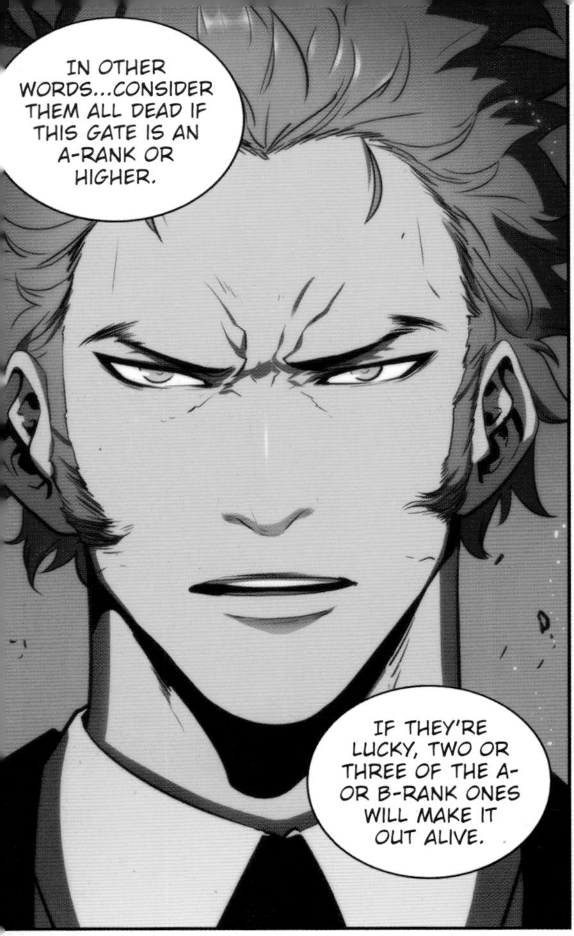
IN OTHER WORDS...CONSIDER THEM ALL DEAD IF THIS GATE IS AN A-RANK OR HIGHER.
IF THEY'RE LUCKY, TWO OR THREE OF THE A- OR B-RANK ONES WILL MAKE IT OUT ALIVE.
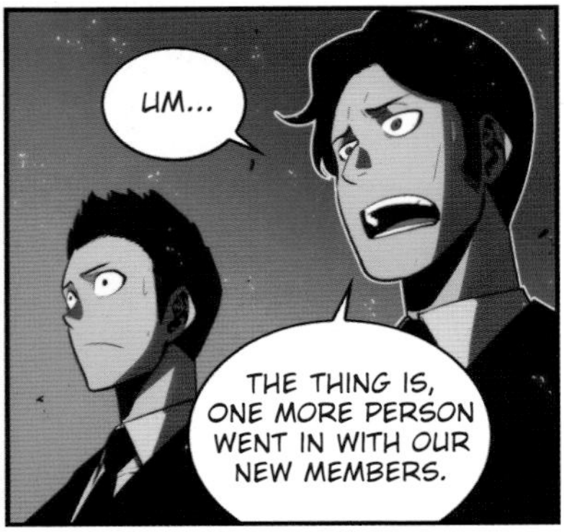
UM...
THE THING IS, ONE MORE PERSON WENT IN WITH OUR NEW MEMBERS.
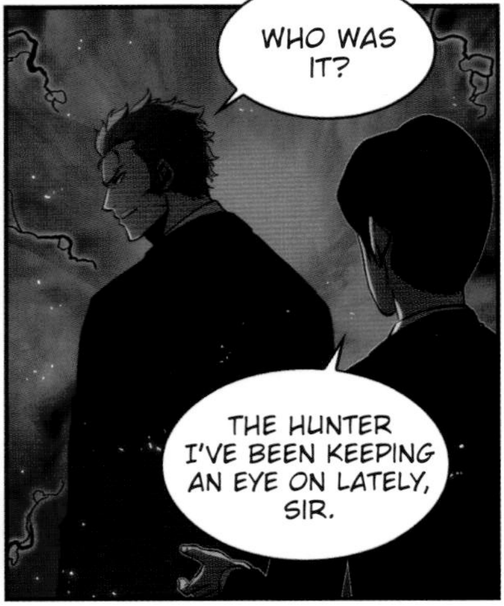
WHO WAS IT?
THE HUNTER I'VE BEEN KEEPING AN EYE ON LATELY, SIR.
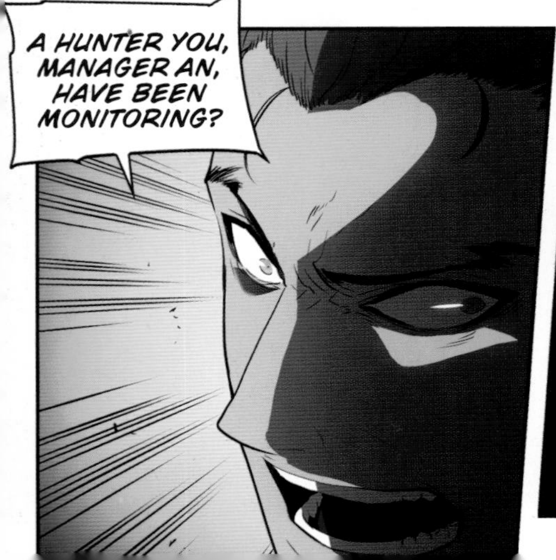
A HUNTER YOU, MANAGER AN, HAVE BEEN MONITORING?
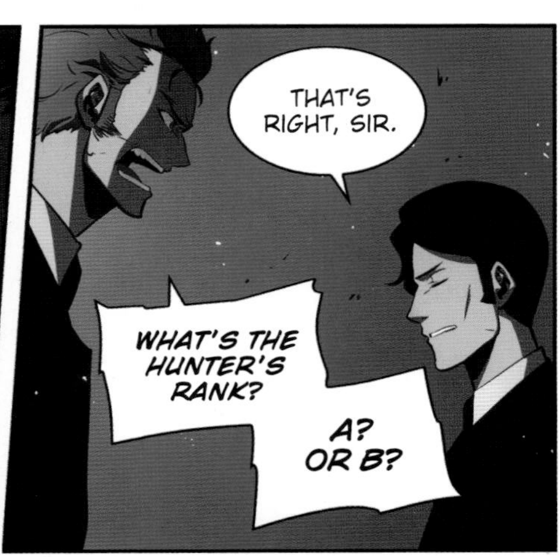
THAT'S RIGHT, SIR.
WHAT'S THE HUNTER'S RANK?
A? OR B?

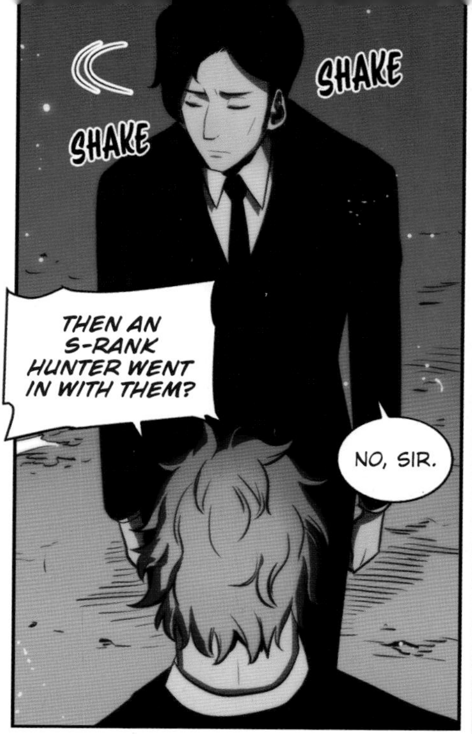
SHAKE
SHAKE
THEN AN S-RANK HUNTER WENT IN WITH THEM?
NO, SIR.
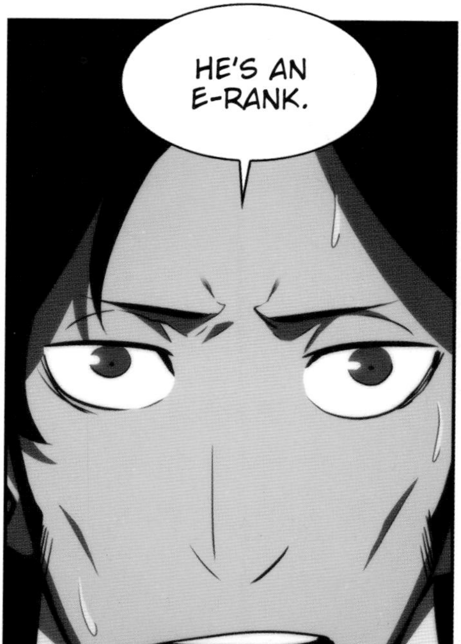
HE'S AN E-RANK.
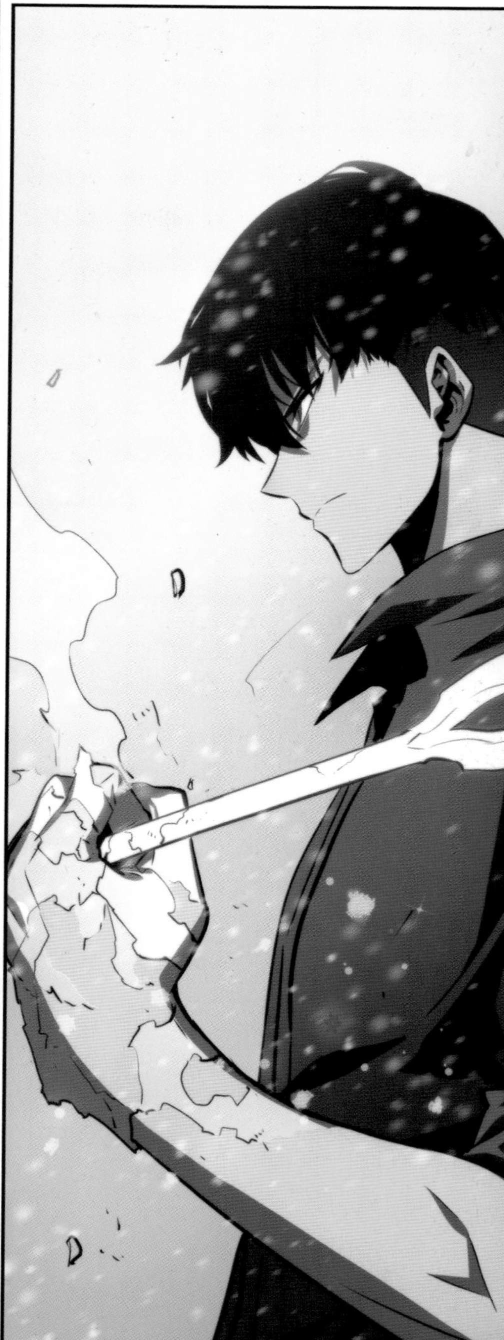

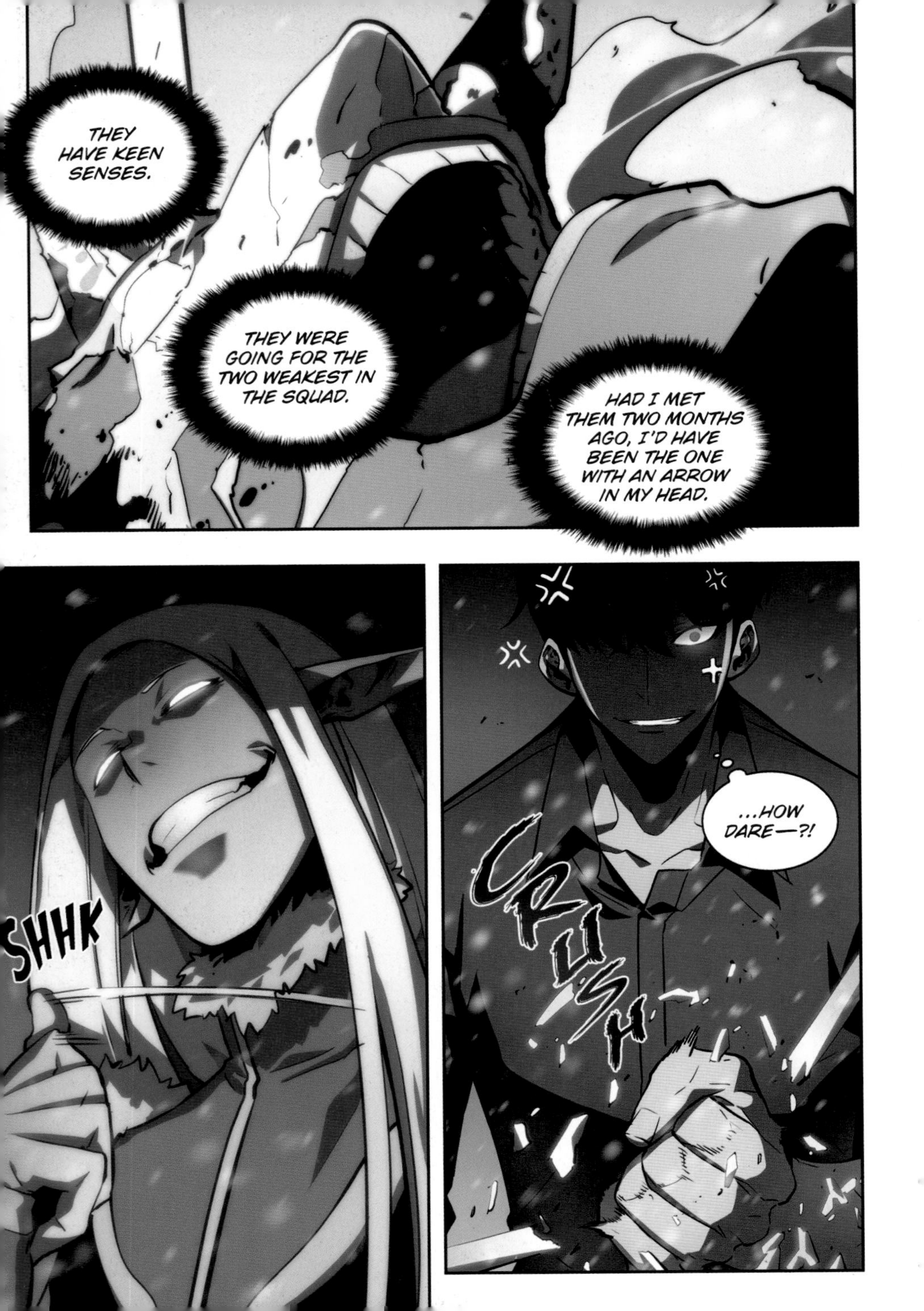
THEY HAVE KEEN SENSES.
THEY WERE GOING FOR THE TWO WEAKEST IN THE SQUAD.
HAD I MET THEM TWO MONTHS AGO, I'D HAVE BEEN THE ONE WITH AN ARROW IN MY HEAD.
SHHK
...HOW DARE—?!
CRUSH

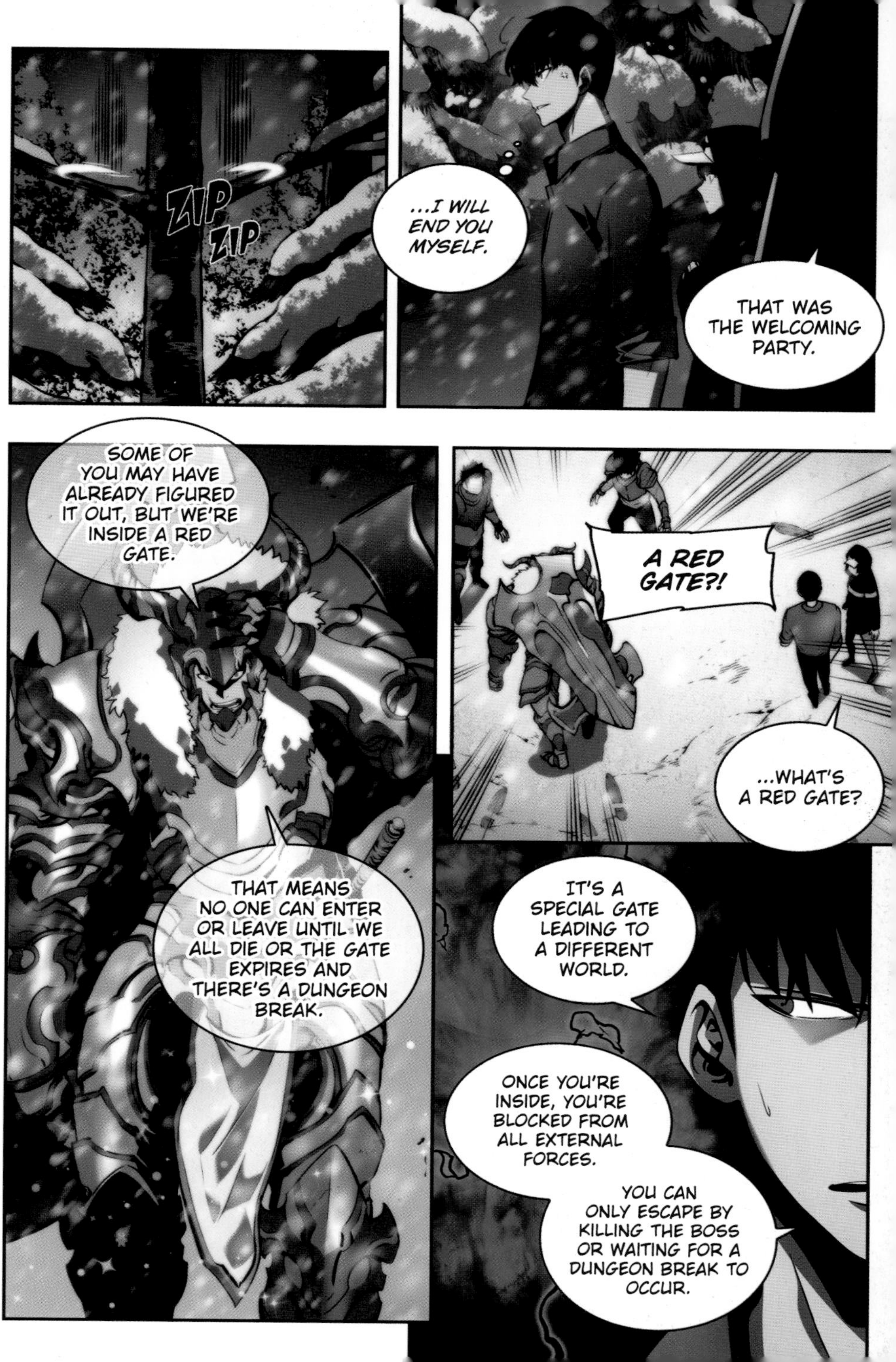
ZIP
ZIP
...I WILL END YOU MYSELF.
THAT WAS THE WELCOMING PARTY.
SOME OF YOU MAY HAVE ALREADY FIGURED IT OUT, BUT WE'RE INSIDE A RED GATE.
THAT MEANS NO ONE CAN ENTER OR LEAVE UNTIL WE ALL DIE OR THE GATE EXPIRES AND THERE'S A DUNGEON BREAK.
A RED GATE?!
...WHAT'S A RED GATE?
IT'S A SPECIAL GATE LEADING TO A DIFFERENT WORLD.
ONCE YOU'RE INSIDE, YOU'RE BLOCKED FROM ALL EXTERNAL FORCES.
YOU CAN ONLY ESCAPE BY KILLING THE BOSS OR WAITING FOR A DUNGEON BREAK TO OCCUR.

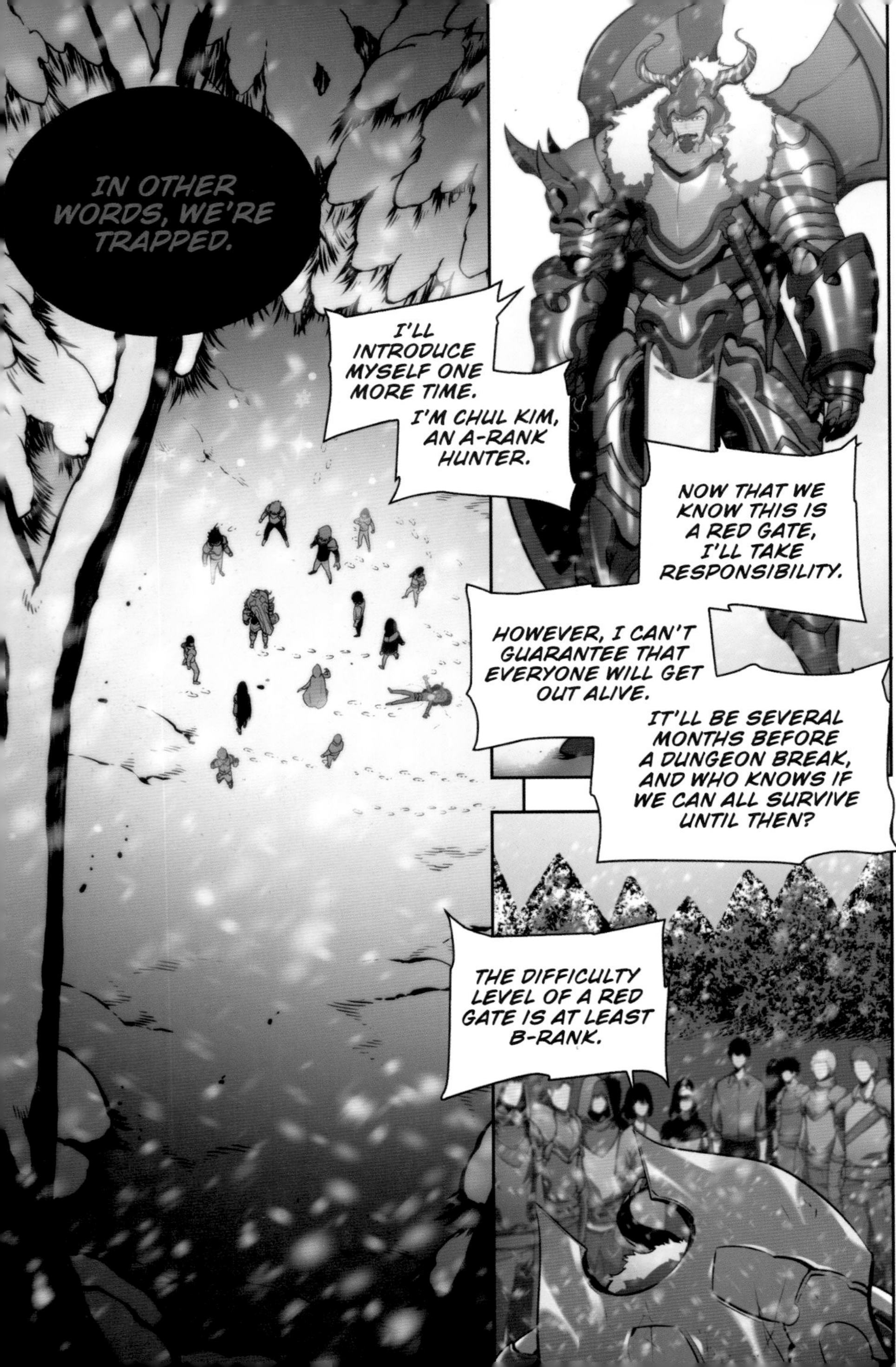
IN OTHER WORDS, WE'RE TRAPPED.
I'LL INTRODUCE MYSELF ONE MORE TIME.
I'M CHUL KIM, AN A-RANK HUNTER.
NOW THAT WE KNOW THIS IS A RED GATE, I'LL TAKE RESPONSIBILITY.
HOWEVER, I CAN'T GUARANTEE THAT EVERYONE WILL GET OUT ALIVE.
IT'LL BE SEVERAL MONTHS BEFORE A DUNGEON BREAK, AND WHO KNOWS IF WE CAN ALL SURVIVE UNTIL THEN?
THE DIFFICULTY LEVEL OF A RED GATE IS AT LEAST B-RANK.

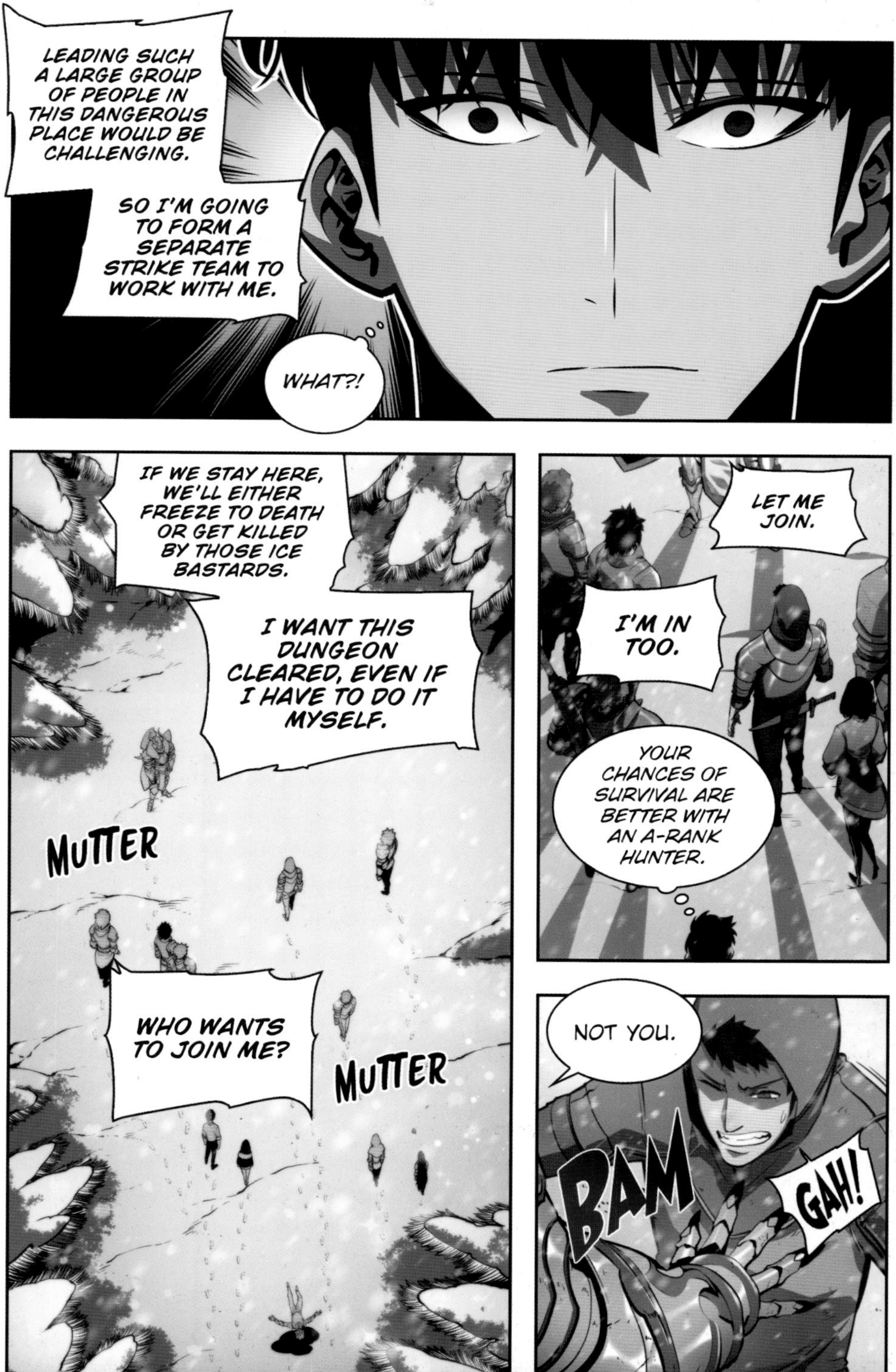
LEADING SUCH A LARGE GROUP OF PEOPLE IN THIS DANGEROUS PLACE WOULD BE CHALLENGING.
SO I'M GOING TO FORM A SEPARATE STRIKE TEAM TO WORK WITH ME.
WHAT?!
IF WE STAY HERE, WE'LL EITHER FREEZE TO DEATH OR GET KILLED BY THOSE ICE BASTARDS.
I WANT THIS DUNGEON CLEARED, EVEN IF I HAVE TO DO IT MYSELF.
MUTTER
WHO WANTS TO JOIN ME?
MUTTER
LET ME JOIN.
I'M IN TOO.
YOUR CHANCES OF SURVIVAL ARE BETTER WITH AN A-RANK HUNTER.
NOT YOU.
BAM
GAH!

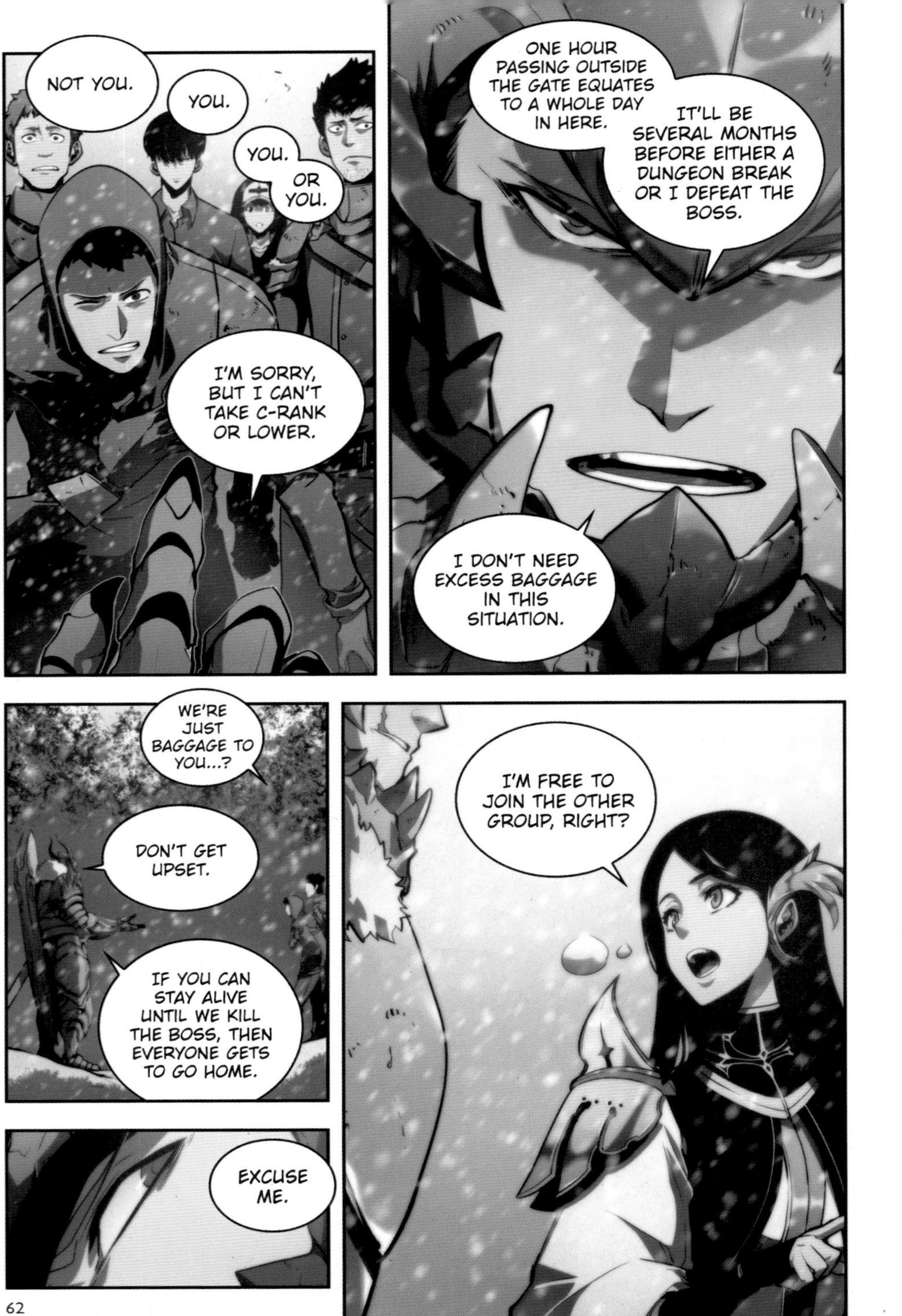
NOT YOU.
YOU.
YOU.
OR YOU.
I'M SORRY, BUT I CAN'T TAKE C-RANK OR LOWER.
ONE HOUR PASSING OUTSIDE THE GATE EQUATES TO A WHOLE DAY IN HERE.
IT'LL BE SEVERAL MONTHS BEFORE EITHER A DUNGEON BREAK OR I DEFEAT THE BOSS.
I DON'T NEED EXCESS BAGGAGE IN THIS SITUATION.
WE'RE JUST BAGGAGE TO YOU...?
DON'T GET UPSET.
IF YOU CAN STAY ALIVE UNTIL WE KILL THE BOSS, THEN EVERYONE GETS TO GO HOME.
EXCUSE ME.
I'M FREE TO JOIN THE OTHER GROUP, RIGHT?

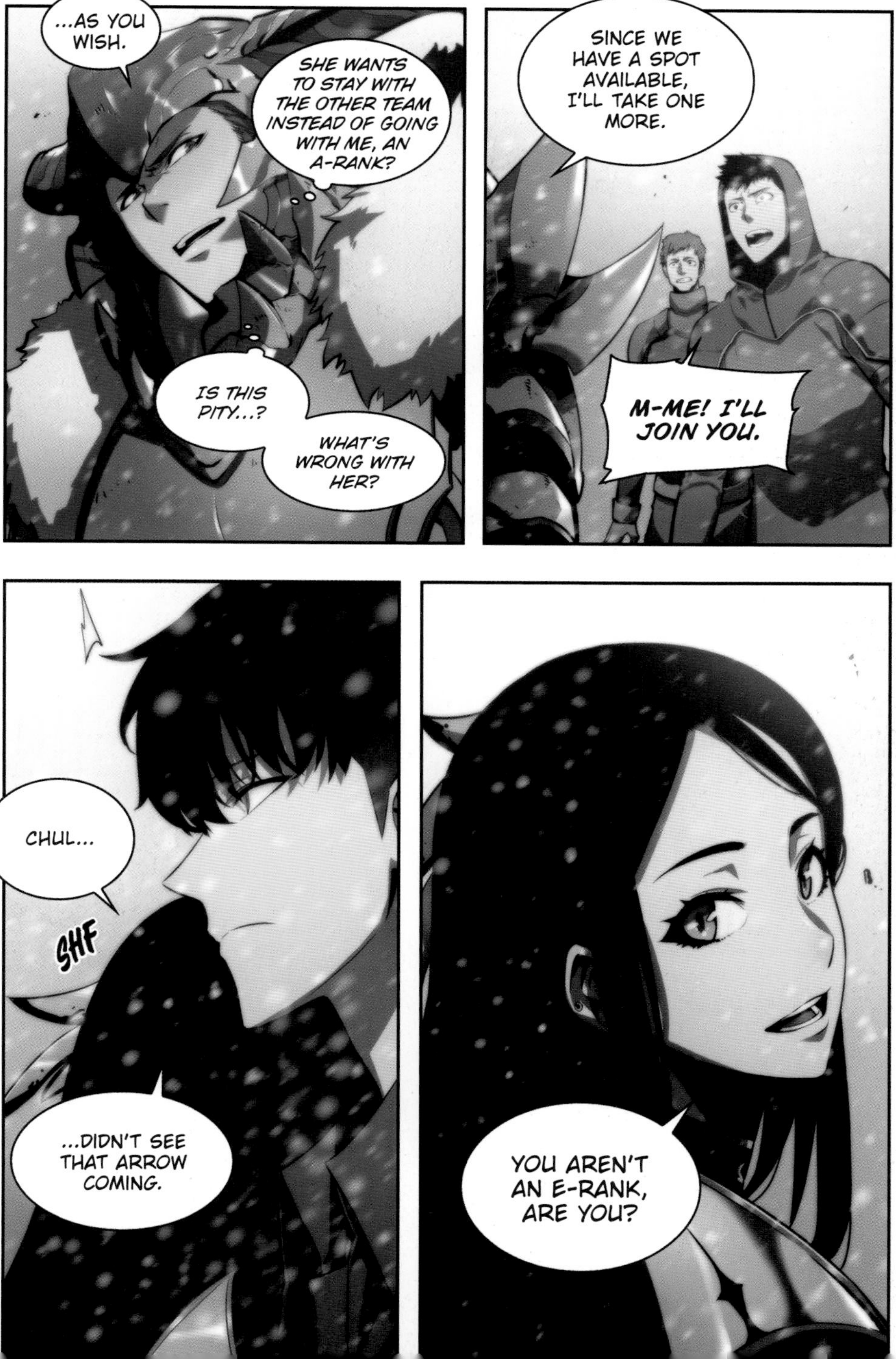
...AS YOU WISH.
SHE WANTS TO STAY WITH THE OTHER TEAM INSTEAD OF GOING WITH ME, AN A-RANK?
IS THIS PITY...?
WHAT'S WRONG WITH HER?
SINCE WE HAVE A SPOT AVAILABLE, I'LL TAKE ONE MORE.
M-ME! I'LL JOIN YOU.
CHUL...
SHF
...DIDN'T SEE THAT ARROW COMING.
YOU AREN'T AN E-RANK, ARE YOU?

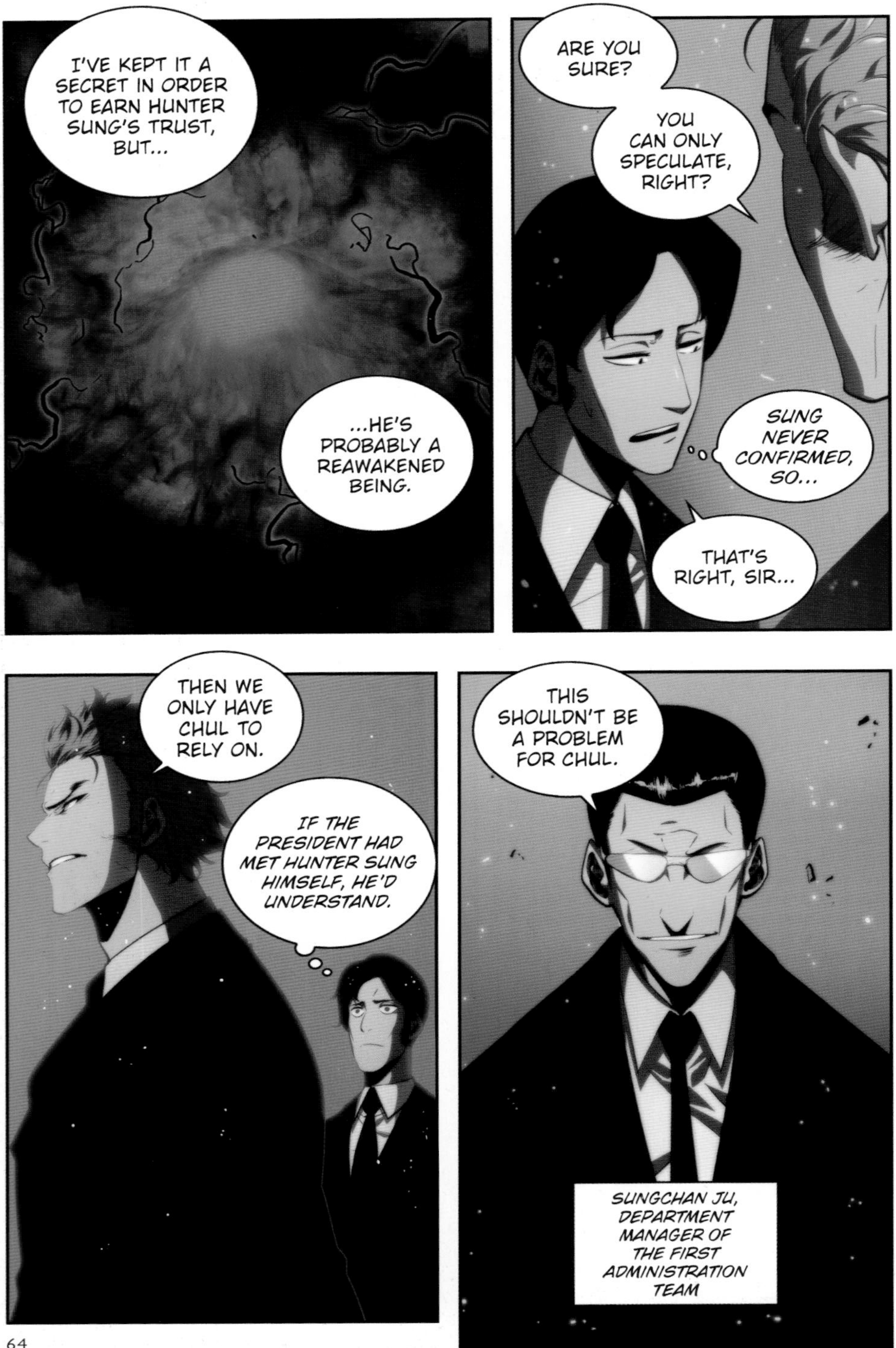
I'VE KEPT IT A SECRET IN ORDER TO EARN HUNTER SUNG'S TRUST, BUT...
...HE'S PROBABLY A REAWAKENED BEING.
ARE YOU SURE?
YOU CAN ONLY SPECULATE, RIGHT?
SUNG NEVER CONFIRMED, SO...
THAT'S RIGHT, SIR...
THEN WE ONLY HAVE CHUL TO RELY ON.
IF THE PRESIDENT HAD MET HUNTER SUNG HIMSELF, HE'D UNDERSTAND.
THIS SHOULDN'T BE A PROBLEM FOR CHUL.
SUNGCHAN JU, DEPARTMENT MANAGER OF THE FIRST ADMINISTRATION TEAM

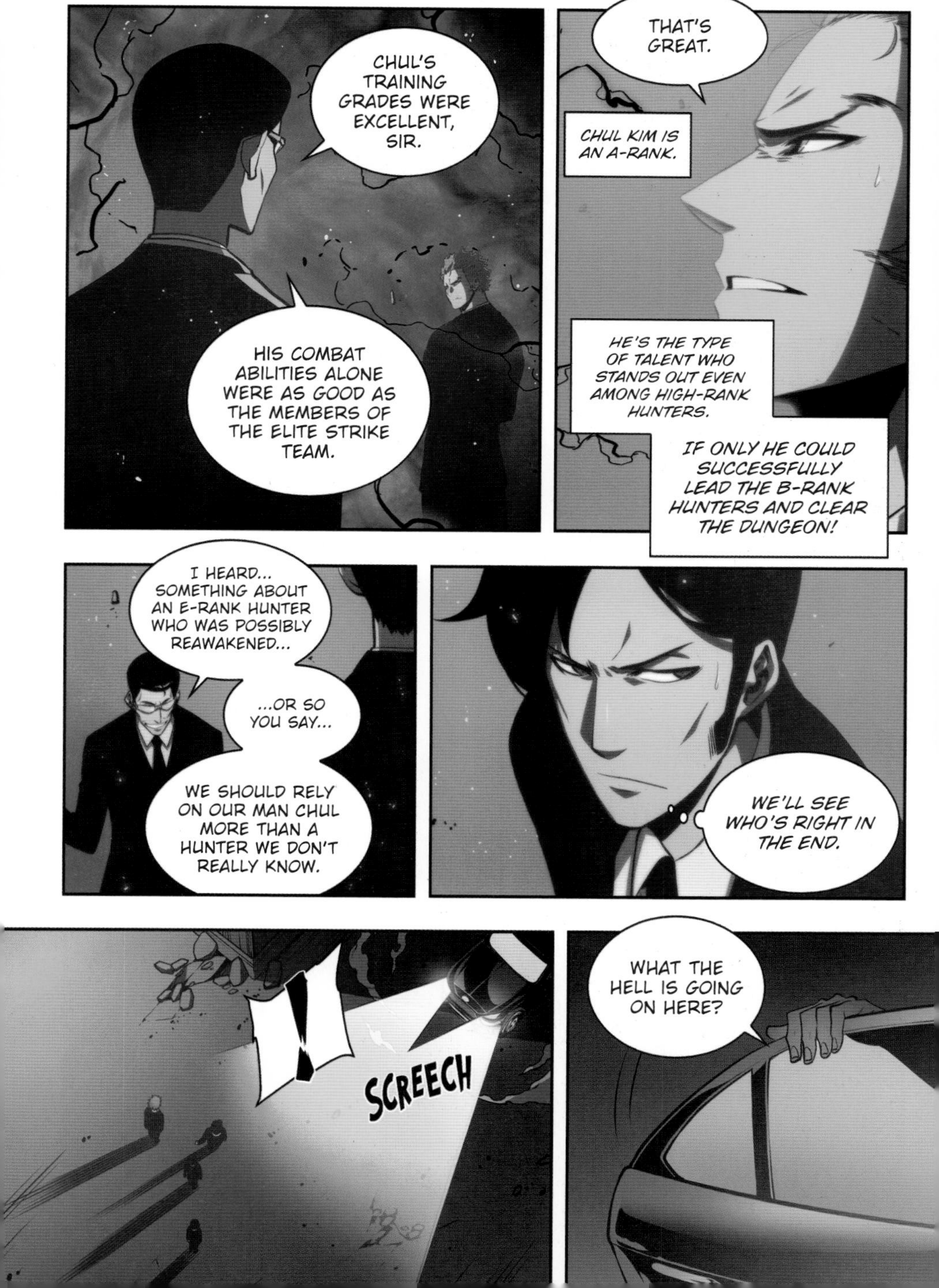
CHUL'S TRAINING GRADES WERE EXCELLENT, SIR.
HIS COMBAT ABILITIES ALONE WERE AS GOOD AS THE MEMBERS OF THE ELITE STRIKE TEAM.
THAT'S GREAT.
CHUL KIM IS AN A-RANK.
HE'S THE TYPE OF TALENT WHO STANDS OUT EVEN AMONG HIGH-RANK HUNTERS.
IF ONLY HE COULD SUCCESSFULLY LEAD THE B-RANK HUNTERS AND CLEAR THE DUNGEON!
I HEARD... SOMETHING ABOUT AN E-RANK HUNTER WHO WAS POSSIBLY REAWAKENED...
...OR SO YOU SAY...
WE SHOULD RELY ON OUR MAN CHUL MORE THAN A HUNTER WE DON'T REALLY KNOW.
WE'LL SEE WHO'S RIGHT IN THE END.
!
SCREECH
WHAT THE HELL IS GOING ON HERE?

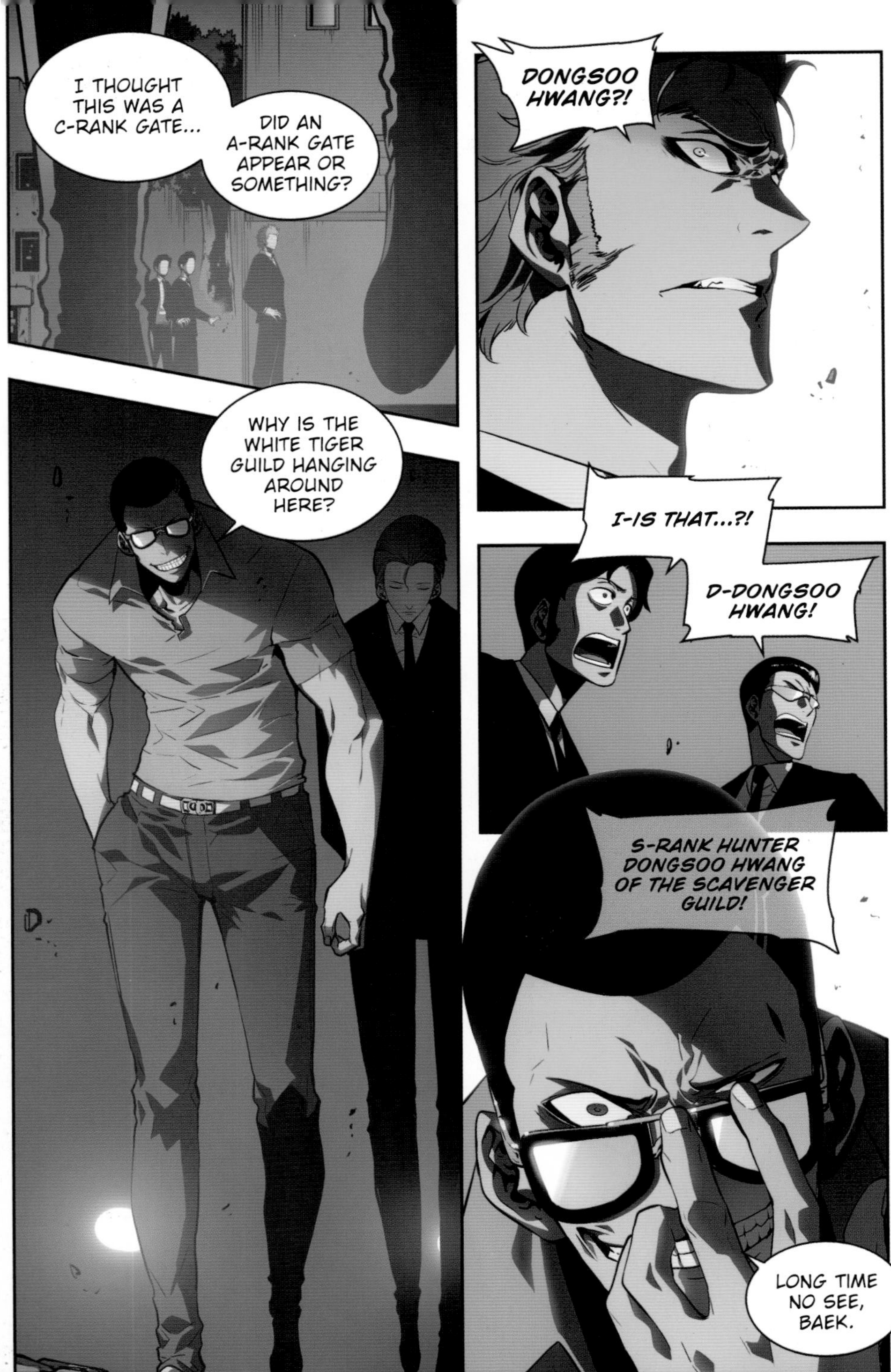
I THOUGHT THIS WAS A C-RANK GATE...
DID AN A-RANK GATE APPEAR OR SOMETHING?
WHY IS THE WHITE TIGER GUILD HANGING AROUND HERE?
DONGSOO HWANG?!
I-IS THAT...?!
D-DONGSOO HWANG!
S-RANK HUNTER DONGSOO HWANG OF THE SCAVENGER GUILD!
LONG TIME NO SEE, BAEK.

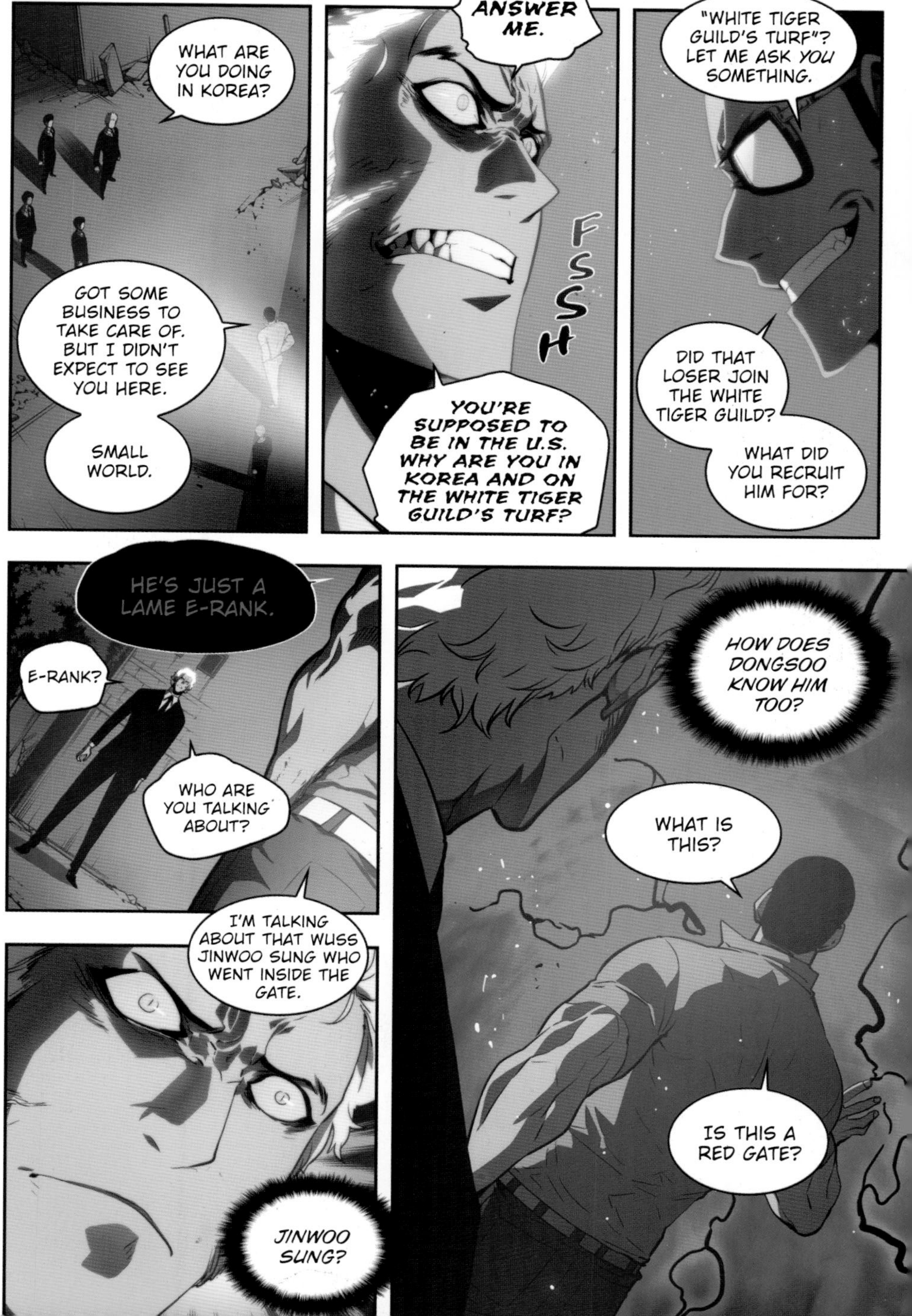
WHAT ARE YOU DOING IN KOREA?
GOT SOME BUSINESS TO TAKE CARE OF. BUT I DIDN'T EXPECT TO SEE YOU HERE.
SMALL WORLD.
ANSWER ME.
FSSH
YOU'RE SUPPOSED TO BE IN THE U.S. WHY ARE YOU IN KOREA AND ON THE WHITE TIGER GUILD'S TURF?
"WHITE TIGER GUILD'S TURF"? LET ME ASK YOU SOMETHING.
DID THAT LOSER JOIN THE WHITE TIGER GUILD?
WHAT DID YOU RECRUIT HIM FOR?
HE'S JUST A LAME E-RANK.
E-RANK?
WHO ARE YOU TALKING ABOUT?
I'M TALKING ABOUT THAT WUSS JINWOO SUNG WHO WENT INSIDE THE GATE.
JINWOO SUNG?
HOW DOES DONGSOO KNOW HIM TOO?
WHAT IS THIS?
IS THIS A RED GATE?

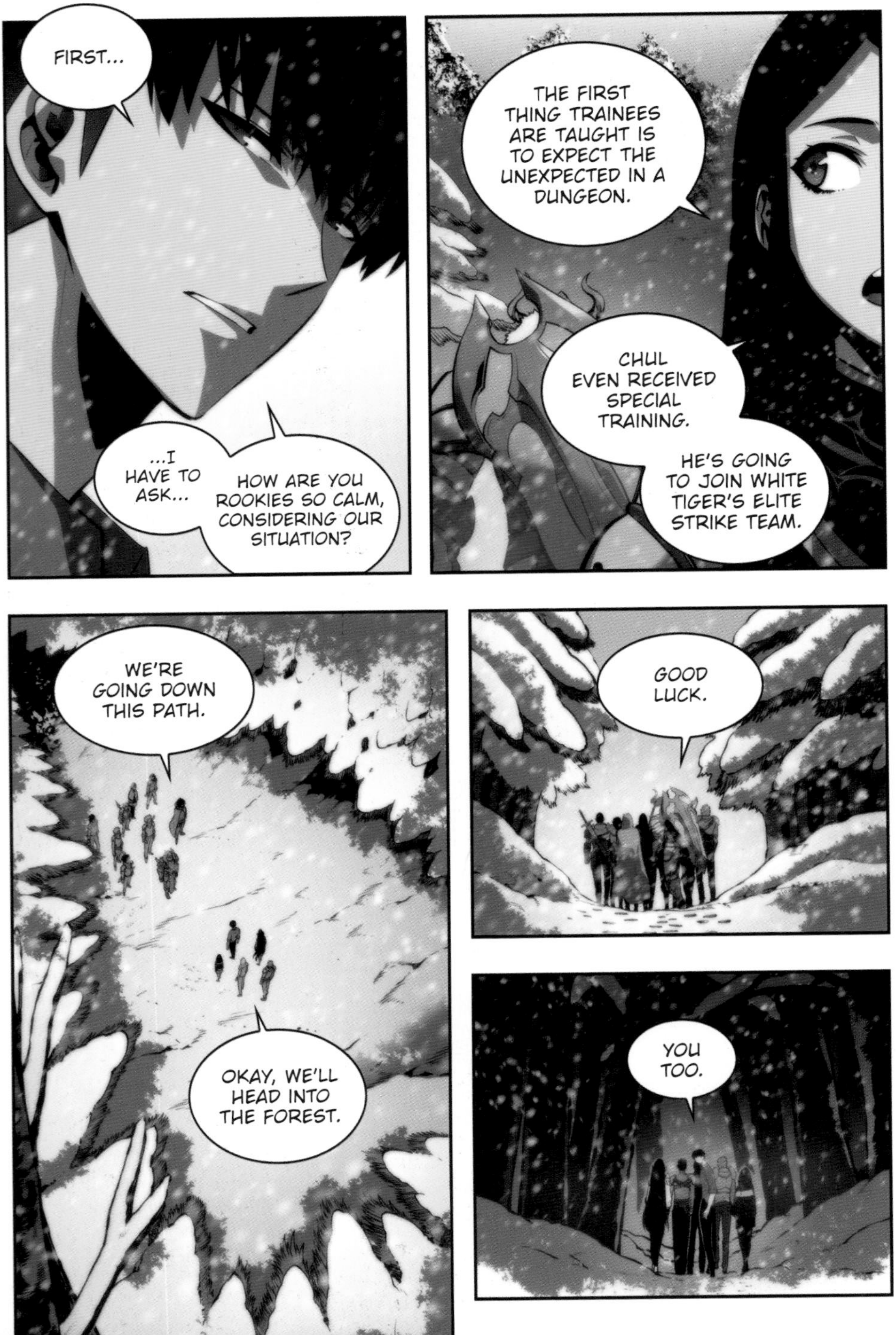
FIRST...
...I HAVE TO ASK...
HOW ARE YOU ROOKIES SO CALM, CONSIDERING OUR SITUATION?
THE FIRST THING TRAINEES ARE TAUGHT IS TO EXPECT THE UNEXPECTED IN A DUNGEON.
CHUL EVEN RECEIVED SPECIAL TRAINING.
HE'S GOING TO JOIN WHITE TIGER'S ELITE STRIKE TEAM.
WE'RE GOING DOWN THIS PATH.
OKAY, WE'LL HEAD INTO THE FOREST.
GOOD LUCK.
YOU TOO.

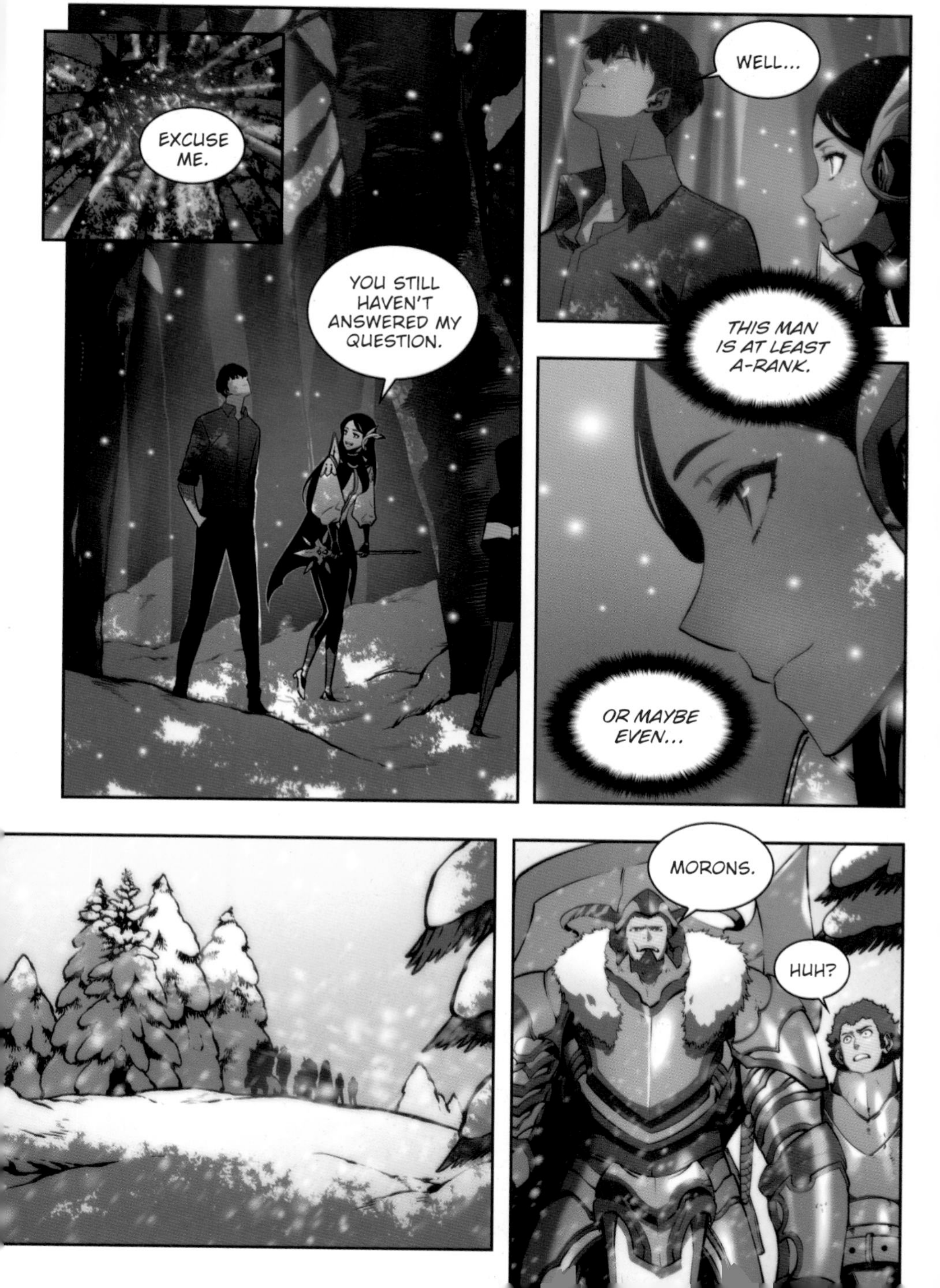
EXCUSE ME.
YOU STILL HAVEN'T ANSWERED MY QUESTION.
WELL...
THIS MAN IS AT LEAST A-RANK.
OR MAYBE EVEN...
MORONS.
HUH?

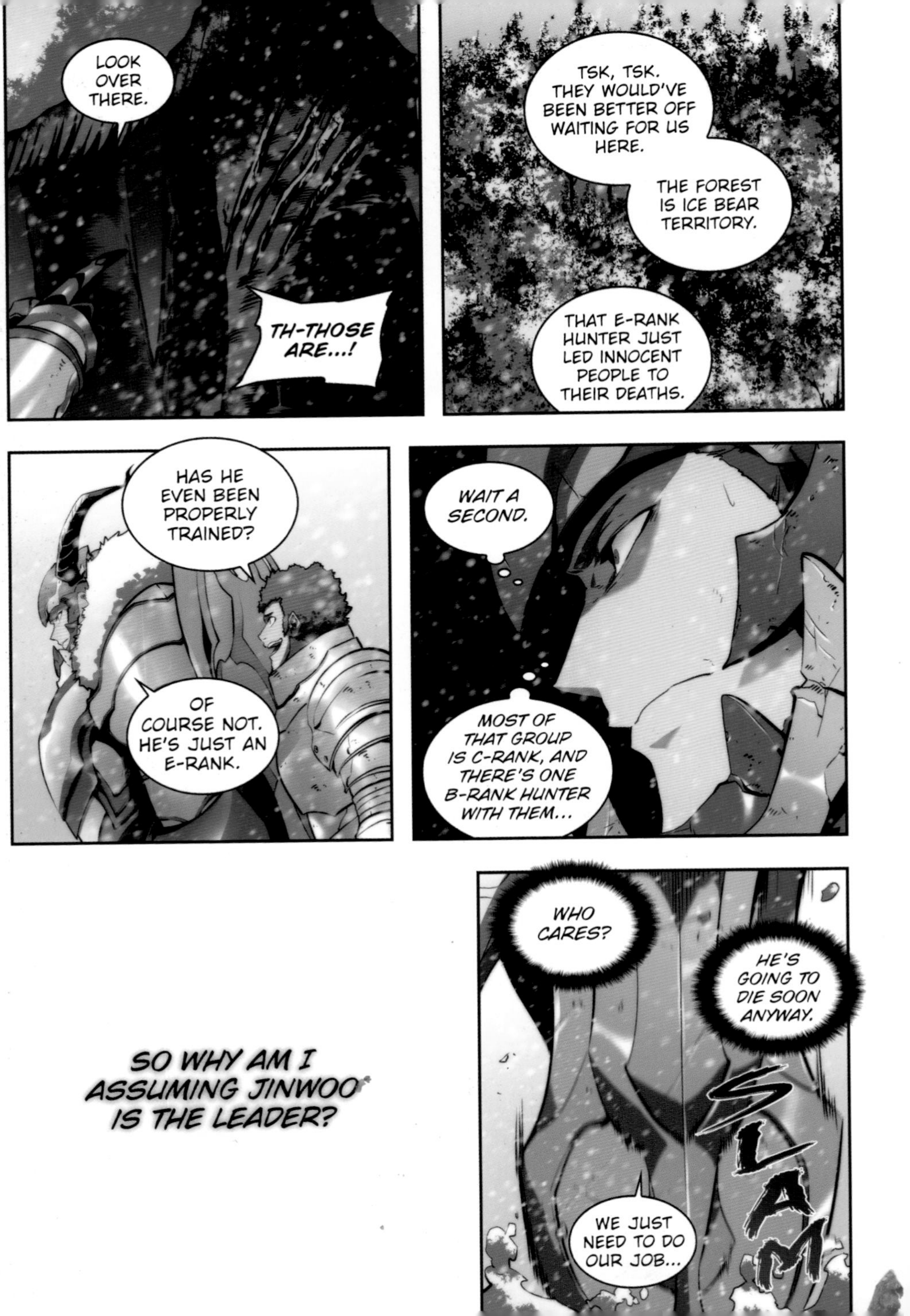
LOOK OVER THERE.
TH-THOSE ARE...!
TSK, TSK. THEY WOULD'VE BEEN BETTER OFF WAITING FOR US HERE.
THE FOREST IS ICE BEAR TERRITORY.
THAT E-RANK HUNTER JUST LED INNOCENT PEOPLE TO THEIR DEATHS.
HAS HE EVEN BEEN PROPERLY TRAINED?
OF COURSE NOT. HE'S JUST AN E-RANK.
WAIT A SECOND.
MOST OF THAT GROUP IS C-RANK, AND THERE'S ONE B-RANK HUNTER WITH THEM...
SO WHY AM I ASSUMING JINWOO IS THE LEADER?
WHO CARES?
HE'S GOING TO DIE SOON ANYWAY.
SLAM
WE JUST NEED TO DO OUR JOB...

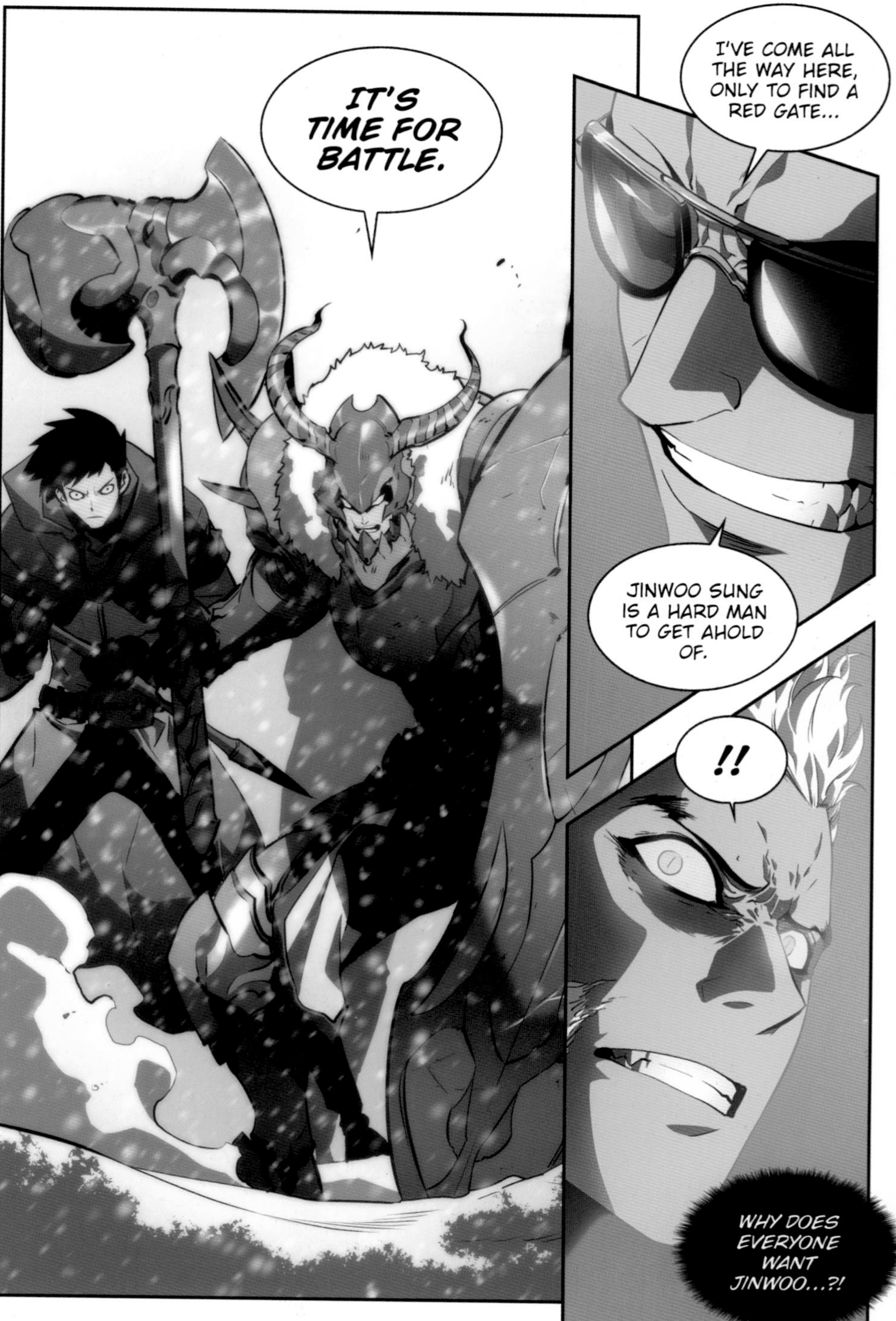
IT'S TIME FOR BATTLE.
I'VE COME ALL THE WAY HERE, ONLY TO FIND A RED GATE...
JINWOO SUNG IS A HARD MAN TO GET AHOLD OF.
!!
WHY DOES EVERYONE WANT JINWOO...?!

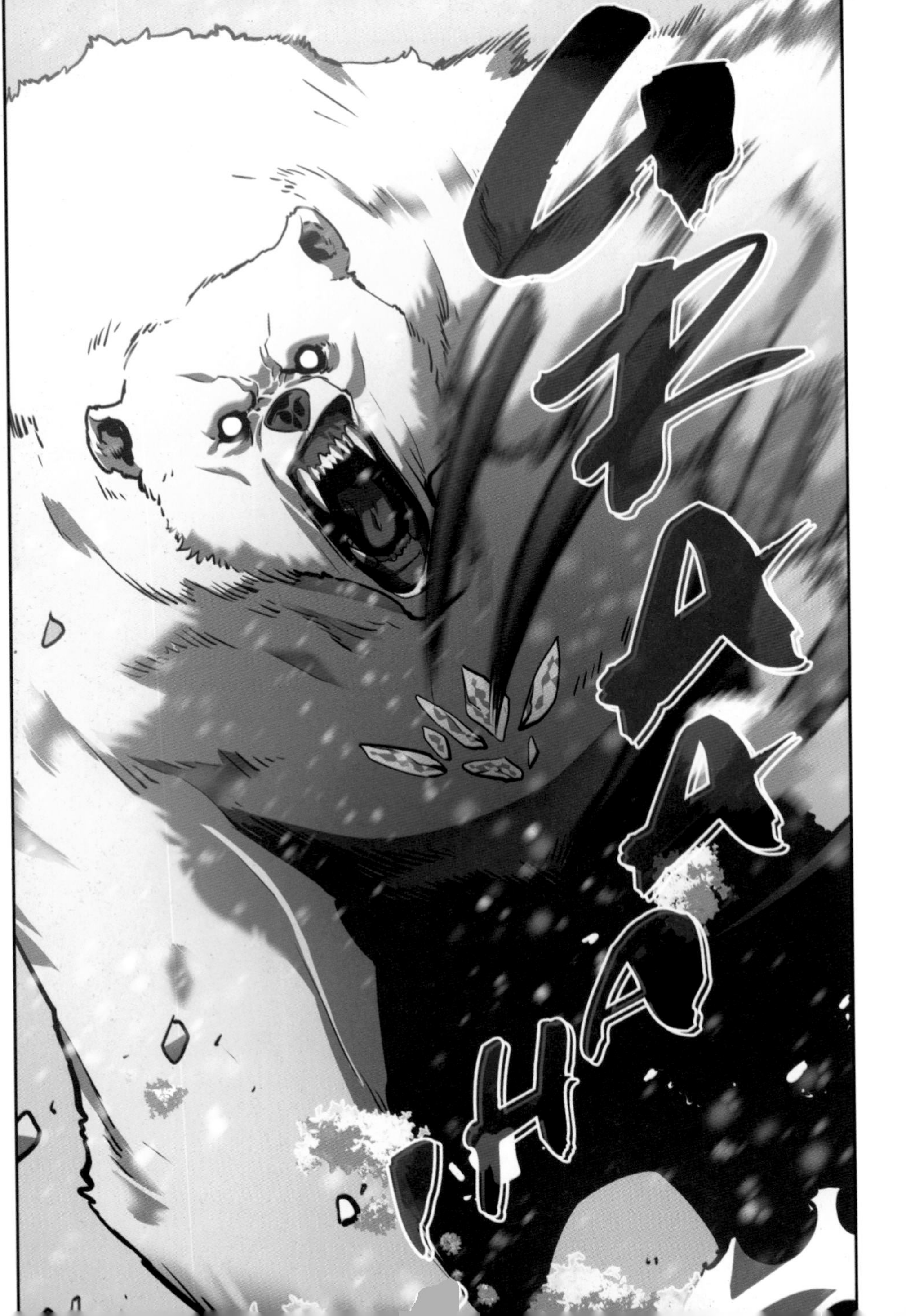
GRAAAH

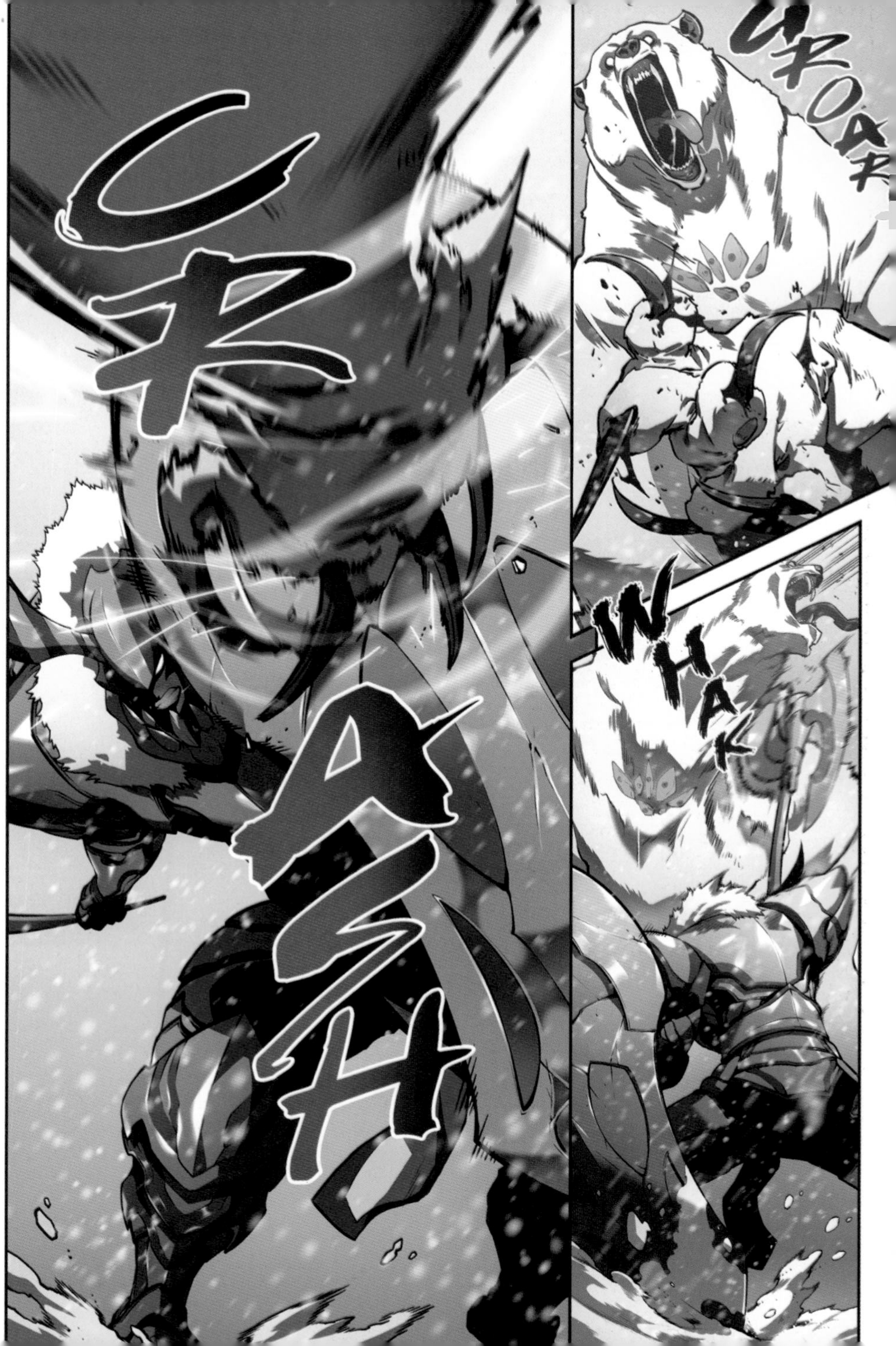
CRASH
UROAR
WHAK

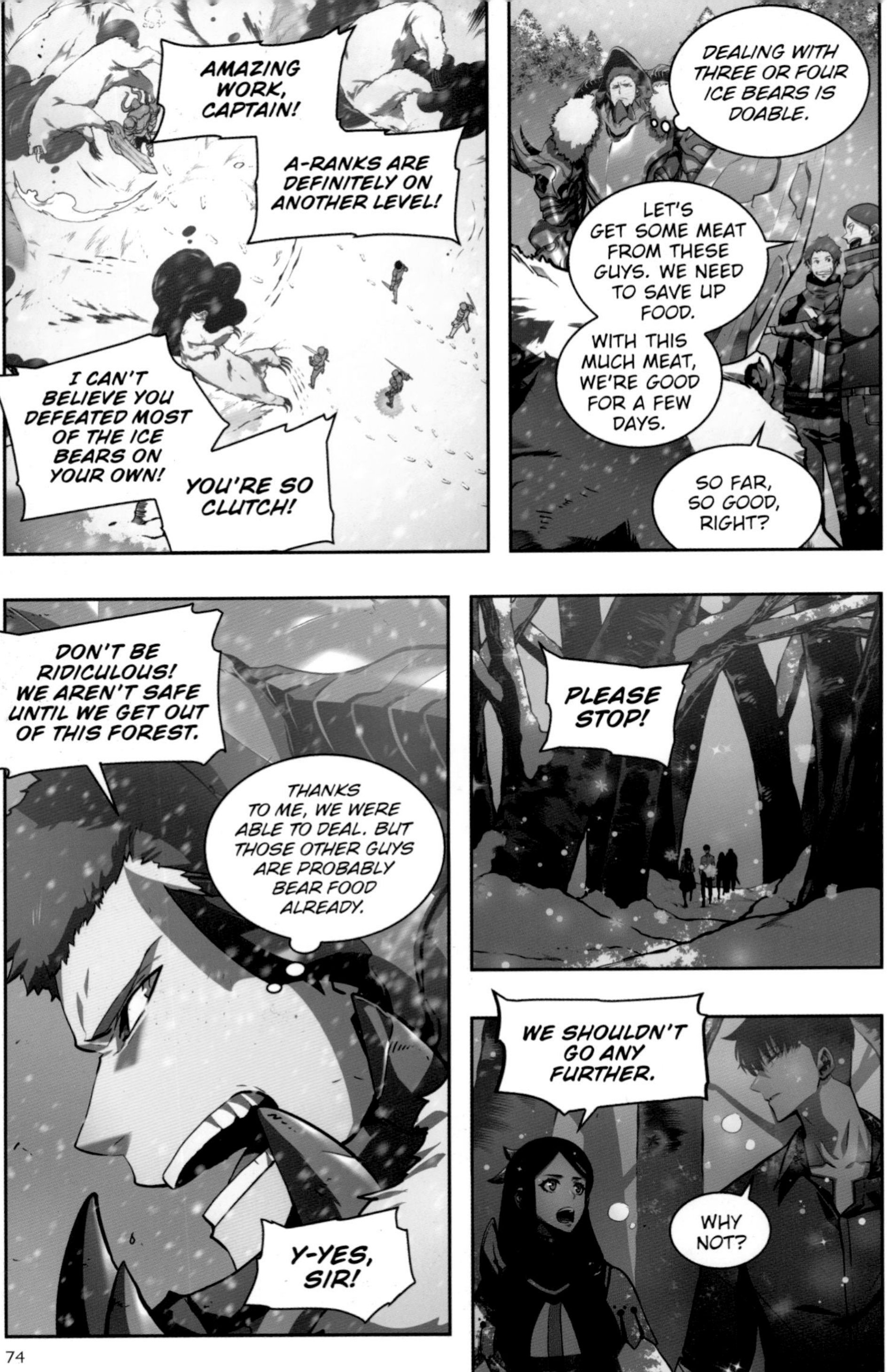
AMAZING WORK, CAPTAIN!
A-RANKS ARE DEFINITELY ON ANOTHER LEVEL!
I CAN'T BELIEVE YOU DEFEATED MOST OF THE ICE BEARS ON YOUR OWN!
YOU'RE SO CLUTCH!
DEALING WITH THREE OR FOUR ICE BEARS IS DOABLE.
LET'S GET SOME MEAT FROM THESE GUYS. WE NEED TO SAVE UP FOOD.
WITH THIS MUCH MEAT, WE'RE GOOD FOR A FEW DAYS.
SO FAR, SO GOOD, RIGHT?
DON'T BE RIDICULOUS! WE AREN'T SAFE UNTIL WE GET OUT OF THIS FOREST.
THANKS TO ME, WE WERE ABLE TO DEAL. BUT THOSE OTHER GUYS ARE PROBABLY BEAR FOOD ALREADY.
Y-YES, SIR!
PLEASE STOP!
WE SHOULDN'T GO ANY FURTHER.
WHY NOT?

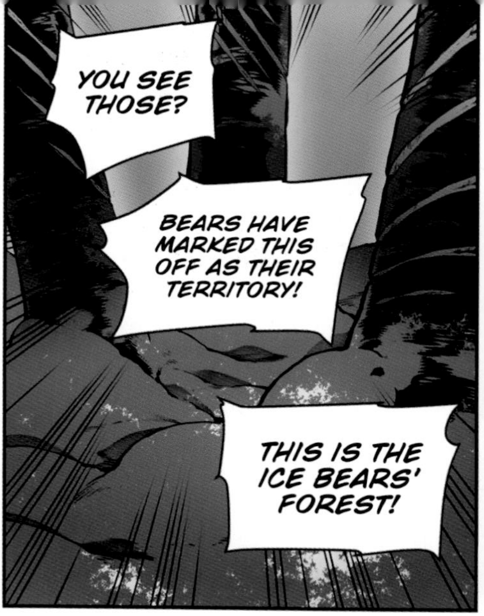
YOU SEE THOSE?
BEARS HAVE MARKED THIS OFF AS THEIR TERRITORY!
THIS IS THE ICE BEARS' FOREST!

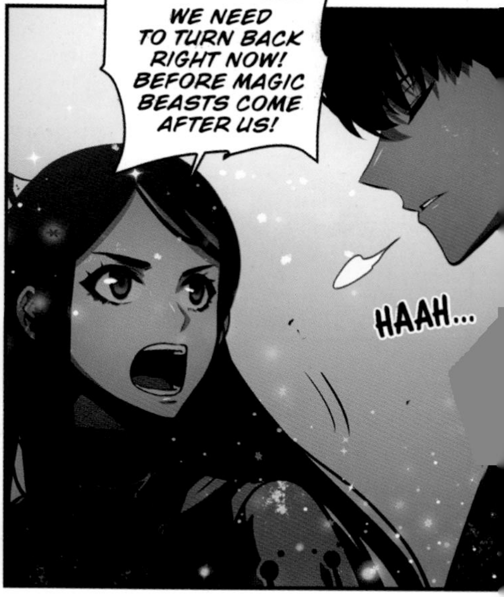
WE NEED TO TURN BACK RIGHT NOW! BEFORE MAGIC BEASTS COME AFTER US!
HAAH...

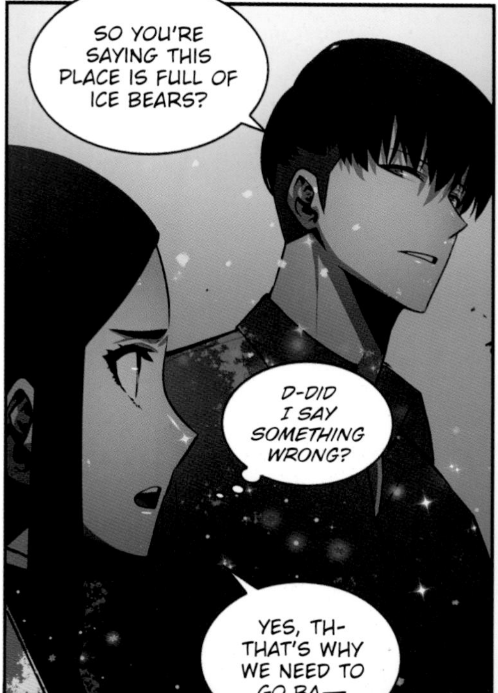
SO YOU'RE SAYING THIS PLACE IS FULL OF ICE BEARS?
D-DID I SAY SOMETHING WRONG?
YES, TH- THAT'S WHY WE NEED TO GO BA—

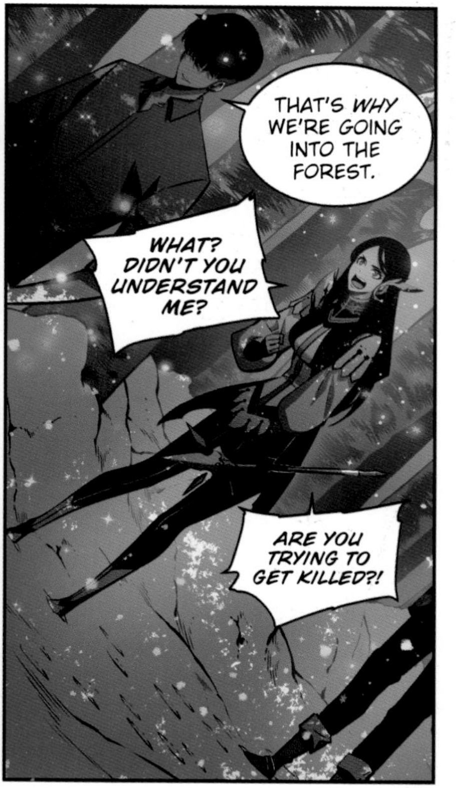
THAT'S WHY WE'RE GOING INTO THE FOREST.
WHAT? DIDN'T YOU UNDERSTAND ME?
ARE YOU TRYING TO GET KILLED?!

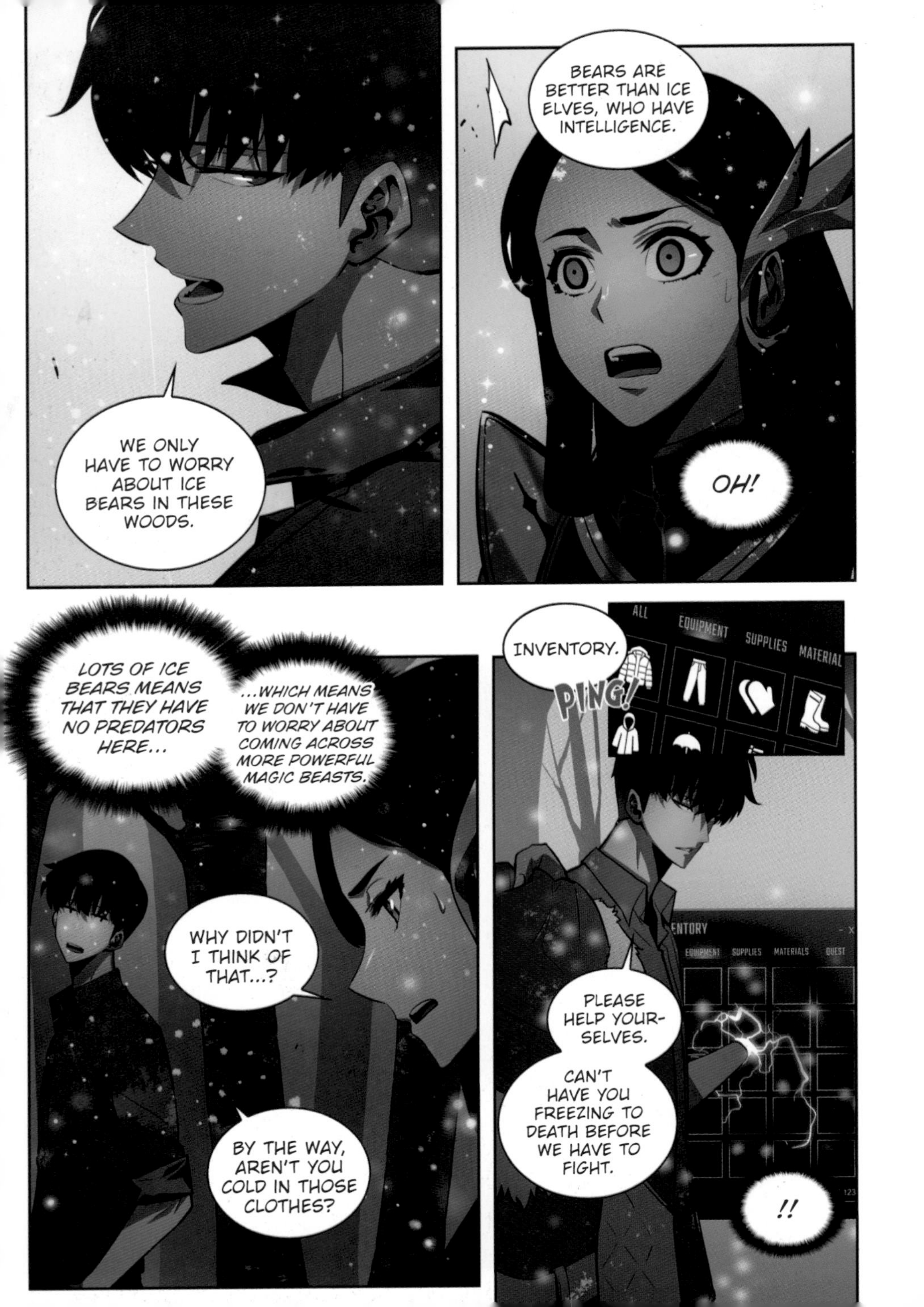

WE ONLY HAVE TO WORRY ABOUT ICE BEARS IN THESE WOODS.
BEARS ARE BETTER THAN ICE ELVES, WHO HAVE INTELLIGENCE.
OH!
LOTS OF ICE BEARS MEANS THAT THEY HAVE NO PREDATORS HERE...
...WHICH MEANS WE DON'T HAVE TO WORRY ABOUT COMING ACROSS MORE POWERFUL MAGIC BEASTS.
WHY DIDN'T I THINK OF THAT...?
BY THE WAY, AREN'T YOU COLD IN THOSE CLOTHES?
INVENTORY.
ALL
EQUIPMENT
SUPPLIES
MATERIAL
PING!
ENTORY
EQUIPMENT
SUPPLIES
MATERIALS
QUEST
PLEASE HELP YOUR-SELVES.
CAN'T HAVE YOU FREEZING TO DEATH BEFORE WE HAVE TO FIGHT.
!!

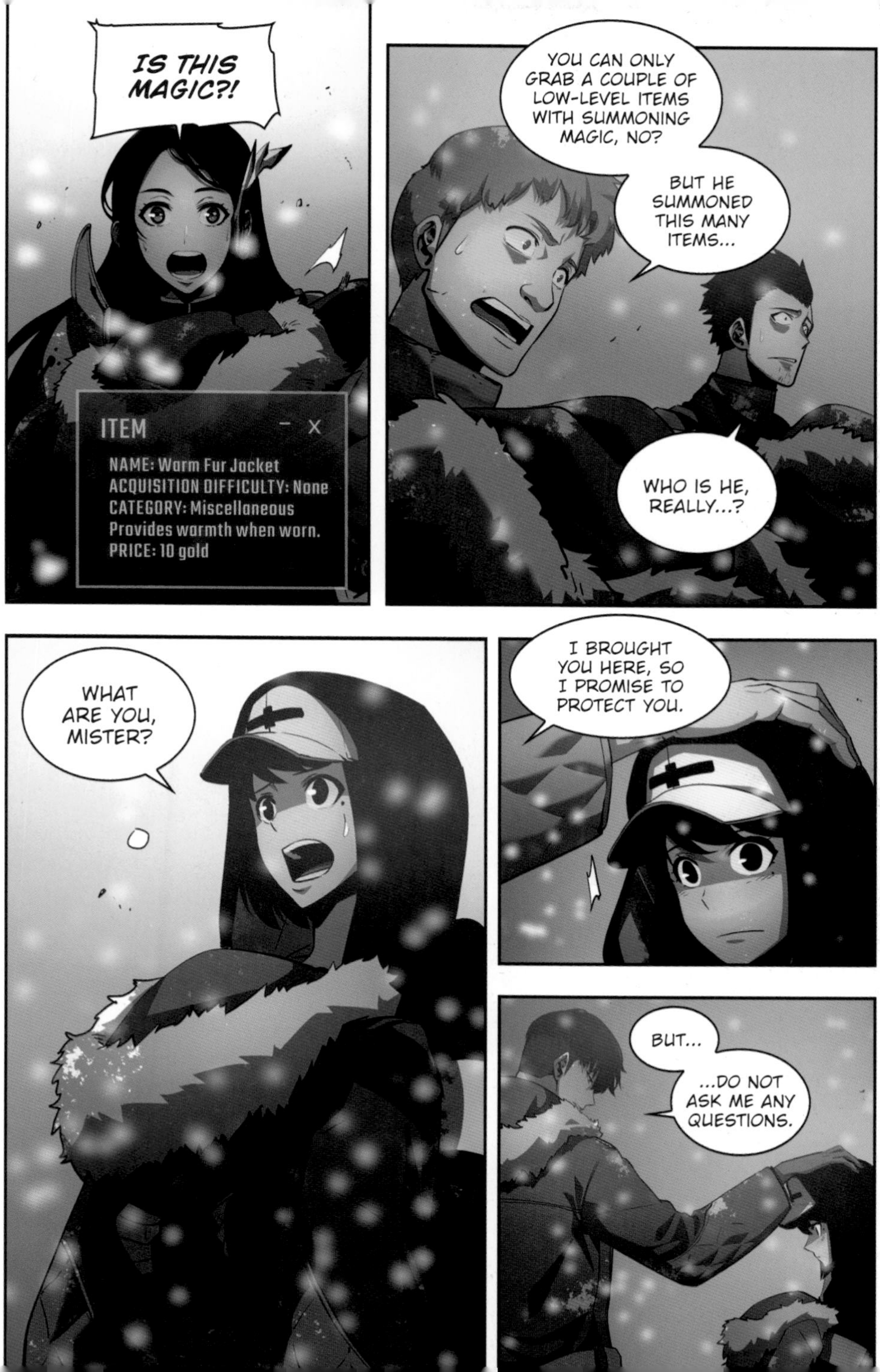
IS THIS MAGIC?!
ITEM
NAME: Warm Fur Jacket
ACQUISITION DIFFICULTY: None
CATEGORY: Miscellaneous
Provides warmth when worn.
PRICE: 10 gold
YOU CAN ONLY GRAB A COUPLE OF LOW-LEVEL ITEMS WITH SUMMONING MAGIC, NO?
BUT HE SUMMONED THIS MANY ITEMS...
WHO IS HE, REALLY...?
WHAT ARE YOU, MISTER?
I BROUGHT YOU HERE, SO I PROMISE TO PROTECT YOU.
BUT...
...DO NOT ASK ME ANY QUESTIONS.

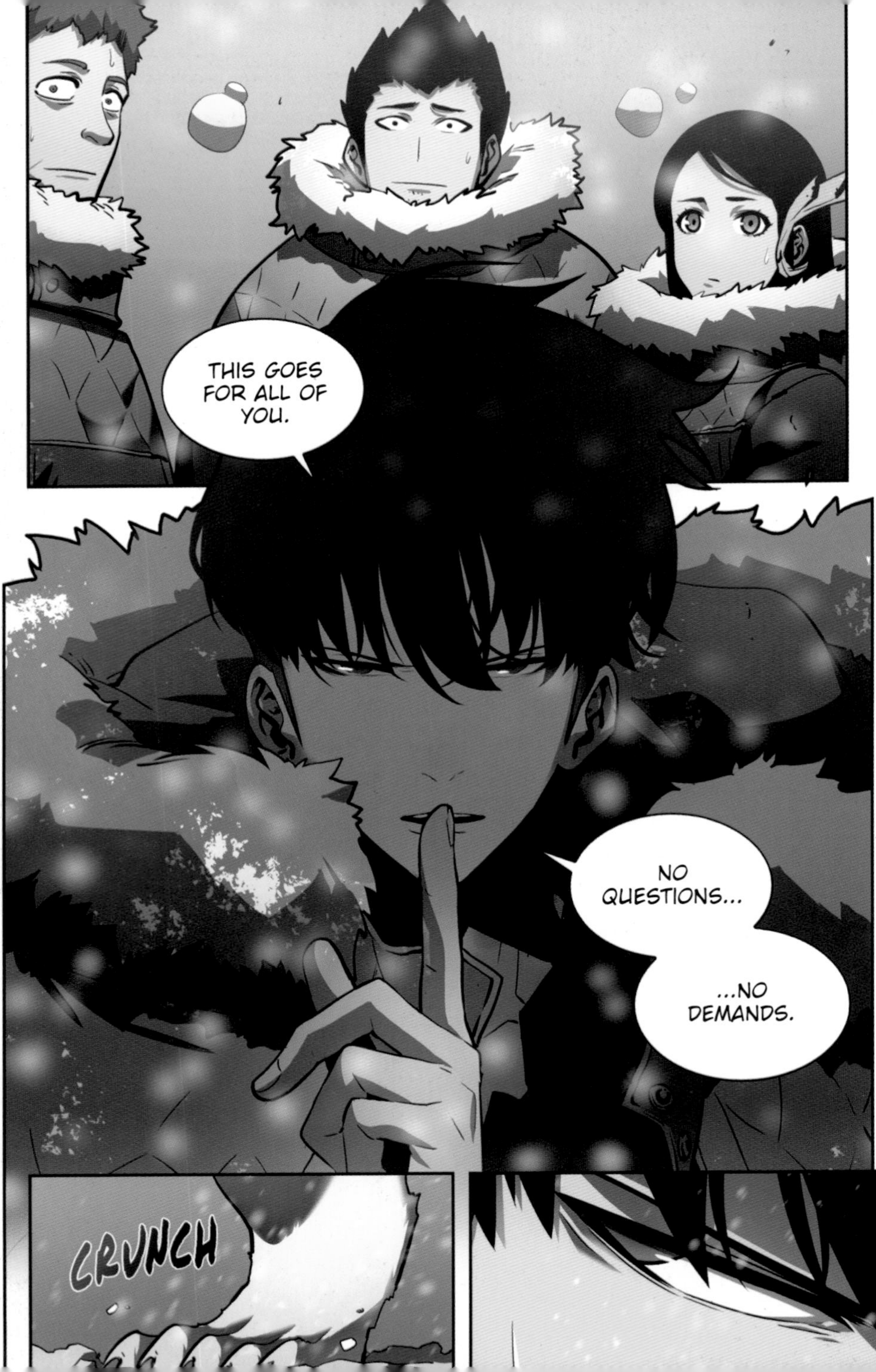
THIS GOES FOR ALL OF YOU.
NO QUESTIONS...
...NO DEMANDS.
CRUNCH

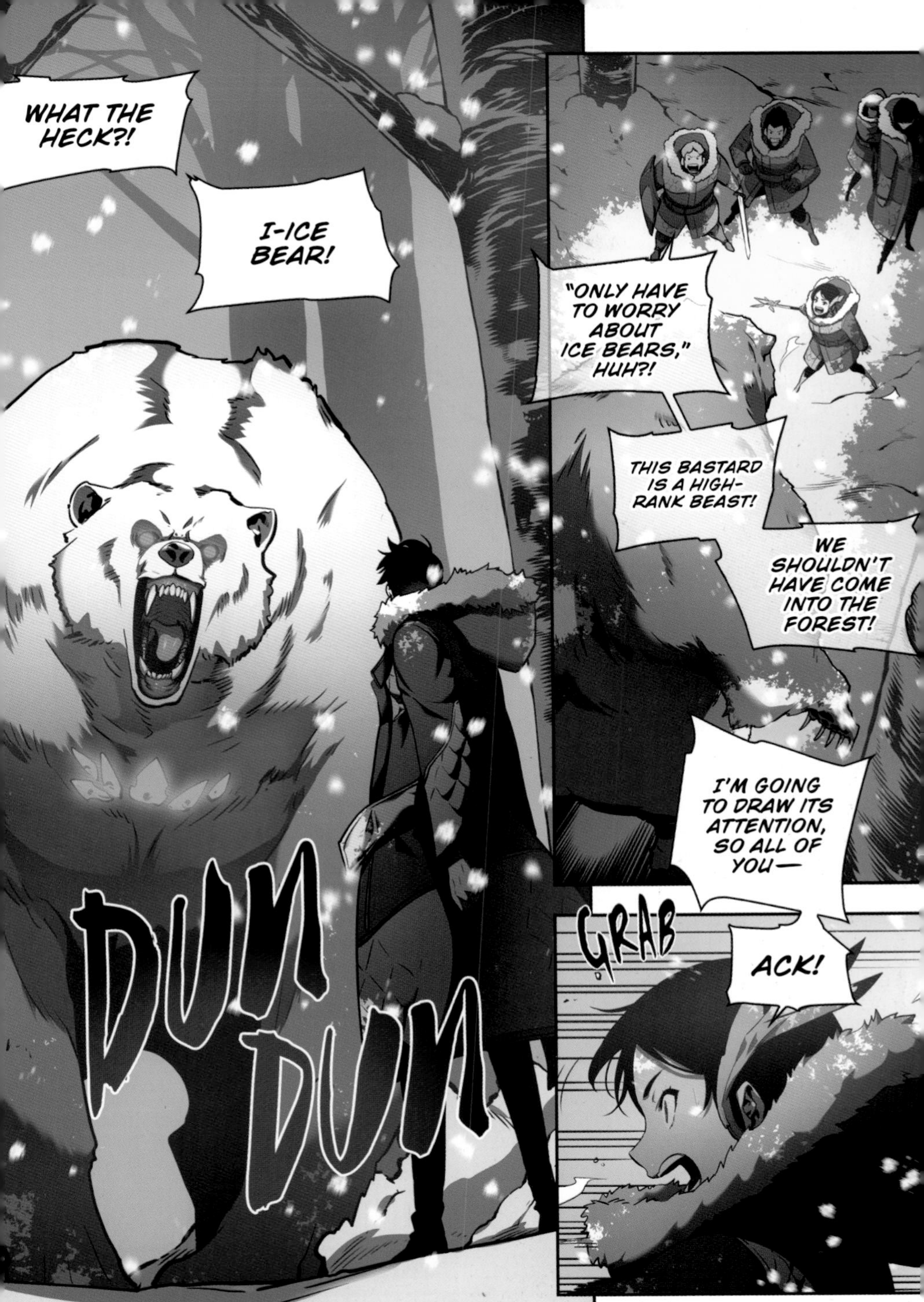
WHAT THE HECK?!
I-ICE BEAR!
DUN DUN
"ONLY HAVE TO WORRY ABOUT ICE BEARS," HUH?!
THIS BASTARD IS A HIGH-RANK BEAST!
WE SHOULDN'T HAVE COME INTO THE FOREST!
I'M GOING TO DRAW ITS ATTENTION, SO ALL OF YOU—
GRAB
ACK!

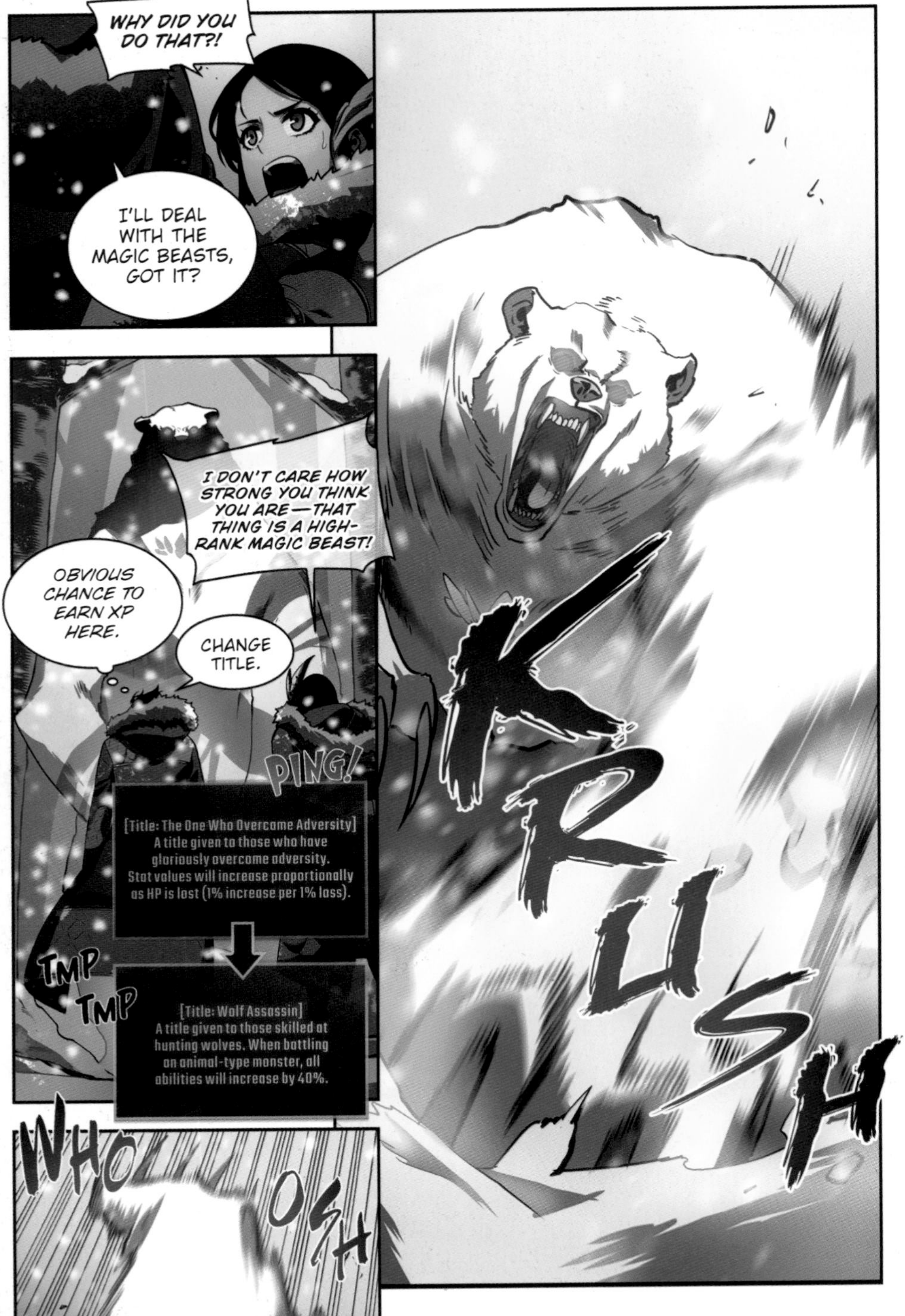
WHY DID YOU DO THAT?!
I'LL DEAL WITH THE MAGIC BEASTS, GOT IT?
I DON'T CARE HOW STRONG YOU THINK YOU ARE—THAT THING IS A HIGH-RANK MAGIC BEAST!
OBVIOUS CHANCE TO EARN XP HERE.
CHANGE TITLE.
PING!
[Title: The One Who Overcame Adversity]
A title given to those who have gloriously overcome adversity.
Stat values will increase proportionally as HP is lost (1% increase per 1% loss).
TMP TMP
[Title: Wolf Assassin]
A title given to those skilled at hunting wolves. When battling an animal-type monster, all abilities will increase by 40%.
KRUSH
WHOOSH

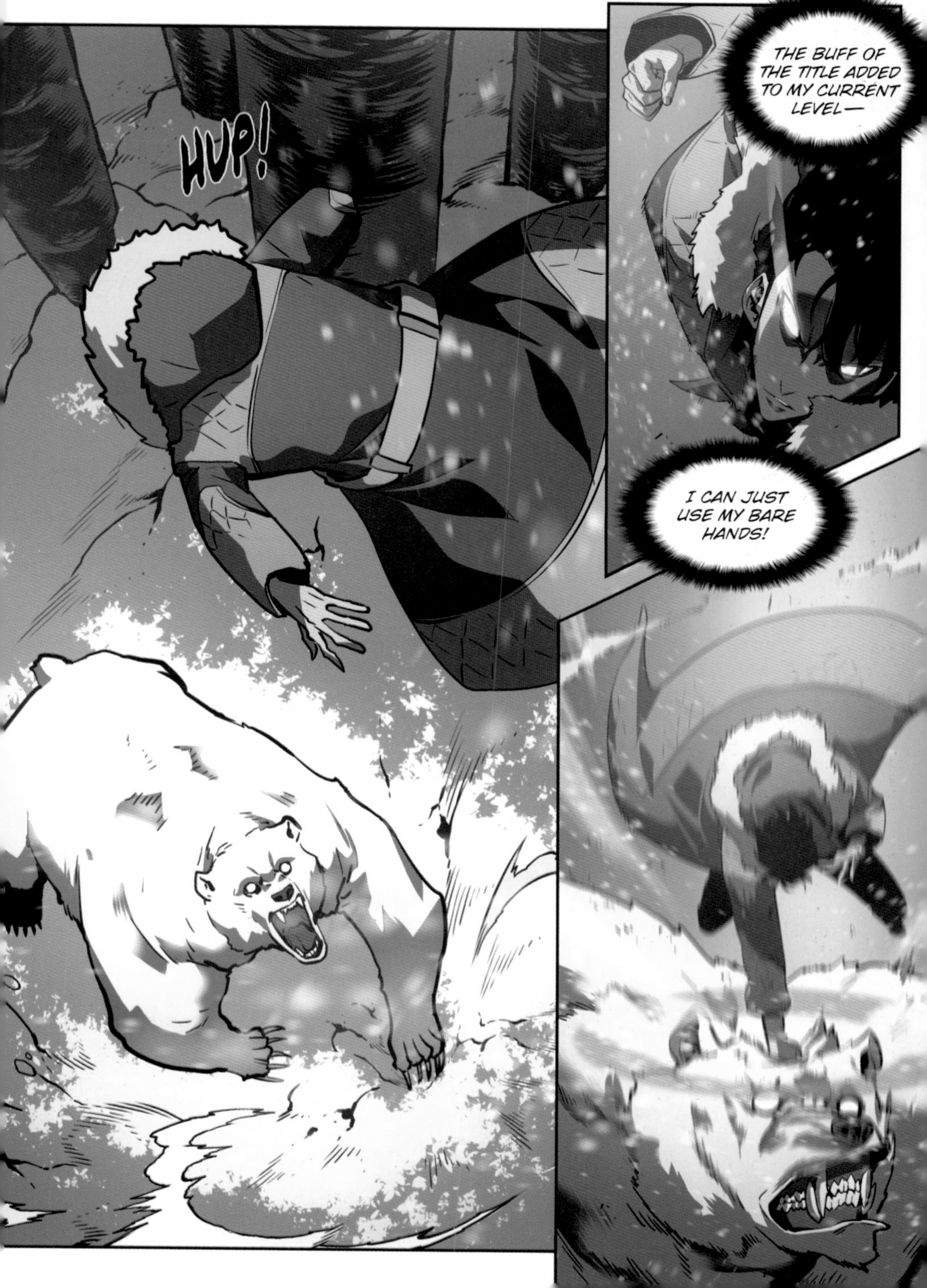
HUP!
THE BUFF OF THE TITLE ADDED TO MY CURRENT LEVEL—
I CAN JUST USE MY BARE HANDS!

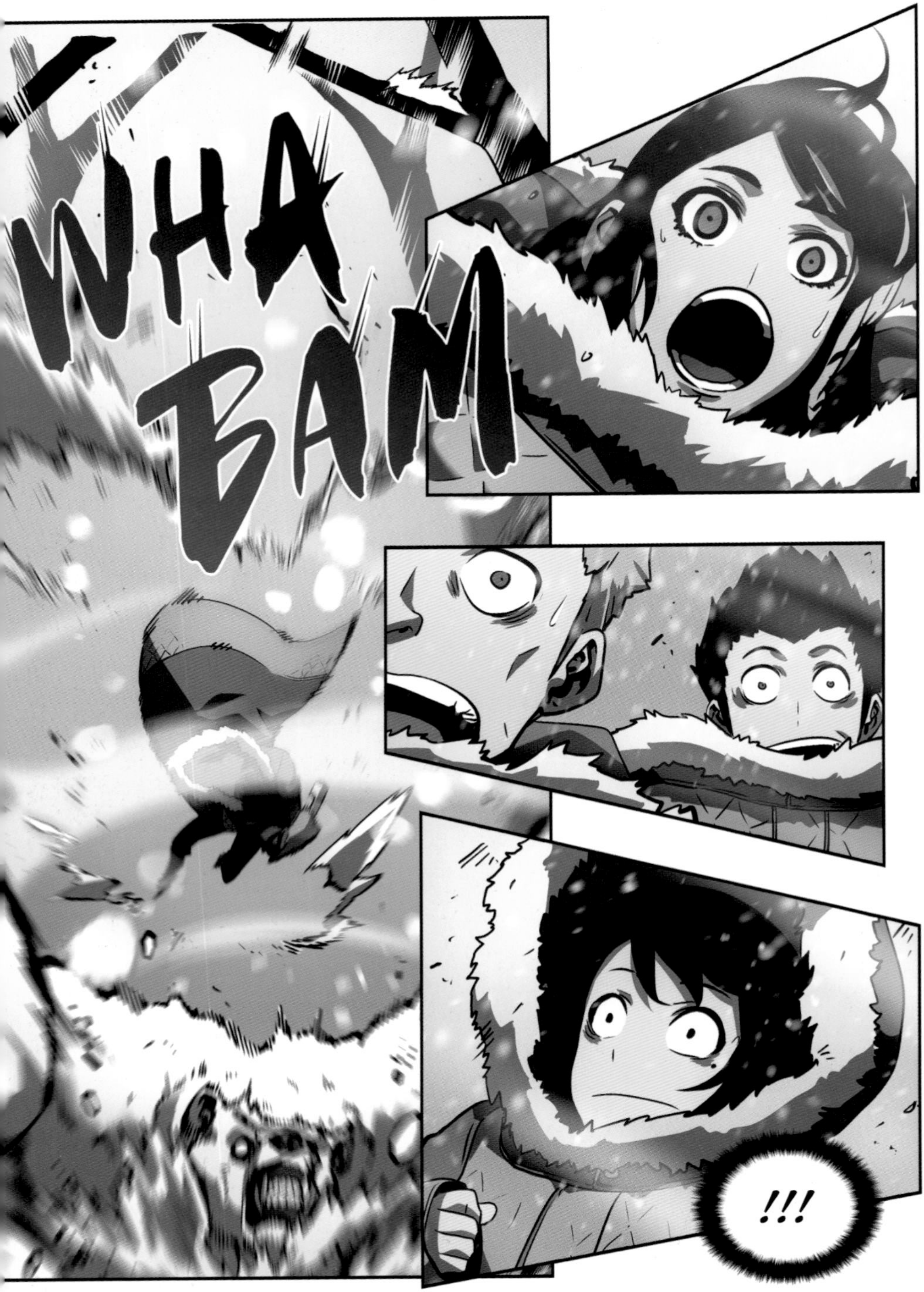
WHA
BAM
!!!

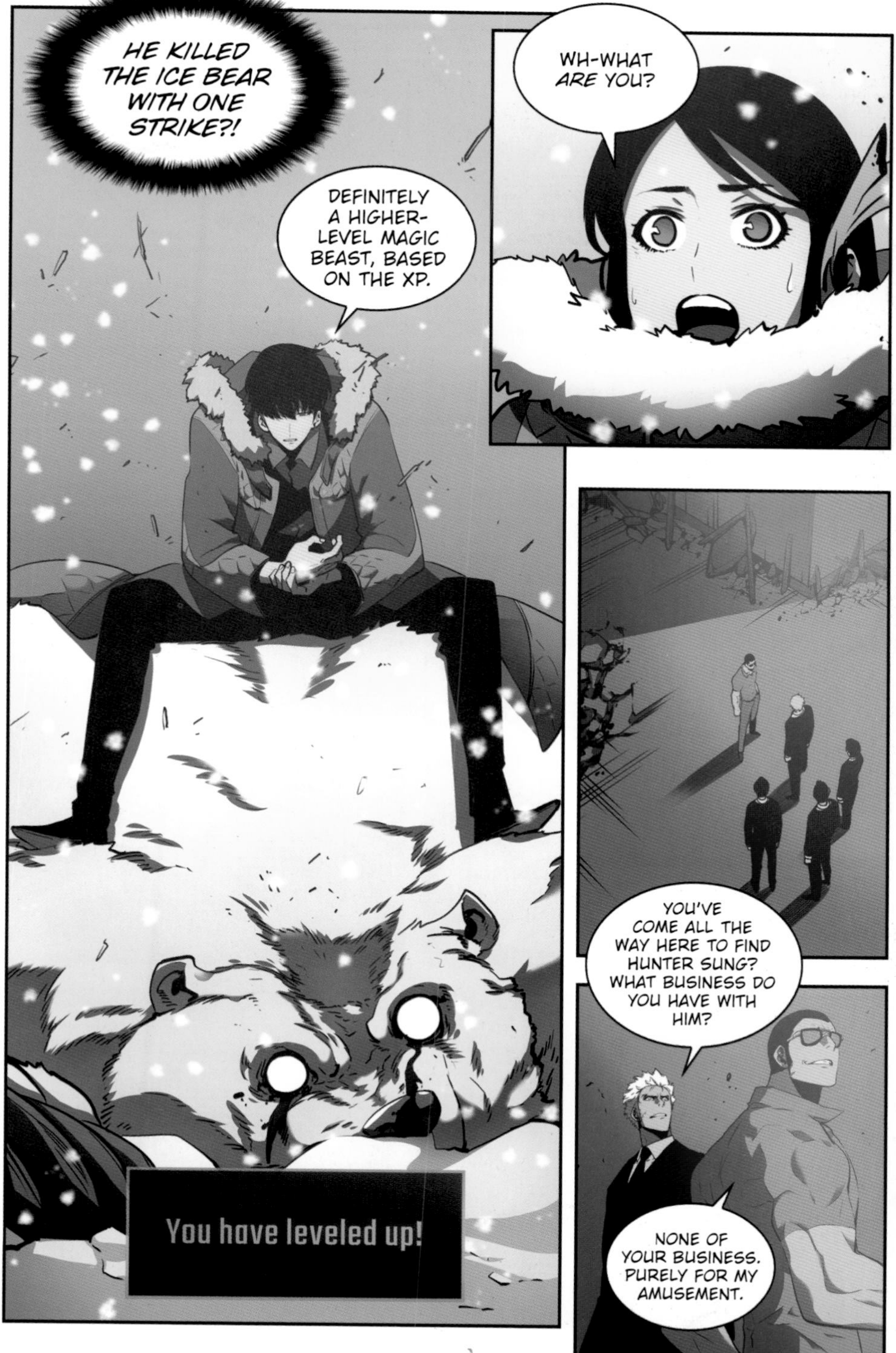
HE KILLED THE ICE BEAR WITH ONE STRIKE?!
DEFINITELY A HIGHER-LEVEL MAGIC BEAST, BASED ON THE XP.
You have leveled up!
WH-WHAT ARE YOU?
YOU'VE COME ALL THE WAY HERE TO FIND HUNTER SUNG? WHAT BUSINESS DO YOU HAVE WITH HIM?
NONE OF YOUR BUSINESS. PURELY FOR MY AMUSEMENT.

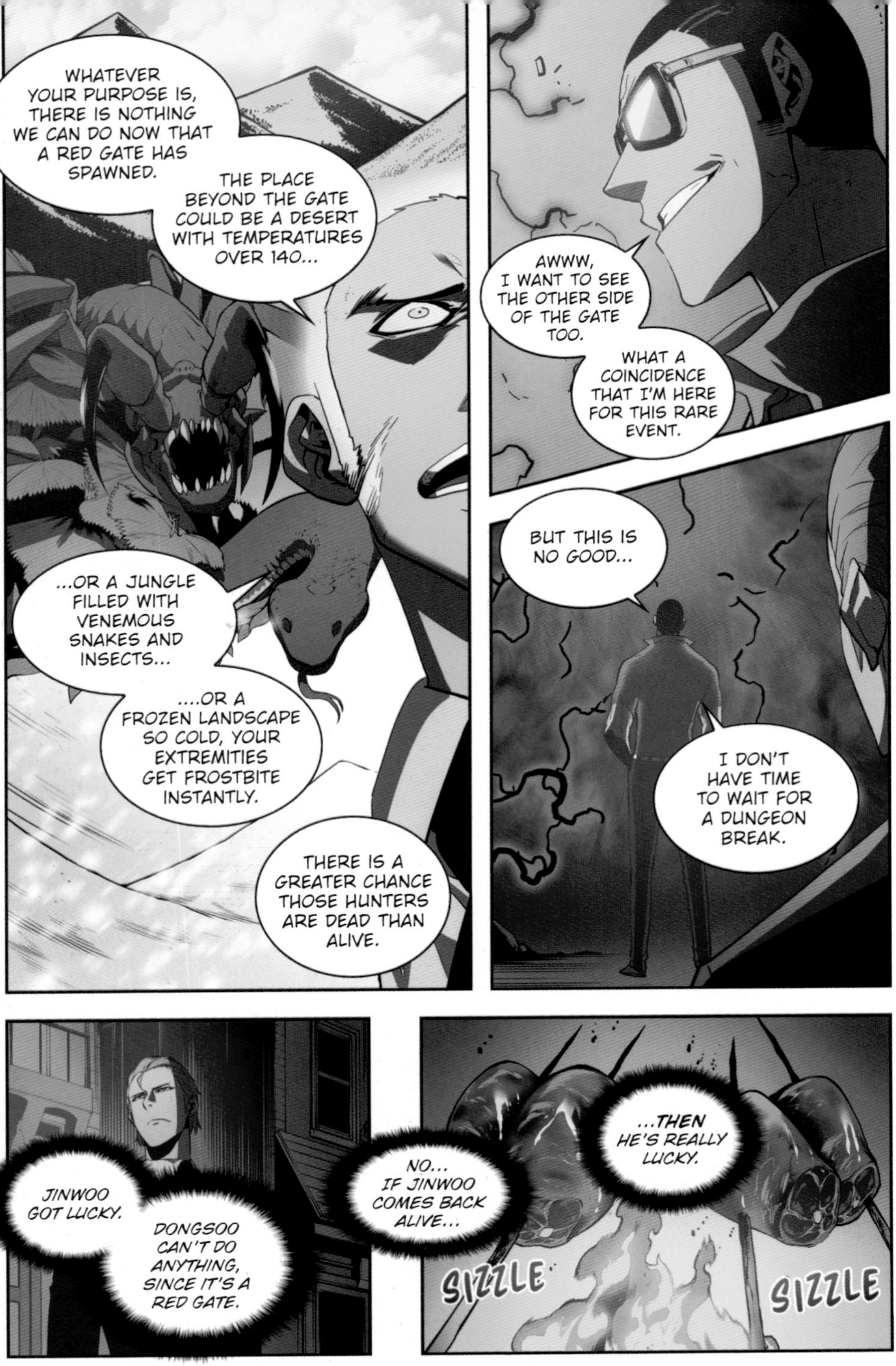

WHATEVER YOUR PURPOSE IS, THERE IS NOTHING WE CAN DO NOW THAT A RED GATE HAS SPAWNED.
THE PLACE BEYOND THE GATE COULD BE A DESERT WITH TEMPERATURES OVER 140...
...OR A JUNGLE FILLED WITH VENEMOUS SNAKES AND INSECTS...
....OR A FROZEN LANDSCAPE SO COLD, YOUR EXTREMITIES GET FROSTBITE INSTANTLY.
THERE IS A GREATER CHANCE THOSE HUNTERS ARE DEAD THAN ALIVE.
AWWW, I WANT TO SEE THE OTHER SIDE OF THE GATE TOO.
WHAT A COINCIDENCE THAT I'M HERE FOR THIS RARE EVENT.
BUT THIS IS NO GOOD...
I DON'T HAVE TIME TO WAIT FOR A DUNGEON BREAK.
JINWOO GOT LUCKY.
DONGSOO CAN'T DO ANYTHING, SINCE IT'S A RED GATE.
NO... IF JINWOO COMES BACK ALIVE...
...THEN HE'S REALLY LUCKY.
SIZZLE
SIZZLE

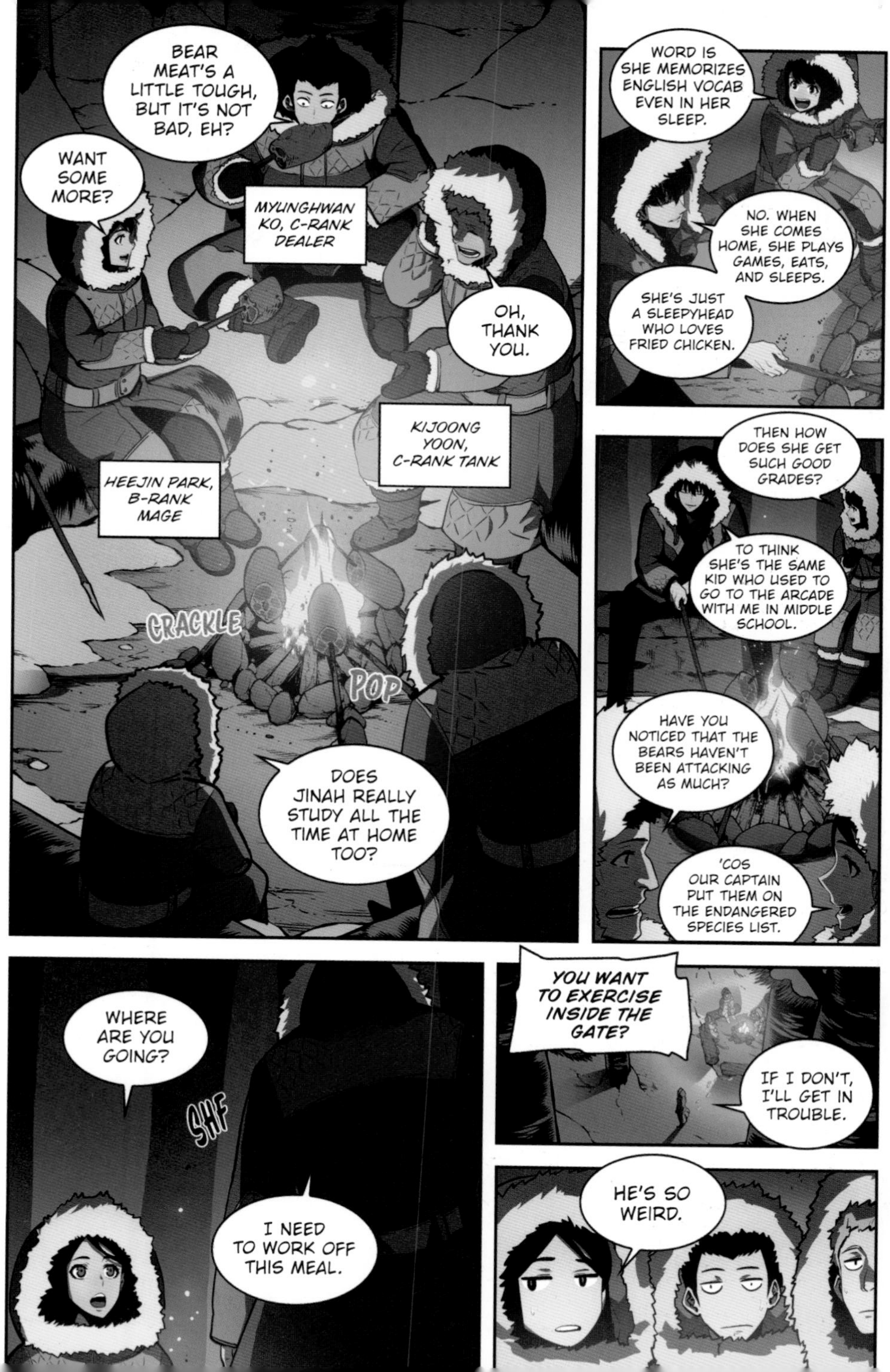
BEAR MEAT'S A LITTLE TOUGH, BUT IT'S NOT BAD, EH?
WANT SOME MORE?
MYUNGHWAN KO, C-RANK DEALER
OH, THANK YOU.
KIJOONG YOON, C-RANK TANK
HEEJIN PARK, B-RANK MAGE
CRACKLE
POP
DOES JINAH REALLY STUDY ALL THE TIME AT HOME TOO?
WORD IS SHE MEMORIZES ENGLISH VOCAB EVEN IN HER SLEEP.
NO. WHEN SHE COMES HOME, SHE PLAYS GAMES, EATS, AND SLEEPS.
SHE'S JUST A SLEEPYHEAD WHO LOVES FRIED CHICKEN.
THEN HOW DOES SHE GET SUCH GOOD GRADES?
TO THINK SHE'S THE SAME KID WHO USED TO GO TO THE ARCADE WITH ME IN MIDDLE SCHOOL.
HAVE YOU NOTICED THAT THE BEARS HAVEN'T BEEN ATTACKING AS MUCH?
'COS OUR CAPTAIN PUT THEM ON THE ENDANGERED SPECIES LIST.
WHERE ARE YOU GOING?
SHF
I NEED TO WORK OFF THIS MEAL.
YOU WANT TO EXERCISE INSIDE THE GATE?
IF I DON'T, I'LL GET IN TROUBLE.
HE'S SO WEIRD.

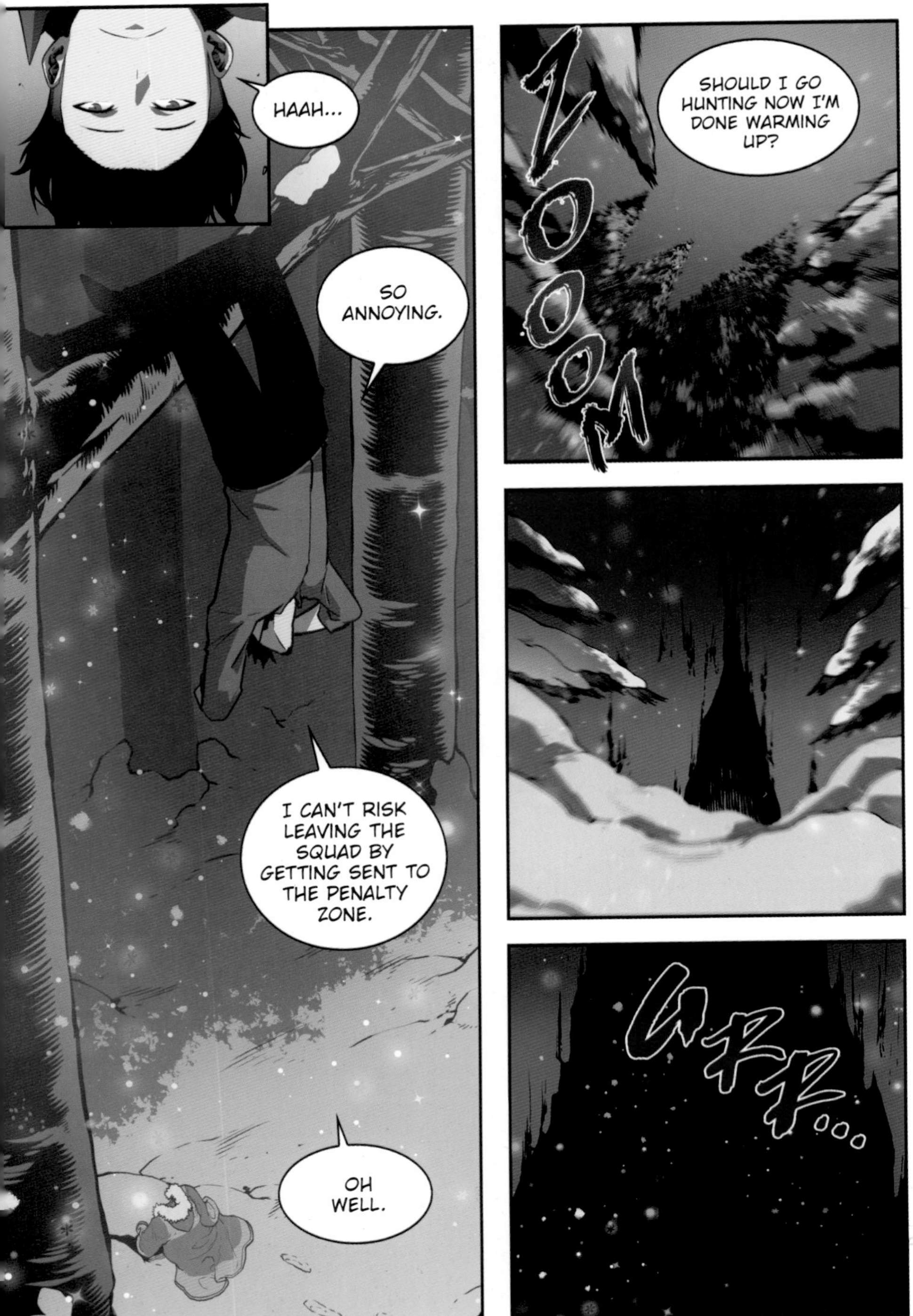
HAAH...
SO ANNOYING.
I CAN'T RISK LEAVING THE SQUAD BY GETTING SENT TO THE PENALTY ZONE.
OH WELL.
ZOOOM
SHOULD I GO HUNTING NOW I'M DONE WARMING UP?
URR...

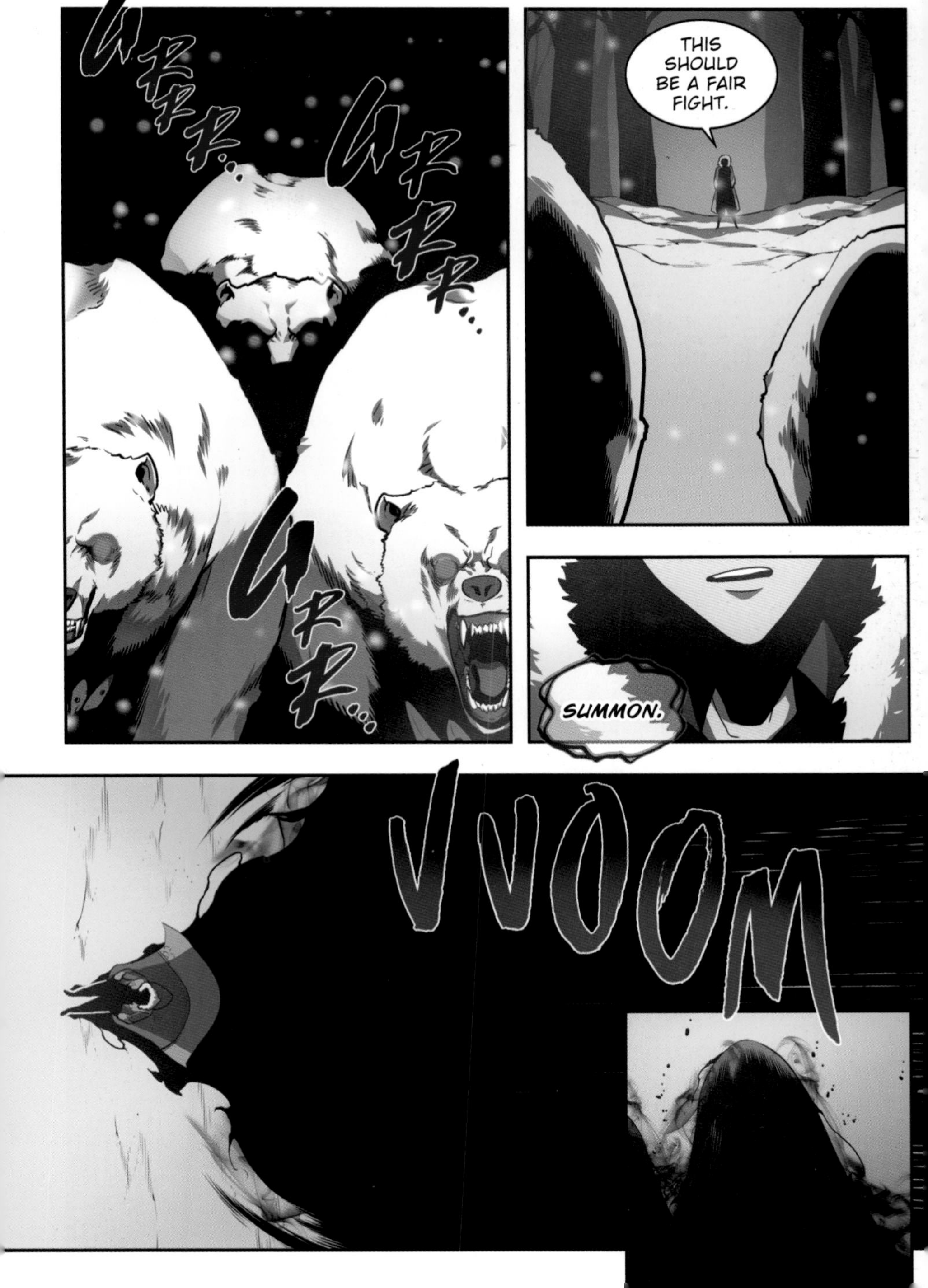
URRR...
URRR...
URRR...
THIS SHOULD BE A FAIR FIGHT.
SUMMON.
VVOOM

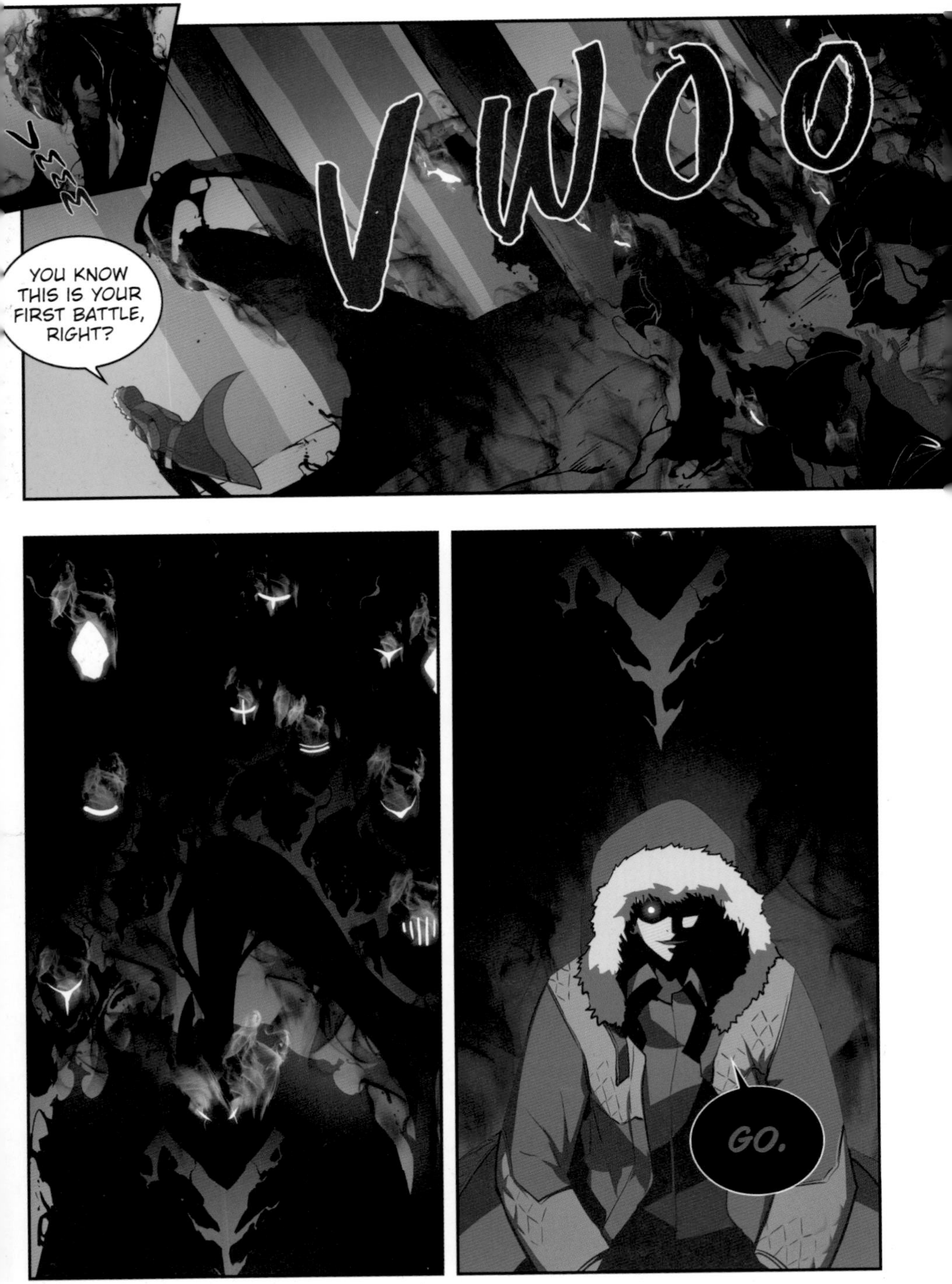
VMMM
VWOO
YOU KNOW THIS IS YOUR FIRST BATTLE, RIGHT?
GO.

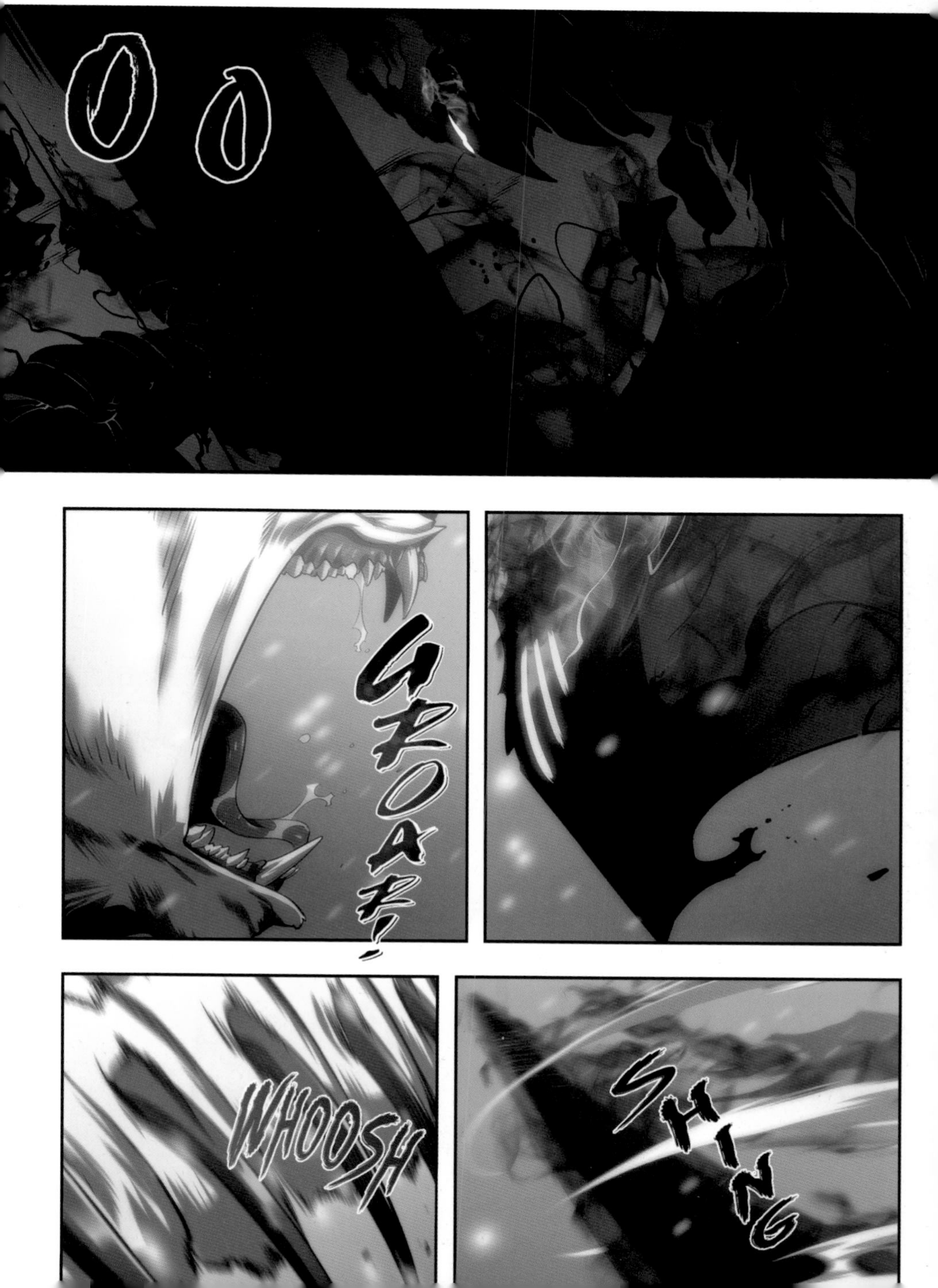
OO
GROAR!
WHOOSH
SHING

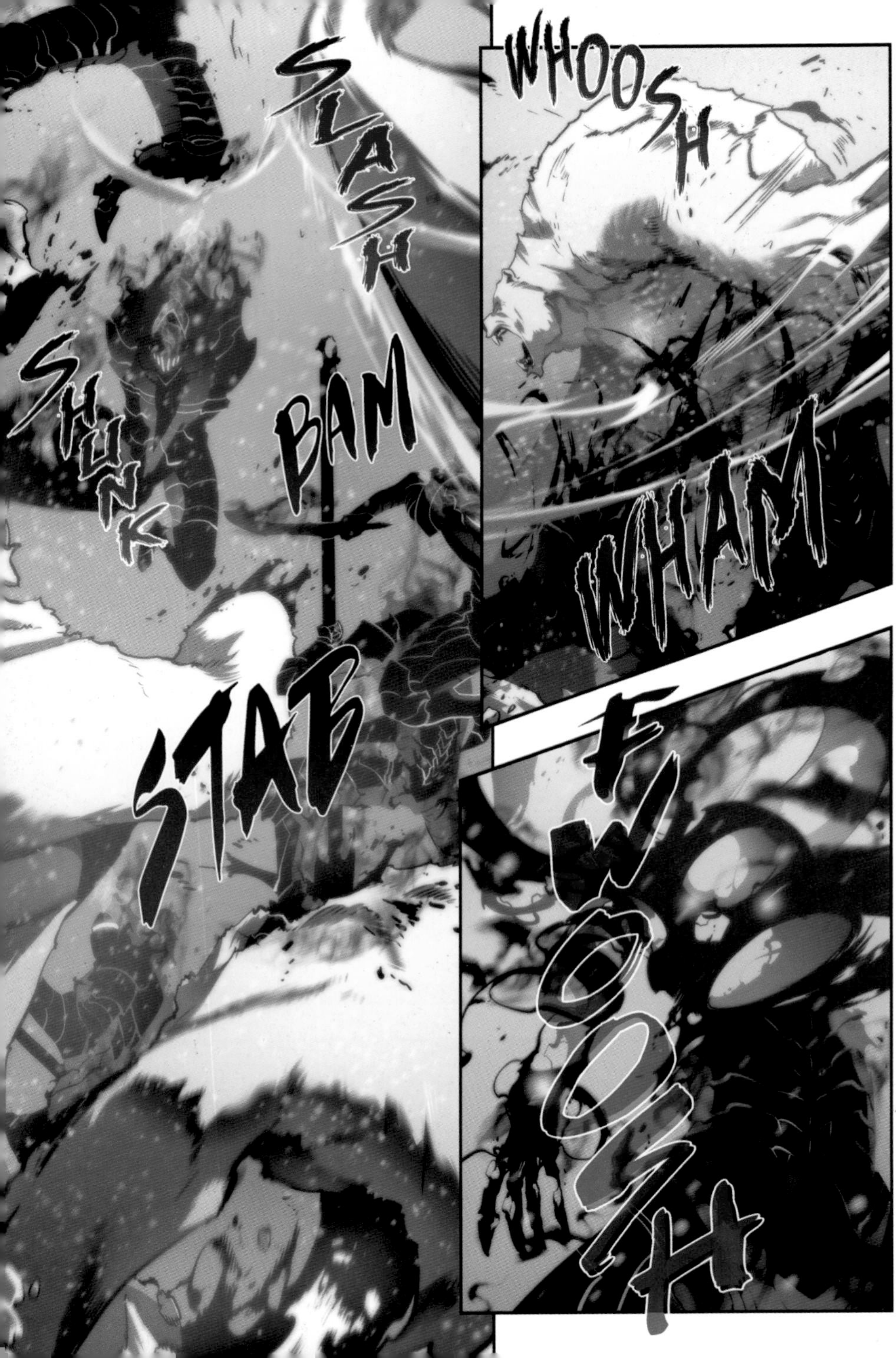
SLASH
SHUNK
BAM
STAB
WHOOSH
WHAM
FWOOOOSH

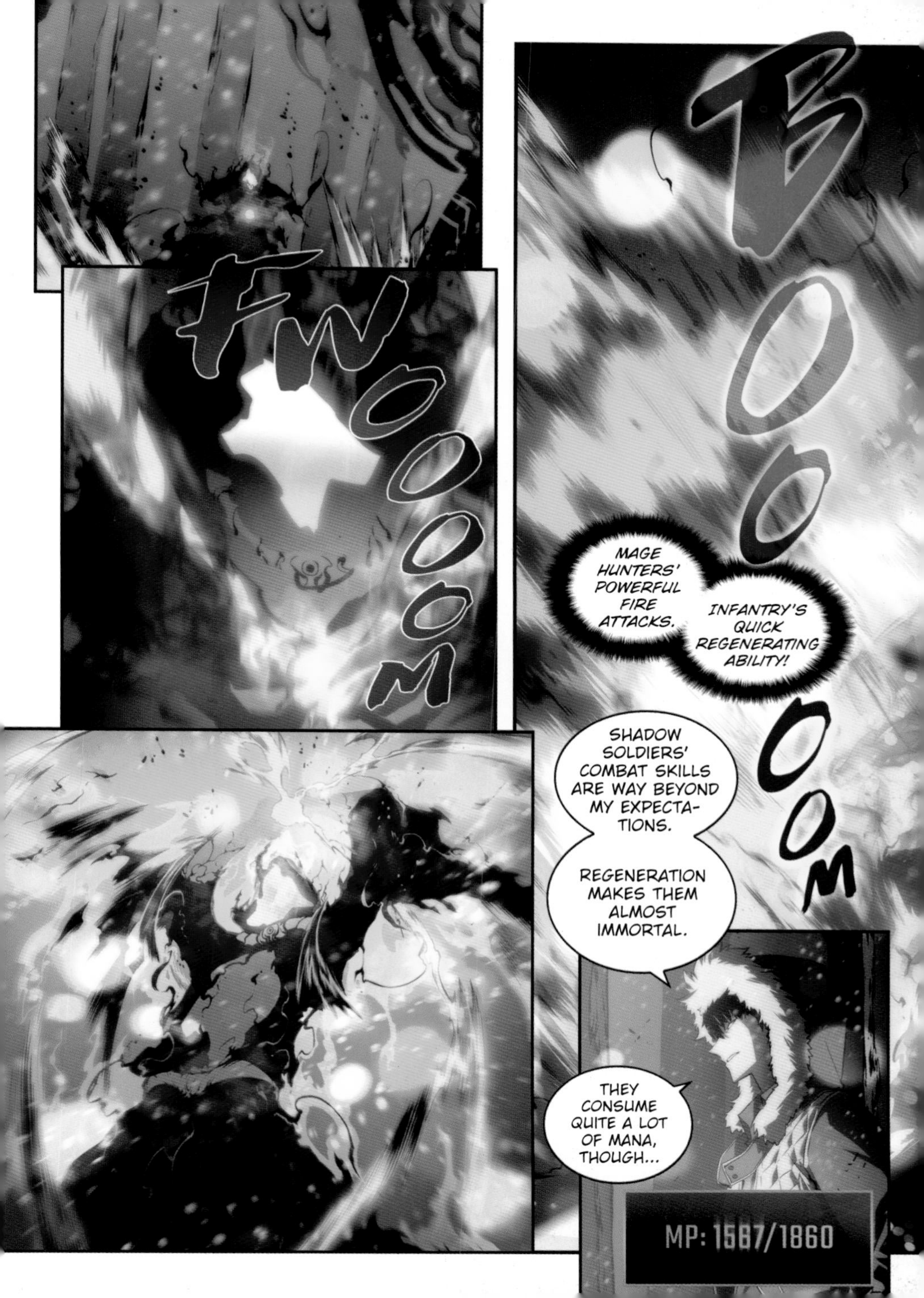
FWOOOOOM
BOOOOOOOM
MAGE HUNTERS' POWERFUL FIRE ATTACKS.
INFANTRY'S QUICK REGENERATING ABILITY!
SHADOW SOLDIERS' COMBAT SKILLS ARE WAY BEYOND MY EXPECTA-TIONS.
REGENERATION MAKES THEM ALMOST IMMORTAL.
THEY CONSUME QUITE A LOT OF MANA, THOUGH...
MP: 1567/1860

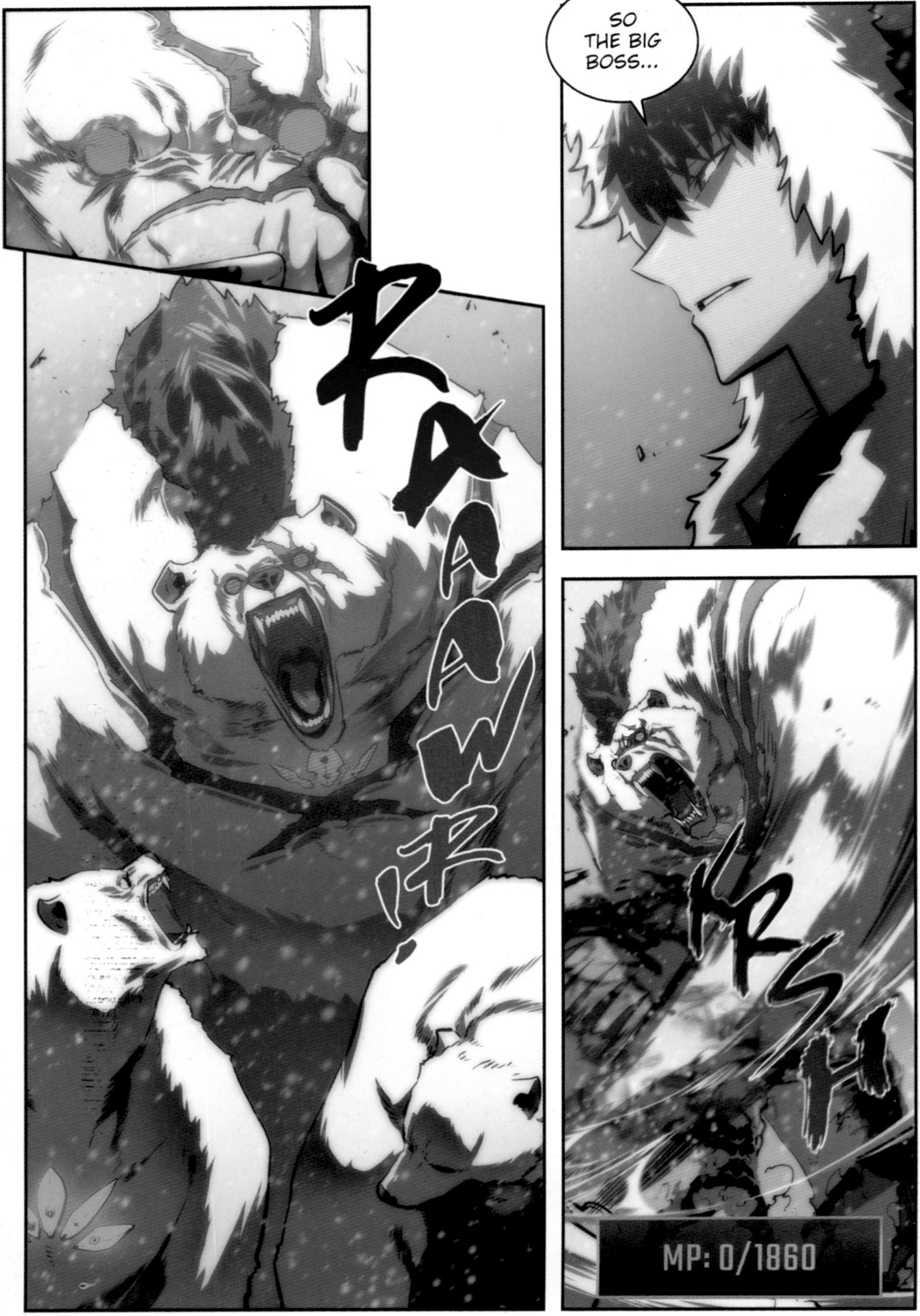
SO THE BIG BOSS...
RAAWR!
KRSH
MP: 0/1860

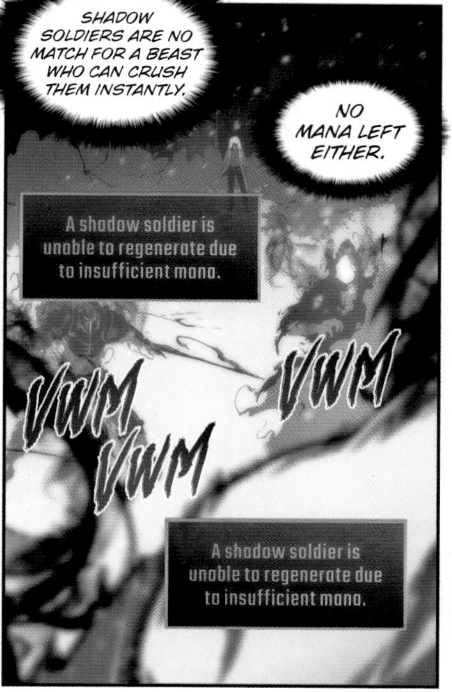
SHADOW SOLDIERS ARE NO MATCH FOR A BEAST WHO CAN CRUSH THEM INSTANTLY.
NO MANA LEFT EITHER.
A shadow soldier is unable to regenerate due to insufficient mana.
VWM
VWM
VWM
A shadow soldier is unable to regenerate due to insufficient mana.
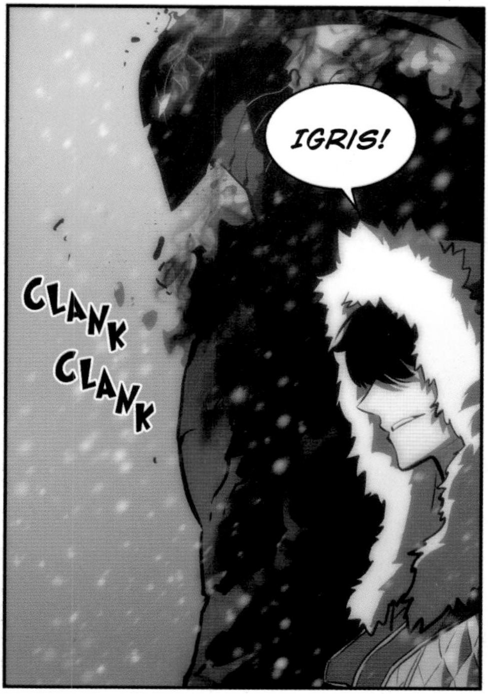
IGRIS!
CLANK
CLANK
CLANK
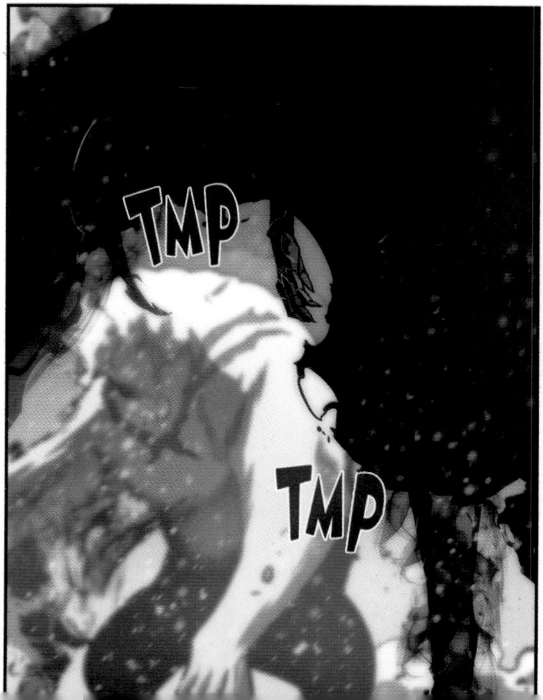
TMP
TMP
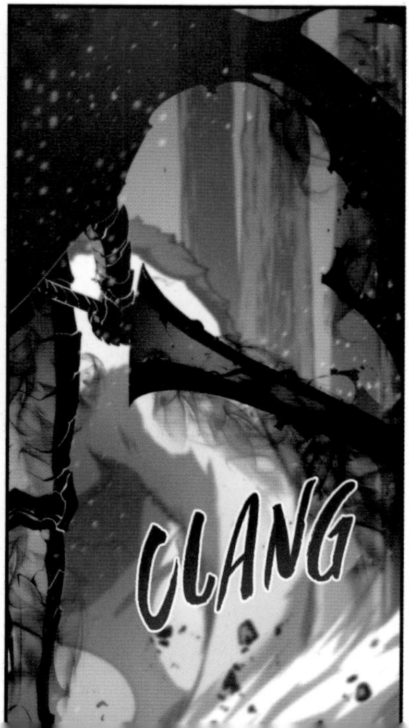
CLANG

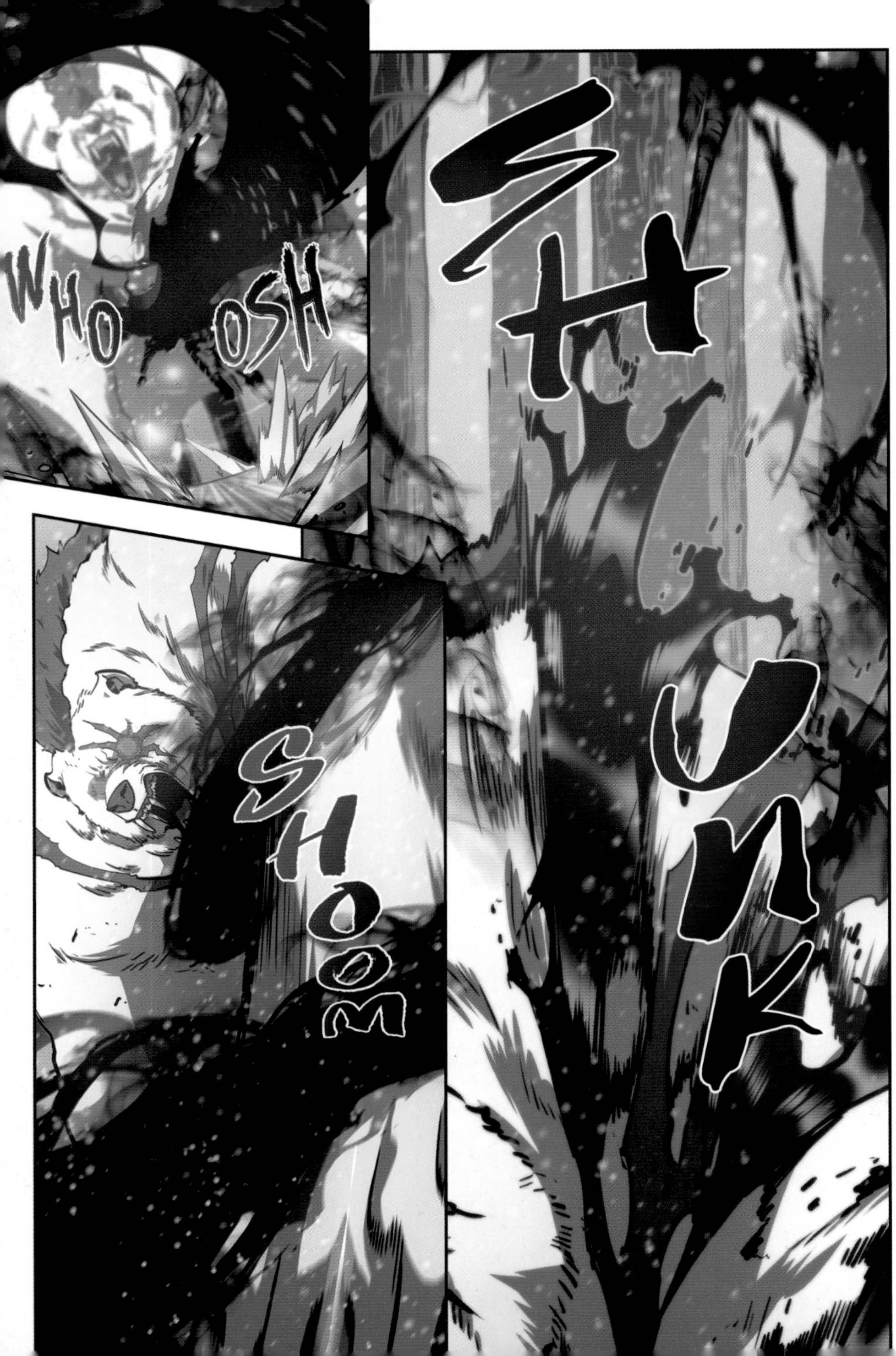
WHOOSH
SHOOM
SHUNK

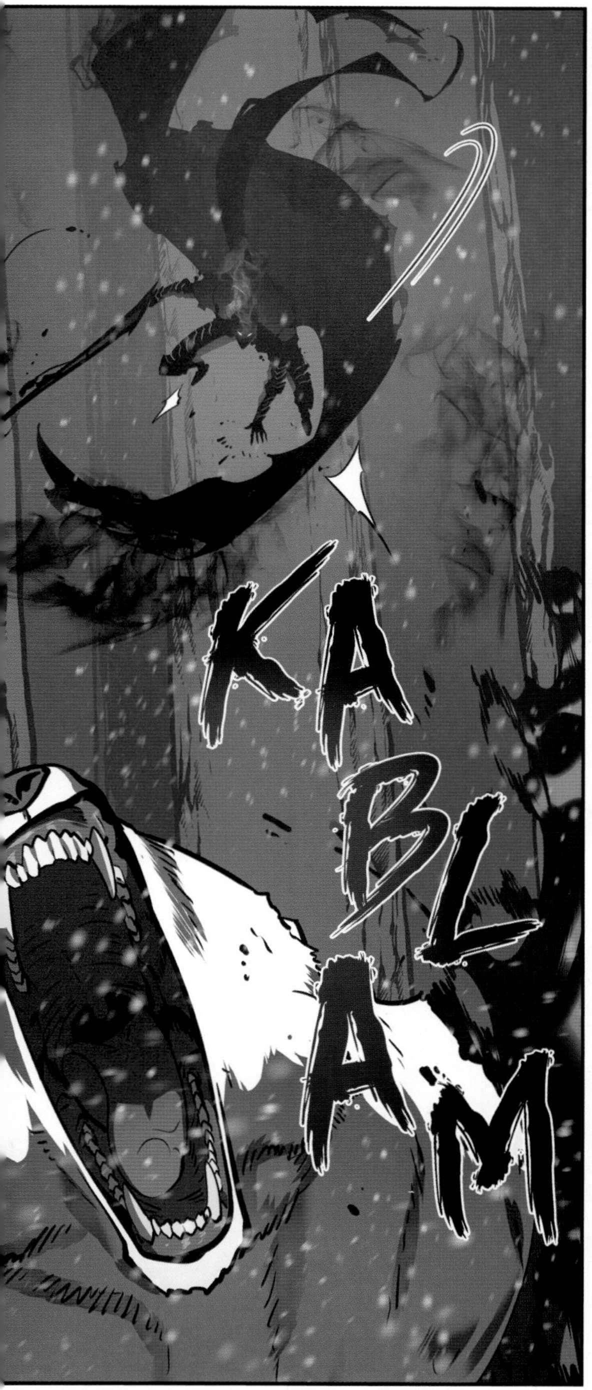
KABLAM
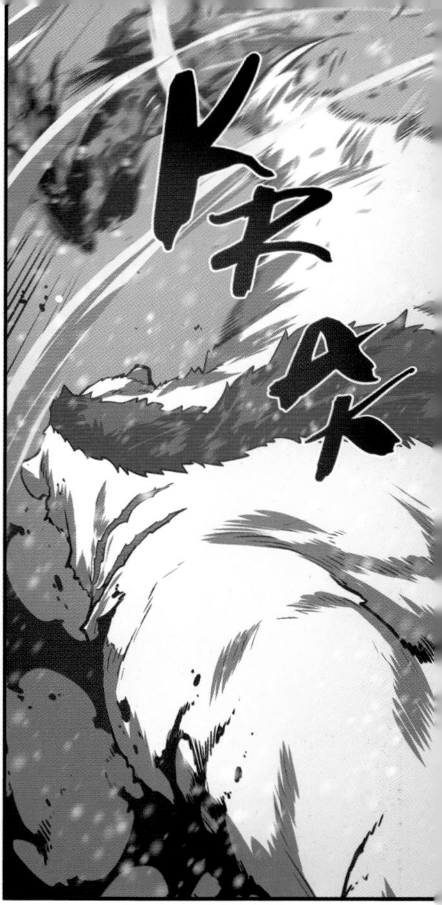
KRAK
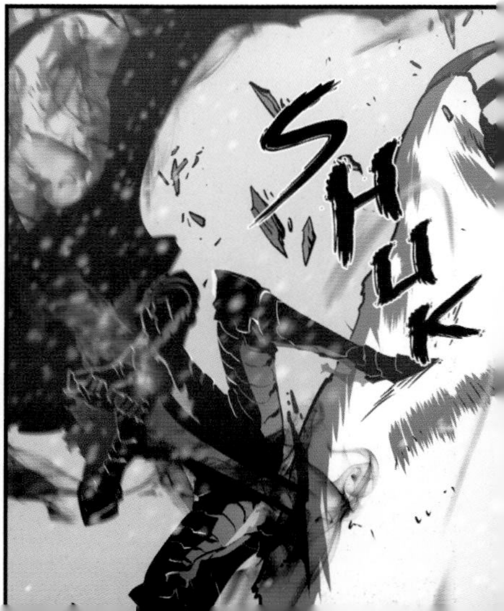
SHUK

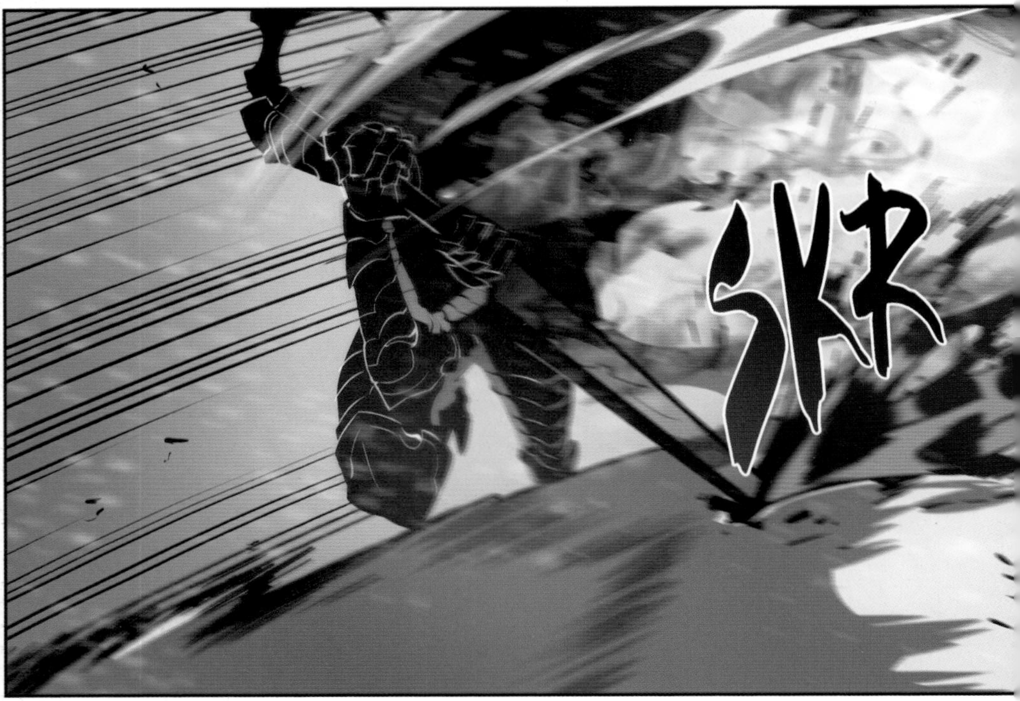
SKR
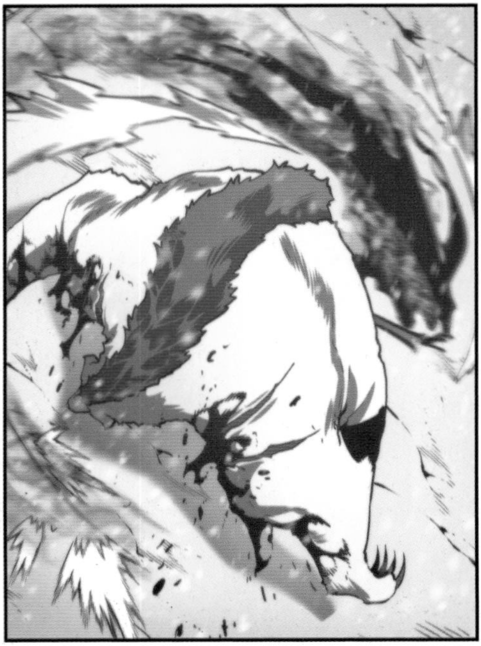
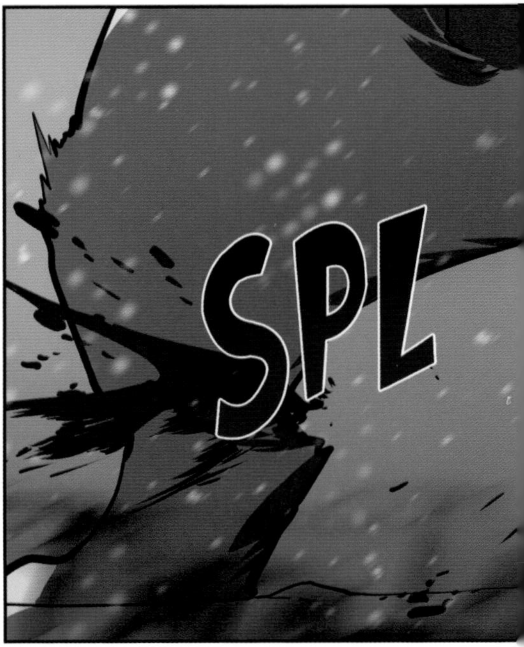
SPL

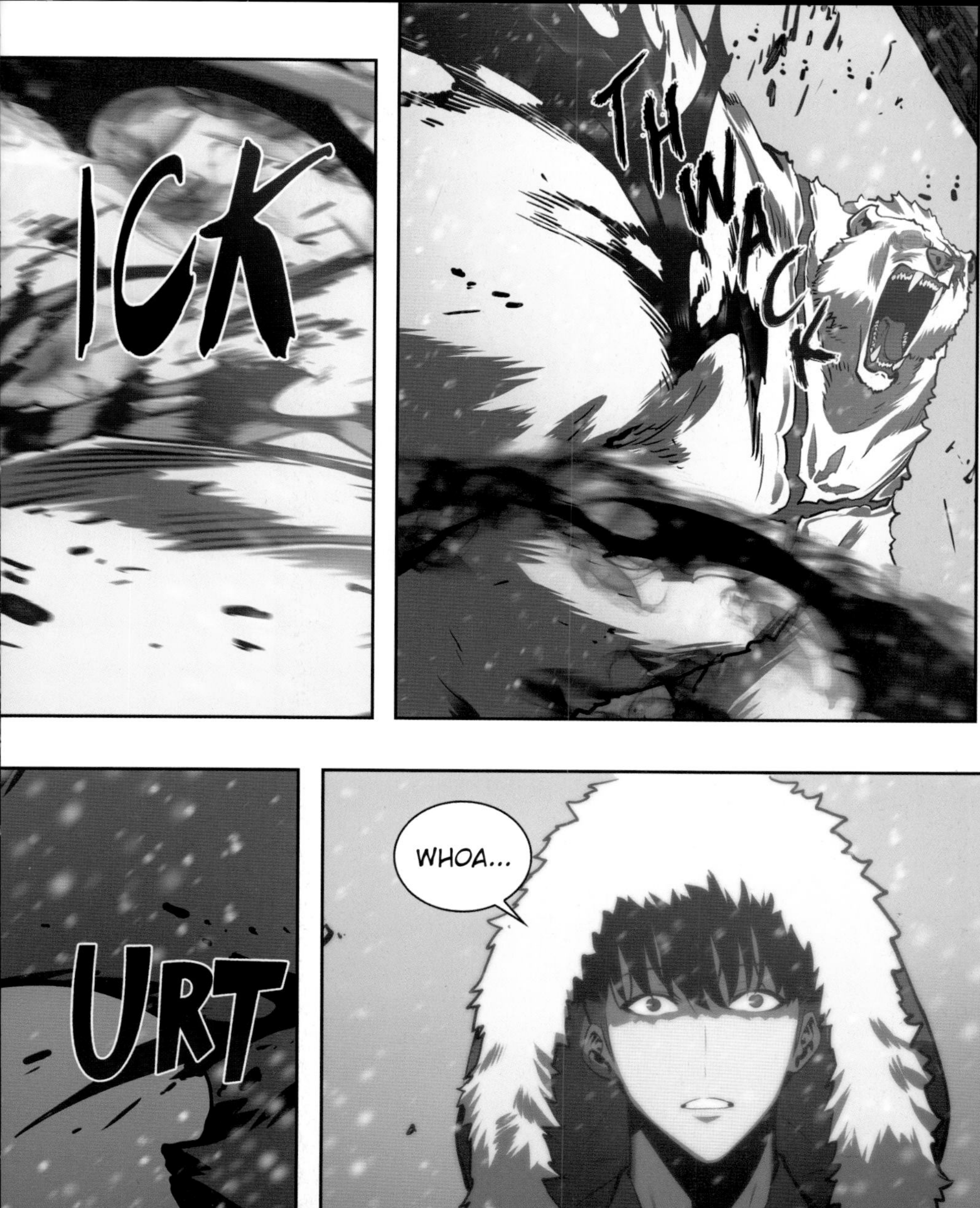
ICK
THWACK
URT
WHOA...

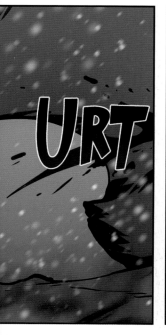

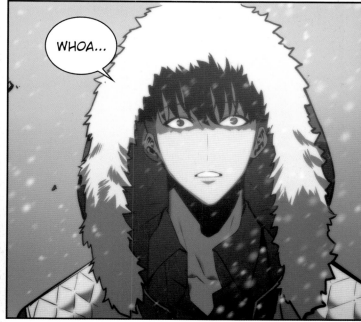

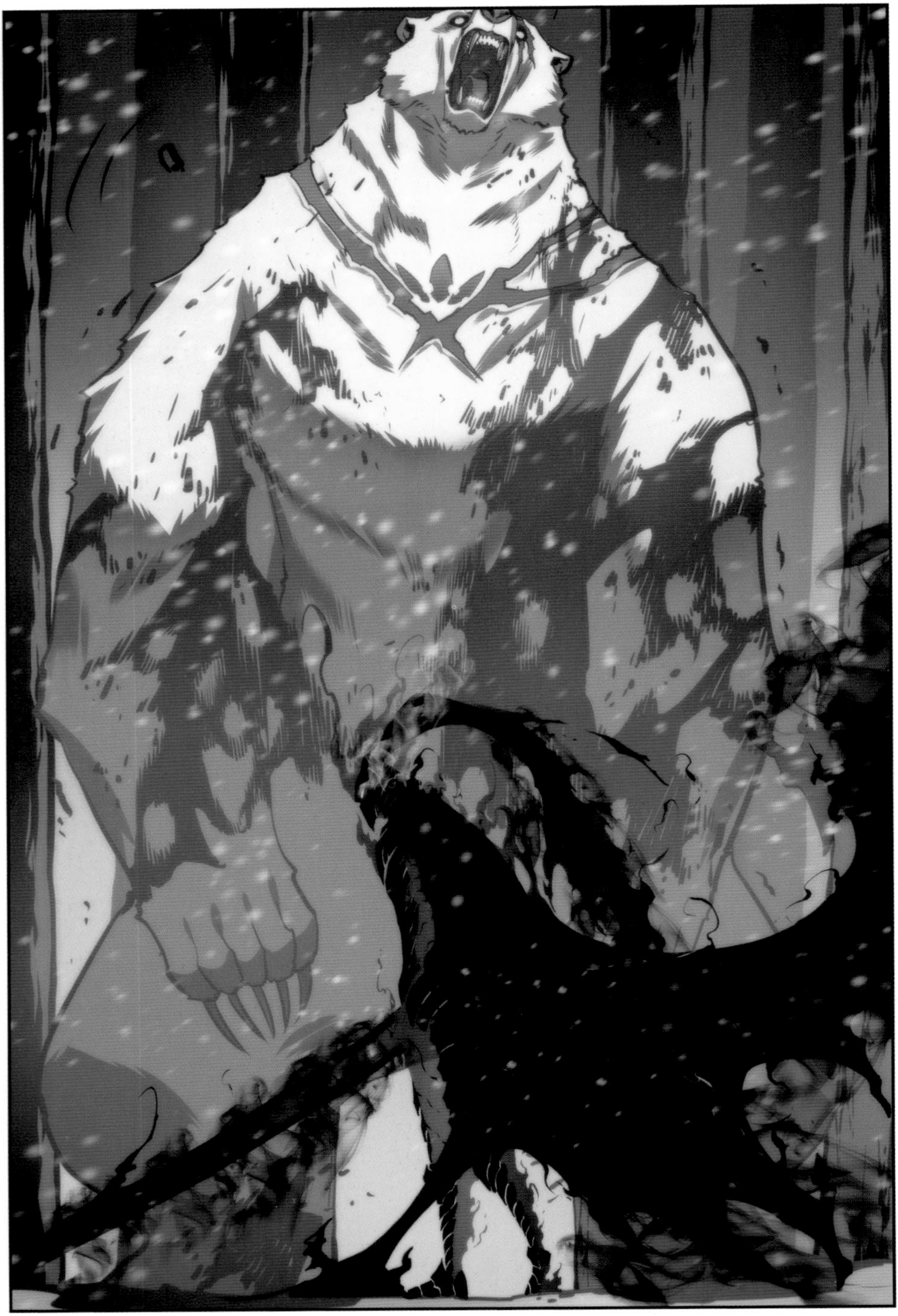

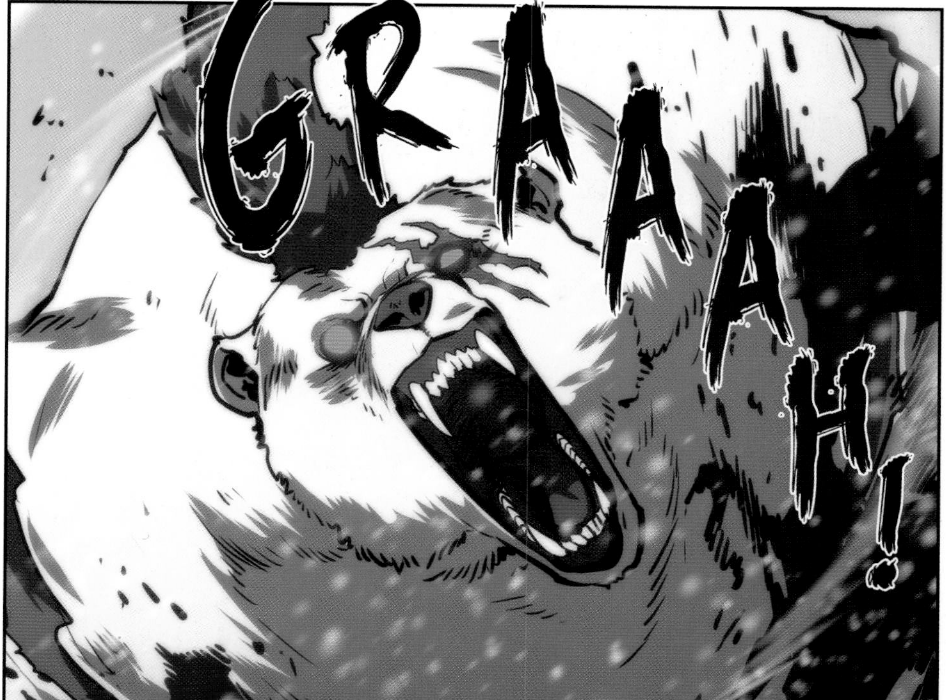
GRAAAH!
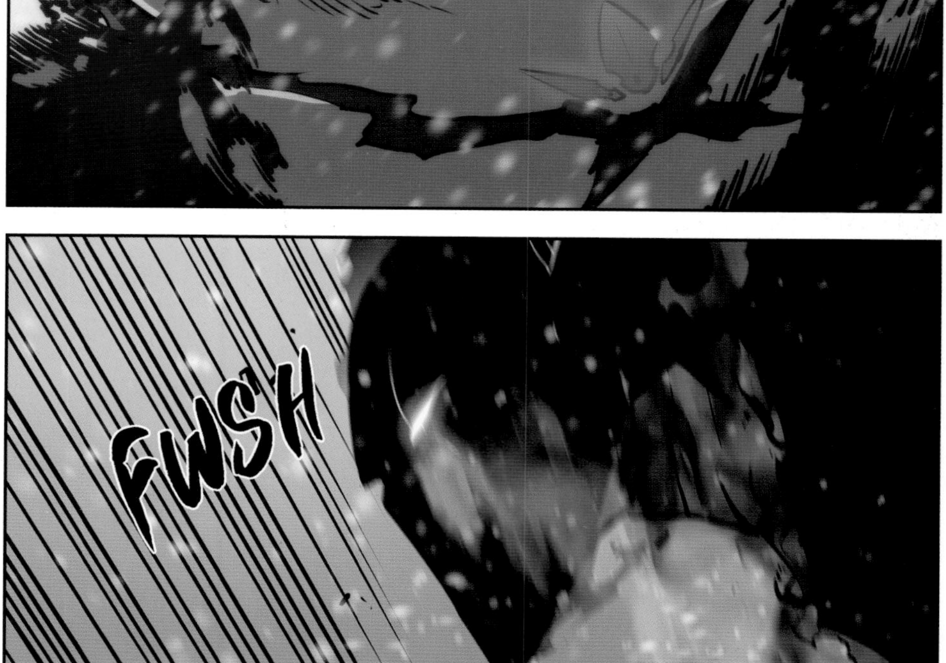
FWSH

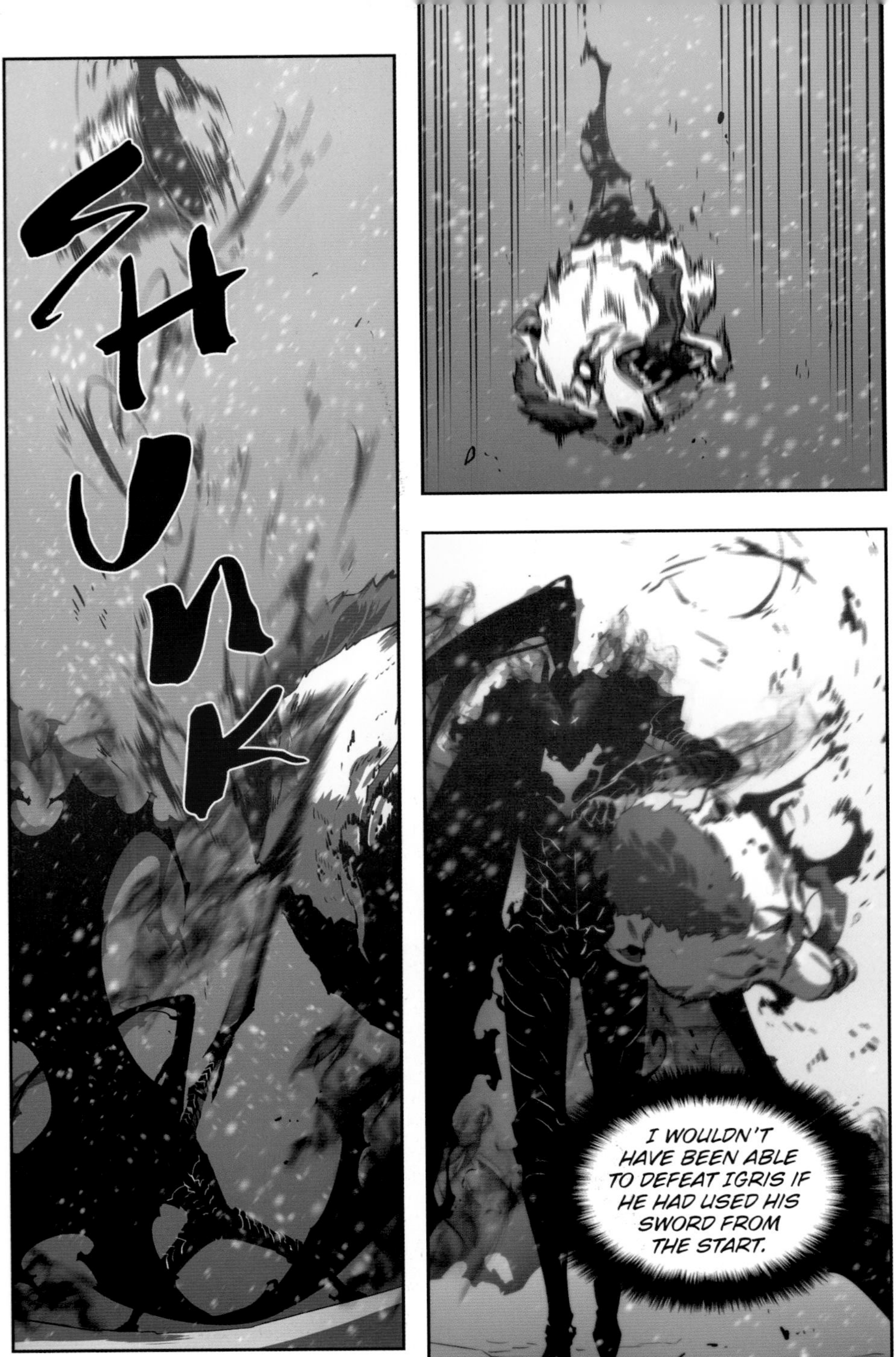
SHUNK
I WOULDN'T HAVE BEEN ABLE TO DEFEAT IGRIS IF HE HAD USED HIS SWORD FROM THE START.

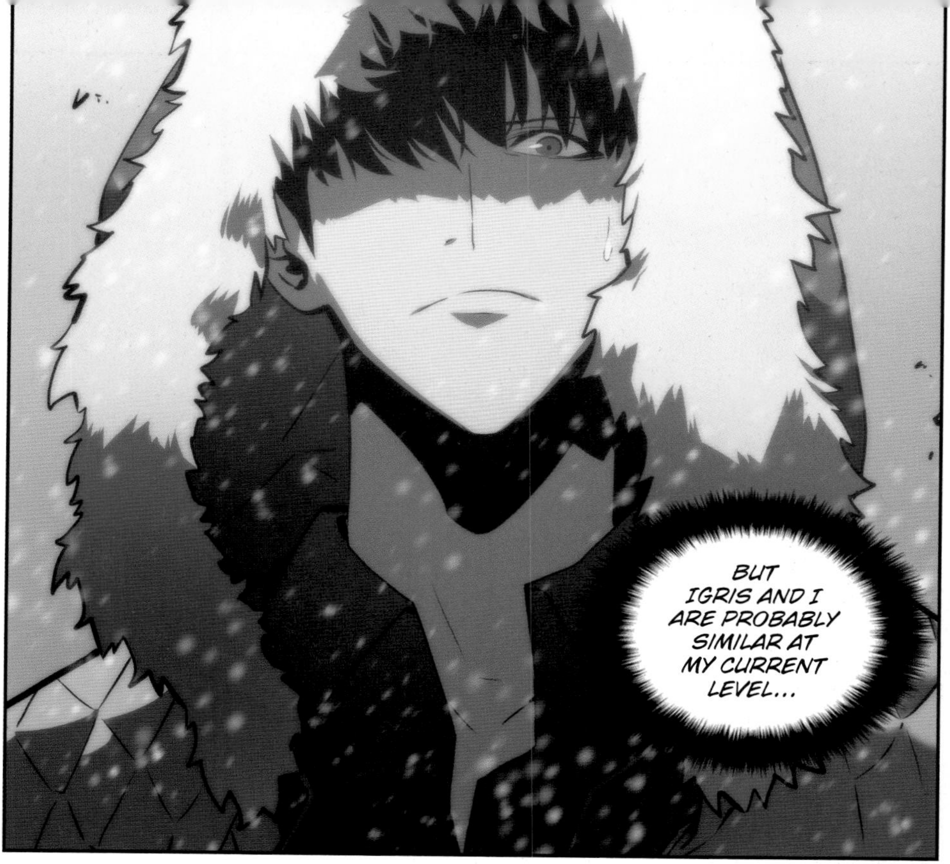
BUT IGRIS AND I ARE PROBABLY SIMILAR AT MY CURRENT LEVEL...
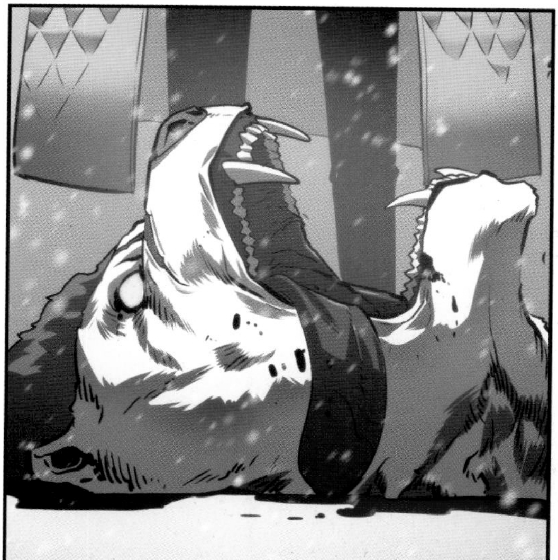
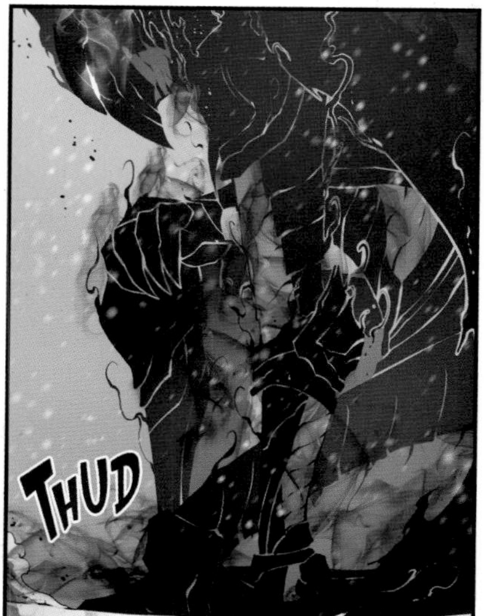
THUD

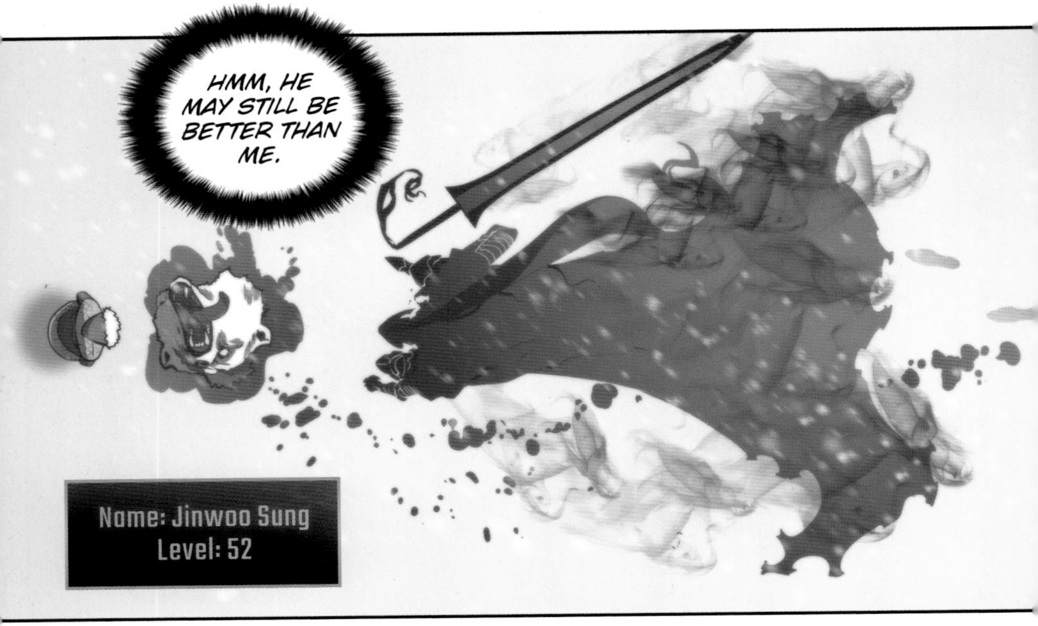
HMM, HE MAY STILL BE BETTER THAN ME.
Name: Jinwoo Sung
Level: 52

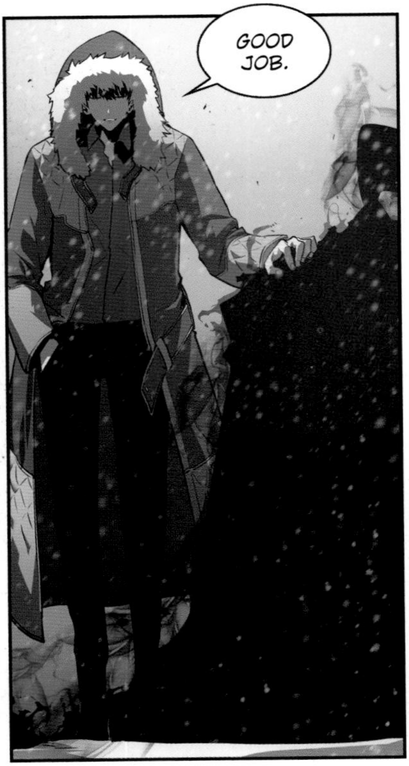
GOOD JOB.

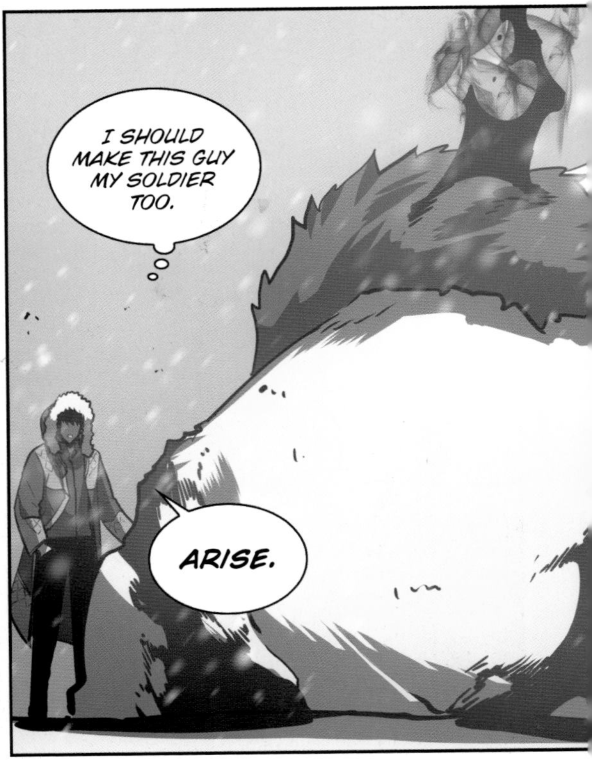
I SHOULD MAKE THIS GUY MY SOLDIER TOO.
ARISE.

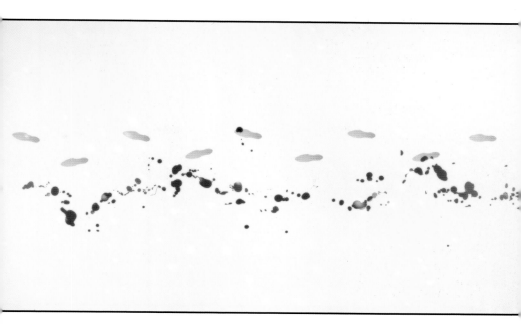

FWOOM

Shadow Extraction
is successful.

GROAR!

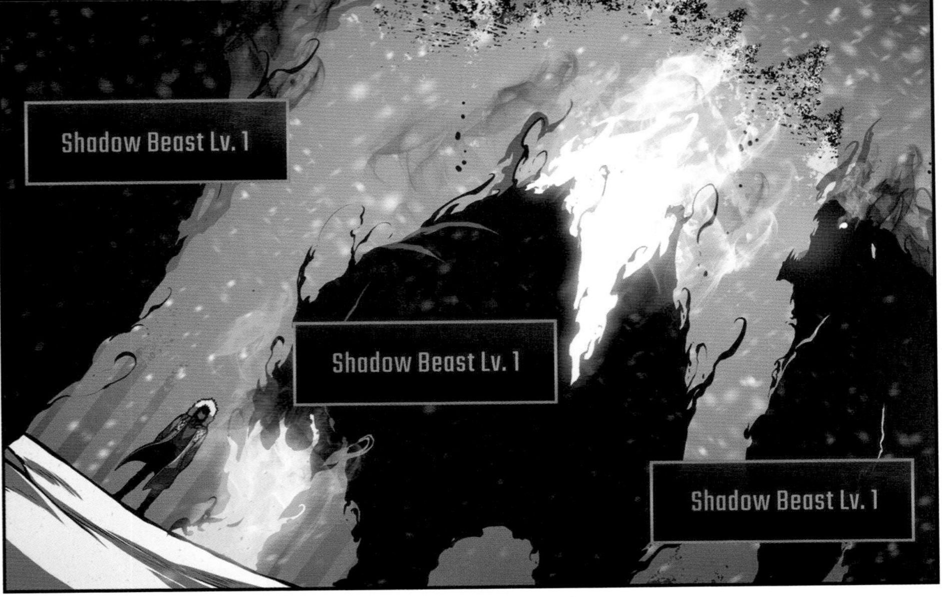
Shadow Beast Lv. 1
Shadow Beast Lv. 1
Shadow Beast Lv. 1

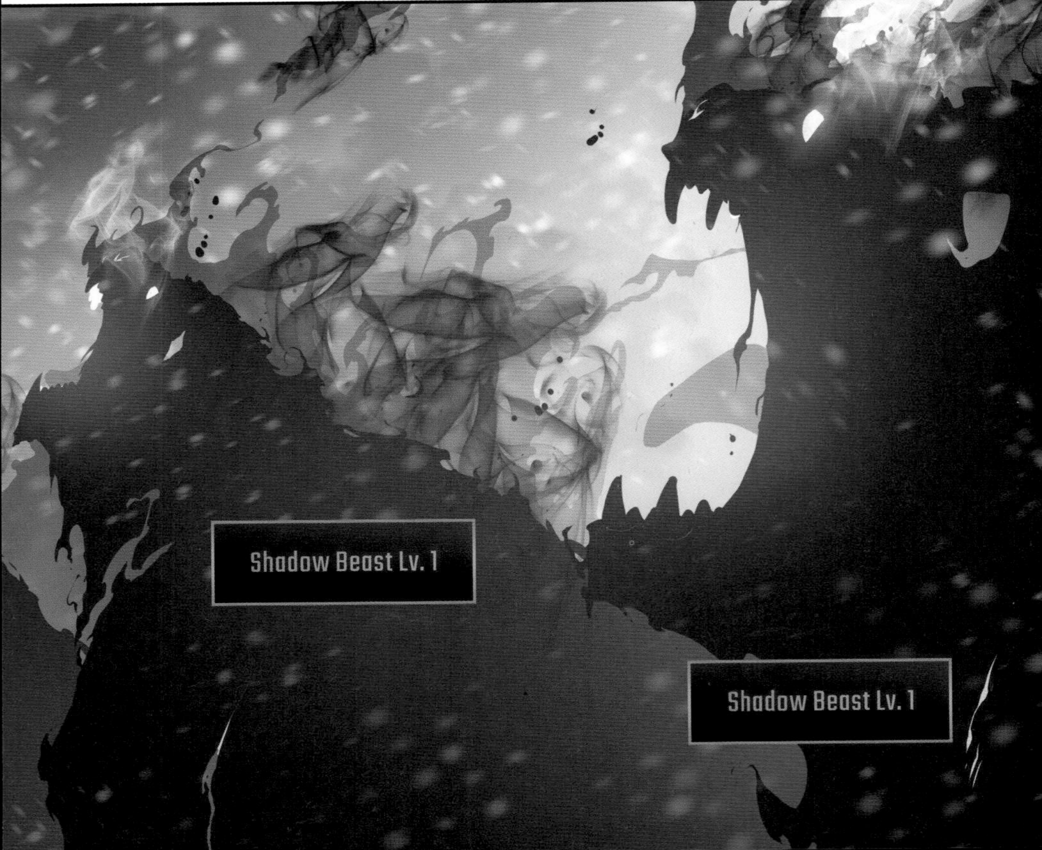
Shadow Beast Lv. 1
Shadow Beast Lv. 1

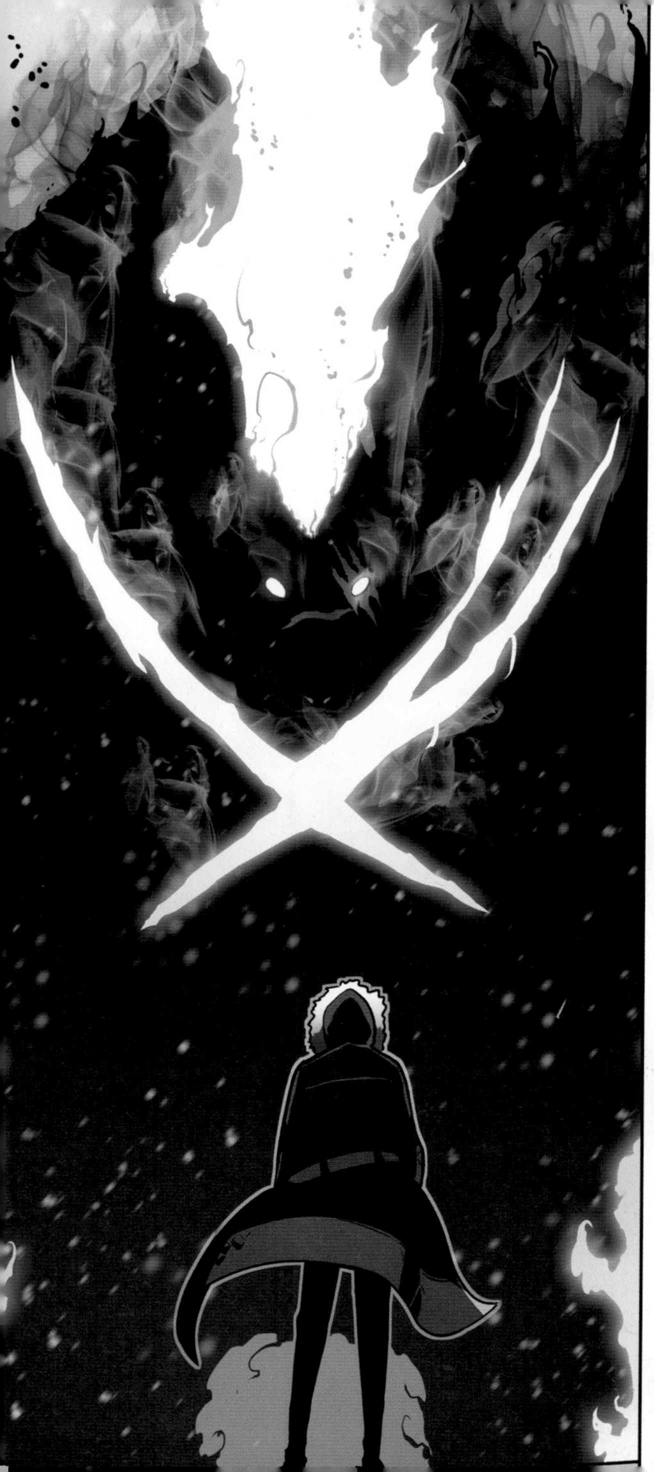
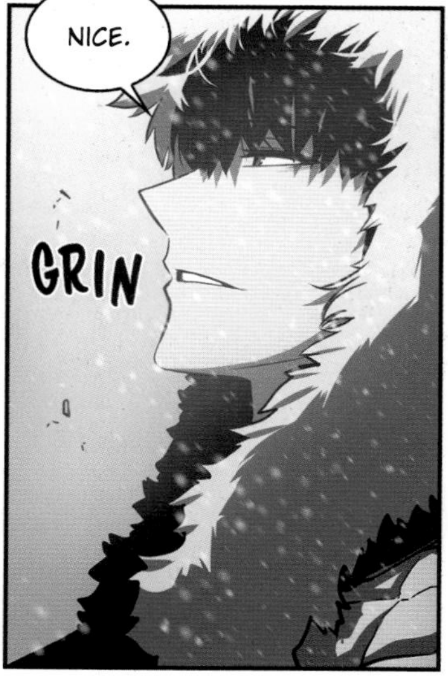
NICE.
GRIN
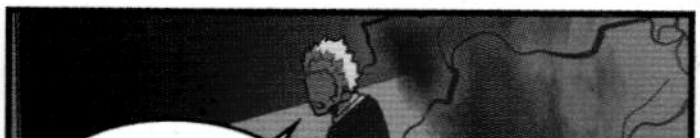
HOW LONG HAS IT BEEN?
ABOUT THREE HOURS... SO THREE DAYS HAVE PASSED INSIDE.
WHO KNOWS HOW MANY ARE STILL ALIVE...
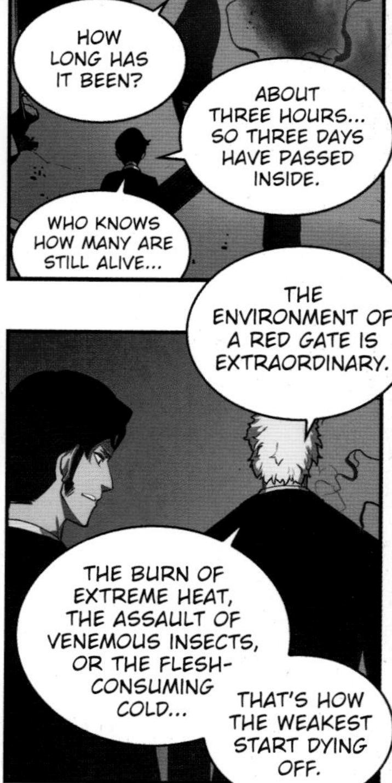
THE ENVIRONMENT OF A RED GATE IS EXTRAORDINARY.
THE BURN OF EXTREME HEAT, THE ASSAULT OF VENEMOUS INSECTS, OR THE FLESH-CONSUMING COLD...
THAT'S HOW THE WEAKEST START DYING OFF.

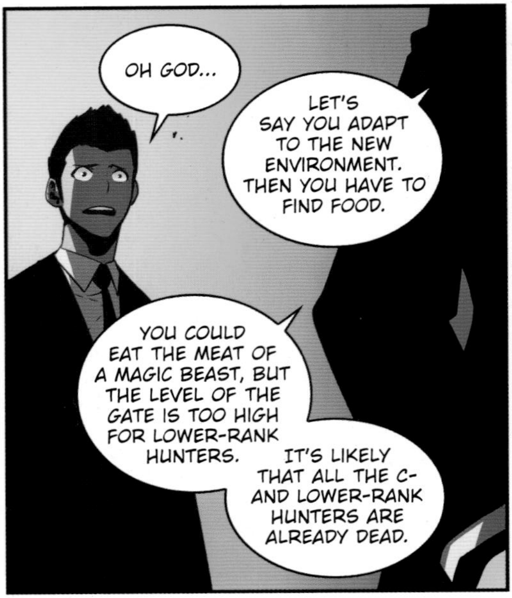
OH GOD...
LET'S SAY YOU ADAPT TO THE NEW ENVIRONMENT. THEN YOU HAVE TO FIND FOOD.
YOU COULD EAT THE MEAT OF A MAGIC BEAST, BUT THE LEVEL OF THE GATE IS TOO HIGH FOR LOWER-RANK HUNTERS.
IT'S LIKELY THAT ALL THE C- AND LOWER-RANK HUNTERS ARE ALREADY DEAD.
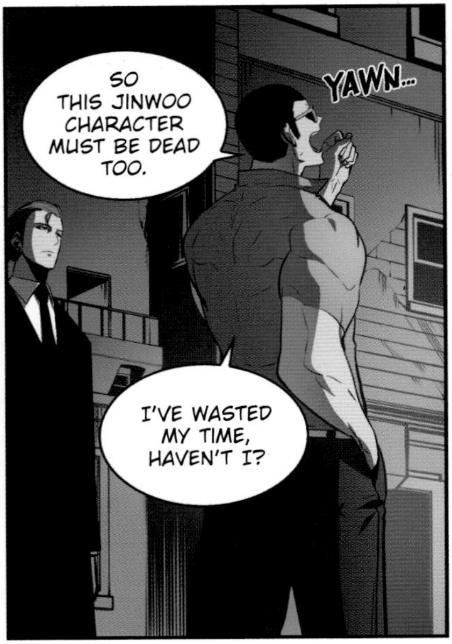
SO THIS JINWOO CHARACTER MUST BE DEAD TOO.
YAWN...
I'VE WASTED MY TIME, HAVEN'T I?
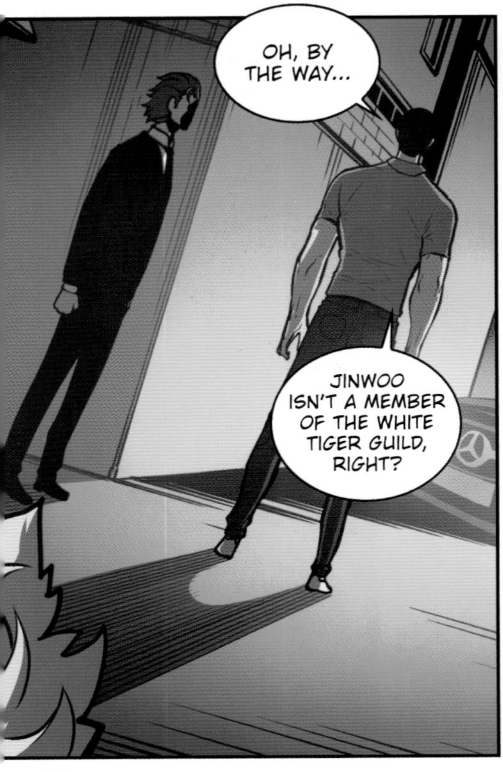
OH, BY THE WAY...
JINWOO ISN'T A MEMBER OF THE WHITE TIGER GUILD, RIGHT?
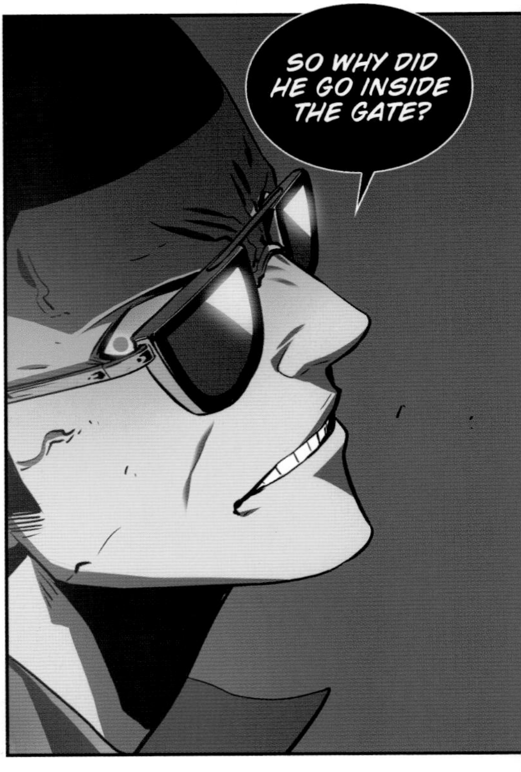
SO WHY DID HE GO INSIDE THE GATE?

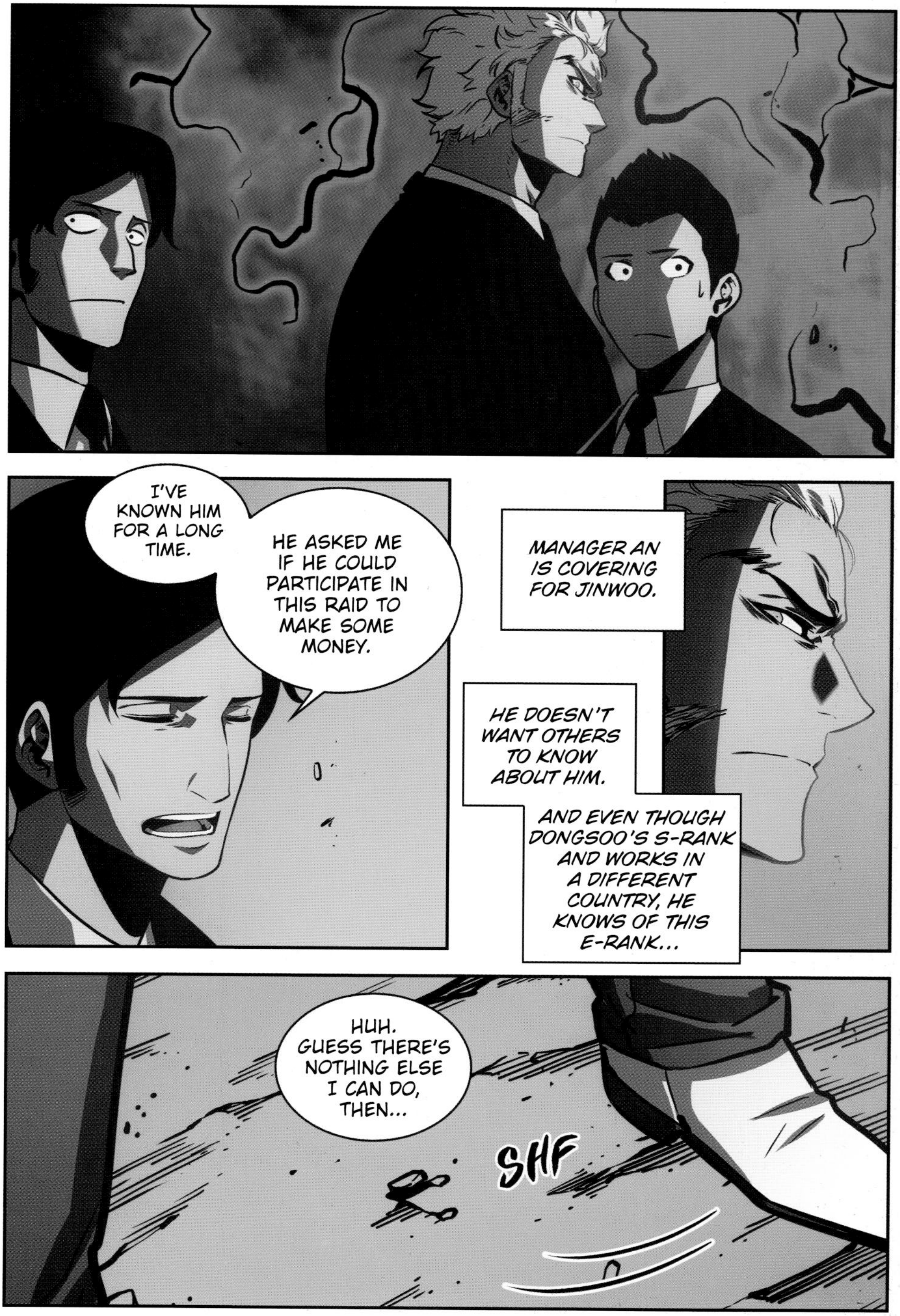
I'VE KNOWN HIM FOR A LONG TIME.
HE ASKED ME IF HE COULD PARTICIPATE IN THIS RAID TO MAKE SOME MONEY.
MANAGER AN IS COVERING FOR JINWOO.
HE DOESN'T WANT OTHERS TO KNOW ABOUT HIM.
AND EVEN THOUGH DONGSOO'S S-RANK AND WORKS IN A DIFFERENT COUNTRY, HE KNOWS OF THIS E-RANK...
HUH. GUESS THERE'S NOTHING ELSE I CAN DO, THEN...
SHF

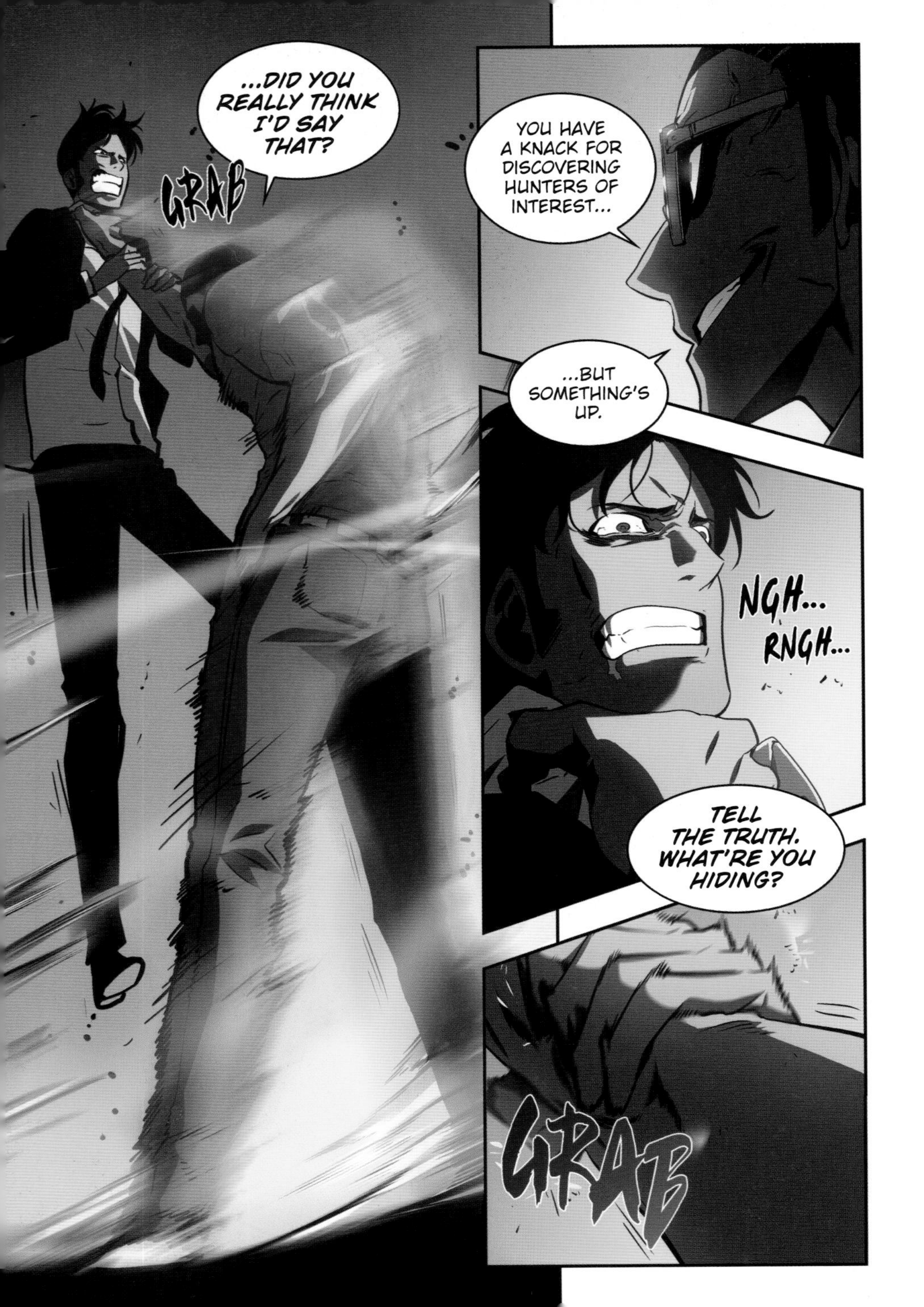
...DID YOU REALLY THINK I'D SAY THAT?
GRAB
YOU HAVE A KNACK FOR DISCOVERING HUNTERS OF INTEREST...
...BUT SOMETHING'S UP.
NGH... RNGH...
TELL THE TRUTH. WHAT'RE YOU HIDING?
GRAB

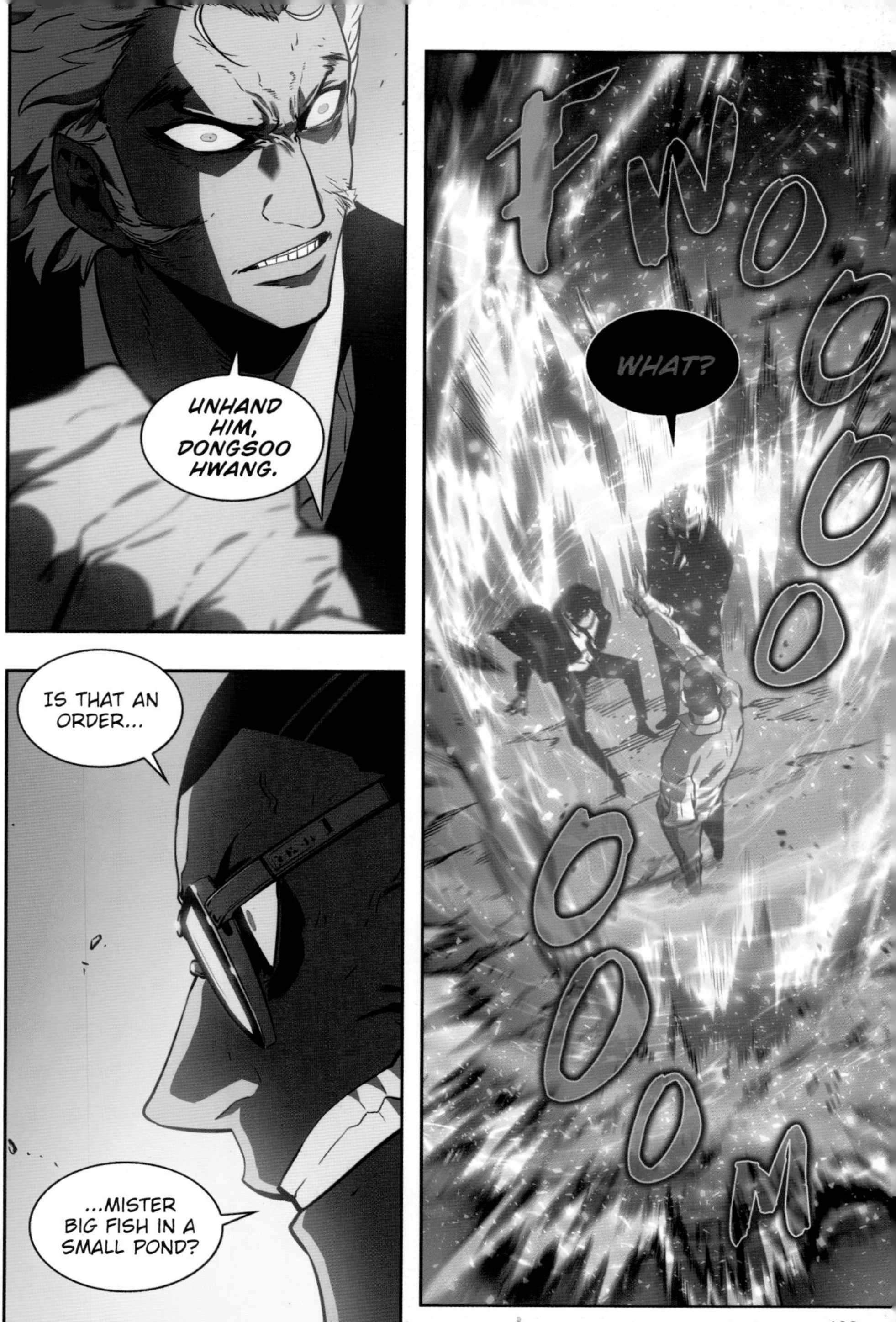
UNHAND HIM, DONGSOO HWANG.
IS THAT AN ORDER...
...MISTER BIG FISH IN A SMALL POND?
FWOOOOOOOOOM
WHAT?

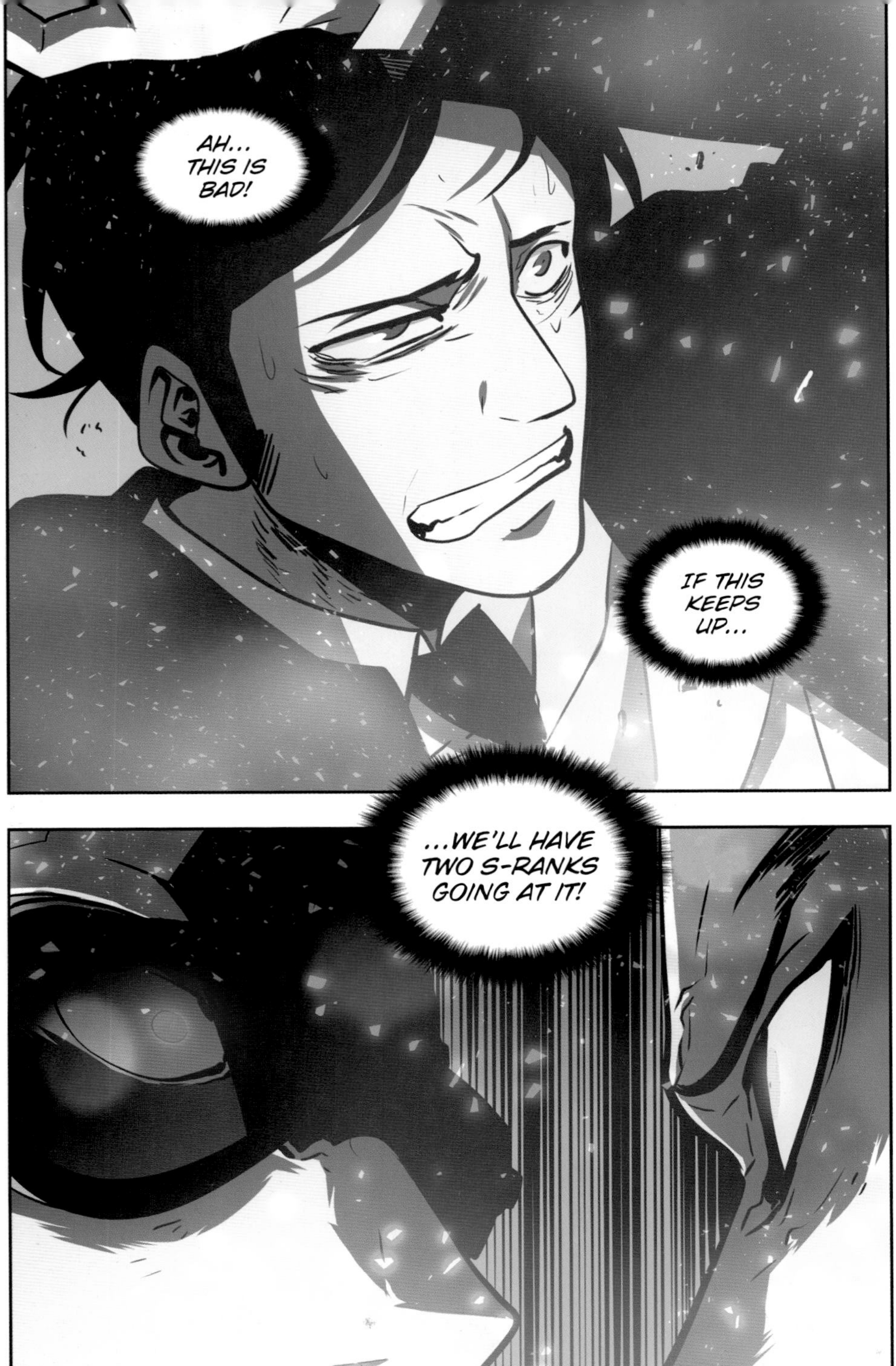
AH... THIS IS BAD!
IF THIS KEEPS UP...
...WE'LL HAVE TWO S-RANKS GOING AT IT!

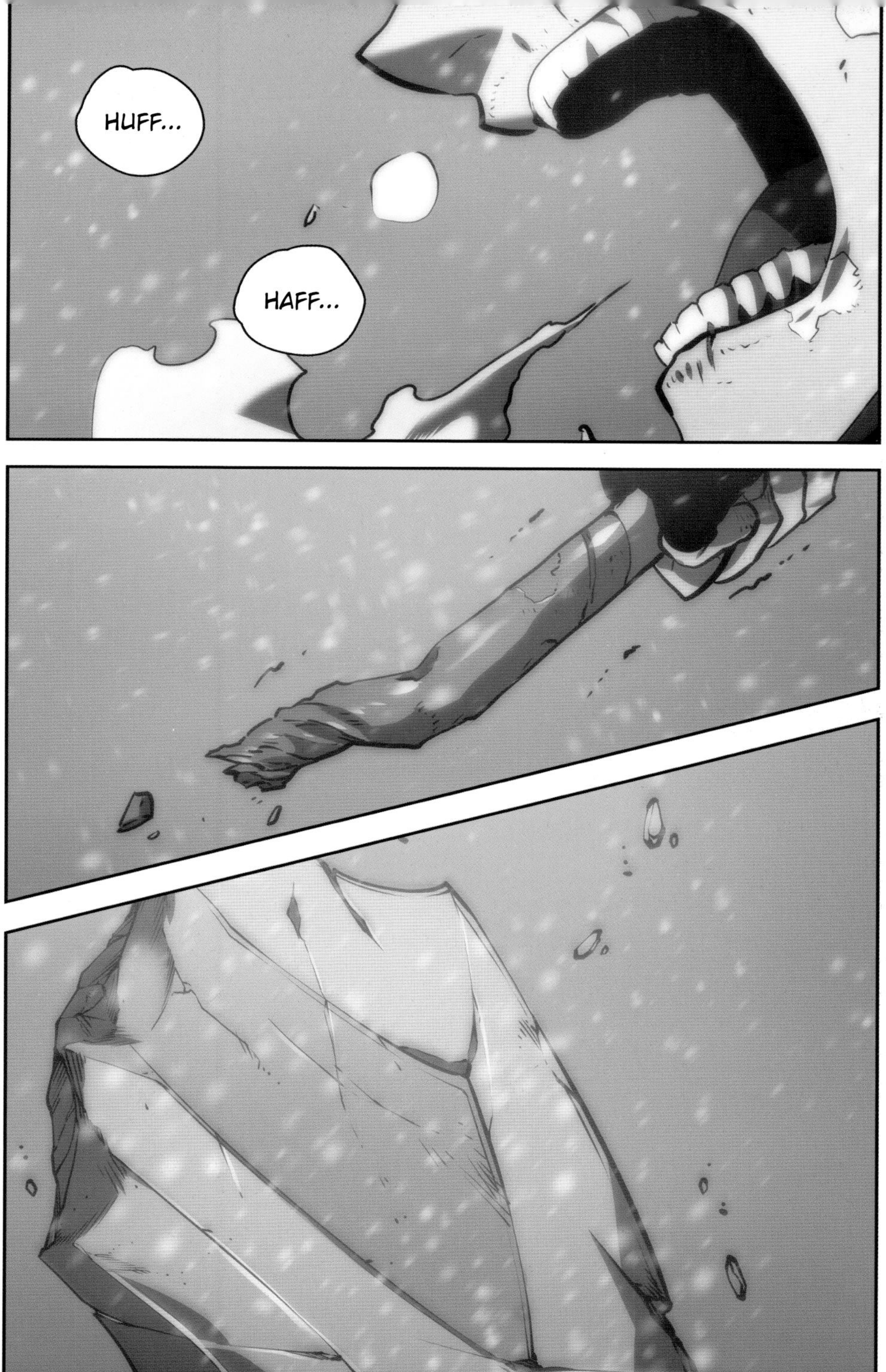
HUFF...
HAFF...

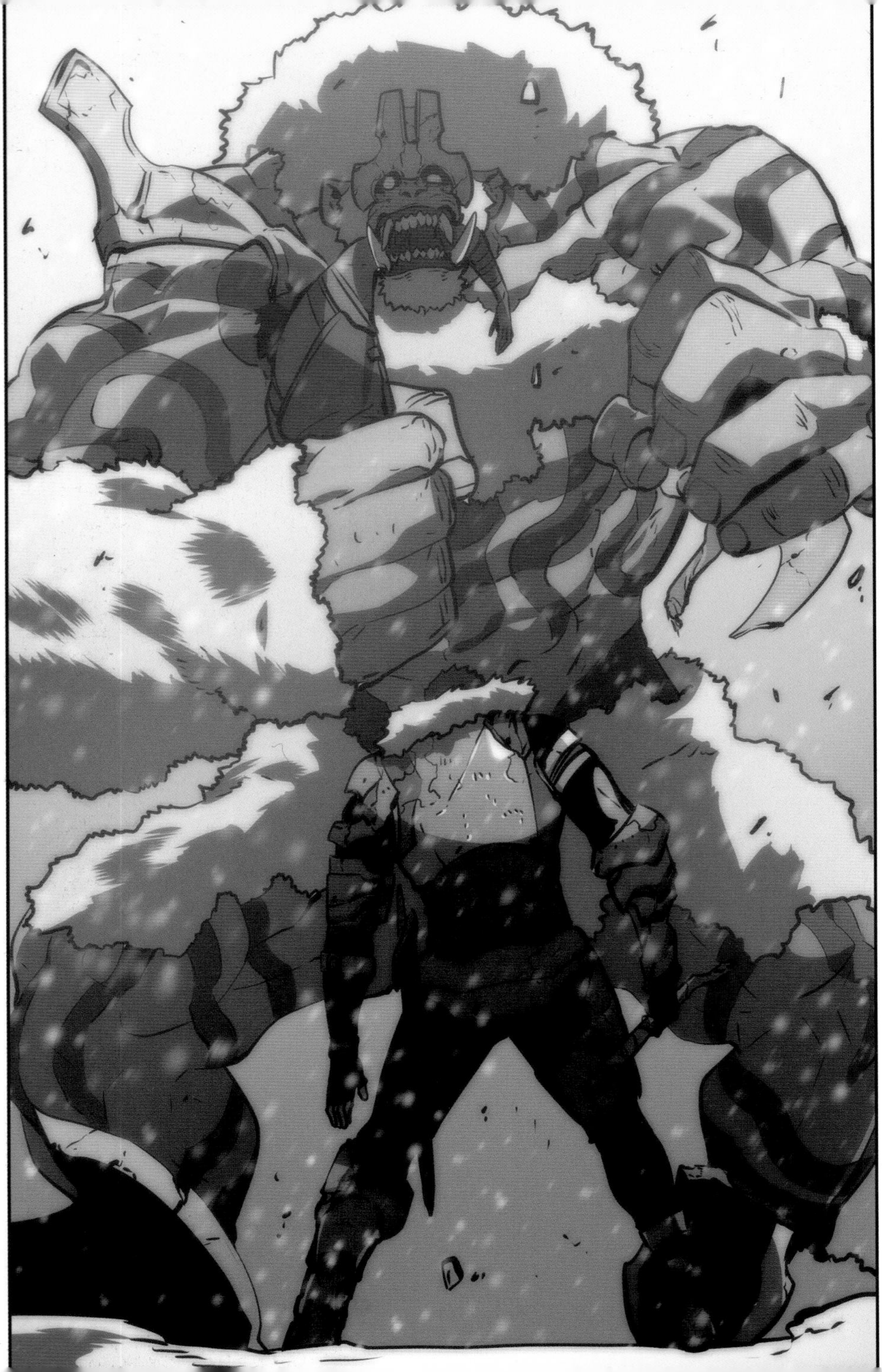

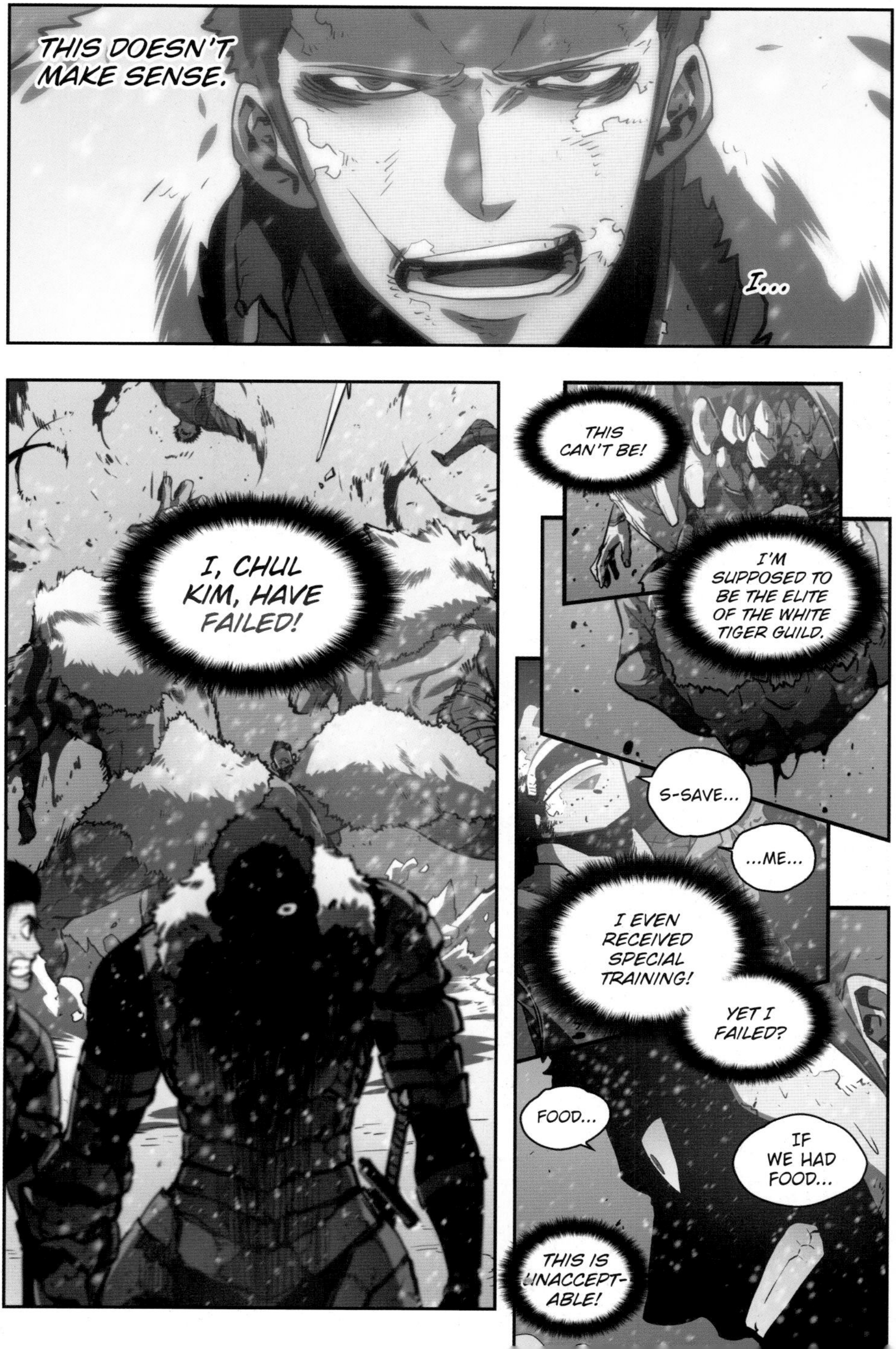
THIS DOESN'T MAKE SENSE.
I...
I, CHUL KIM, HAVE FAILED!
THIS CAN'T BE!
I'M SUPPOSED TO BE THE ELITE OF THE WHITE TIGER GUILD.
S-SAVE...
...ME...
I EVEN RECEIVED SPECIAL TRAINING!
YET I FAILED?
FOOD...
IF WE HAD FOOD...
THIS IS UNACCEPT-ABLE!

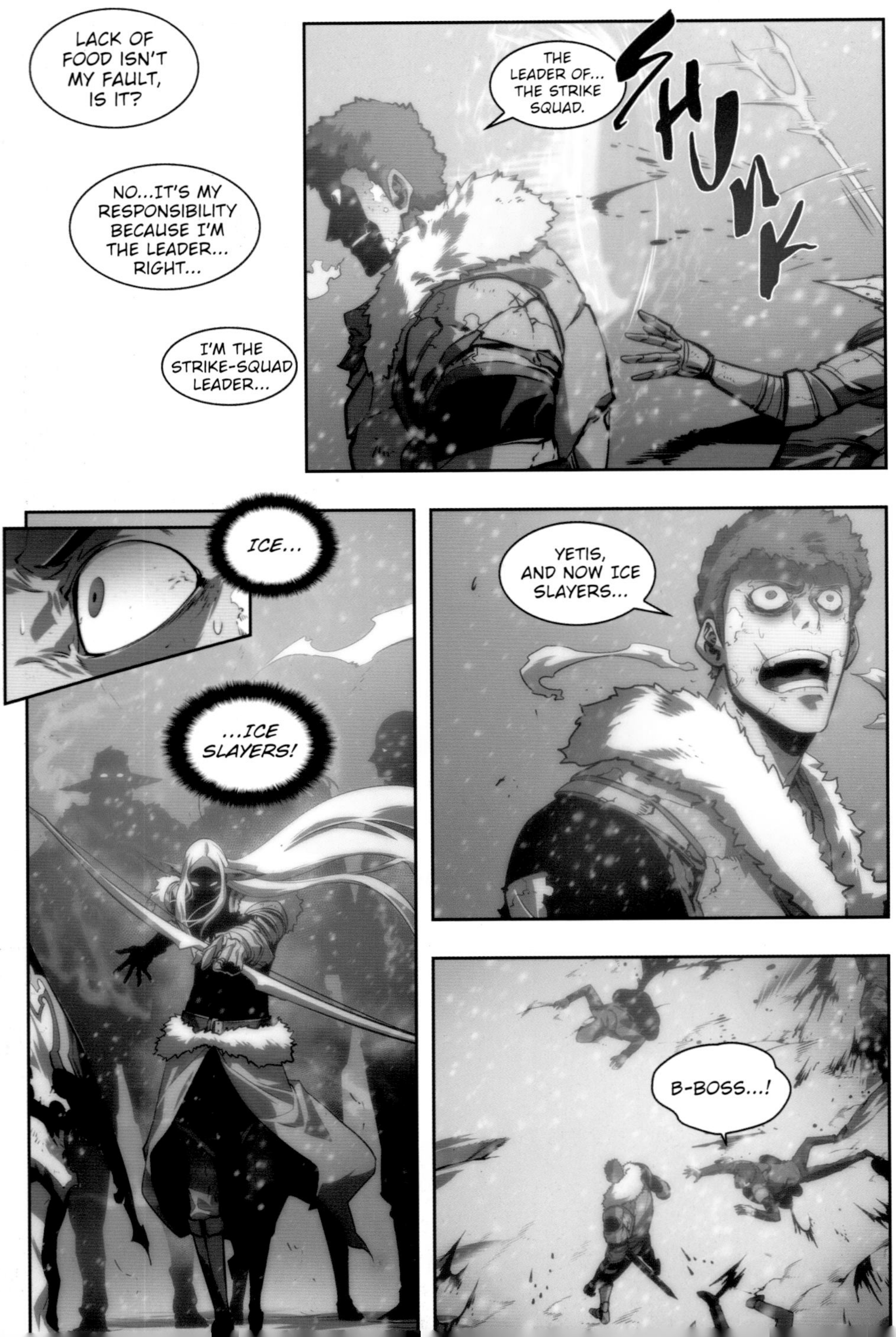
LACK OF FOOD ISN'T MY FAULT, IS IT?
NO...IT'S MY RESPONSIBILITY BECAUSE I'M THE LEADER... RIGHT...
I'M THE STRIKE-SQUAD LEADER...
THE LEADER OF... THE STRIKE SQUAD.
SHUNK
ICE...
...ICE SLAYERS!
YETIS, AND NOW ICE SLAYERS...
B-BOSS...!

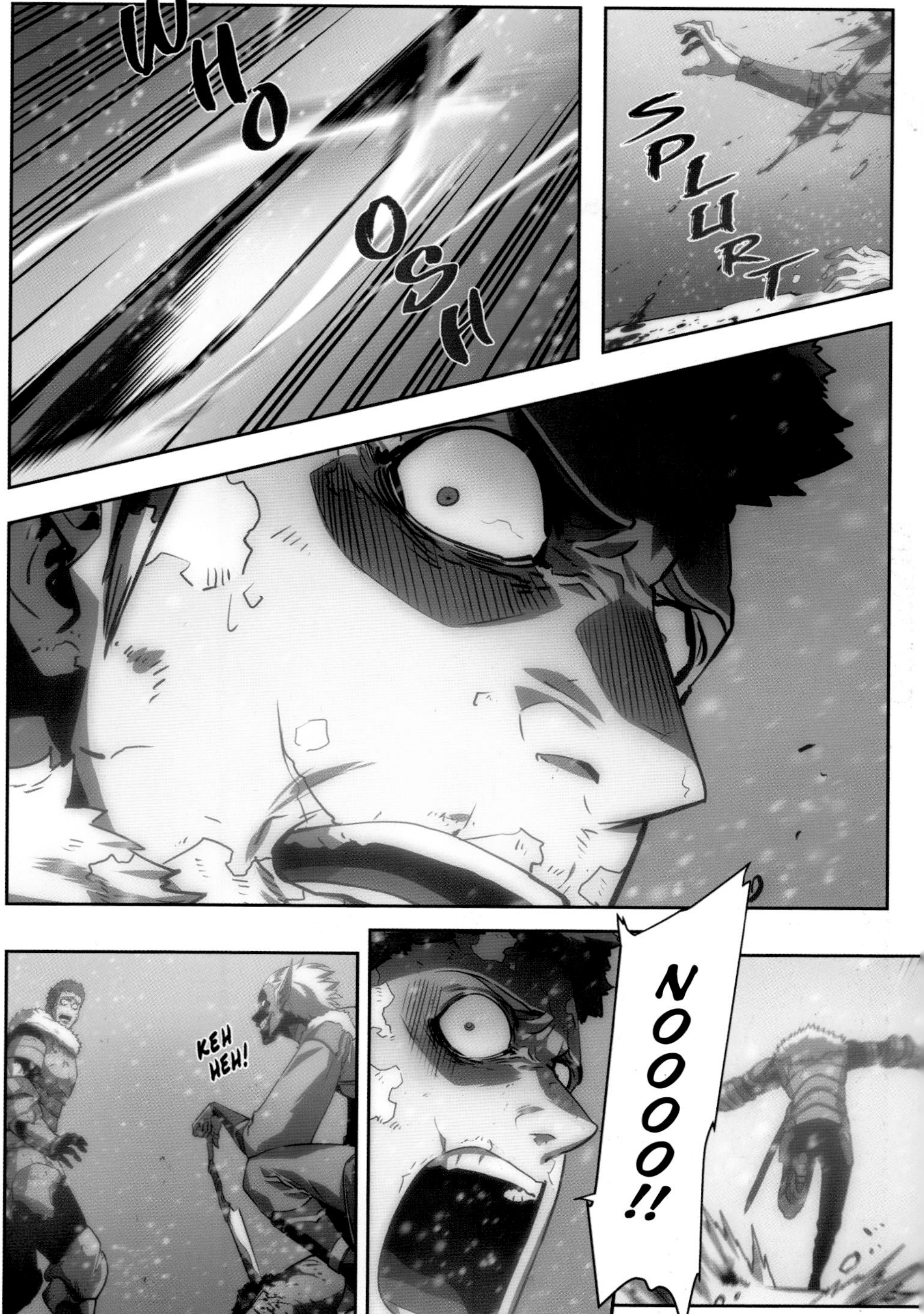
WHOOOSH
SPLURT
KEH HEH!
NOOOOOO!!

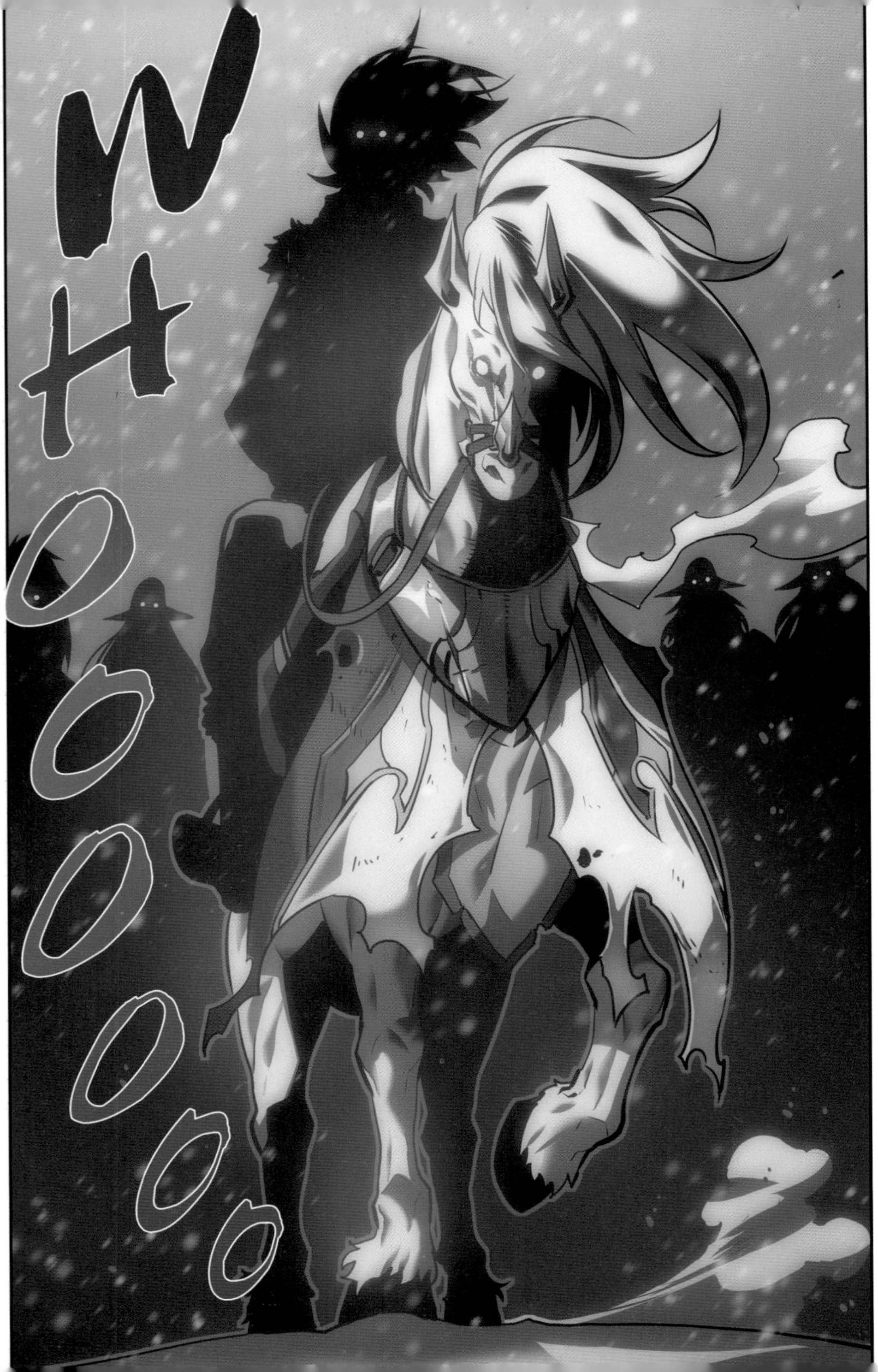
WHOOOOOOO

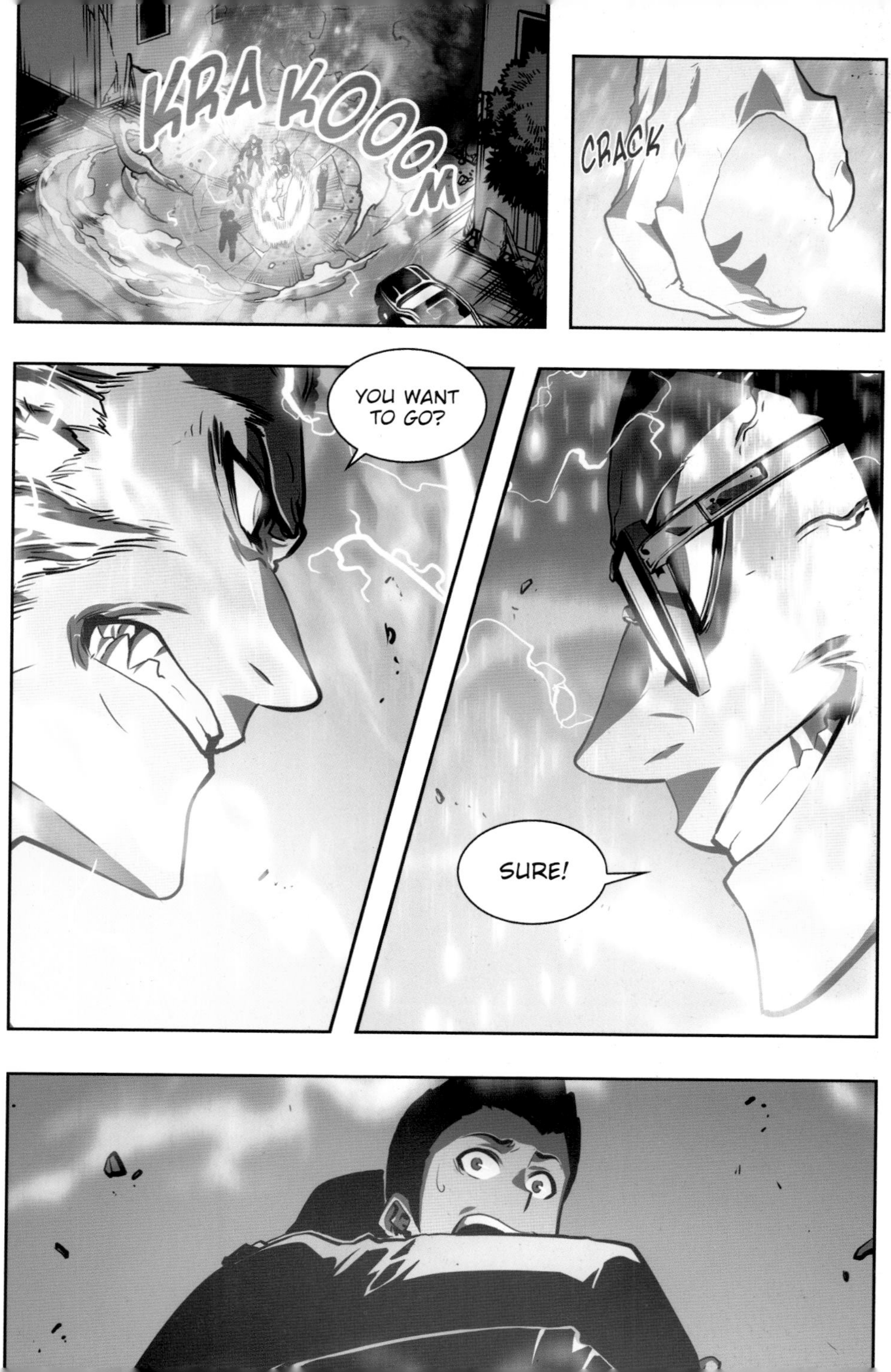
KRA KOOOM
CRACK
YOU WANT TO GO?
SURE!

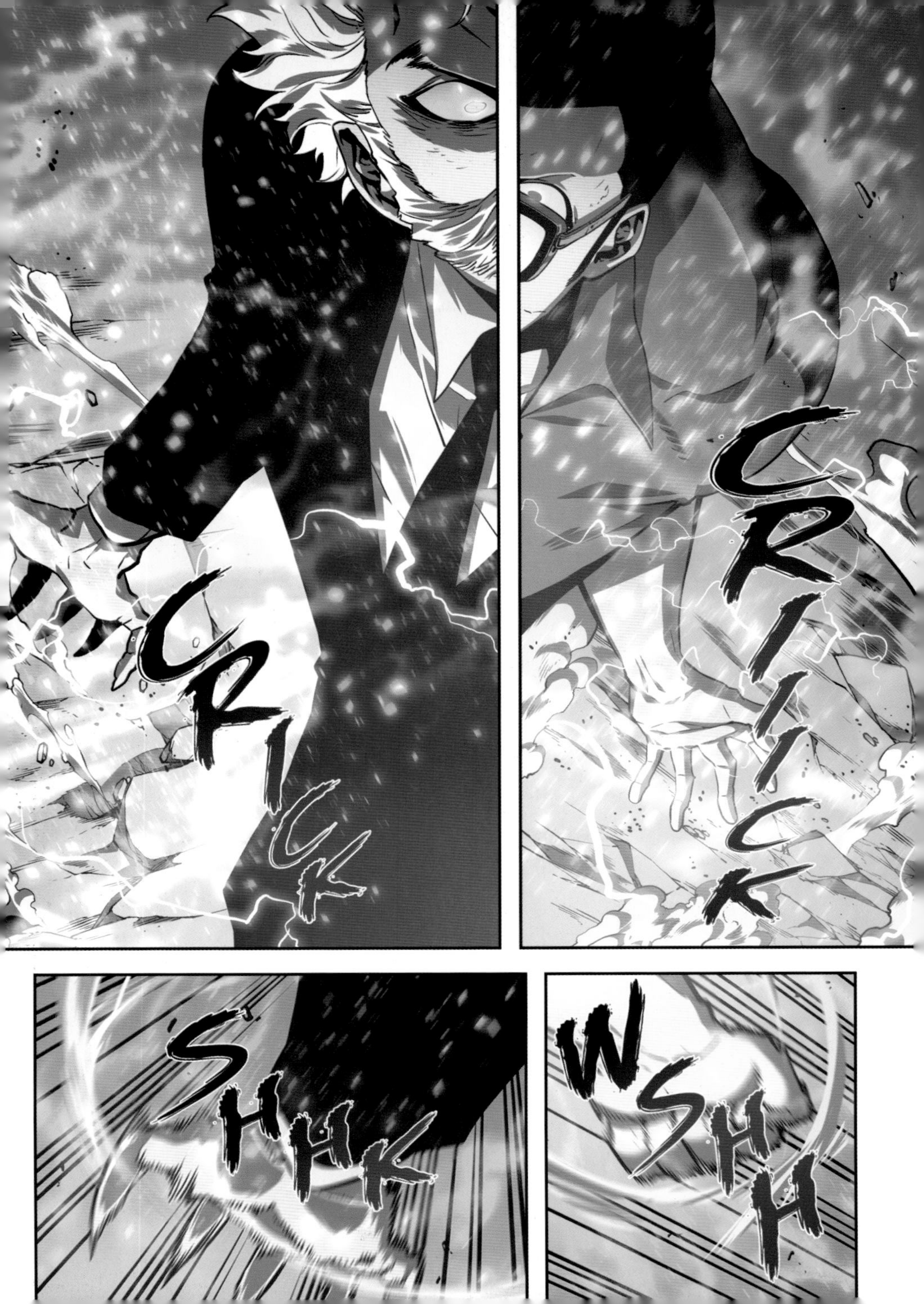
CRICK
CRIIICK
SHHK
WSHH

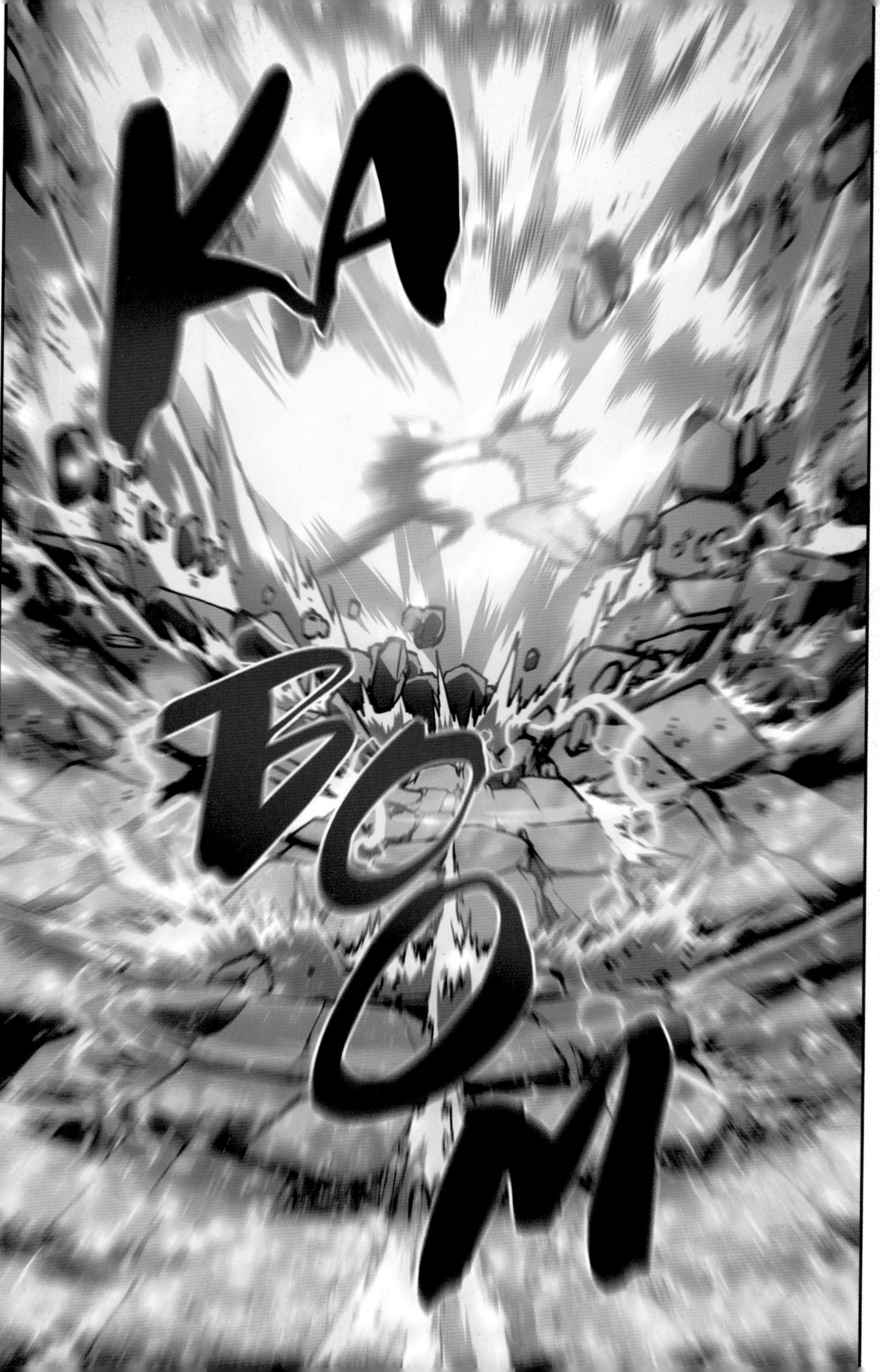
KA
BOOM

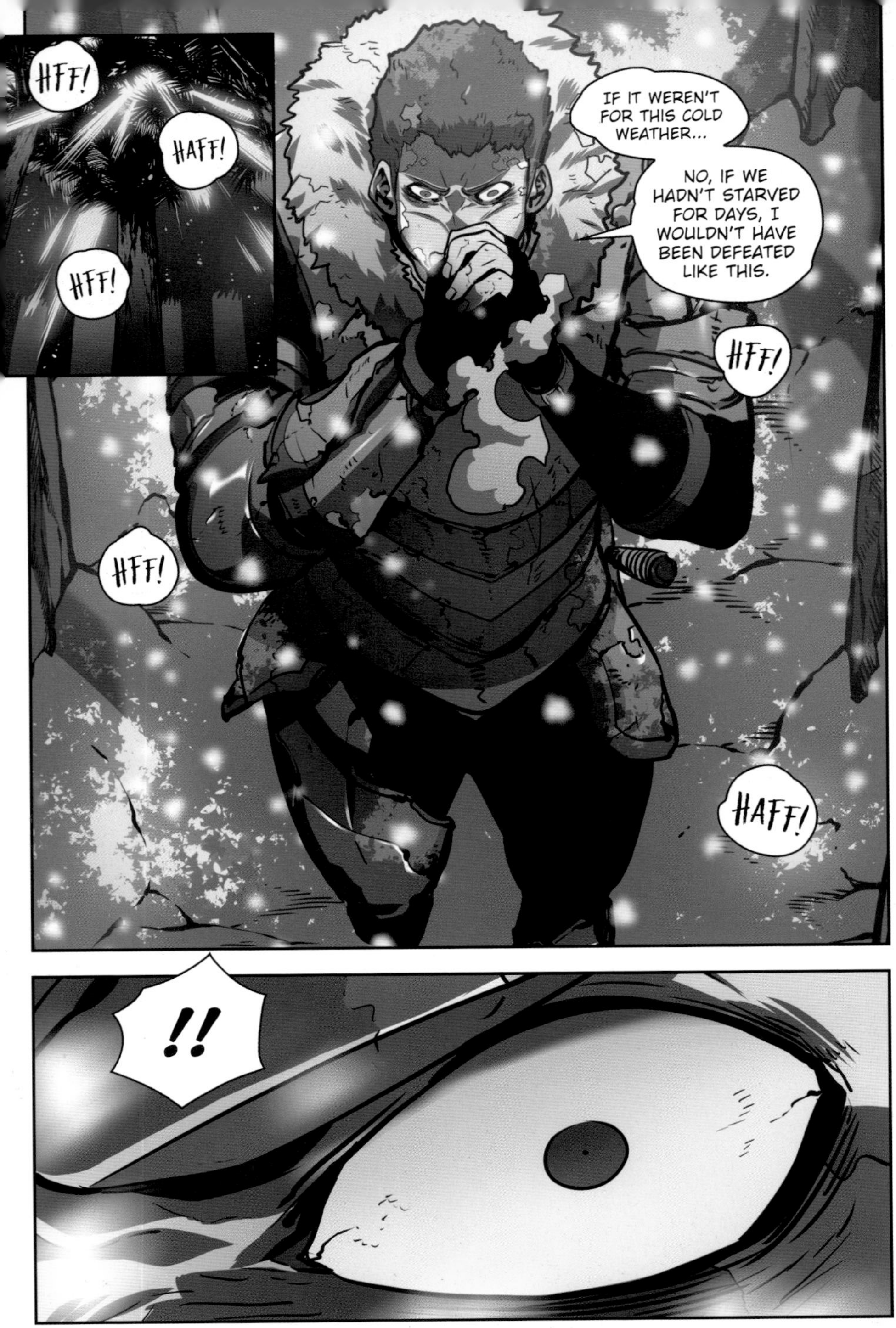
HFF!
HAFF!
HFF!
IF IT WEREN'T FOR THIS COLD WEATHER...
NO, IF WE HADN'T STARVED FOR DAYS, I WOULDN'T HAVE BEEN DEFEATED LIKE THIS.
HFF!
HFF!
HAFF!
!!

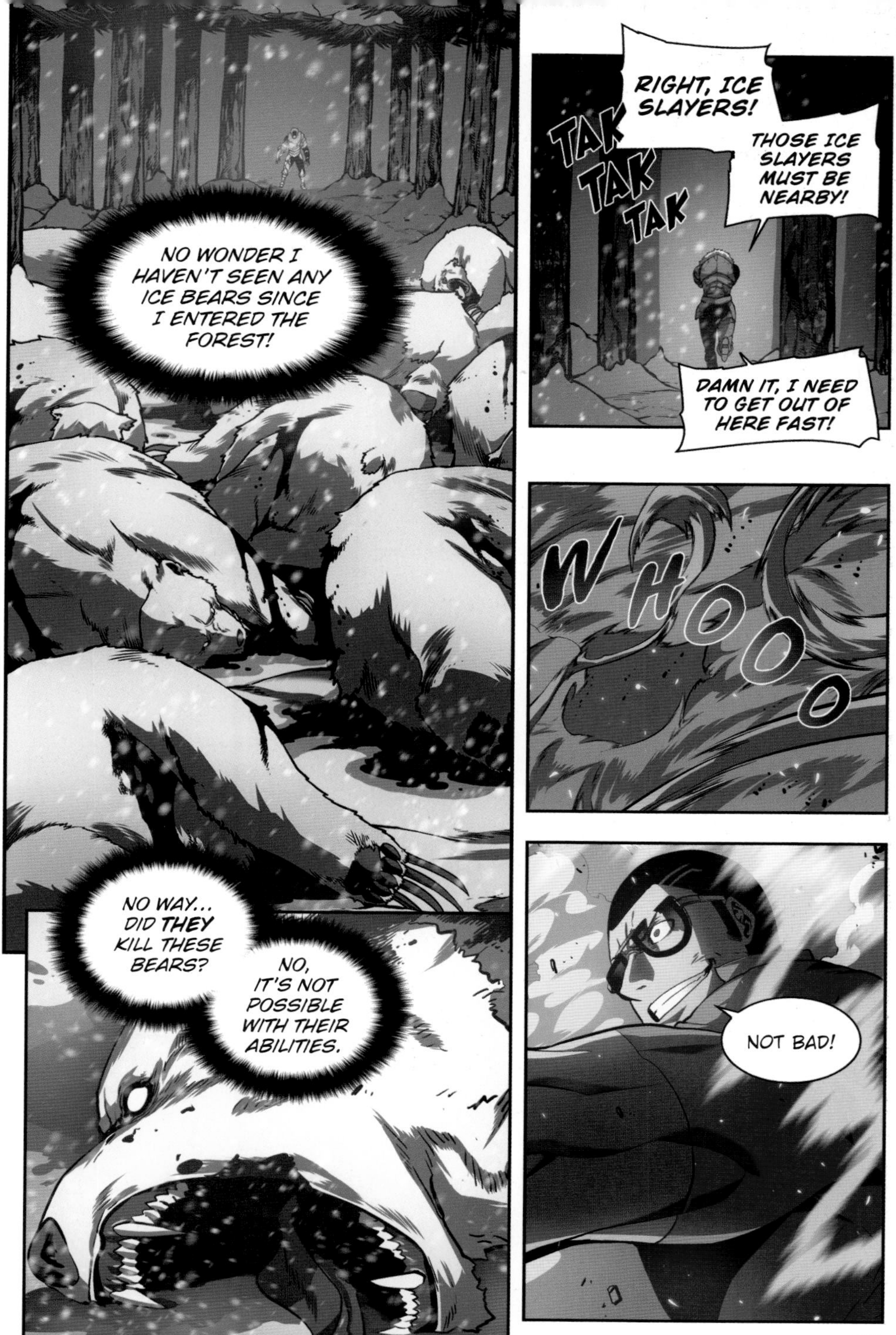
NO WONDER I HAVEN'T SEEN ANY ICE BEARS SINCE I ENTERED THE FOREST!
NO WAY... DID THEY KILL THESE BEARS?
NO, IT'S NOT POSSIBLE WITH THEIR ABILITIES.
RIGHT, ICE SLAYERS!
TAK TAK TAK
THOSE ICE SLAYERS MUST BE NEARBY!
DAMN IT, I NEED TO GET OUT OF HERE FAST!
WHOOOO
NOT BAD!

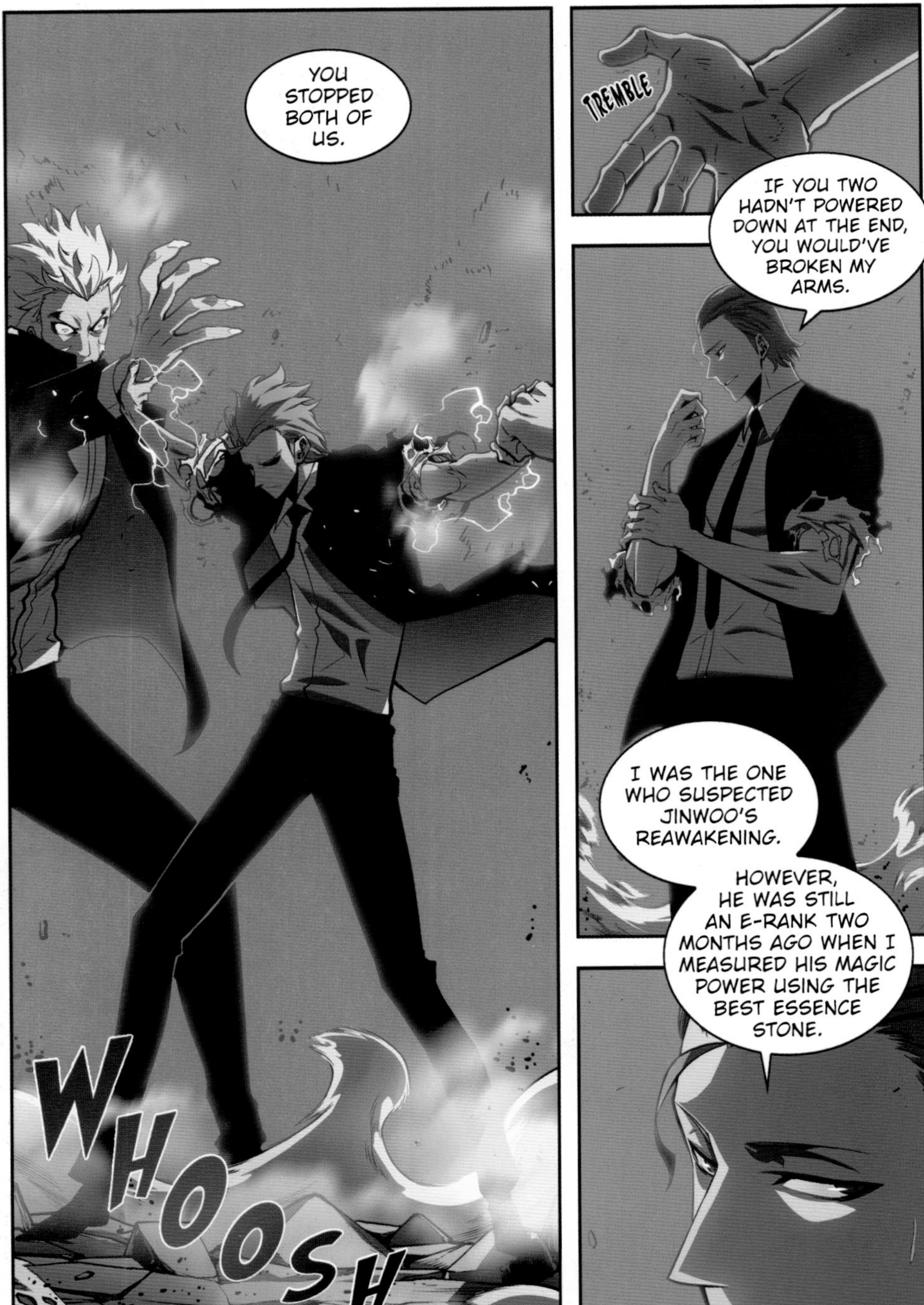
YOU STOPPED BOTH OF US.
WHOOSH
TREMBLE
IF YOU TWO HADN'T POWERED DOWN AT THE END, YOU WOULD'VE BROKEN MY ARMS.
I WAS THE ONE WHO SUSPECTED JINWOO'S REAWAKENING.
HOWEVER, HE WAS STILL AN E-RANK TWO MONTHS AGO WHEN I MEASURED HIS MAGIC POWER USING THE BEST ESSENCE STONE.

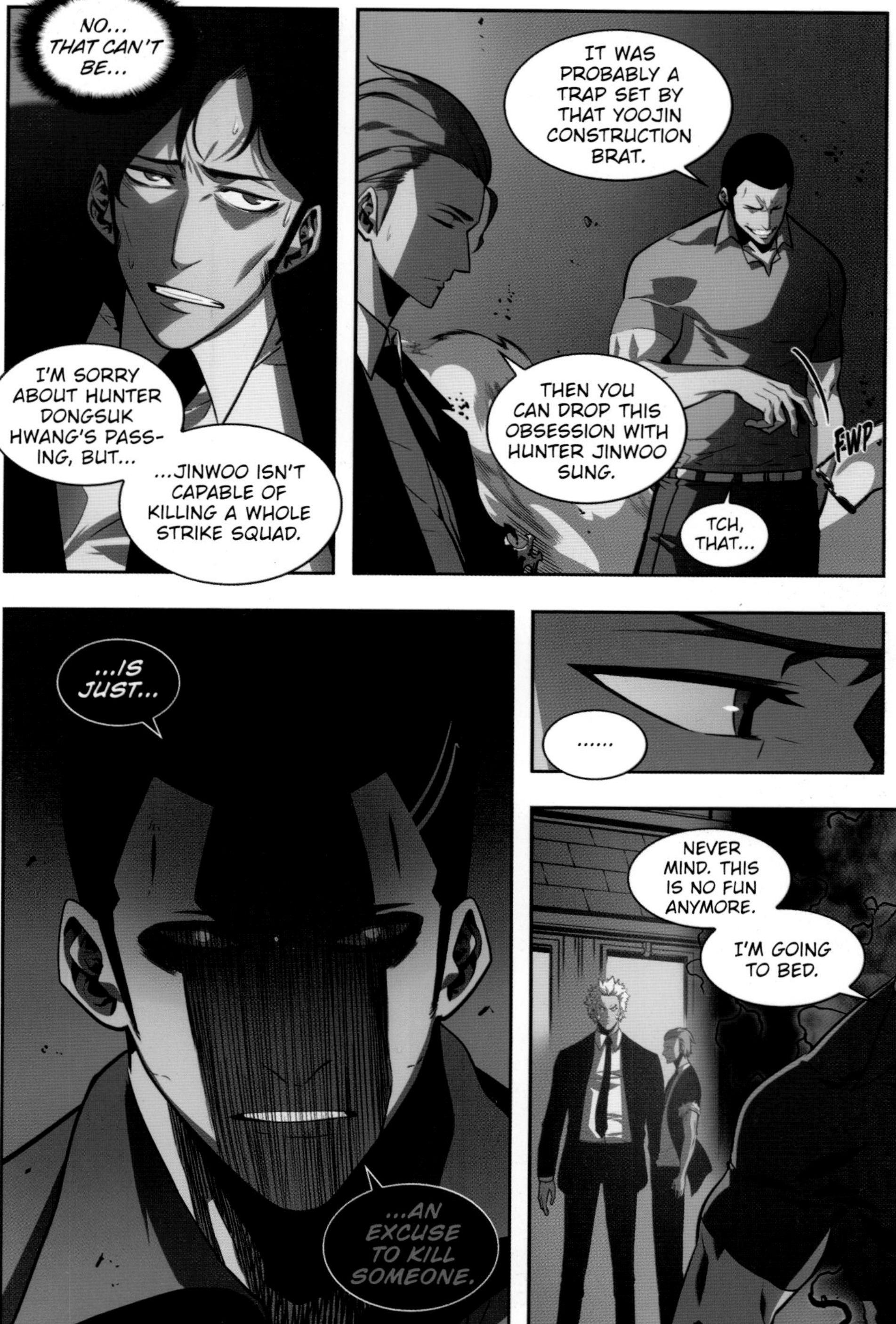
NO... THAT CAN'T BE...
I'M SORRY ABOUT HUNTER DONGSUK HWANG'S PASS-ING, BUT...
...JINWOO ISN'T CAPABLE OF KILLING A WHOLE STRIKE SQUAD.
IT WAS PROBABLY A TRAP SET BY THAT YOOJIN CONSTRUCTION BRAT.
THEN YOU CAN DROP THIS OBSESSION WITH HUNTER JINWOO SUNG.
FWP
TCH, THAT...
...IS JUST...
...AN EXCUSE TO KILL SOMEONE.
......
NEVER MIND. THIS IS NO FUN ANYMORE.
I'M GOING TO BED.

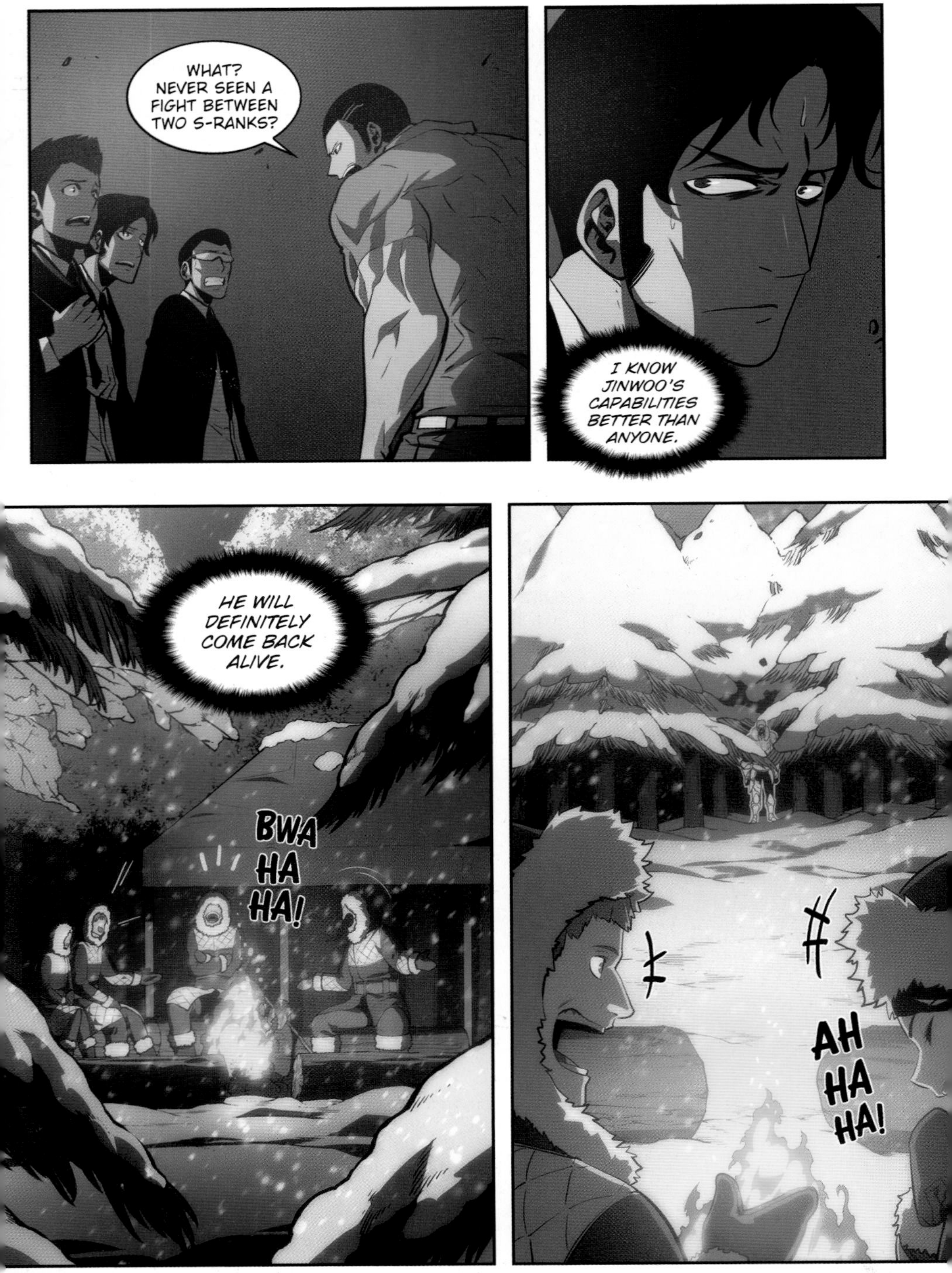
WHAT? NEVER SEEN A FIGHT BETWEEN TWO S-RANKS?
I KNOW JINWOO'S CAPABILITIES BETTER THAN ANYONE.
HE WILL DEFINITELY COME BACK ALIVE.
BWA HA HA!
AH HA HA!

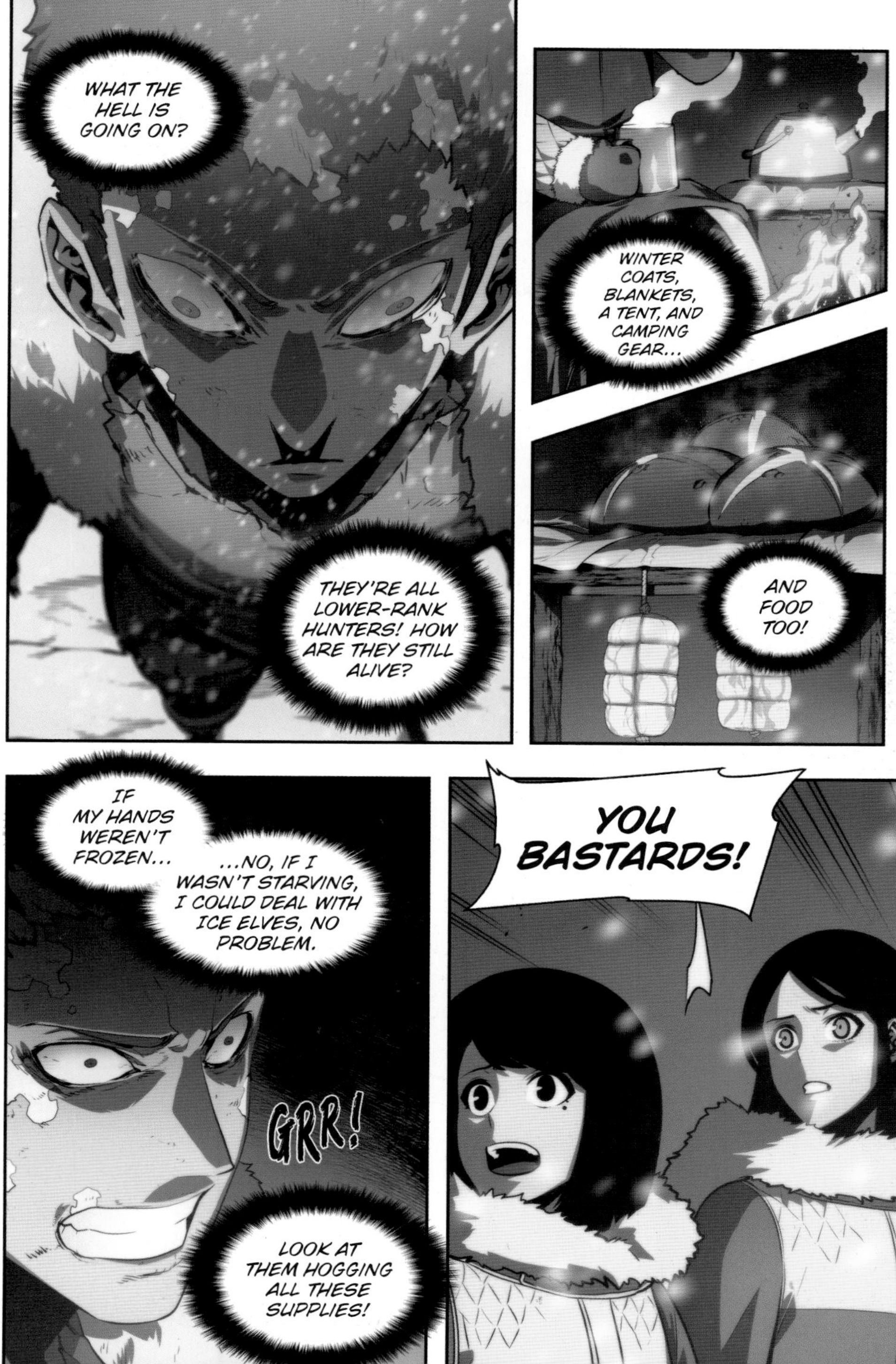
WHAT THE HELL IS GOING ON?
THEY'RE ALL LOWER-RANK HUNTERS! HOW ARE THEY STILL ALIVE?
WINTER COATS, BLANKETS, A TENT, AND CAMPING GEAR...
AND FOOD TOO!
IF MY HANDS WEREN'T FROZEN...
...NO, IF I WASN'T STARVING, I COULD DEAL WITH ICE ELVES, NO PROBLEM.
GRR!
LOOK AT THEM HOGGING ALL THESE SUPPLIES!
YOU BASTARDS!

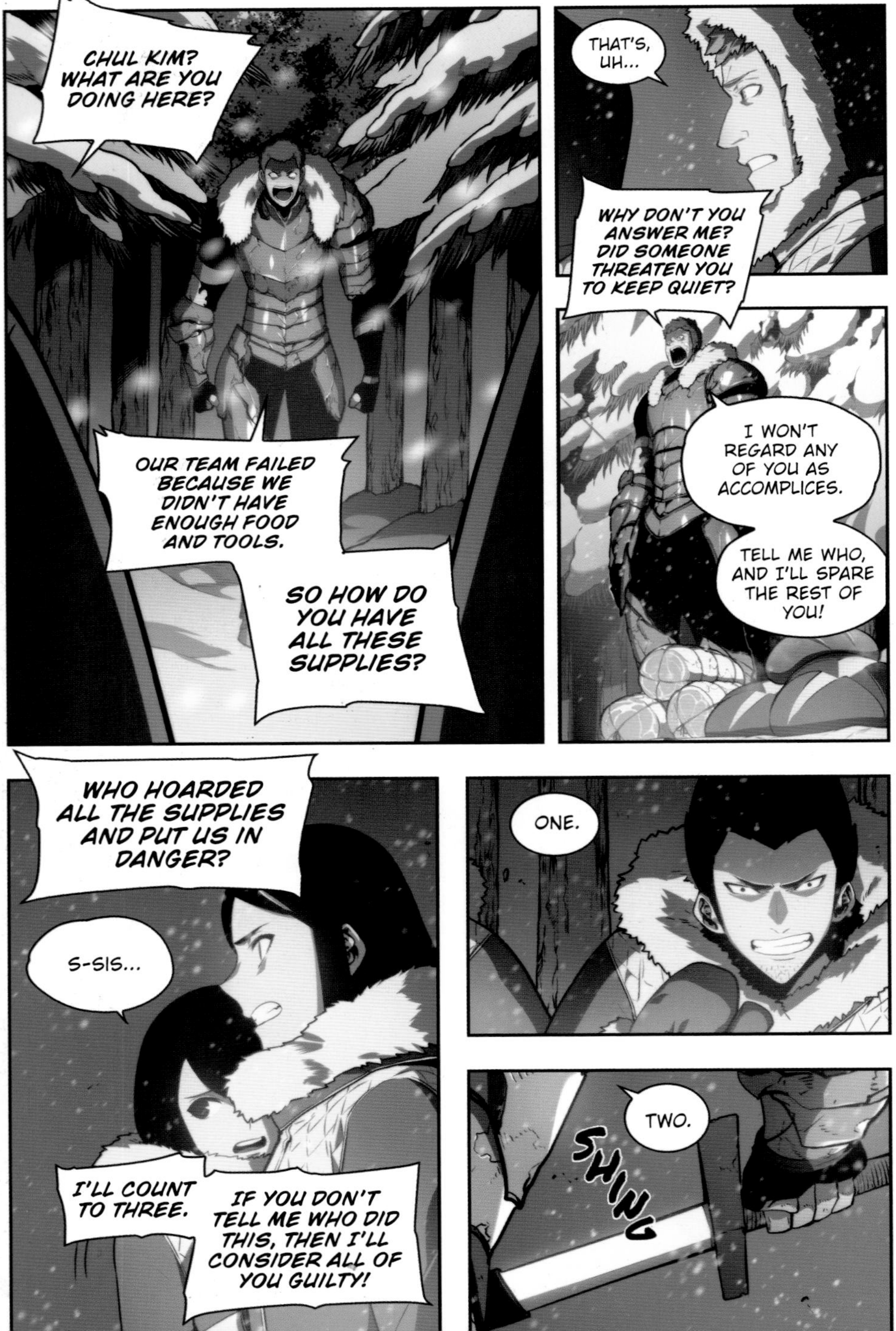
CHUL KIM? WHAT ARE YOU DOING HERE?
OUR TEAM FAILED BECAUSE WE DIDN'T HAVE ENOUGH FOOD AND TOOLS.
SO HOW DO YOU HAVE ALL THESE SUPPLIES?
THAT'S, UH...
WHY DON'T YOU ANSWER ME? DID SOMEONE THREATEN YOU TO KEEP QUIET?
I WON'T REGARD ANY OF YOU AS ACCOMPLICES.
TELL ME WHO, AND I'LL SPARE THE REST OF YOU!
WHO HOARDED ALL THE SUPPLIES AND PUT US IN DANGER?
S-SIS...
I'LL COUNT TO THREE.
IF YOU DON'T TELL ME WHO DID THIS, THEN I'LL CONSIDER ALL OF YOU GUILTY!
ONE.
TWO.
SHING

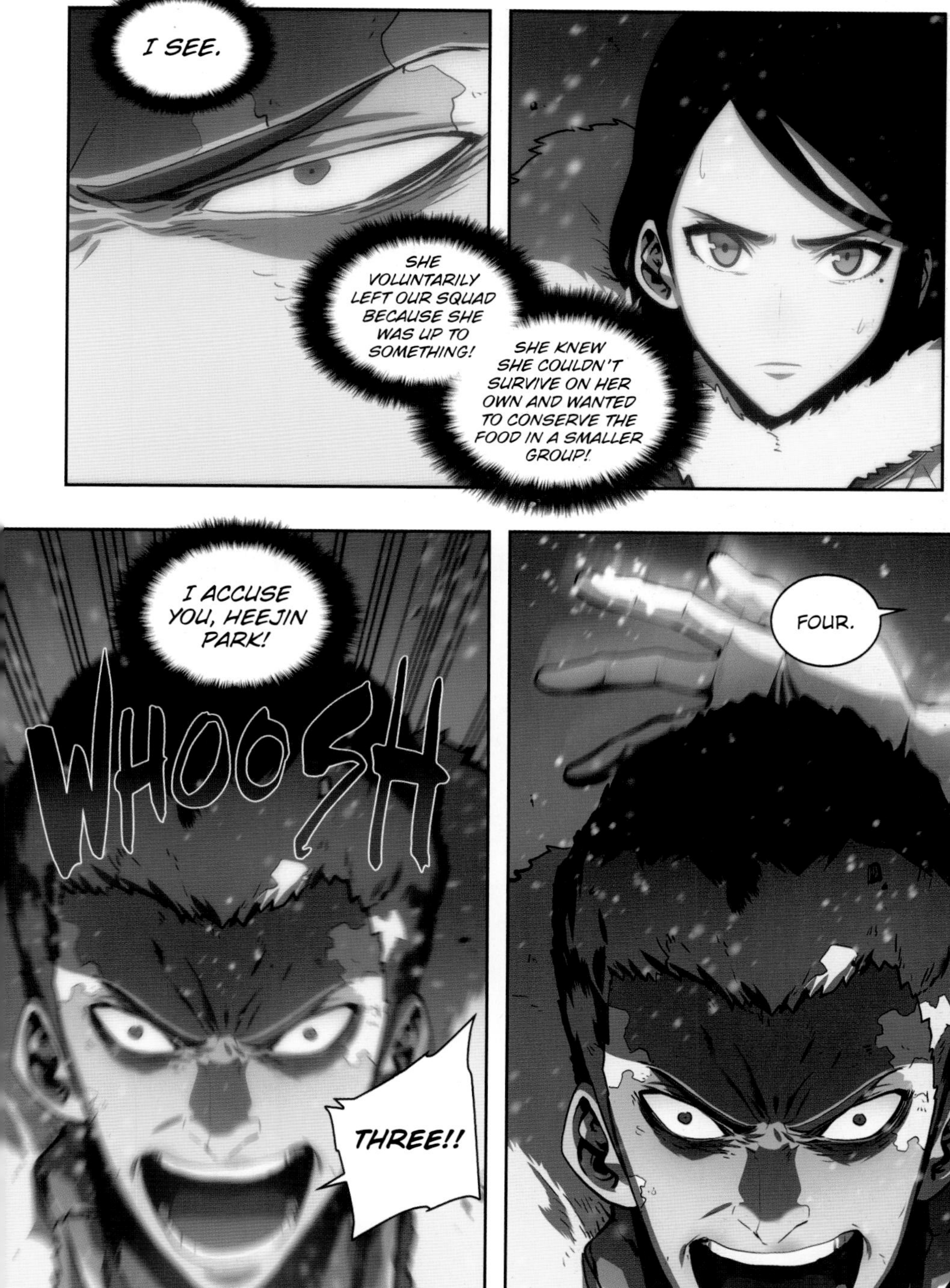
I SEE.
SHE VOLUNTARILY LEFT OUR SQUAD BECAUSE SHE WAS UP TO SOMETHING!
SHE KNEW SHE COULDN'T SURVIVE ON HER OWN AND WANTED TO CONSERVE THE FOOD IN A SMALLER GROUP!
I ACCUSE YOU, HEEJIN PARK!
WHOOSH
THREE!!
FOUR.

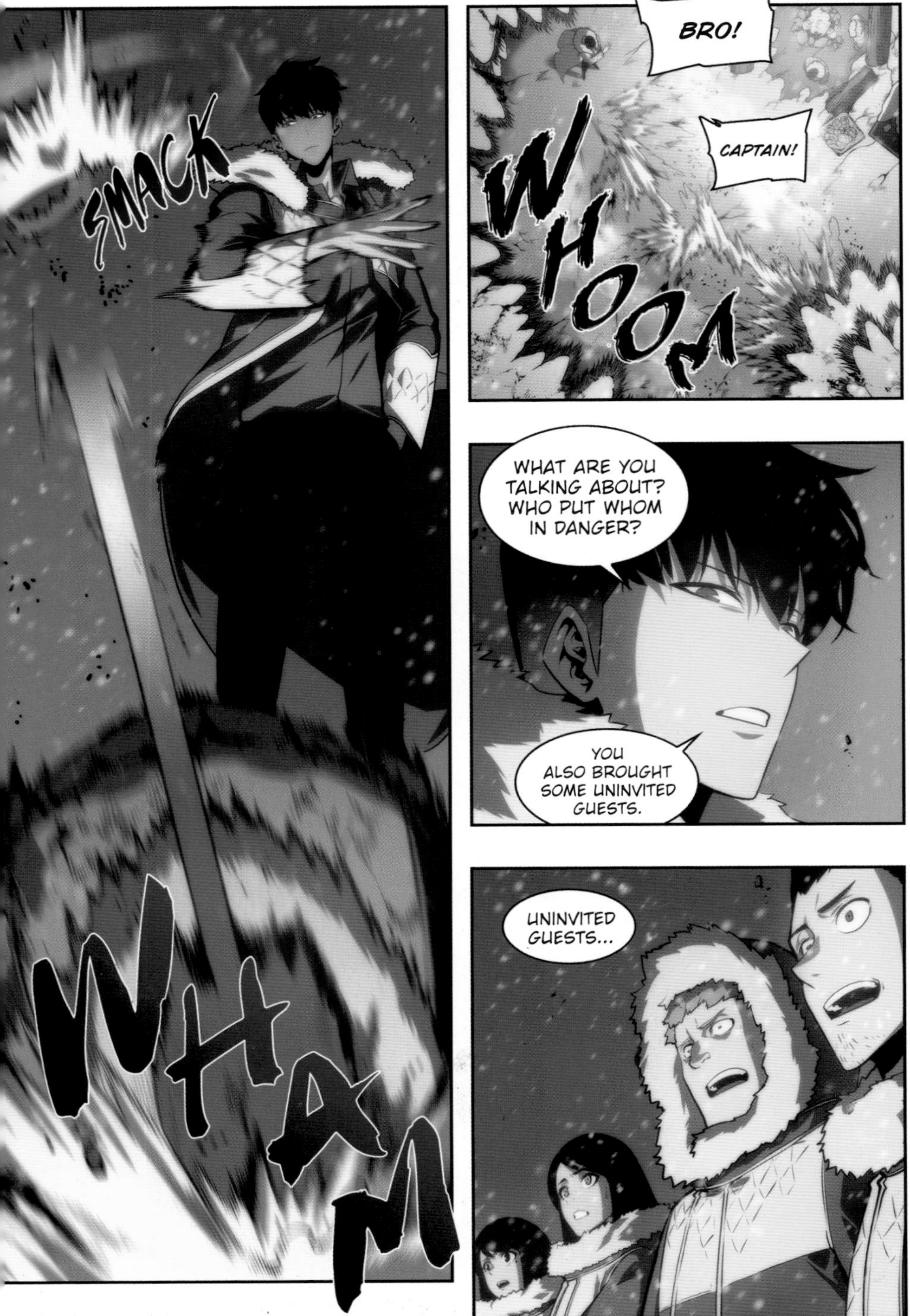
SMACK
WHAM
BRO!
CAPTAIN!
WHOOM
WHAT ARE YOU TALKING ABOUT? WHO PUT WHOM IN DANGER?
YOU ALSO BROUGHT SOME UNINVITED GUESTS.
UNINVITED GUESTS...

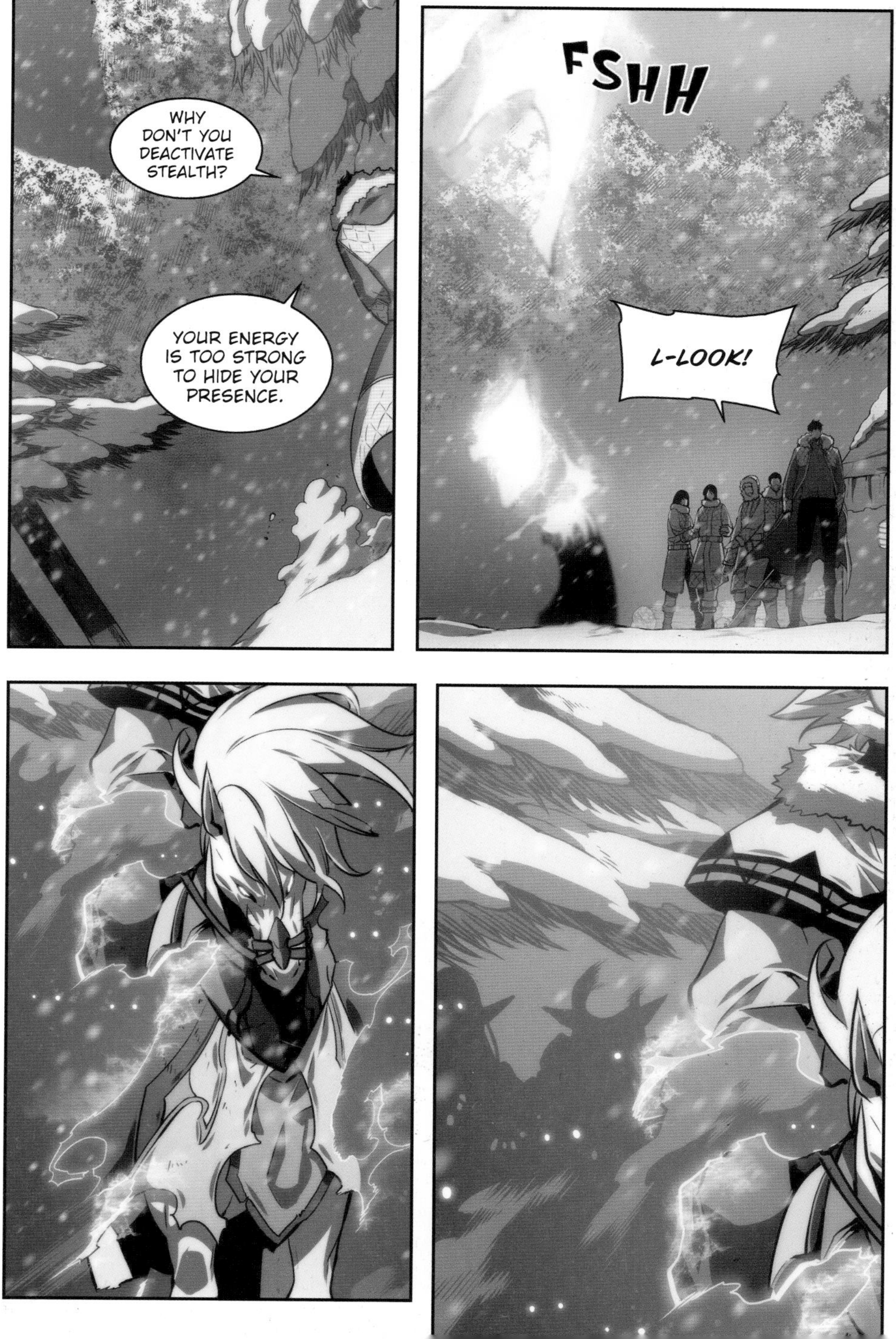
WHY DON'T YOU DEACTIVATE STEALTH?
YOUR ENERGY IS TOO STRONG TO HIDE YOUR PRESENCE.
FSHH
L-LOOK!

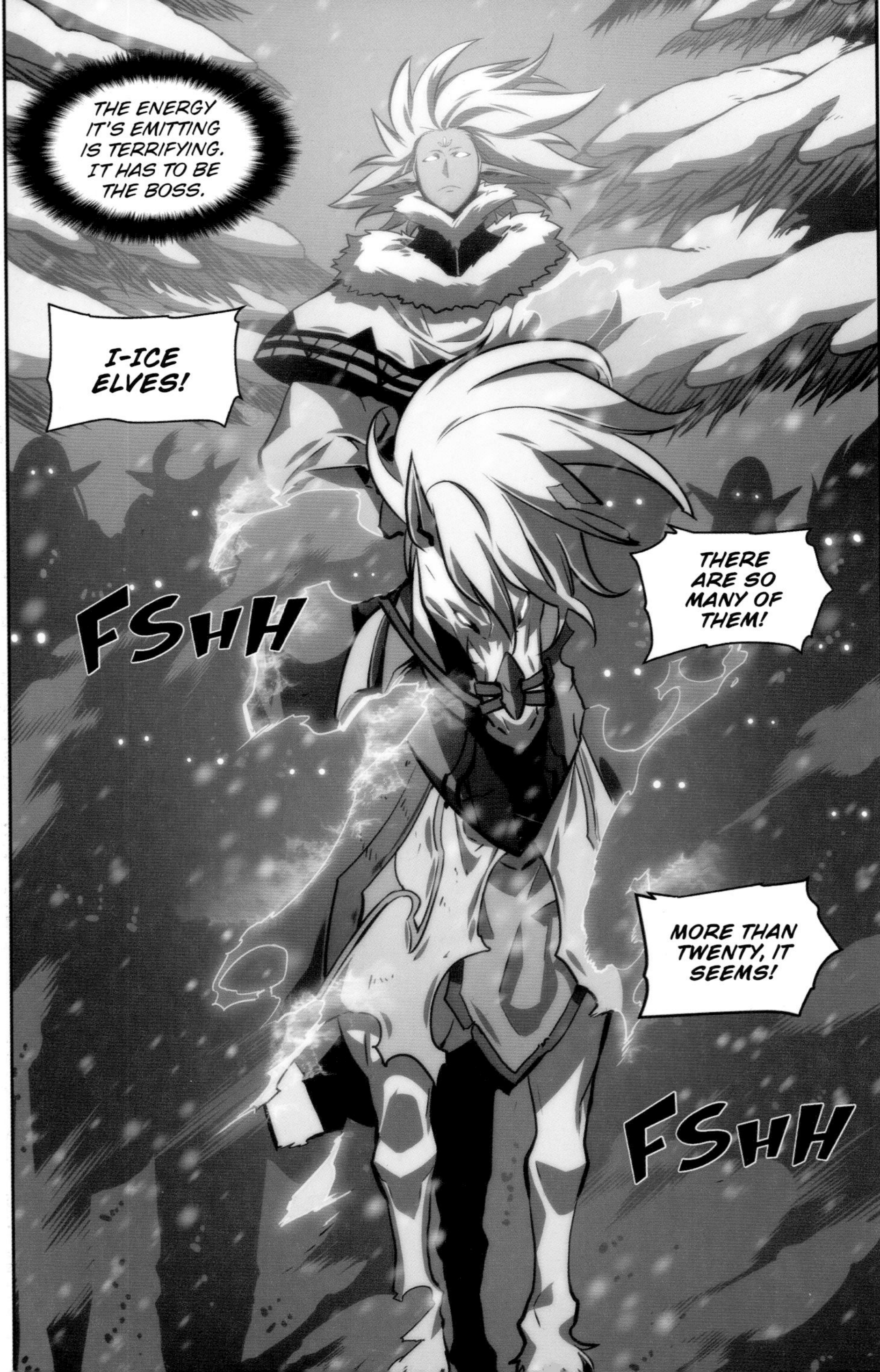
THE ENERGY IT'S EMITTING IS TERRIFYING. IT HAS TO BE THE BOSS.
I-ICE ELVES!
FSHH
THERE ARE SO MANY OF THEM!
MORE THAN TWENTY, IT SEEMS!
FSHH

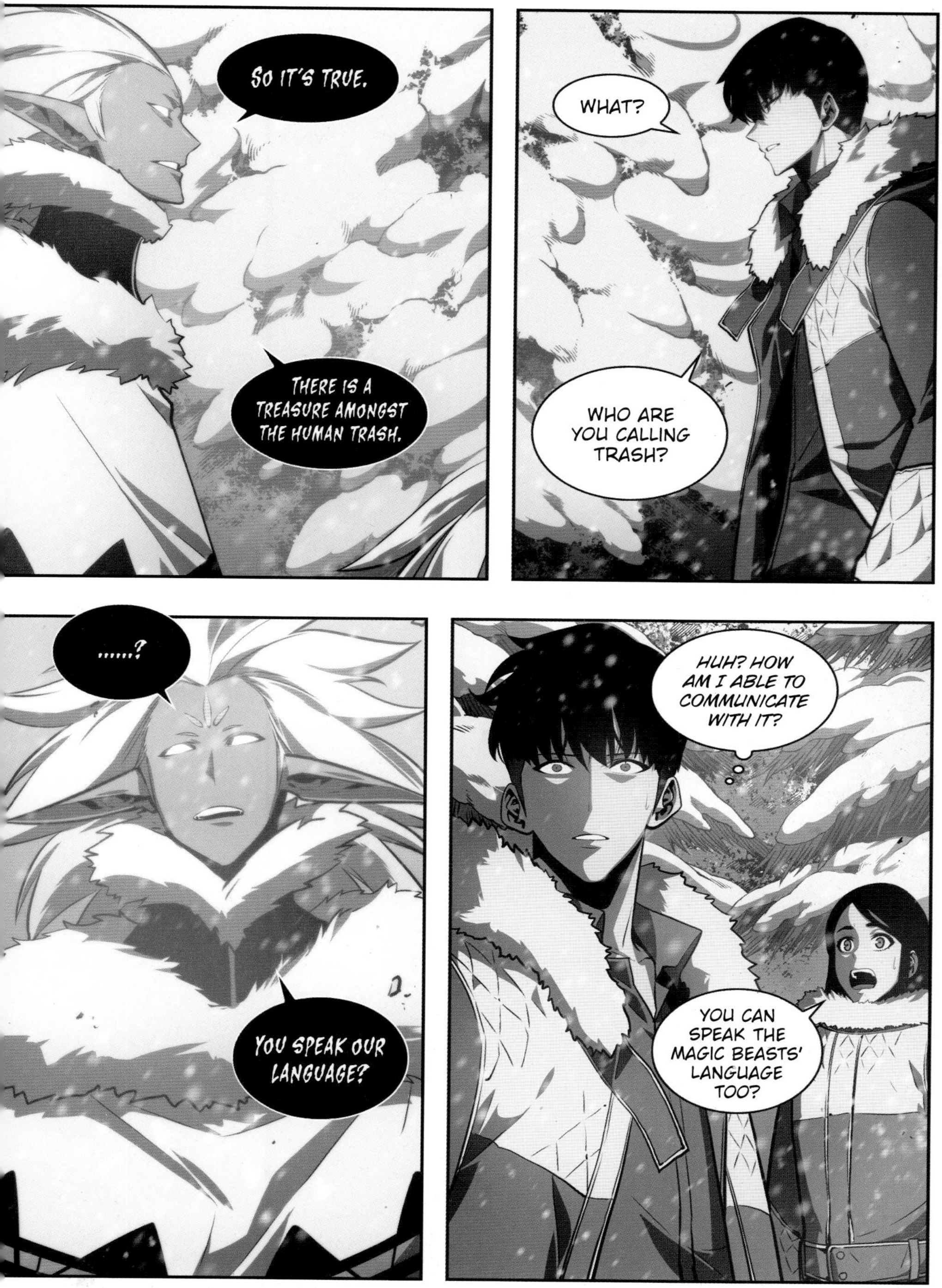
So it's true.
There is a treasure amongst the human trash.
WHAT?
WHO ARE YOU CALLING TRASH?
......?
You speak our language?
HUH? HOW AM I ABLE TO COMMUNICATE WITH IT?
YOU CAN SPEAK THE MAGIC BEASTS' LANGUAGE TOO?

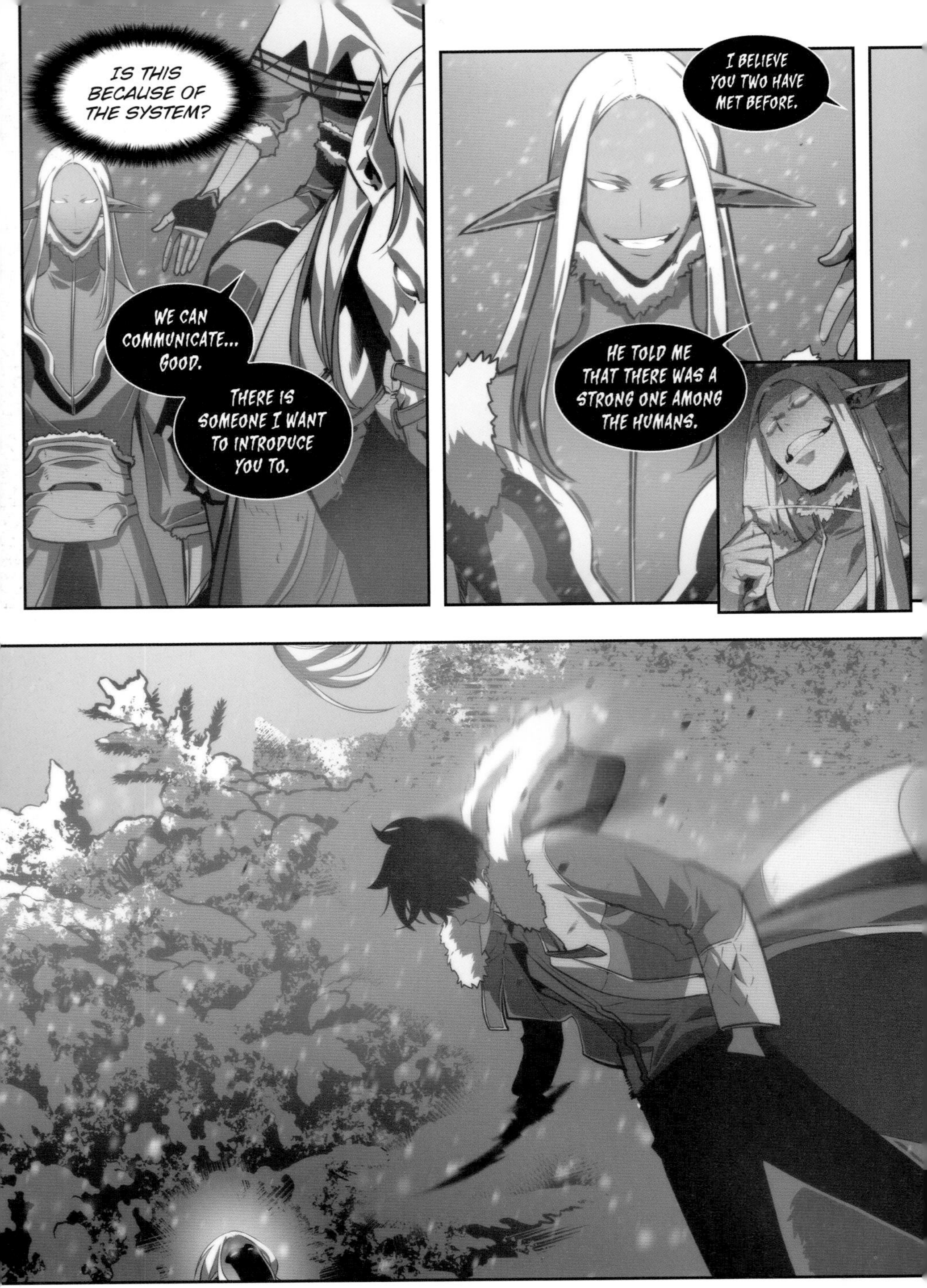
IS THIS BECAUSE OF THE SYSTEM?
WE CAN COMMUNICATE... GOOD.
THERE IS SOMEONE I WANT TO INTRODUCE YOU TO.
I BELIEVE YOU TWO HAVE MET BEFORE.
HE TOLD ME THAT THERE WAS A STRONG ONE AMONG THE HUMANS.

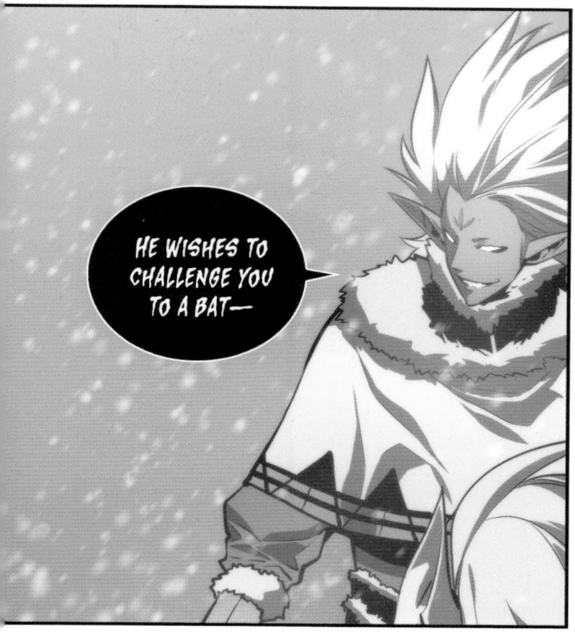
HE WISHES TO CHALLENGE YOU TO A BAT—

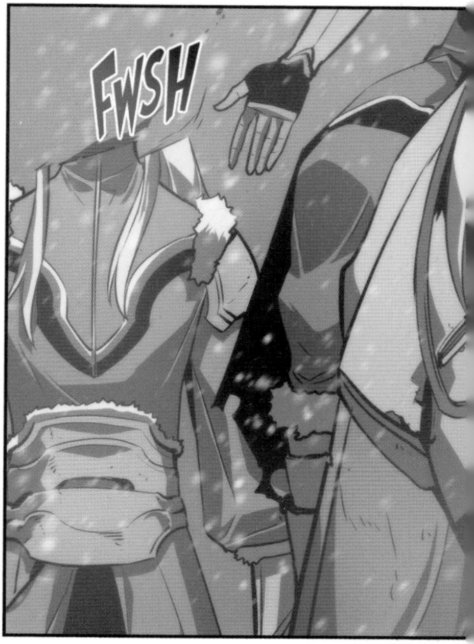
FWSH

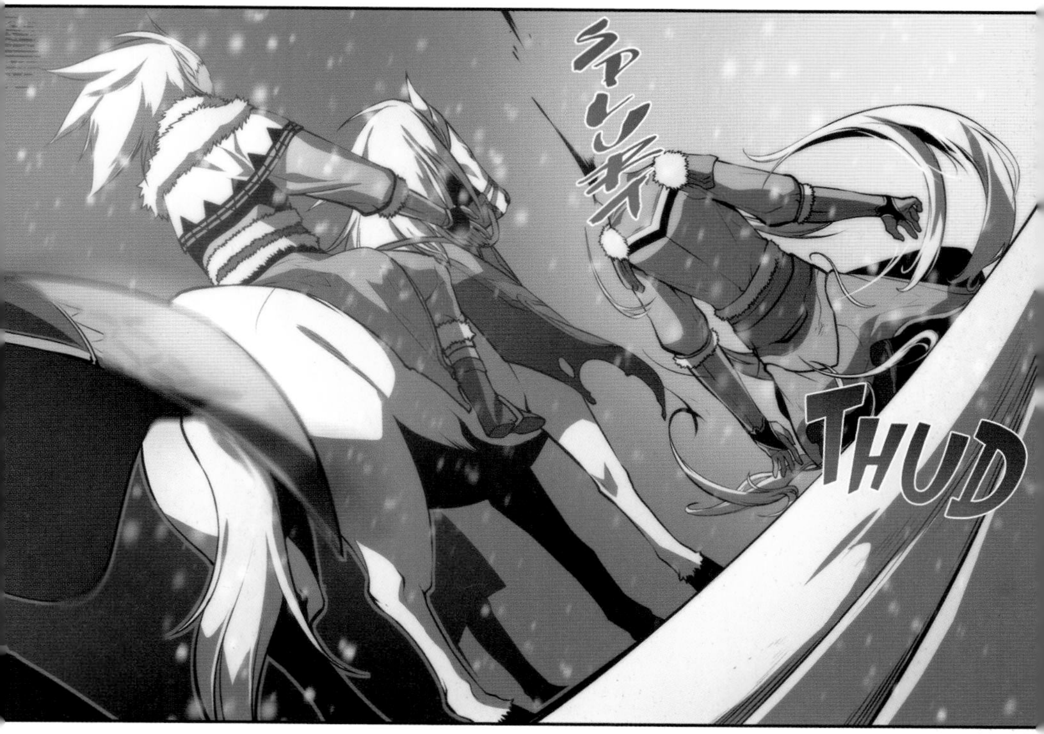
THUD

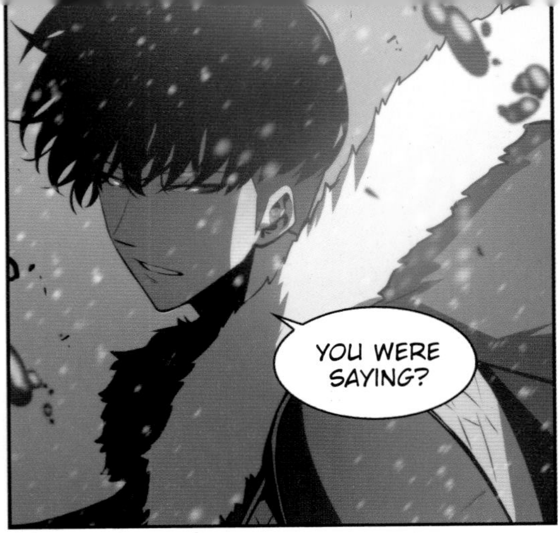
YOU WERE SAYING?

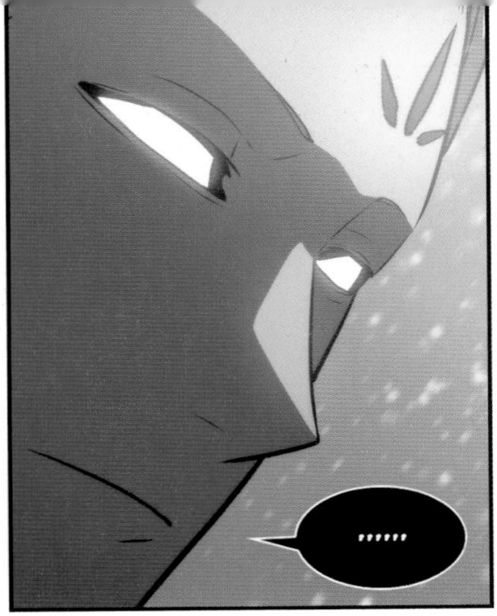
……

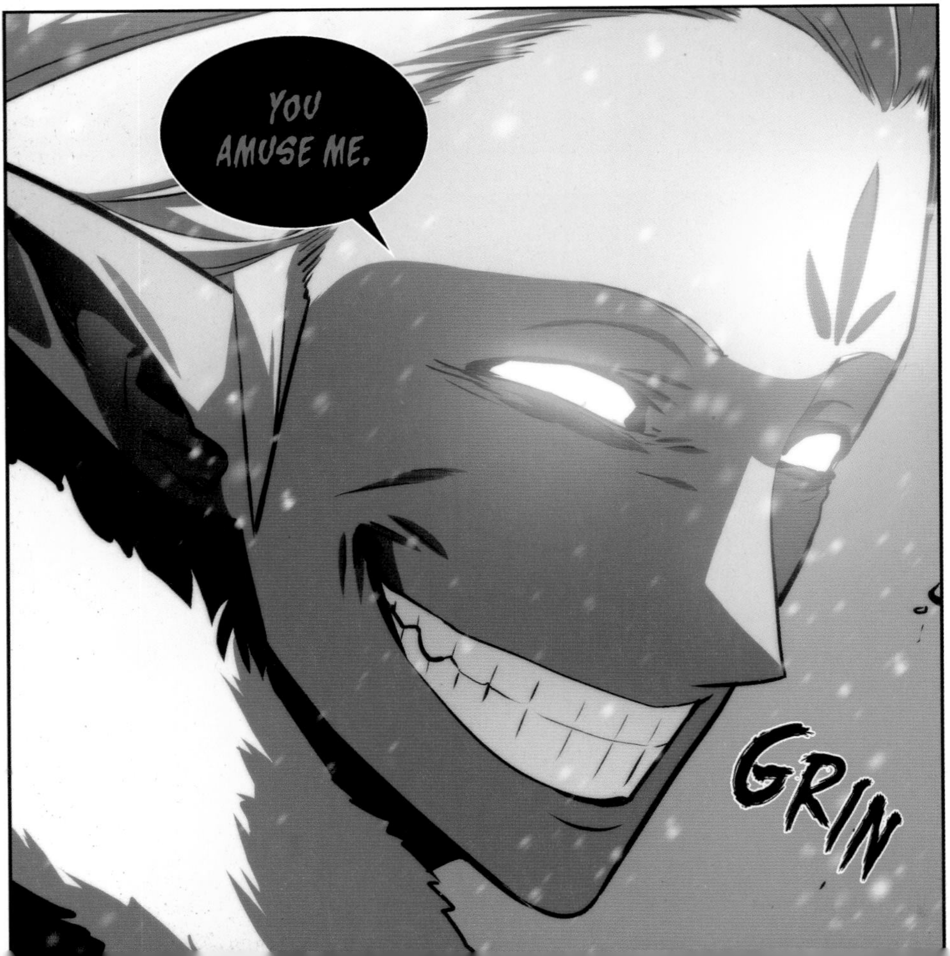
YOU AMUSE ME.
GRIN

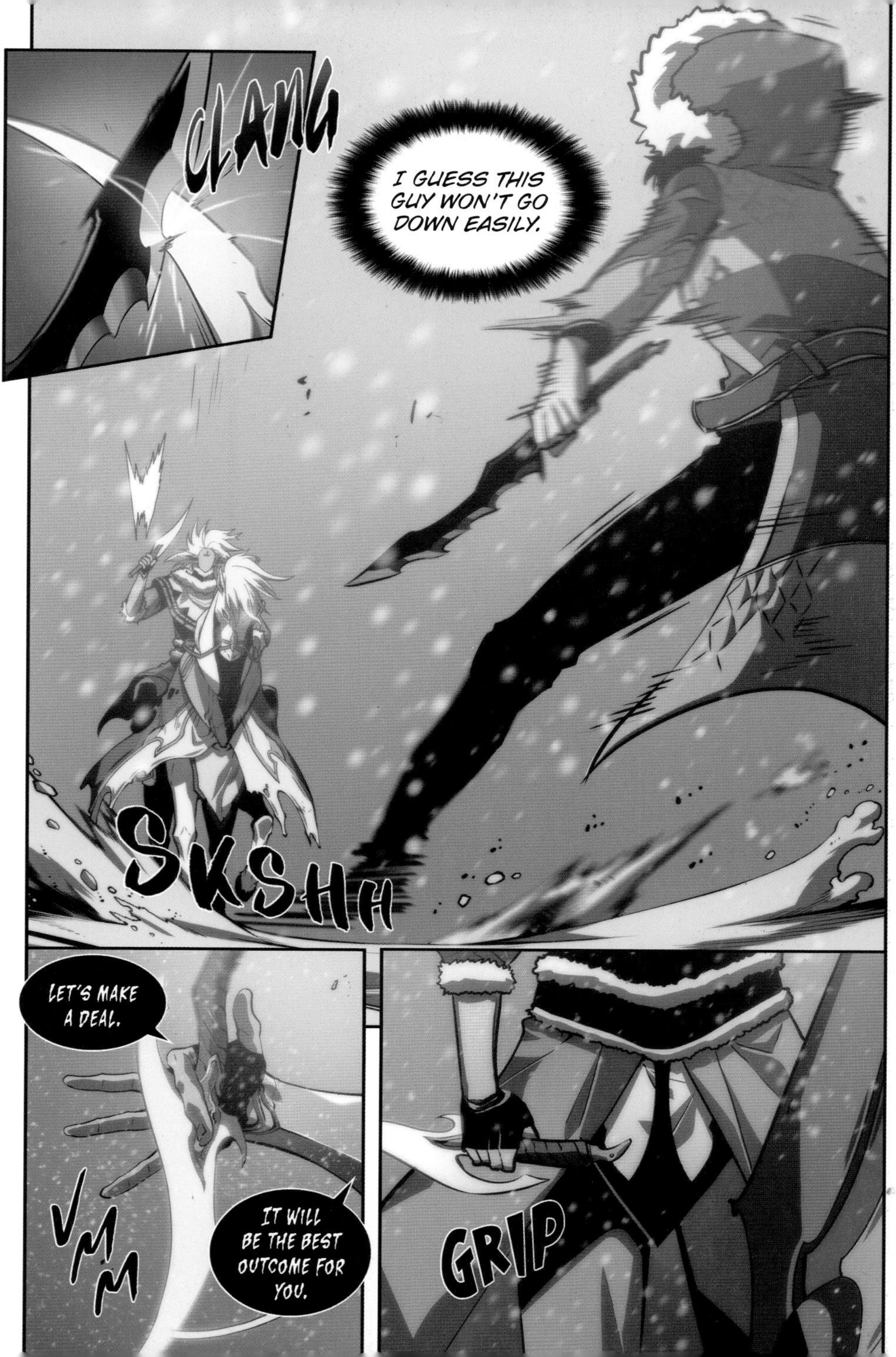
CLANG
I GUESS THIS GUY WON'T GO DOWN EASILY.
SKSHH
LET'S MAKE A DEAL.
VMM
IT WILL BE THE BEST OUTCOME FOR YOU.
GRIP

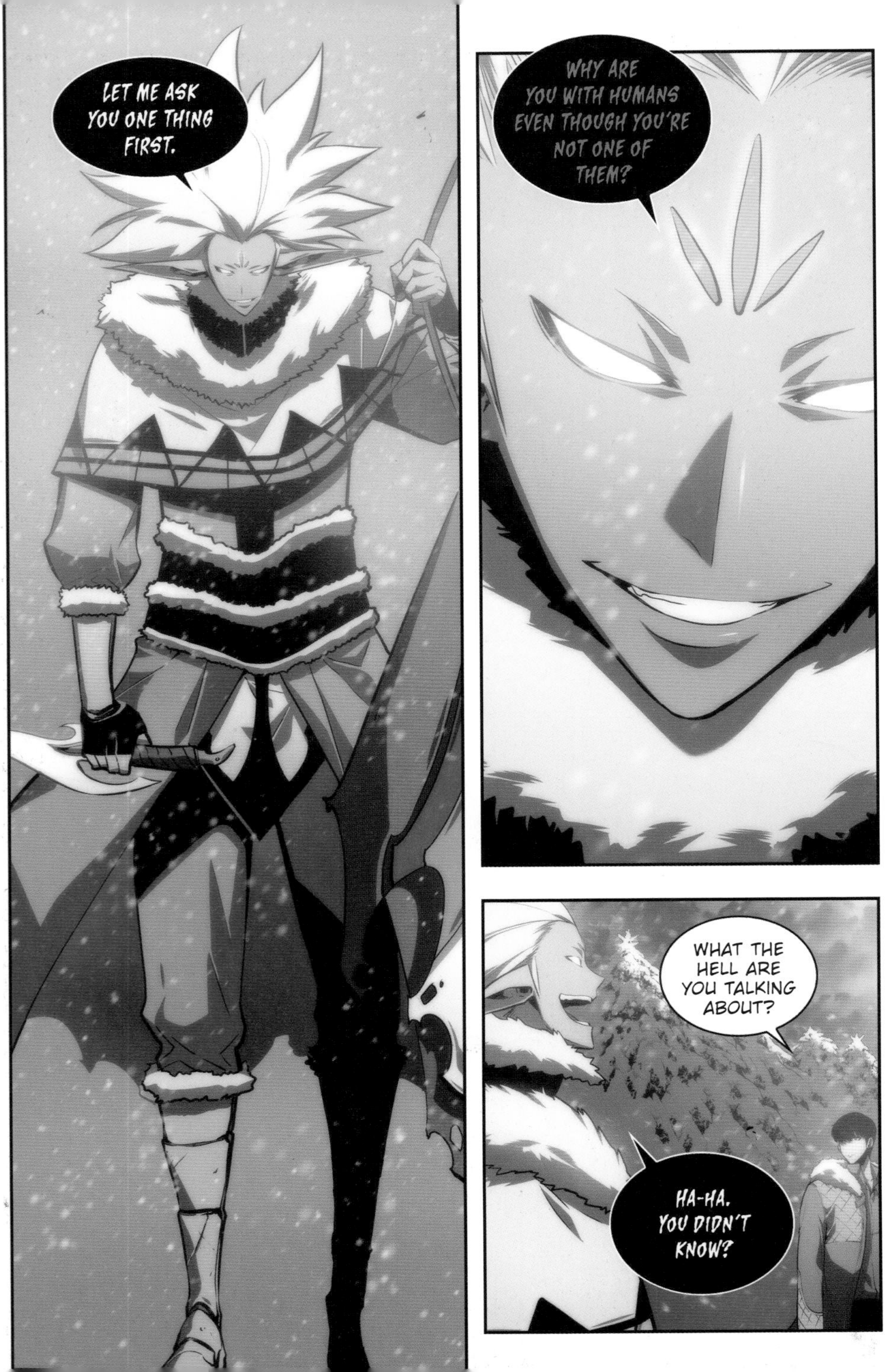
LET ME ASK YOU ONE THING FIRST.
WHY ARE YOU WITH HUMANS EVEN THOUGH YOU'RE NOT ONE OF THEM?
WHAT THE HELL ARE YOU TALKING ABOUT?
HA-HA. YOU DIDN'T KNOW?

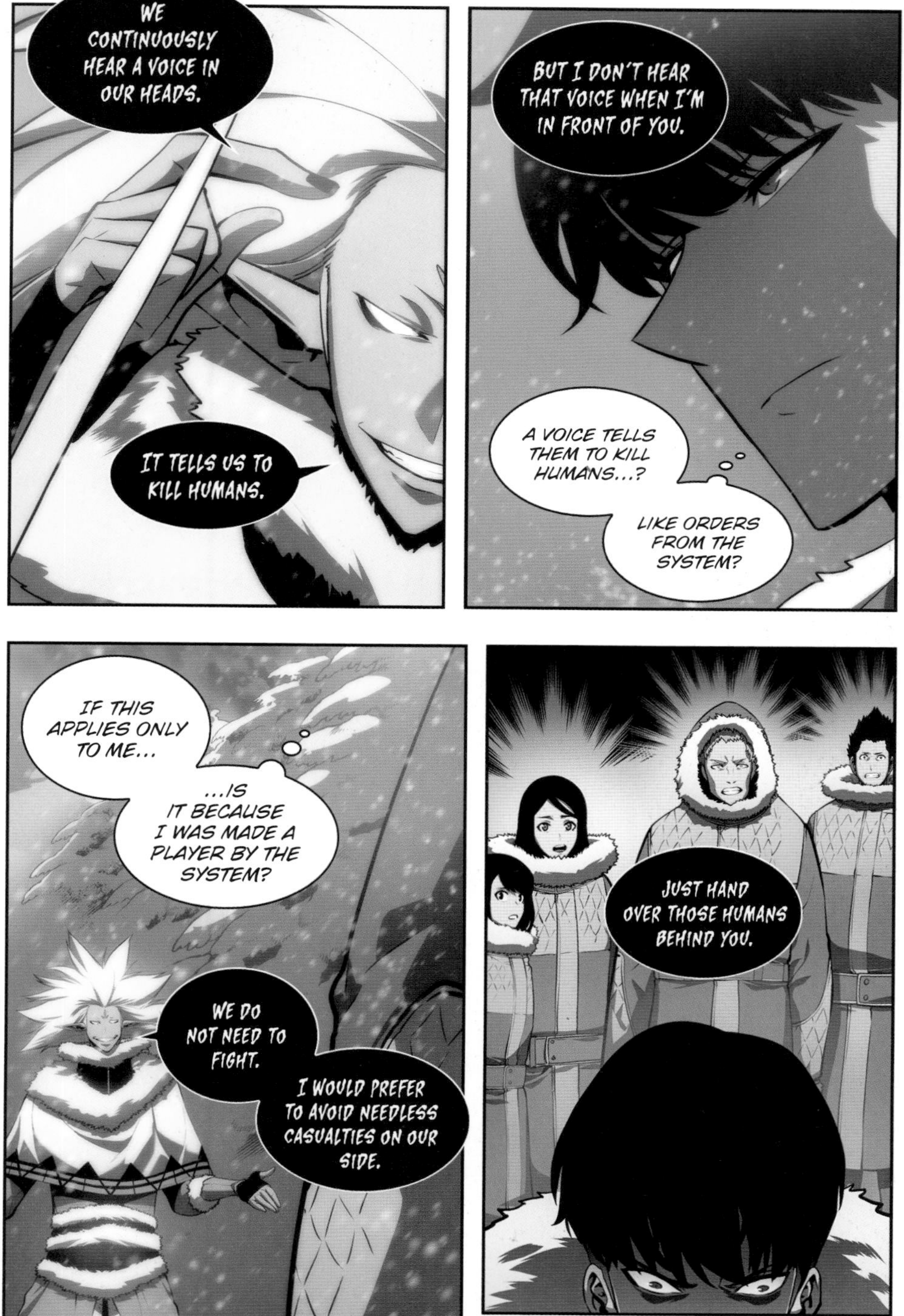

WE CONTINUOUSLY HEAR A VOICE IN OUR HEADS.
IT TELLS US TO KILL HUMANS.
BUT I DON'T HEAR THAT VOICE WHEN I'M IN FRONT OF YOU.
A VOICE TELLS THEM TO KILL HUMANS...?
LIKE ORDERS FROM THE SYSTEM?
IF THIS APPLIES ONLY TO ME...
...IS IT BECAUSE I WAS MADE A PLAYER BY THE SYSTEM?
WE DO NOT NEED TO FIGHT.
I WOULD PREFER TO AVOID NEEDLESS CASUALTIES ON OUR SIDE.
JUST HAND OVER THOSE HUMANS BEHIND YOU.

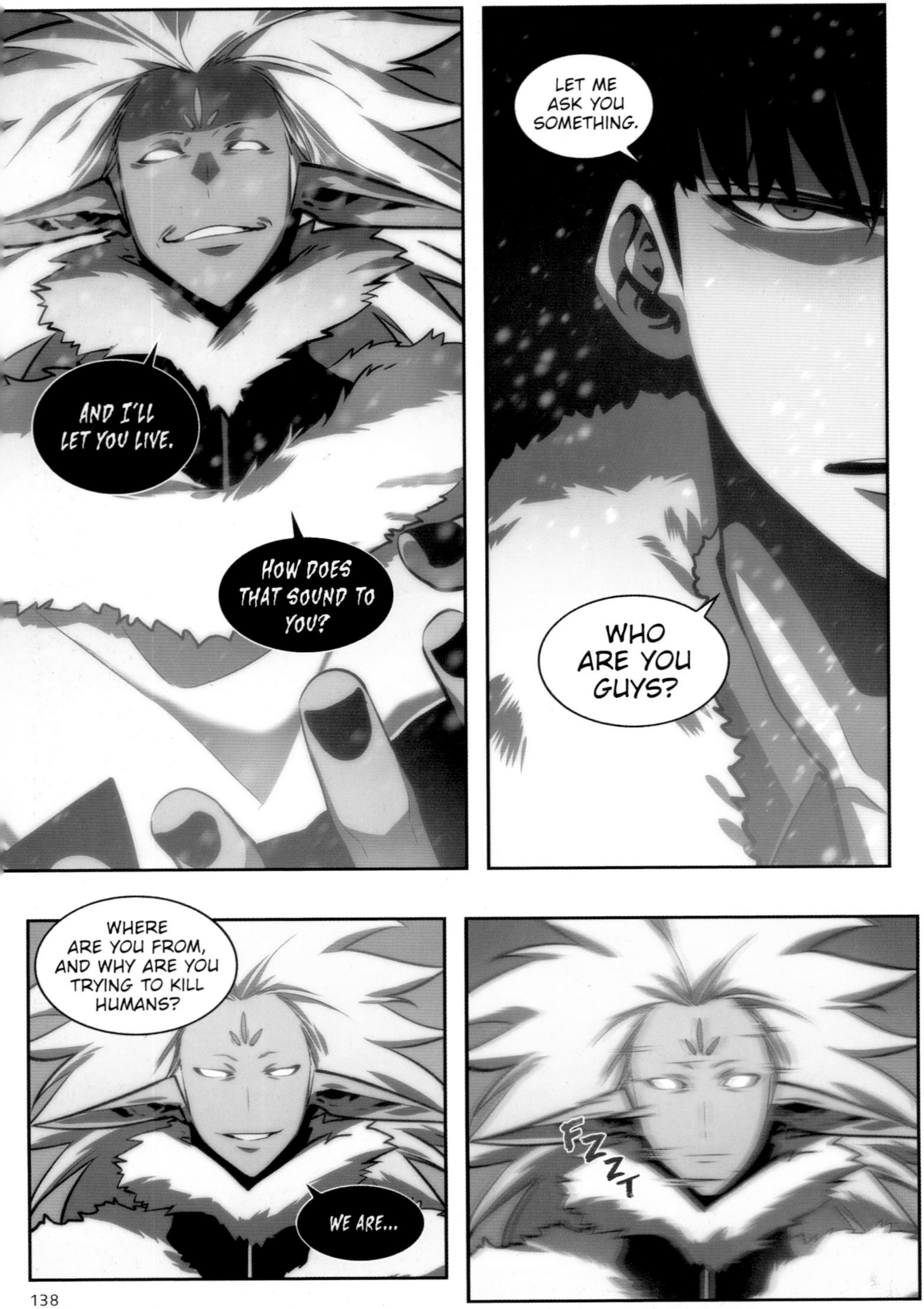
AND I'LL LET YOU LIVE.
HOW DOES THAT SOUND TO YOU?
LET ME ASK YOU SOMETHING.
WHO ARE YOU GUYS?
WHERE ARE YOU FROM, AND WHY ARE YOU TRYING TO KILL HUMANS?
WE ARE...
FZZZT

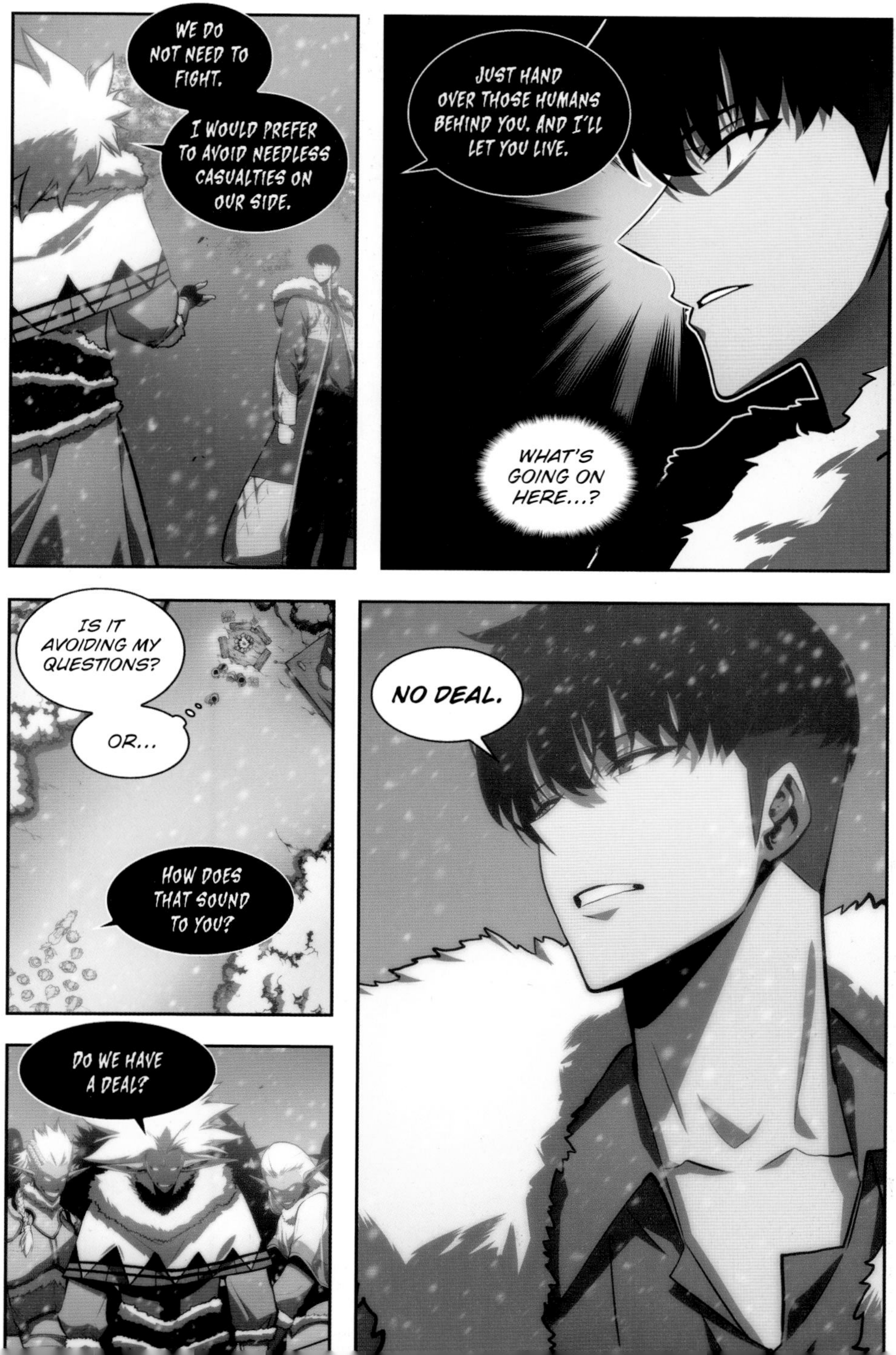
WE DO NOT NEED TO FIGHT.
I WOULD PREFER TO AVOID NEEDLESS CASUALTIES ON OUR SIDE.
JUST HAND OVER THOSE HUMANS BEHIND YOU. AND I'LL LET YOU LIVE.
WHAT'S GOING ON HERE...?
IS IT AVOIDING MY QUESTIONS?
OR...
HOW DOES THAT SOUND TO YOU?
DO WE HAVE A DEAL?
NO DEAL.

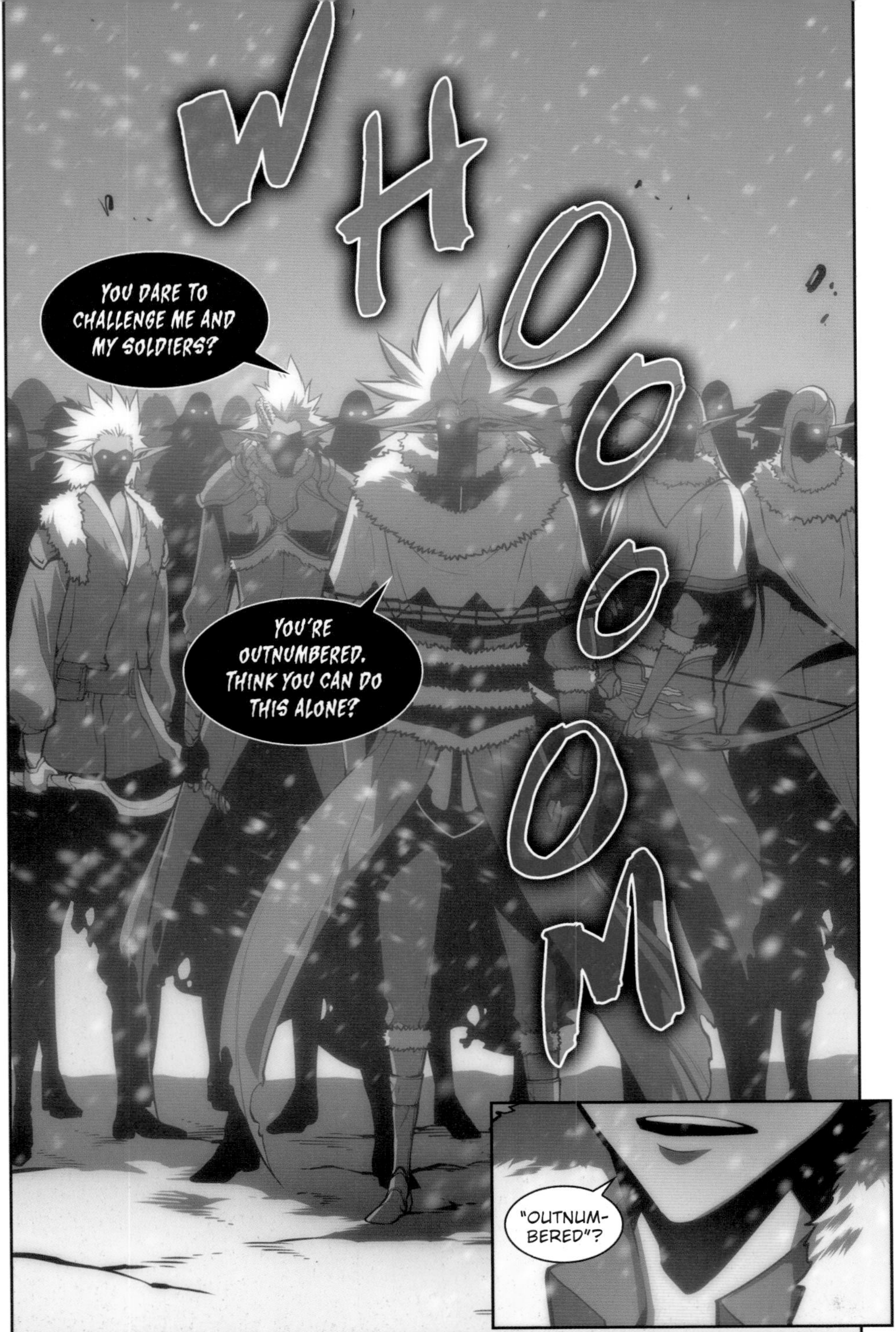
WHOOOOOM
YOU DARE TO CHALLENGE ME AND MY SOLDIERS?
YOU'RE OUTNUMBERED. THINK YOU CAN DO THIS ALONE?
"OUTNUM-BERED"?

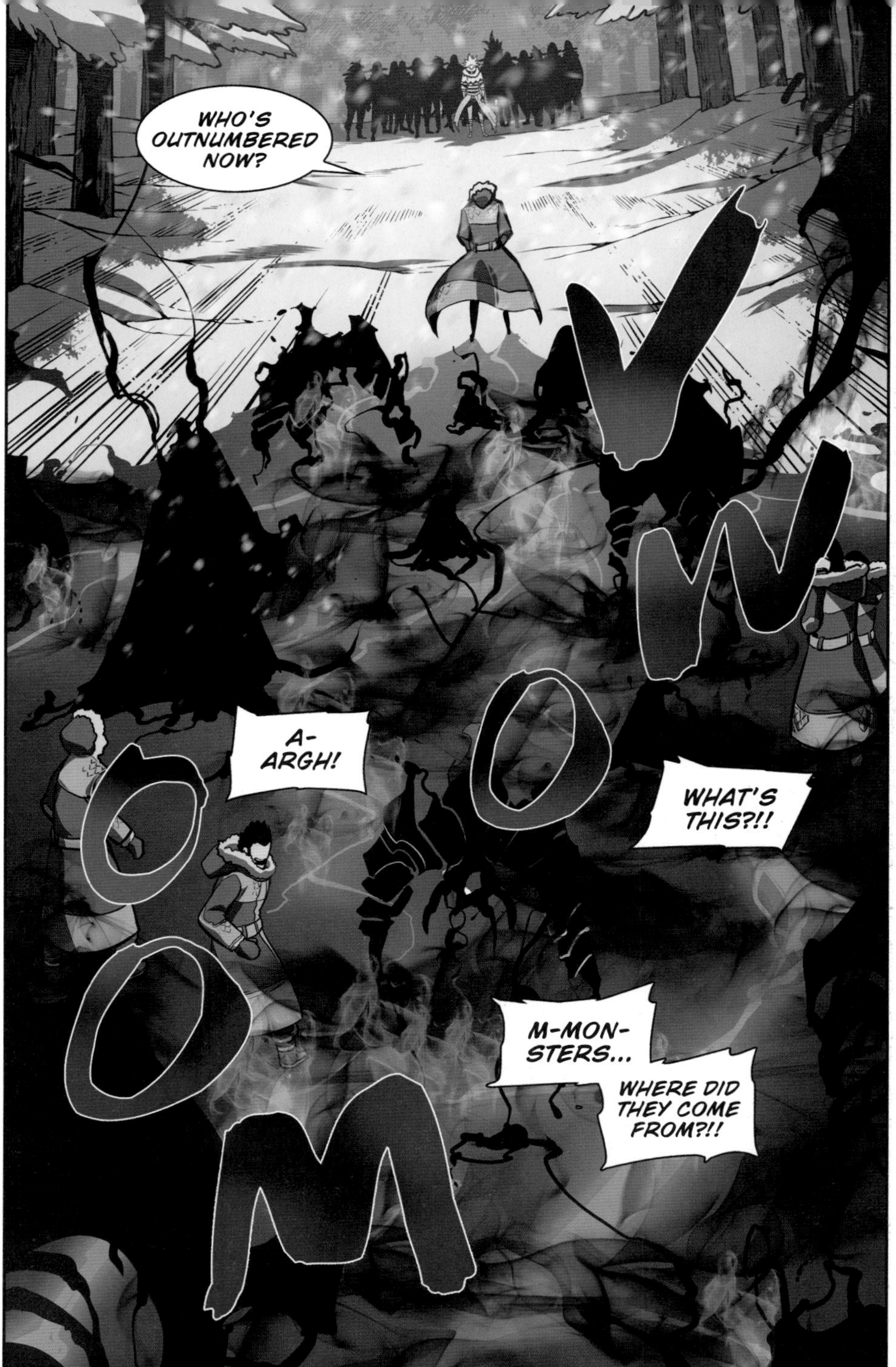
WHO'S OUTNUMBERED NOW?
VWOOOM
A-ARGH!
WHAT'S THIS?!!
M-MON-STERS...
WHERE DID THEY COME FROM?!!

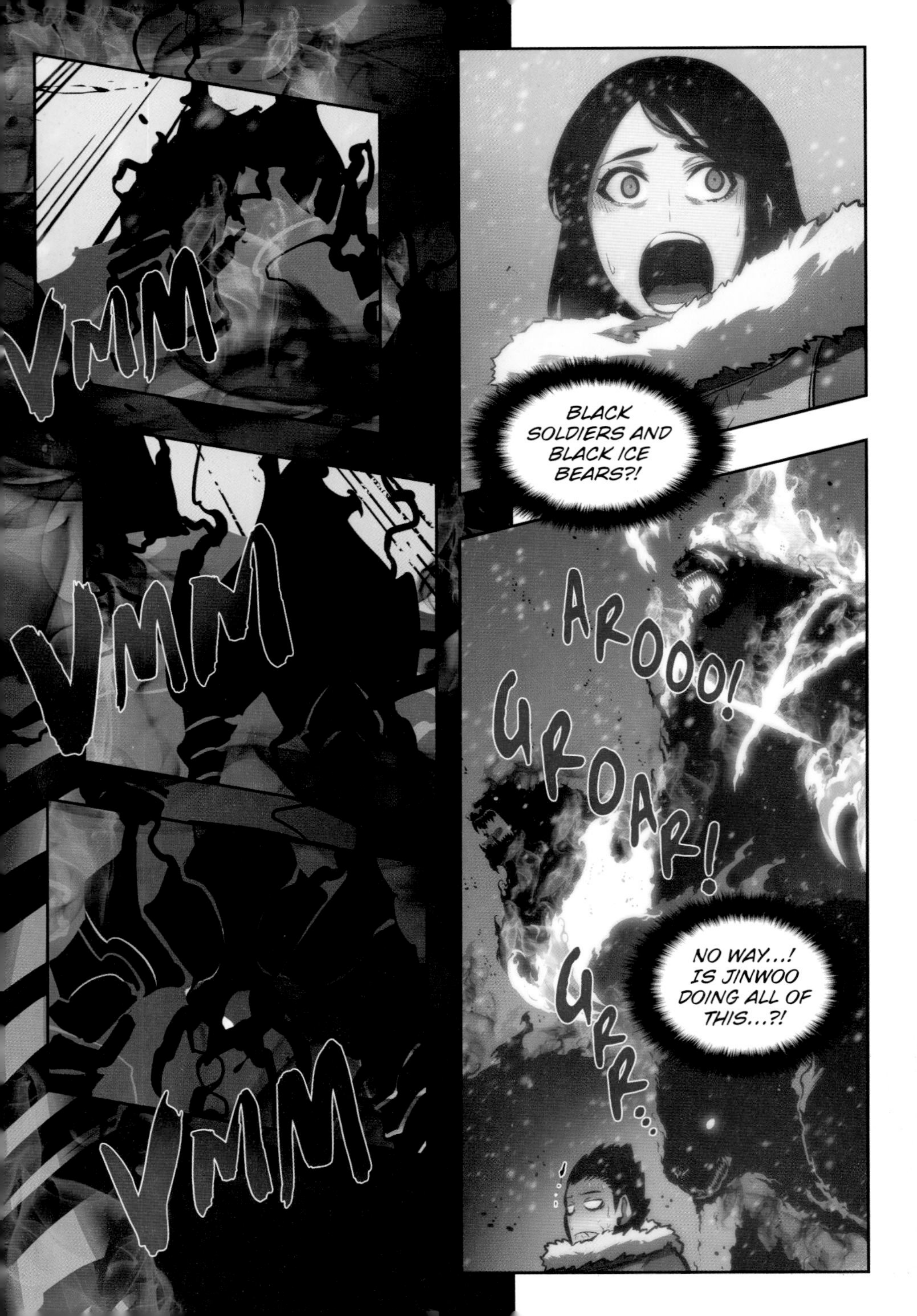
VMM
VMM
VMM
BLACK SOLDIERS AND BLACK ICE BEARS?!
AROOO!
GROAR!
GRR...
NO WAY...! IS JINWOO DOING ALL OF THIS...?!

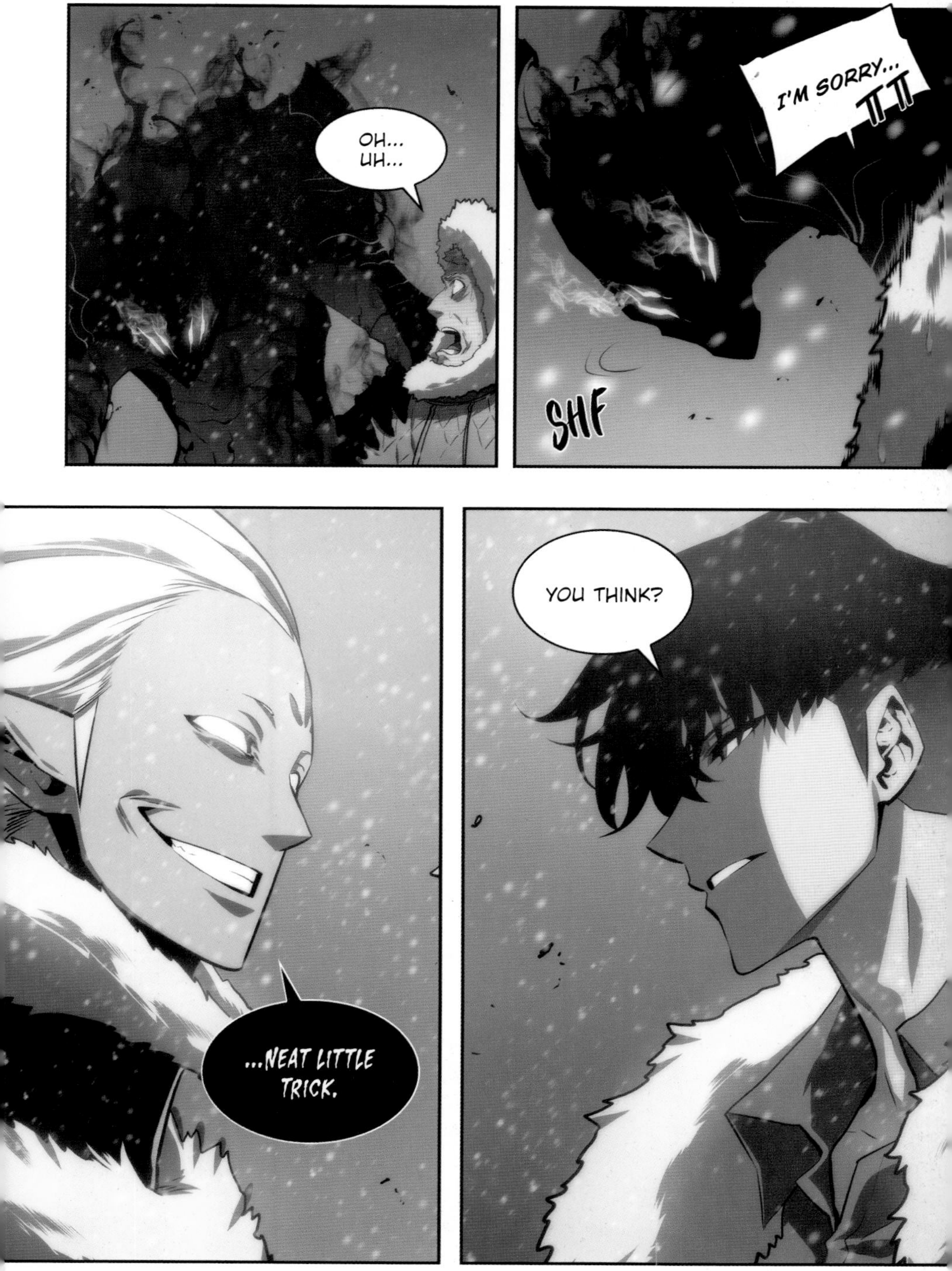
OH... UH...
I'M SORRY...
SHF
...NEAT LITTLE TRICK.
YOU THINK?

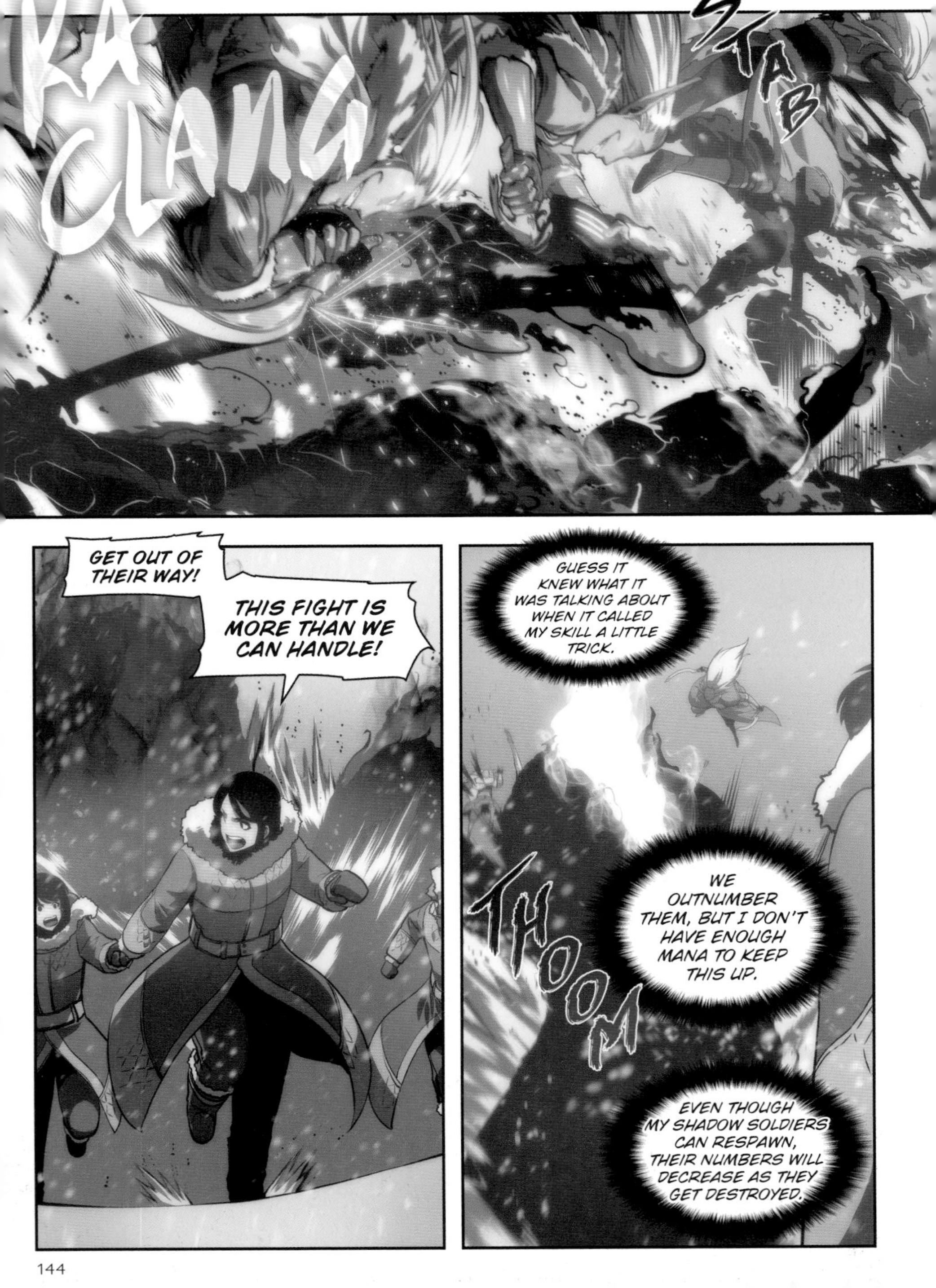
KA CLANG
STAB
GET OUT OF THEIR WAY!
THIS FIGHT IS MORE THAN WE CAN HANDLE!
GUESS IT KNEW WHAT IT WAS TALKING ABOUT WHEN IT CALLED MY SKILL A LITTLE TRICK.
THOOM
WE OUTNUMBER THEM, BUT I DON'T HAVE ENOUGH MANA TO KEEP THIS UP.
EVEN THOUGH MY SHADOW SOLDIERS CAN RESPAWN, THEIR NUMBERS WILL DECREASE AS THEY GET DESTROYED.

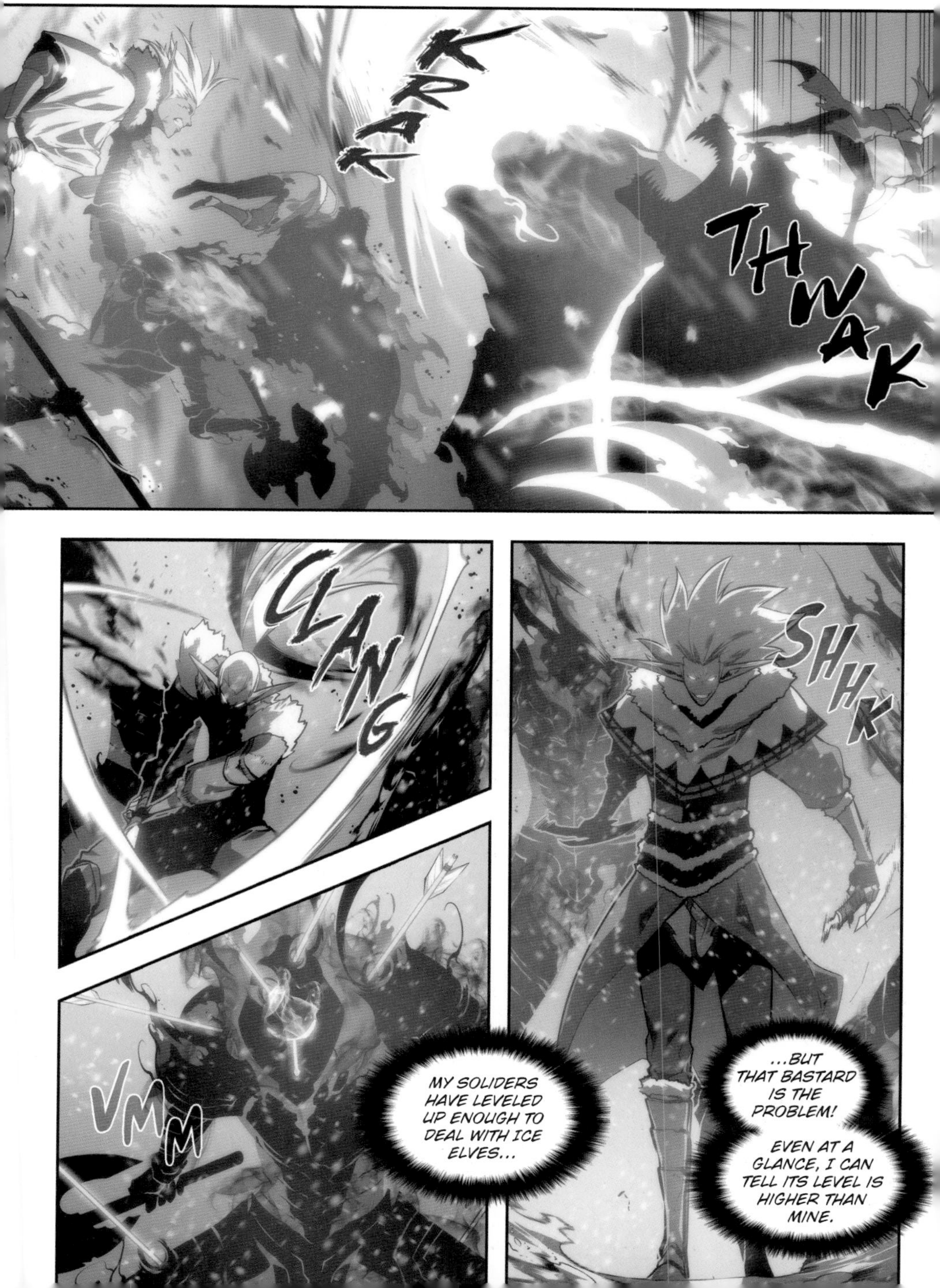
KRAK
THWAK
CLANG
SHHK
VMM
MY SOLIDERS HAVE LEVELED UP ENOUGH TO DEAL WITH ICE ELVES...
...BUT THAT BASTARD IS THE PROBLEM!
EVEN AT A GLANCE, I CAN TELL ITS LEVEL IS HIGHER THAN MINE.

EVEN IF IGRIS AND I FIGHT IT TOGETHER, IT'LL BE A CHALLENGE...

ORDINARY SOLDIERS ARE NO MATCH FOR IT.

IF ONLY...

...I HAD A MORE POWERFUL SOLDIER!

MY NAME IS BARCA.

WHAT'S YOURS?

JINWOO SUNG.

CLANG

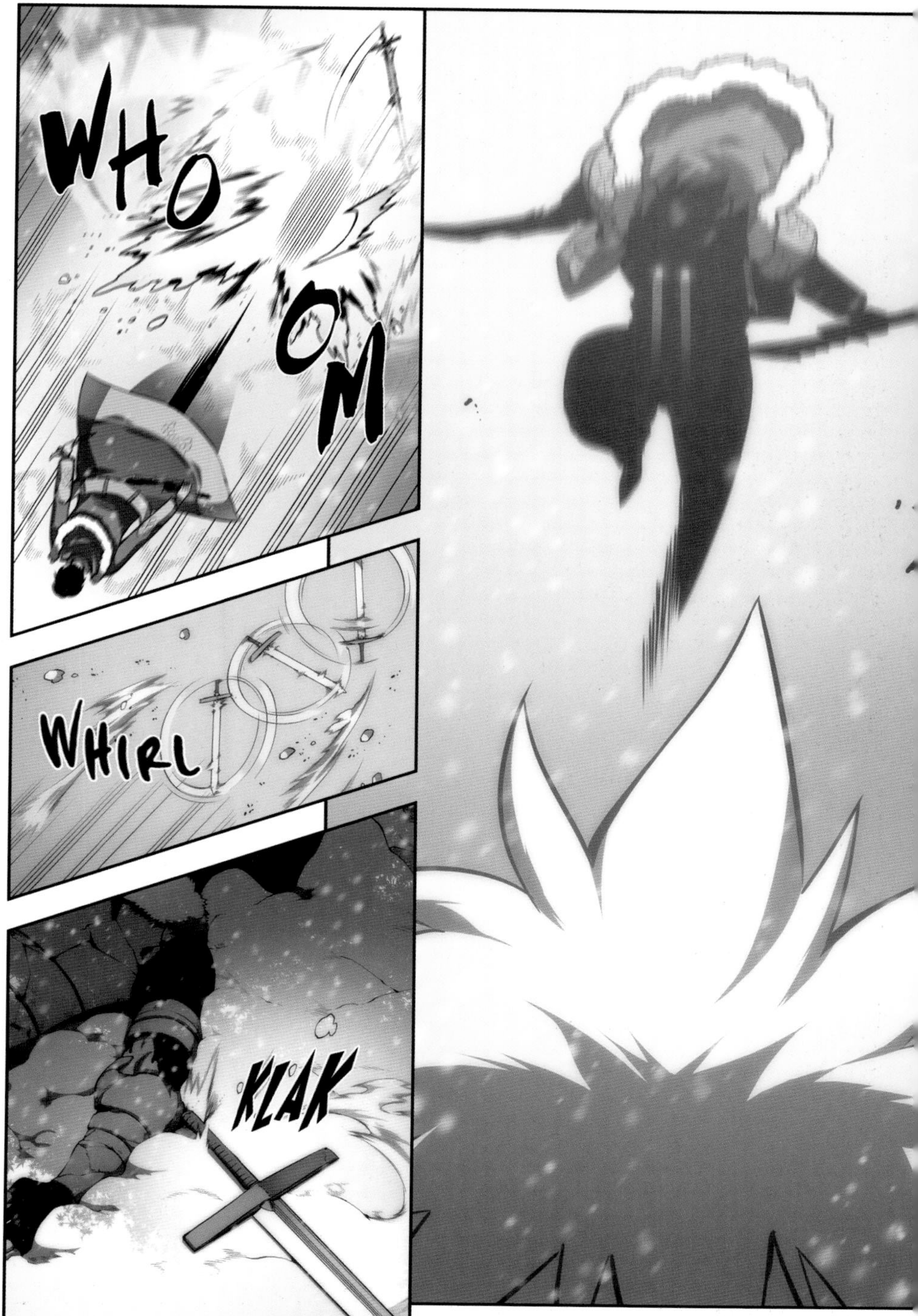
WHOOM
WHIRL
KLAK

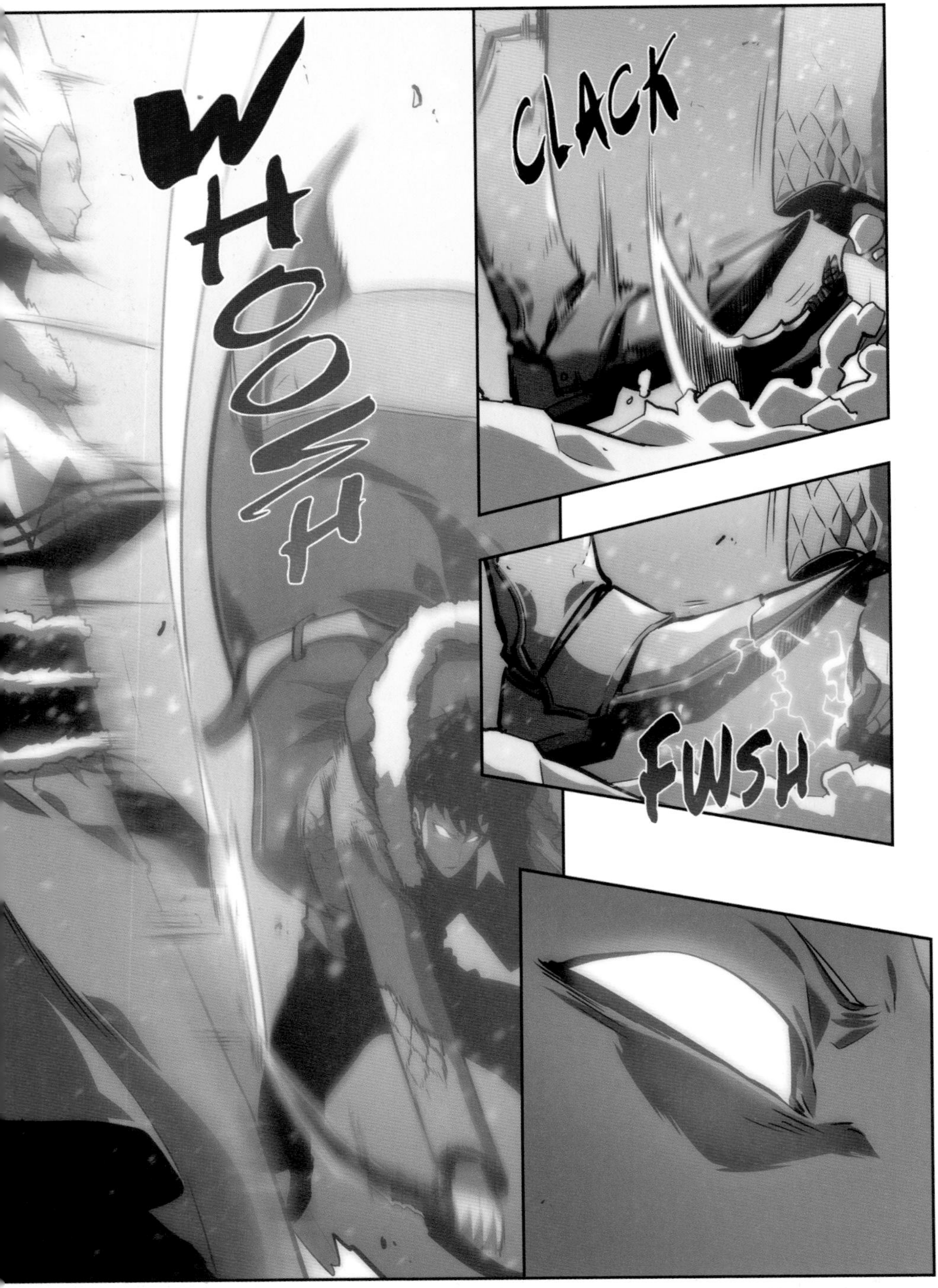
WHOOSH
CLACK
FWSH

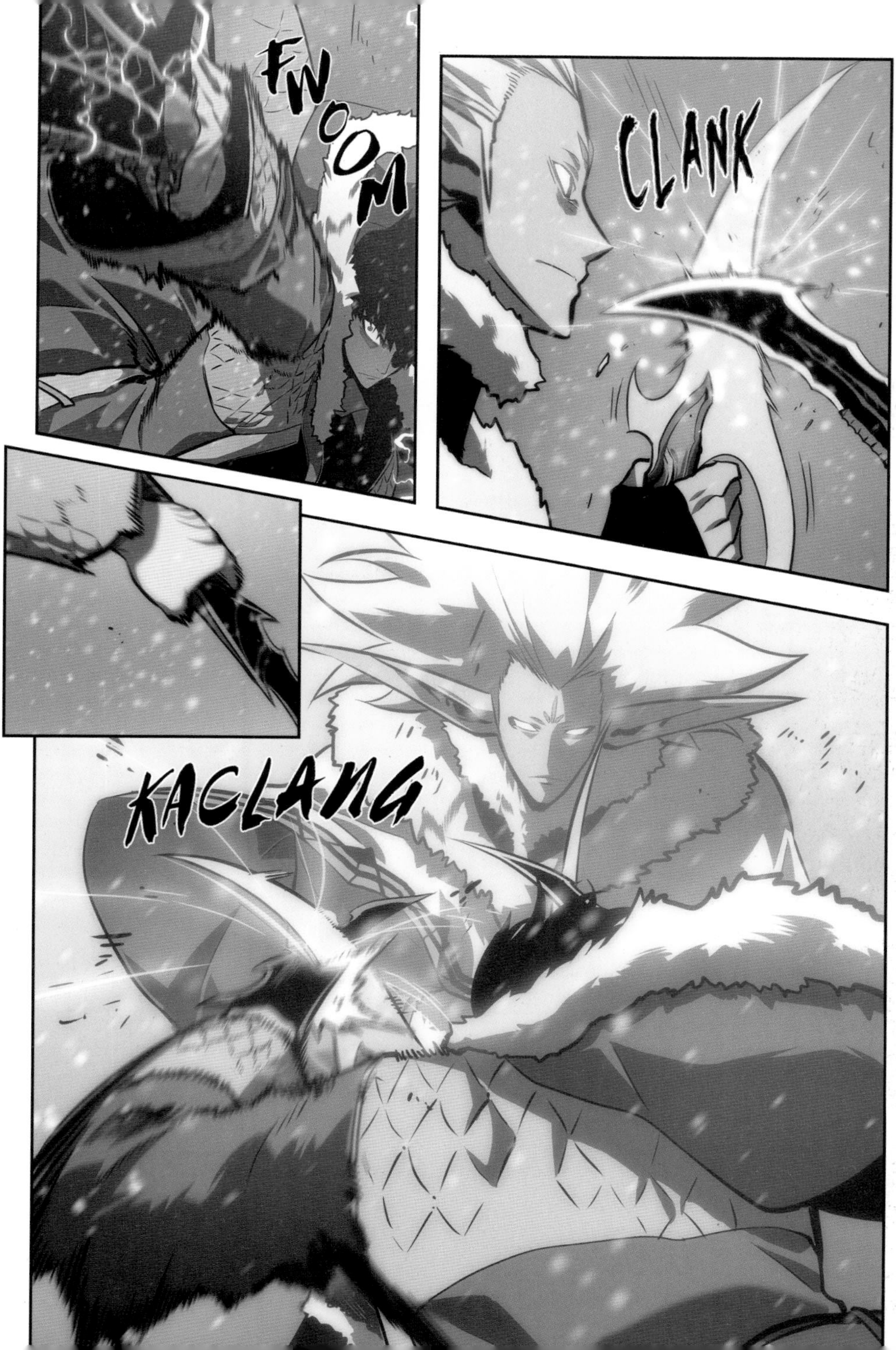
FWOOM
CLANK
KACLANG

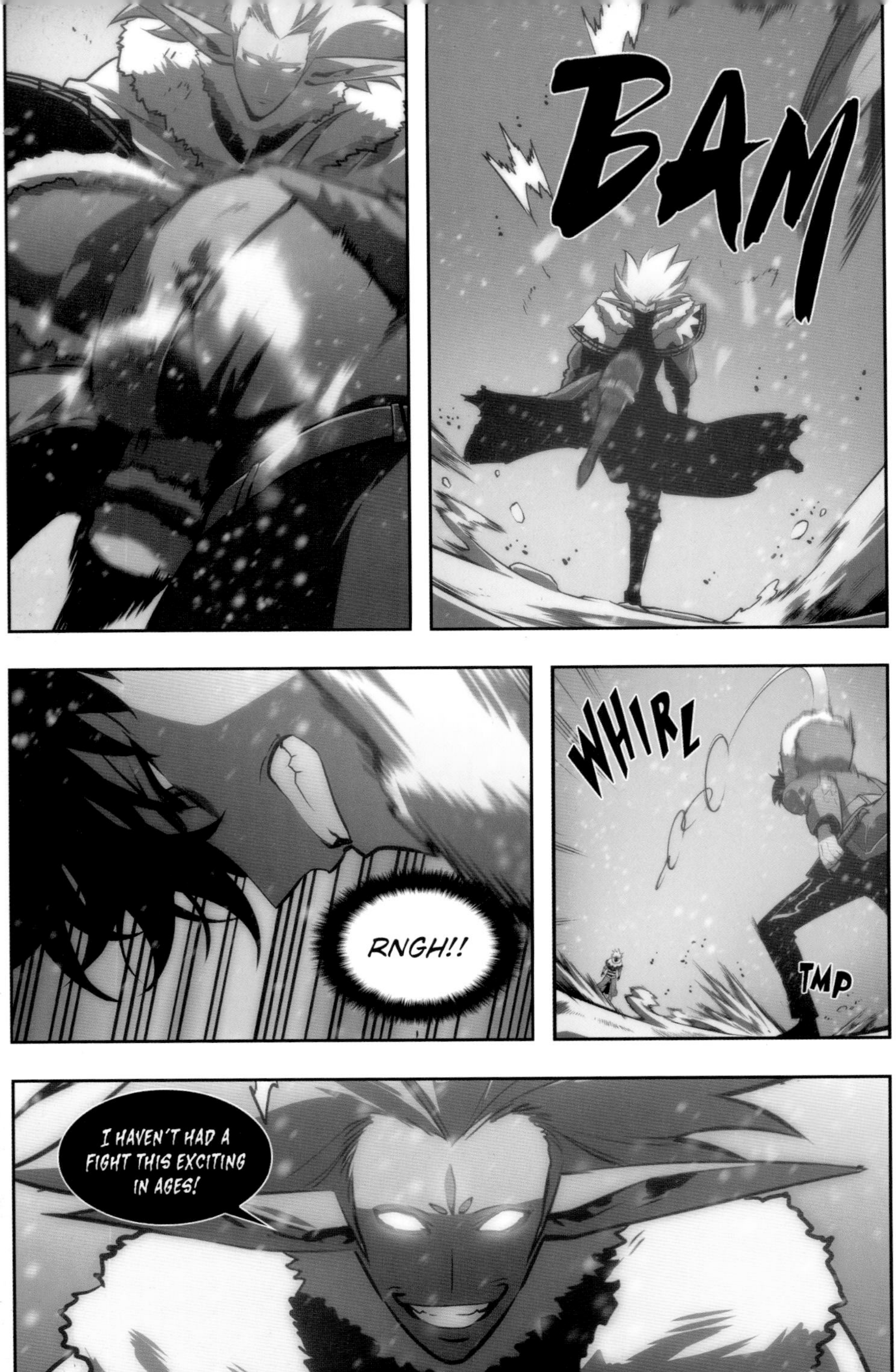
BAM
RNGH!!
WHIRL
TMP
I HAVEN'T HAD A FIGHT THIS EXCITING IN AGES!

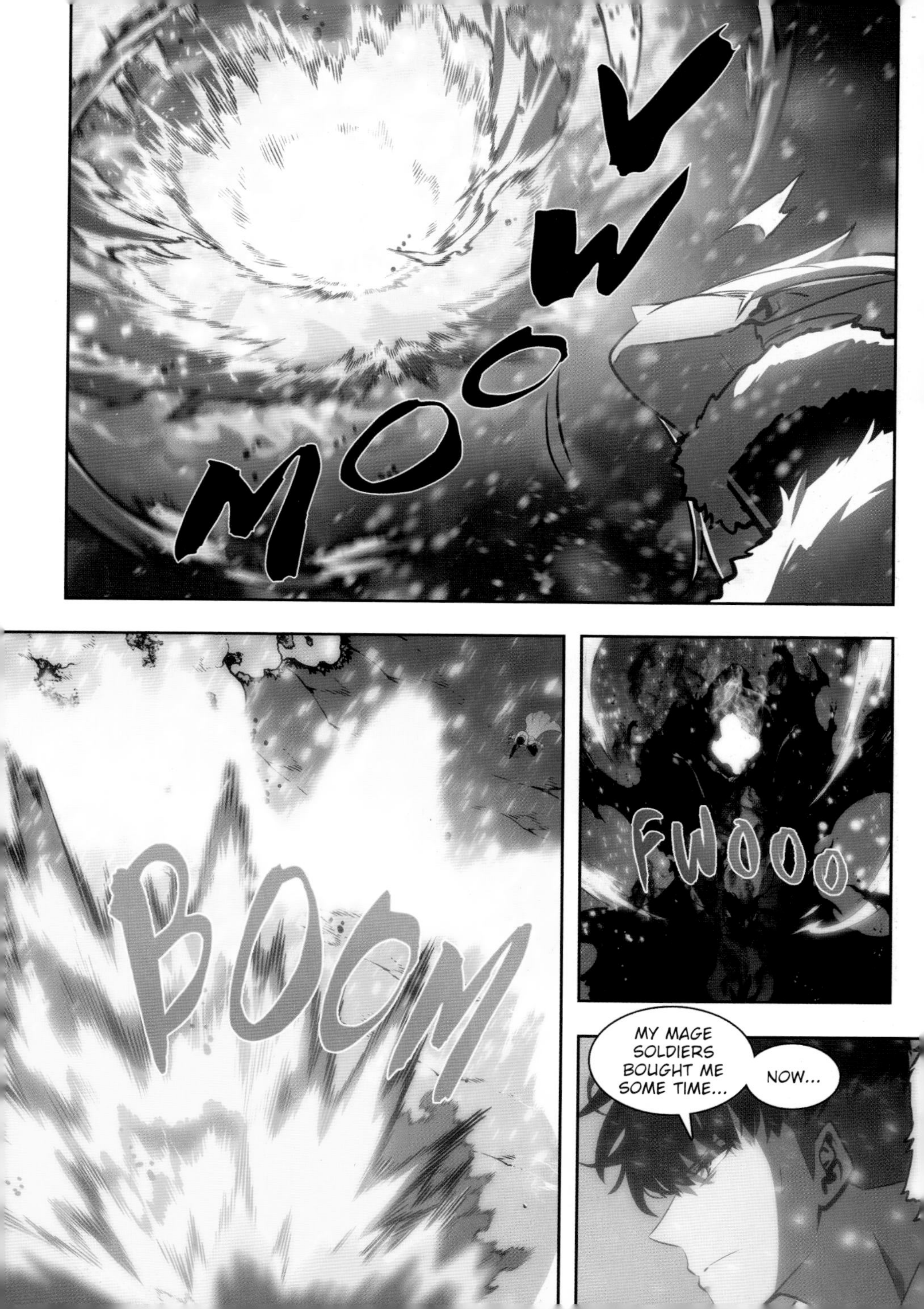
MOOOWV
BOOM
FWOOO
MY MAGE SOLDIERS BOUGHT ME SOME TIME...
NOW...

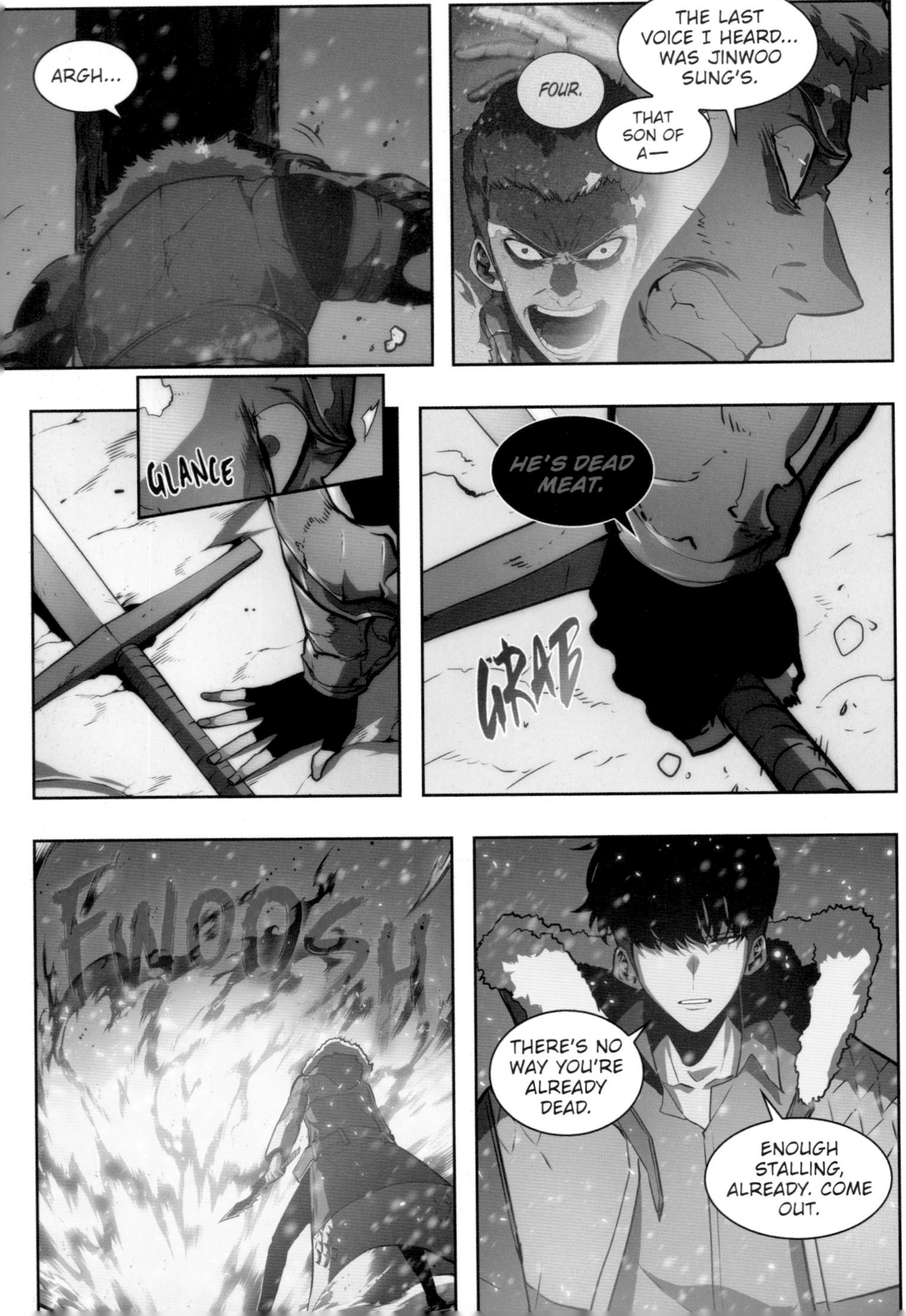
ARGH...
FOUR.
THAT SON OF A—
THE LAST VOICE I HEARD... WAS JINWOO SUNG'S.
GLANCE
HE'S DEAD MEAT.
GRAB
FWOOSH
THERE'S NO WAY YOU'RE ALREADY DEAD.
ENOUGH STALLING, ALREADY. COME OUT.

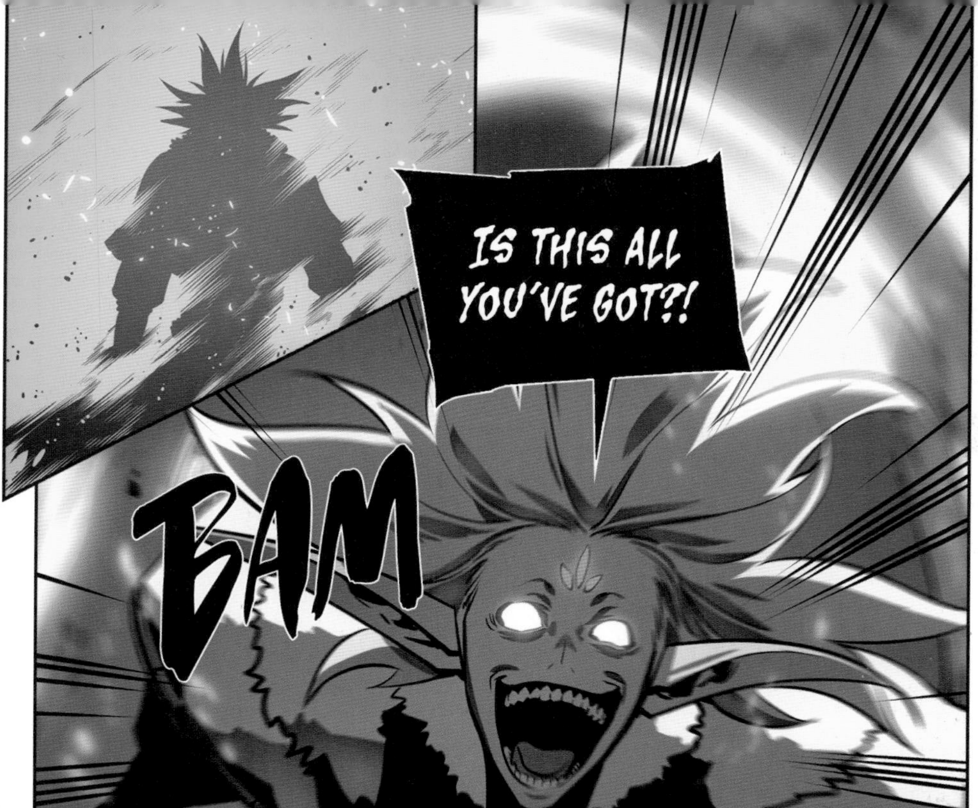
IS THIS ALL YOU'VE GOT?!
BAM
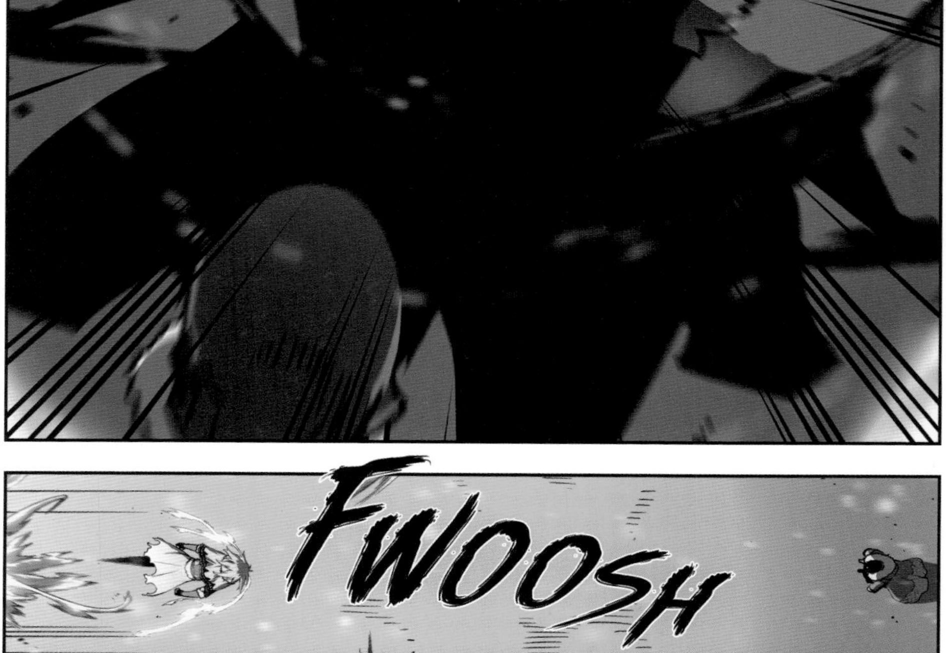
FWOOSH

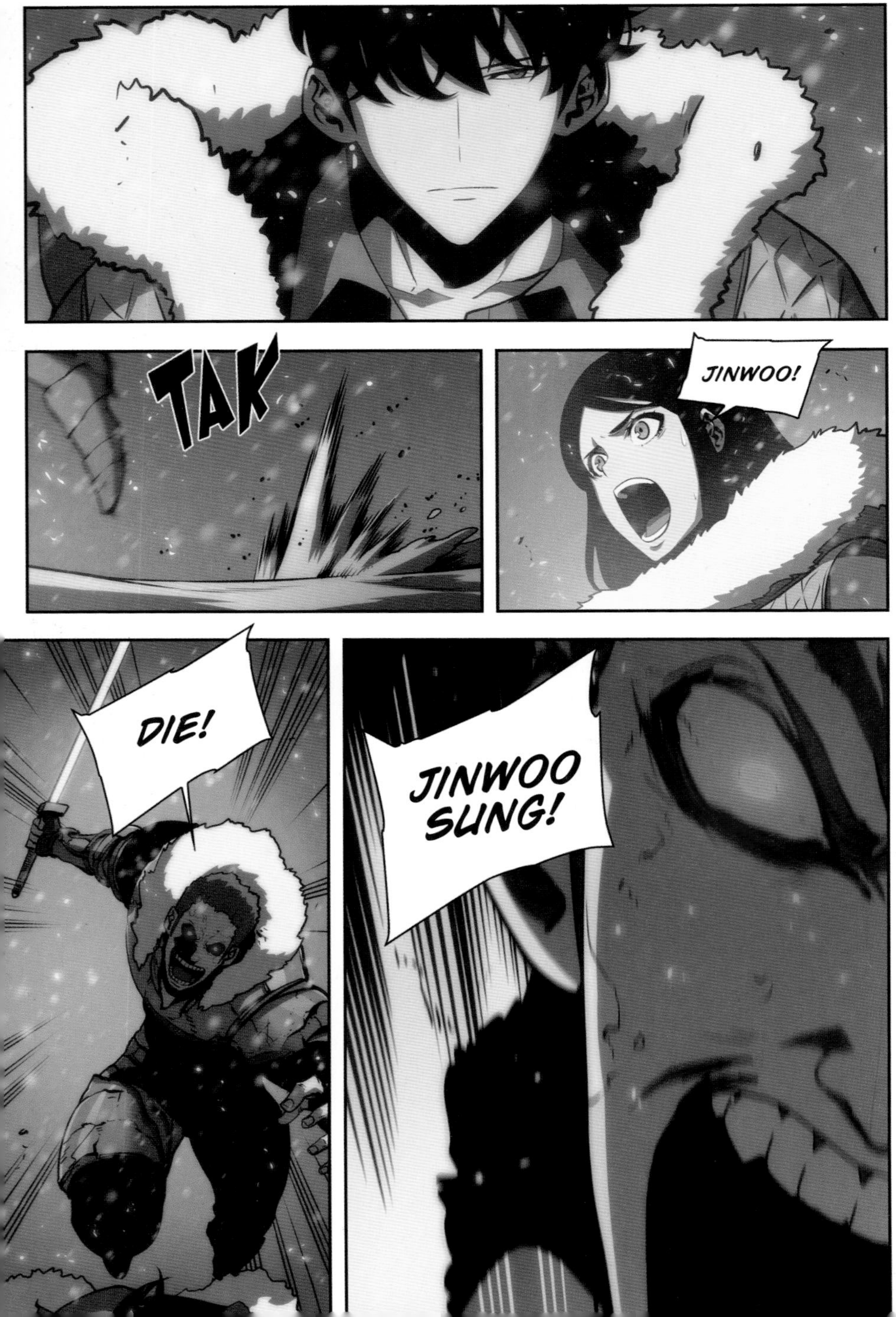
TAK
JINWOO!
DIE!
JINWOO SUNG!

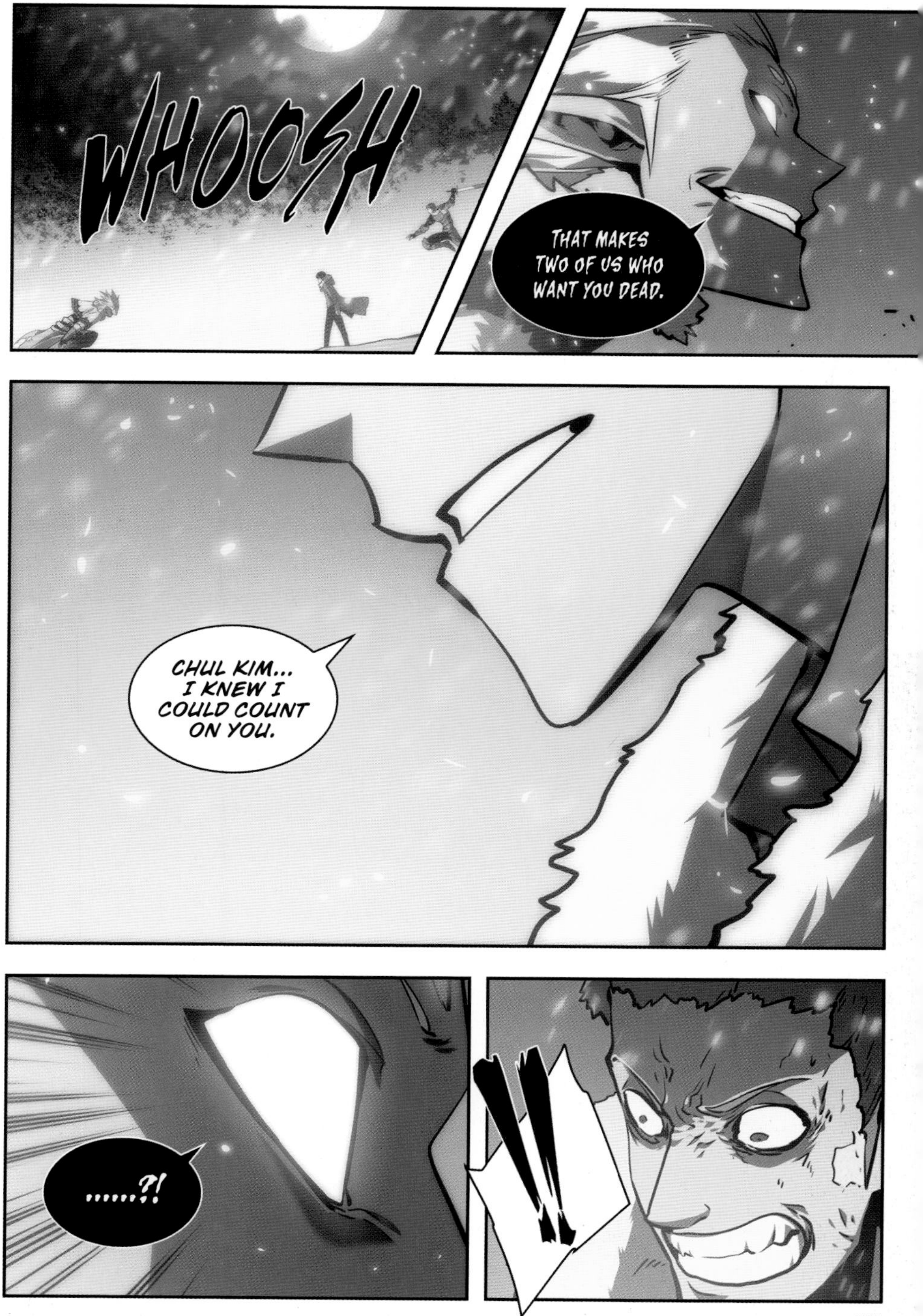
WHOOSH
THAT MAKES TWO OF US WHO WANT YOU DEAD.
CHUL KIM... I KNEW I COULD COUNT ON YOU.
......?!
!!

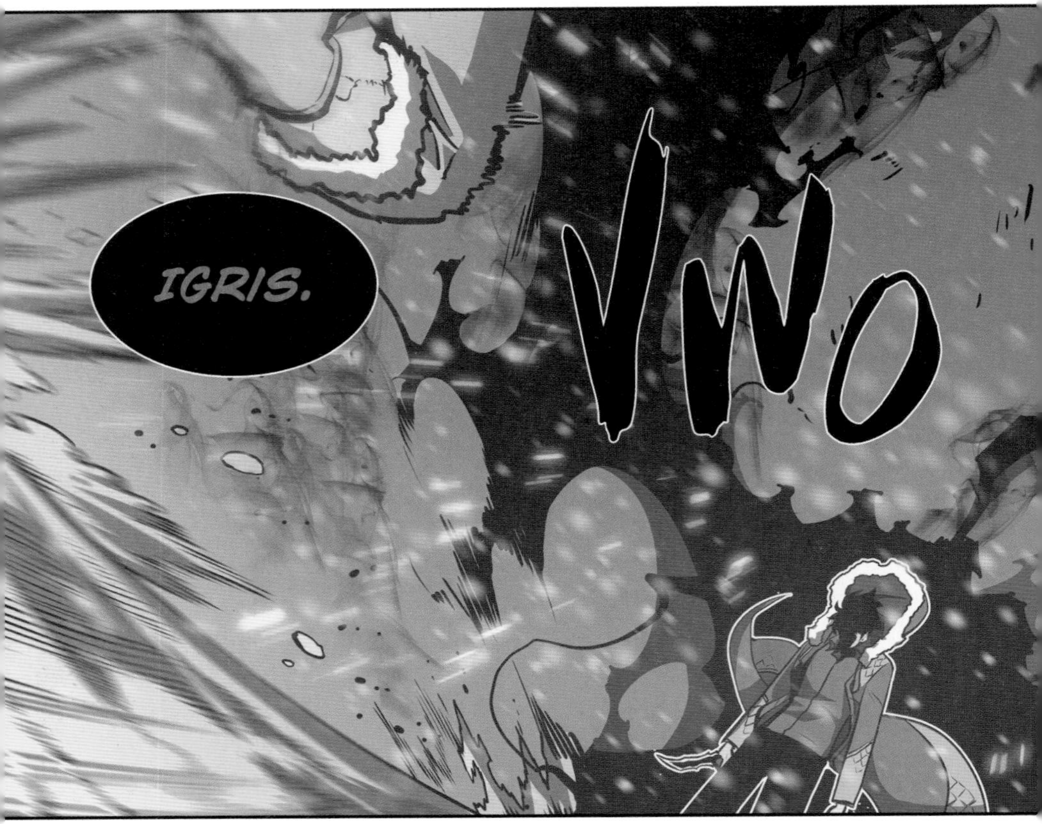
IGRIS.
VWO

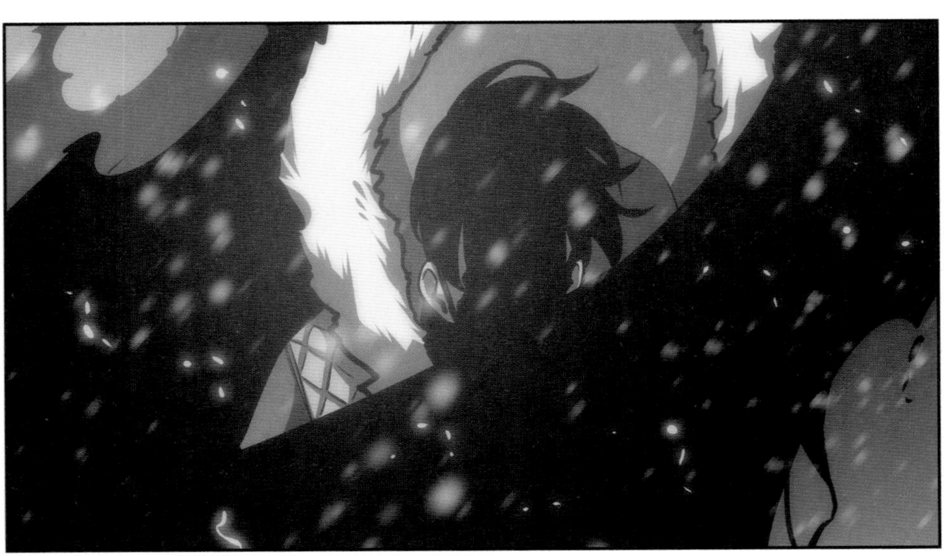

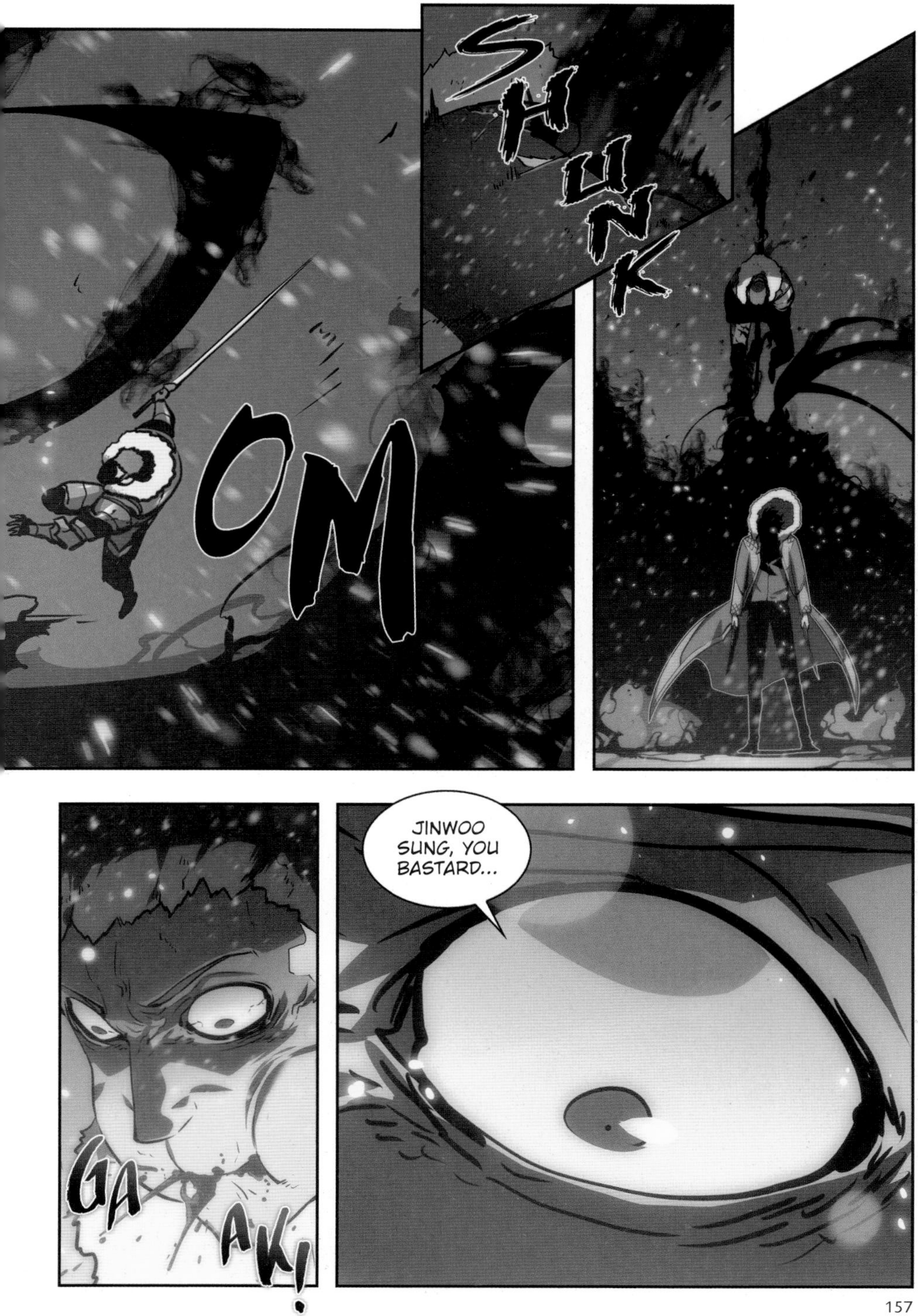
OM
SHUNK
GA
AK!
JINWOO SUNG, YOU BASTARD...

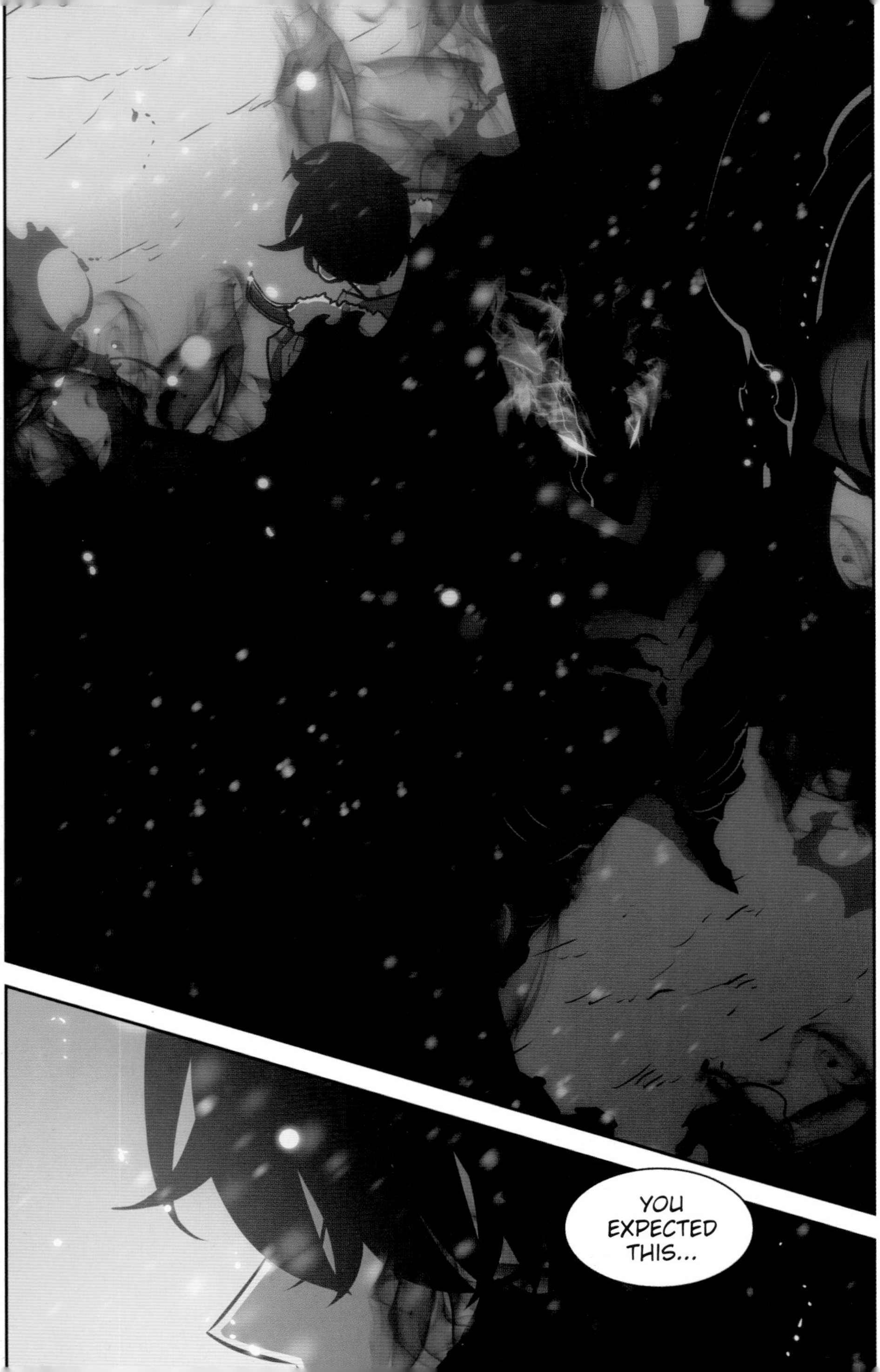
YOU EXPECTED THIS...

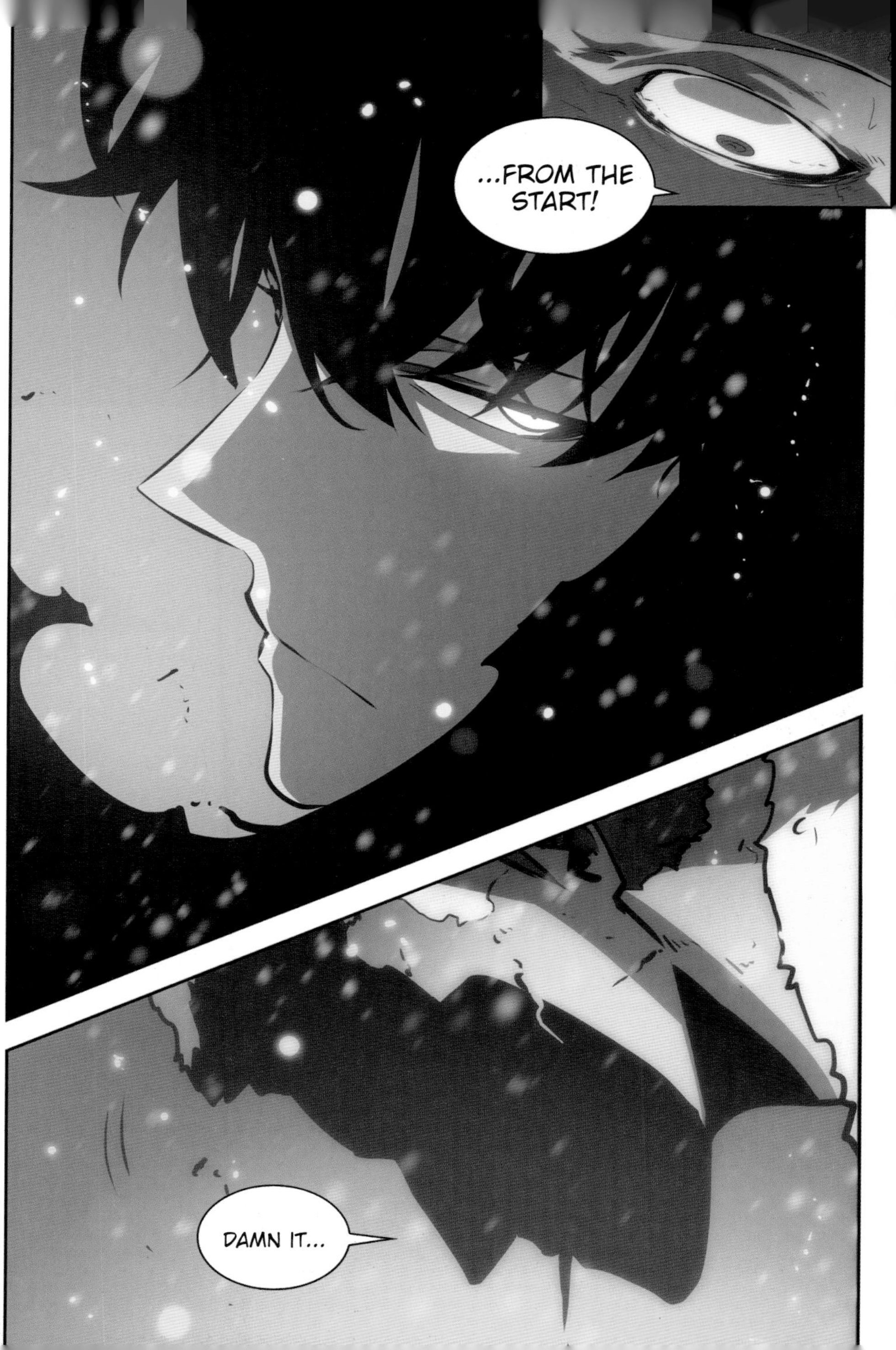
...FROM THE START!
DAMN IT...

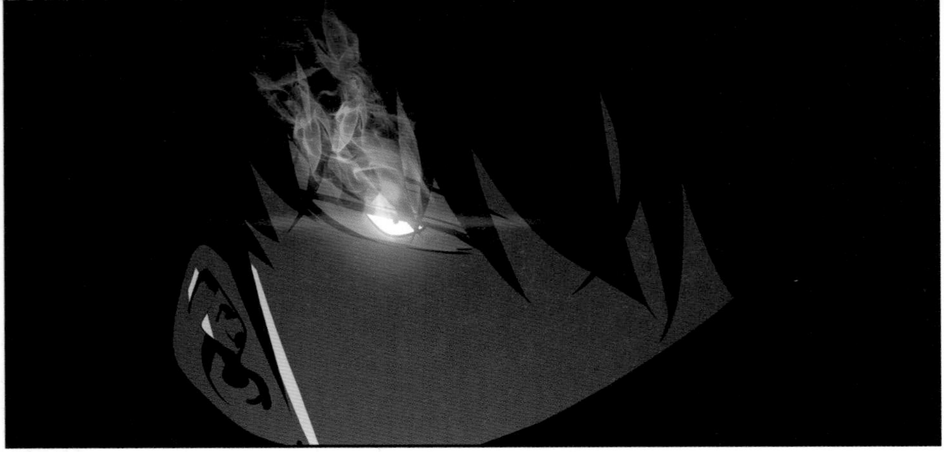

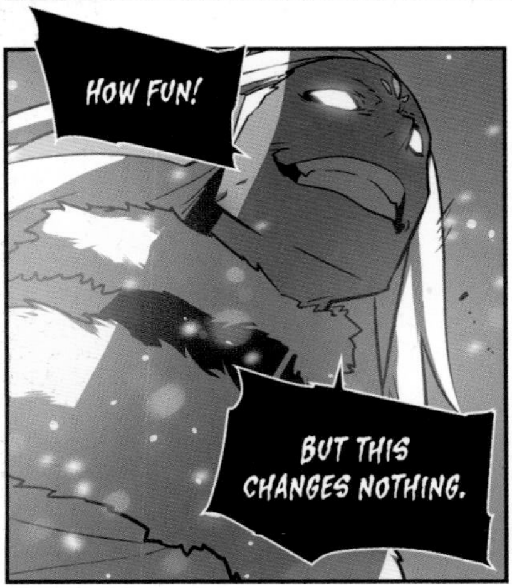
HOW FUN!
BUT THIS CHANGES NOTHING.

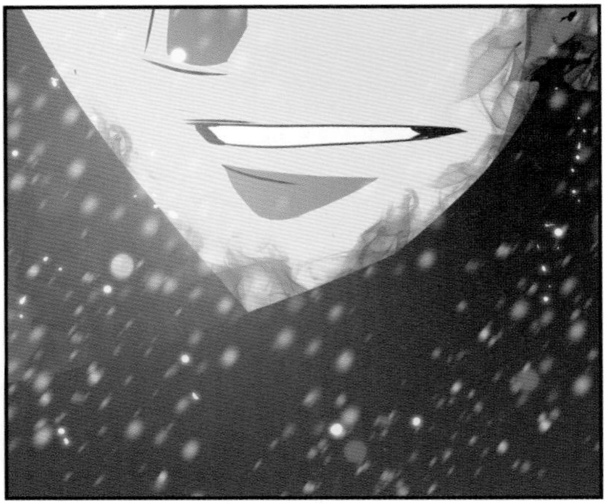

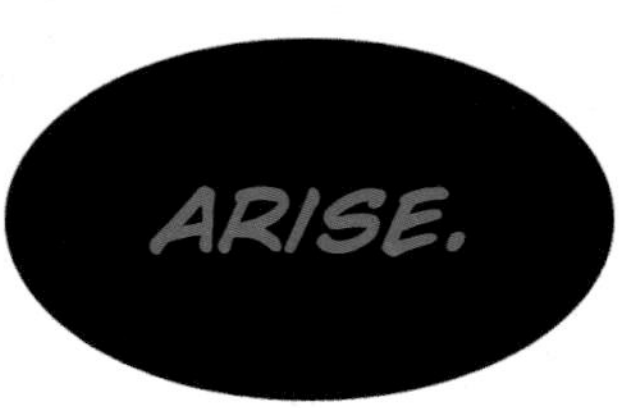
ARISE.

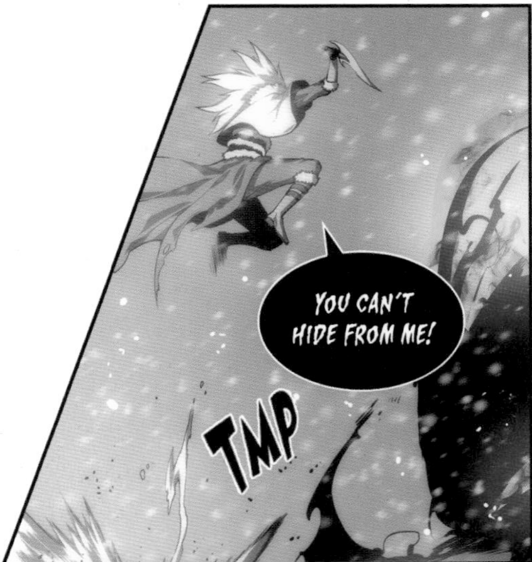
YOU CAN'T HIDE FROM ME!
TMP

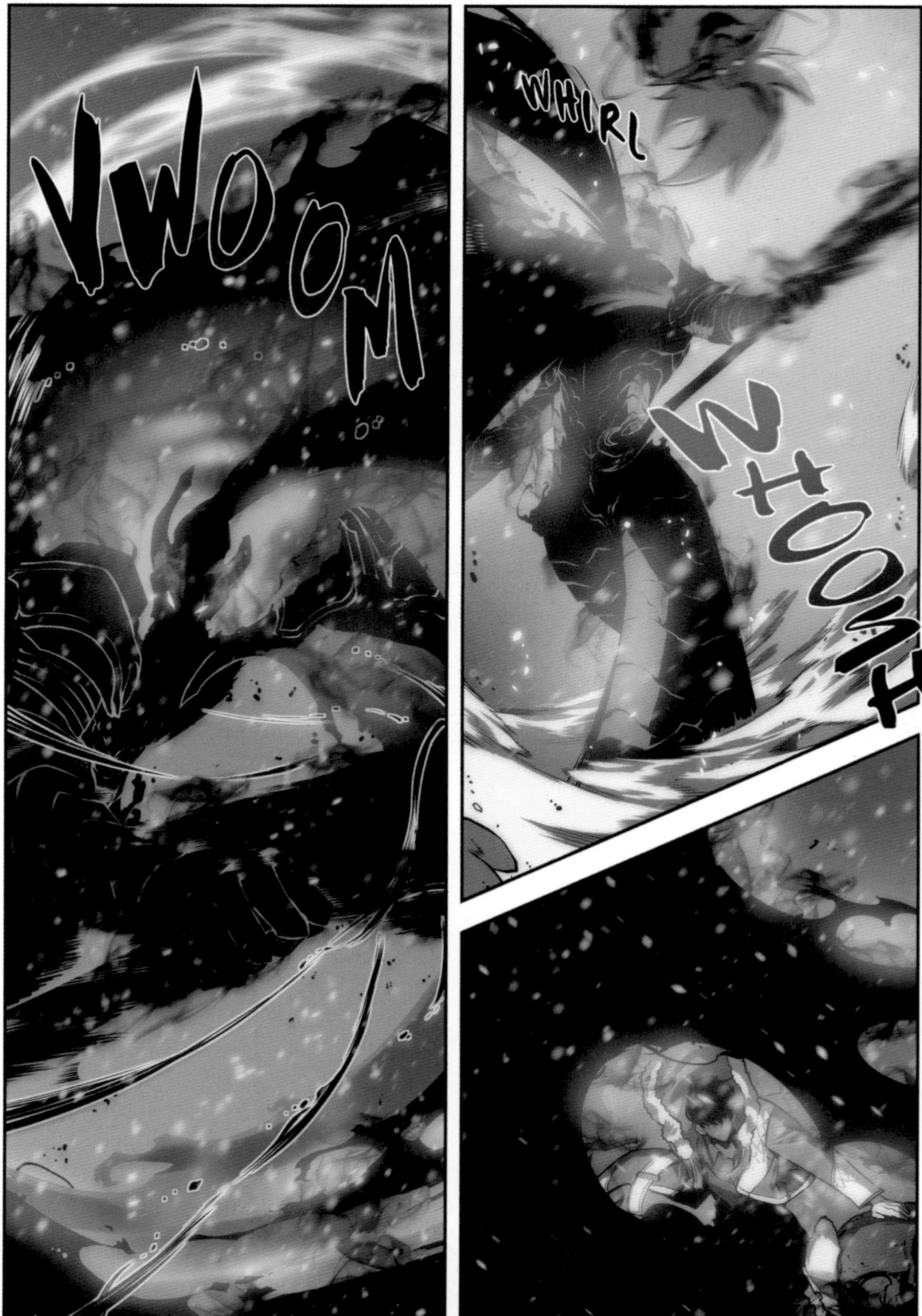
VWOOM
WHIRL
WHOOSH

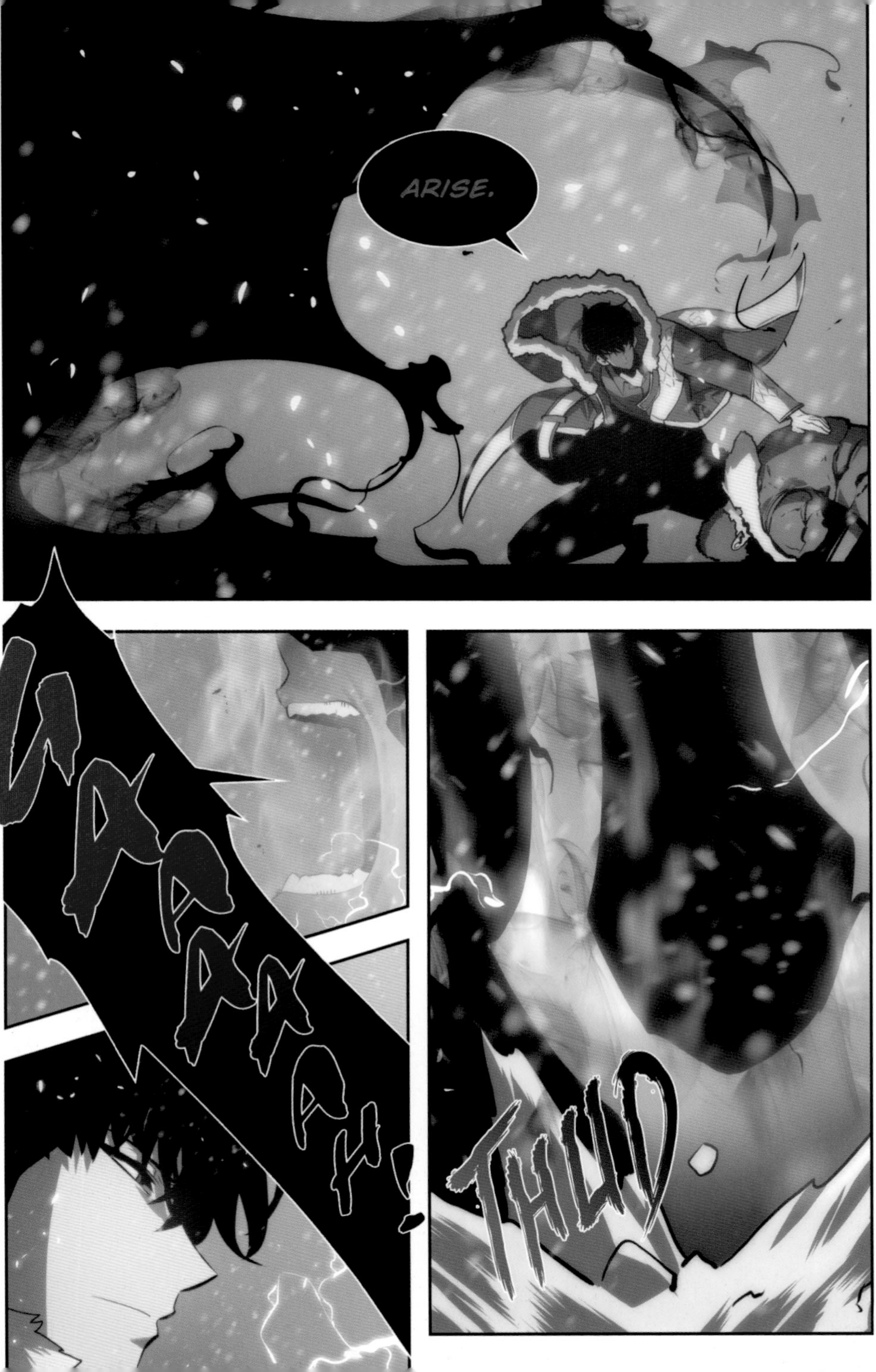
ARISE.
UAAAAAH!
THUD

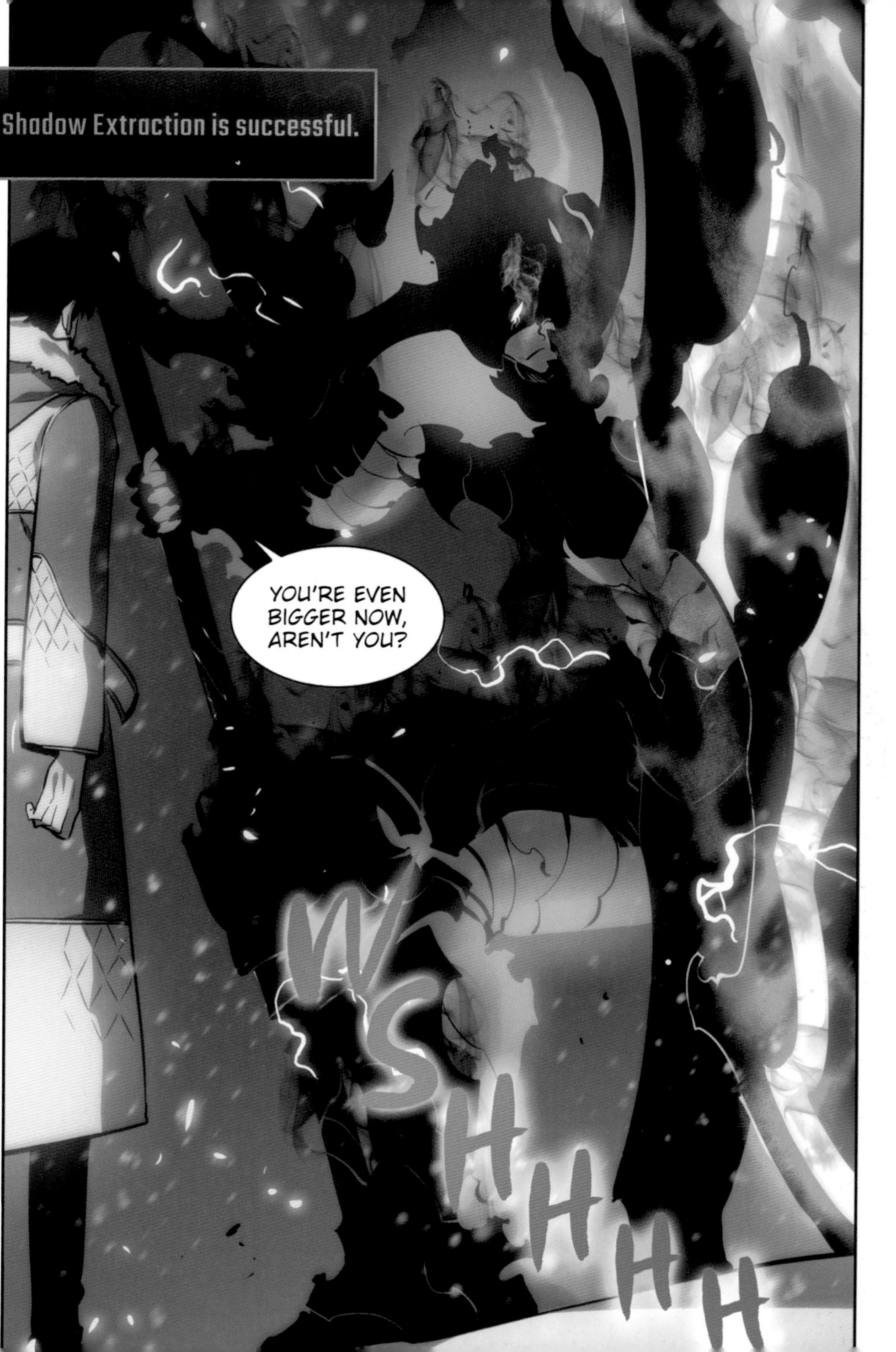
Shadow Extraction is successful.
YOU'RE EVEN BIGGER NOW, AREN'T YOU?
WSHHHHH

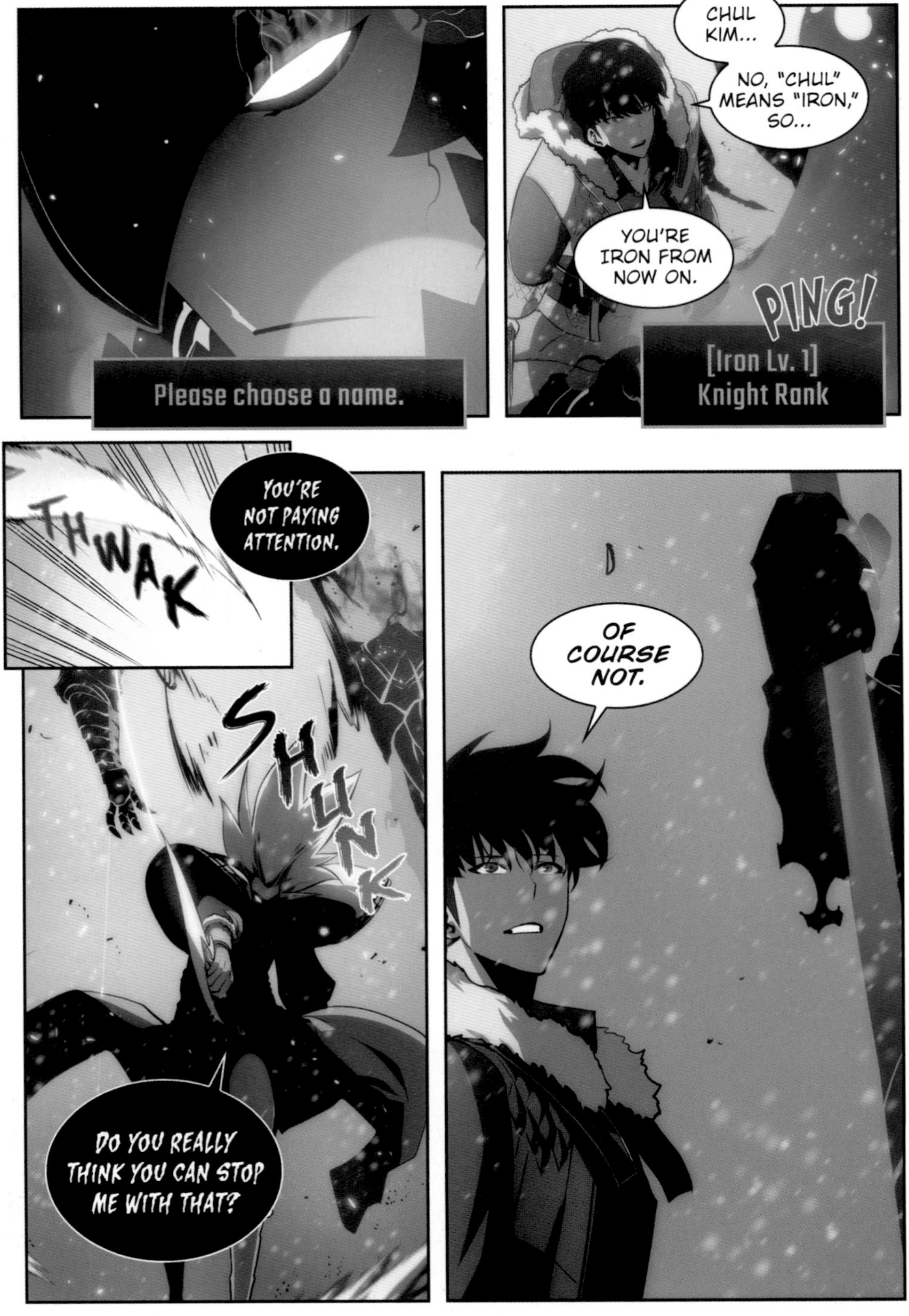
Please choose a name.
CHUL KIM...
NO, "CHUL" MEANS "IRON," SO...
YOU'RE IRON FROM NOW ON.
PING!
[Iron Lv. 1] Knight Rank
THWAK
YOU'RE NOT PAYING ATTENTION.
SHUNK
DO YOU REALLY THINK YOU CAN STOP ME WITH THAT?
OF COURSE NOT.

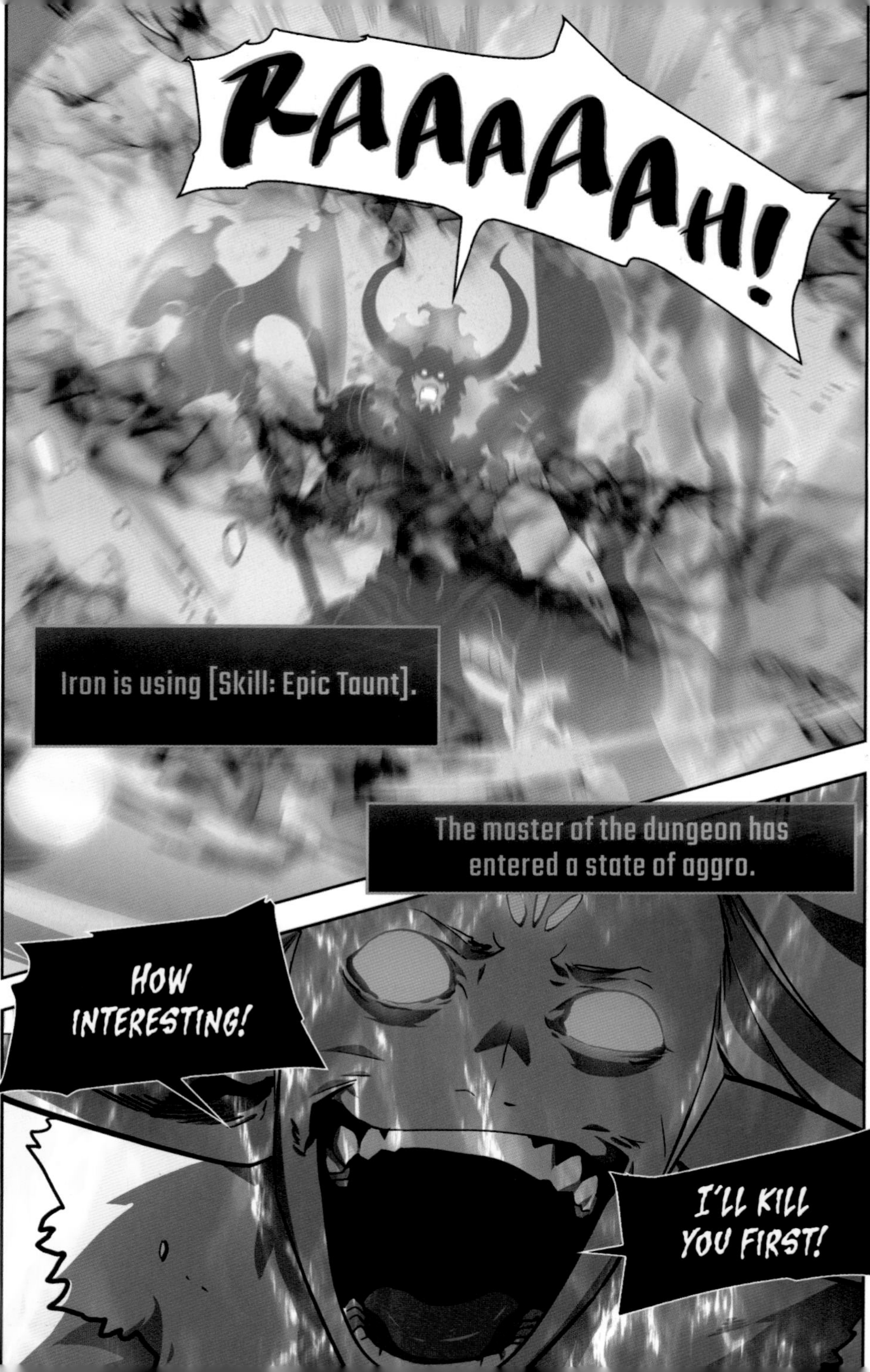
RAAAAAAH!
Iron is using [Skill: Epic Taunt].
The master of the dungeon has entered a state of aggro.
HOW INTERESTING!
I'LL KILL YOU FIRST!

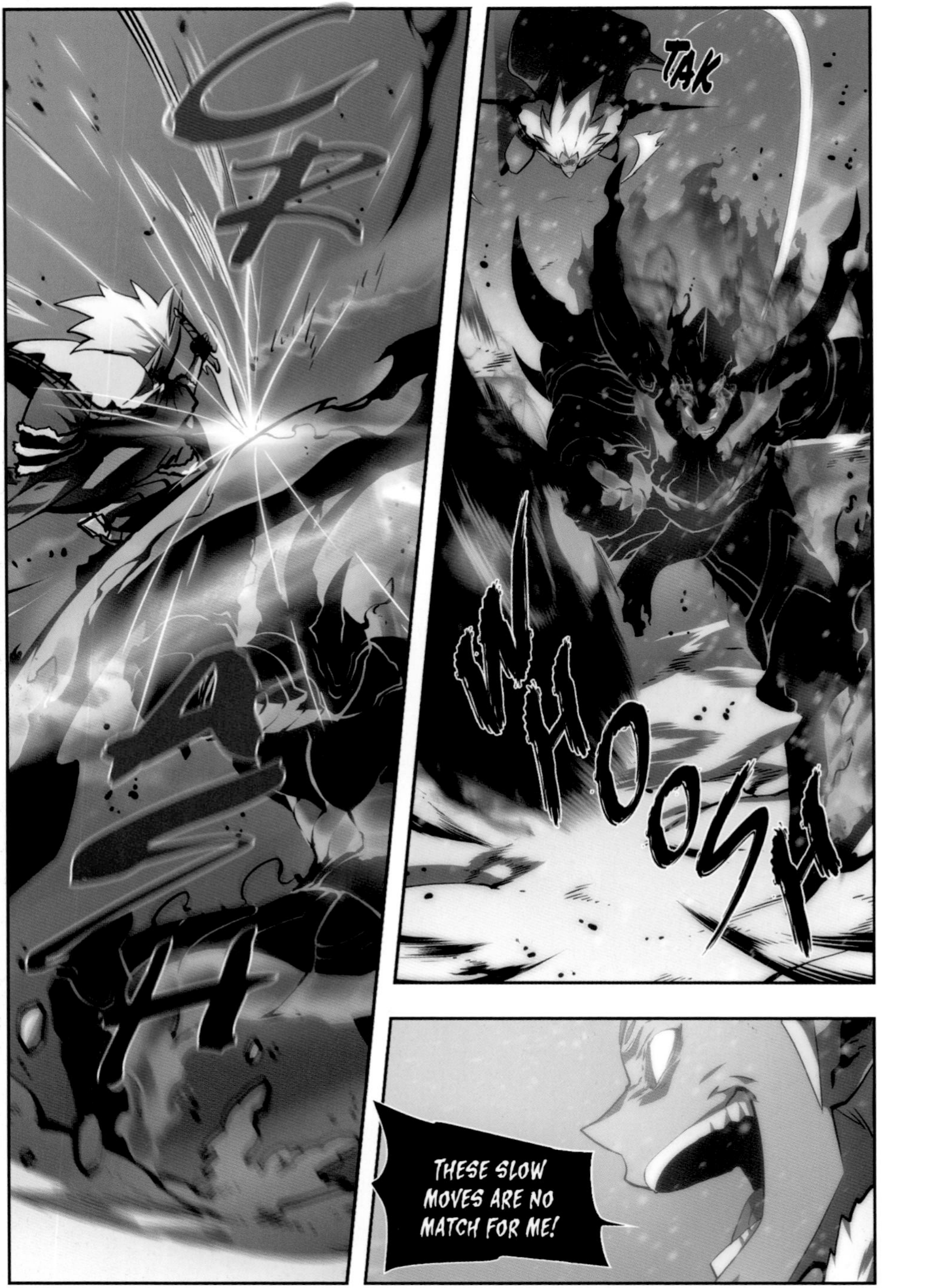
CRASH
TAK
WHOOSH
THESE SLOW MOVES ARE NO MATCH FOR ME!

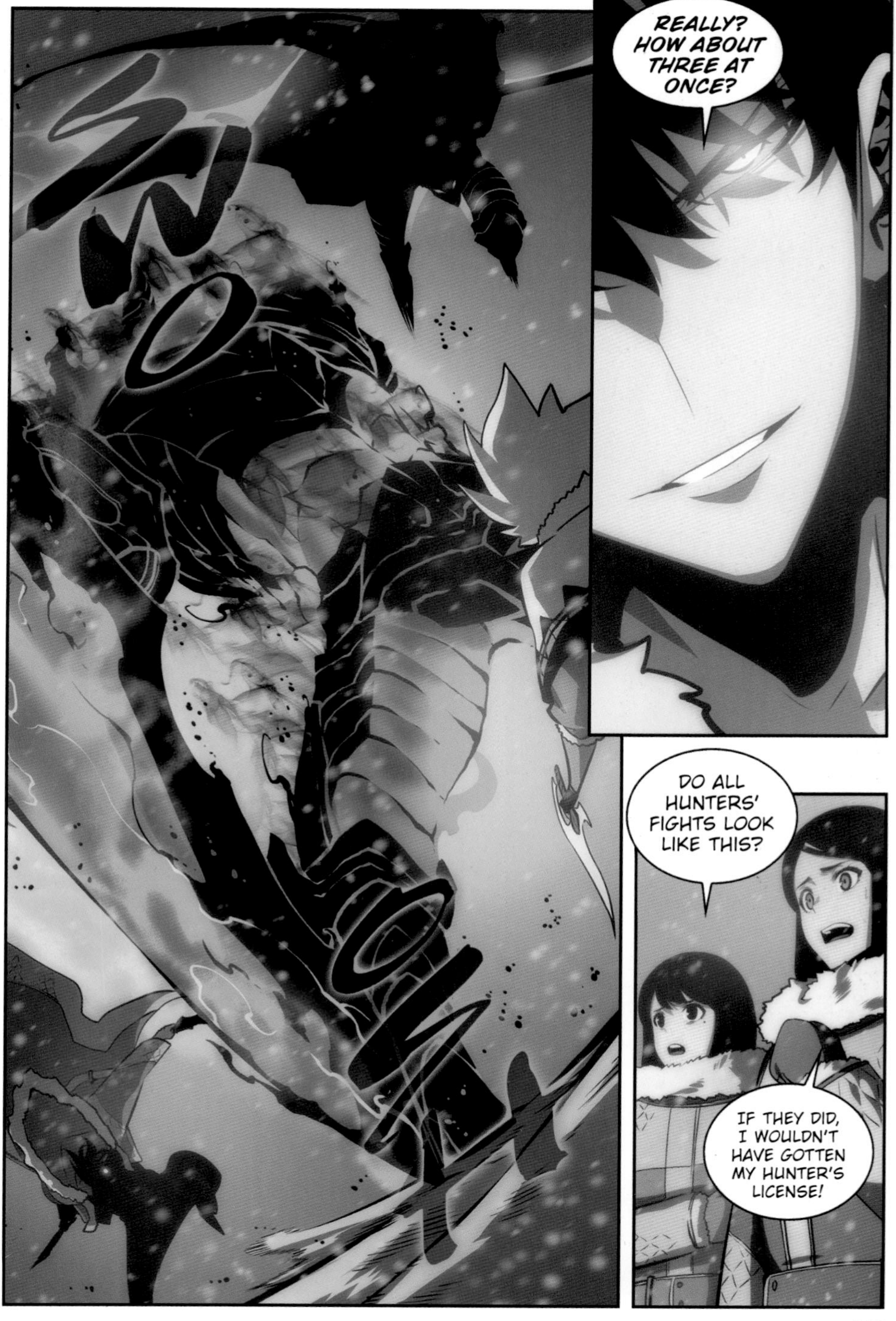
REALLY? HOW ABOUT THREE AT ONCE?
DO ALL HUNTERS' FIGHTS LOOK LIKE THIS?
IF THEY DID, I WOULDN'T HAVE GOTTEN MY HUNTER'S LICENSE!

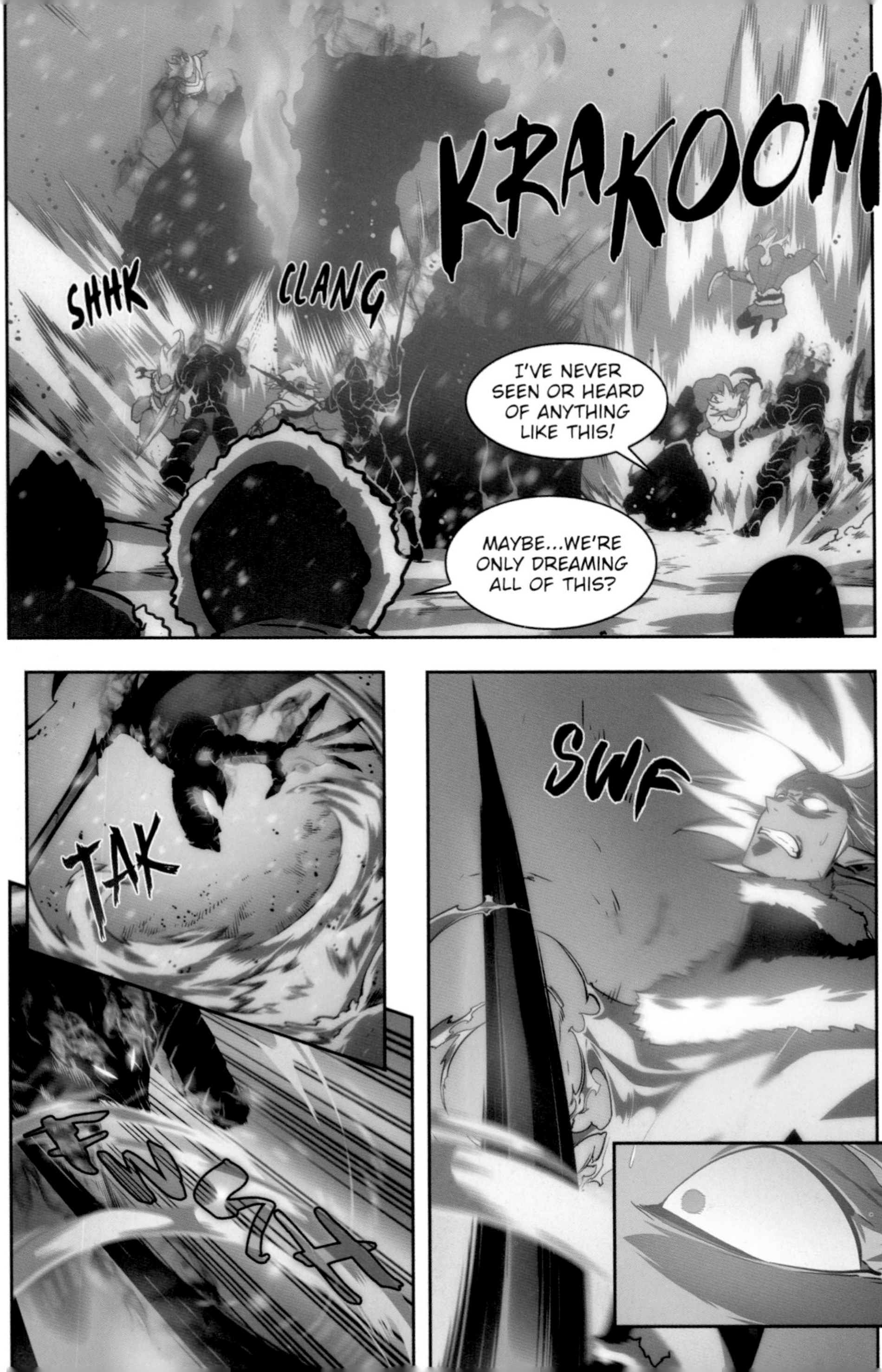
KRAKOOM
SHHK
CLANG
I'VE NEVER SEEN OR HEARD OF ANYTHING LIKE THIS!
MAYBE...WE'RE ONLY DREAMING ALL OF THIS?
TAK
SWF

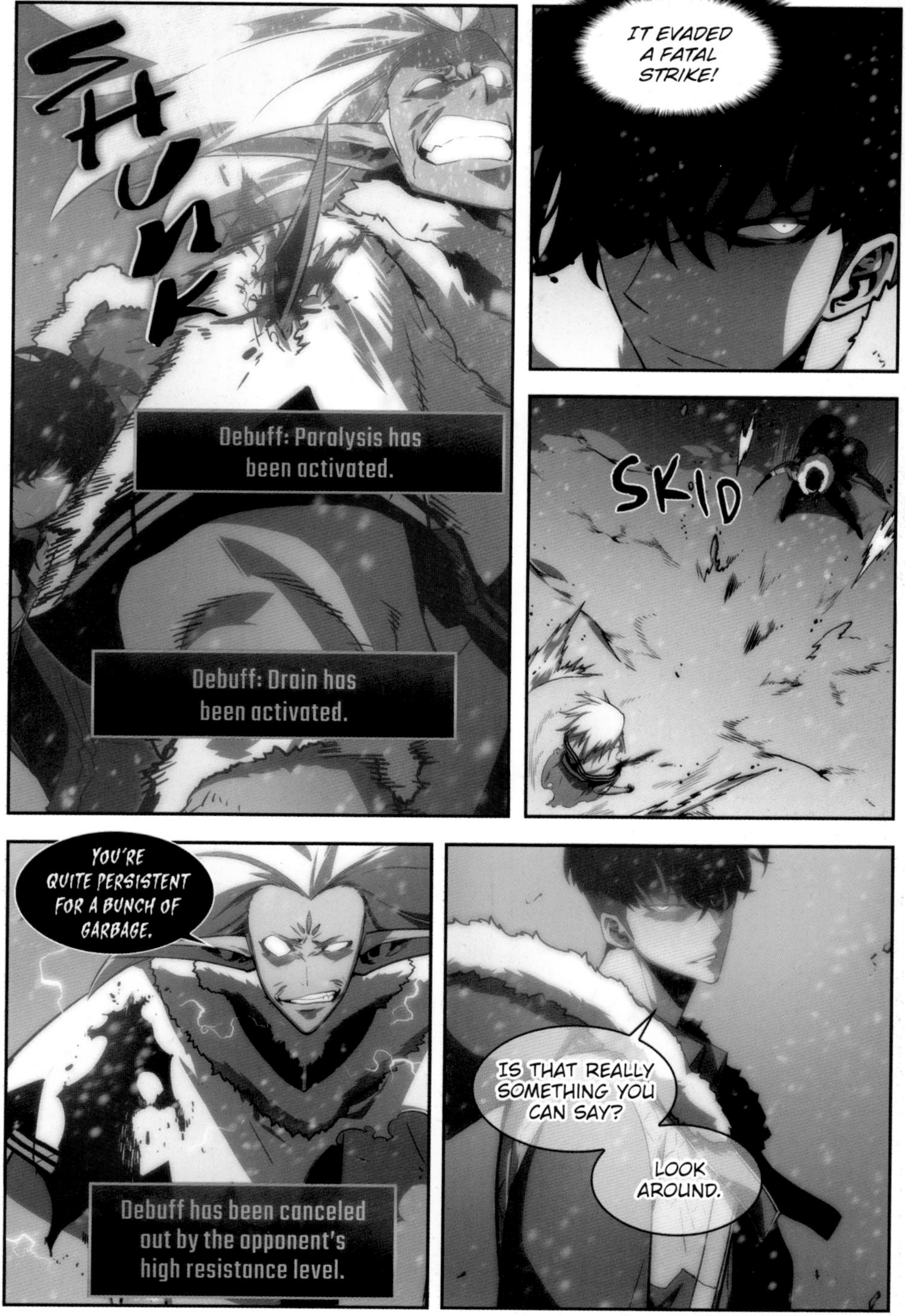
SHUNK
Debuff: Paralysis has been activated.
Debuff: Drain has been activated.
IT EVADED A FATAL STRIKE!
SKID
YOU'RE QUITE PERSISTENT FOR A BUNCH OF GARBAGE.
Debuff has been canceled out by the opponent's high resistance level.
IS THAT REALLY SOMETHING YOU CAN SAY?
LOOK AROUND.

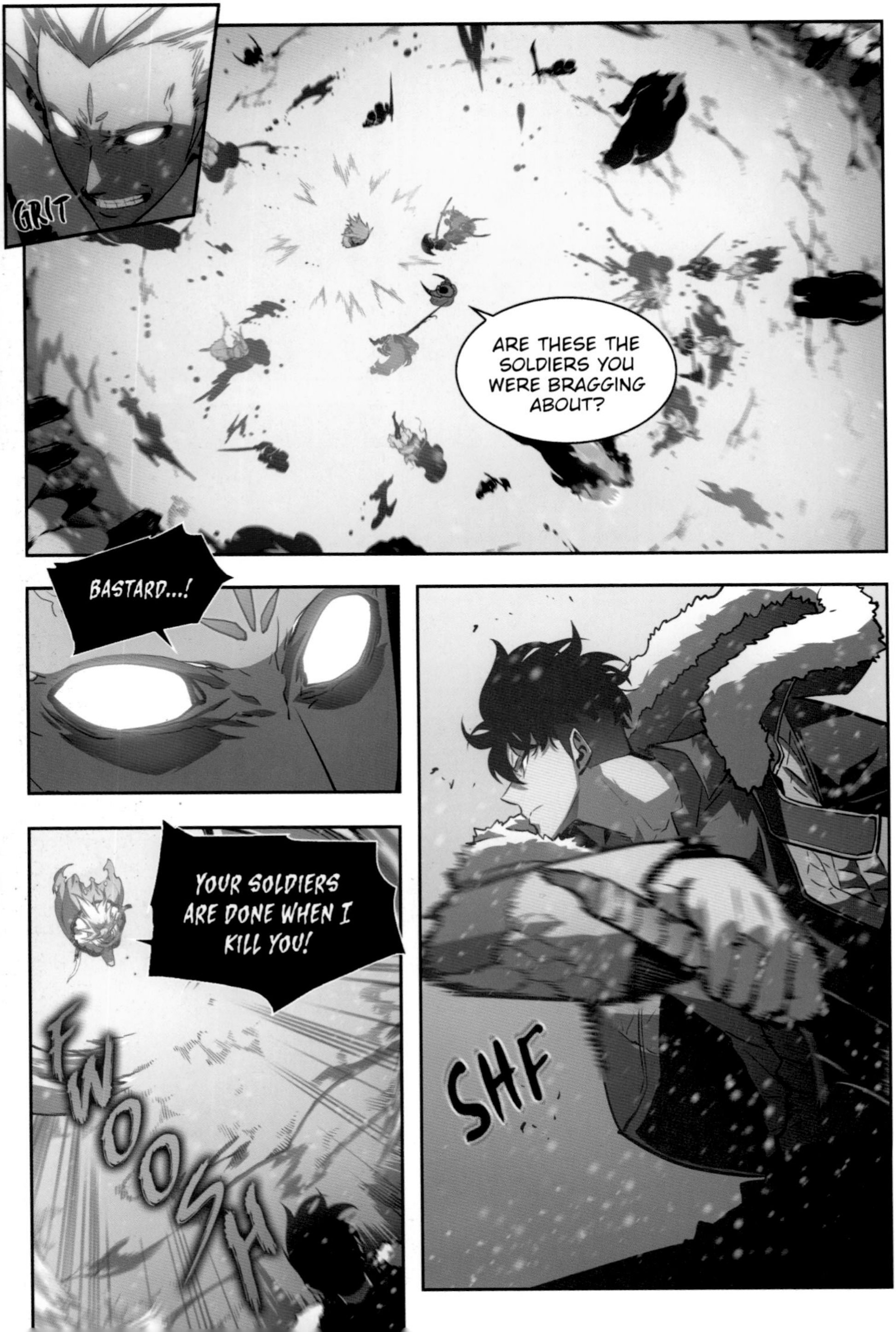
GRIT
ARE THESE THE SOLDIERS YOU WERE BRAGGING ABOUT?
BASTARD...!
YOUR SOLDIERS ARE DONE WHEN I KILL YOU!
FWOOSH
SHF

THROWING AWAY YOUR WEAPON? HOW FOO—

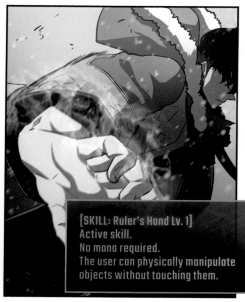

[SKILL: Ruler's Hand Lv. 1]
Active skill.
No mana required.
The user can physically manipulate objects without touching them.

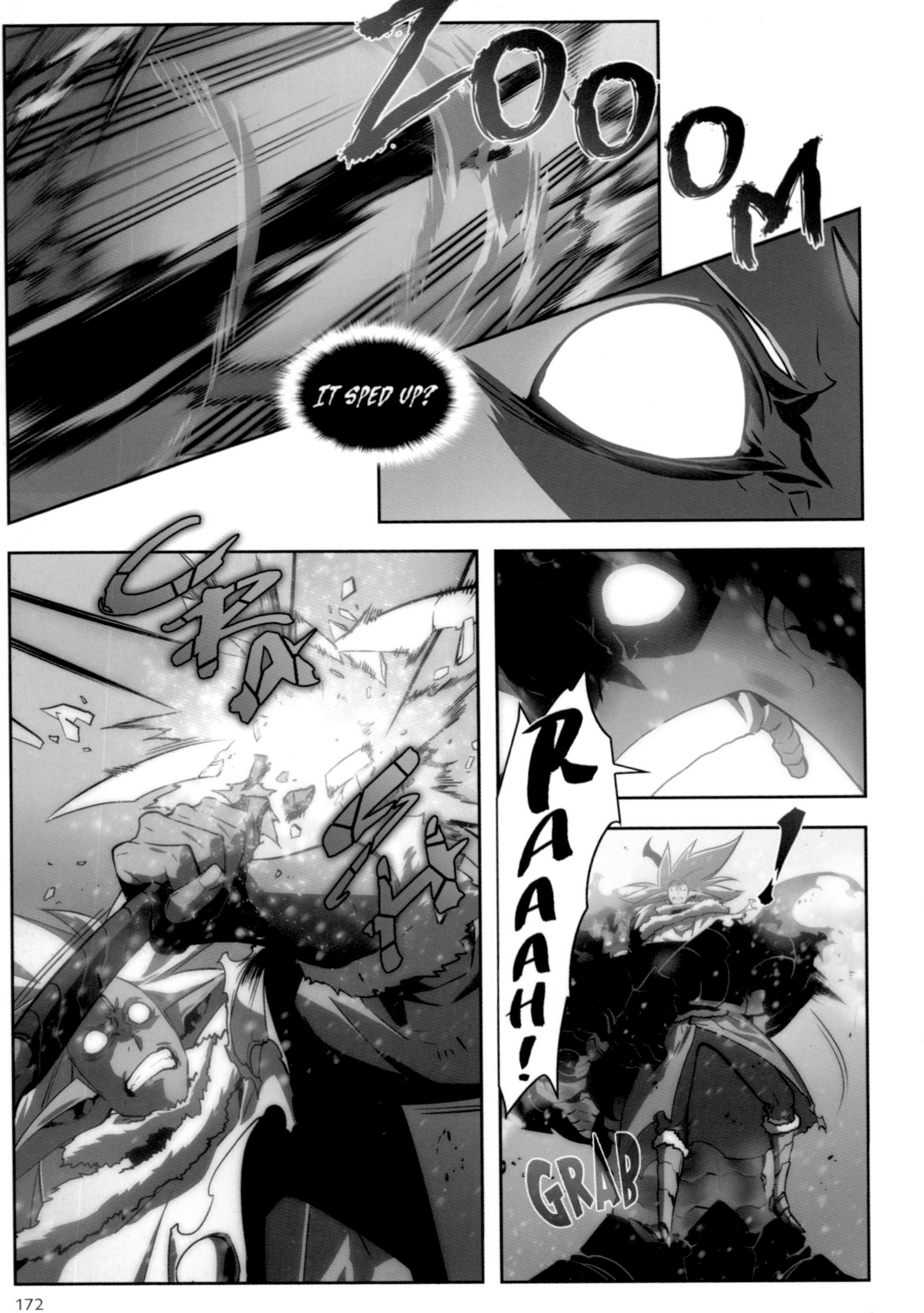
ZOOOM
IT SPED UP?
CRASH
RAAAH!!
!
GRAB

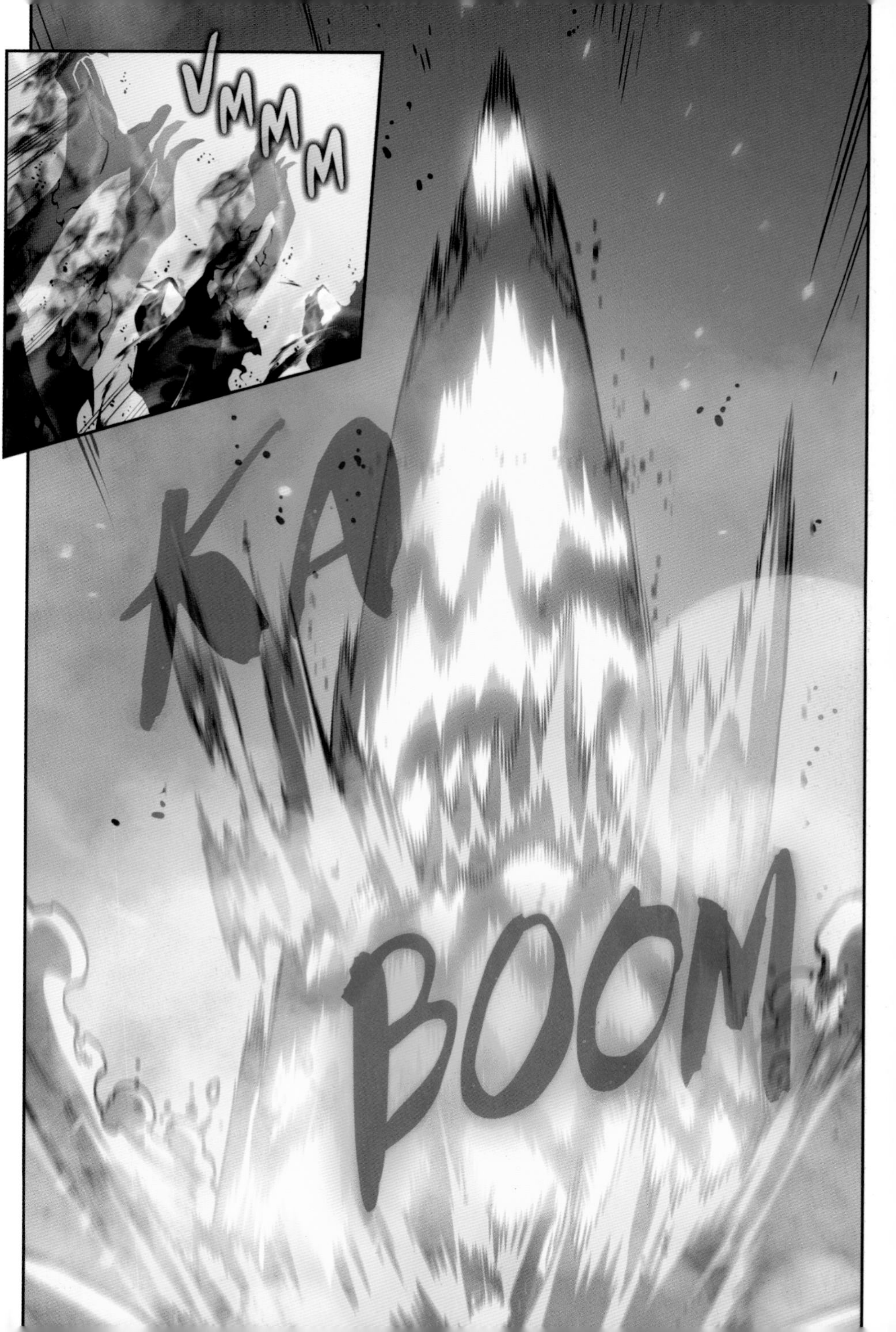
VMMM
KA
BOOM

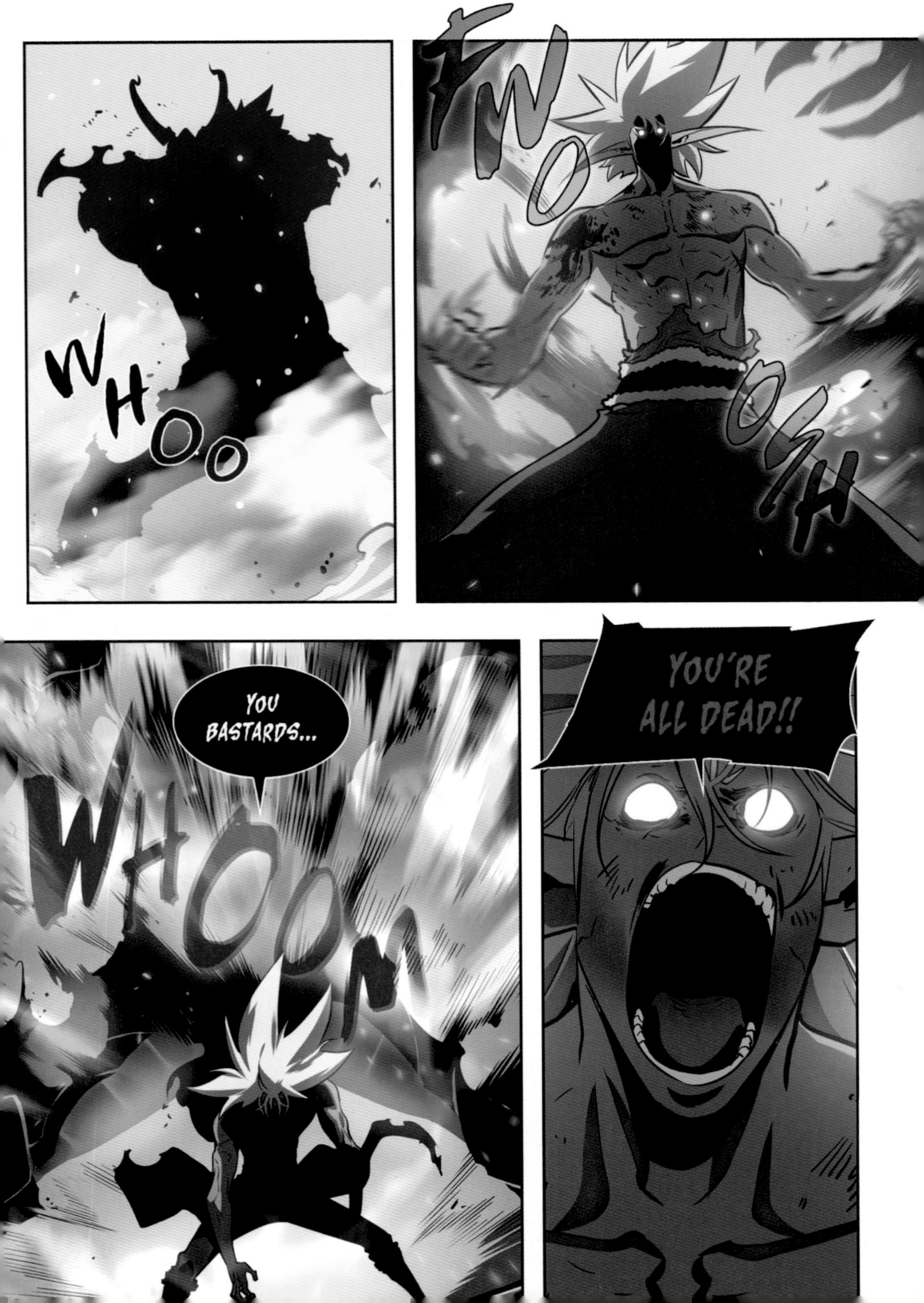
WHOOO
FWOOSH
YOU BASTARDS...
WHOOM
YOU'RE ALL DEAD!!

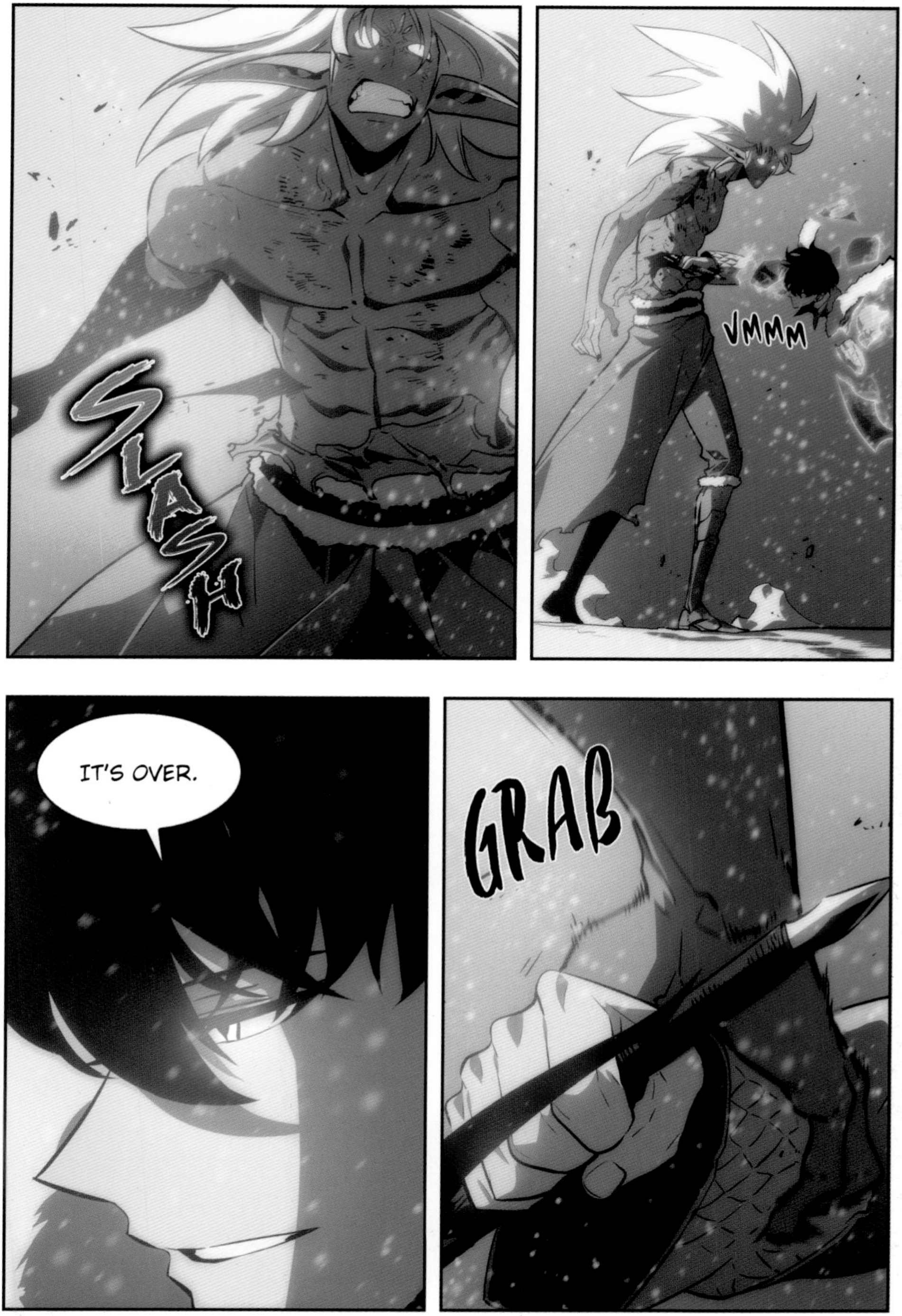
SLASH
VMMM
IT'S OVER.
GRAB

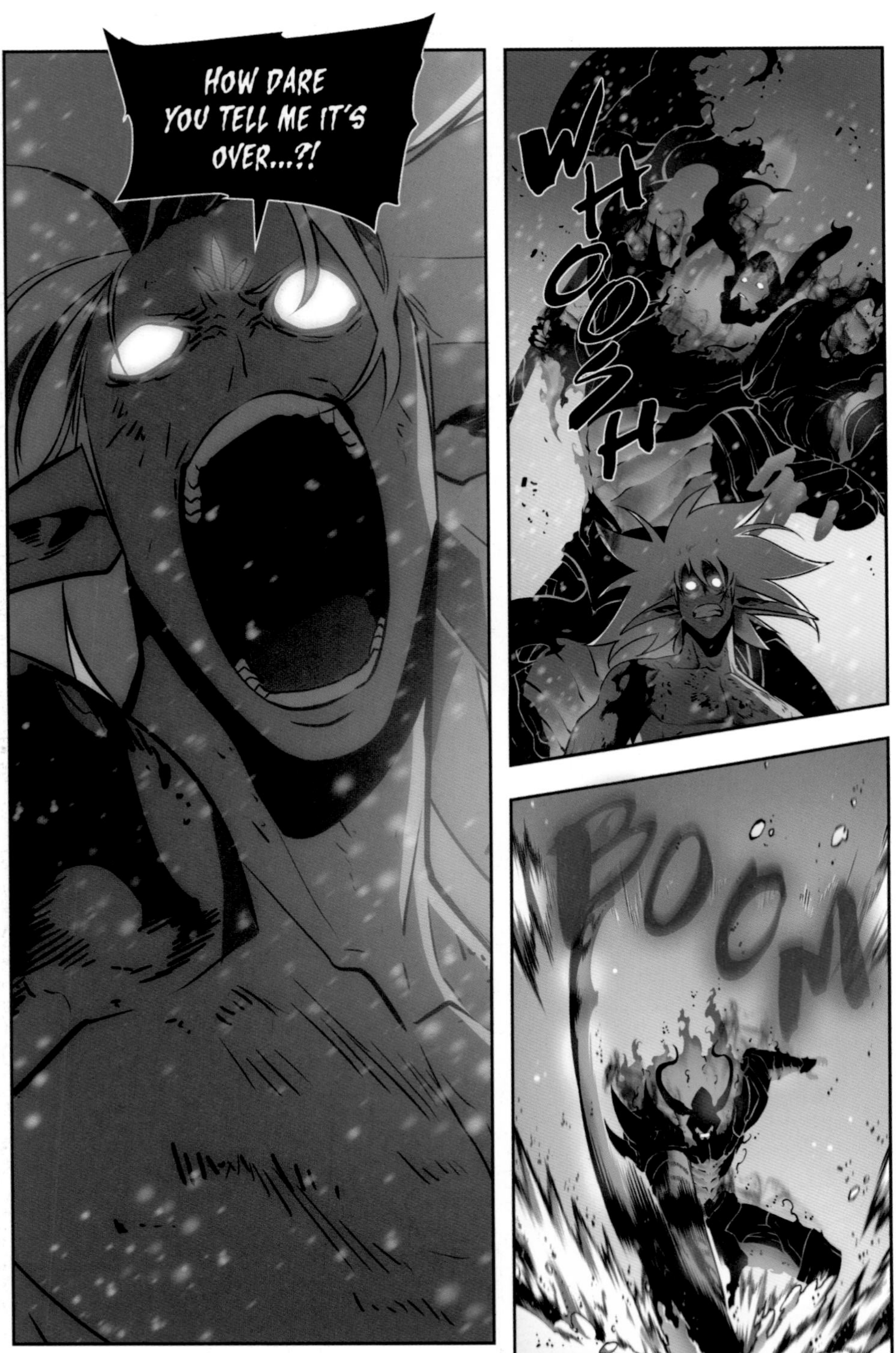
HOW DARE YOU TELL ME IT'S OVER...?!
WHOOSH
BOOM

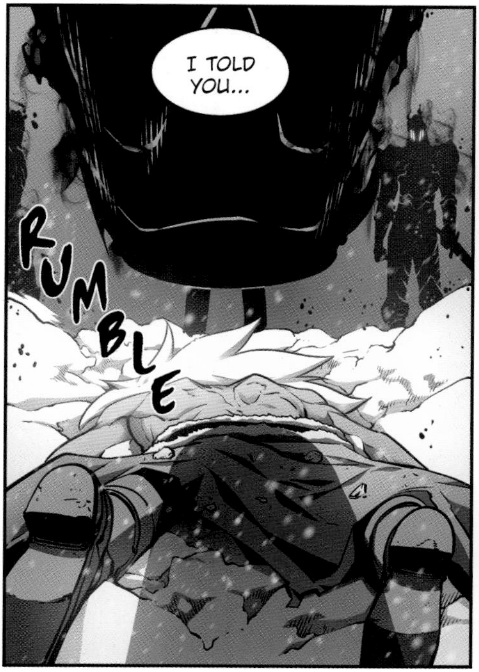
I TOLD YOU...
RUMBLE
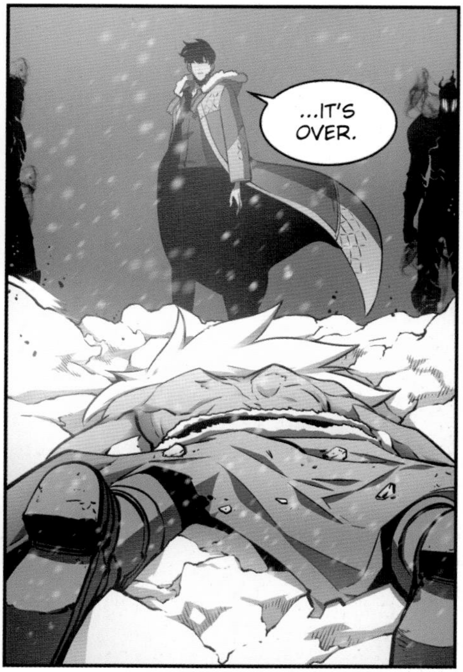
...IT'S OVER.
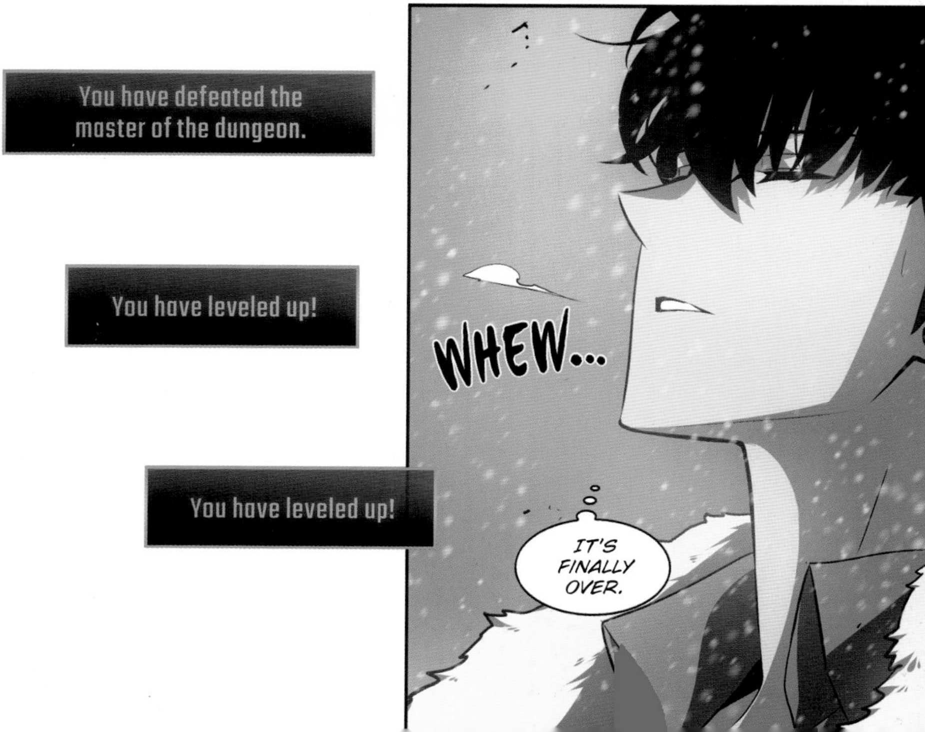
You have defeated the master of the dungeon.
You have leveled up!
You have leveled up!
WHEW...
IT'S FINALLY OVER.

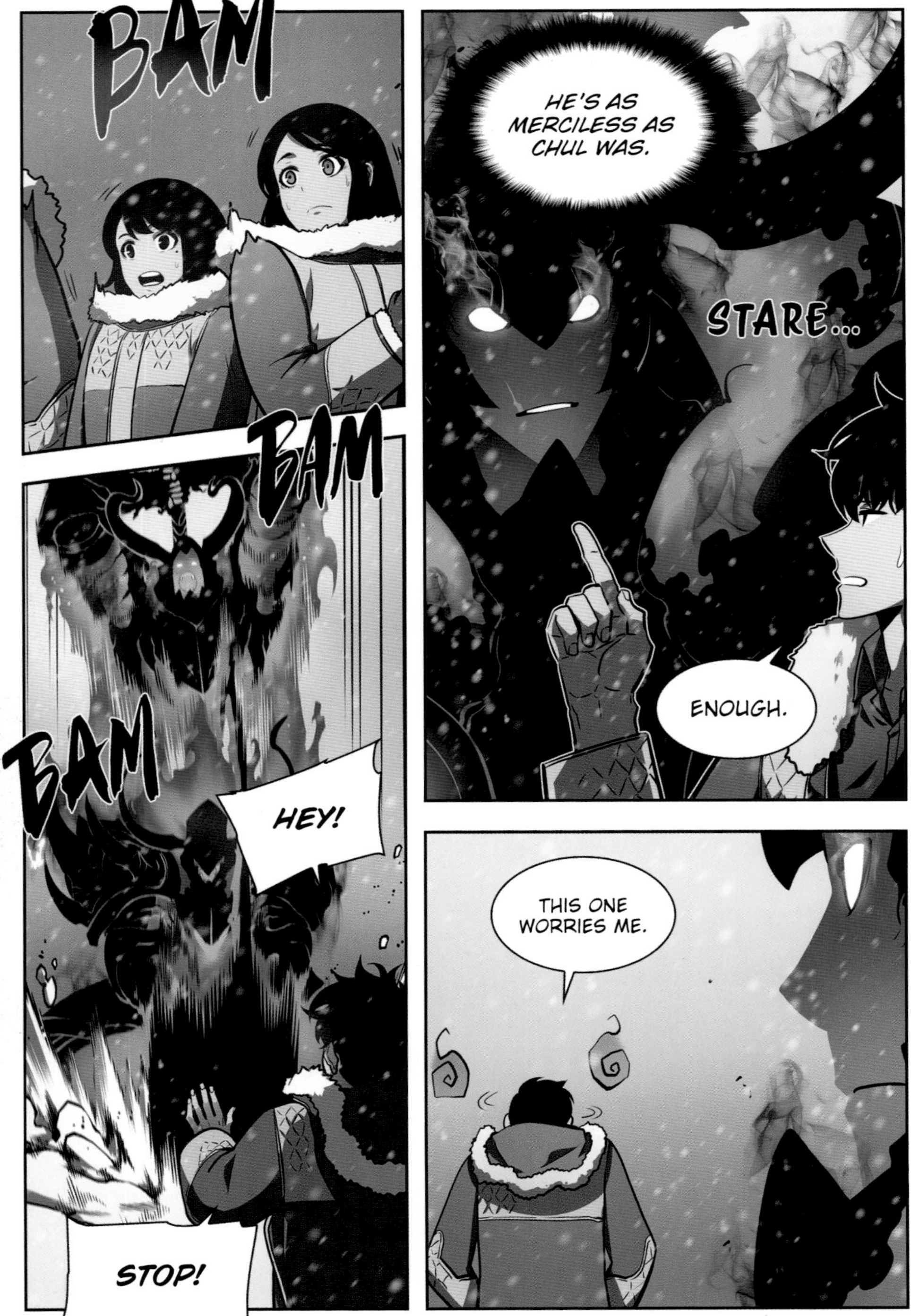
BAM
BAM
BAM
HEY!
STOP!
HE'S AS MERCILESS AS CHUL WAS.
STARE...
ENOUGH.
THIS ONE WORRIES ME.

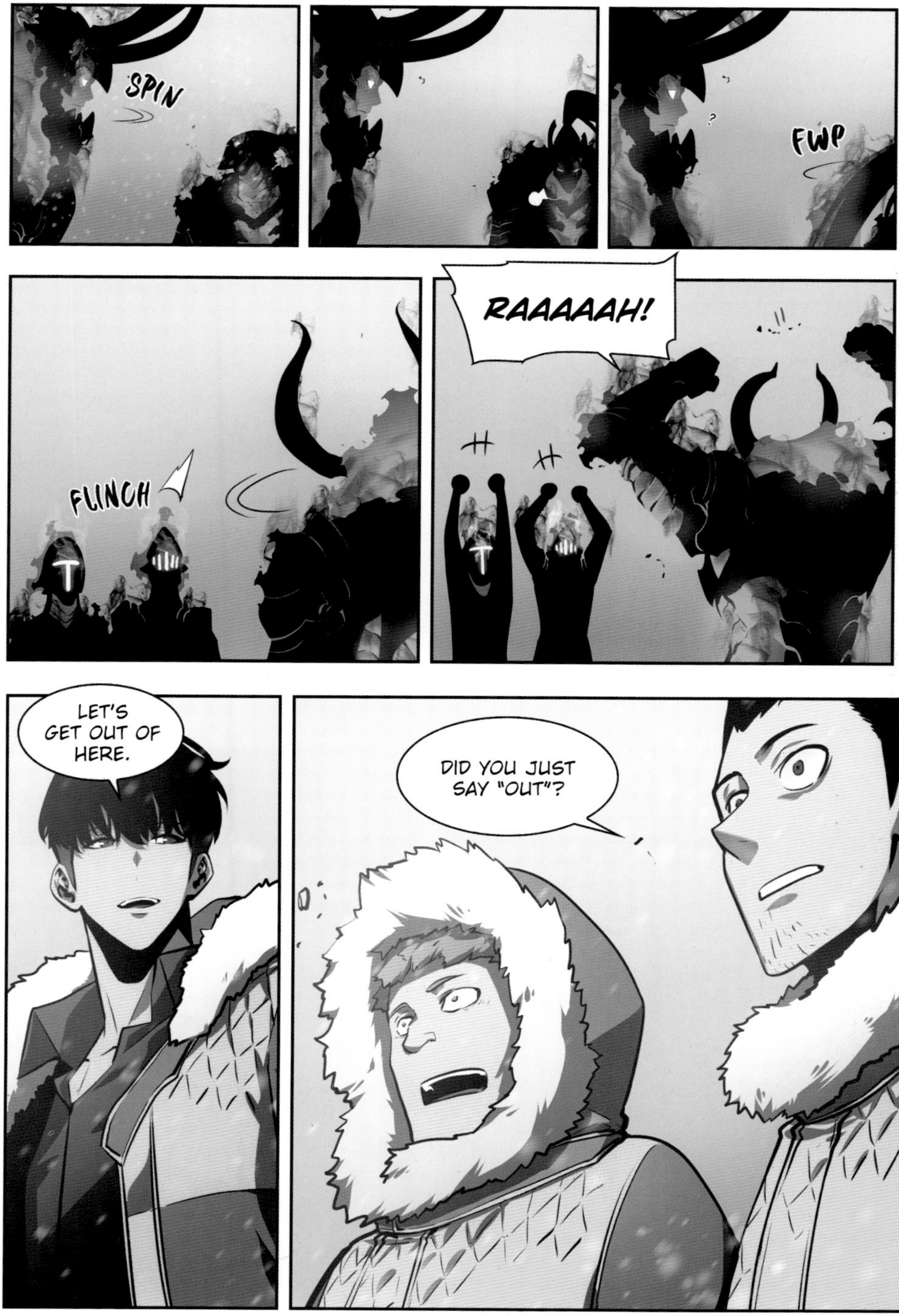

SPIN
FWP
FLINCH
RAAAAAH!
LET'S GET OUT OF HERE.
DID YOU JUST SAY "OUT"?

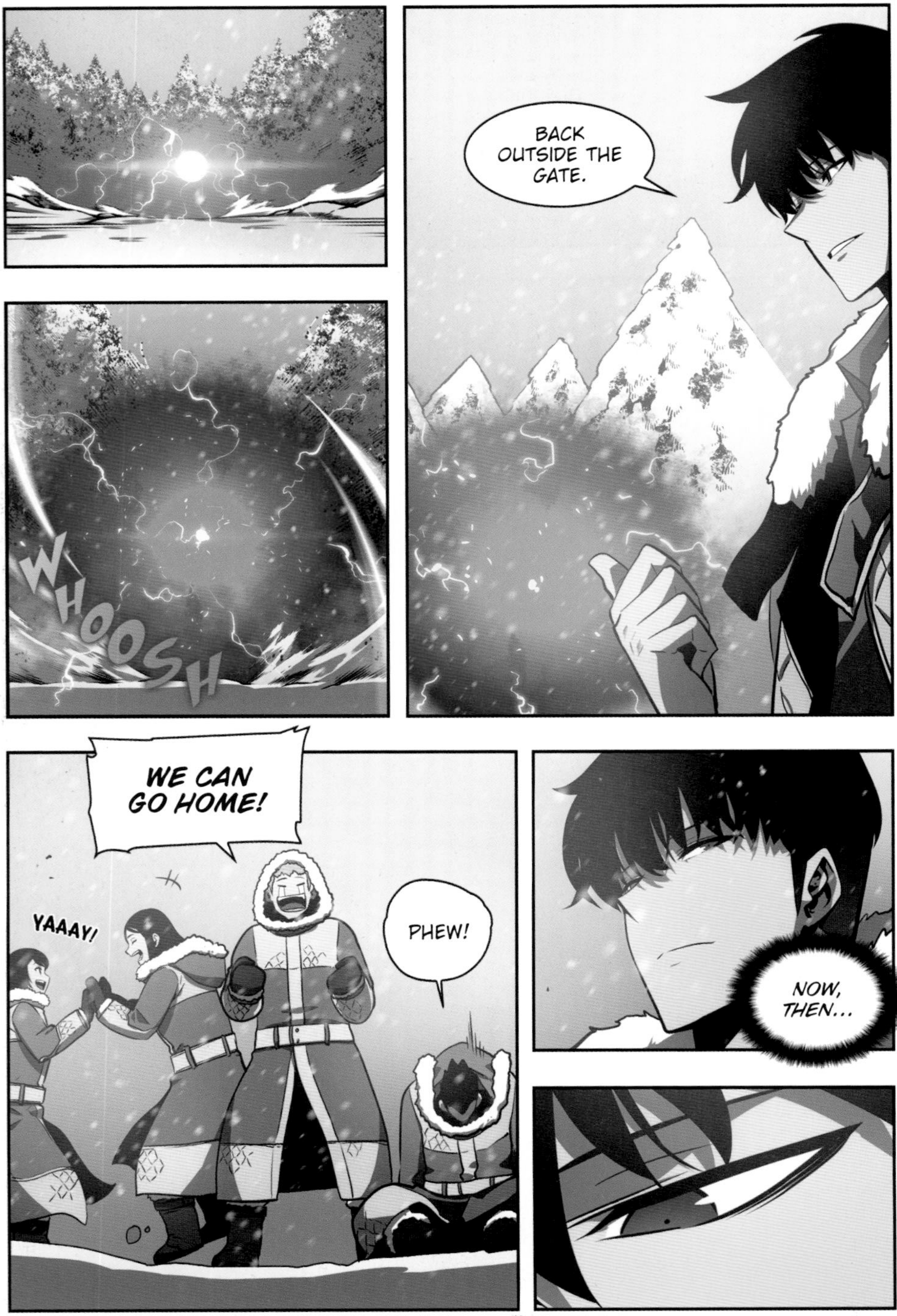
WHOOSH
BACK OUTSIDE THE GATE.
WE CAN GO HOME!
YAAAY!
PHEW!
NOW, THEN...

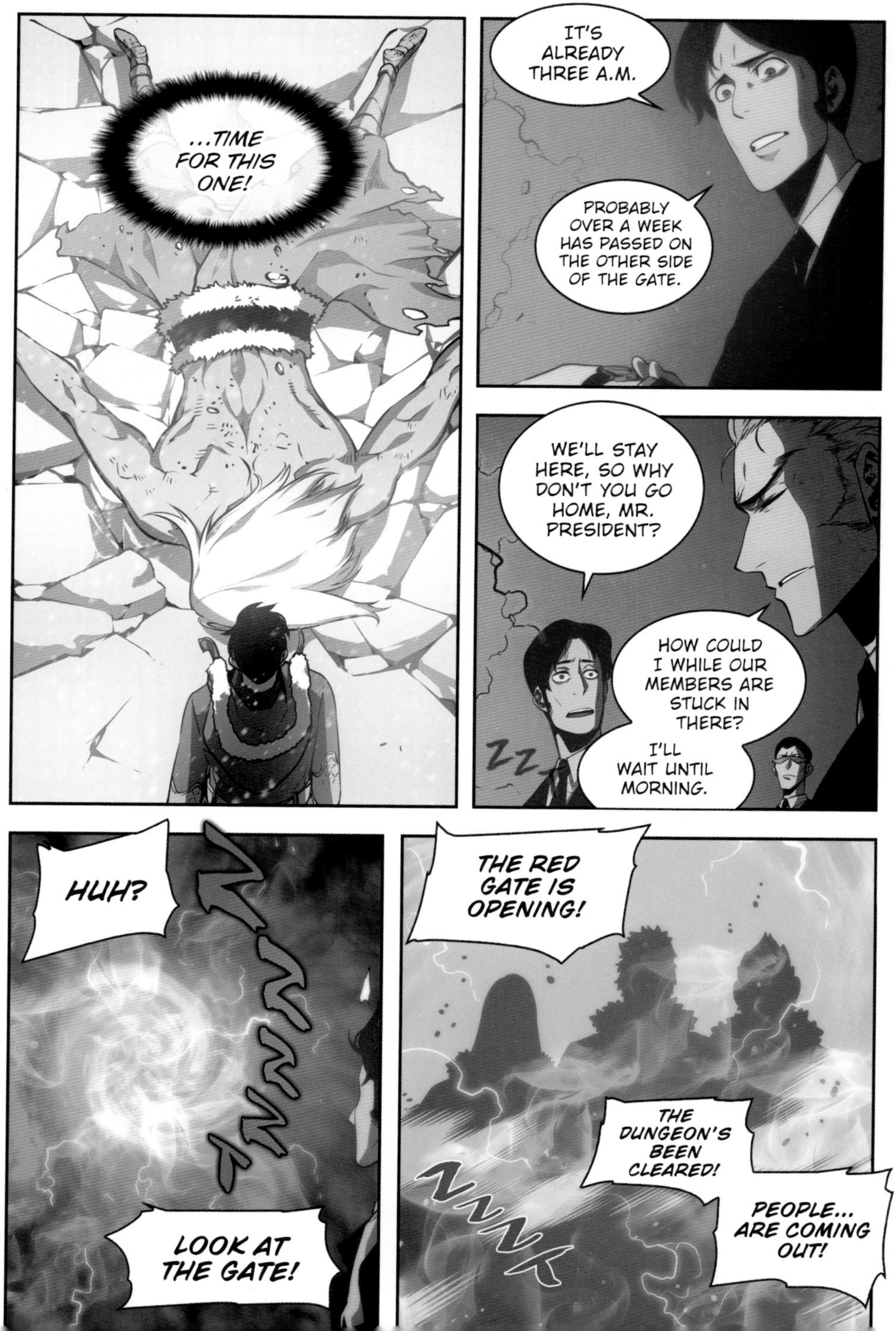
...TIME FOR THIS ONE!
IT'S ALREADY THREE A.M.
PROBABLY OVER A WEEK HAS PASSED ON THE OTHER SIDE OF THE GATE.
WE'LL STAY HERE, SO WHY DON'T YOU GO HOME, MR. PRESIDENT?
ZZ
HOW COULD I WHILE OUR MEMBERS ARE STUCK IN THERE?
I'LL WAIT UNTIL MORNING.
HUH?
NNNNK
LOOK AT THE GATE!
THE RED GATE IS OPENING!
THE DUNGEON'S BEEN CLEARED!
NNNK
PEOPLE... ARE COMING OUT!

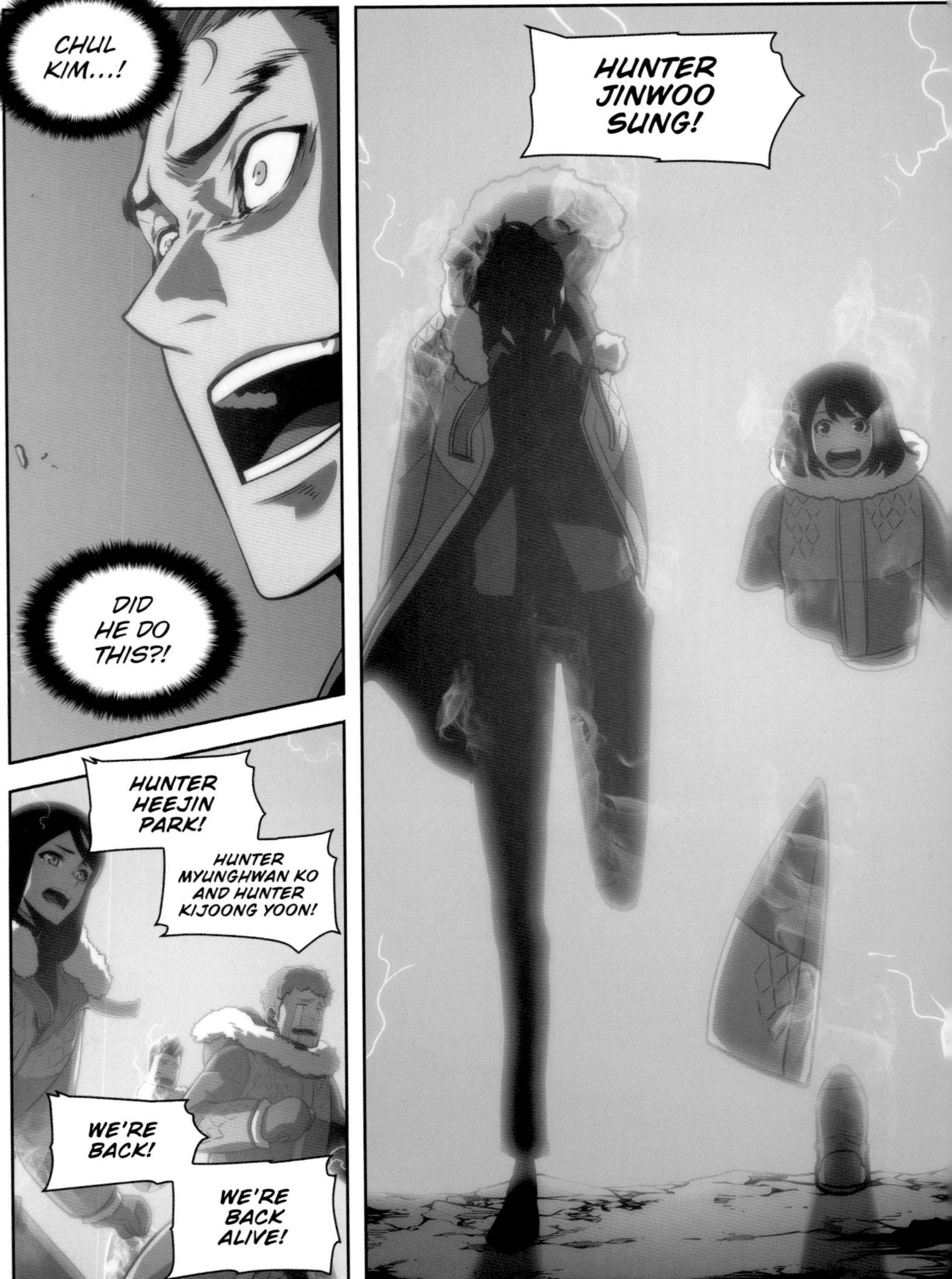
CHUL KIM...!
DID HE DO THIS?!
HUNTER HEEJIN PARK!
HUNTER MYUNGHWAN KO AND HUNTER KIJOONG YOON!
WE'RE BACK!
WE'RE BACK ALIVE!
HUNTER JINWOO SUNG!

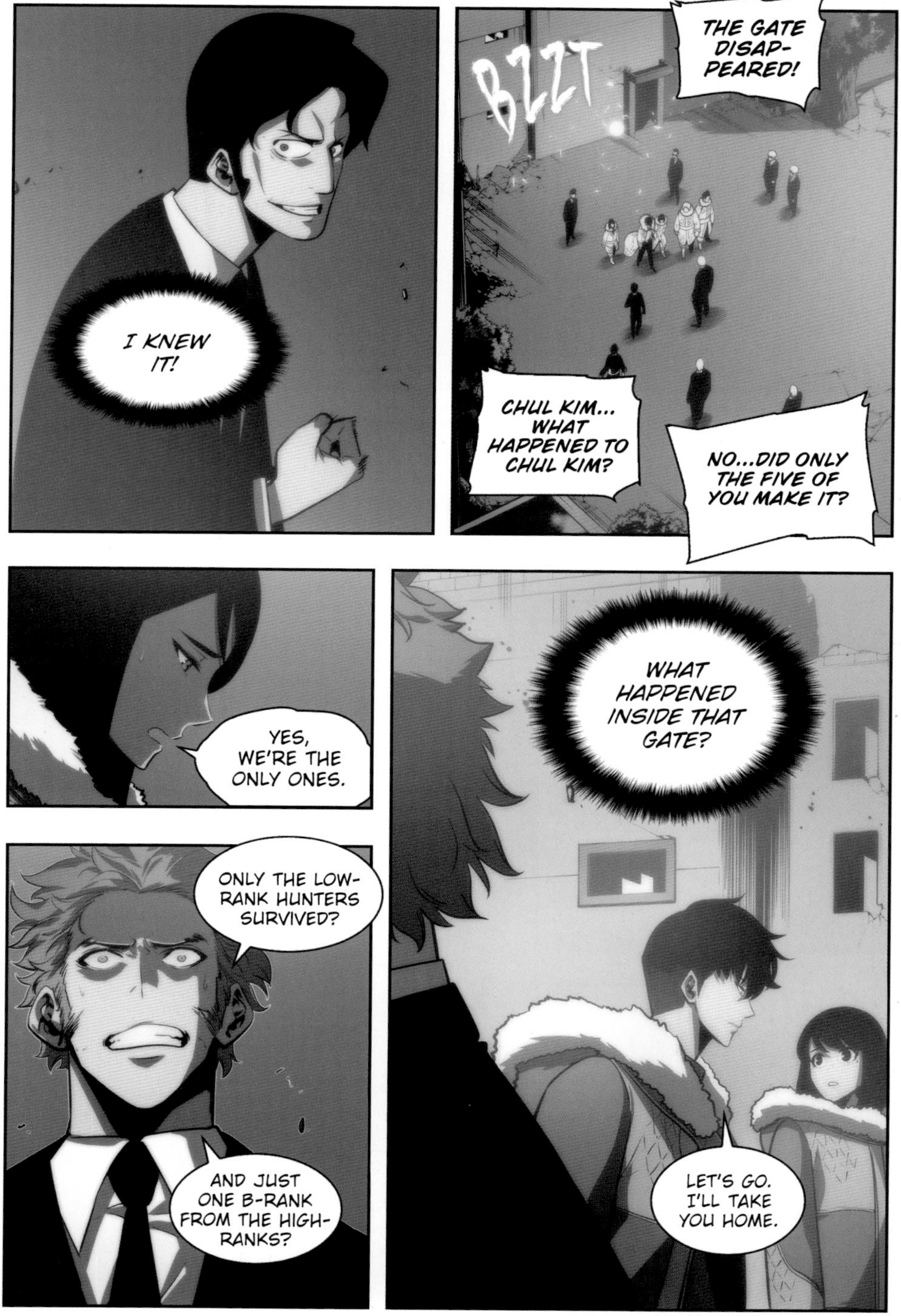
I KNEW IT!
BZZT
THE GATE DISAPPEARED!
CHUL KIM... WHAT HAPPENED TO CHUL KIM?
NO...DID ONLY THE FIVE OF YOU MAKE IT?
YES, WE'RE THE ONLY ONES.
ONLY THE LOW-RANK HUNTERS SURVIVED?
AND JUST ONE B-RANK FROM THE HIGH-RANKS?
WHAT HAPPENED INSIDE THAT GATE?
LET'S GO. I'LL TAKE YOU HOME.

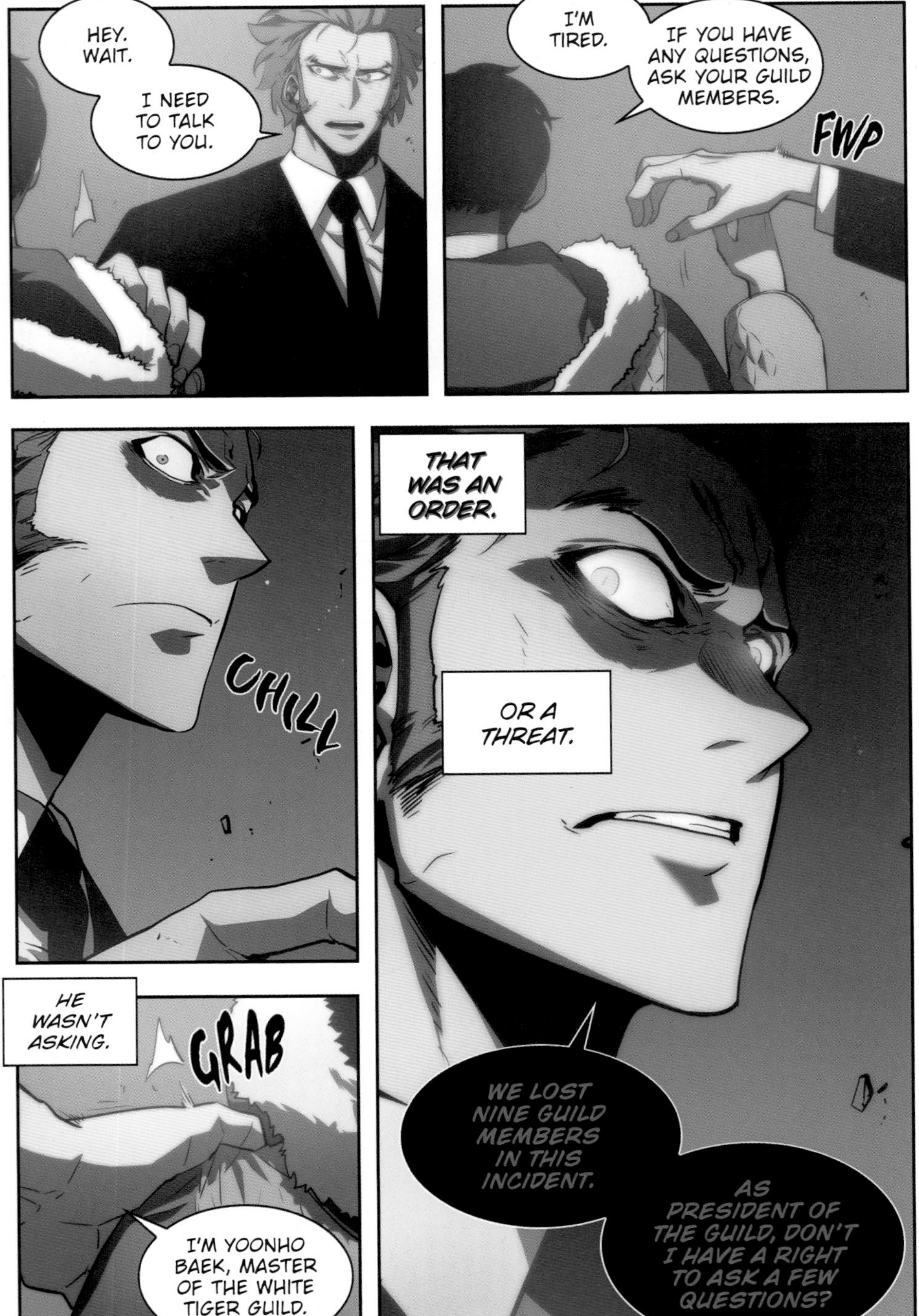
HEY. WAIT.
I NEED TO TALK TO YOU.
I'M TIRED.
IF YOU HAVE ANY QUESTIONS, ASK YOUR GUILD MEMBERS.
FWP
CHILL
THAT WAS AN ORDER.
OR A THREAT.
HE WASN'T ASKING.
GRAB
I'M YOONHO BAEK, MASTER OF THE WHITE TIGER GUILD.
WE LOST NINE GUILD MEMBERS IN THIS INCIDENT.
AS PRESIDENT OF THE GUILD, DON'T I HAVE A RIGHT TO ASK A FEW QUESTIONS?

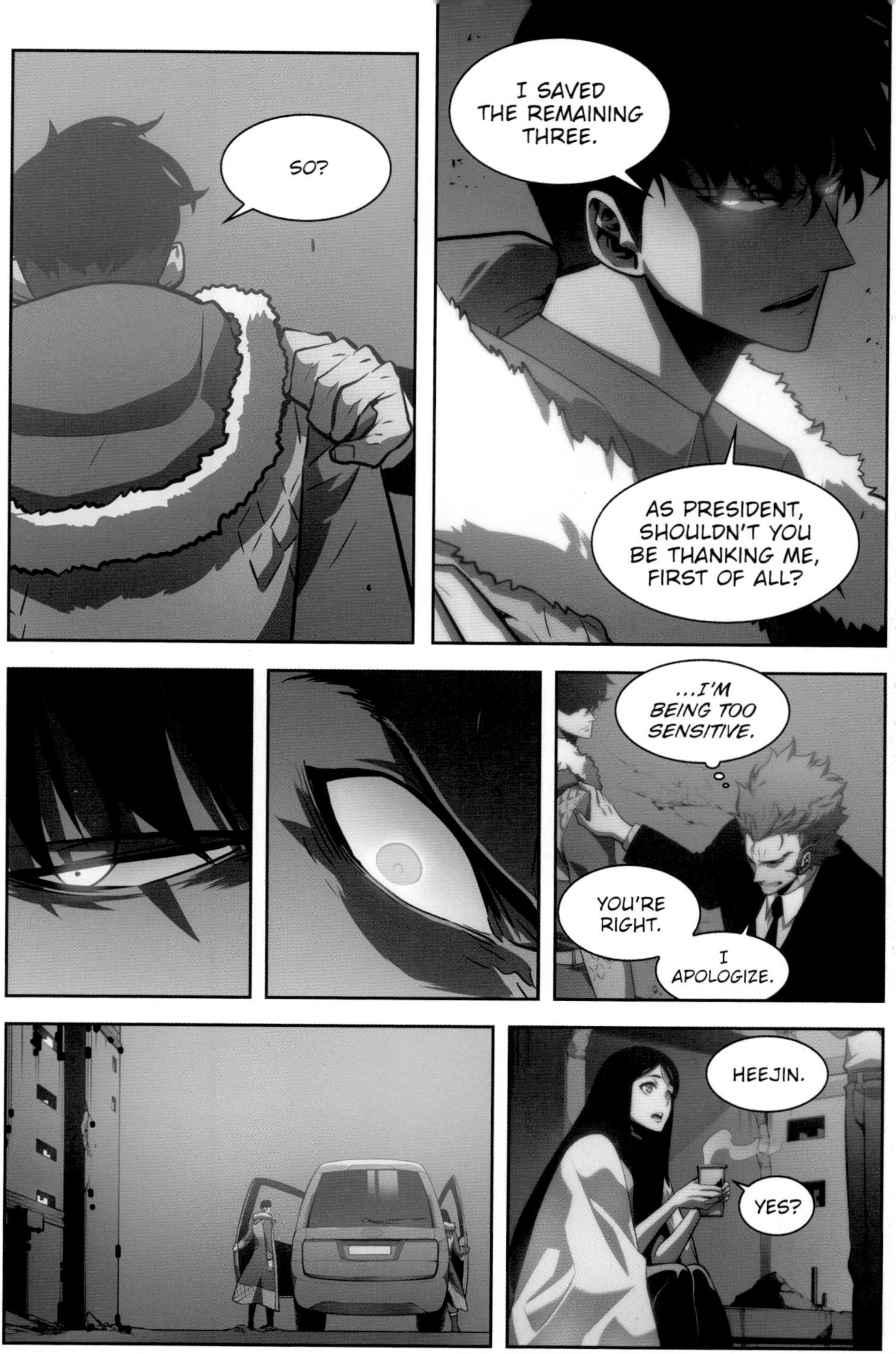
SO?
I SAVED THE REMAINING THREE.
AS PRESIDENT, SHOULDN'T YOU BE THANKING ME, FIRST OF ALL?
...I'M BEING TOO SENSITIVE.
YOU'RE RIGHT.
I APOLOGIZE.
HEEJIN.
YES?

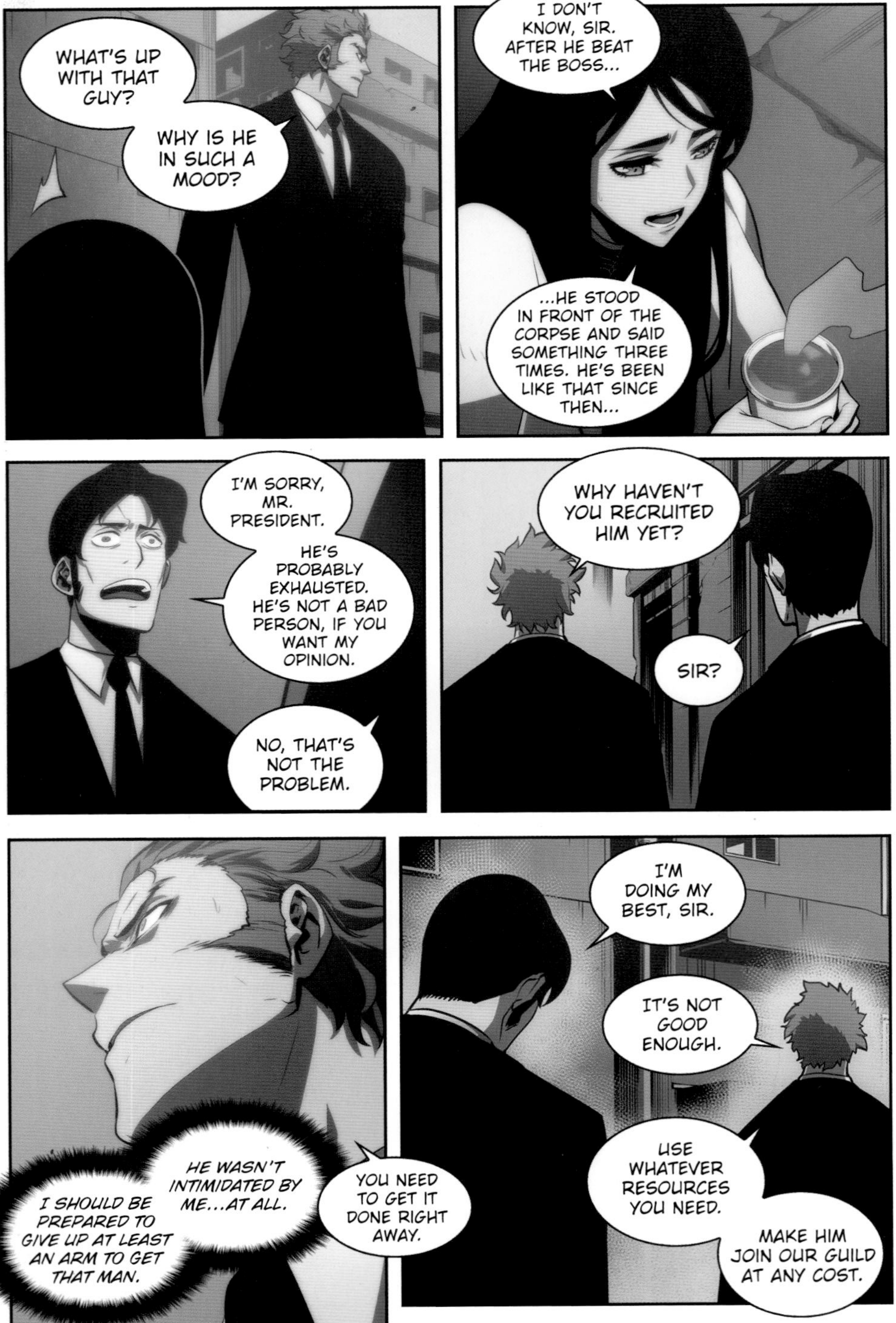
WHAT'S UP WITH THAT GUY?
WHY IS HE IN SUCH A MOOD?
I DON'T KNOW, SIR. AFTER HE BEAT THE BOSS...
...HE STOOD IN FRONT OF THE CORPSE AND SAID SOMETHING THREE TIMES. HE'S BEEN LIKE THAT SINCE THEN...
I'M SORRY, MR. PRESIDENT.
HE'S PROBABLY EXHAUSTED. HE'S NOT A BAD PERSON, IF YOU WANT MY OPINION.
NO, THAT'S NOT THE PROBLEM.
WHY HAVEN'T YOU RECRUITED HIM YET?
SIR?
HE WASN'T INTIMIDATED BY ME...AT ALL.
I SHOULD BE PREPARED TO GIVE UP AT LEAST AN ARM TO GET THAT MAN.
YOU NEED TO GET IT DONE RIGHT AWAY.
I'M DOING MY BEST, SIR.
IT'S NOT GOOD ENOUGH.
USE WHATEVER RESOURCES YOU NEED.
MAKE HIM JOIN OUR GUILD AT ANY COST.

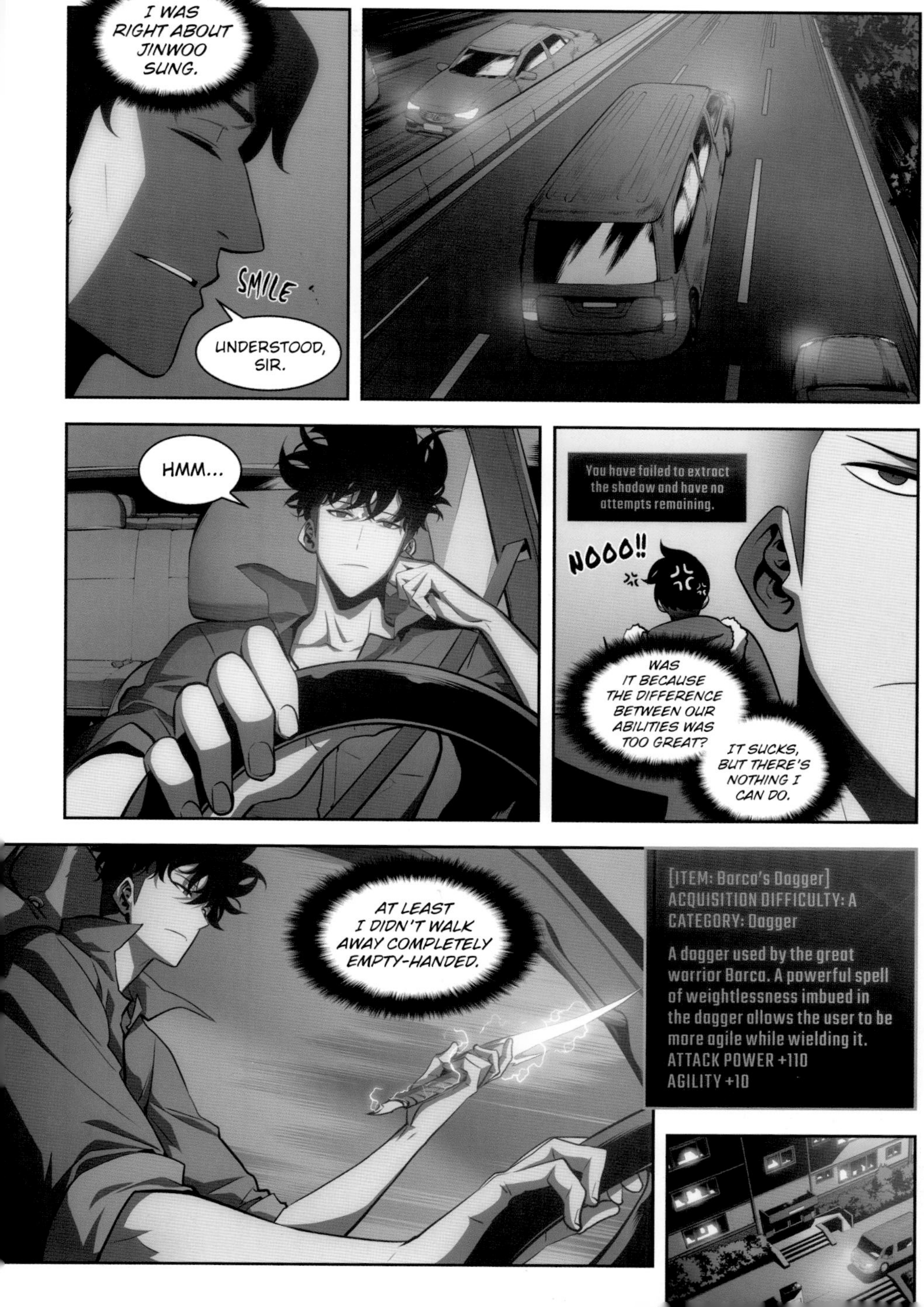
I WAS RIGHT ABOUT JINWOO SUNG.
SMILE
UNDERSTOOD, SIR.
HMM...
You have failed to extract the shadow and have no attempts remaining.
NOOO!!
WAS IT BECAUSE THE DIFFERENCE BETWEEN OUR ABILITIES WAS TOO GREAT?
IT SUCKS, BUT THERE'S NOTHING I CAN DO.
AT LEAST I DIDN'T WALK AWAY COMPLETELY EMPTY-HANDED.
[ITEM: Barca's Dagger]
ACQUISITION DIFFICULTY: A
CATEGORY: Dagger
A dagger used by the great warrior Barca. A powerful spell of weightlessness imbued in the dagger allows the user to be more agile while wielding it.
ATTACK POWER +110
AGILITY +10

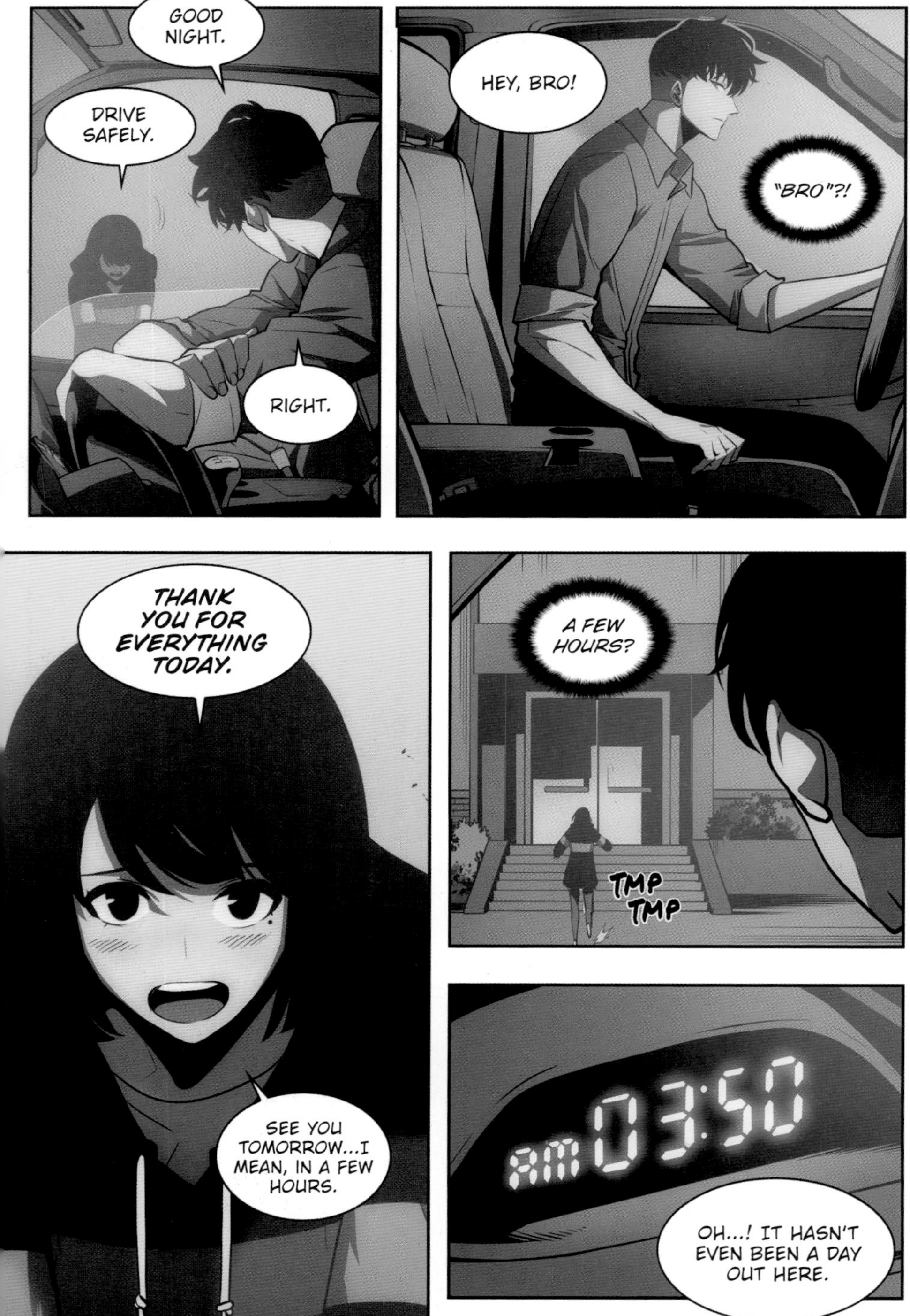
GOOD NIGHT.
DRIVE SAFELY.
RIGHT.
HEY, BRO!
"BRO"?!
THANK YOU FOR EVERYTHING TODAY.
SEE YOU TOMORROW...I MEAN, IN A FEW HOURS.
A FEW HOURS?
TMP TMP
AM 03:50
OH...! IT HASN'T EVEN BEEN A DAY OUT HERE.

SO IT'S BACK TO RAIDS WITH JINHO STARTING TODAY?

TURN

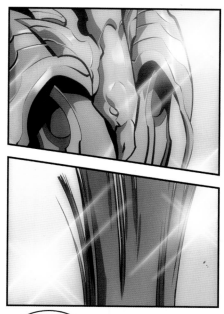

IT'S OKAY, BOSS. YOU DO ENOUGH FOR ME. I CAN WALK IF I HAVE TO!

LET'S GO!

DID YOU TAKE A CAB WITH THAT ON?

THIS IS SO LIKE YOU...

I WAS GONNA PICK YOU UP TODAY.

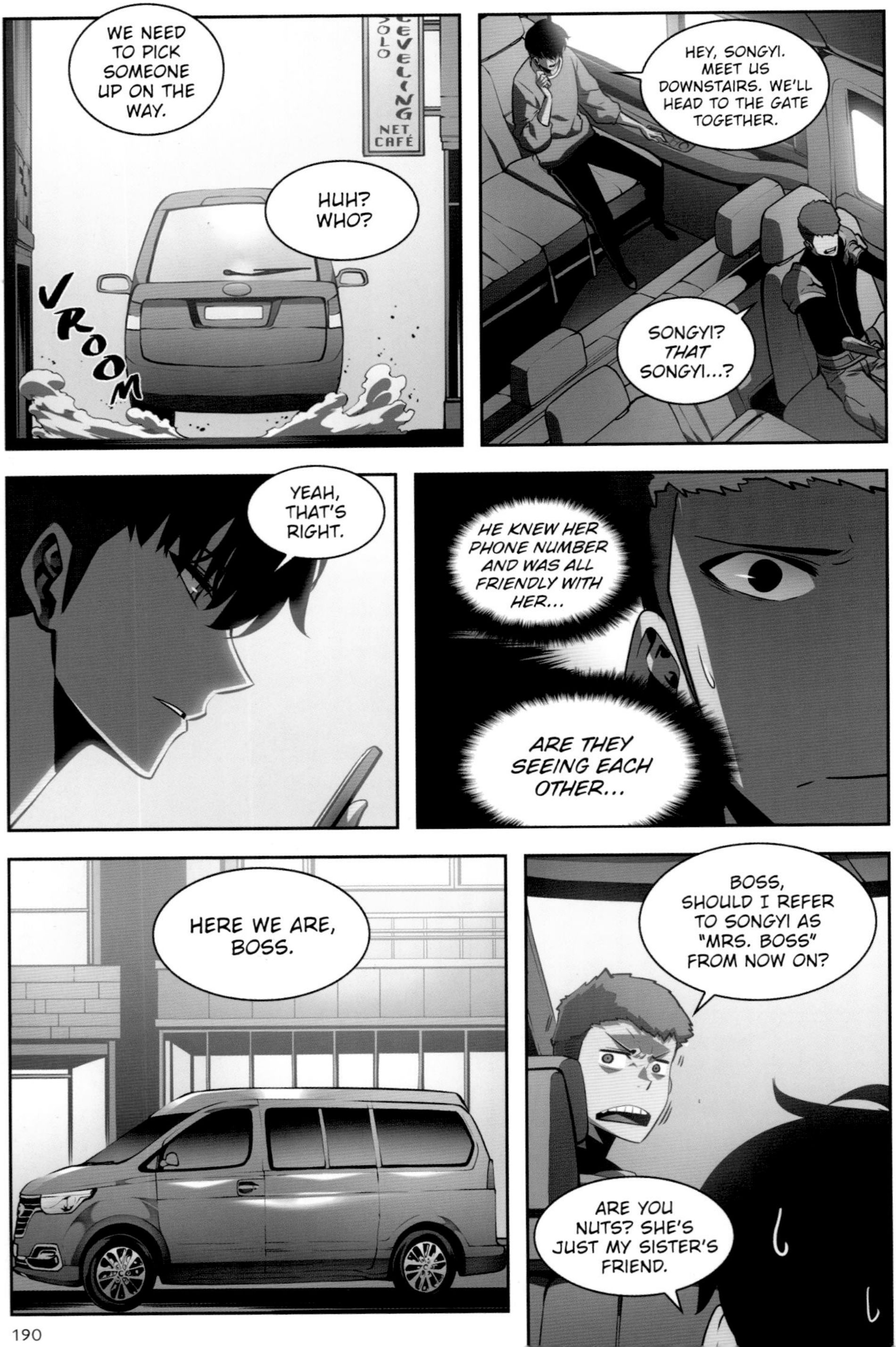
WE NEED TO PICK SOMEONE UP ON THE WAY.
SOLO LEVELING NET. CAFÉ
HUH? WHO?
VROOM
HEY, SONGYI. MEET US DOWNSTAIRS. WE'LL HEAD TO THE GATE TOGETHER.
SONGYI? THAT SONGYI...?
YEAH, THAT'S RIGHT.
HE KNEW HER PHONE NUMBER AND WAS ALL FRIENDLY WITH HER...
ARE THEY SEEING EACH OTHER...
HERE WE ARE, BOSS.
BOSS, SHOULD I REFER TO SONGYI AS "MRS. BOSS" FROM NOW ON?
ARE YOU NUTS? SHE'S JUST MY SISTER'S FRIEND.

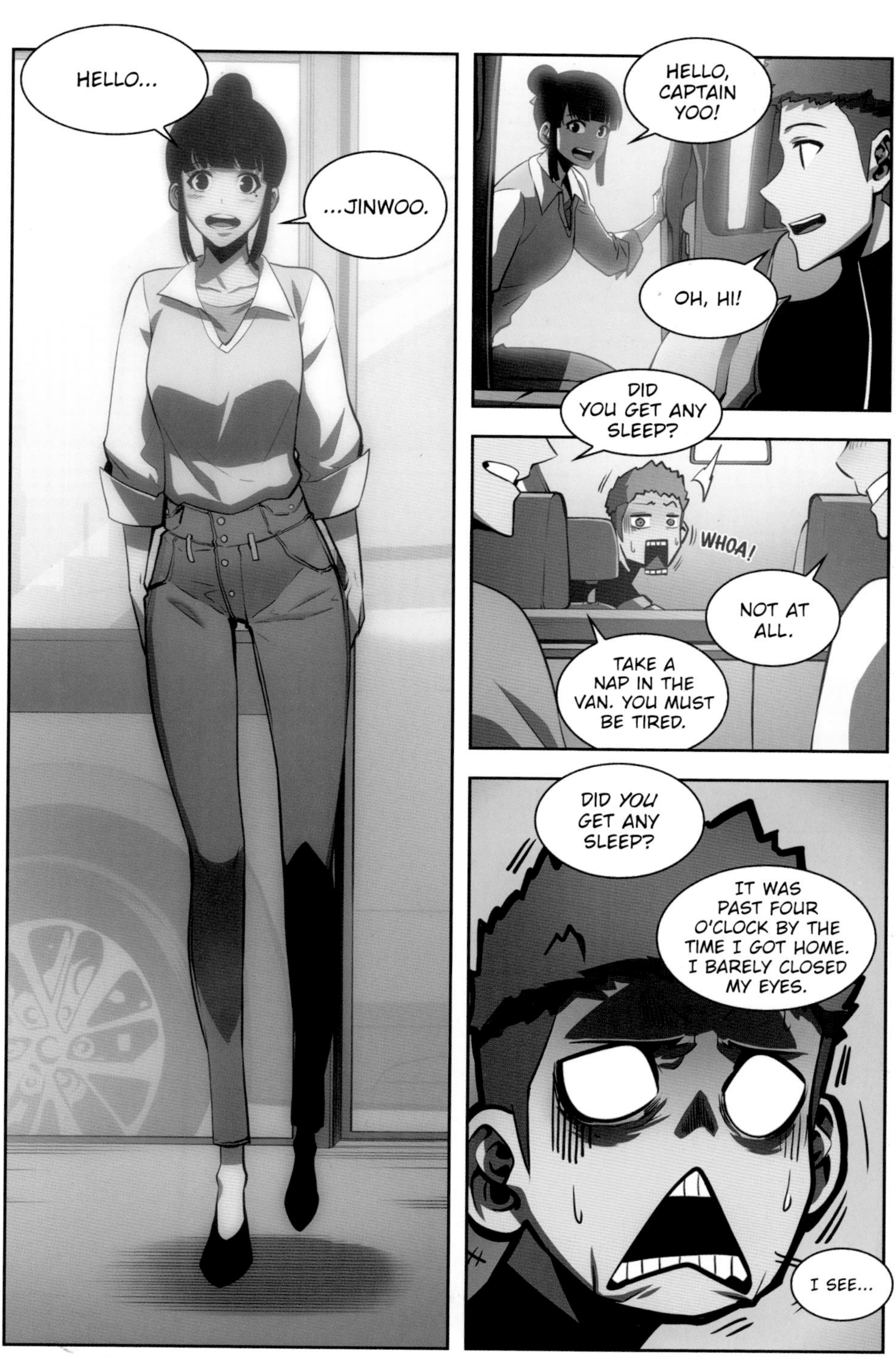
HELLO...
...JINWOO.
HELLO, CAPTAIN YOO!
OH, HI!
DID YOU GET ANY SLEEP?
WHOA!
NOT AT ALL.
TAKE A NAP IN THE VAN. YOU MUST BE TIRED.
DID YOU GET ANY SLEEP?
IT WAS PAST FOUR O'CLOCK BY THE TIME I GOT HOME. I BARELY CLOSED MY EYES.
I SEE...

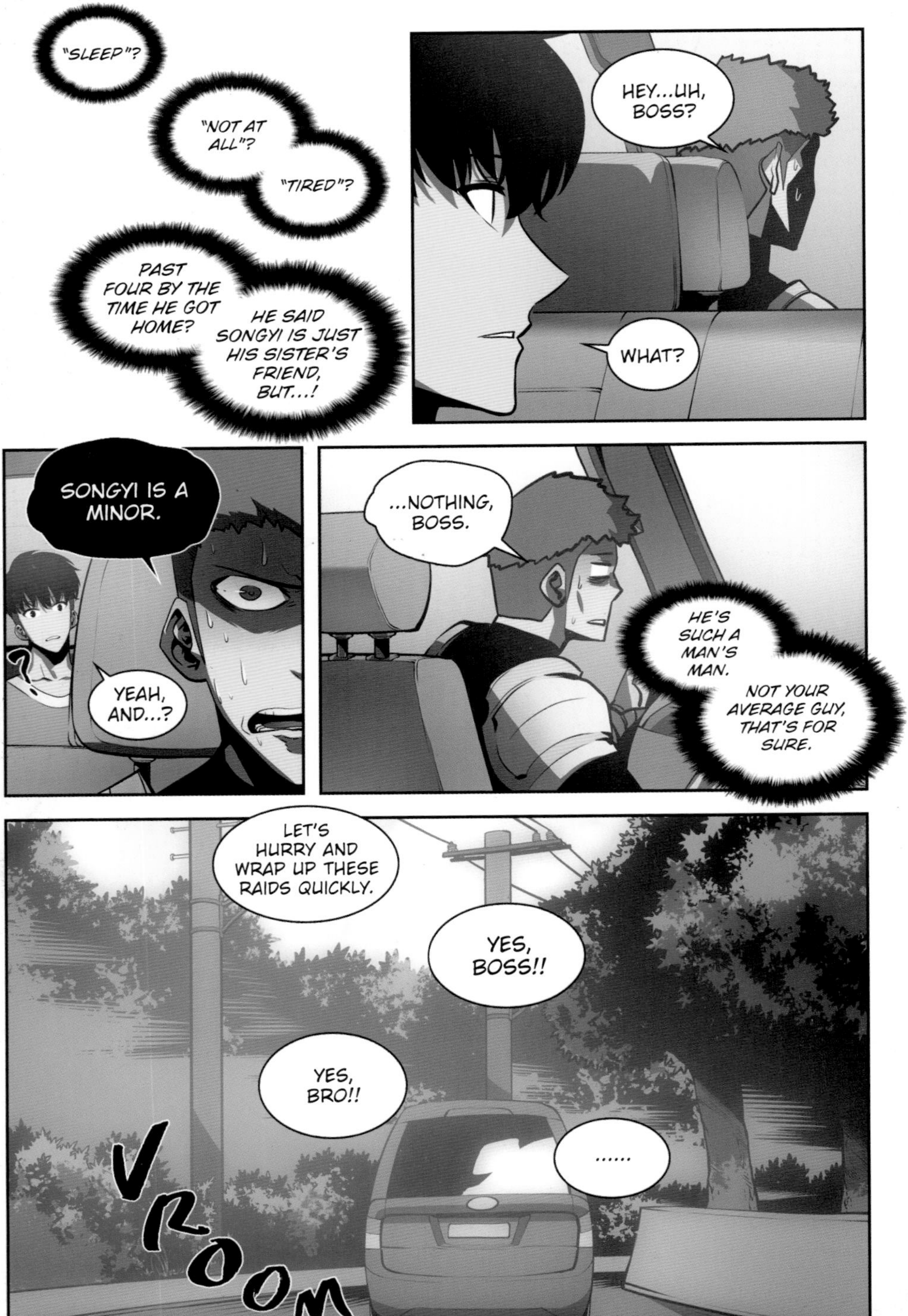
"SLEEP"?
"NOT AT ALL"?
"TIRED"?
PAST FOUR BY THE TIME HE GOT HOME?
HE SAID SONGYI IS JUST HIS SISTER'S FRIEND, BUT...!
HEY...UH, BOSS?
WHAT?
SONGYI IS A MINOR.
YEAH, AND...?
...NOTHING, BOSS.
HE'S SUCH A MAN'S MAN.
NOT YOUR AVERAGE GUY, THAT'S FOR SURE.
LET'S HURRY AND WRAP UP THESE RAIDS QUICKLY.
YES, BOSS!!
YES, BRO!!
......
VROOM

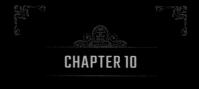

## CHAPTER 10

# Conquering the Demon's Castle

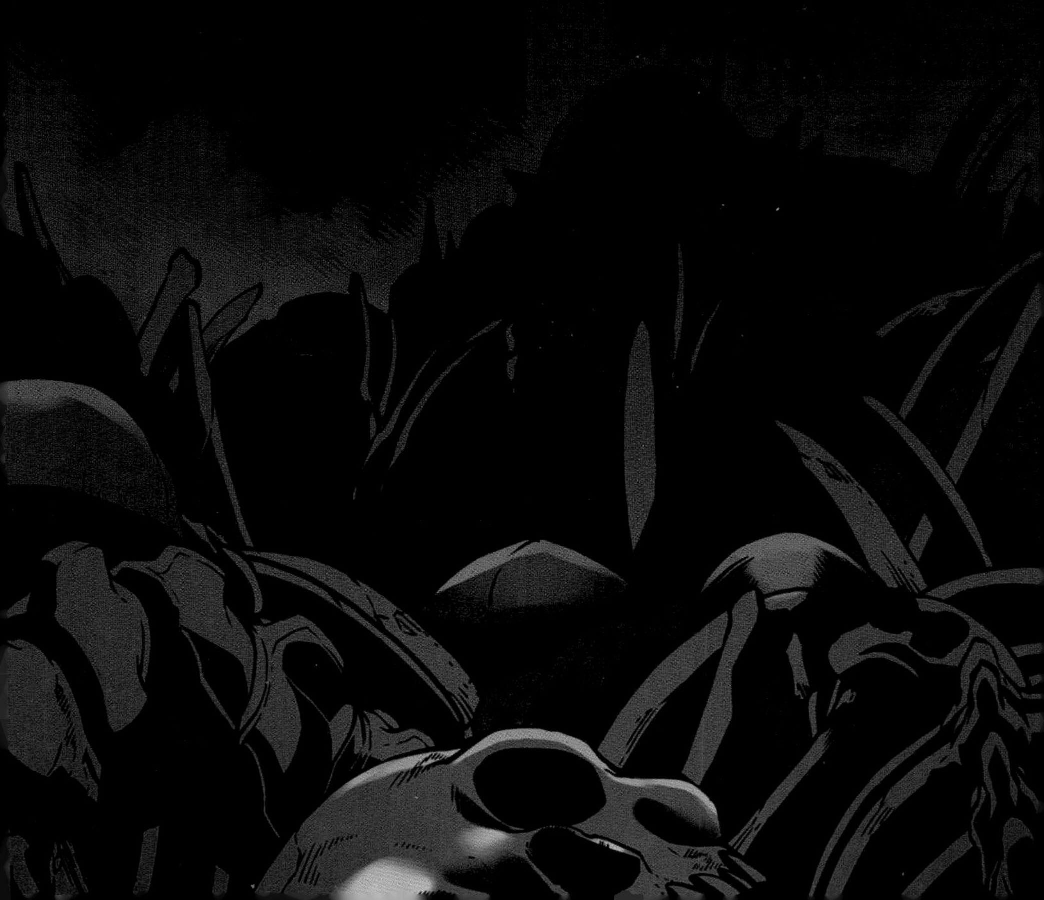

Solo Leveling

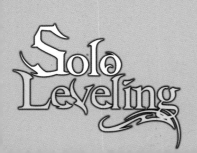

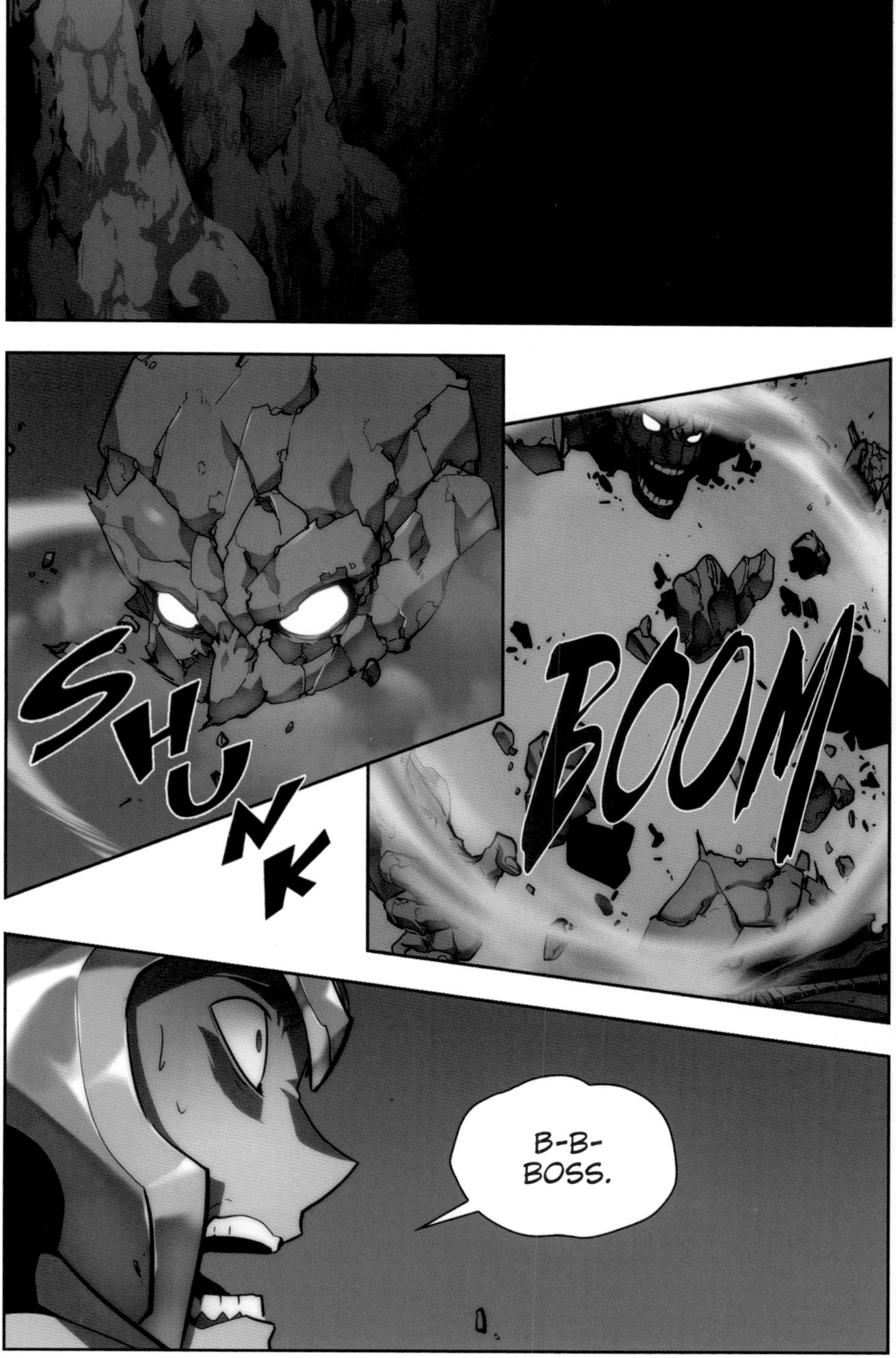
SHUNK
BOOM
B-B-BOSS.

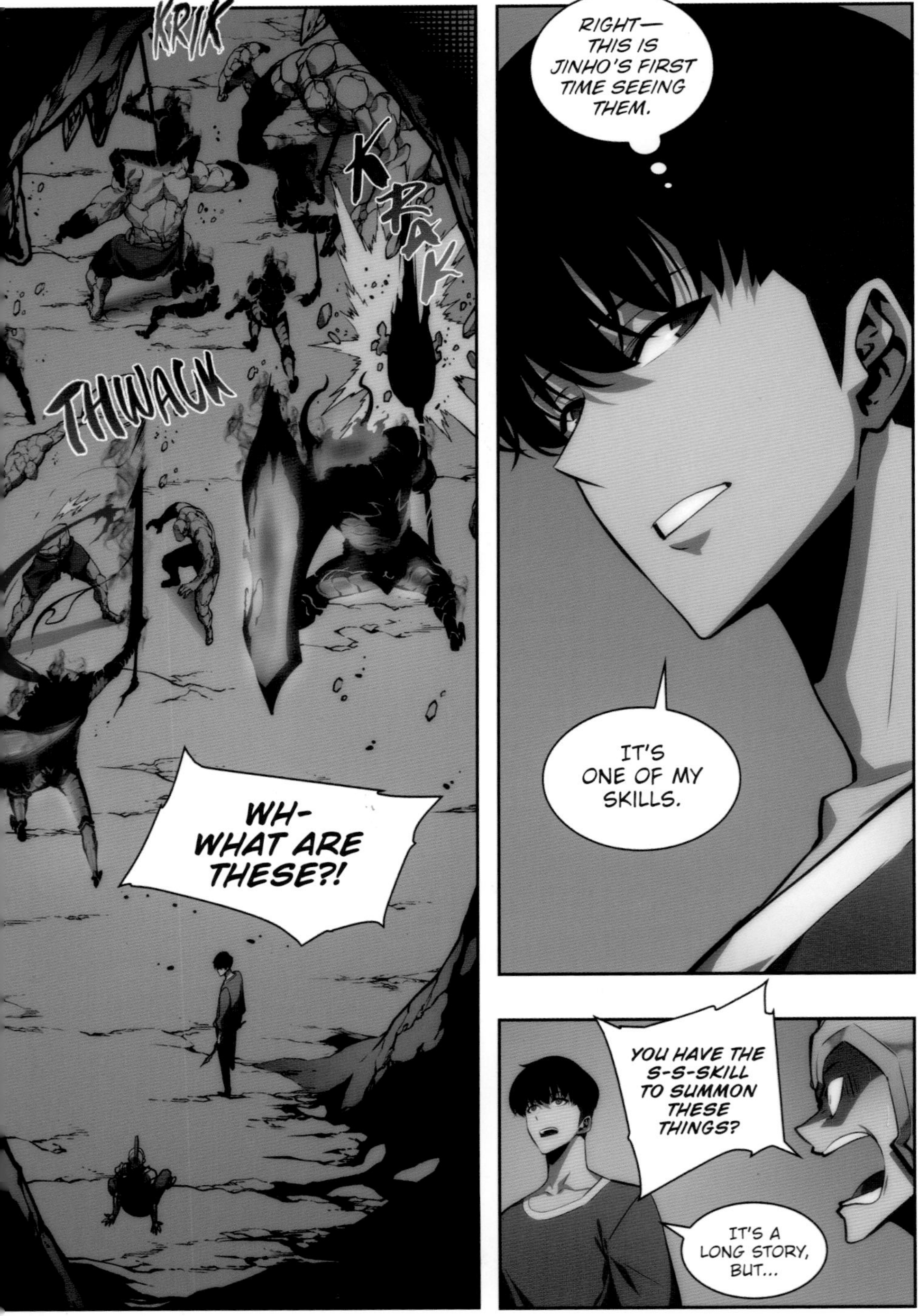
KRIK
KRAK
THWACK
WH- WHAT ARE THESE?!
RIGHT— THIS IS JINHO'S FIRST TIME SEEING THEM.
IT'S ONE OF MY SKILLS.
YOU HAVE THE S-S-SKILL TO SUMMON THESE THINGS?
IT'S A LONG STORY, BUT...

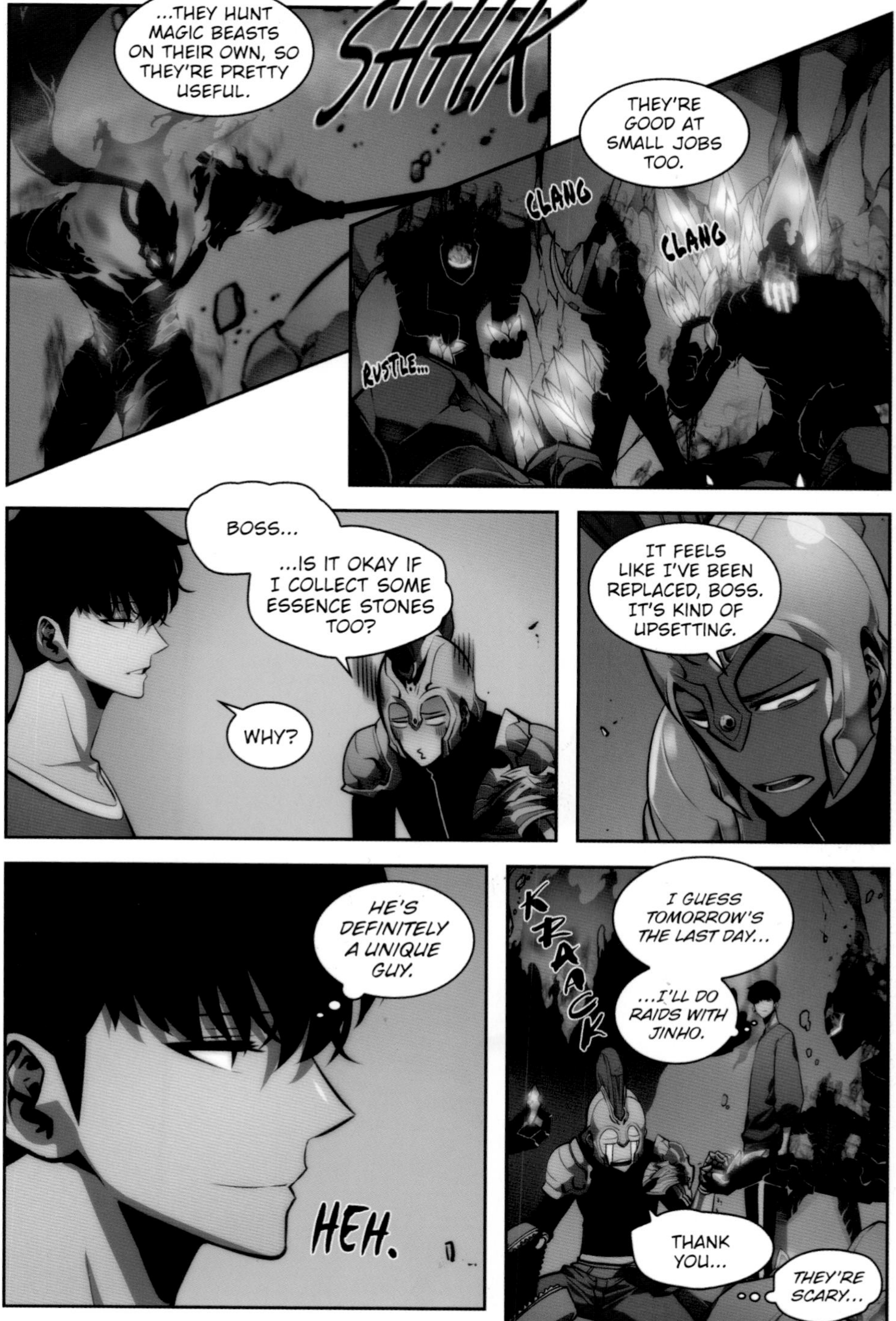
...THEY HUNT MAGIC BEASTS ON THEIR OWN, SO THEY'RE PRETTY USEFUL.
SHHK
THEY'RE GOOD AT SMALL JOBS TOO.
CLANG
CLANG
RUSTLE...
BOSS...
...IS IT OKAY IF I COLLECT SOME ESSENCE STONES TOO?
WHY?
IT FEELS LIKE I'VE BEEN REPLACED, BOSS. IT'S KIND OF UPSETTING.
HE'S DEFINITELY A UNIQUE GUY.
HEH.
KRAACK
I GUESS TOMORROW'S THE LAST DAY...
...I'LL DO RAIDS WITH JINHO.
THANK YOU...
THEY'RE SCARY...

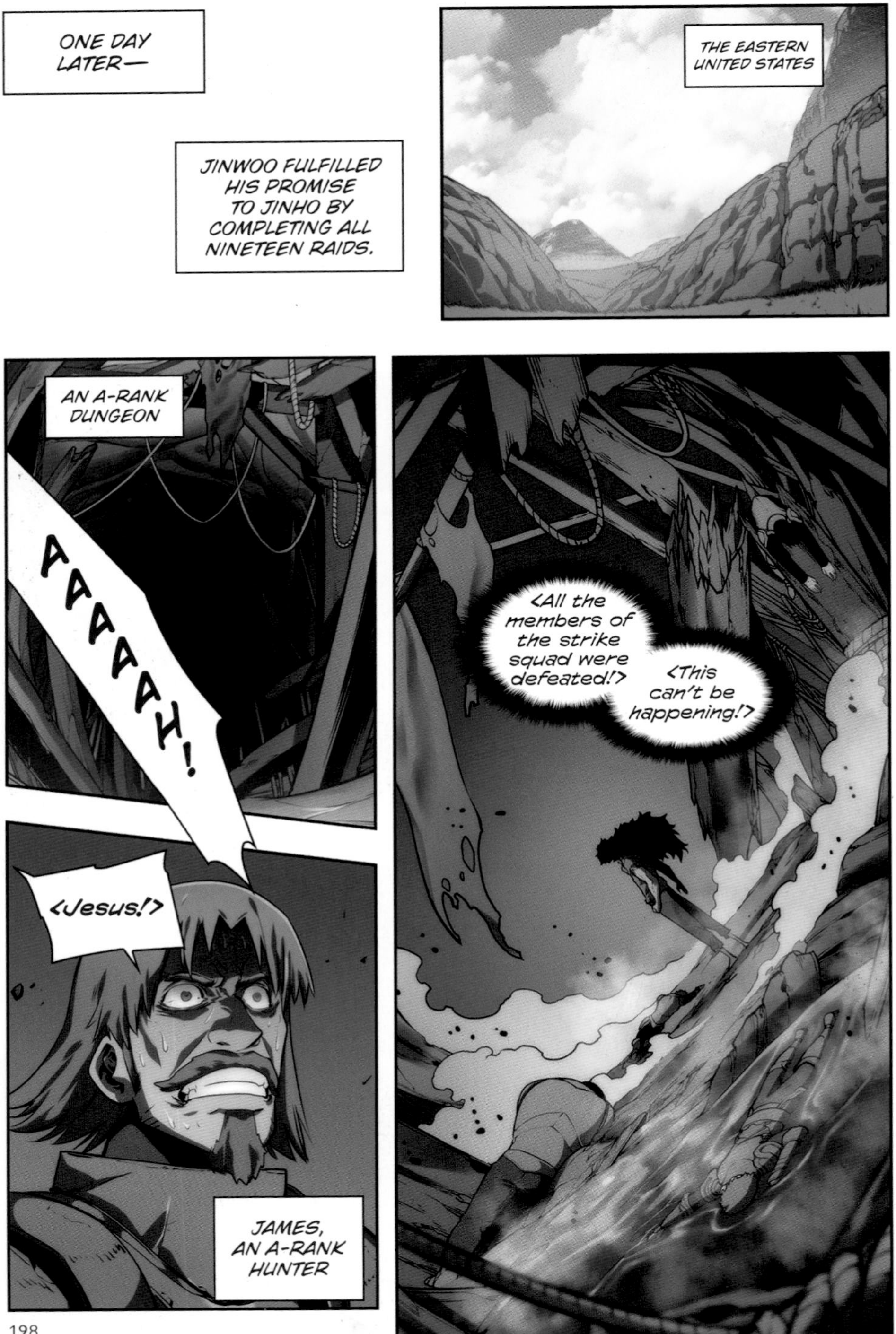
ONE DAY LATER—
JINWOO FULFILLED HIS PROMISE TO JINHO BY COMPLETING ALL NINETEEN RAIDS.
THE EASTERN UNITED STATES
AN A-RANK DUNGEON
AAAAAH!
<Jesus!>
JAMES, AN A-RANK HUNTER
<All the members of the strike squad were defeated!>
<This can't be happening!>

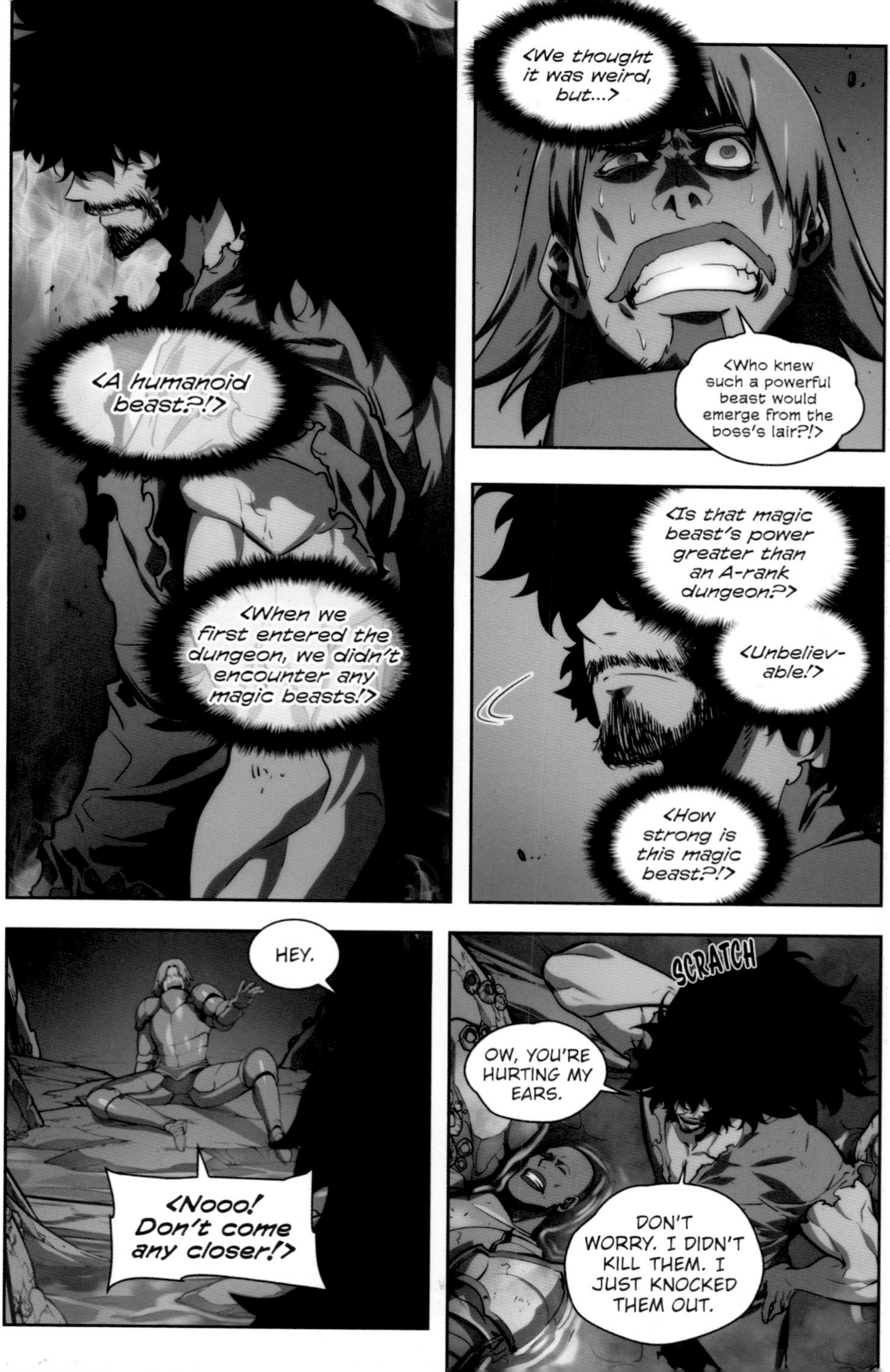
<A humanoid beast?!>
<When we first entered the dungeon, we didn't encounter any magic beasts!>
<We thought it was weird, but...>
<Who knew such a powerful beast would emerge from the boss's lair?!>
<Is that magic beast's power greater than an A-rank dungeon?>
<Unbeliev-able!>
<How strong is this magic beast?!>
HEY.
<Nooo! Don't come any closer!>
SCRATCH
OW, YOU'RE HURTING MY EARS.
DON'T WORRY. I DIDN'T KILL THEM. I JUST KNOCKED THEM OUT.

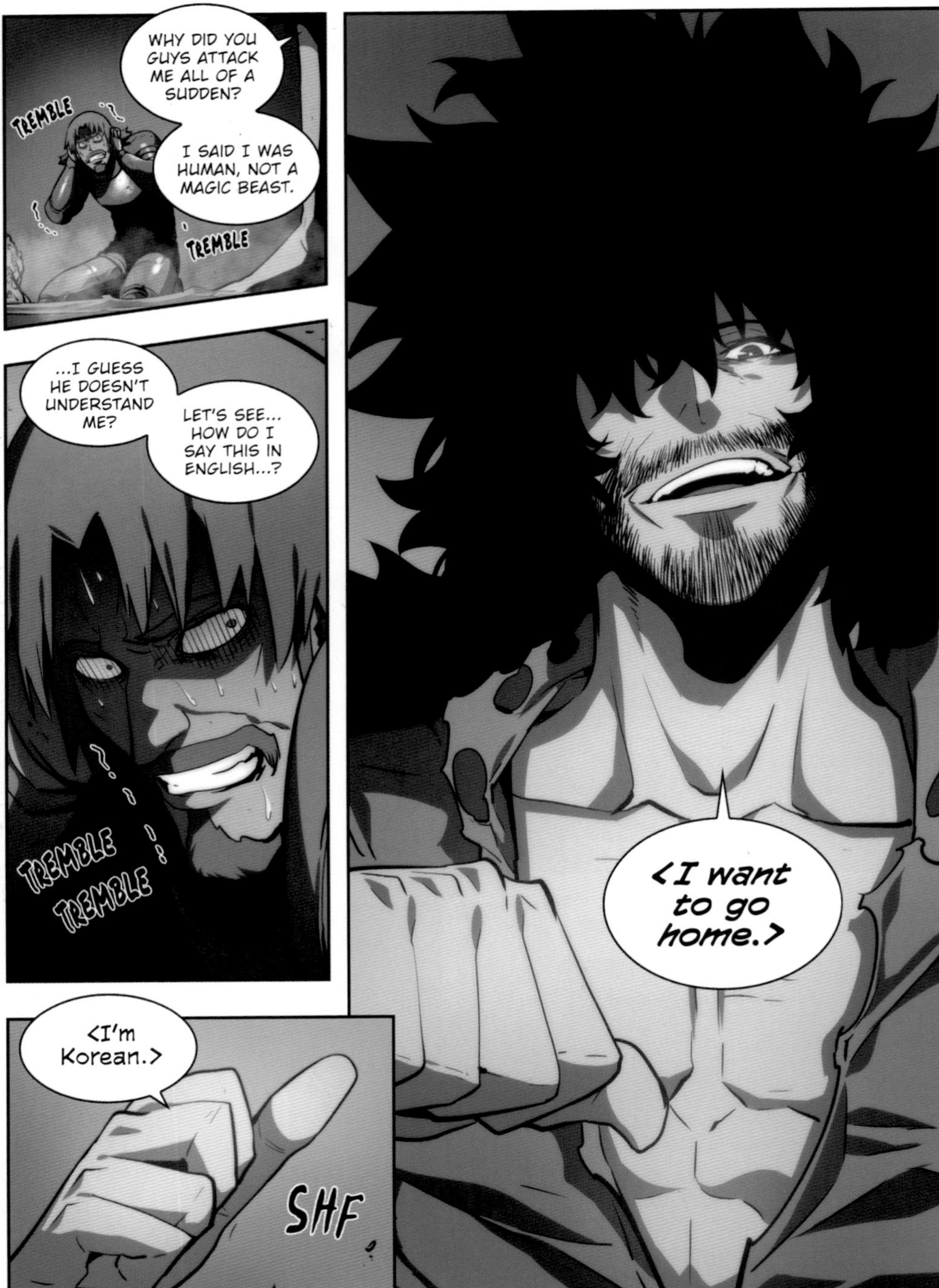
WHY DID YOU GUYS ATTACK ME ALL OF A SUDDEN?
TREMBLE
?
I SAID I WAS HUMAN, NOT A MAGIC BEAST.
TREMBLE
...I GUESS HE DOESN'T UNDERSTAND ME?
LET'S SEE... HOW DO I SAY THIS IN ENGLISH...?
TREMBLE TREMBLE
<I'm Korean.>
SHF
<I want to go home.>

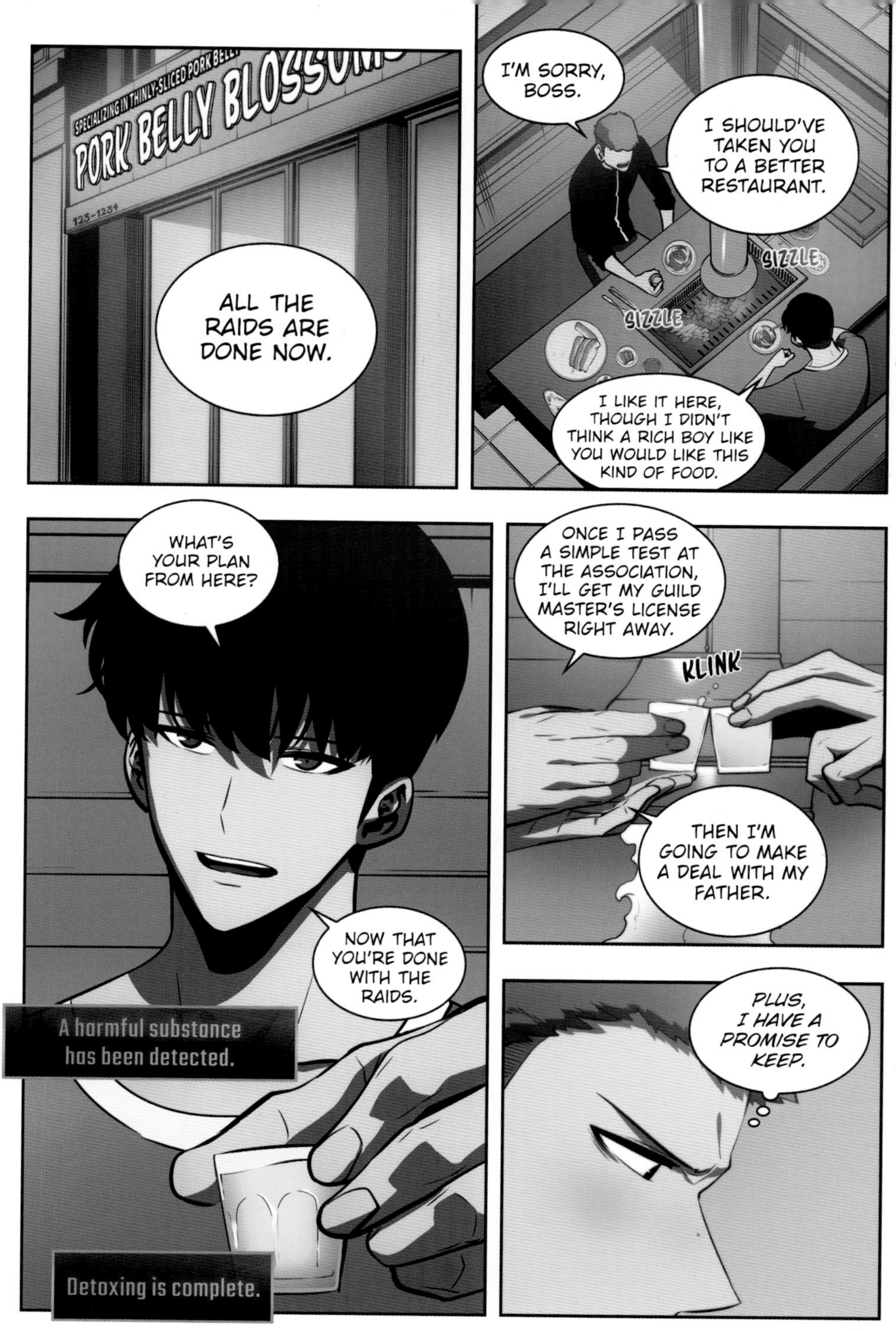

SPECIALIZING IN THINLY-SLICED PORK BELLY
PORK BELLY BLOSSOMS
123-1234
ALL THE RAIDS ARE DONE NOW.
I'M SORRY, BOSS.
I SHOULD'VE TAKEN YOU TO A BETTER RESTAURANT.
SIZZLE
SIZZLE
I LIKE IT HERE, THOUGH I DIDN'T THINK A RICH BOY LIKE YOU WOULD LIKE THIS KIND OF FOOD.
WHAT'S YOUR PLAN FROM HERE?
NOW THAT YOU'RE DONE WITH THE RAIDS.
A harmful substance has been detected.
Detoxing is complete.
ONCE I PASS A SIMPLE TEST AT THE ASSOCIATION, I'LL GET MY GUILD MASTER'S LICENSE RIGHT AWAY.
KLINK
THEN I'M GOING TO MAKE A DEAL WITH MY FATHER.
PLUS, I HAVE A PROMISE TO KEEP.

IT'D BE GREAT TO OWN A 30 BILLION WON BUILDING, BUT...

...THAT WOULD BE LIKE ICING ON THE CAKE.

MY MAIN GOAL WAS LEVELING UP.

SINCE I'VE ALREADY REACHED MY GOAL, I DON'T NEED TO HANG WITH HIM ANYMORE.

**STATUS** — X

NAME: Jinwoo Sung   LEVEL: 61
JOB: Shadow Monarch
TITLE: The One Who Overcame Adversity (and 1 other)

HP: 13001          MP: 1677
FATIGUE: 0

STRENGTH: 142      STAMINA: 101
AGILITY: 121       INTELLECT: 89
PERCEPTION: 103    AP: 0

Physical Damage Decrease: 46%

BUT...

CHEW CHEW

WHAT ARE YOU GOING TO DO NEXT, BOSS?

**ITEM** — X

[ITEM: Castle Door Key]
ACQUISITION DIFFICULTY: A
CATEGORY: Key

This key unlocks the door to the Demon's Castle. You can acquire this only when you kill the gatekeeper.

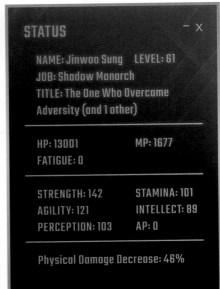

YOU WON'T BE ABLE TO REACH ME FOR A WHILE.

CLENCH

THERE'S SOMEWHERE I NEED TO BE.

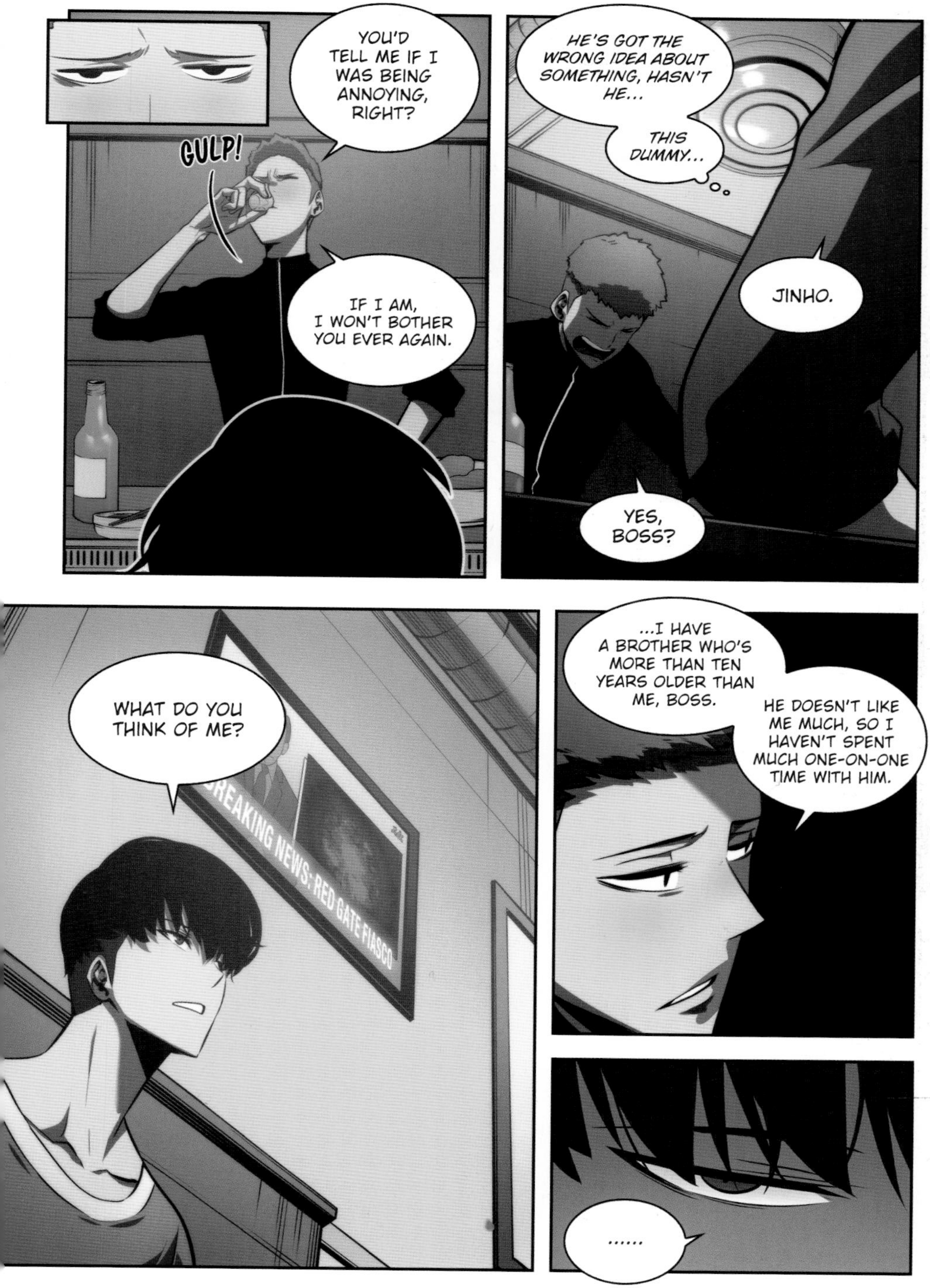
YOU'D TELL ME IF I WAS BEING ANNOYING, RIGHT?
GULP!
IF I AM, I WON'T BOTHER YOU EVER AGAIN.
HE'S GOT THE WRONG IDEA ABOUT SOMETHING, HASN'T HE...
THIS DUMMY...
JINHO.
YES, BOSS?
WHAT DO YOU THINK OF ME?
BREAKING NEWS: RED GATE FIASCO
...I HAVE A BROTHER WHO'S MORE THAN TEN YEARS OLDER THAN ME, BOSS.
HE DOESN'T LIKE ME MUCH, SO I HAVEN'T SPENT MUCH ONE-ON-ONE TIME WITH HIM.
......

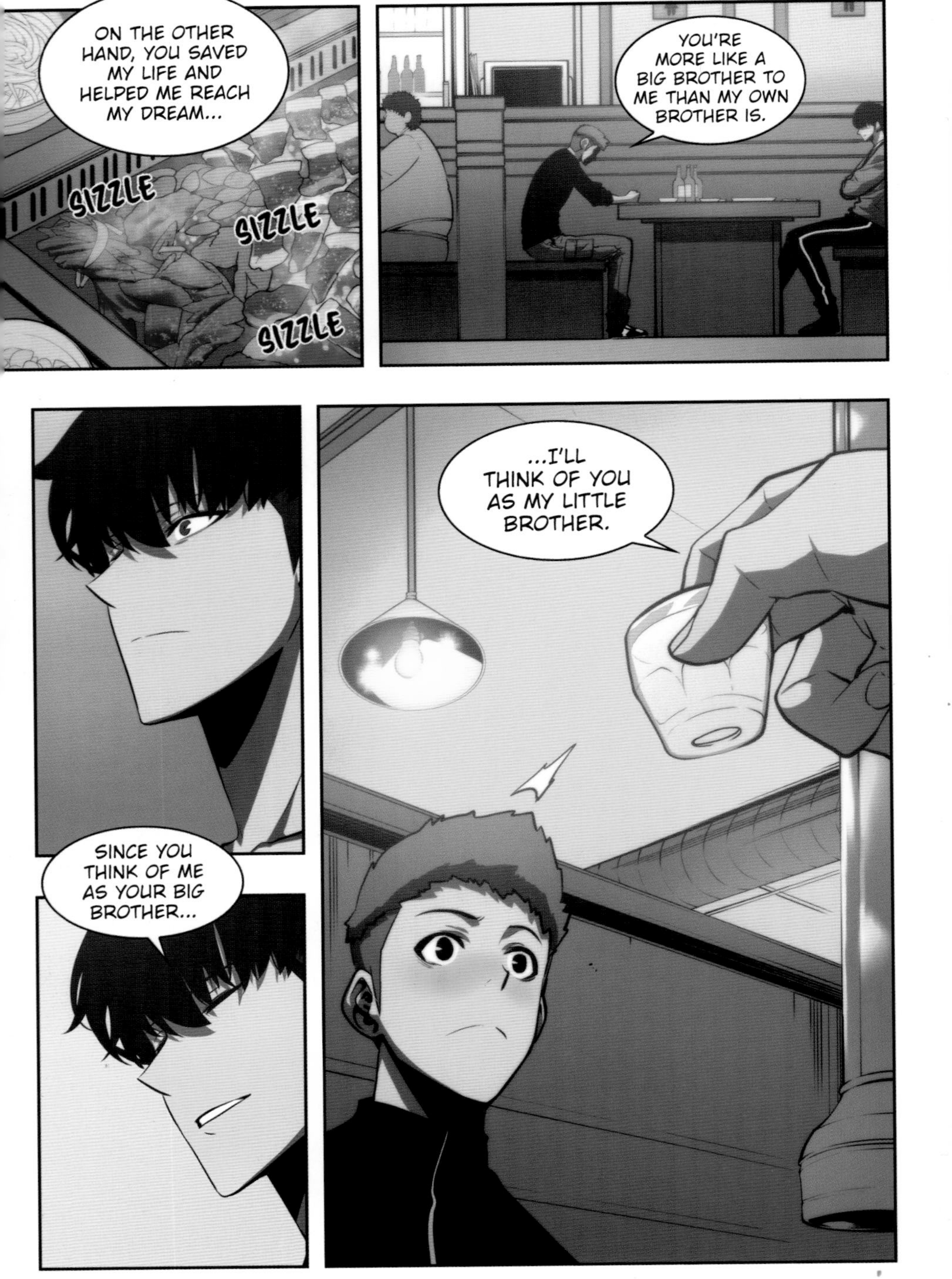
ON THE OTHER HAND, YOU SAVED MY LIFE AND HELPED ME REACH MY DREAM...
SIZZLE
SIZZLE
SIZZLE
YOU'RE MORE LIKE A BIG BROTHER TO ME THAN MY OWN BROTHER IS.
SINCE YOU THINK OF ME AS YOUR BIG BROTHER...
...I'LL THINK OF YOU AS MY LITTLE BROTHER.

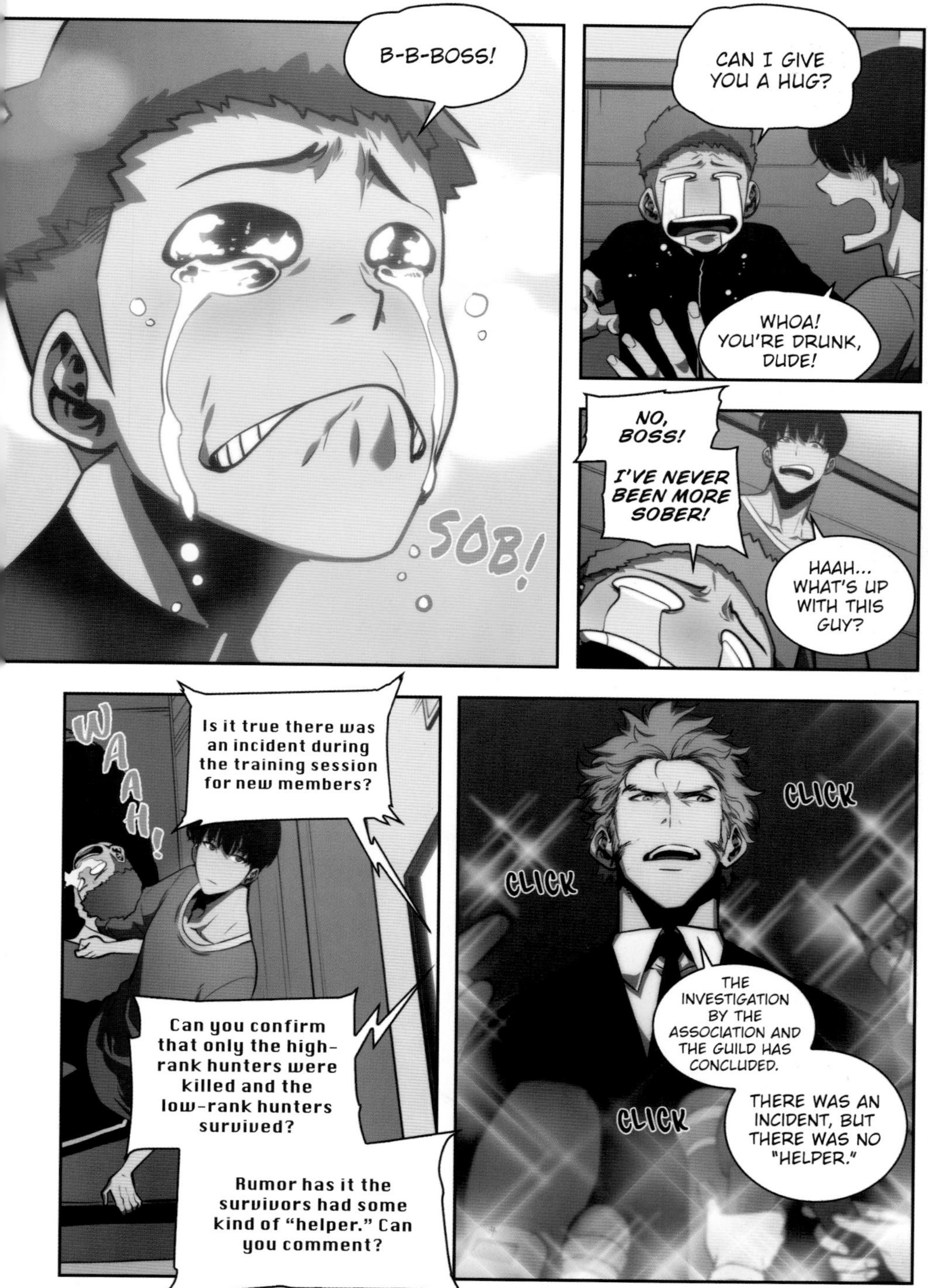
B-B-BOSS!
SOB!
CAN I GIVE YOU A HUG?
WHOA! YOU'RE DRUNK, DUDE!
NO, BOSS!
I'VE NEVER BEEN MORE SOBER!
HAAH... WHAT'S UP WITH THIS GUY?
WAAAH!
Is it true there was an incident during the training session for new members?
Can you confirm that only the high-rank hunters were killed and the low-rank hunters survived?
Rumor has it the survivors had some kind of "helper." Can you comment?
CLICK
CLICK
THE INVESTIGATION BY THE ASSOCIATION AND THE GUILD HAS CONCLUDED.
CLICK
THERE WAS AN INCIDENT, BUT THERE WAS NO "HELPER."

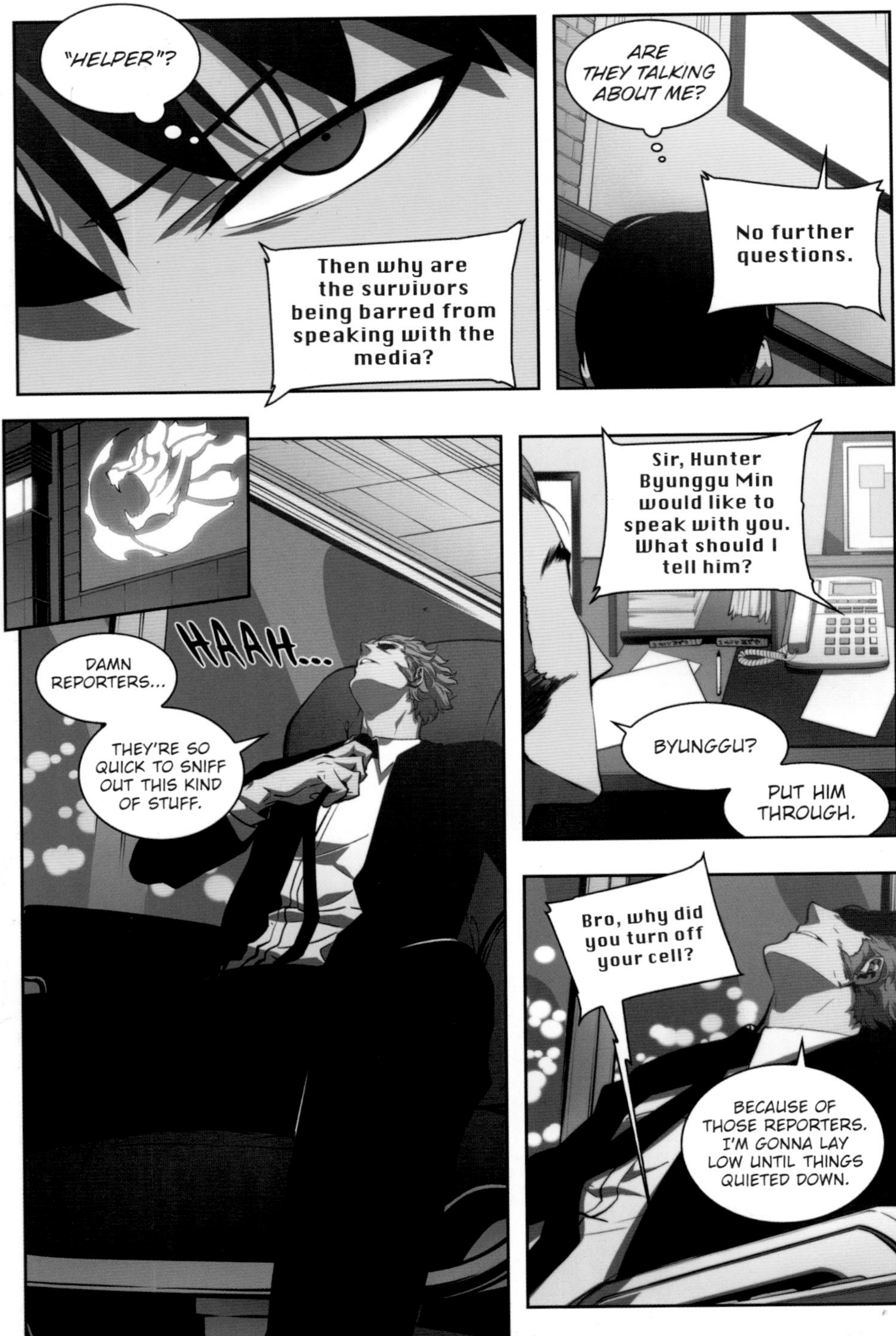
"HELPER"?
Then why are the survivors being barred from speaking with the media?
ARE THEY TALKING ABOUT ME?
No further questions.
HAAAH...
DAMN REPORTERS...
THEY'RE SO QUICK TO SNIFF OUT THIS KIND OF STUFF.
Sir, Hunter Byunggu Min would like to speak with you. What should I tell him?
BYUNGGU?
PUT HIM THROUGH.
Bro, why did you turn off your cell?
BECAUSE OF THOSE REPORTERS. I'M GONNA LAY LOW UNTIL THINGS QUIETED DOWN.

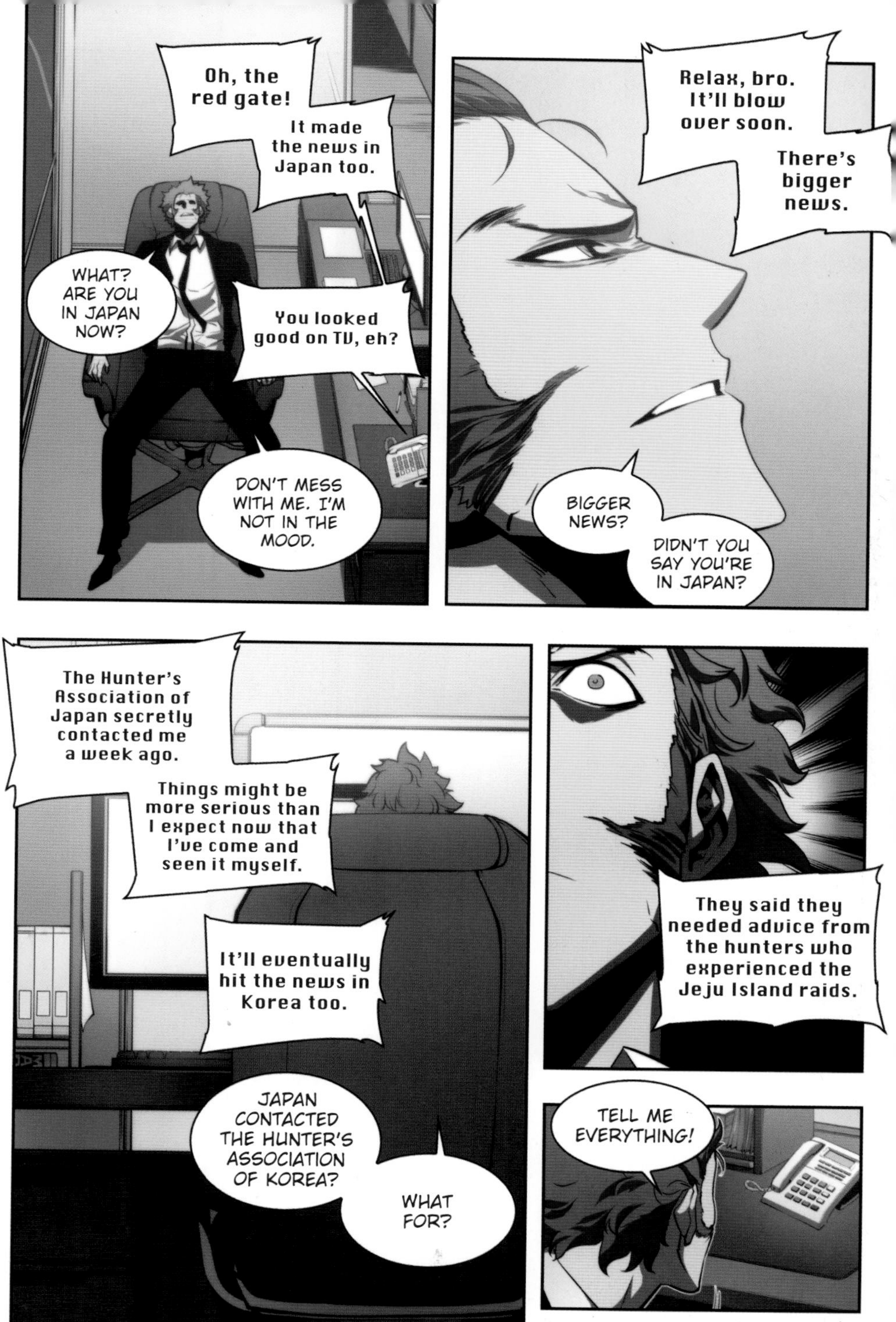
Oh, the red gate!
It made the news in Japan too.
WHAT? ARE YOU IN JAPAN NOW?
You looked good on TV, eh?
DON'T MESS WITH ME. I'M NOT IN THE MOOD.
Relax, bro. It'll blow over soon.
There's bigger news.
BIGGER NEWS?
DIDN'T YOU SAY YOU'RE IN JAPAN?
The Hunter's Association of Japan secretly contacted me a week ago.
Things might be more serious than I expect now that I've come and seen it myself.
It'll eventually hit the news in Korea too.
JAPAN CONTACTED THE HUNTER'S ASSOCIATION OF KOREA?
WHAT FOR?
They said they needed advice from the hunters who experienced the Jeju Island raids.
TELL ME EVERYTHING!

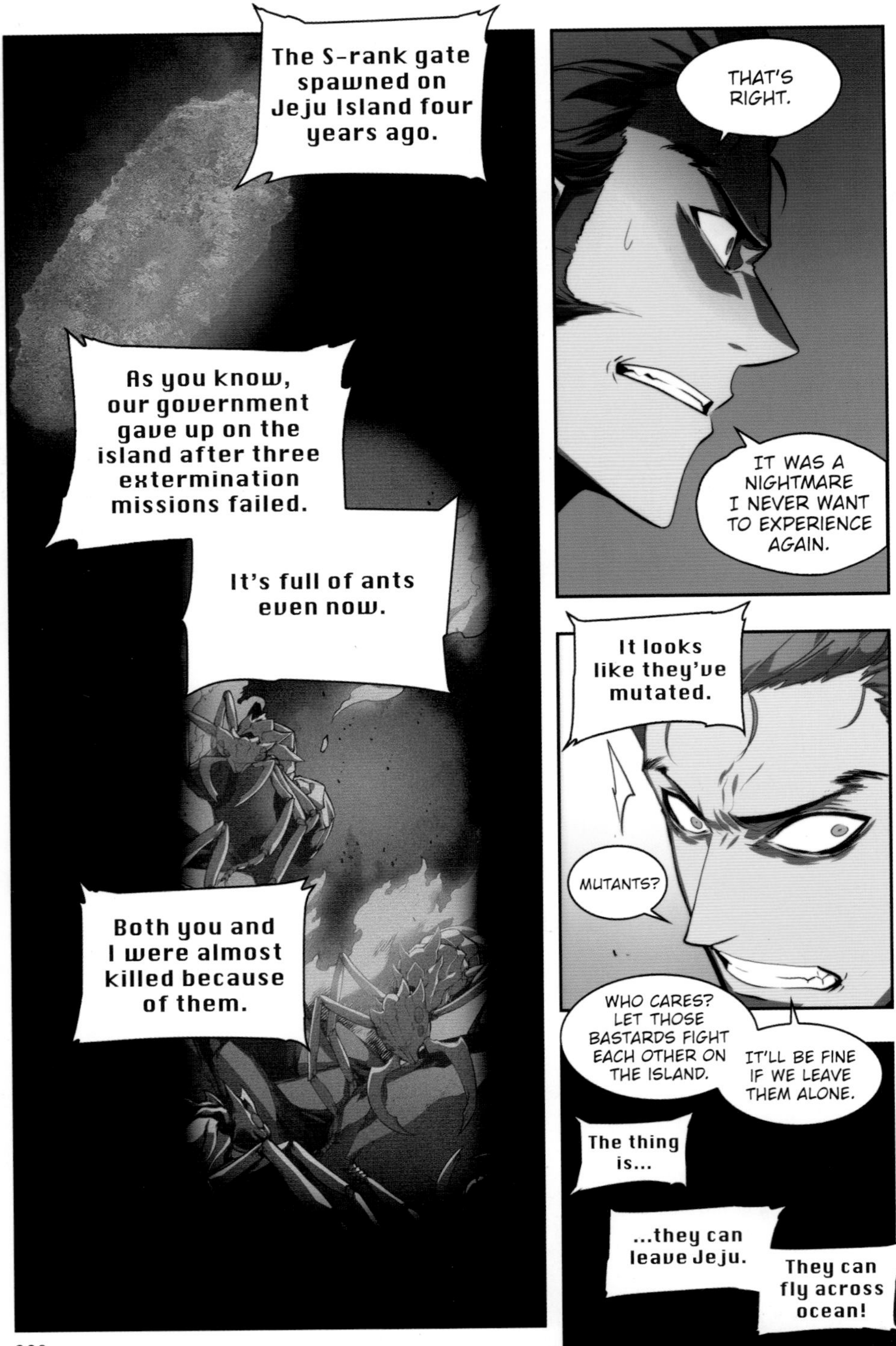
The S-rank gate spawned on Jeju Island four years ago.
As you know, our government gave up on the island after three extermination missions failed.
It's full of ants even now.
Both you and I were almost killed because of them.
THAT'S RIGHT.
IT WAS A NIGHTMARE I NEVER WANT TO EXPERIENCE AGAIN.
It looks like they've mutated.
MUTANTS?
WHO CARES? LET THOSE BASTARDS FIGHT EACH OTHER ON THE ISLAND.
IT'LL BE FINE IF WE LEAVE THEM ALONE.
The thing is...
...they can leave Jeju.
They can fly across ocean!

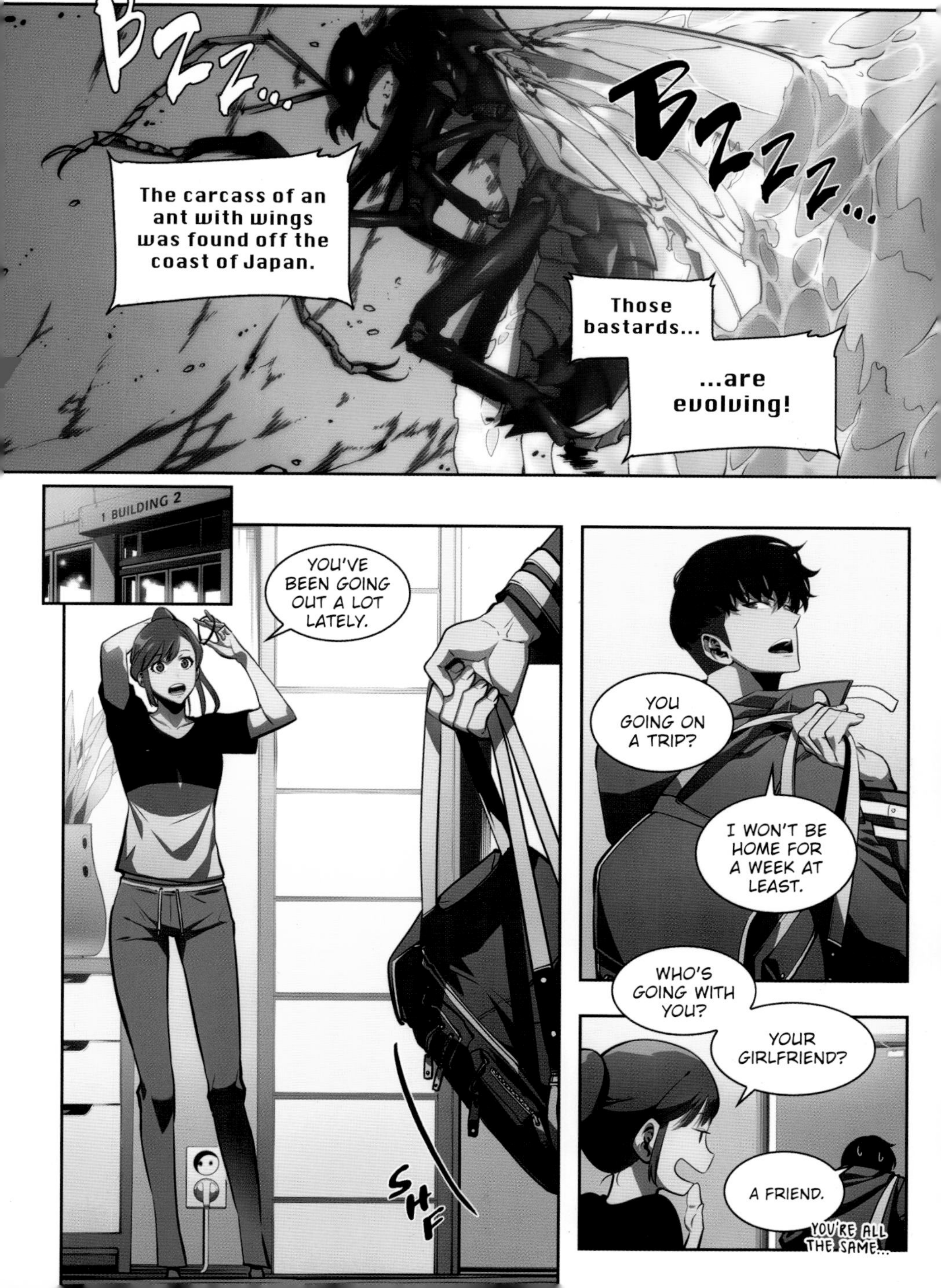
BZZ...
The carcass of an ant with wings was found off the coast of Japan.
BZZZZ...
Those bastards...
...are evolving!
1 BUILDING 2
YOU'VE BEEN GOING OUT A LOT LATELY.
SHF
YOU GOING ON A TRIP?
I WON'T BE HOME FOR A WEEK AT LEAST.
WHO'S GOING WITH YOU?
YOUR GIRLFRIEND?
A FRIEND.
YOU'RE ALL THE SAME...

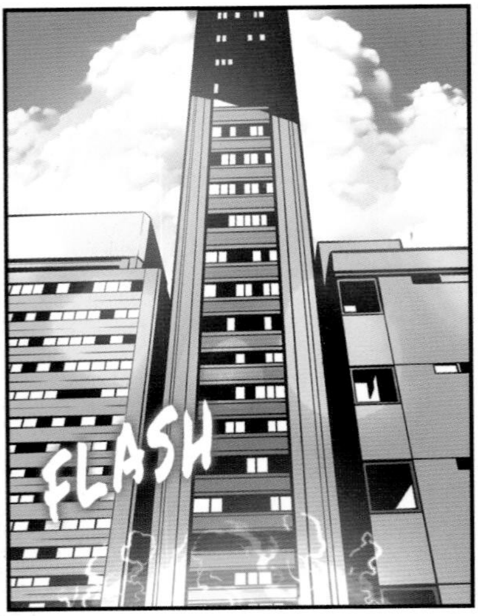
FLASH

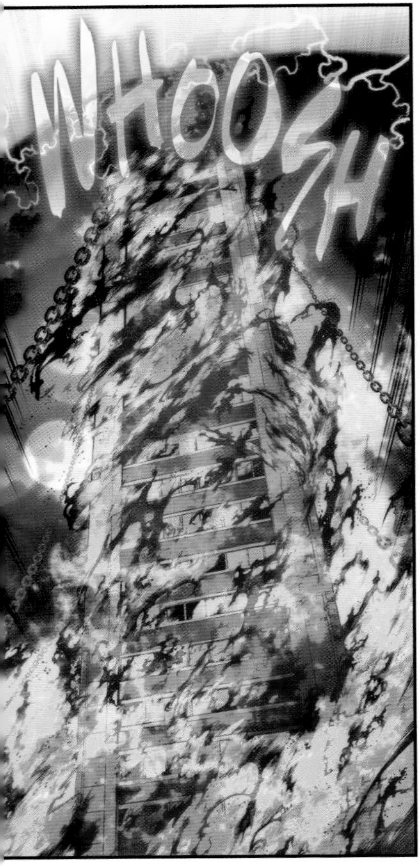
WHOOSH

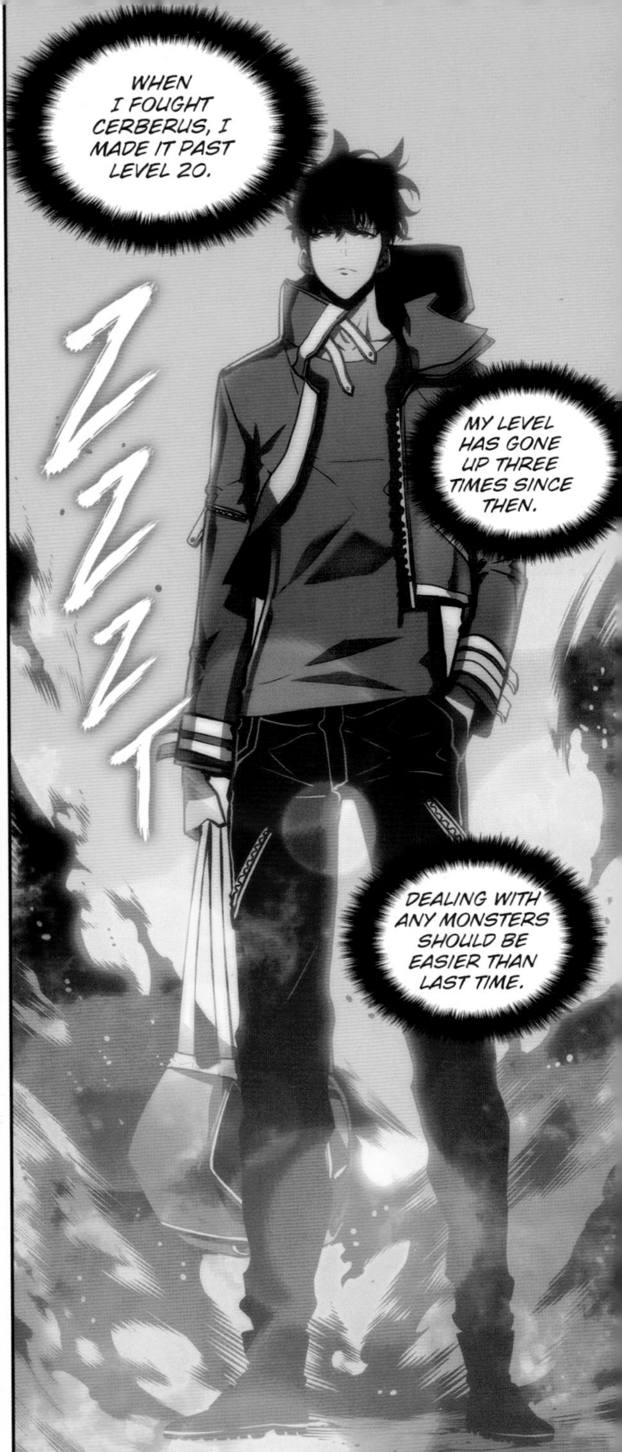
WHEN I FOUGHT CERBERUS, I MADE IT PAST LEVEL 20.
ZZZZT
MY LEVEL HAS GONE UP THREE TIMES SINCE THEN.
DEALING WITH ANY MONSTERS SHOULD BE EASIER THAN LAST TIME.

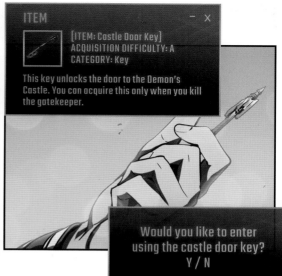

ITEM — X

[ITEM: Castle Door Key]
ACQUISITION DIFFICULTY: A
CATEGORY: Key

This key unlocks the door to the Demon's
Castle. You can acquire this only when you kill
the gatekeeper.

Would you like to enter
using the castle door key?
Y / N

A new quest has arrived.

WHAT'S
THIS?

NO
MONSTERS...
IS THIS JUST
A HALL?

IS THE
EXIT ON
THE OTHER
SIDE...?

PING!

QUEST

[Quest: Collect Demon Souls! (1)]

The Demon's Castle is filled with demons. Defeat the demons and collect their souls to acquire special re[...]

Quest Clear Requirement:
10,000 demon souls

Rewards:
- 1. Your choice of any 1 it[...]
- 2. +20 Ability Points
- 3. Mystery reward

A QUEST. IT'S BEEN A WHILE.

THE REWARDS ARE INCREDIBLE, HUH?

A STAT BONUS, AND ANY ITEM FROM THE SHOP TO BOOT.

BOOM

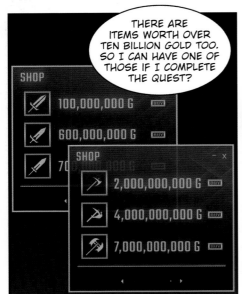

THERE ARE ITEMS WORTH OVER TEN BILLION GOLD TOO. SO I CAN HAVE ONE OF THOSE IF I COMPLETE THE QUEST?

SHOP

100,000,000 G

600,000,000 G

7[...]

SHOP        — X

2,000,000,000 G

4,000,000,000 G

7,000,000,000 G

BUT HIGH-LEVEL REWARDS MEANS THE DIFFICULTY LEVEL OF THE QUEST IS HIGH TOO...

CREAK

I DON'T SEE A SINGLE MONSTER.

WHAT THE...?

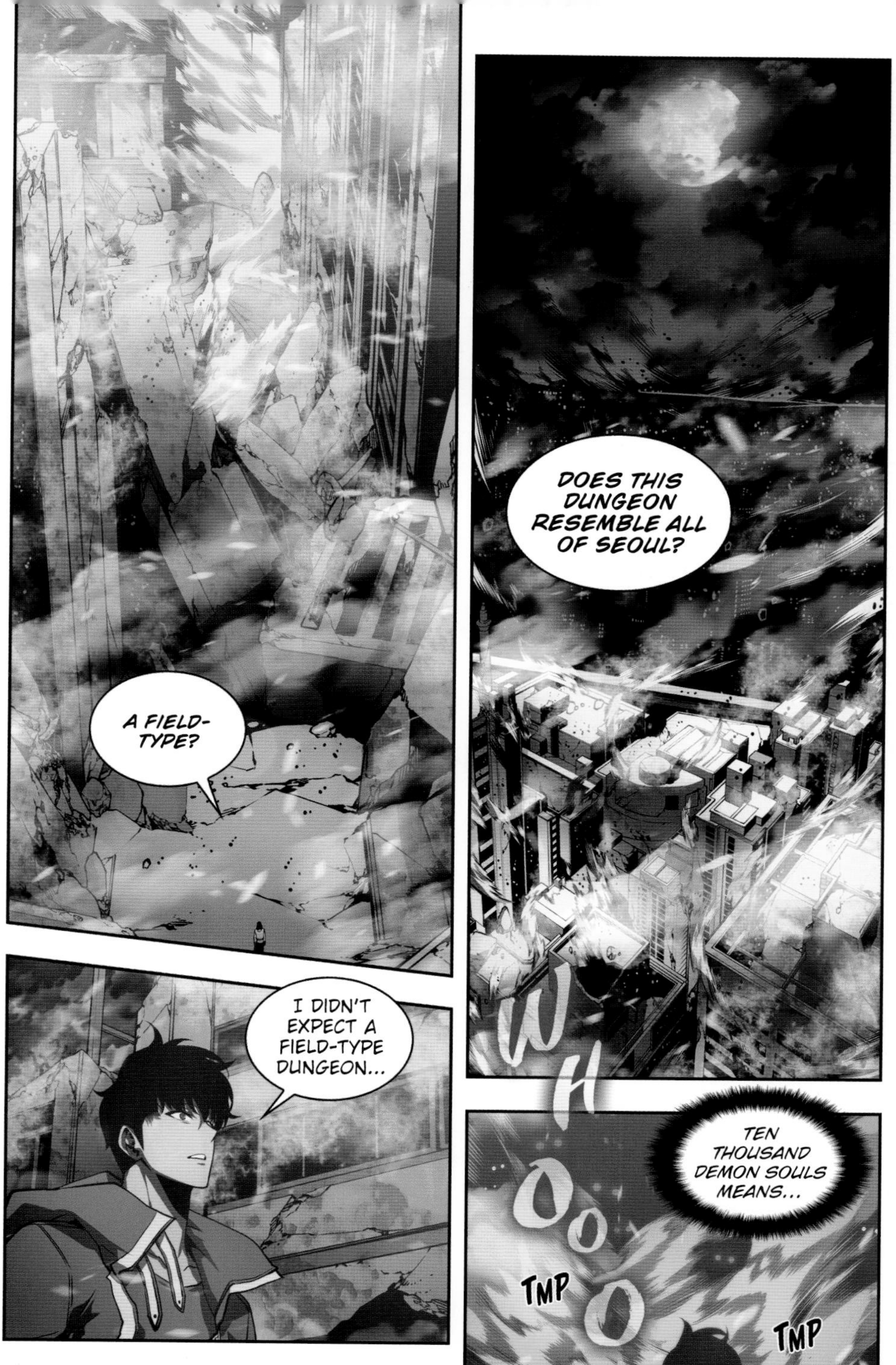
A FIELD-TYPE?
I DIDN'T EXPECT A FIELD-TYPE DUNGEON...
DOES THIS DUNGEON RESEMBLE ALL OF SEOUL?
WHOOO
TEN THOUSAND DEMON SOULS MEANS...
TMP
TMP

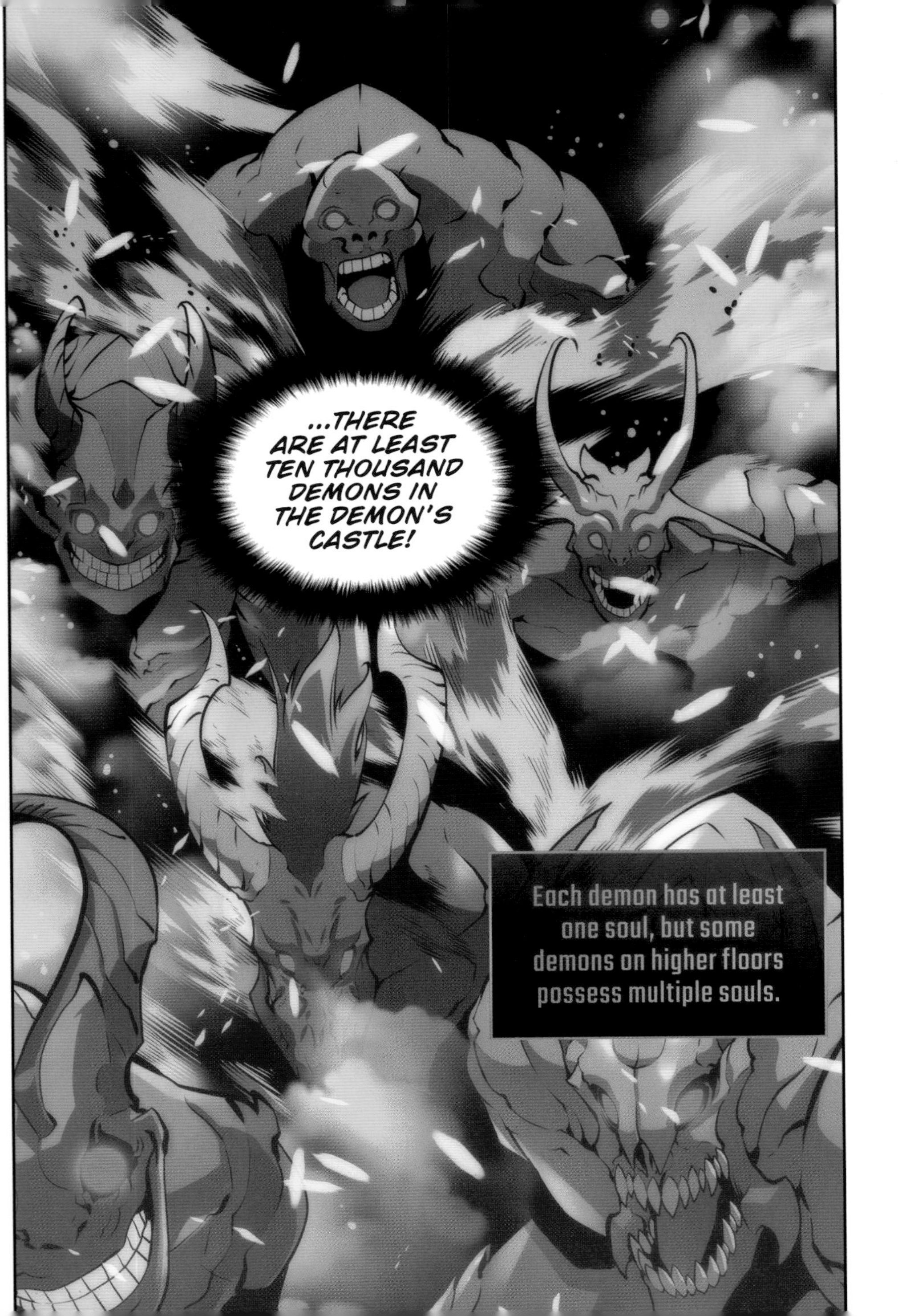
...THERE ARE AT LEAST TEN THOUSAND DEMONS IN THE DEMON'S CASTLE!
Each demon has at least one soul, but some demons on higher floors possess multiple souls.

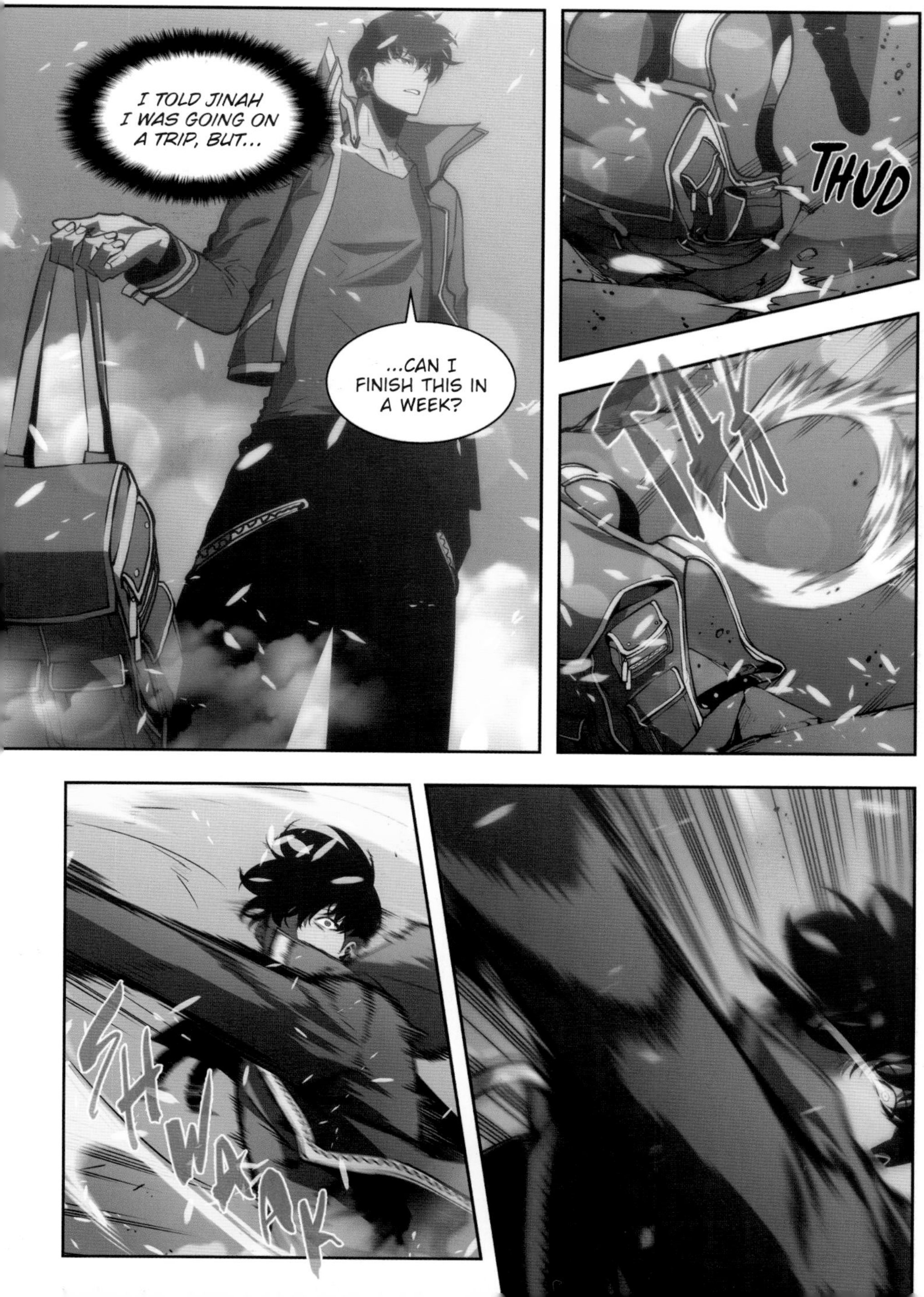
I TOLD JINAH I WAS GOING ON A TRIP, BUT...
...CAN I FINISH THIS IN A WEEK?
THUD
SHWAAK

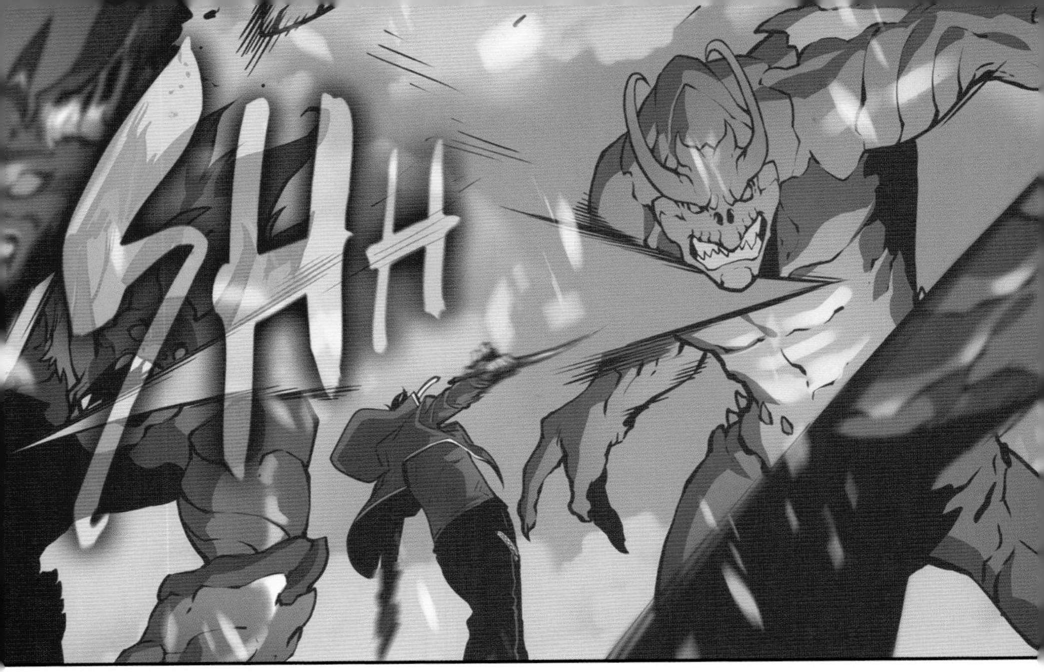
SHH

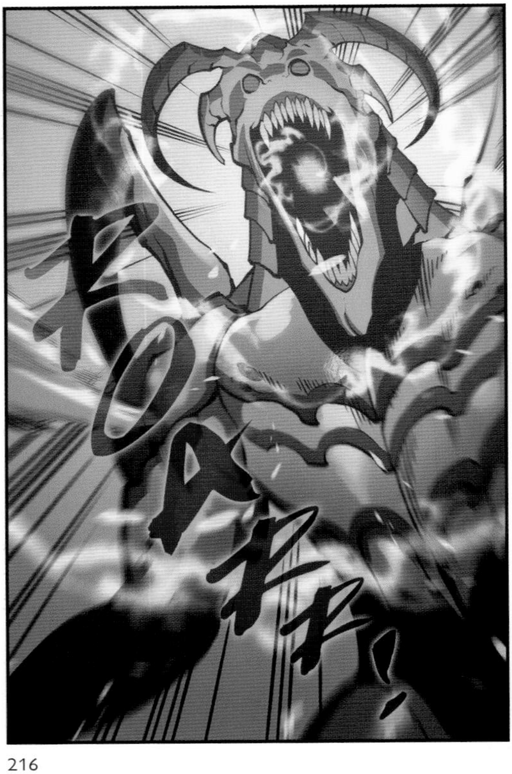

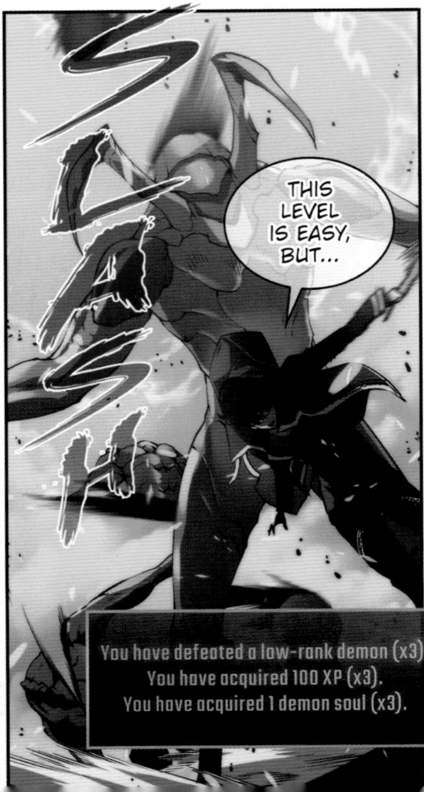
SLASH
THIS LEVEL IS EASY, BUT...
You have defeated a low-rank demon (x3).
You have acquired 100 XP (x3).
You have acquired 1 demon soul (x3).

Experience points needed to level up: 59,700

THE SYSTEM IS EVEN SHOWING XP NOW?

HOW CONVENIENT.

IT'S A RACE AGAINST TIME FROM HERE!

SOORiM Traditional Korean Restauran

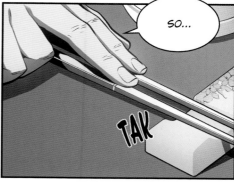

SO...

TAK

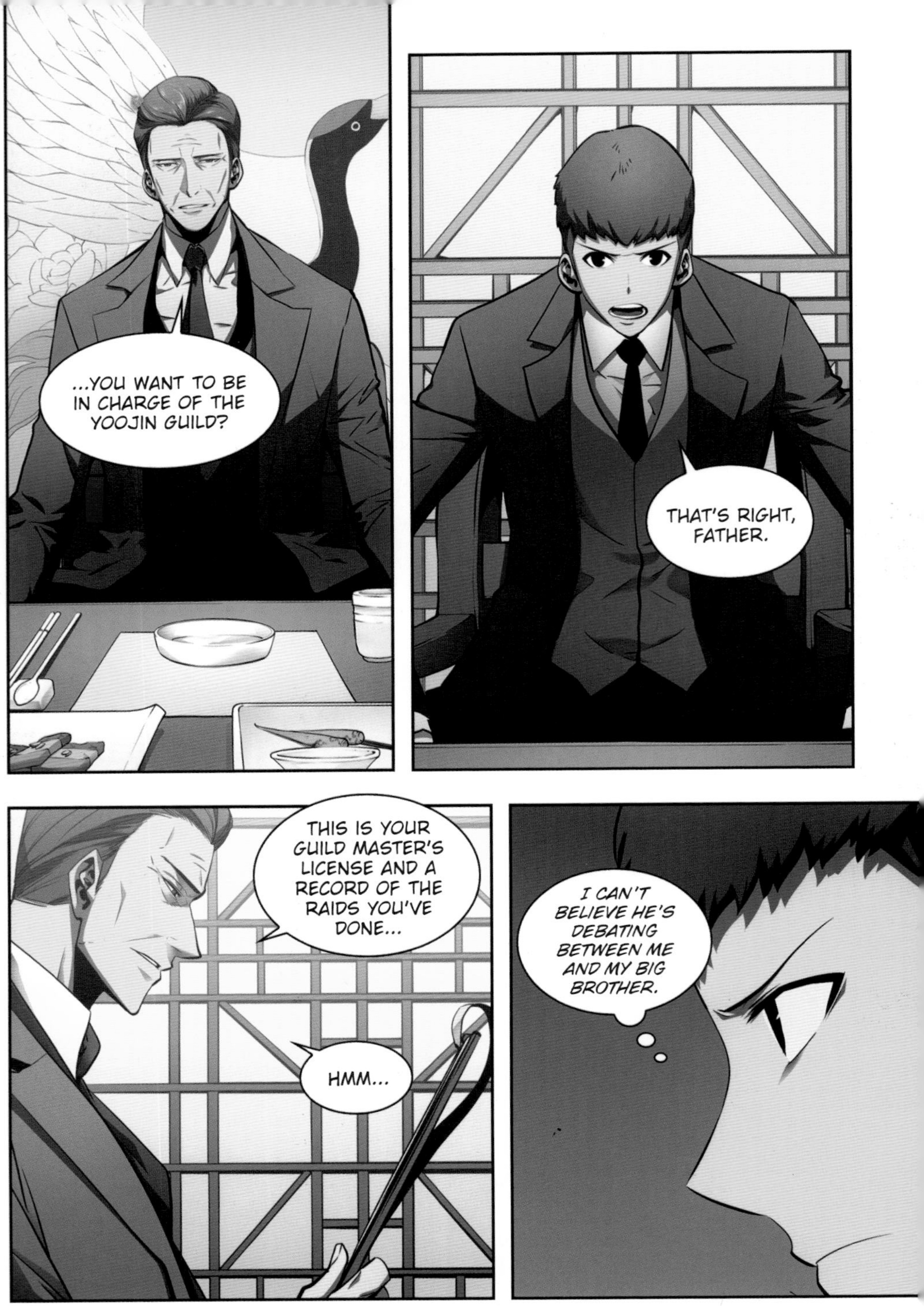
...YOU WANT TO BE IN CHARGE OF THE YOOJIN GUILD?
THAT'S RIGHT, FATHER.
THIS IS YOUR GUILD MASTER'S LICENSE AND A RECORD OF THE RAIDS YOU'VE DONE...
HMM...
I CAN'T BELIEVE HE'S DEBATING BETWEEN ME AND MY BIG BROTHER.

AS YOU ALREADY KNOW, IT'S TOO RISKY TO HAND OVER THAT KIND OF POWER TO SOMEONE OUTSIDE OF THE FAMILY AND—

ENOUGH.

I WANT TO INTRODUCE YOU TO SOMEONE.

?

PLEASE COME IN.

SLIIIDE

THIS IS HUNTER MYUNGHWAN KO.

HELLO.

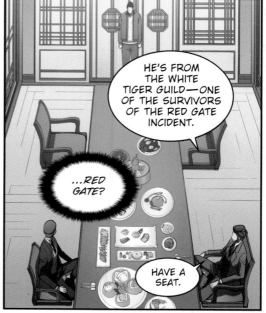

HE'S FROM THE WHITE TIGER GUILD—ONE OF THE SURVIVORS OF THE RED GATE INCIDENT.

...RED GATE?

HAVE A SEAT.

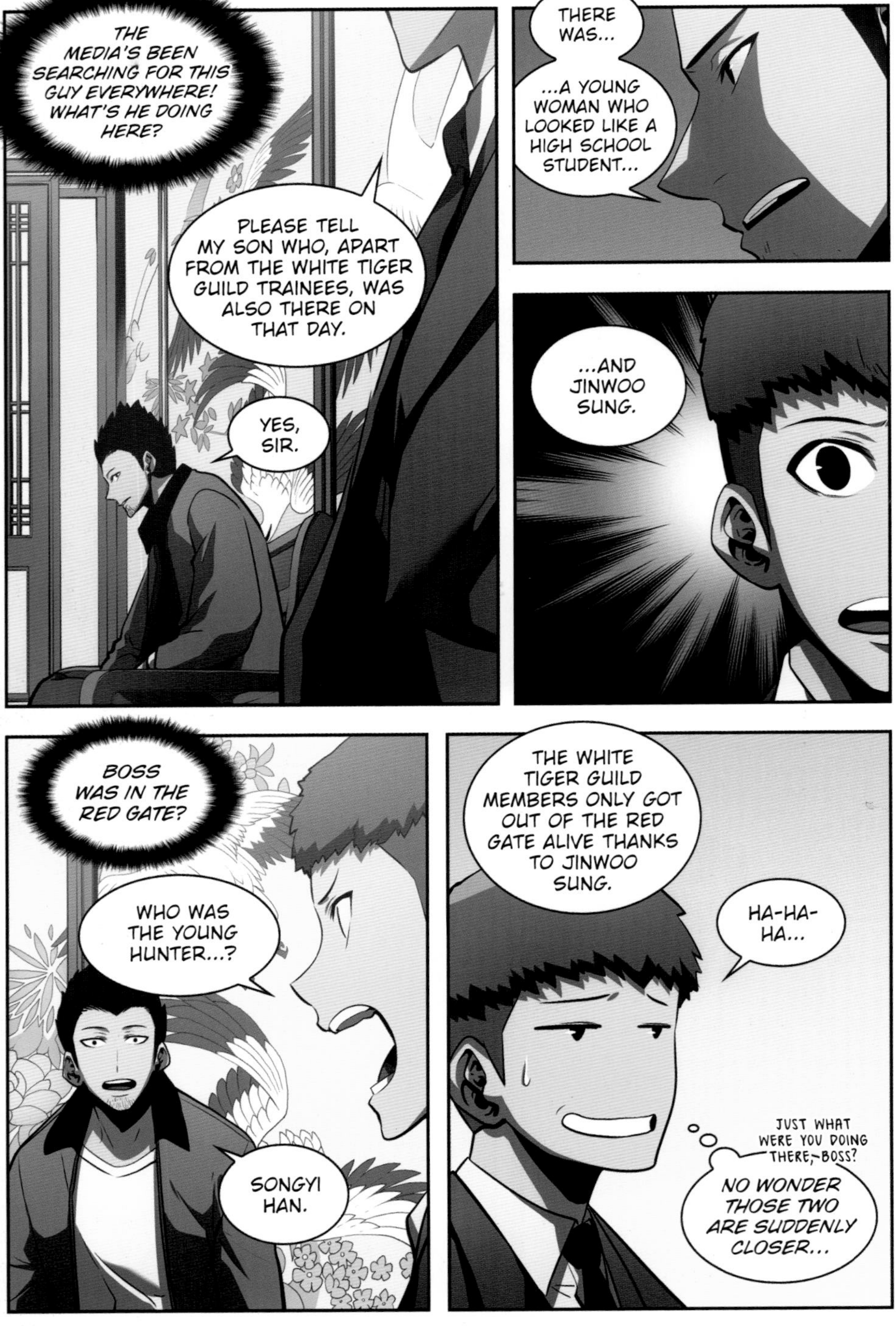
THE MEDIA'S BEEN SEARCHING FOR THIS GUY EVERYWHERE! WHAT'S HE DOING HERE?
PLEASE TELL MY SON WHO, APART FROM THE WHITE TIGER GUILD TRAINEES, WAS ALSO THERE ON THAT DAY.
YES, SIR.
THERE WAS...
...A YOUNG WOMAN WHO LOOKED LIKE A HIGH SCHOOL STUDENT...
...AND JINWOO SUNG.
BOSS WAS IN THE RED GATE?
WHO WAS THE YOUNG HUNTER...?
SONGYI HAN.
THE WHITE TIGER GUILD MEMBERS ONLY GOT OUT OF THE RED GATE ALIVE THANKS TO JINWOO SUNG.
HA-HA-HA...
JUST WHAT WERE YOU DOING THERE, BOSS?
NO WONDER THOSE TWO ARE SUDDENLY CLOSER...

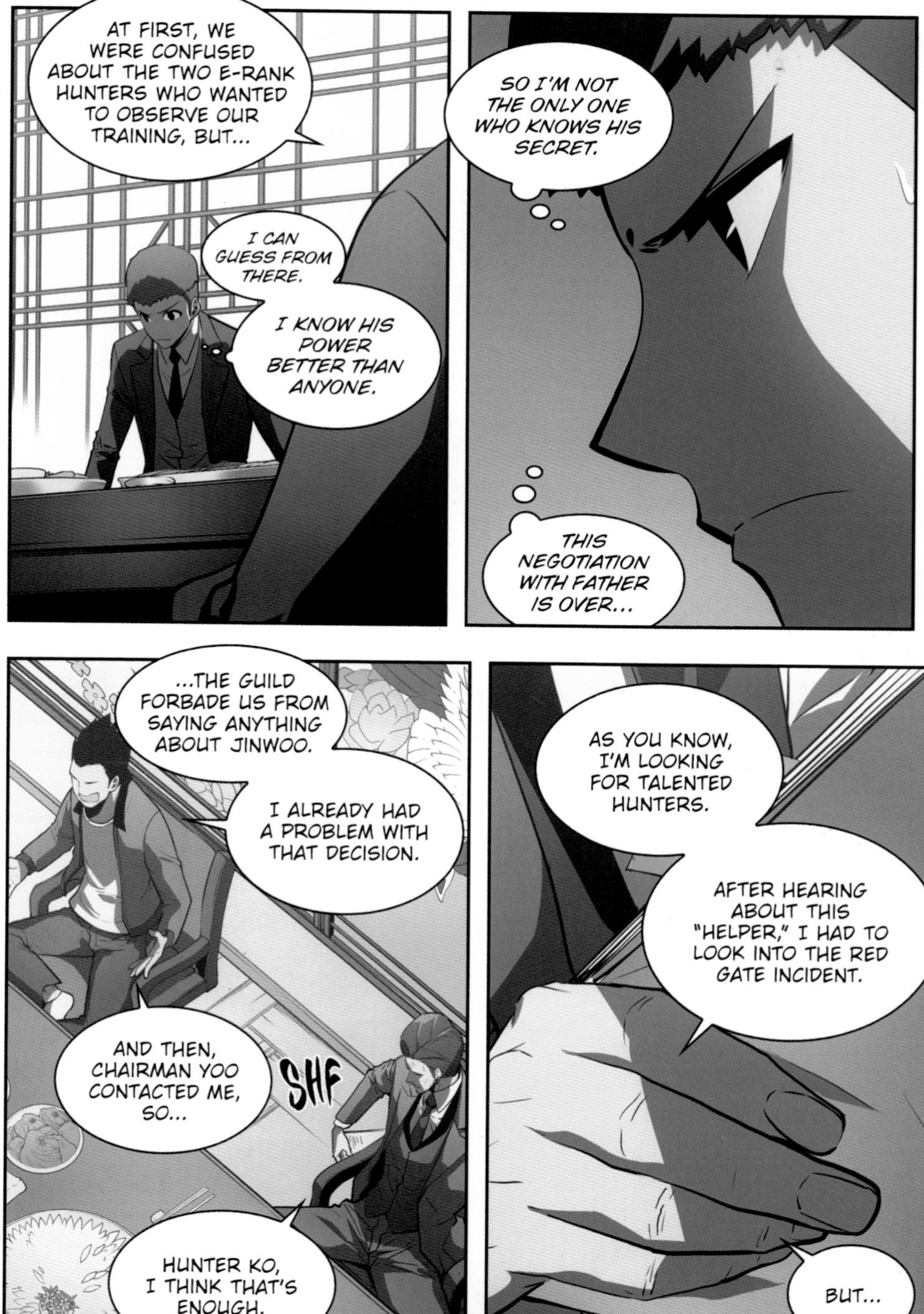
AT FIRST, WE WERE CONFUSED ABOUT THE TWO E-RANK HUNTERS WHO WANTED TO OBSERVE OUR TRAINING, BUT...
I CAN GUESS FROM THERE.
I KNOW HIS POWER BETTER THAN ANYONE.
SO I'M NOT THE ONLY ONE WHO KNOWS HIS SECRET.
THIS NEGOTIATION WITH FATHER IS OVER...
...THE GUILD FORBADE US FROM SAYING ANYTHING ABOUT JINWOO.
I ALREADY HAD A PROBLEM WITH THAT DECISION.
AND THEN, CHAIRMAN YOO CONTACTED ME, SO...
SHF
HUNTER KO, I THINK THAT'S ENOUGH.
AS YOU KNOW, I'M LOOKING FOR TALENTED HUNTERS.
AFTER HEARING ABOUT THIS "HELPER," I HAD TO LOOK INTO THE RED GATE INCIDENT.
BUT...

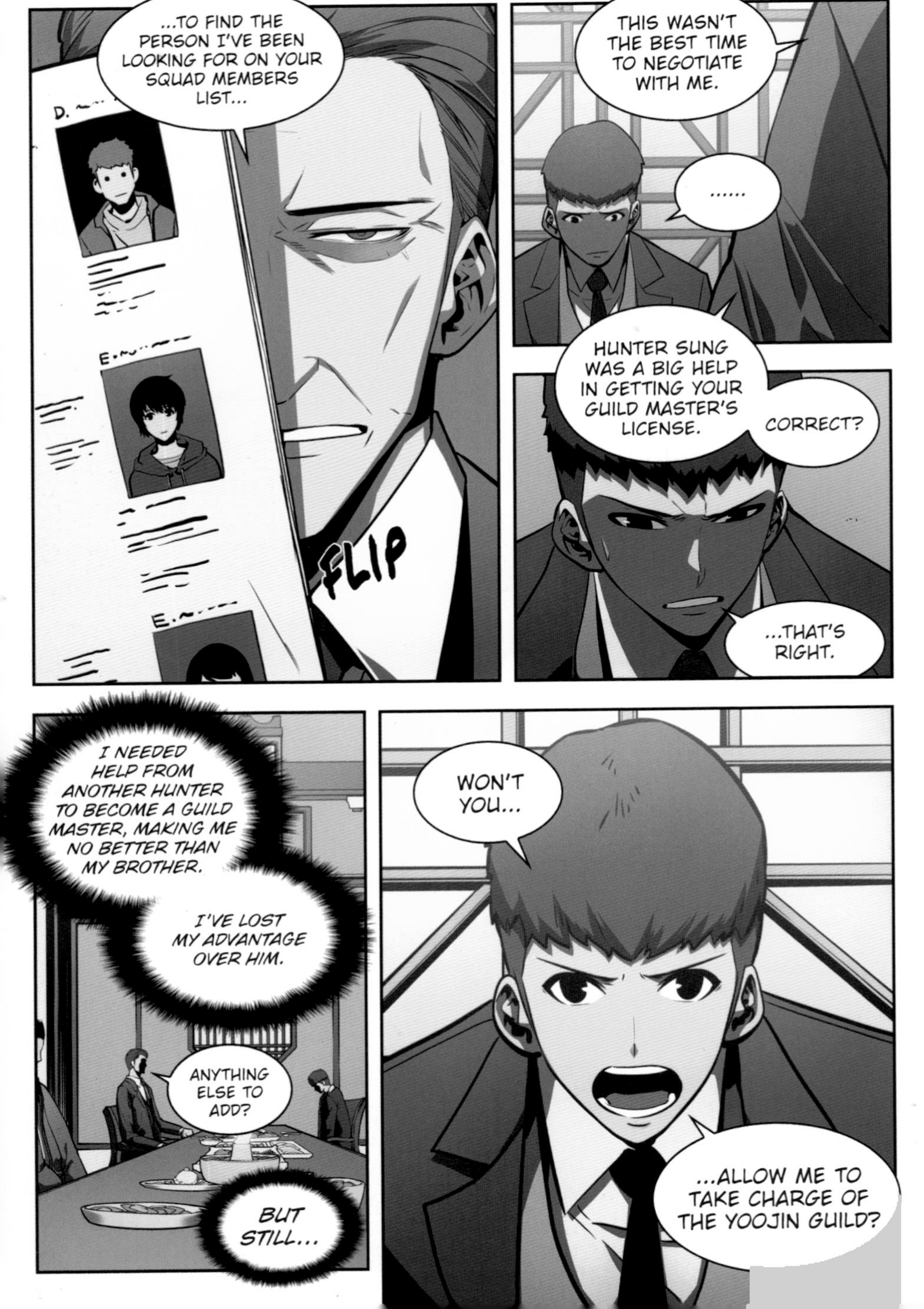
...TO FIND THE PERSON I'VE BEEN LOOKING FOR ON YOUR SQUAD MEMBERS LIST...
FLIP
THIS WASN'T THE BEST TIME TO NEGOTIATE WITH ME.
......
HUNTER SUNG WAS A BIG HELP IN GETTING YOUR GUILD MASTER'S LICENSE.
CORRECT?
...THAT'S RIGHT.
I NEEDED HELP FROM ANOTHER HUNTER TO BECOME A GUILD MASTER, MAKING ME NO BETTER THAN MY BROTHER.
I'VE LOST MY ADVANTAGE OVER HIM.
ANYTHING ELSE TO ADD?
BUT STILL...
WON'T YOU...
...ALLOW ME TO TAKE CHARGE OF THE YOOJIN GUILD?

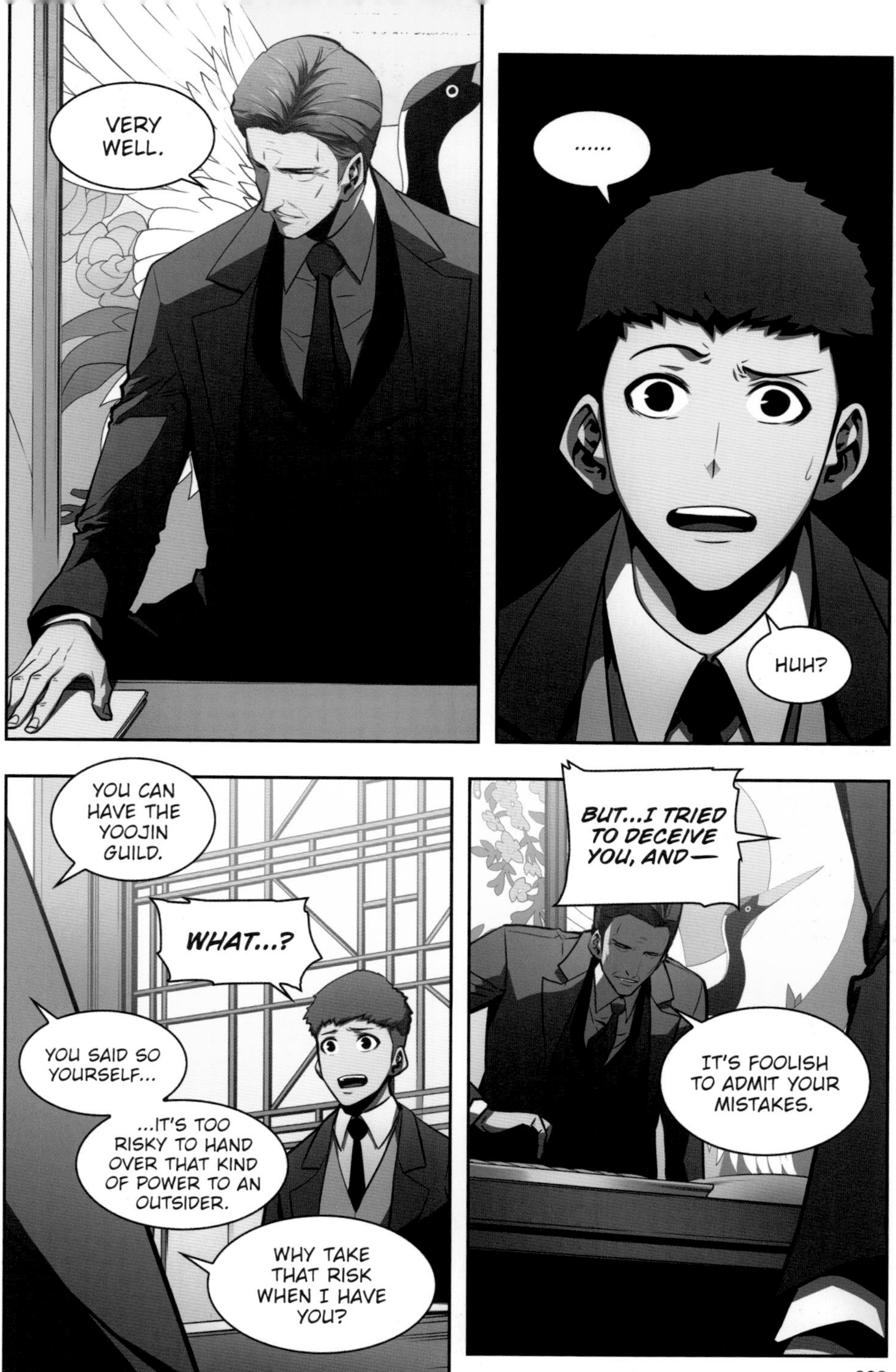
VERY WELL.
......
HUH?
YOU CAN HAVE THE YOOJIN GUILD.
WHAT...?
YOU SAID SO YOURSELF...
...IT'S TOO RISKY TO HAND OVER THAT KIND OF POWER TO AN OUTSIDER.
WHY TAKE THAT RISK WHEN I HAVE YOU?
BUT...I TRIED TO DECEIVE YOU, AND—
IT'S FOOLISH TO ADMIT YOUR MISTAKES.

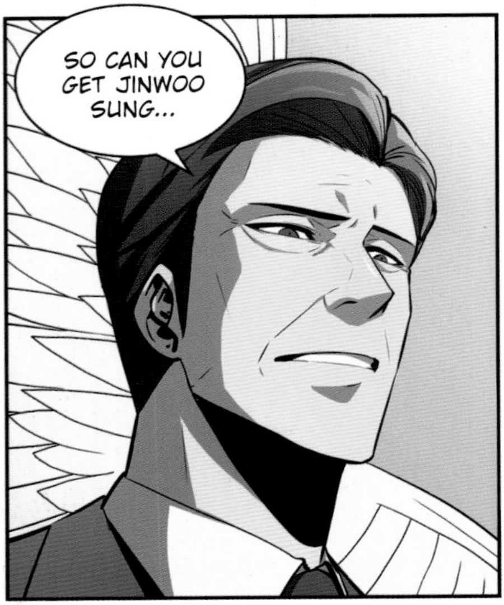
SO CAN YOU GET JINWOO SUNG...
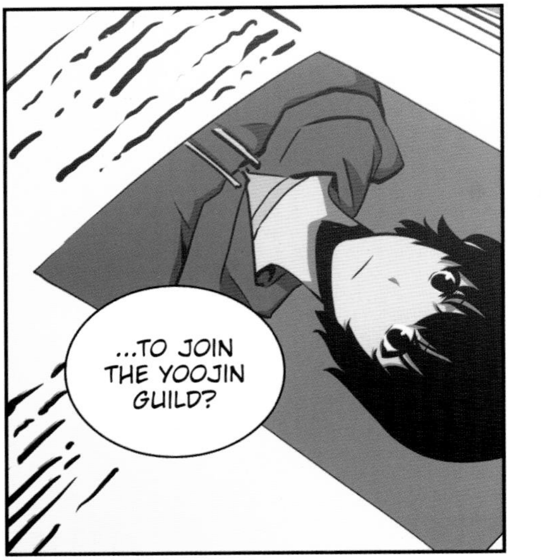
...TO JOIN THE YOOJIN GUILD?
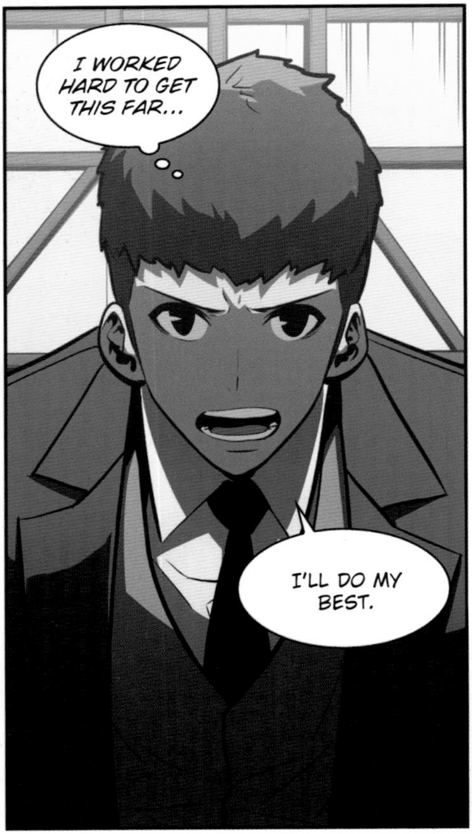
I WORKED HARD TO GET THIS FAR...
I'LL DO MY BEST.
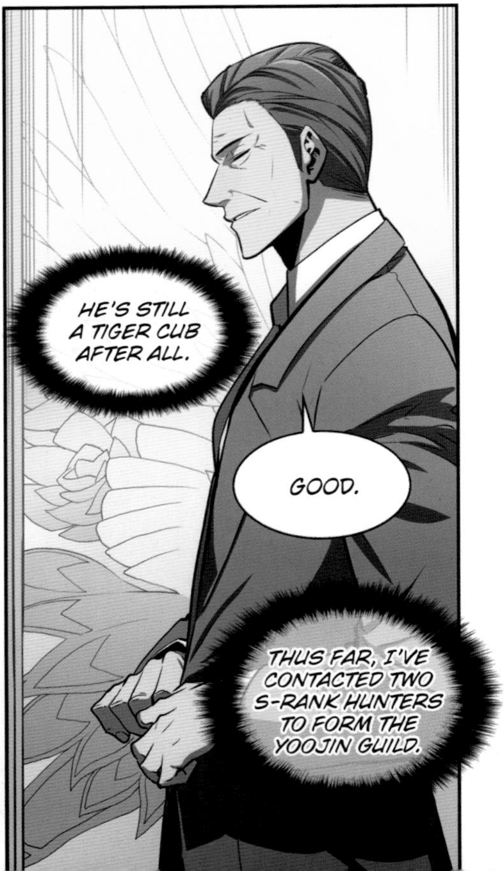
HE'S STILL A TIGER CUB AFTER ALL.
GOOD.
THUS FAR, I'VE CONTACTED TWO S-RANK HUNTERS TO FORM THE YOOJIN GUILD.

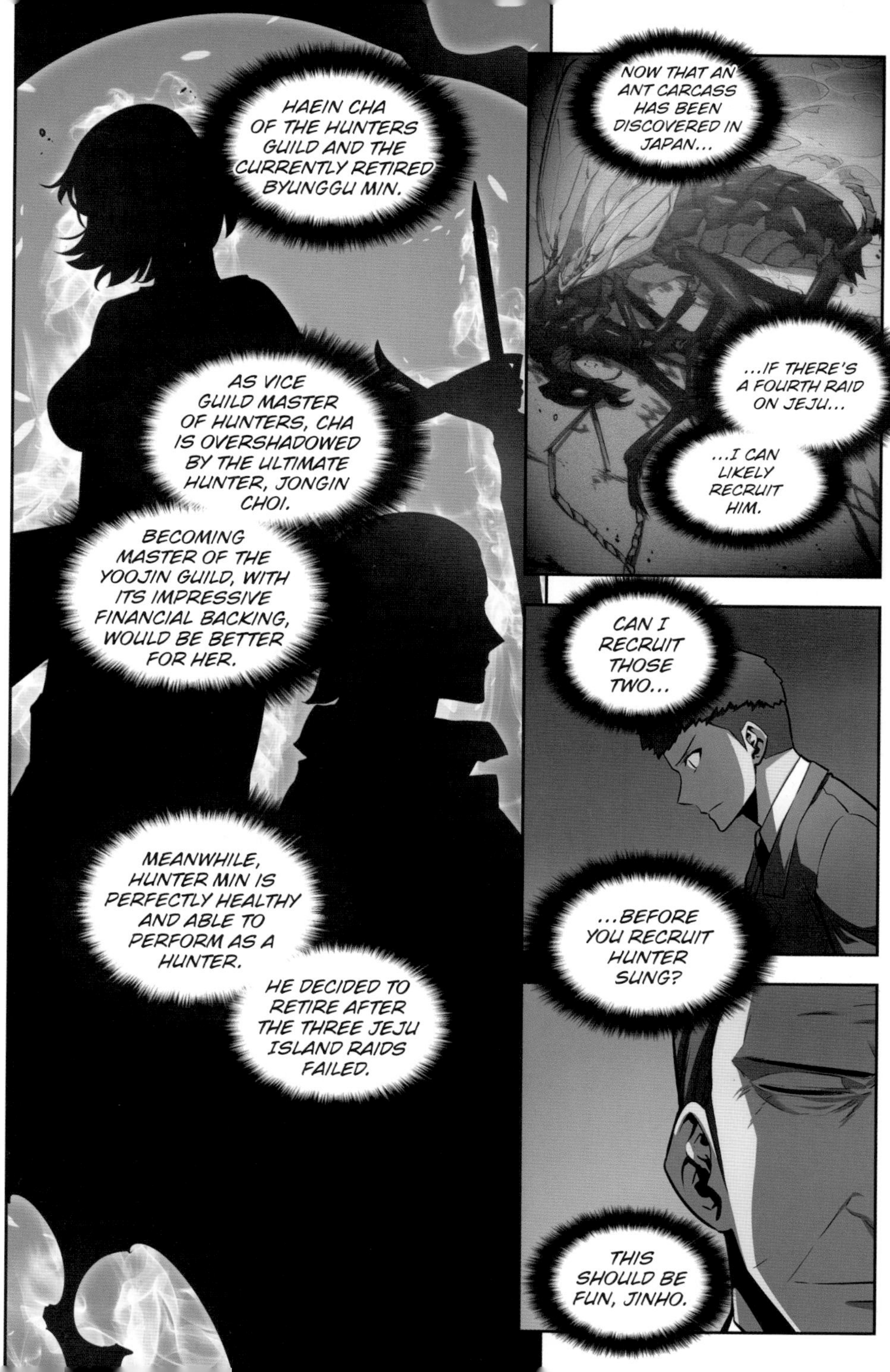
HAEIN CHA OF THE HUNTERS GUILD AND THE CURRENTLY RETIRED BYUNGGU MIN.
AS VICE GUILD MASTER OF HUNTERS, CHA IS OVERSHADOWED BY THE ULTIMATE HUNTER, JONGIN CHOI.
BECOMING MASTER OF THE YOOJIN GUILD, WITH ITS IMPRESSIVE FINANCIAL BACKING, WOULD BE BETTER FOR HER.
MEANWHILE, HUNTER MIN IS PERFECTLY HEALTHY AND ABLE TO PERFORM AS A HUNTER.
HE DECIDED TO RETIRE AFTER THE THREE JEJU ISLAND RAIDS FAILED.
NOW THAT AN ANT CARCASS HAS BEEN DISCOVERED IN JAPAN...
...IF THERE'S A FOURTH RAID ON JEJU...
...I CAN LIKELY RECRUIT HIM.
CAN I RECRUIT THOSE TWO...
...BEFORE YOU RECRUIT HUNTER SUNG?
THIS SHOULD BE FUN, JINHO.

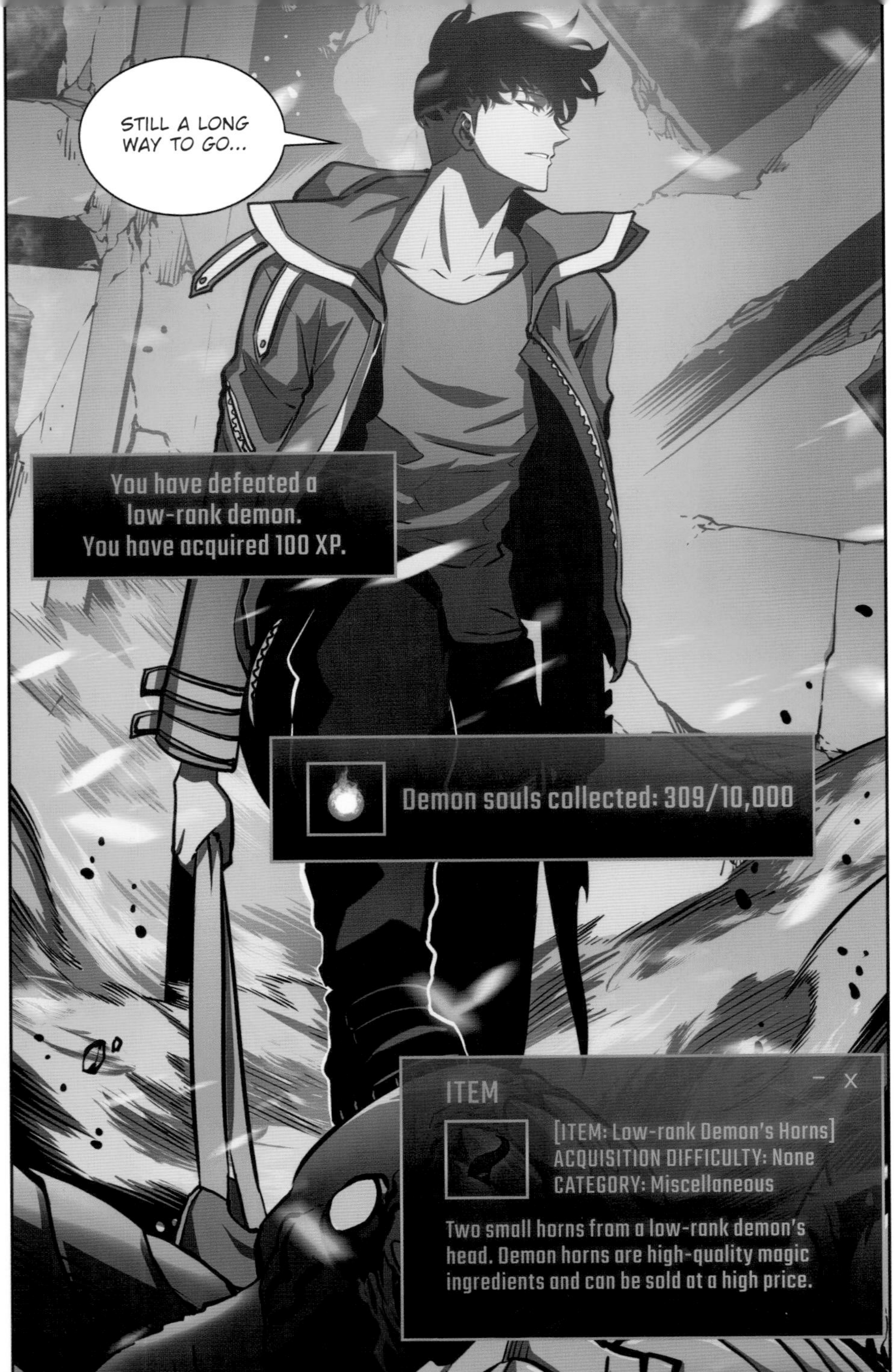
STILL A LONG WAY TO GO...
You have defeated a low-rank demon. You have acquired 100 XP.
Demon souls collected: 309/10,000
ITEM
[ITEM: Low-rank Demon's Horns]
ACQUISITION DIFFICULTY: None
CATEGORY: Miscellaneous
Two small horns from a low-rank demon's head. Demon horns are high-quality magic ingredients and can be sold at a high price.

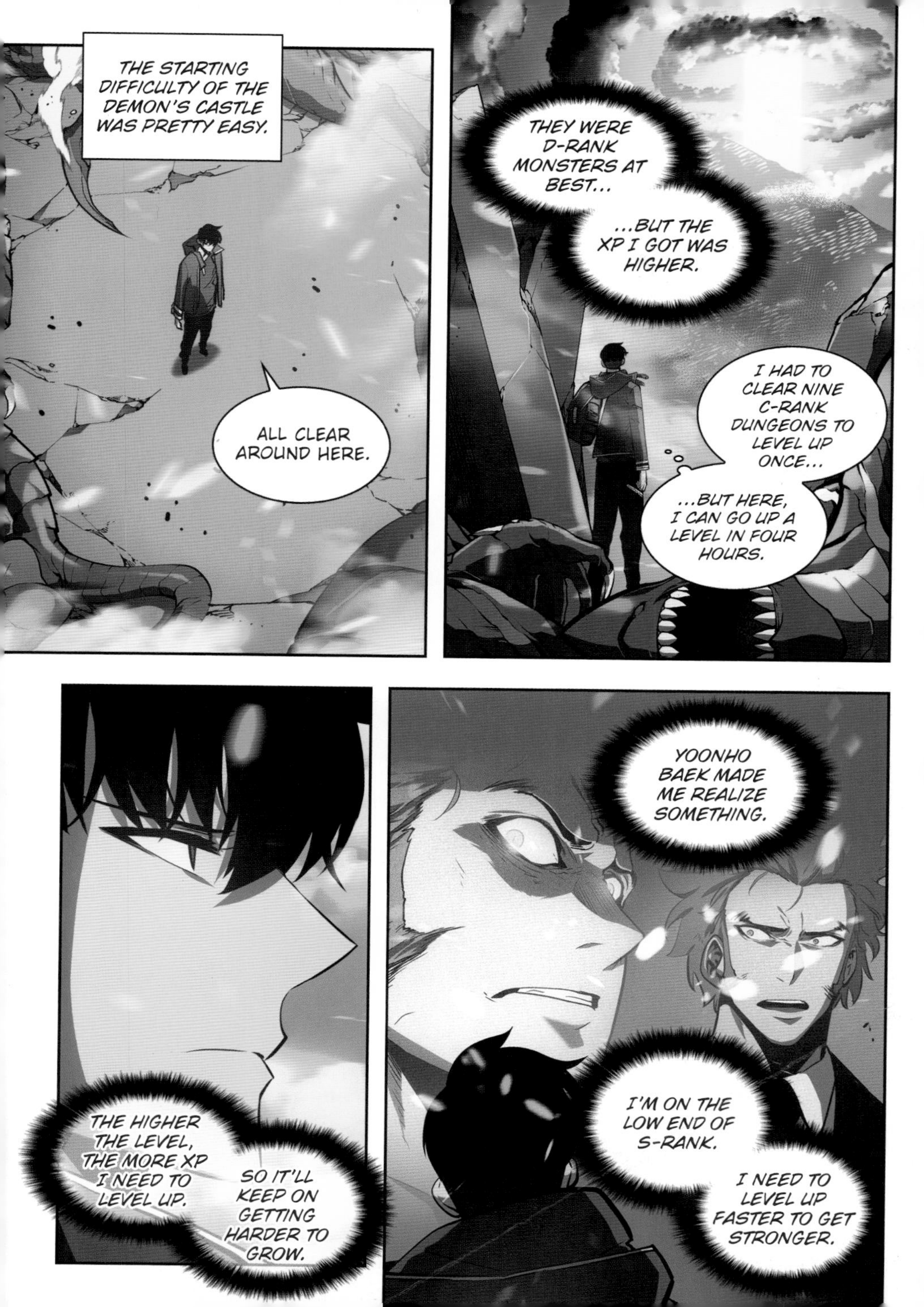
THE STARTING DIFFICULTY OF THE DEMON'S CASTLE WAS PRETTY EASY.
ALL CLEAR AROUND HERE.
THEY WERE D-RANK MONSTERS AT BEST...
...BUT THE XP I GOT WAS HIGHER.
I HAD TO CLEAR NINE C-RANK DUNGEONS TO LEVEL UP ONCE...
...BUT HERE, I CAN GO UP A LEVEL IN FOUR HOURS.
THE HIGHER THE LEVEL, THE MORE XP I NEED TO LEVEL UP.
SO IT'LL KEEP ON GETTING HARDER TO GROW.
YOONHO BAEK MADE ME REALIZE SOMETHING.
I'M ON THE LOW END OF S-RANK.
I NEED TO LEVEL UP FASTER TO GET STRONGER.

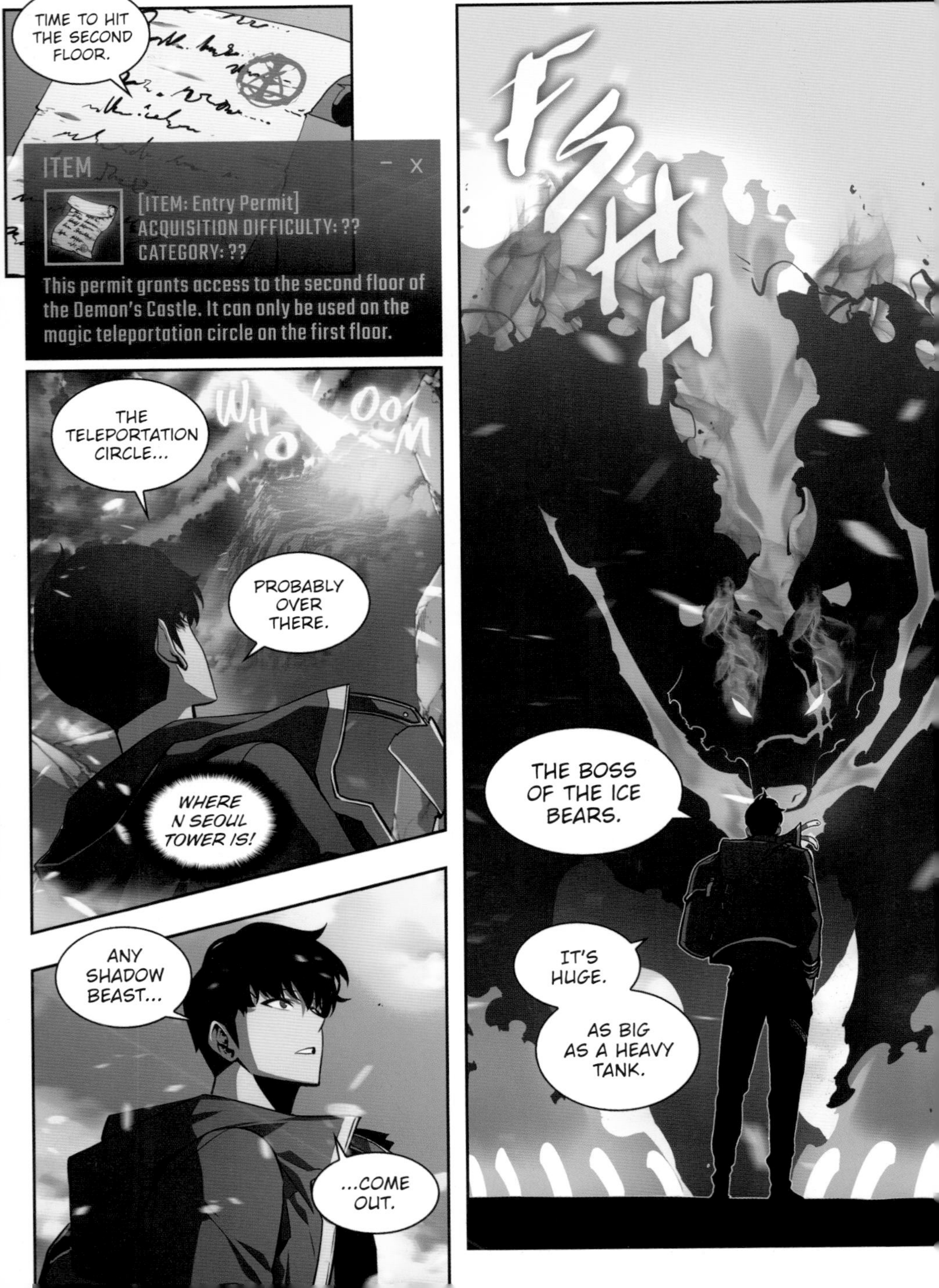
TIME TO HIT THE SECOND FLOOR.
ITEM
[ITEM: Entry Permit]
ACQUISITION DIFFICULTY: ??
CATEGORY: ??
This permit grants access to the second floor of the Demon's Castle. It can only be used on the magic teleportation circle on the first floor.
THE TELEPORTATION CIRCLE...
WHOOOM
PROBABLY OVER THERE.
WHERE N SEOUL TOWER IS!
ANY SHADOW BEAST...
...COME OUT.
FSHHH
THE BOSS OF THE ICE BEARS.
IT'S HUGE.
AS BIG AS A HEAVY TANK.

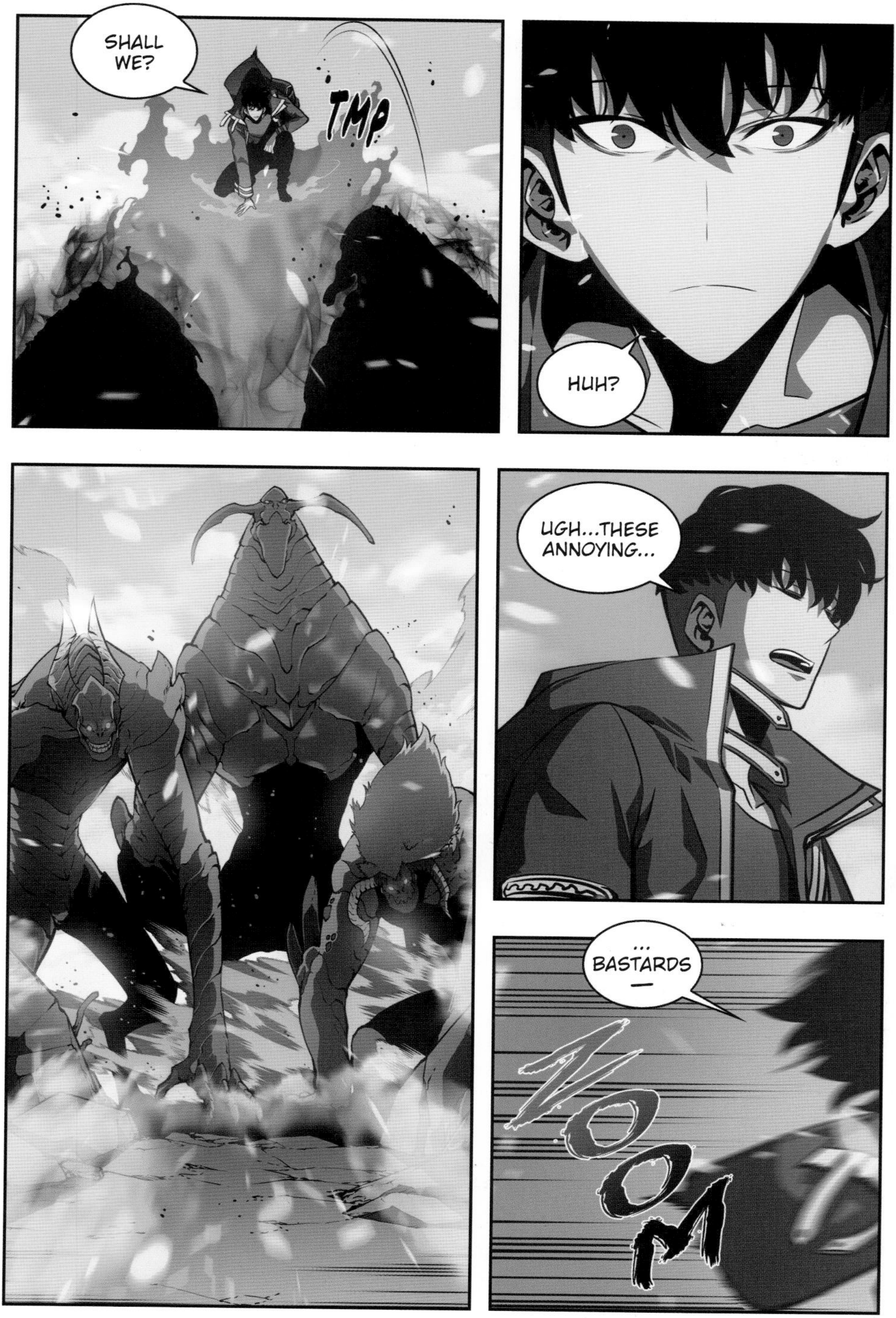
SHALL WE?
TMP
HUH?
UGH...THESE ANNOYING...
...BASTARDS—
ZOOM

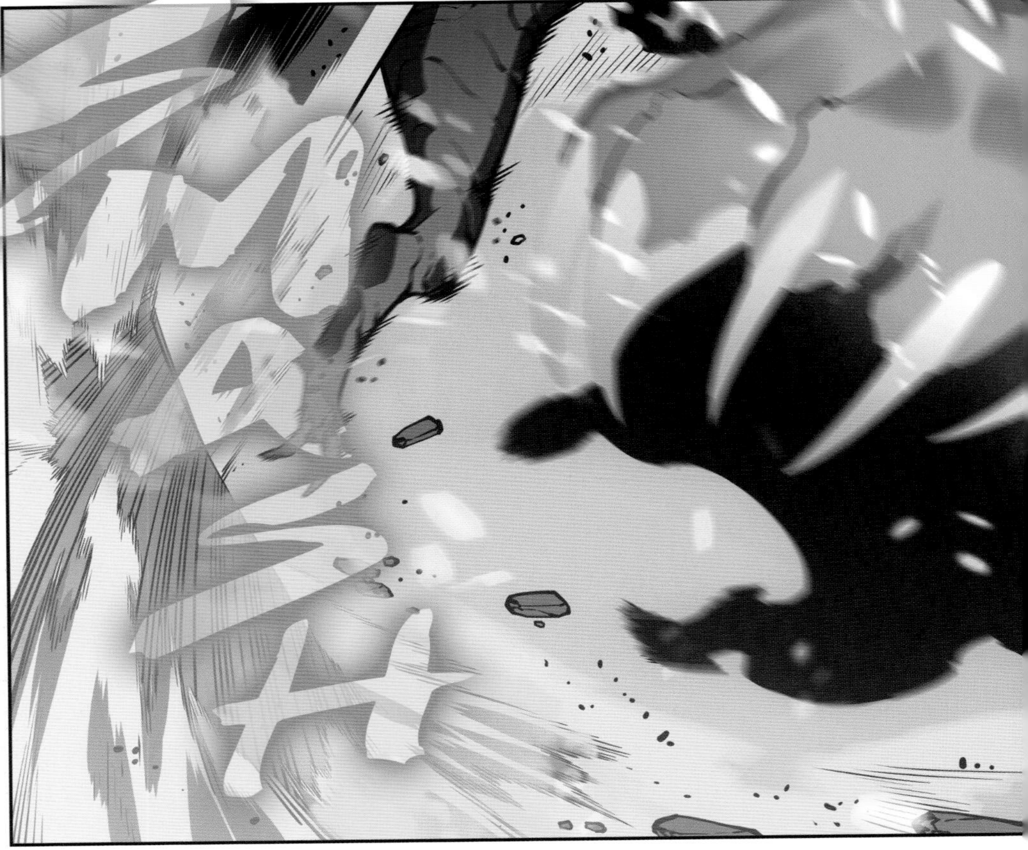

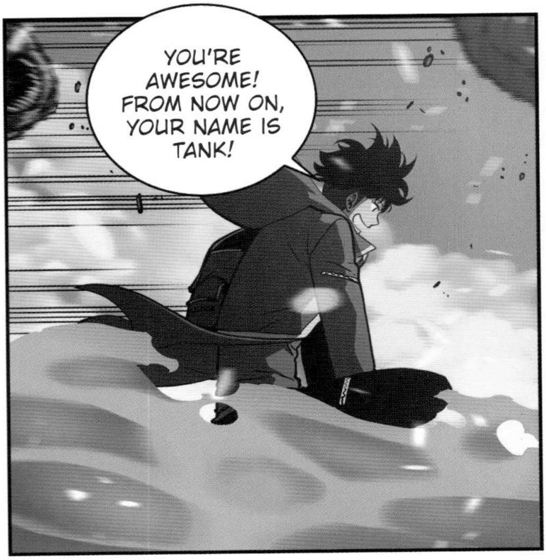
YOU'RE AWESOME! FROM NOW ON, YOUR NAME IS TANK!

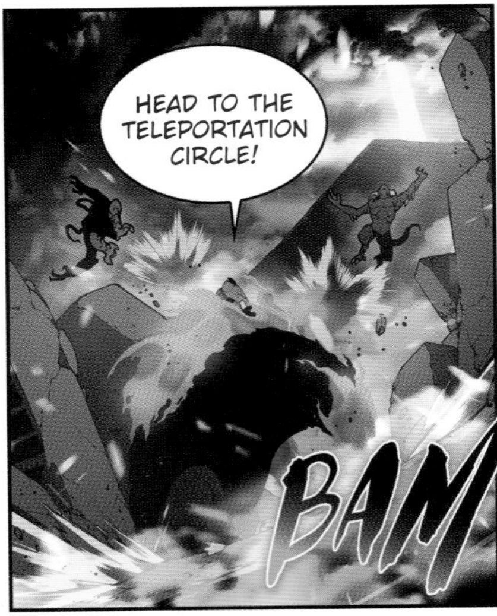
HEAD TO THE TELEPORTATION CIRCLE!
BAM

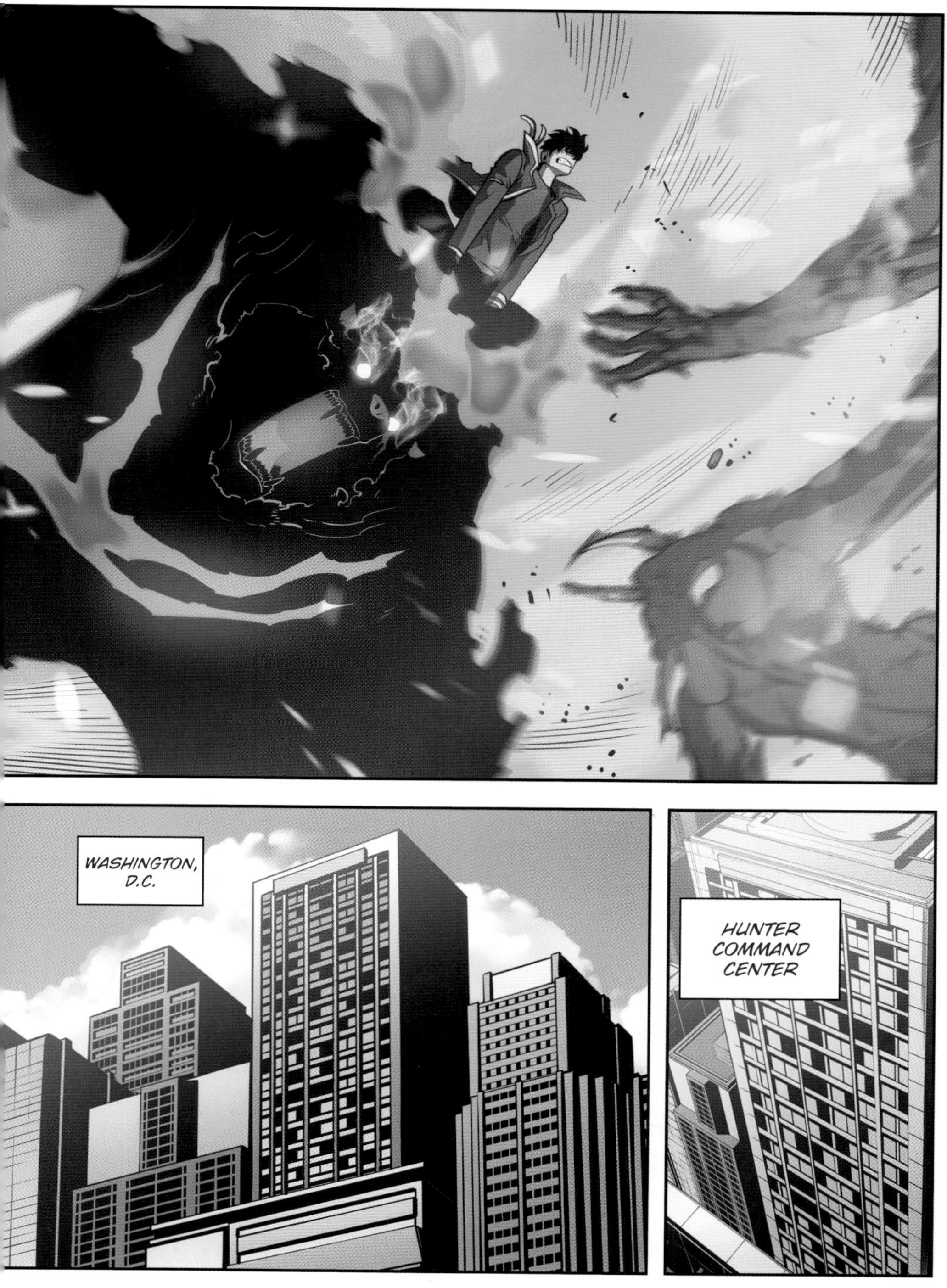
WASHINGTON, D.C.
HUNTER COMMAND CENTER

<Is that him?>

<Yes, sir.>

ASSISTANT DIRECTOR (A.D.) OF HUNTER COMMAND CENTER

<Who is he?>

<He insists he's a Korean hunter.>

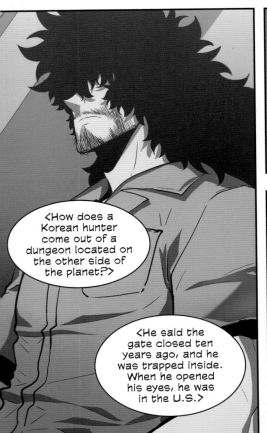

<How does a Korean hunter come out of a dungeon located on the other side of the planet?>

<He said the gate closed ten years ago, and he was trapped inside. When he opened his eyes, he was in the U.S.>

IT WAS AN UNPRECE-DENTED DISCOVERY.

A HUMAN FOUND INSIDE A DUNGEON. A STRIKE SQUAD WITH SEVERAL A-RANK HUNTERS WERE HELPLESS AGAINST HIM.

<Don't just stand there.>

<Go pry more information out of him.>

<Sir, we're investigating the possibility that this may be a magic beast possessing a human's memories.>

<We need an S-rank hunter at least. Otherwise, all of Washington, D.C. may be in danger, sir.>

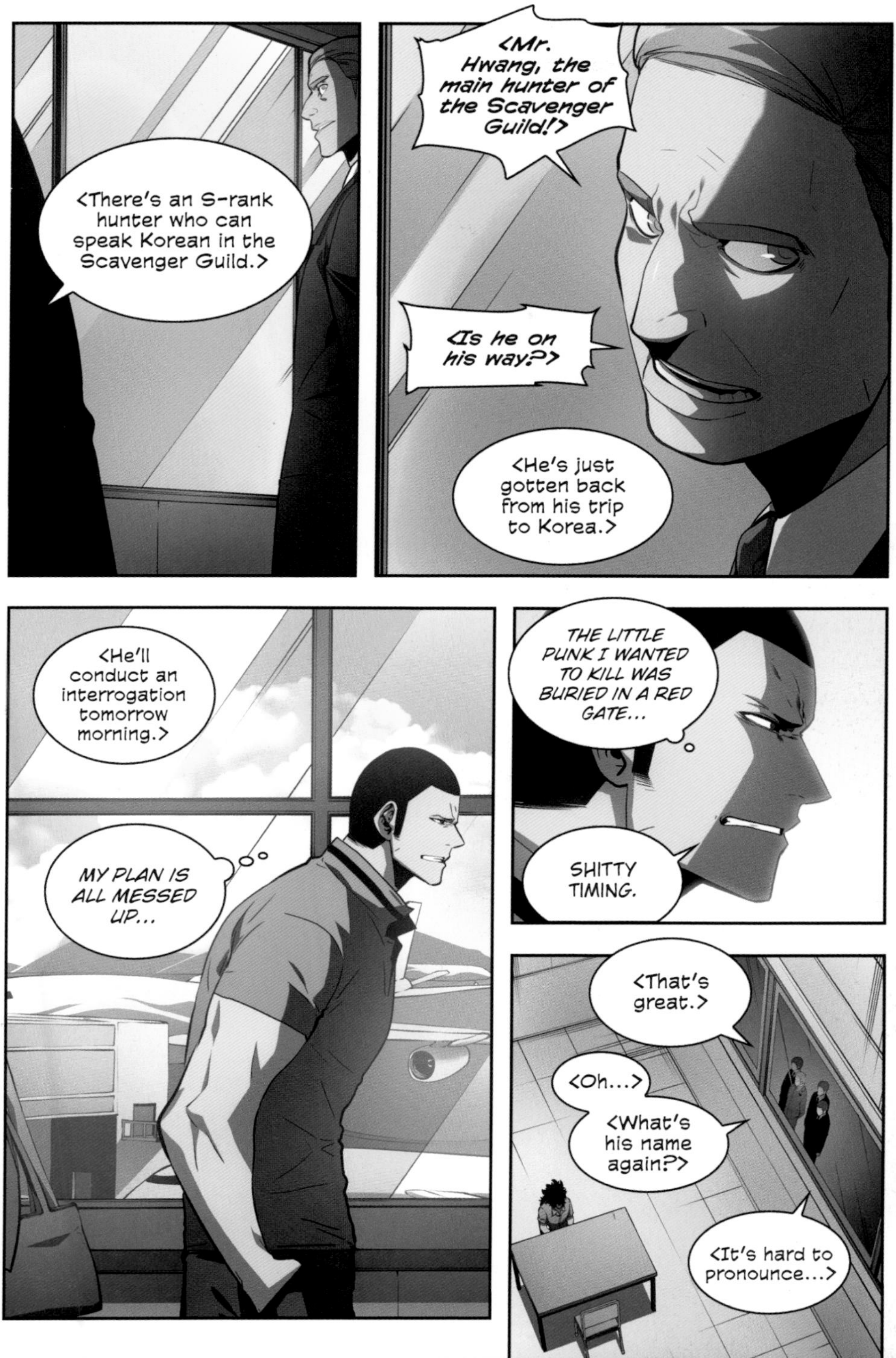
<There's an S-rank hunter who can speak Korean in the Scavenger Guild.>
<Mr. Hwang, the main hunter of the Scavenger Guild!>
<Is he on his way?>
<He's just gotten back from his trip to Korea.>
<He'll conduct an interrogation tomorrow morning.>
MY PLAN IS ALL MESSED UP...
THE LITTLE PUNK I WANTED TO KILL WAS BURIED IN A RED GATE...
SHITTY TIMING.
<That's great.>
<Oh...>
<What's his name again?>
<It's hard to pronounce...>

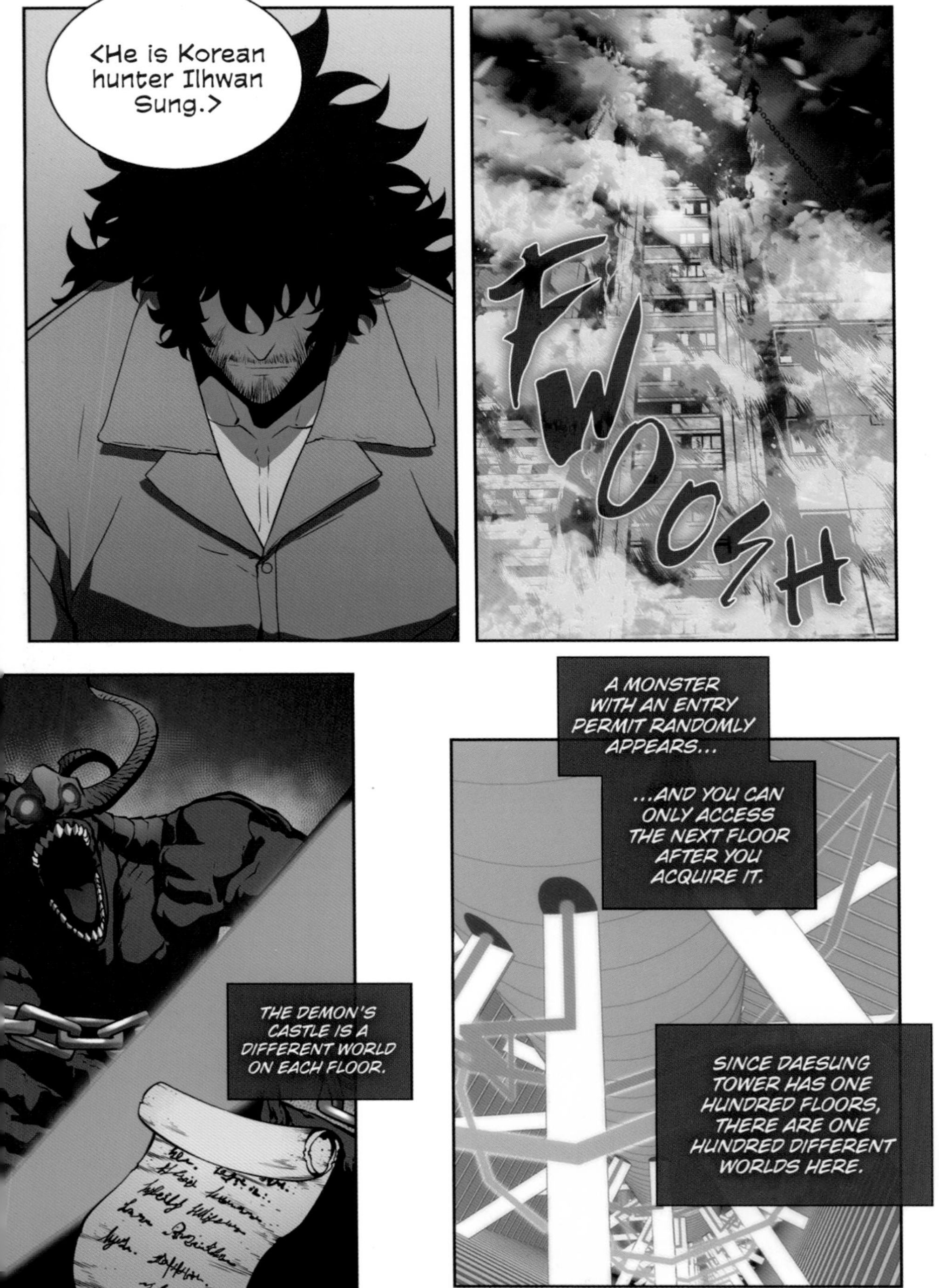
<He is Korean hunter Ilhwan Sung.>
FWOOSH
THE DEMON'S CASTLE IS A DIFFERENT WORLD ON EACH FLOOR.
A MONSTER WITH AN ENTRY PERMIT RANDOMLY APPEARS...
...AND YOU CAN ONLY ACCESS THE NEXT FLOOR AFTER YOU ACQUIRE IT.
SINCE DAESUNG TOWER HAS ONE HUNDRED FLOORS, THERE ARE ONE HUNDRED DIFFERENT WORLDS HERE.

2F...

3F...

4F...

27F.

HE PICKED UP SPEED THE HIGHER HE WENT.

SLASH

You have defeated a mid-rank demon.
You have acquired 300 XP.
You have acquired 1 demon soul.

The level of [Skill: Ruler's Hand] has increased.

MID-RANK DEMONS ARE JUST AS POWERFUL AS MID- TO HIGH-C-RANK MAGIC BEASTS?

THE LEVEL OF HIGH-RANK DEMONS WILL PROBABLY INCREASE EXPONENTIALLY.

THERE'S A BIG DIFFERENCE BETWEEN AN A-RANK HUNTER AND AN S-RANK HUNTER TOO.

Demon souls collected:
2,116/10,000

THE PROBLEM— IT WAS A RACE AGAINST TIME.

IF THERE ARE REALLY A HUNDRED FLOORS HERE, I MAY NOT BE ABLE TO REACH THE TOP FLOOR IN A WEEK.

WHEN HE FIRST ACQUIRED THE DEMON CASTLE'S KEY TWO MONTHS AGO, JINWOO HAD FEARED THE DUNGEON MIGHT BE S-RANK.

BUT THAT ANXIETY BEGAN TO FADE OVER TIME AS THE BATTLES WERE MUCH EASIER THAN HE EXPECTED.

47F...

48F...

49F...

50F.

Demon souls collected:
2,581/10,000

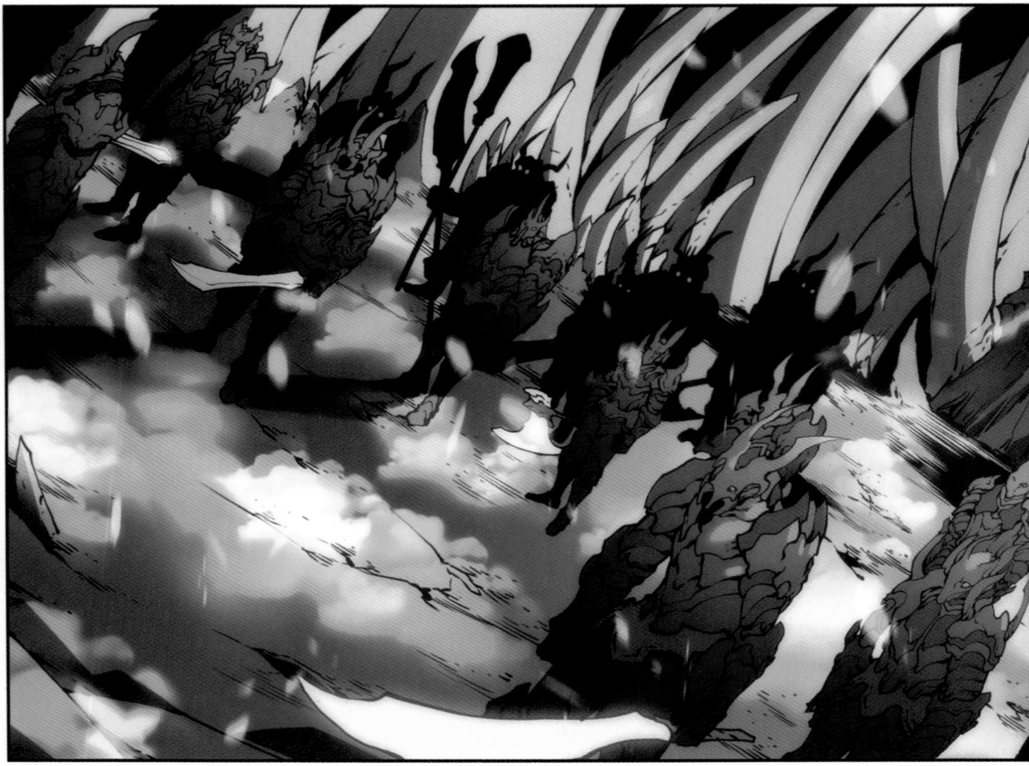

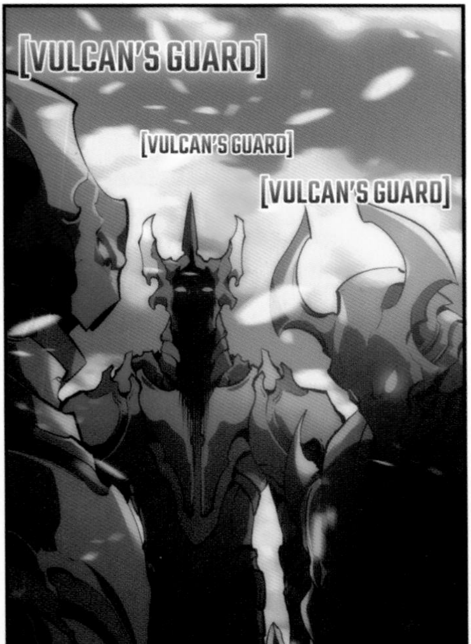
[VULCAN'S GUARD]
[VULCAN'S GUARD]
[VULCAN'S GUARD]

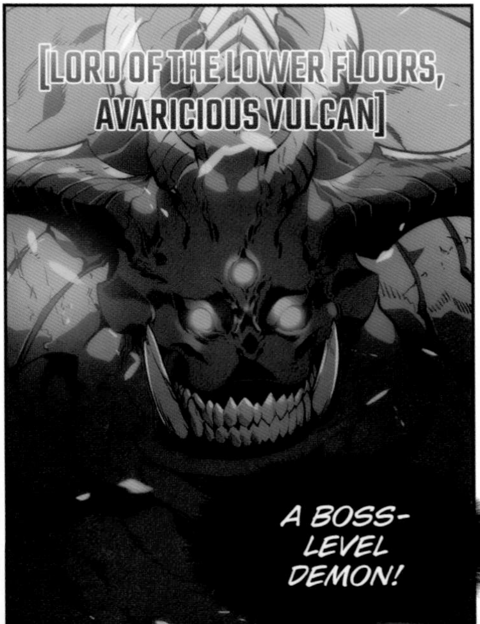
[LORD OF THE LOWER FLOORS, AVARICIOUS VULCAN]
A BOSS-LEVEL DEMON!

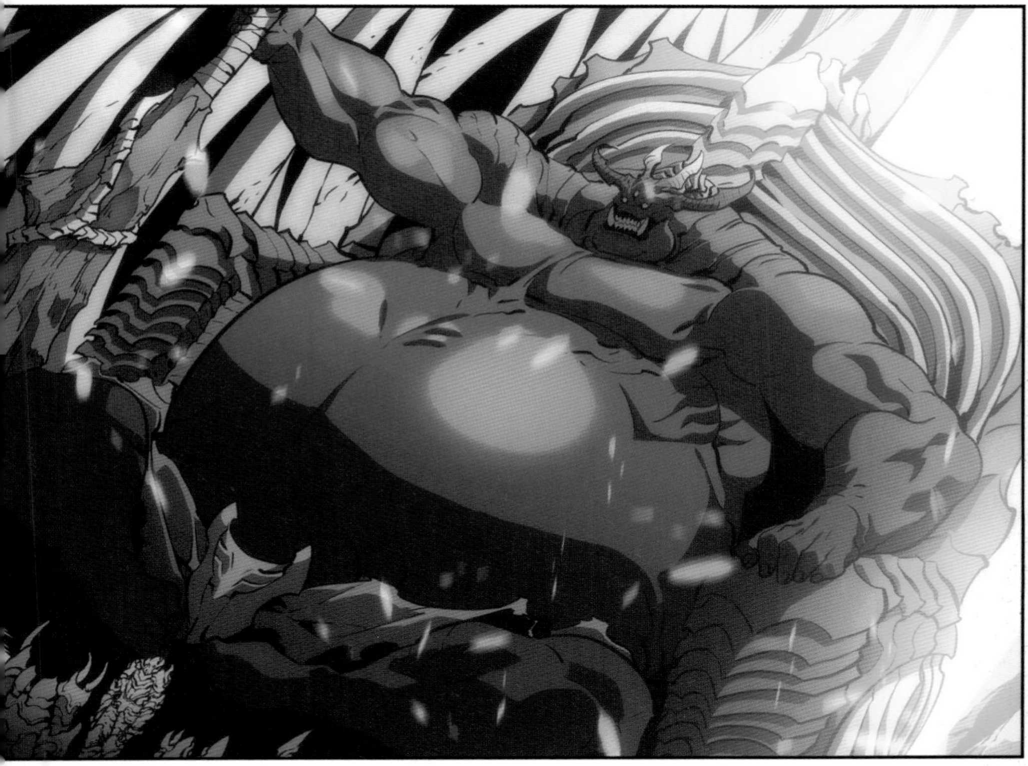
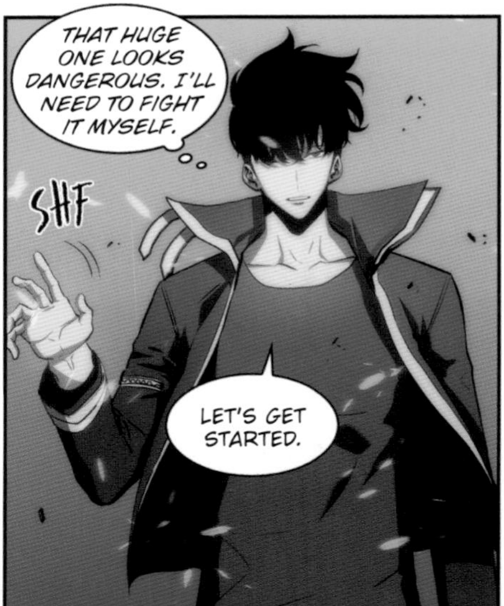
THAT HUGE ONE LOOKS DANGEROUS. I'LL NEED TO FIGHT IT MYSELF.
SHF
LET'S GET STARTED.
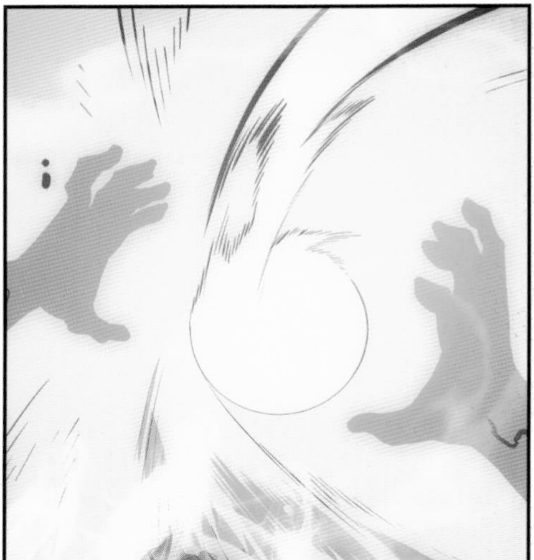

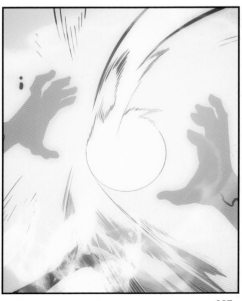

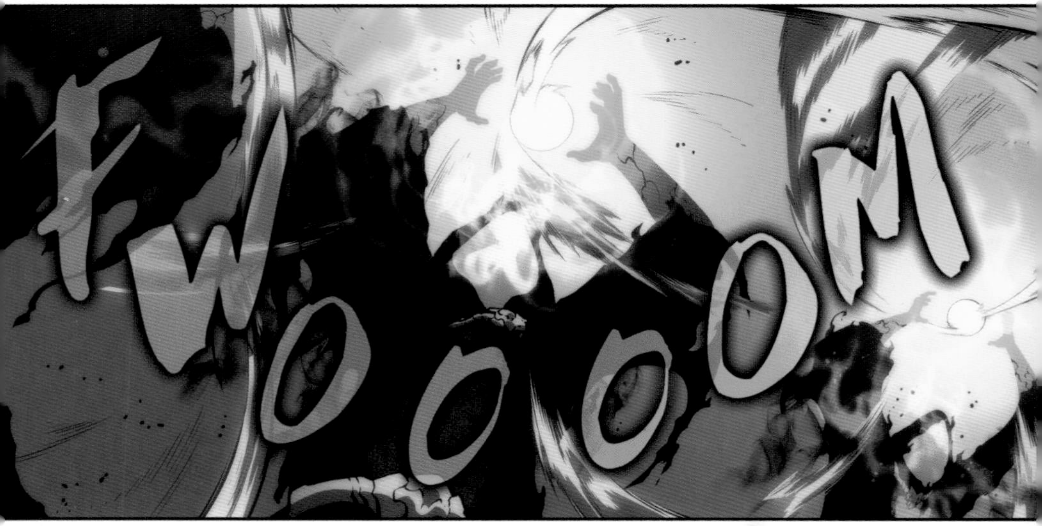
FWOOOOOM
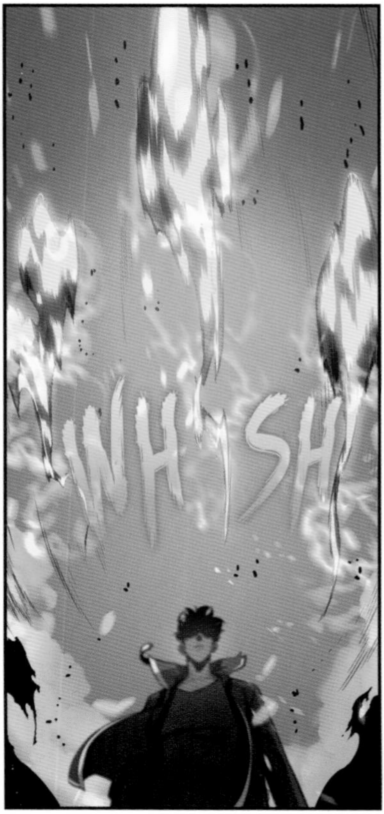
WHISH
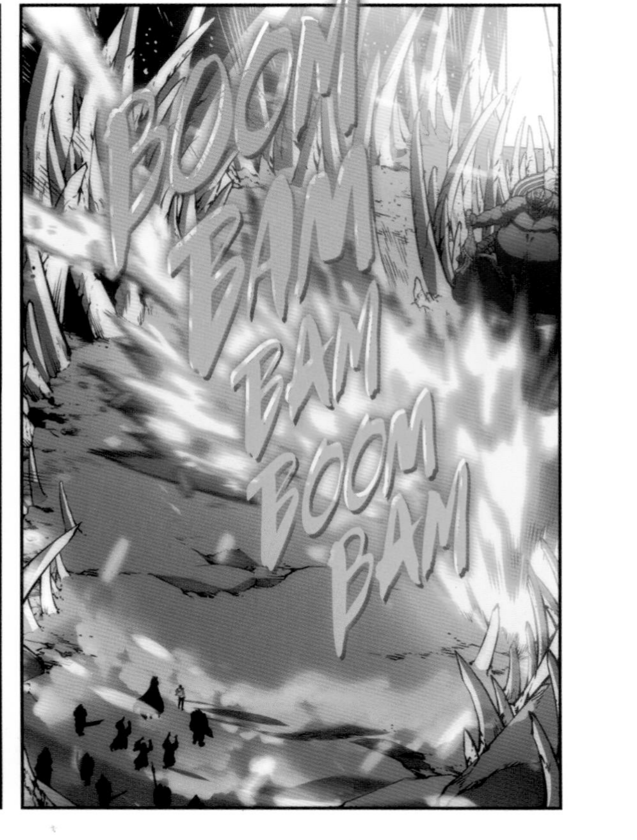
BOOM
BAM
BAM
BOOM
BAM

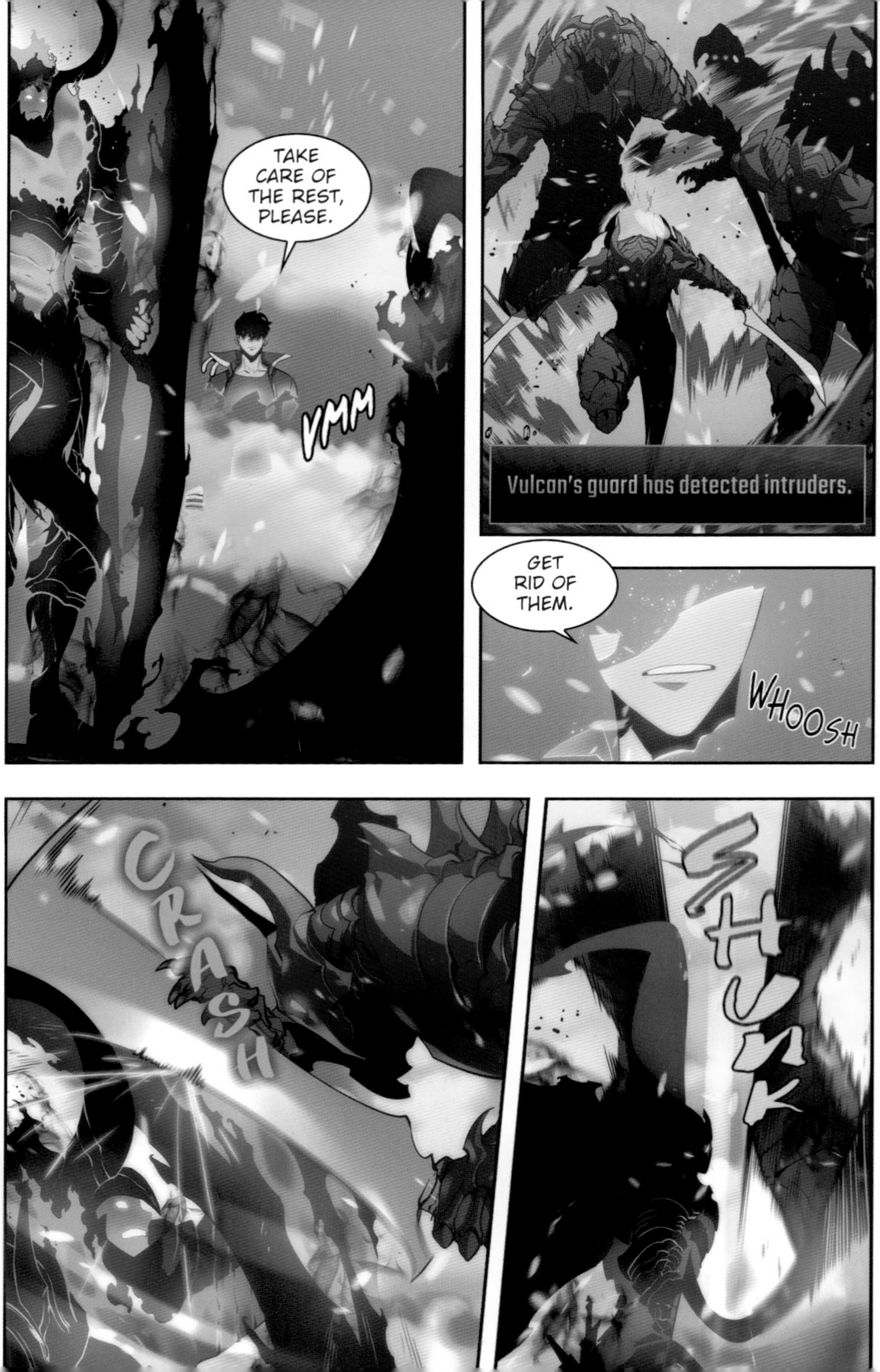
TAKE CARE OF THE REST, PLEASE.
VMM
Vulcan's guard has detected intruders.
GET RID OF THEM.
WHOOSH
CRASH
SHUNK

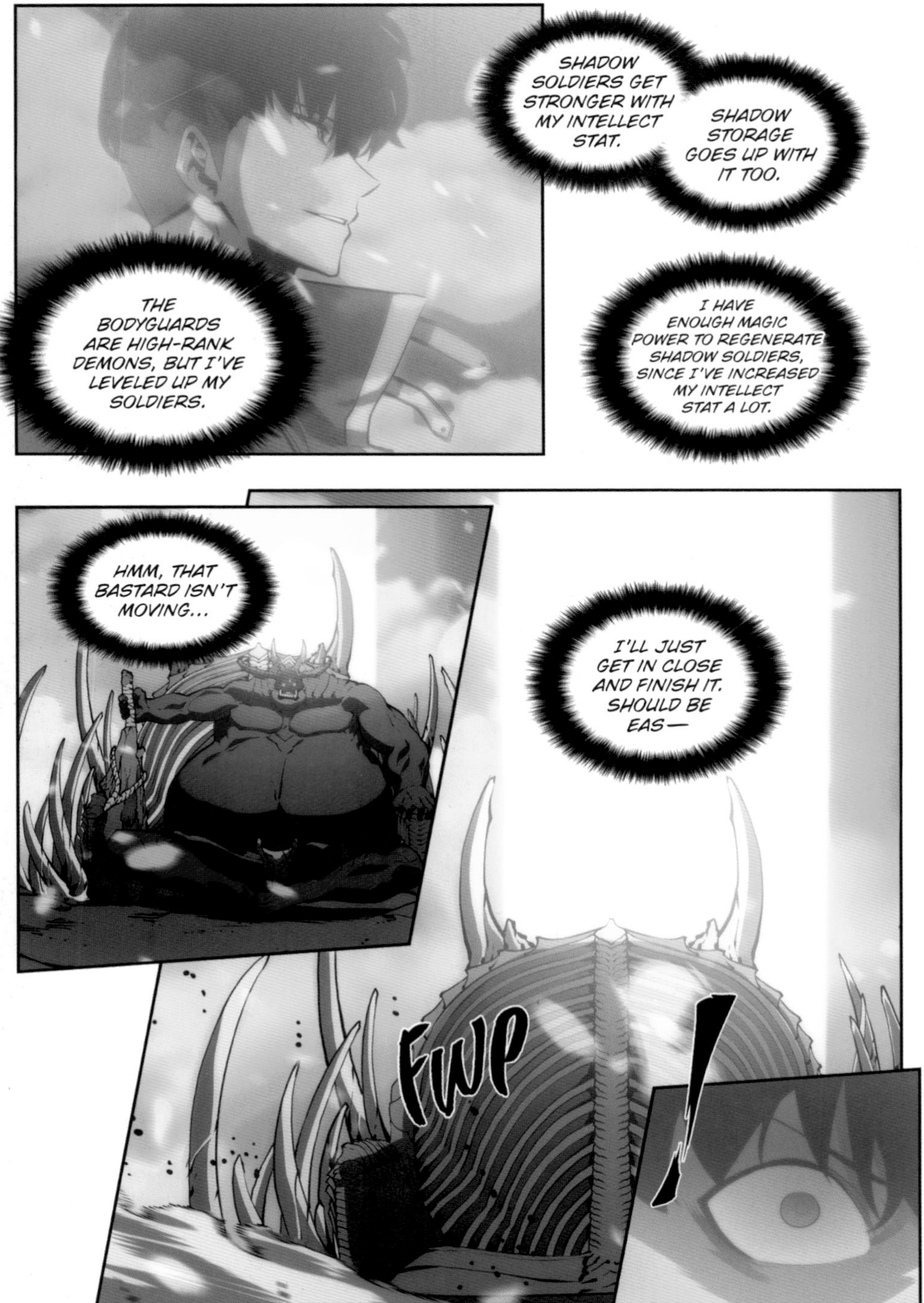
SHADOW SOLDIERS GET STRONGER WITH MY INTELLECT STAT.
SHADOW STORAGE GOES UP WITH IT TOO.
THE BODYGUARDS ARE HIGH-RANK DEMONS, BUT I'VE LEVELED UP MY SOLDIERS.
I HAVE ENOUGH MAGIC POWER TO REGENERATE SHADOW SOLDIERS, SINCE I'VE INCREASED MY INTELLECT STAT A LOT.
HMM, THAT BASTARD ISN'T MOVING...
I'LL JUST GET IN CLOSE AND FINISH IT. SHOULD BE EAS—
FWP
!

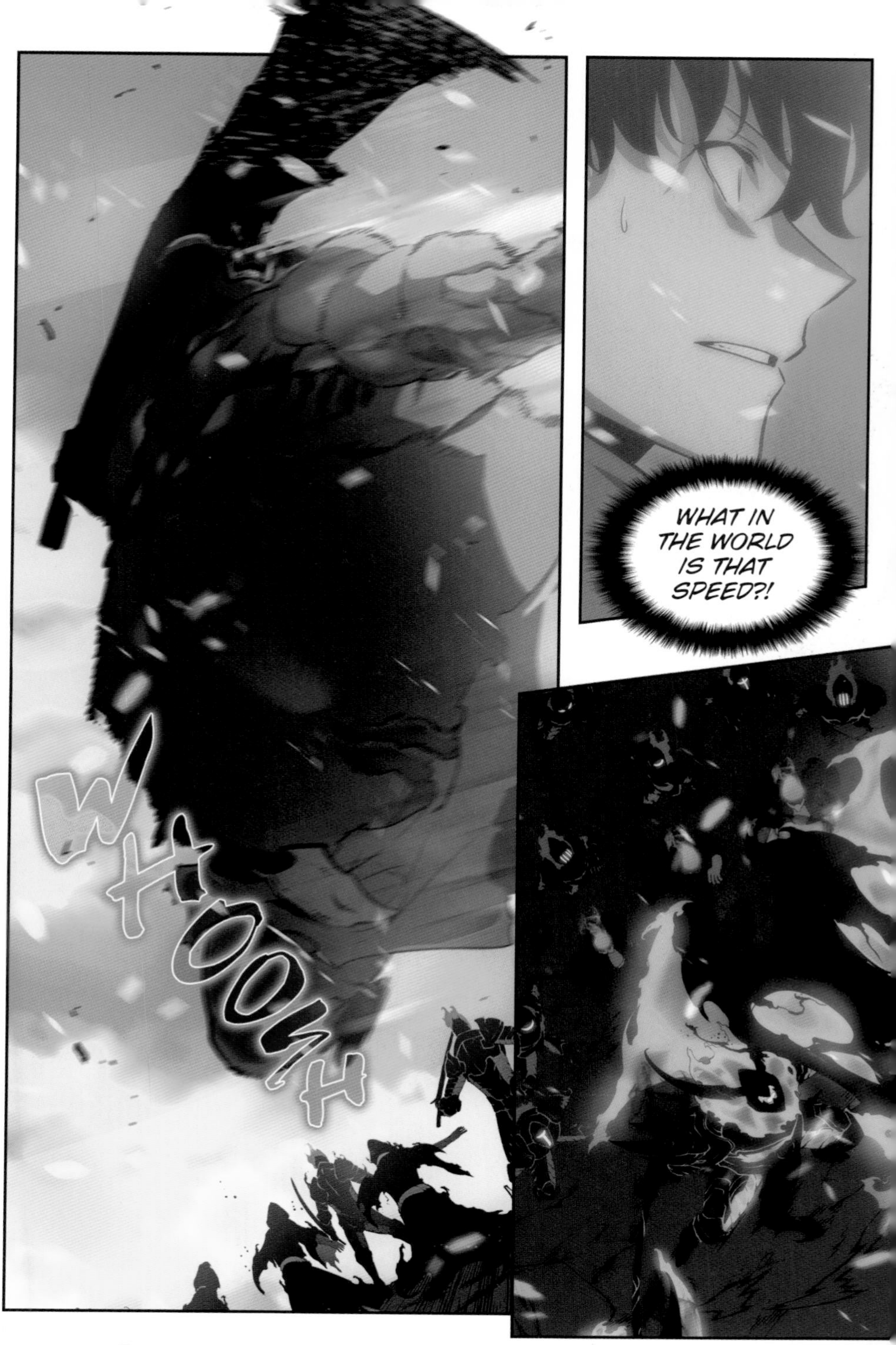
WHOOSH
WHAT IN THE WORLD IS THAT SPEED?!

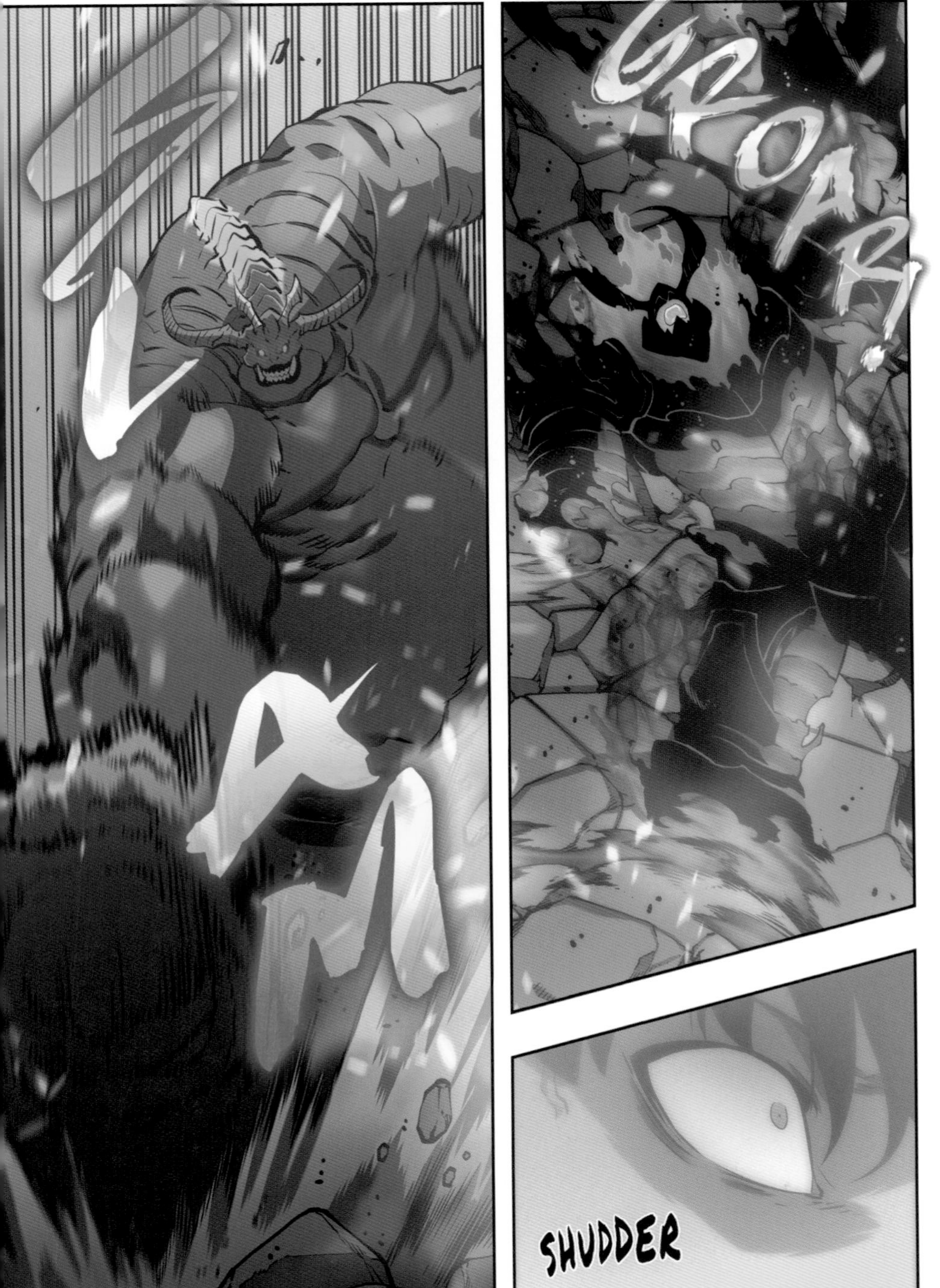
GROAR!
SHUDDER

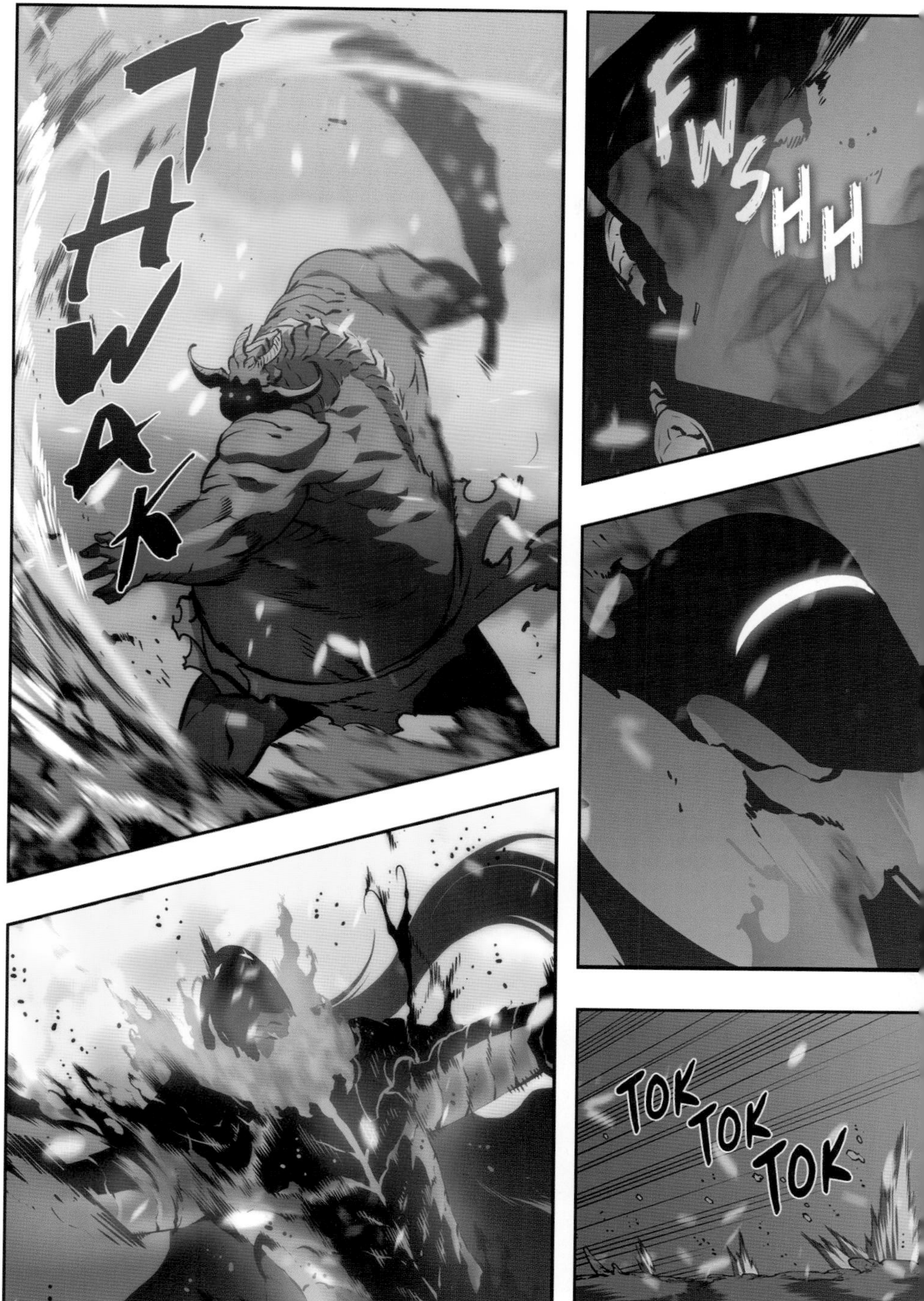
THWAK
FWSHH
TOK TOK TOK

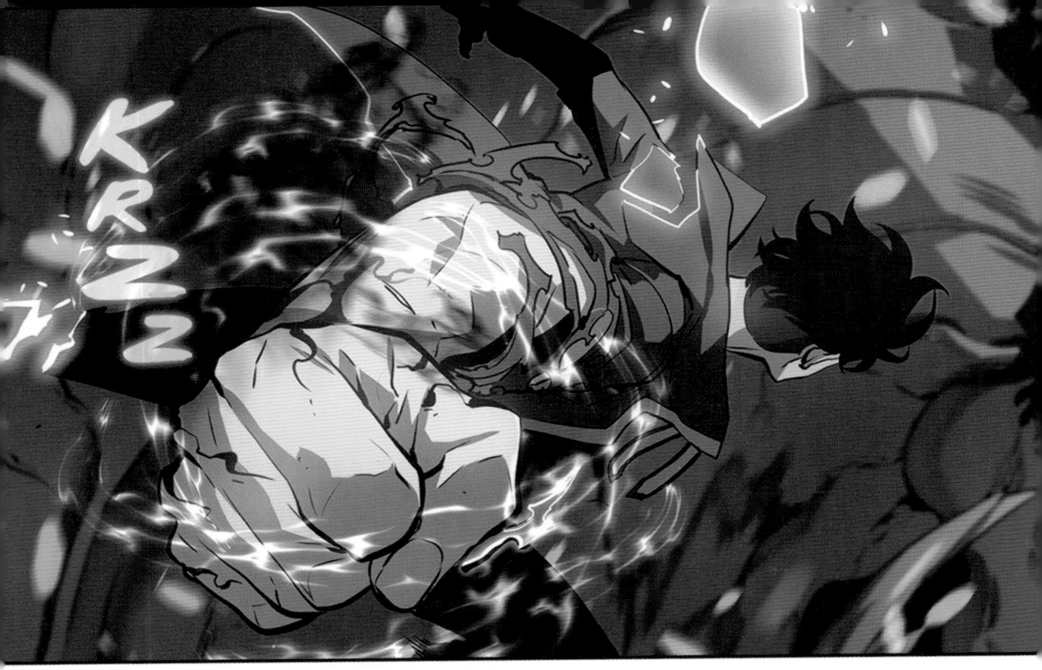
KRZZ
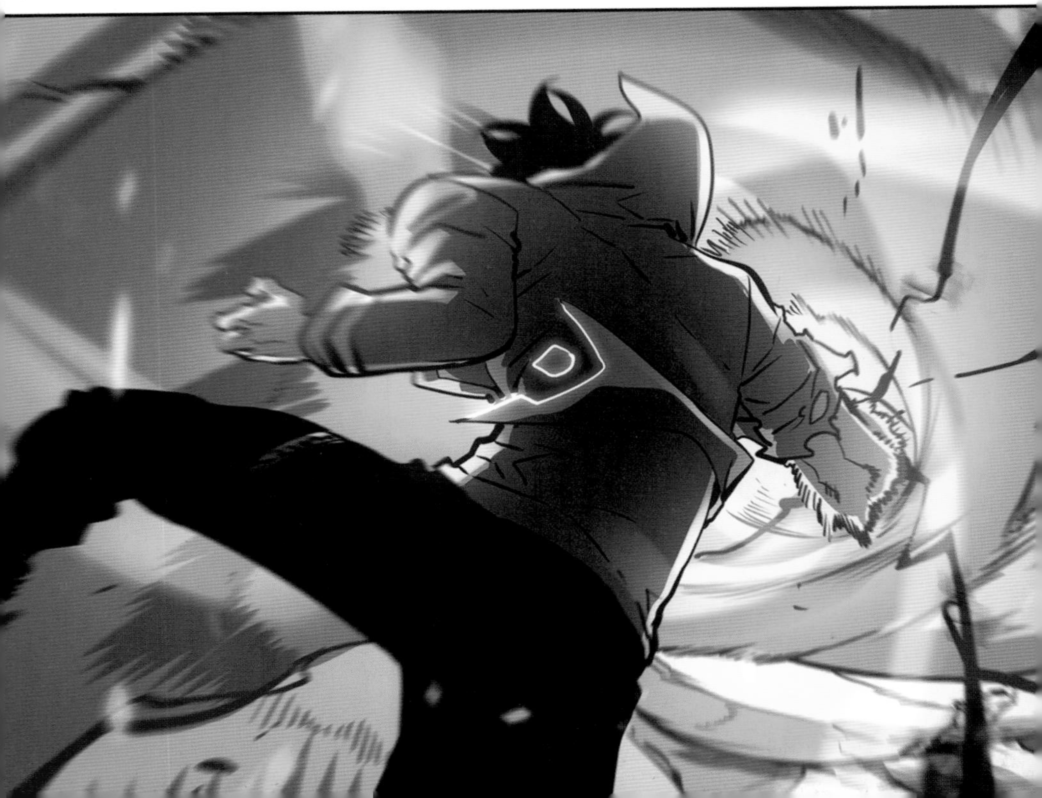

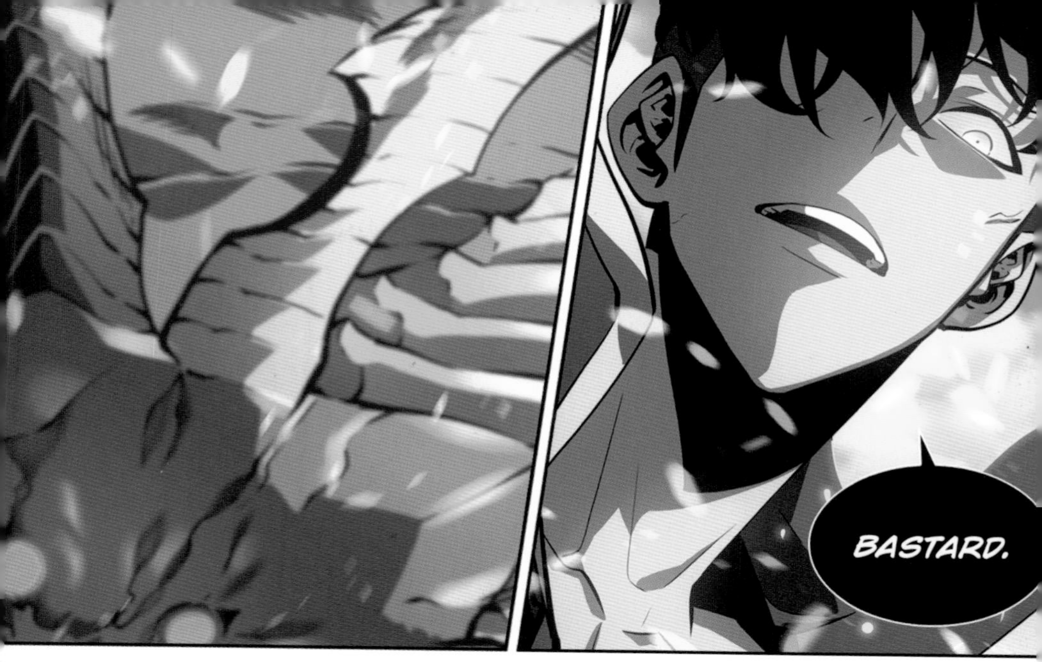
BASTARD.

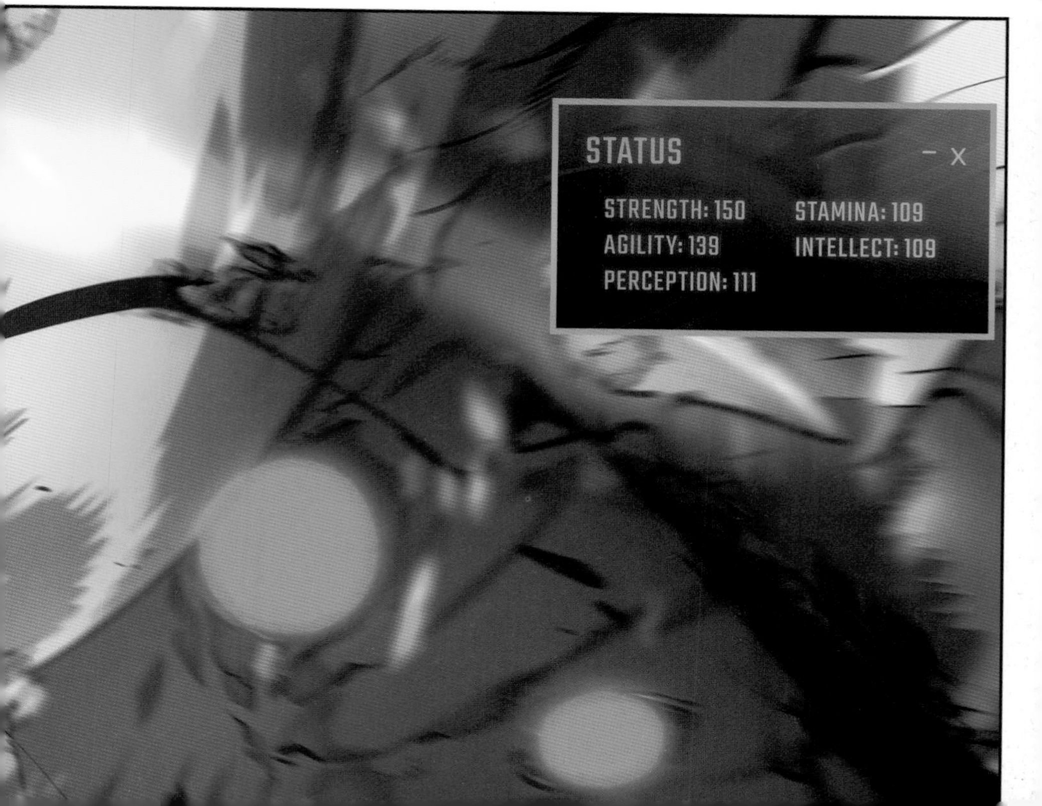
STATUS
STRENGTH: 150
STAMINA: 109
AGILITY: 139
INTELLECT: 109
PERCEPTION: 111

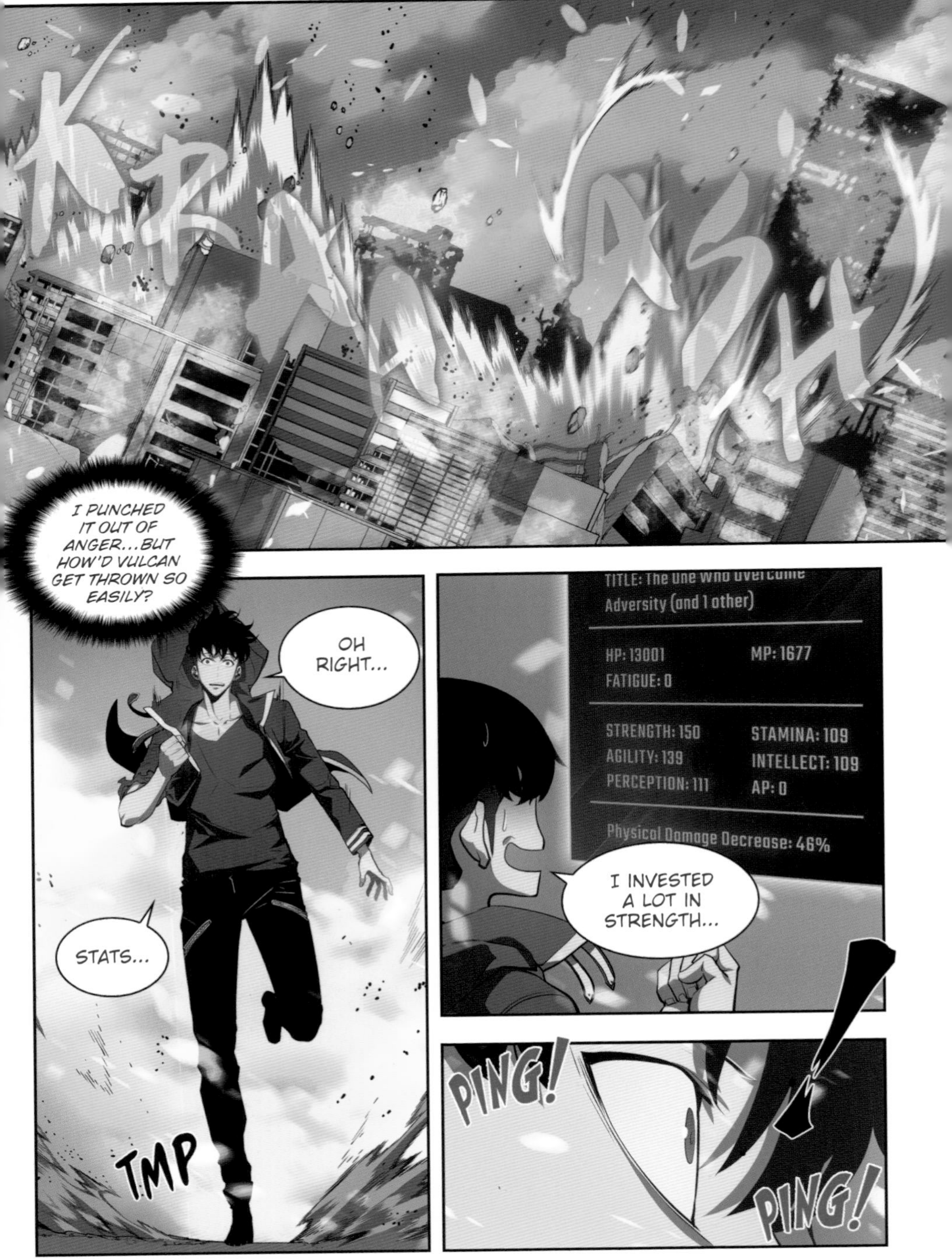
KRASH
I PUNCHED IT OUT OF ANGER...BUT HOW'D VULCAN GET THROWN SO EASILY?
OH RIGHT...
STATS...
TMP
TITLE: The One Who Overcame Adversity (and 1 other)
HP: 13001
MP: 1677
FATIGUE: 0
STRENGTH: 150
STAMINA: 109
AGILITY: 139
INTELLECT: 109
PERCEPTION: 111
AP: 0
Physical Damage Decrease: 46%
I INVESTED A LOT IN STRENGTH...
PING!
PING!

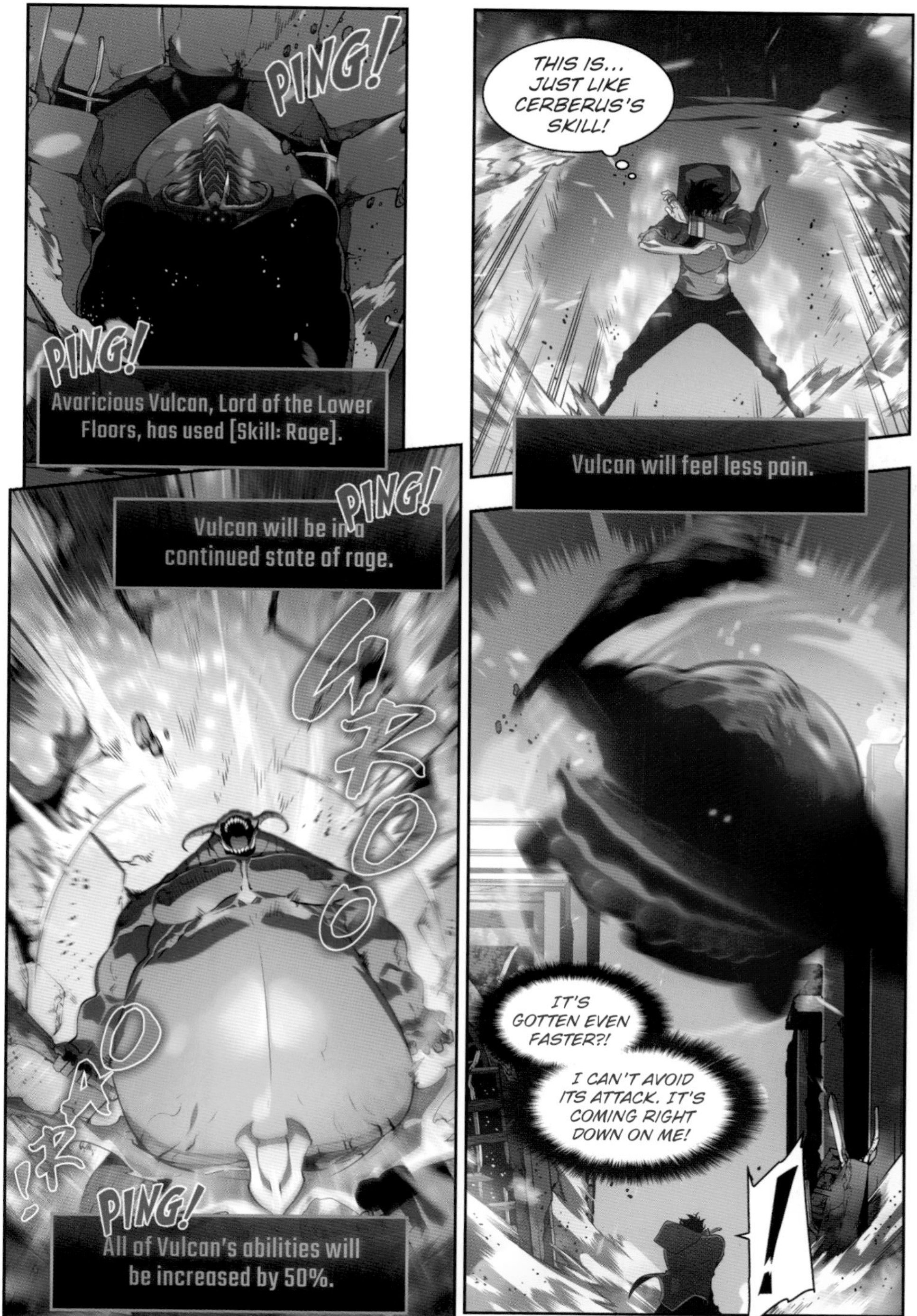
PING!
PING!
Avaricious Vulcan, Lord of the Lower Floors, has used [Skill: Rage].
THIS IS... JUST LIKE CERBERUS'S SKILL!
Vulcan will feel less pain.
PING!
Vulcan will be in a continued state of rage.
WROOO
PING!
All of Vulcan's abilities will be increased by 50%.
IT'S GOTTEN EVEN FASTER?!
I CAN'T AVOID ITS ATTACK. IT'S COMING RIGHT DOWN ON ME!
!

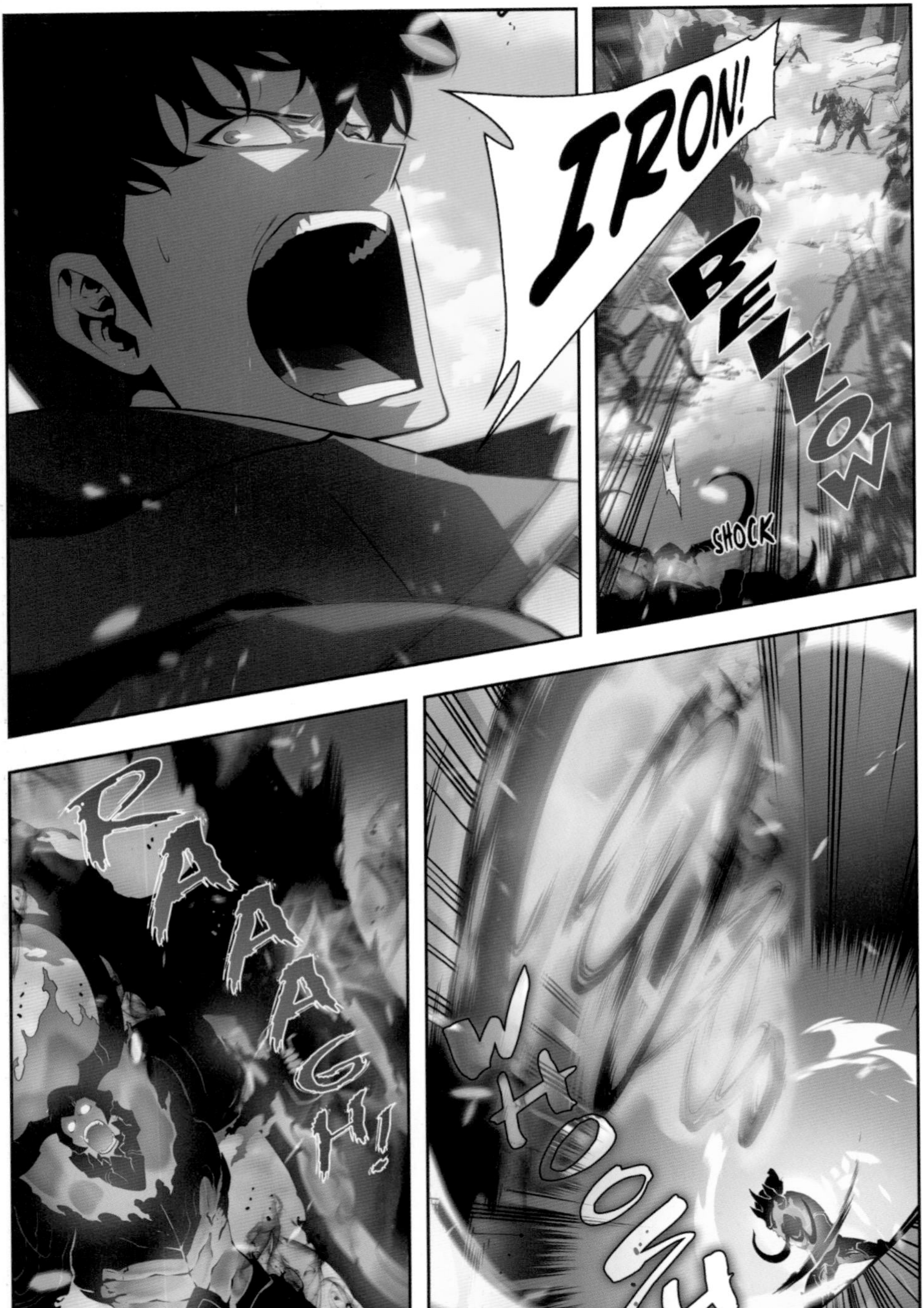
IRON!
BELLOW
SHOCK
RAAAGH!
WHOOOSH

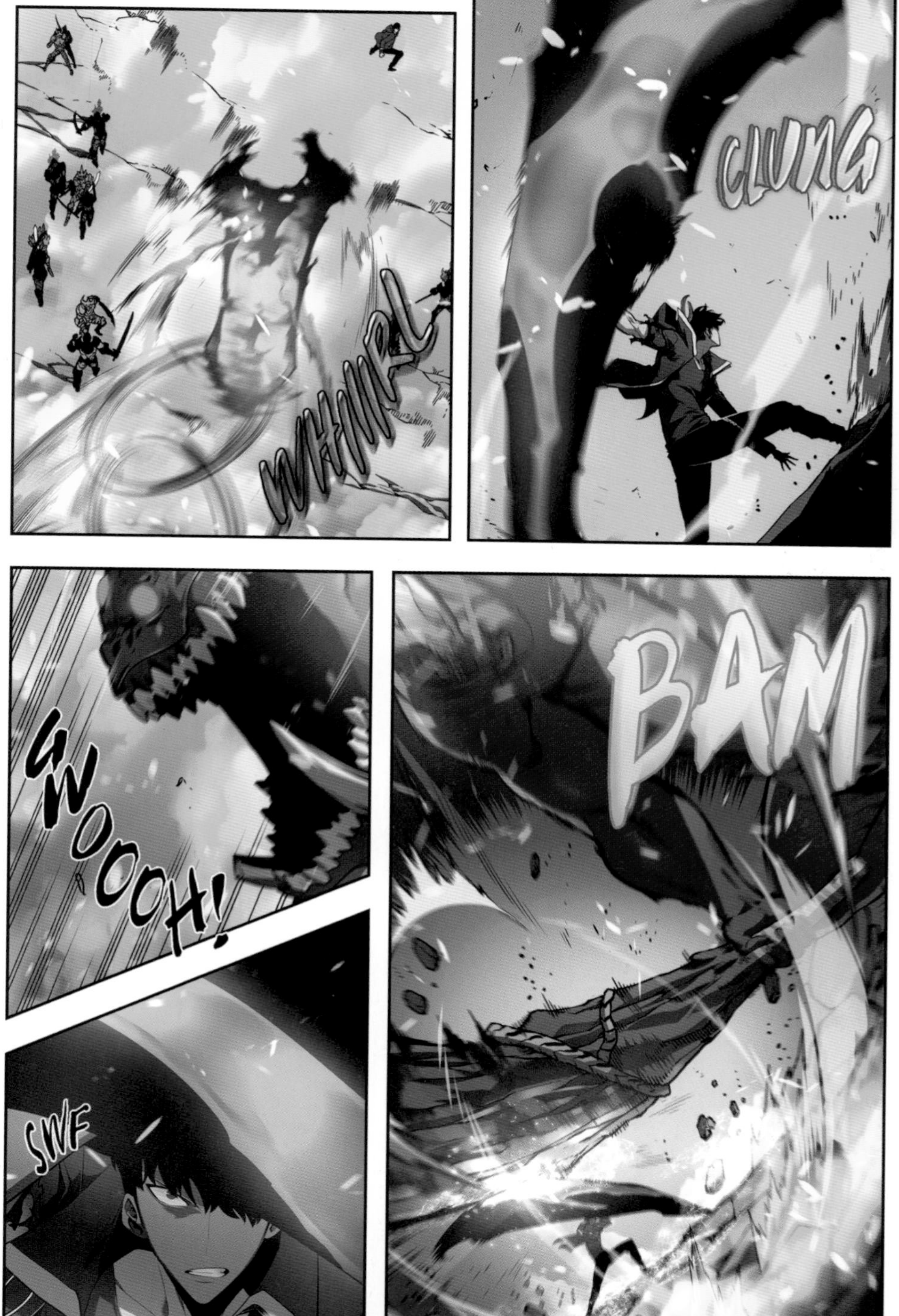
WHIIRL
CLUNG
WOOOOH!
SWF
BAM

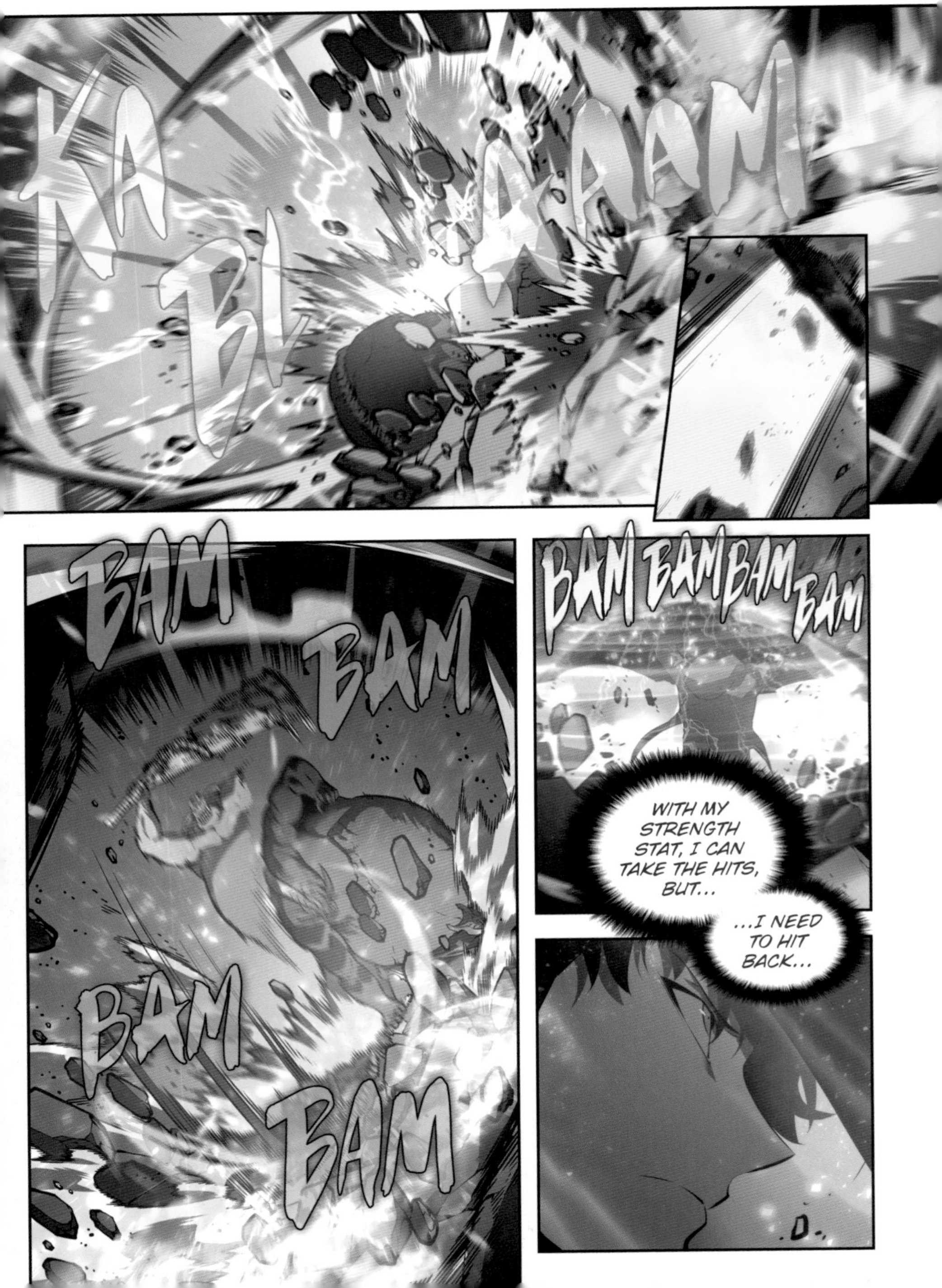
KA BLAAAAM
BAM
BAM
BAM
BAM
BAM BAM BAM BAM
WITH MY STRENGTH STAT, I CAN TAKE THE HITS, BUT...
...I NEED TO HIT BACK...

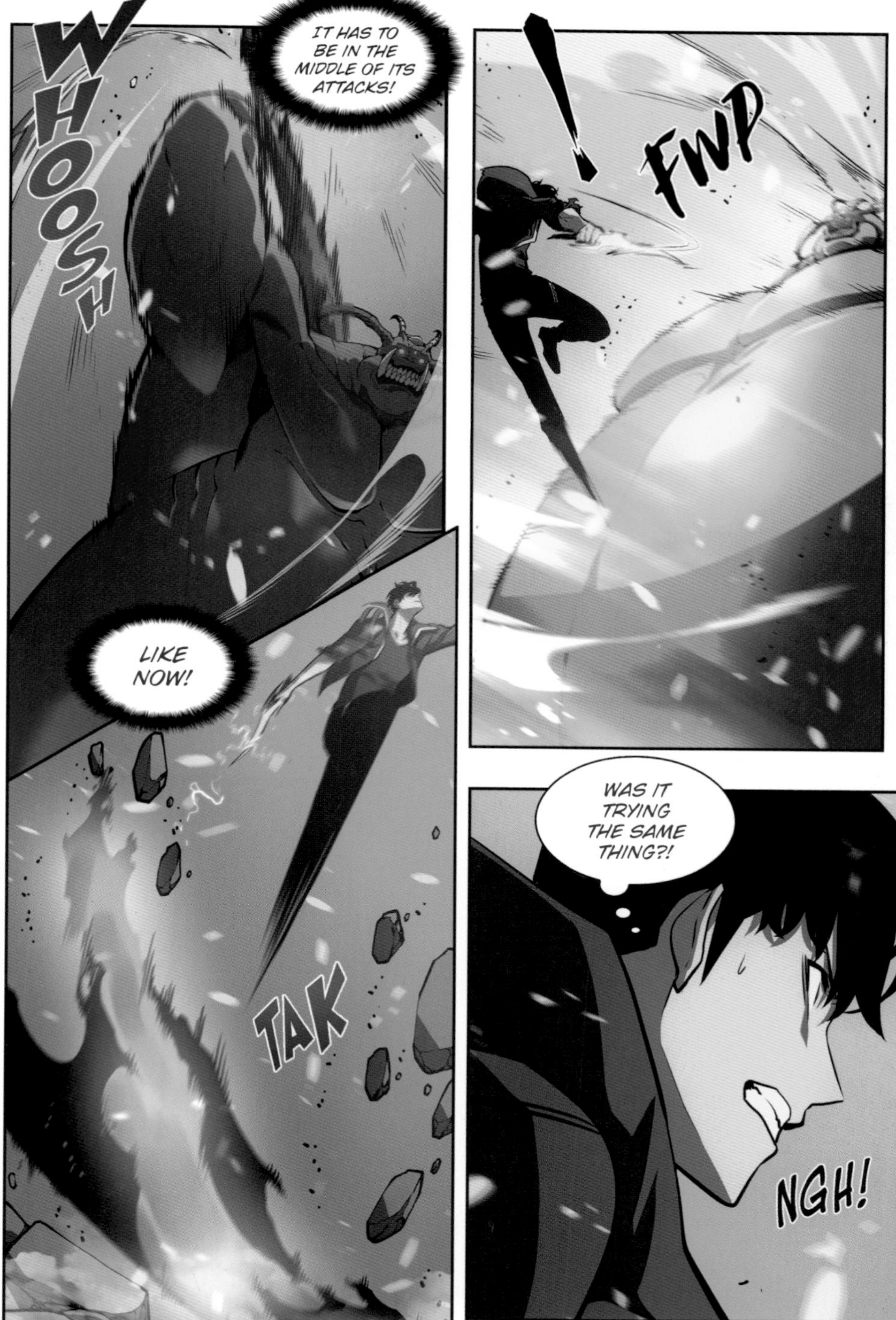

WHOOSH
IT HAS TO BE IN THE MIDDLE OF ITS ATTACKS!
!
FWP
LIKE NOW!
TAK
WAS IT TRYING THE SAME THING?!
NGH!

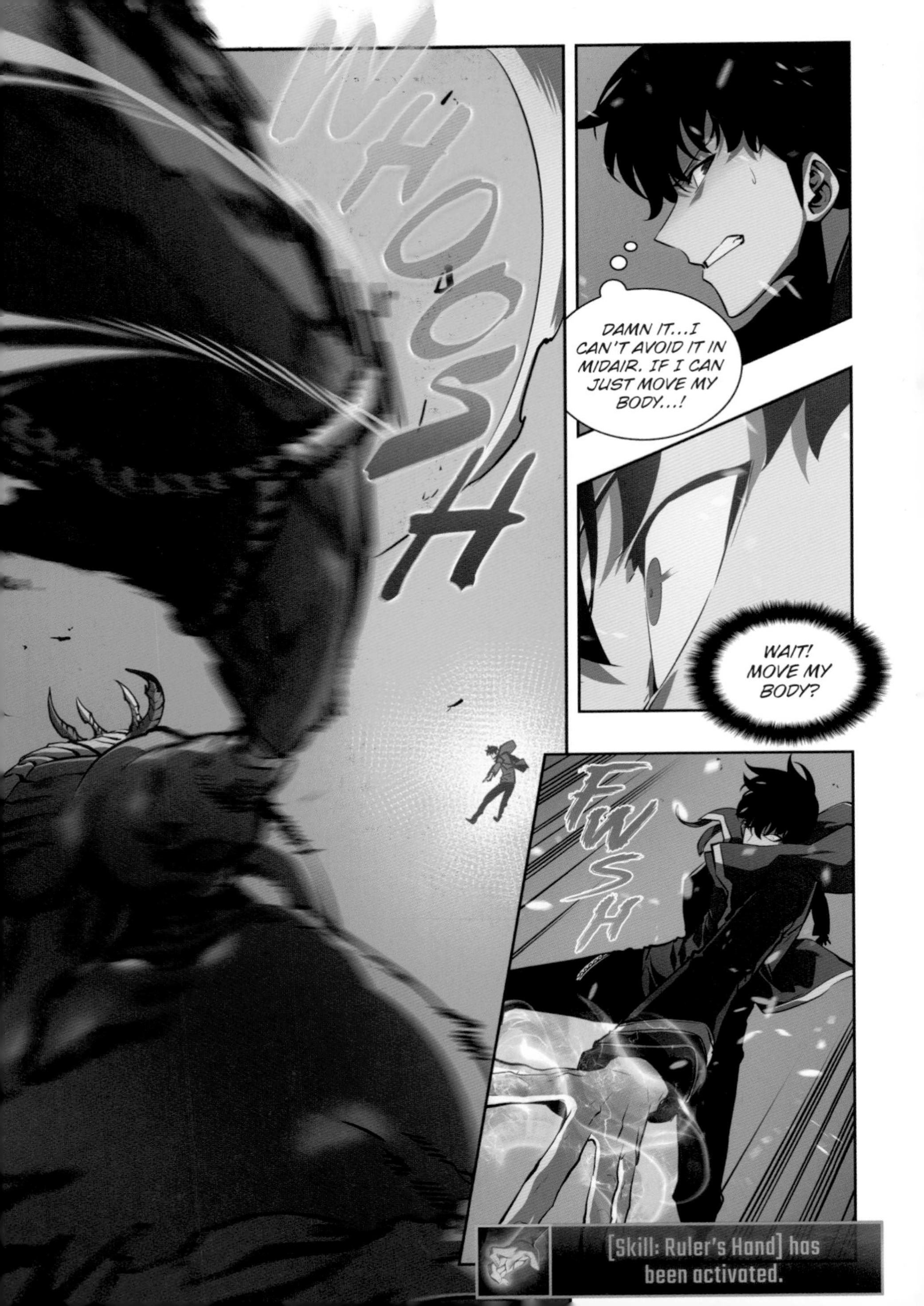
WHOOOSH
DAMN IT...I CAN'T AVOID IT IN MIDAIR. IF I CAN JUST MOVE MY BODY...!
WAIT! MOVE MY BODY?
FWSH
[Skill: Ruler's Hand] has been activated.

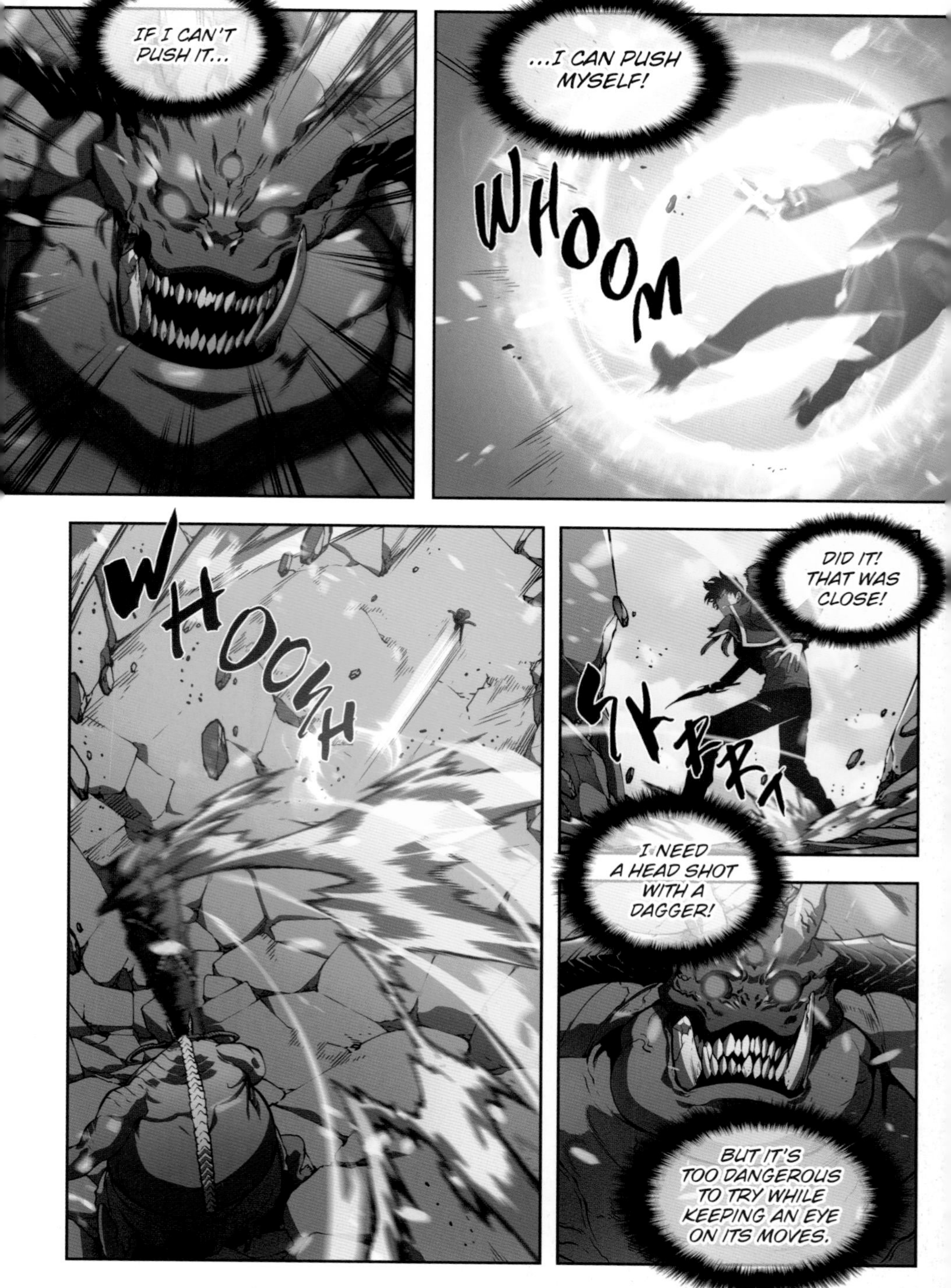
IF I CAN'T PUSH IT...
...I CAN PUSH MYSELF!
WHOOM
WHOOSH
DID IT! THAT WAS CLOSE!
SKRRT
I NEED A HEAD SHOT WITH A DAGGER!
BUT IT'S TOO DANGEROUS TO TRY WHILE KEEPING AN EYE ON ITS MOVES.

I NEED A TRAP...

...IT CAN'T AVOID...

I NEED TO IMMOBILIZE THIS DEMON FIRST.

GRIN

THAT'S IT!

TAK TAK TAK

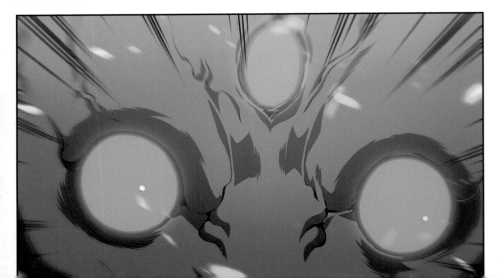

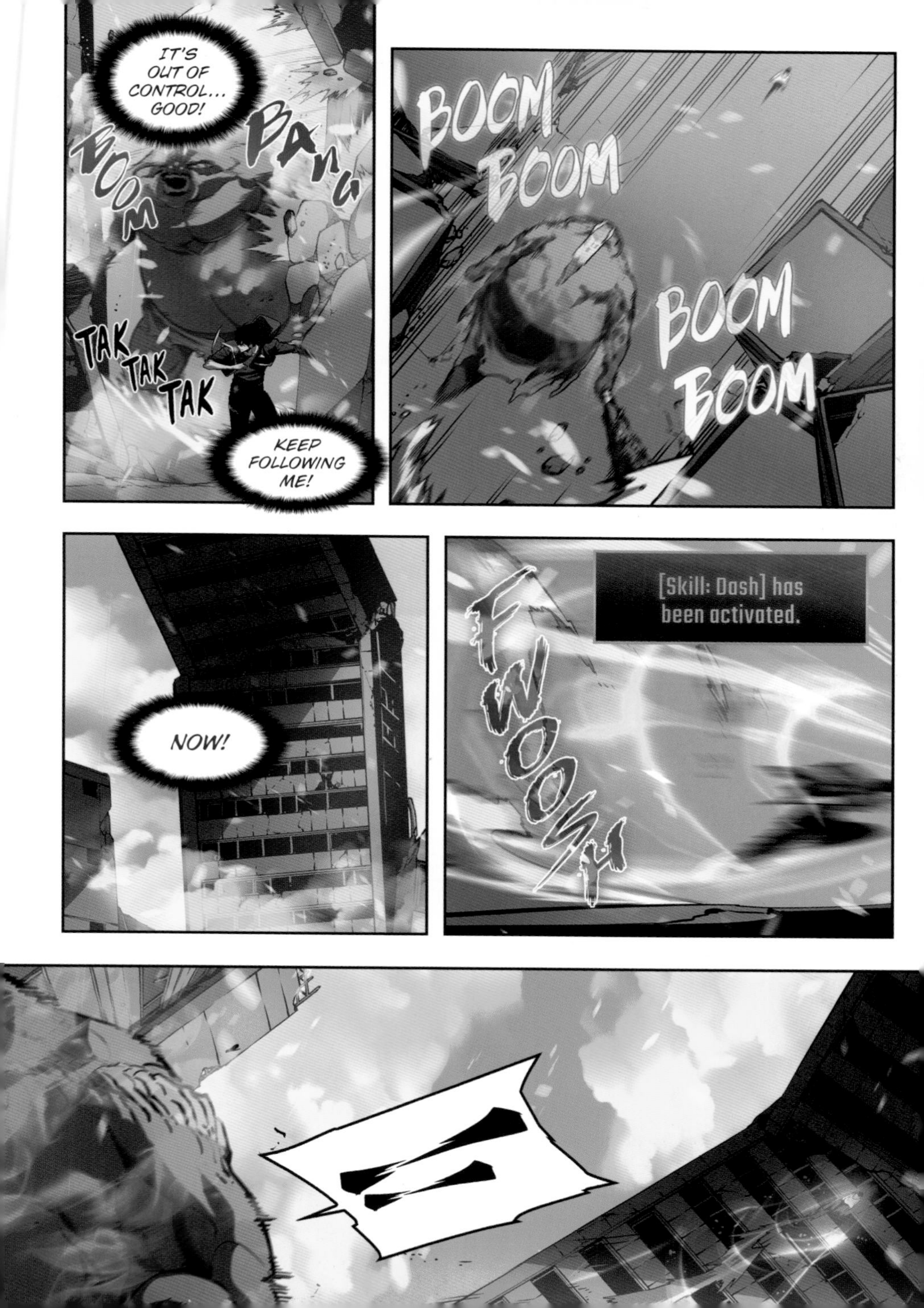
IT'S OUT OF CONTROL... GOOD!
BOOM
BANG
TAK TAK TAK
KEEP FOLLOWING ME!
BOOM BOOM
BOOM BOOM
NOW!
[Skill: Dash] has been activated.
FWOOSH
!!

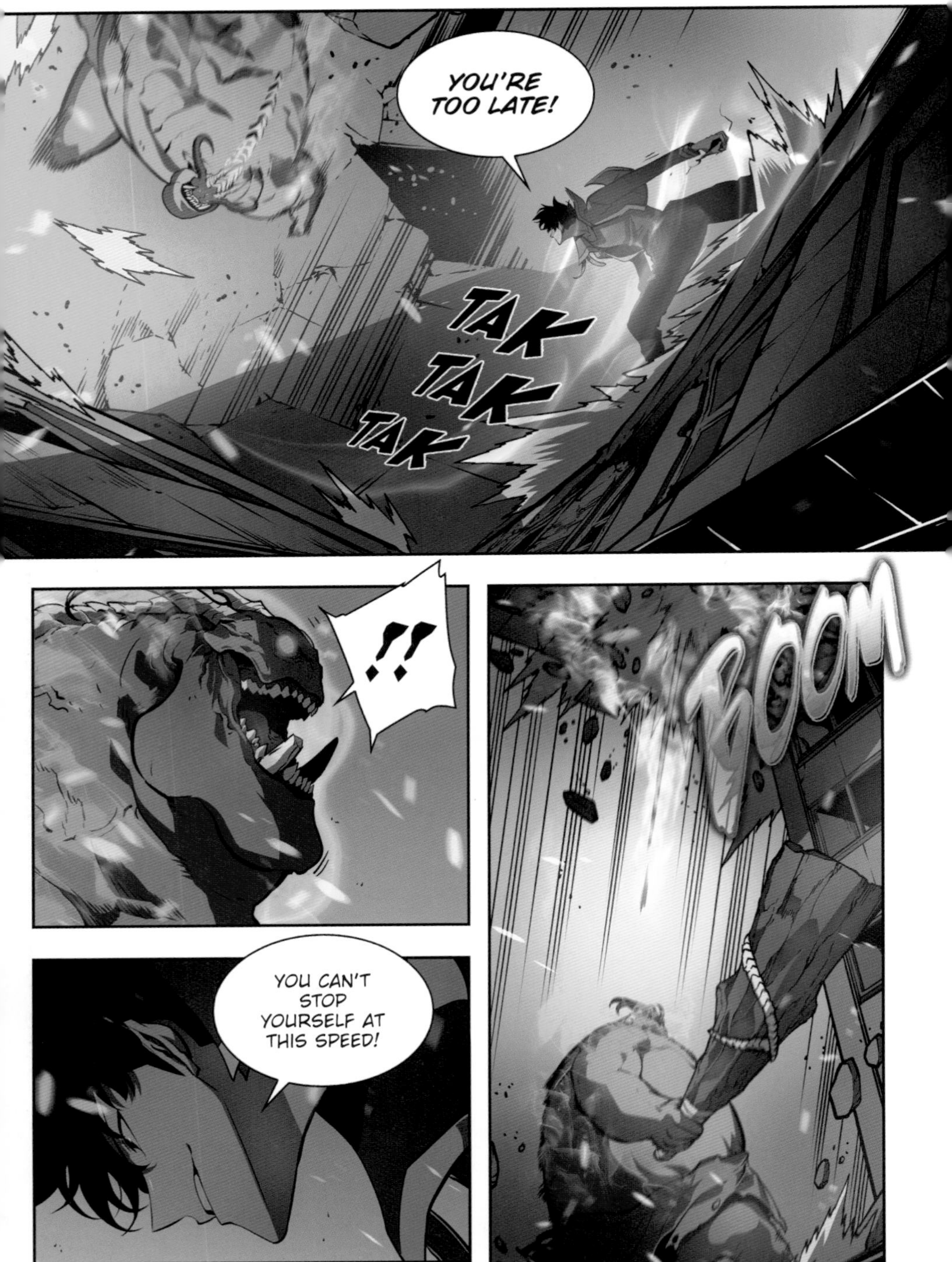
YOU'RE TOO LATE!
TAK
TAK
TAK
!?
YOU CAN'T STOP YOURSELF AT THIS SPEED!
BOOM

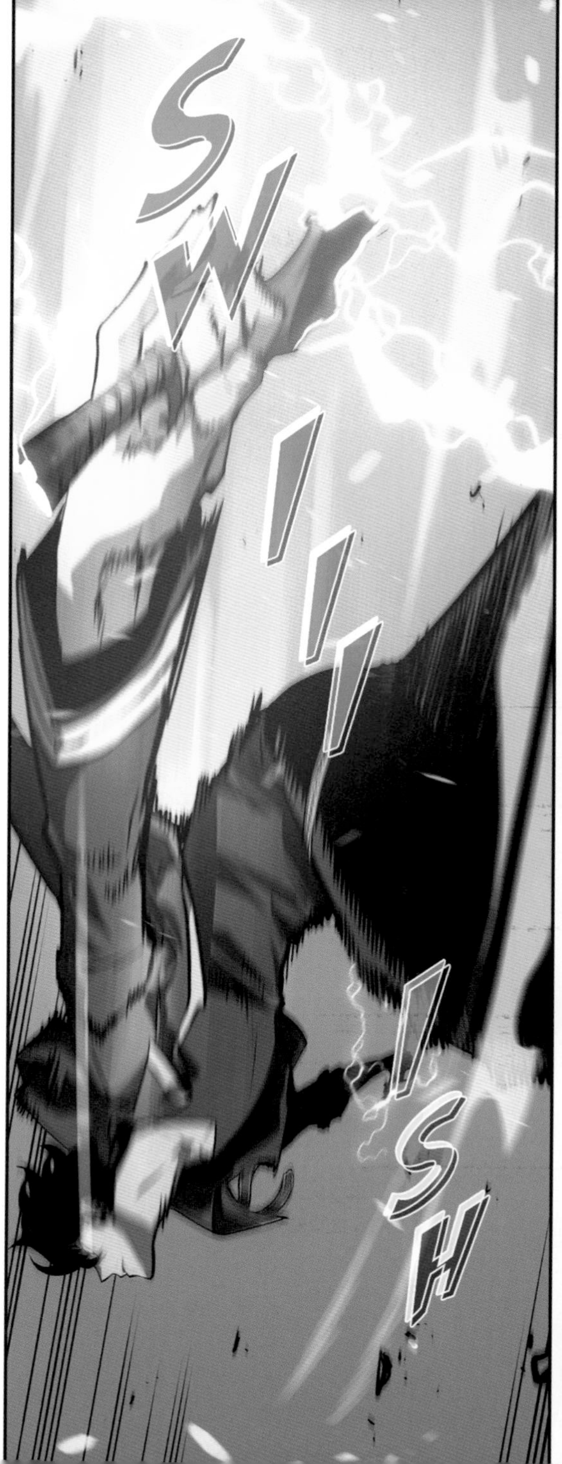
SWIIIISH
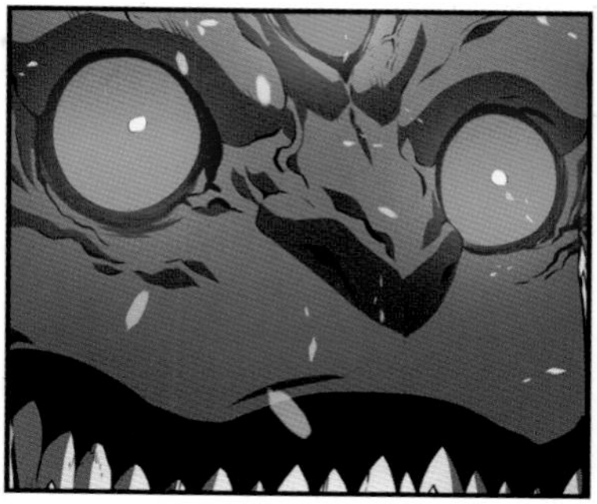
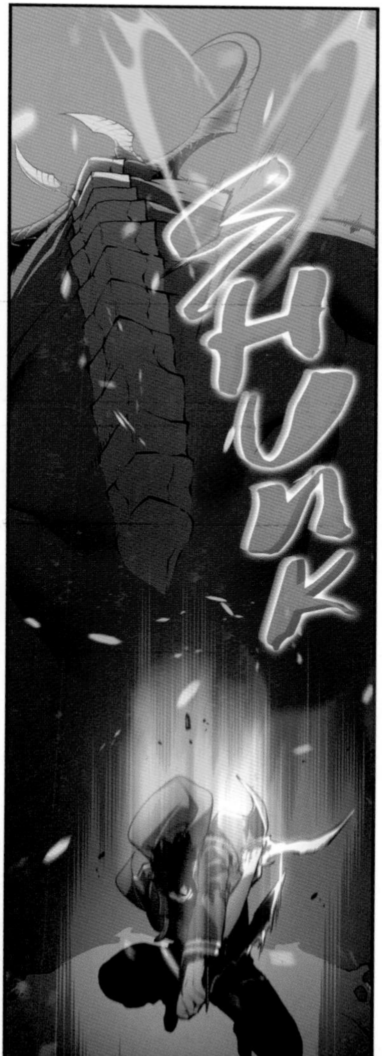
SHUNK

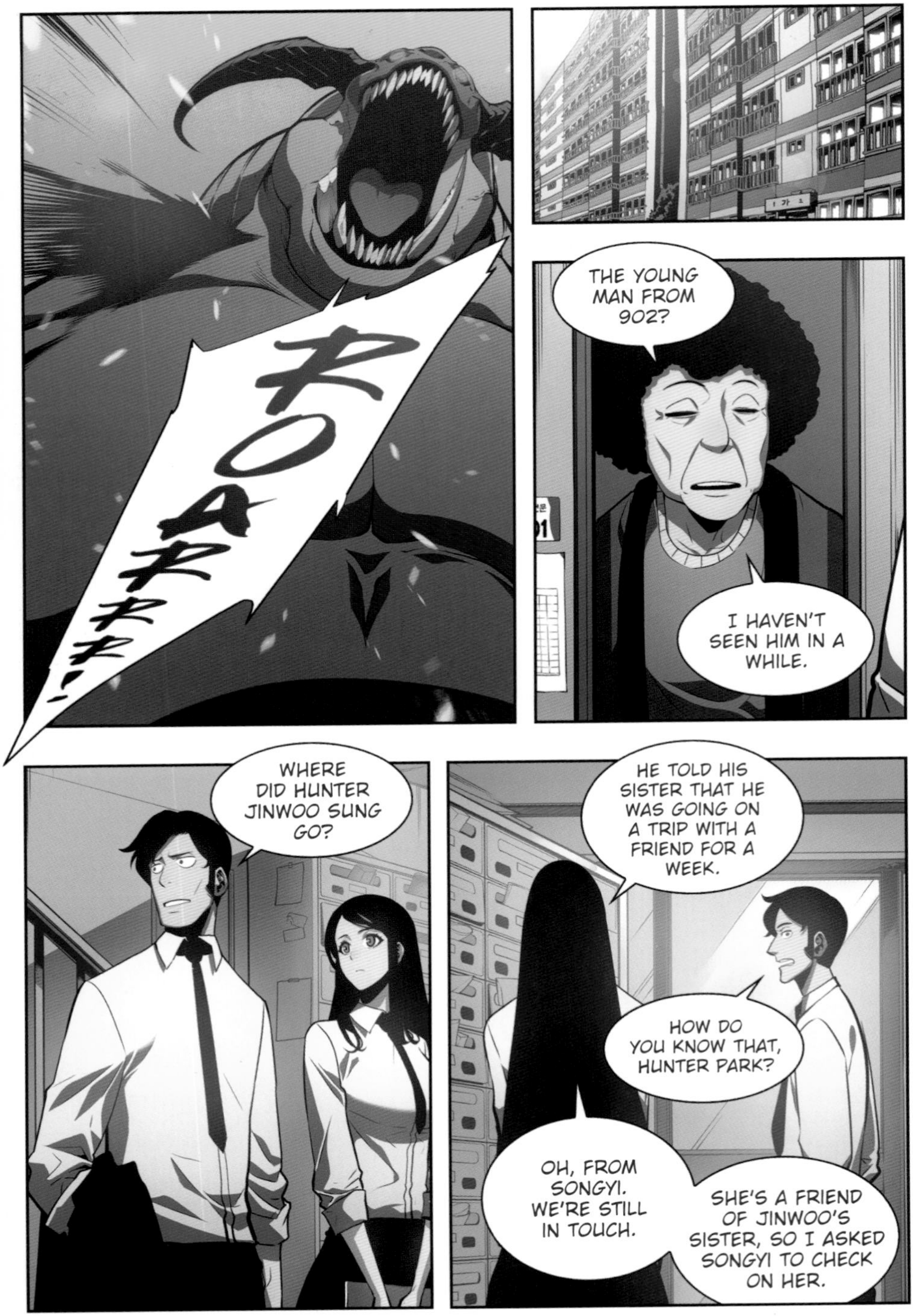
ROARRR!!
THE YOUNG MAN FROM 902?
I HAVEN'T SEEN HIM IN A WHILE.
WHERE DID HUNTER JINWOO SUNG GO?
HE TOLD HIS SISTER THAT HE WAS GOING ON A TRIP WITH A FRIEND FOR A WEEK.
HOW DO YOU KNOW THAT, HUNTER PARK?
OH, FROM SONGYI. WE'RE STILL IN TOUCH.
SHE'S A FRIEND OF JINWOO'S SISTER, SO I ASKED SONGYI TO CHECK ON HER.

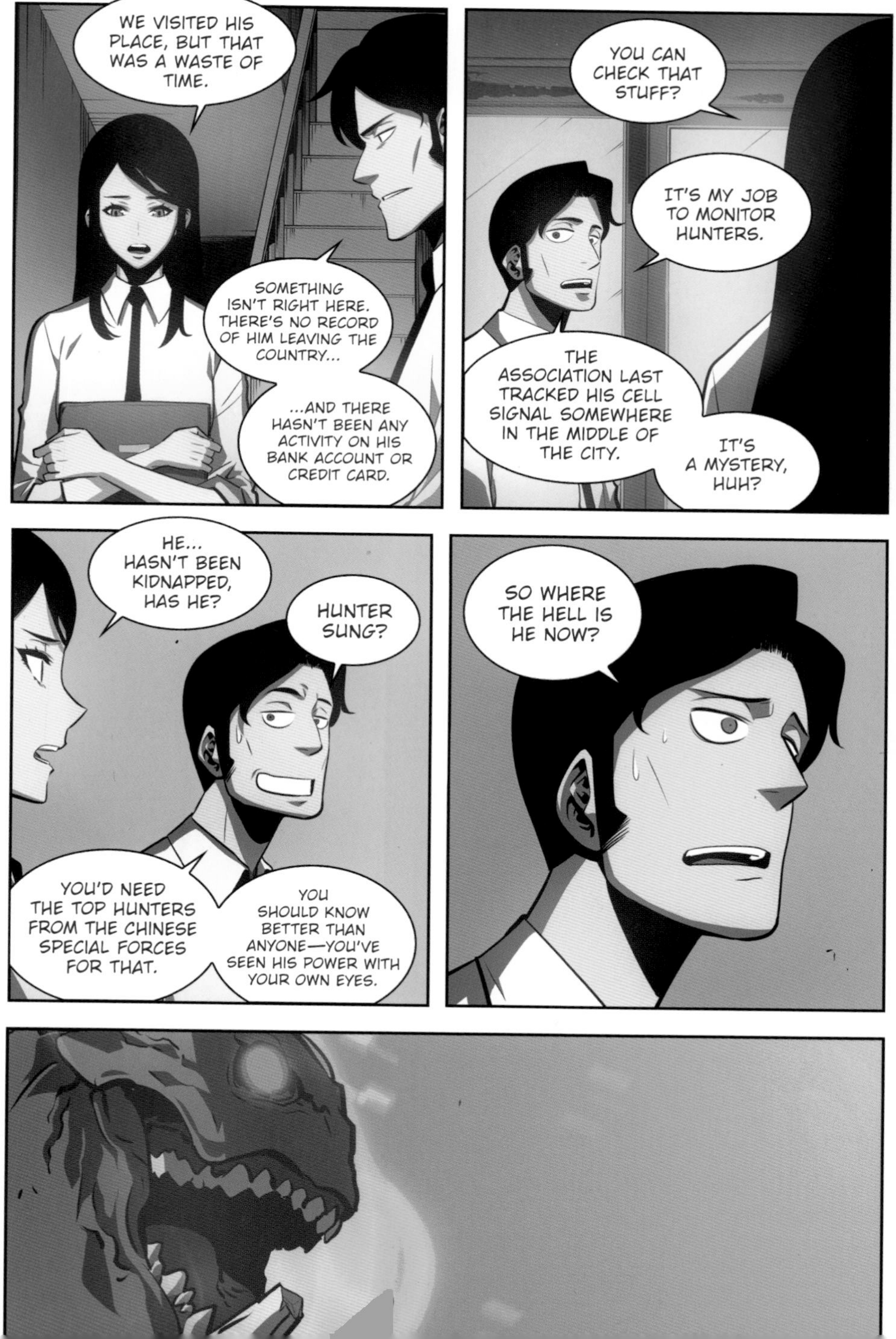
WE VISITED HIS PLACE, BUT THAT WAS A WASTE OF TIME.
SOMETHING ISN'T RIGHT HERE. THERE'S NO RECORD OF HIM LEAVING THE COUNTRY...
...AND THERE HASN'T BEEN ANY ACTIVITY ON HIS BANK ACCOUNT OR CREDIT CARD.
YOU CAN CHECK THAT STUFF?
IT'S MY JOB TO MONITOR HUNTERS.
THE ASSOCIATION LAST TRACKED HIS CELL SIGNAL SOMEWHERE IN THE MIDDLE OF THE CITY.
IT'S A MYSTERY, HUH?
HE... HASN'T BEEN KIDNAPPED, HAS HE?
HUNTER SUNG?
YOU'D NEED THE TOP HUNTERS FROM THE CHINESE SPECIAL FORCES FOR THAT.
YOU SHOULD KNOW BETTER THAN ANYONE—YOU'VE SEEN HIS POWER WITH YOUR OWN EYES.
SO WHERE THE HELL IS HE NOW?

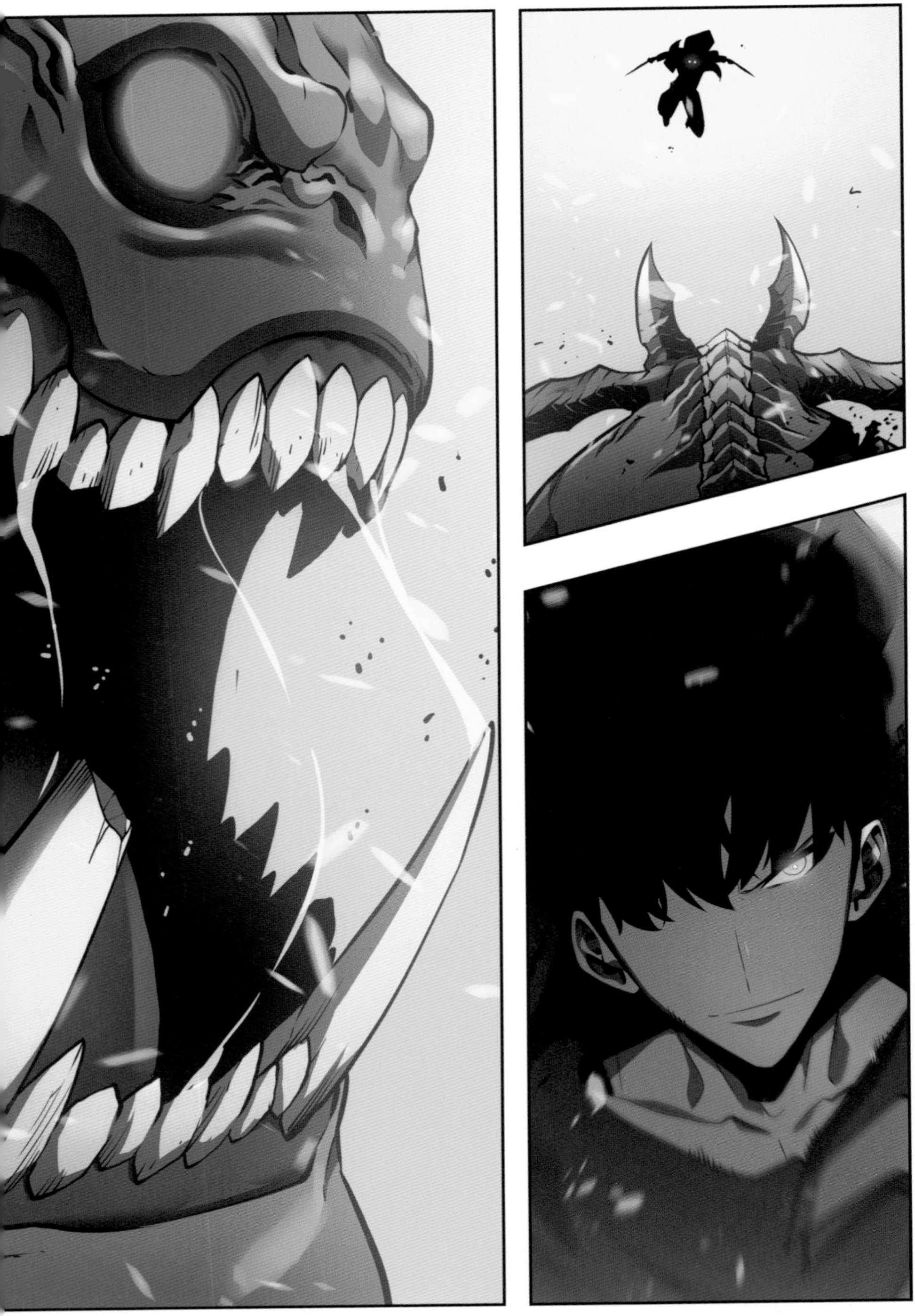

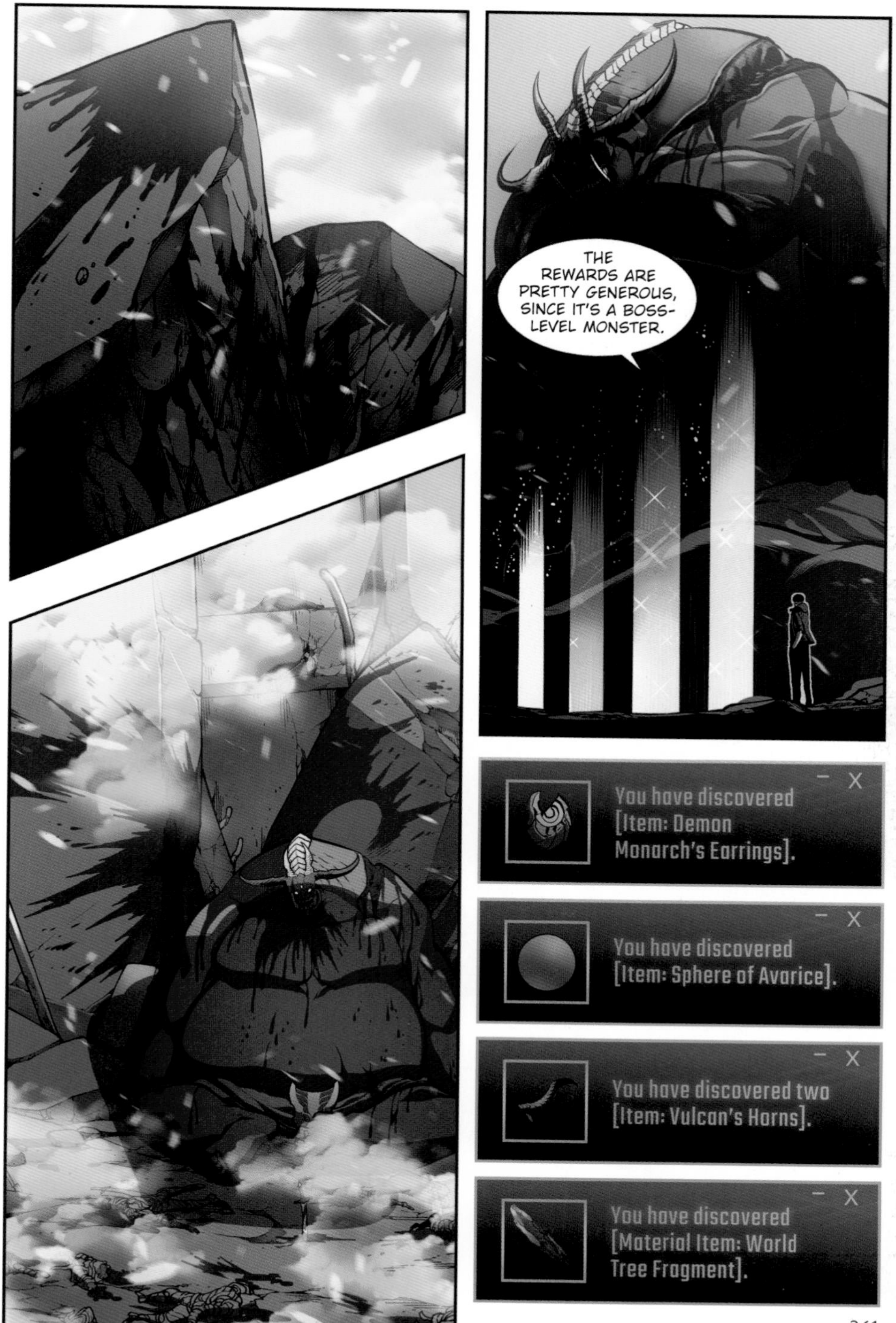
THE REWARDS ARE PRETTY GENEROUS, SINCE IT'S A BOSS-LEVEL MONSTER.
You have discovered [Item: Demon Monarch's Earrings].
You have discovered [Item: Sphere of Avarice].
You have discovered two [Item: Vulcan's Horns].
You have discovered [Material Item: World Tree Fragment].

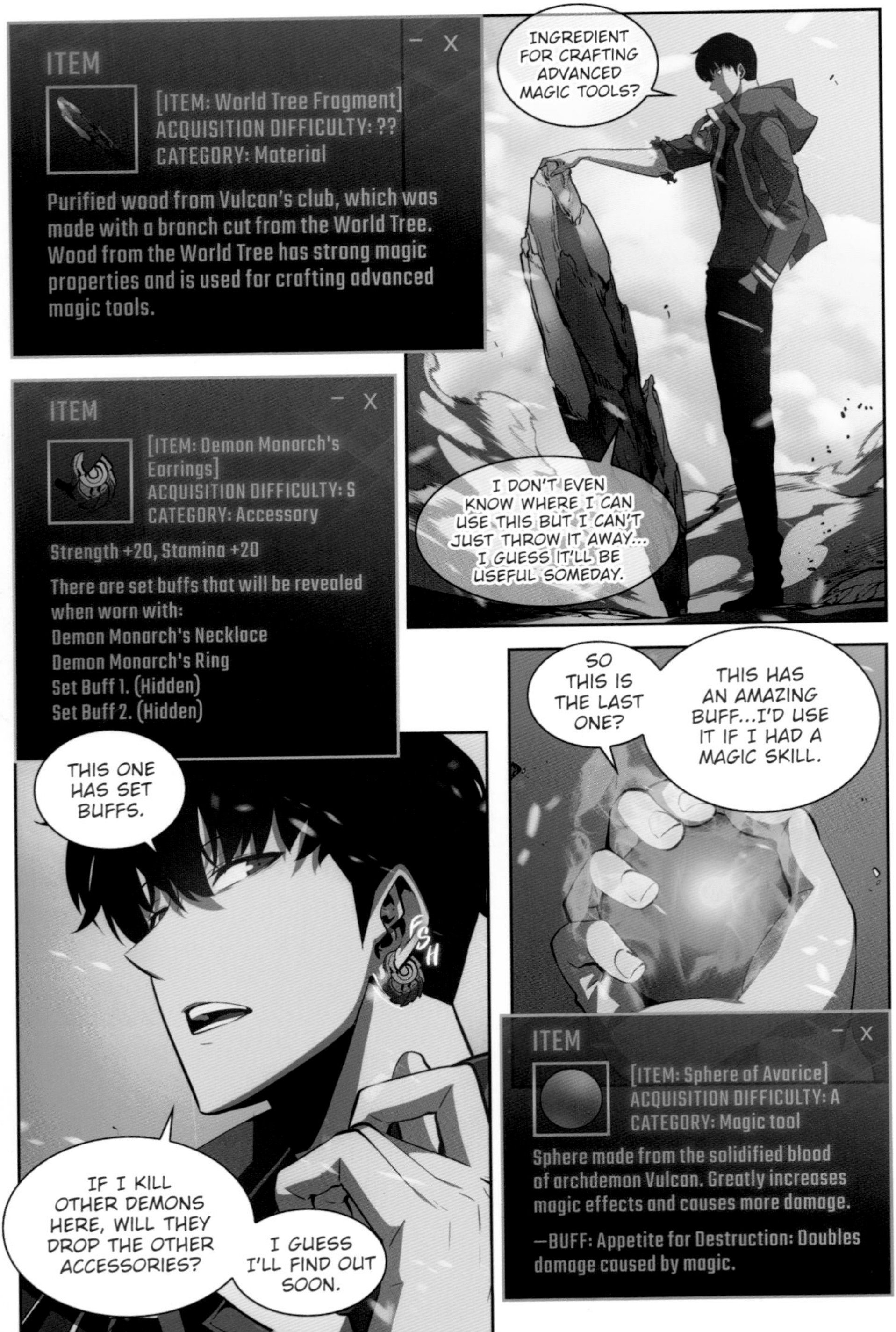
ITEM
[ITEM: World Tree Fragment]
ACQUISITION DIFFICULTY: ??
CATEGORY: Material
Purified wood from Vulcan's club, which was made with a branch cut from the World Tree. Wood from the World Tree has strong magic properties and is used for crafting advanced magic tools.
INGREDIENT FOR CRAFTING ADVANCED MAGIC TOOLS?
I DON'T EVEN KNOW WHERE I CAN USE THIS BUT I CAN'T JUST THROW IT AWAY... I GUESS IT'LL BE USEFUL SOMEDAY.
ITEM
[ITEM: Demon Monarch's Earrings]
ACQUISITION DIFFICULTY: S
CATEGORY: Accessory
Strength +20, Stamina +20
There are set buffs that will be revealed when worn with:
Demon Monarch's Necklace
Demon Monarch's Ring
Set Buff 1. (Hidden)
Set Buff 2. (Hidden)
THIS ONE HAS SET BUFFS.
FSH
IF I KILL OTHER DEMONS HERE, WILL THEY DROP THE OTHER ACCESSORIES?
I GUESS I'LL FIND OUT SOON.
SO THIS IS THE LAST ONE?
THIS HAS AN AMAZING BUFF...I'D USE IT IF I HAD A MAGIC SKILL.
ITEM
[ITEM: Sphere of Avarice]
ACQUISITION DIFFICULTY: A
CATEGORY: Magic tool
Sphere made from the solidified blood of archdemon Vulcan. Greatly increases magic effects and causes more damage.
—BUFF: Appetite for Destruction: Doubles damage caused by magic.

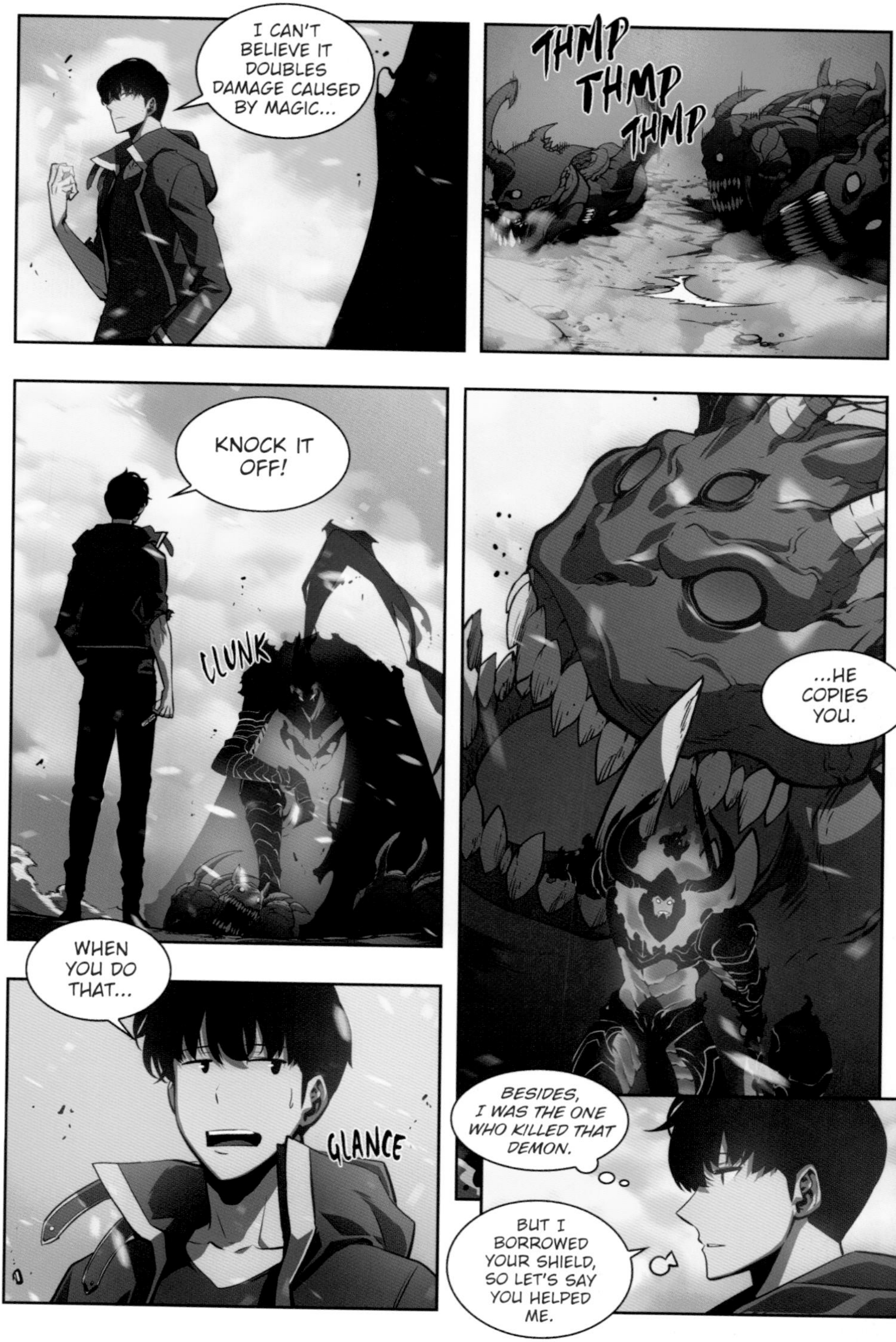

I CAN'T BELIEVE IT DOUBLES DAMAGE CAUSED BY MAGIC...
THMP THMP THMP
KNOCK IT OFF!
CLUNK
...HE COPIES YOU.
WHEN YOU DO THAT...
GLANCE
BESIDES, I WAS THE ONE WHO KILLED THAT DEMON.
BUT I BORROWED YOUR SHIELD, SO LET'S SAY YOU HELPED ME.

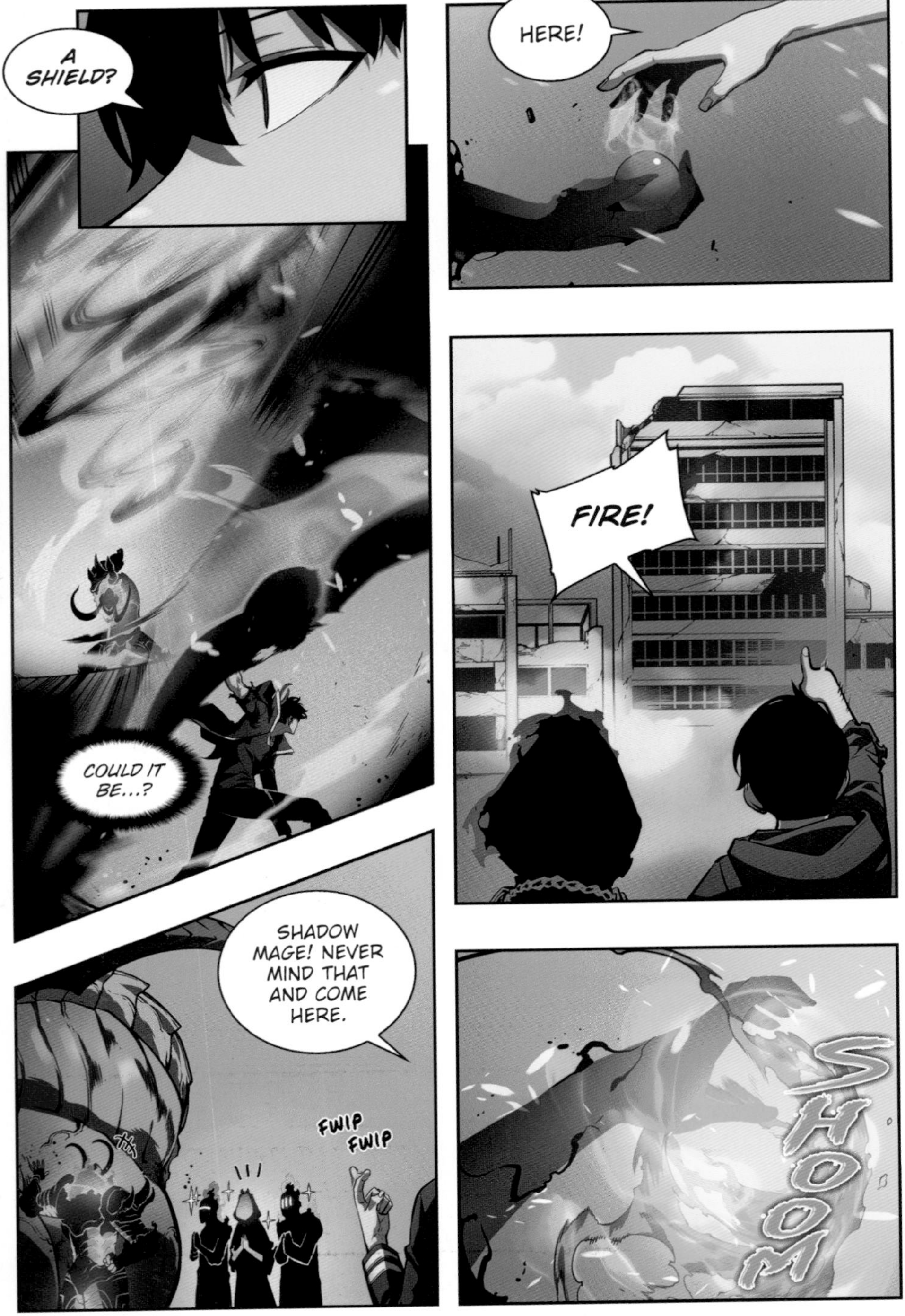
A SHIELD?
HERE!
COULD IT BE...?
FIRE!
SHADOW MAGE! NEVER MIND THAT AND COME HERE.
FWIP FWIP
SHOOM

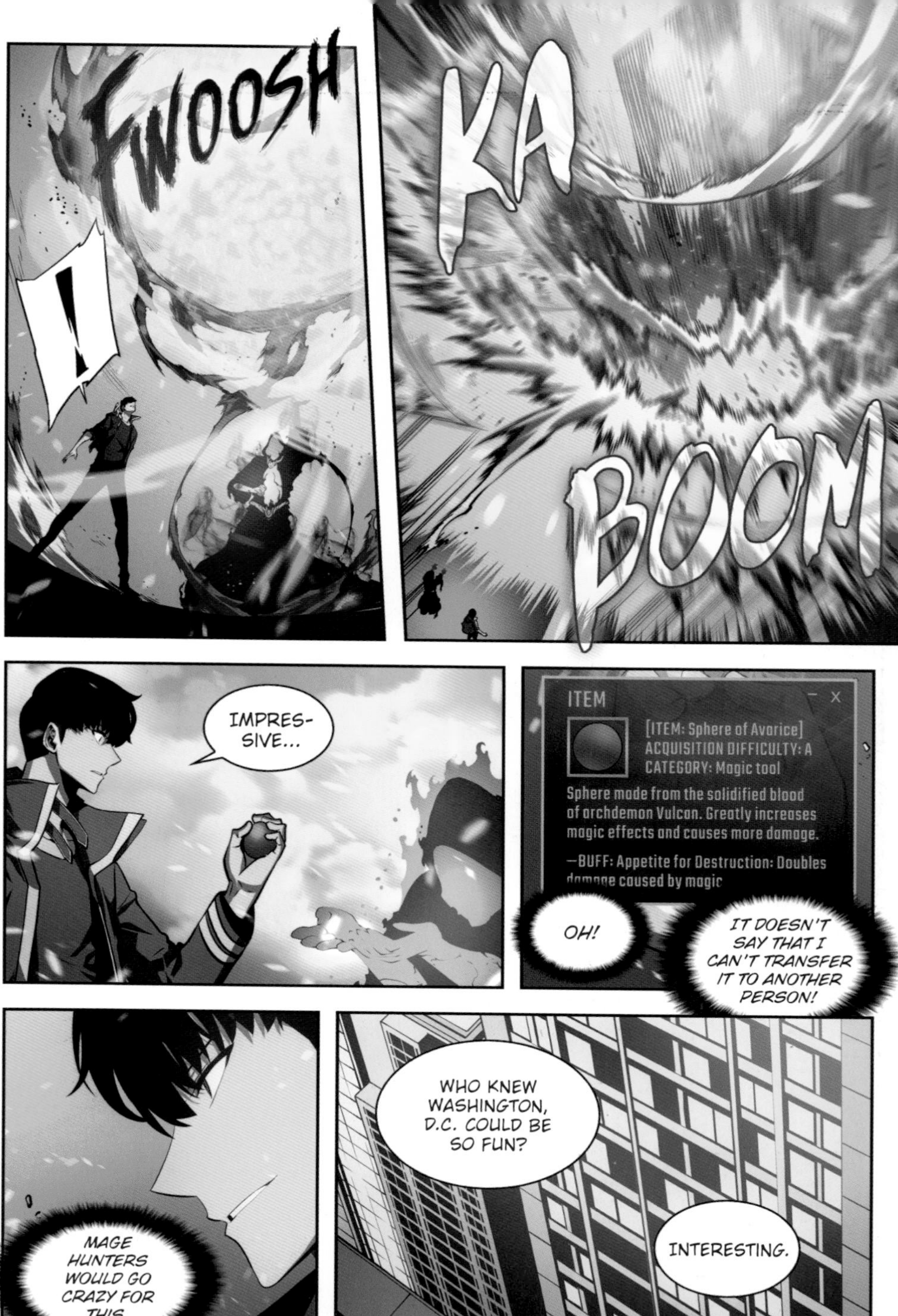
FWOOSH
!
KA
BOOM
IMPRESSIVE...
ITEM
[ITEM: Sphere of Avarice]
ACQUISITION DIFFICULTY: A
CATEGORY: Magic tool
Sphere made from the solidified blood of archdemon Vulcan. Greatly increases magic effects and causes more damage.
—BUFF: Appetite for Destruction: Doubles damage caused by magic
OH!
IT DOESN'T SAY THAT I CAN'T TRANSFER IT TO ANOTHER PERSON!
MAGE HUNTERS WOULD GO CRAZY FOR THIS.
WHO KNEW WASHINGTON, D.C. COULD BE SO FUN?
INTERESTING.

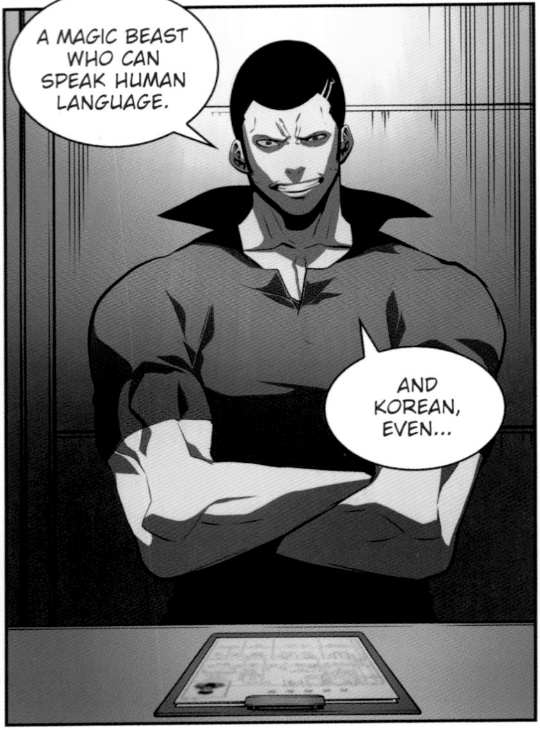
A MAGIC BEAST WHO CAN SPEAK HUMAN LANGUAGE.
AND KOREAN, EVEN...
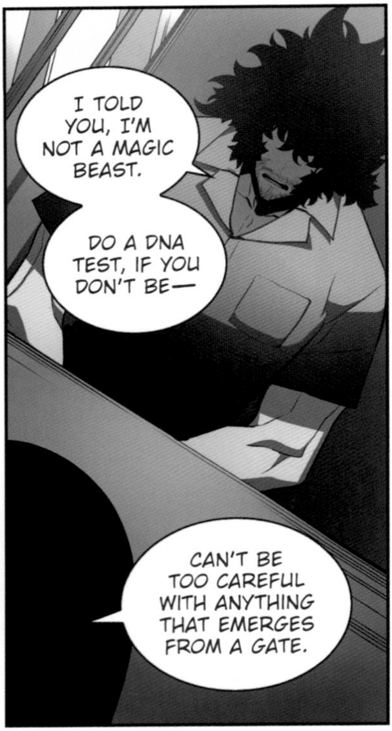
I TOLD YOU, I'M NOT A MAGIC BEAST.
DO A DNA TEST, IF YOU DON'T BE—
CAN'T BE TOO CAREFUL WITH ANYTHING THAT EMERGES FROM A GATE.
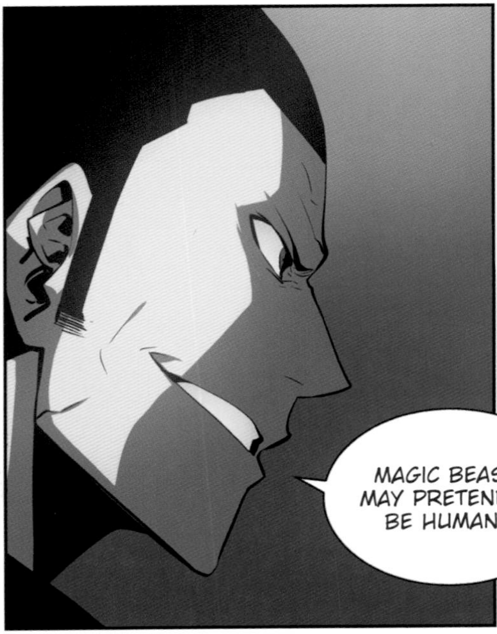
MAGIC BEASTS MAY PRETEND TO BE HUMAN...
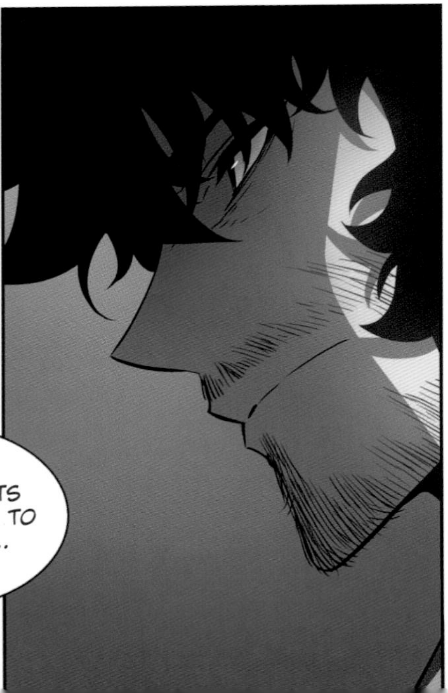

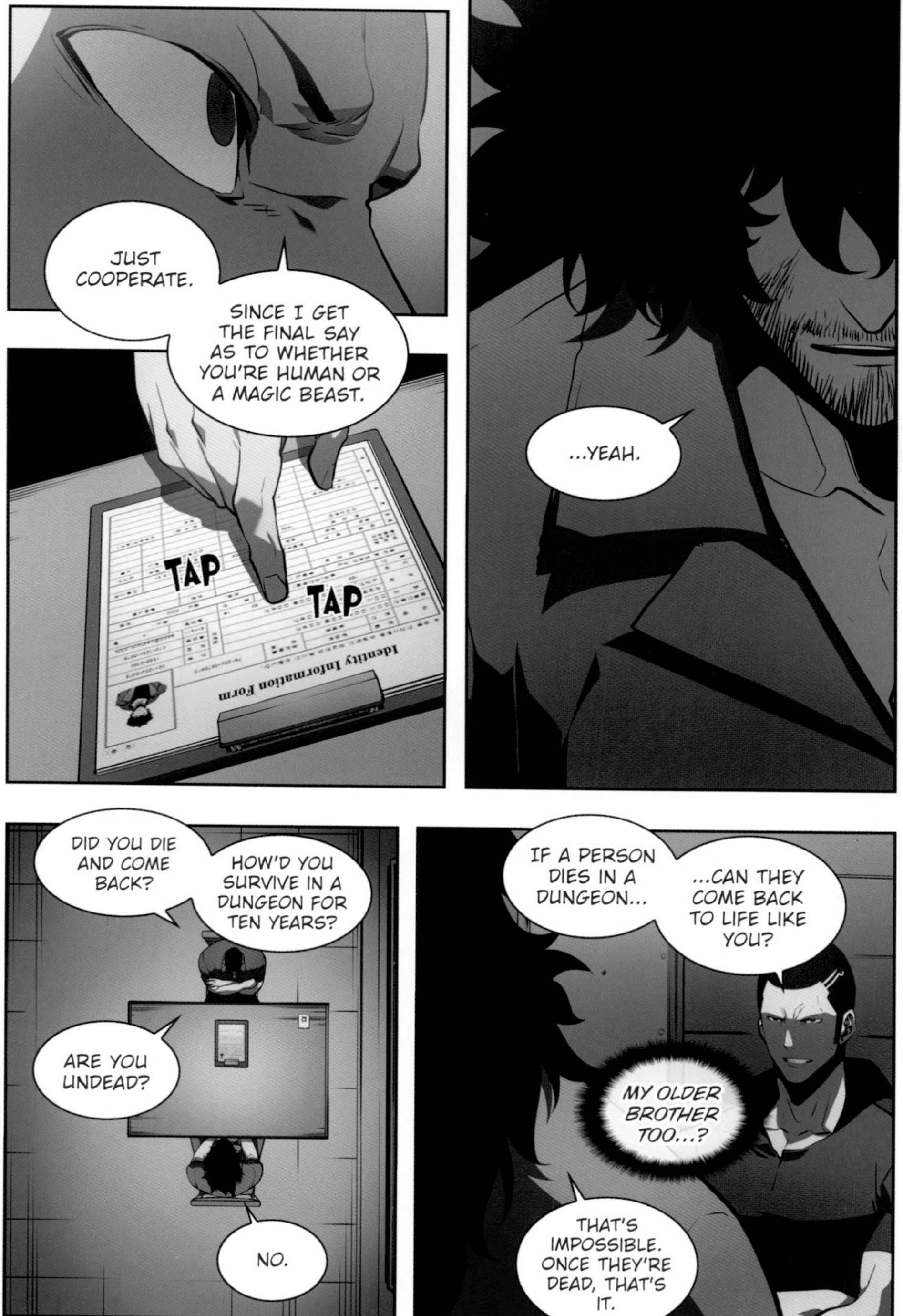
JUST COOPERATE.
SINCE I GET THE FINAL SAY AS TO WHETHER YOU'RE HUMAN OR A MAGIC BEAST.
TAP
TAP
Identity Information Form
...YEAH.
DID YOU DIE AND COME BACK?
HOW'D YOU SURVIVE IN A DUNGEON FOR TEN YEARS?
ARE YOU UNDEAD?
NO.
IF A PERSON DIES IN A DUNGEON...
...CAN THEY COME BACK TO LIFE LIKE YOU?
MY OLDER BROTHER TOO...?
THAT'S IMPOSSIBLE. ONCE THEY'RE DEAD, THAT'S IT.

LET ME ASK YOU SOMETHING.

...I ASK THE QUESTIONS HERE.

HOW MUCH DO YOU KNOW ABOUT GATES AND MAGIC BEASTS?

......

<Assistant director...>

<Shh.>

ARE YOU SAYING YOU HAVE AN ANSWER?

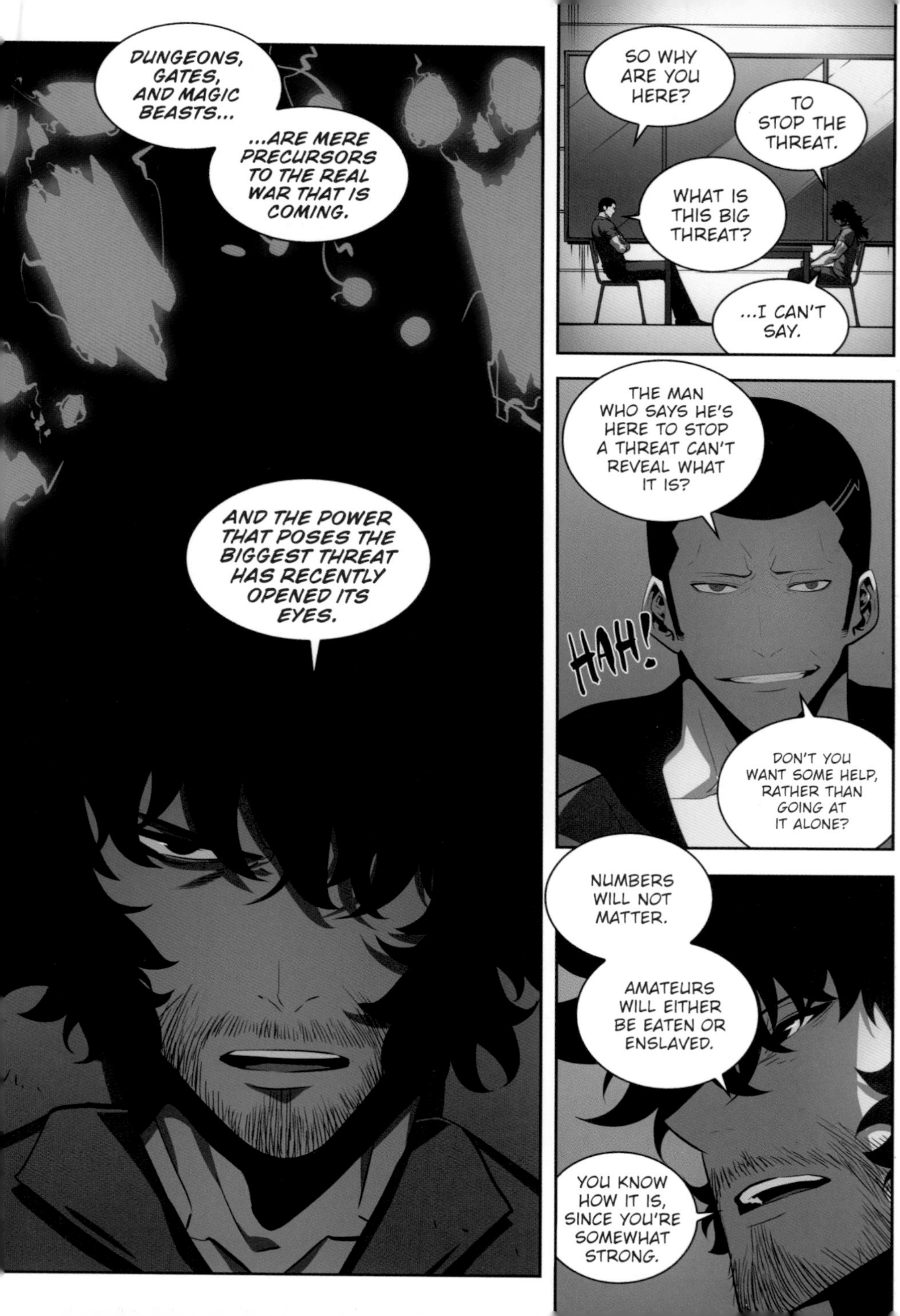
DUNGEONS, GATES, AND MAGIC BEASTS...
...ARE MERE PRECURSORS TO THE REAL WAR THAT IS COMING.
AND THE POWER THAT POSES THE BIGGEST THREAT HAS RECENTLY OPENED ITS EYES.
SO WHY ARE YOU HERE?
TO STOP THE THREAT.
WHAT IS THIS BIG THREAT?
...I CAN'T SAY.
THE MAN WHO SAYS HE'S HERE TO STOP A THREAT CAN'T REVEAL WHAT IT IS?
HAH!
DON'T YOU WANT SOME HELP, RATHER THAN GOING AT IT ALONE?
NUMBERS WILL NOT MATTER.
AMATEURS WILL EITHER BE EATEN OR ENSLAVED.
YOU KNOW HOW IT IS, SINCE YOU'RE SOMEWHAT STRONG.

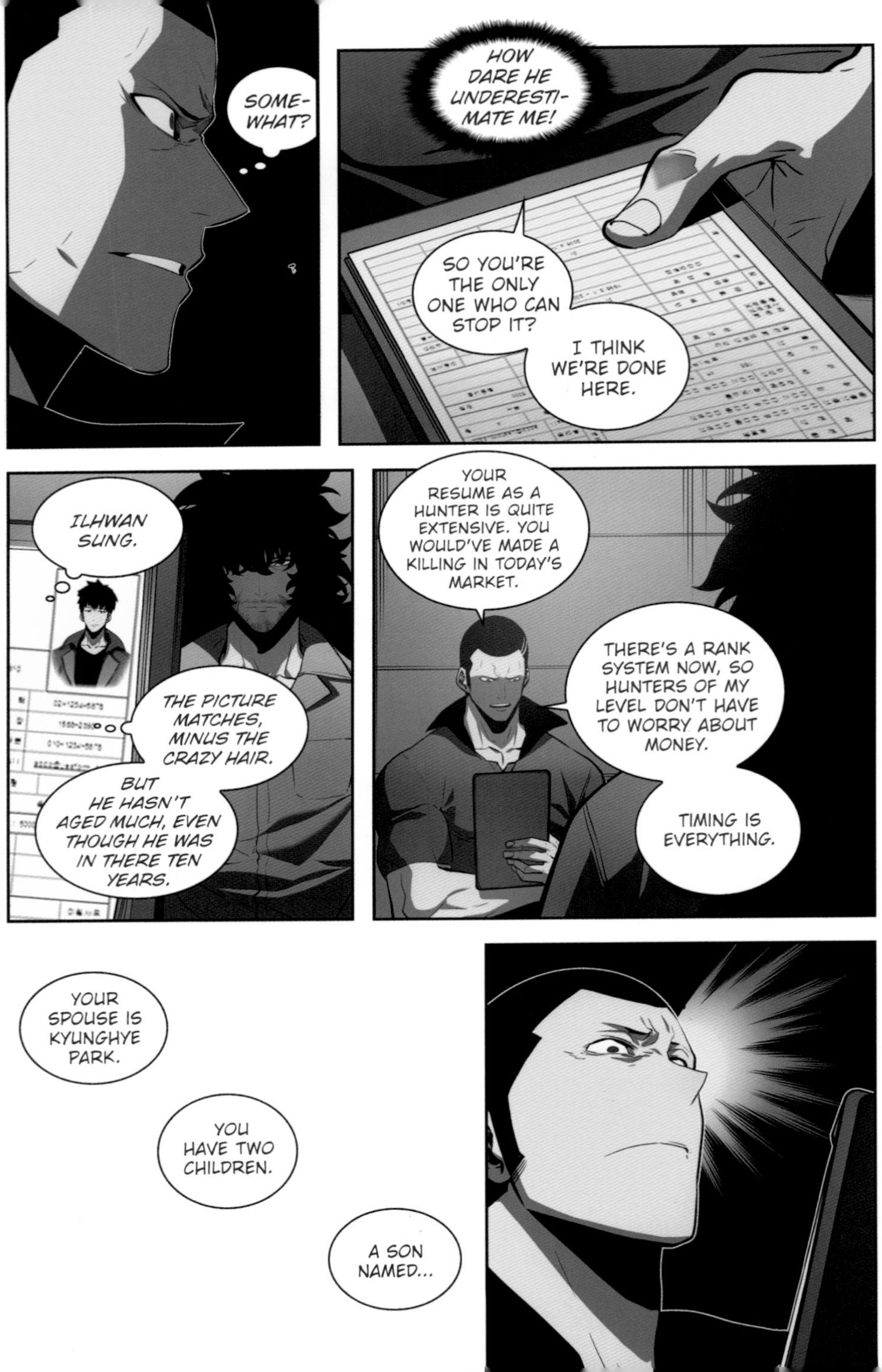
SOME-WHAT?
HOW DARE HE UNDERESTI-MATE ME!
SO YOU'RE THE ONLY ONE WHO CAN STOP IT?
I THINK WE'RE DONE HERE.
ILHWAN SUNG.
THE PICTURE MATCHES, MINUS THE CRAZY HAIR.
BUT HE HASN'T AGED MUCH, EVEN THOUGH HE WAS IN THERE TEN YEARS.
YOUR RESUME AS A HUNTER IS QUITE EXTENSIVE. YOU WOULD'VE MADE A KILLING IN TODAY'S MARKET.
THERE'S A RANK SYSTEM NOW, SO HUNTERS OF MY LEVEL DON'T HAVE TO WORRY ABOUT MONEY.
TIMING IS EVERYTHING.
YOUR SPOUSE IS KYUNGHYE PARK.
YOU HAVE TWO CHILDREN.
A SON NAMED...

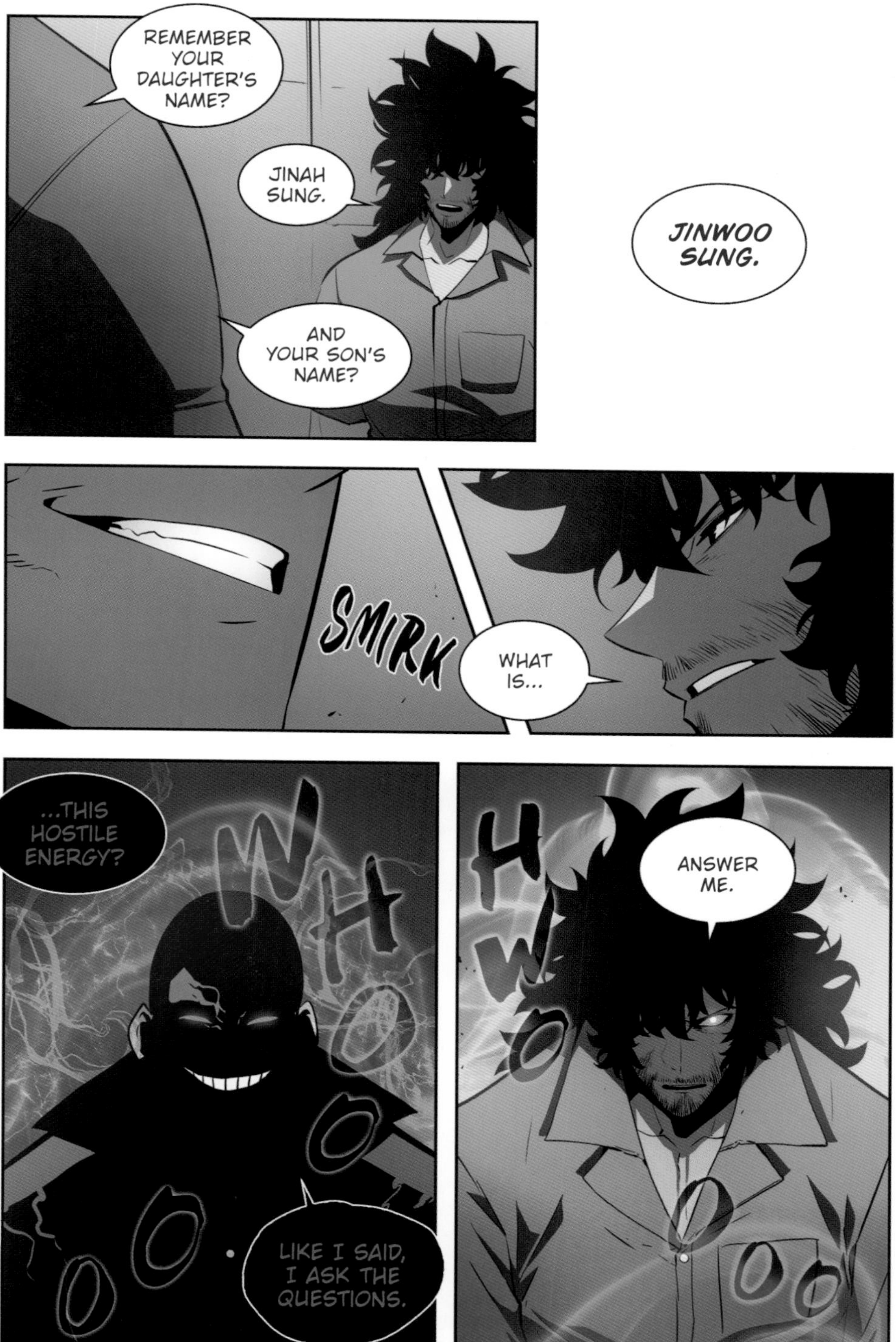
REMEMBER YOUR DAUGHTER'S NAME?
JINAH SUNG.
AND YOUR SON'S NAME?
JINWOO SUNG.
SMIRK
WHAT IS...
...THIS HOSTILE ENERGY?
LIKE I SAID, I ASK THE QUESTIONS.
ANSWER ME.

IF I DON'T WANT TO ANSWER?

I GUESS I'LL HAVE TO FORCE YOU TO TALK.

YOU'VE BEEN RUDE FROM THE START.

PERHAPS HEAVEN IS GIVING ME A SECOND CHANCE.

...I SEE. YOU'RE A MAGIC BEAST, THEN.

BEEP

&lt;Assistant director, this man is a magic beast.&gt;

&lt;It's preparing to attack. You must evacuate.&gt;

&lt;What? W-w-wait!&gt;

I JUST CAME BACK FROM KOREA.

SO I KNOW EXACTLY WHAT'S HAPPENED TO YOUR SON.

VROOM

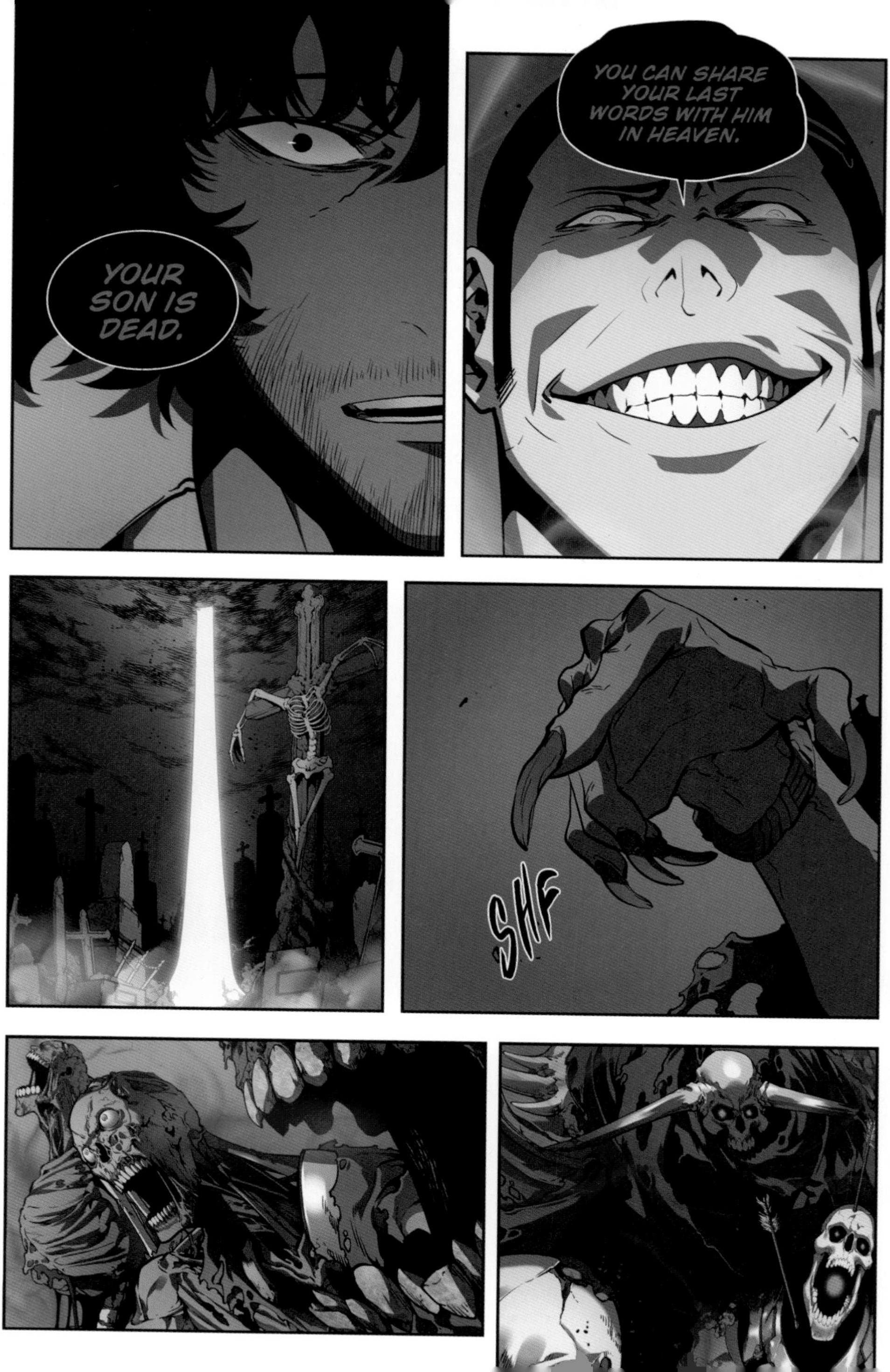
YOUR SON IS DEAD.
YOU CAN SHARE YOUR LAST WORDS WITH HIM IN HEAVEN.
SHF

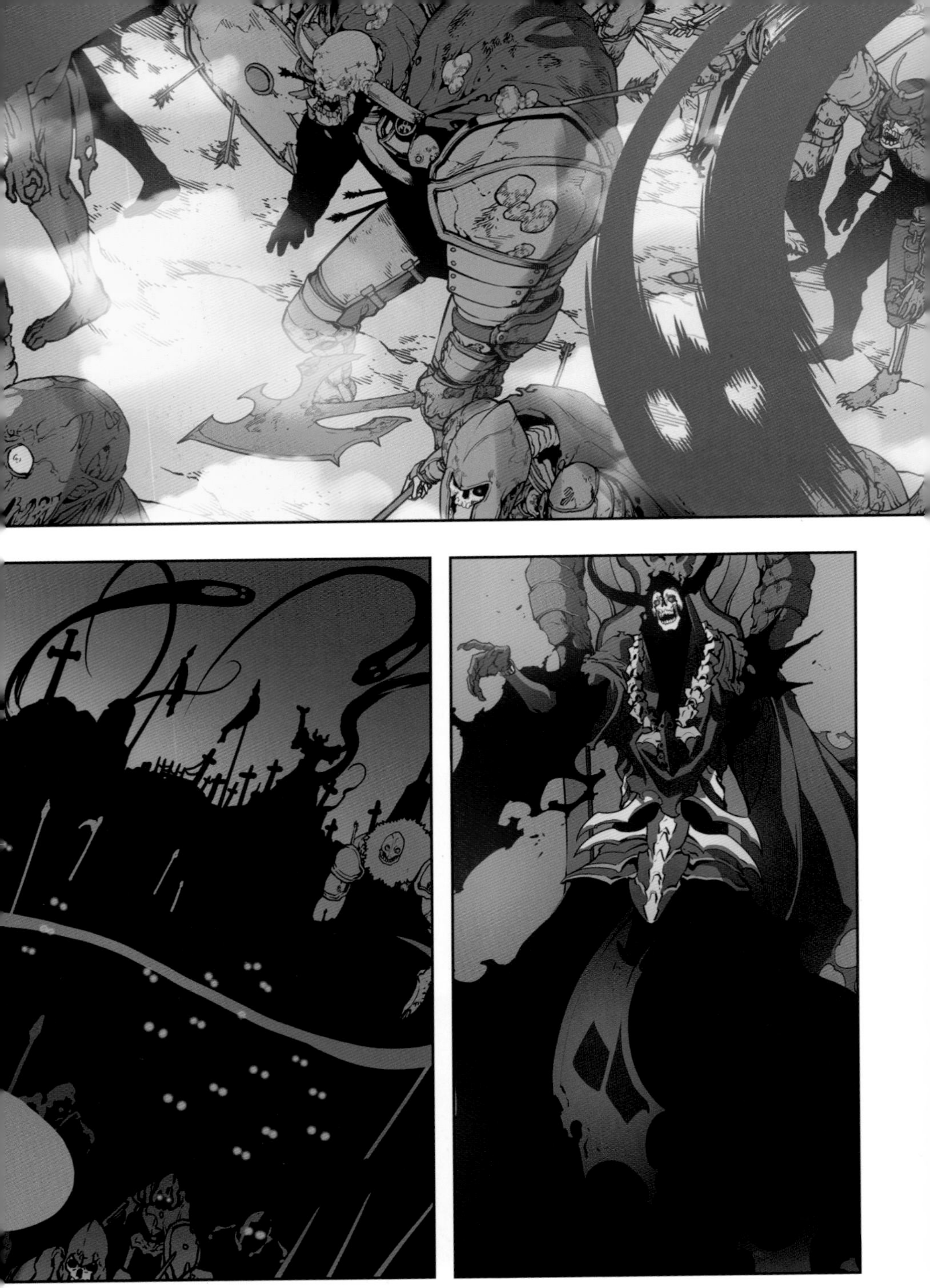

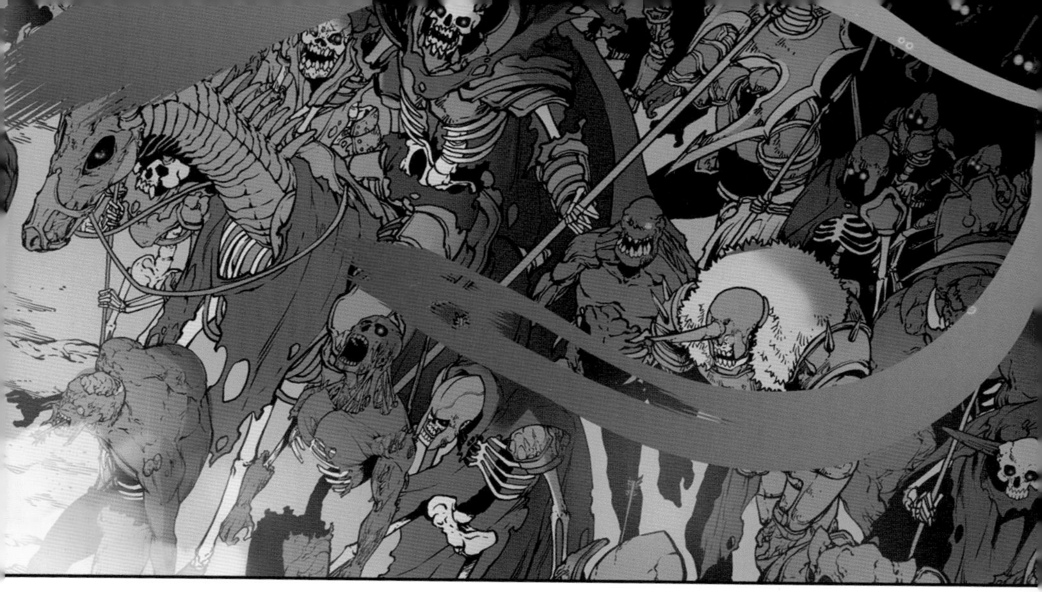

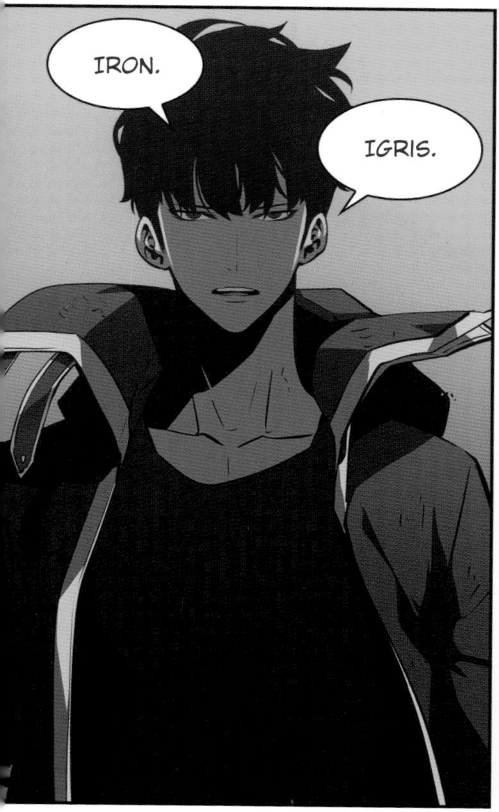
IRON.
IGRIS.

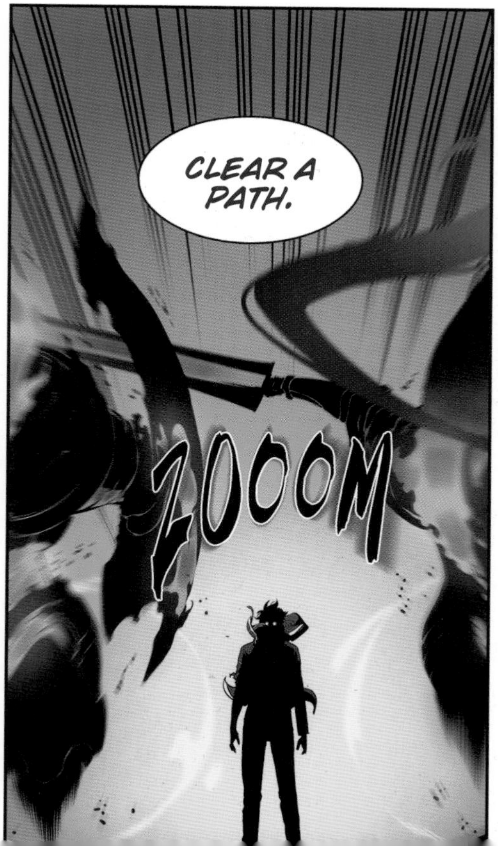
CLEAR A PATH.
ZOOOM

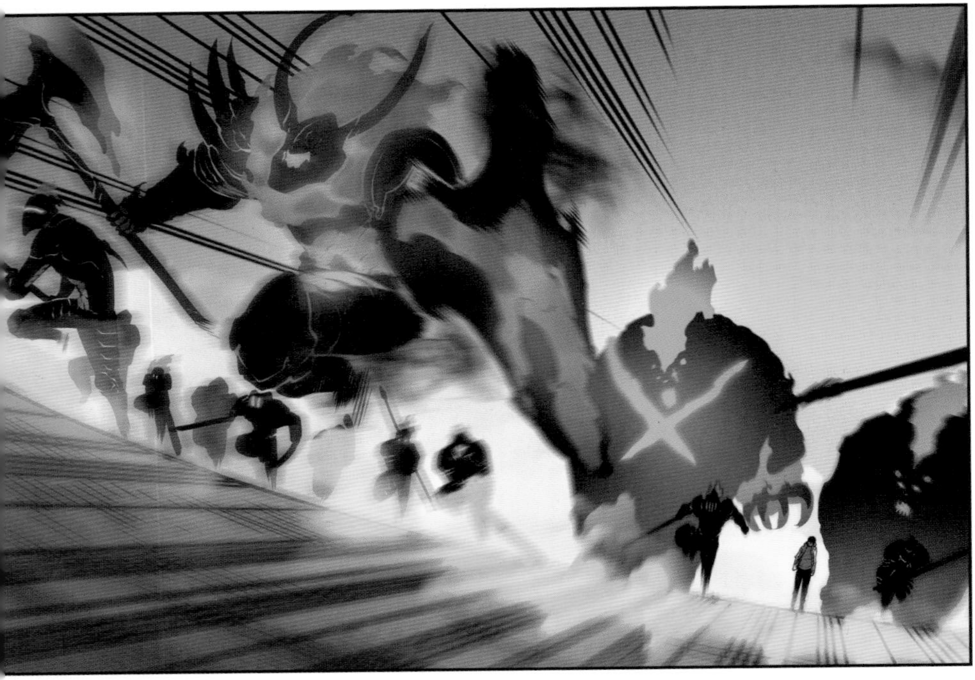
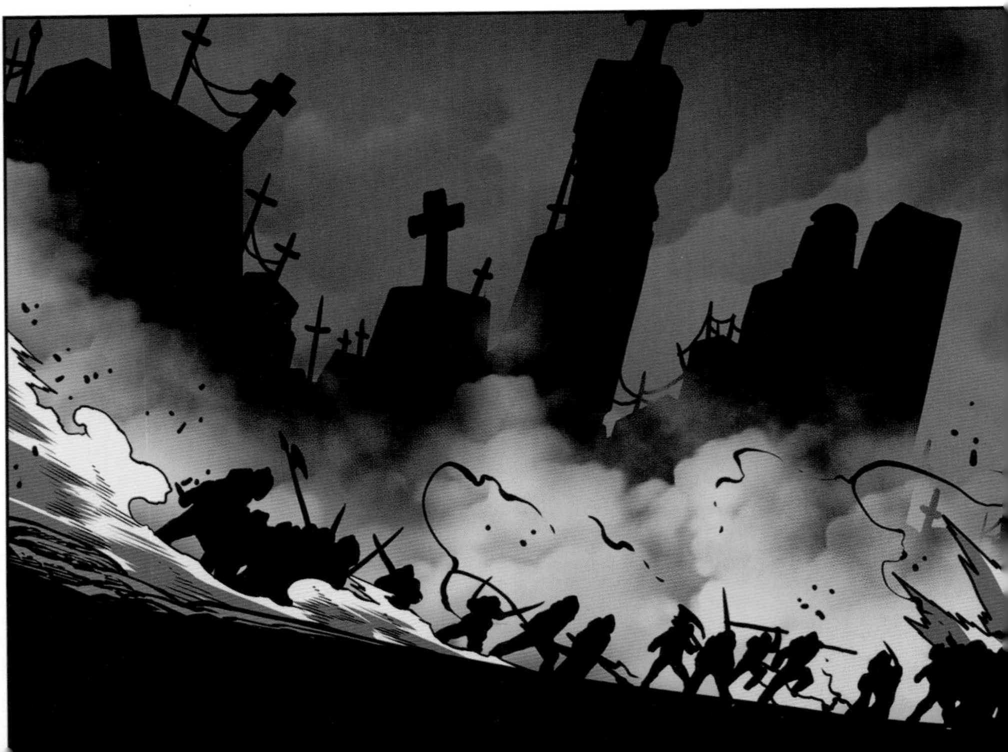

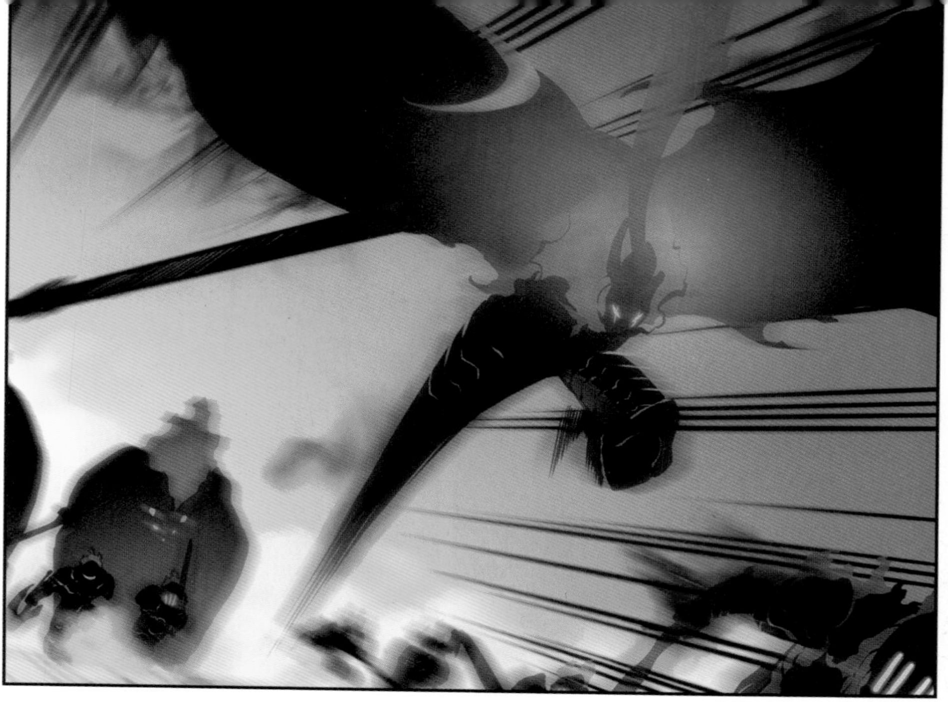

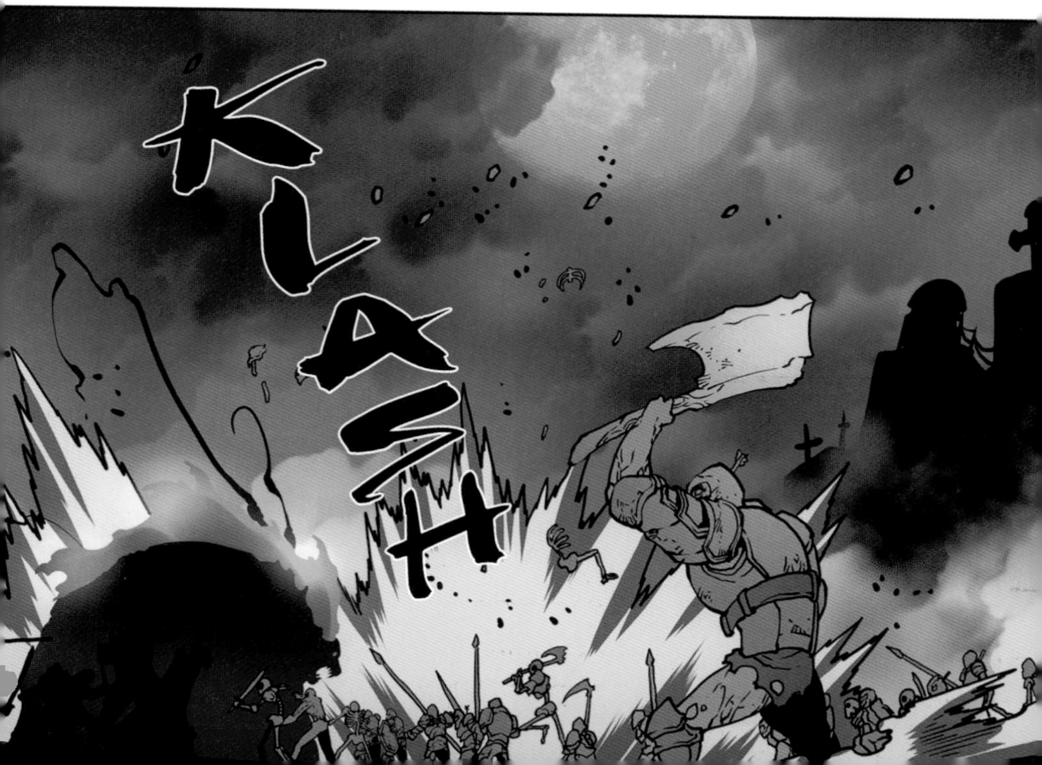
KLASH

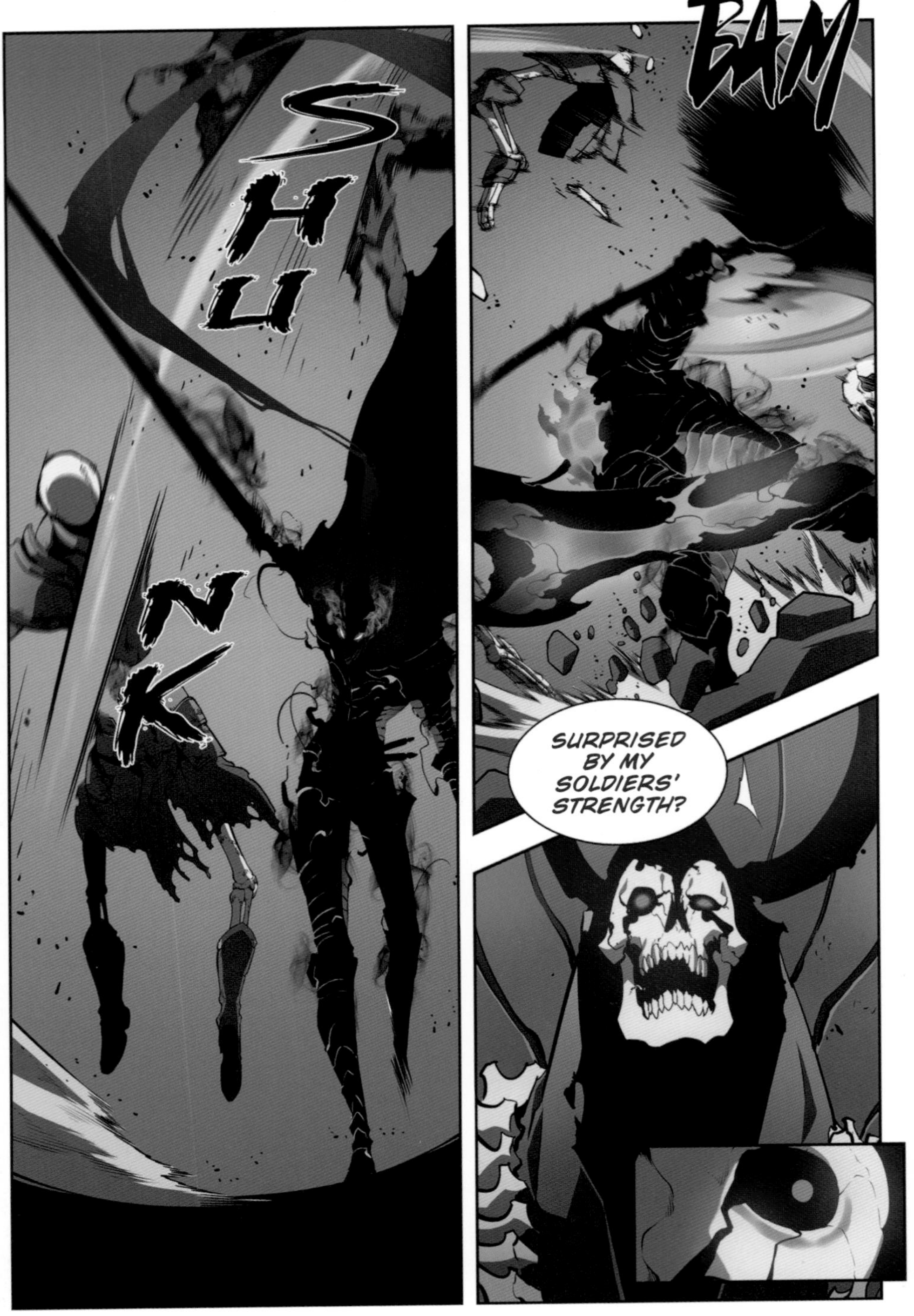
SHUNK
BAM
SURPRISED BY MY SOLDIERS' STRENGTH?

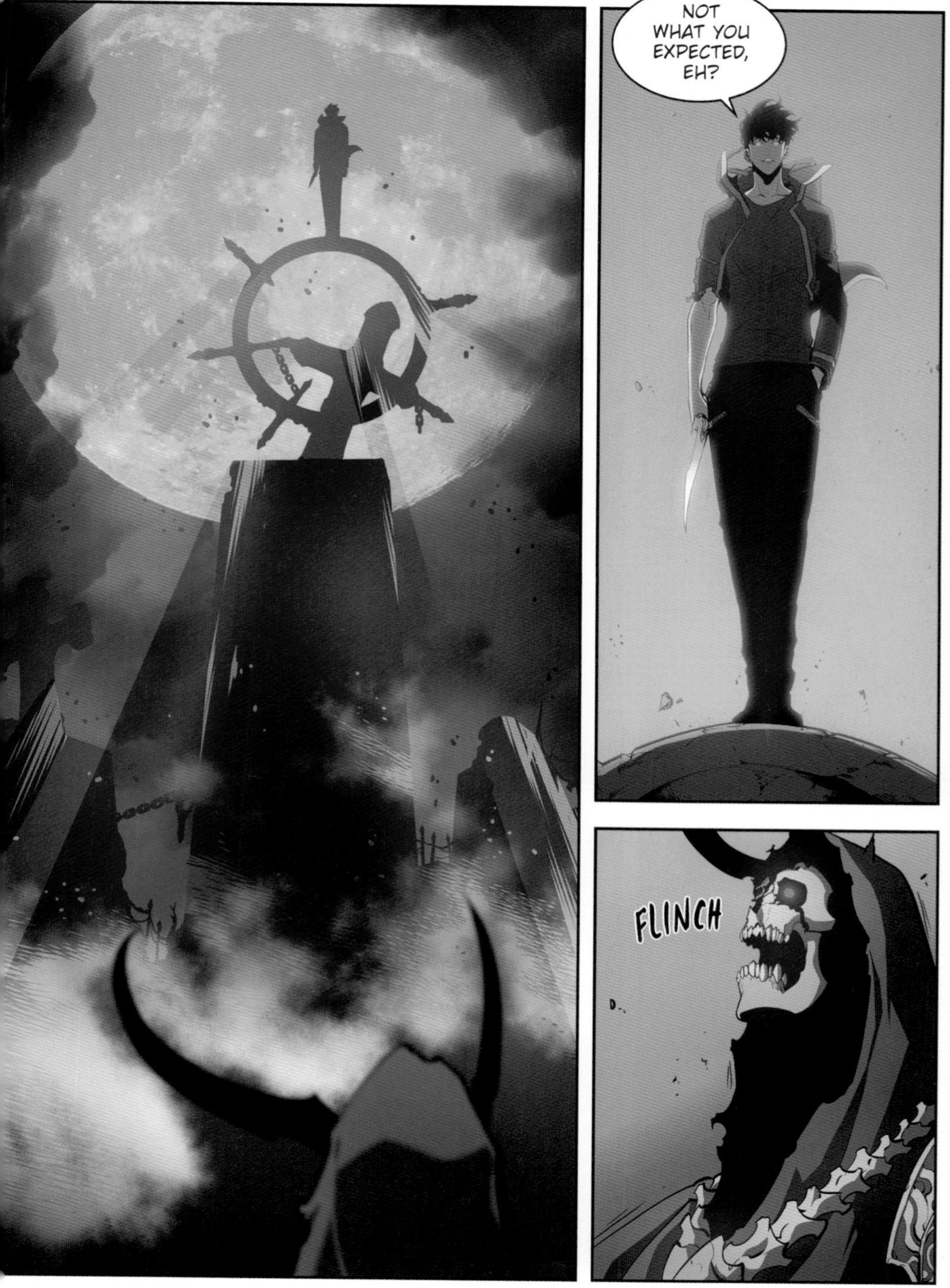
NOT WHAT YOU EXPECTED, EH?
FLINCH
D-..

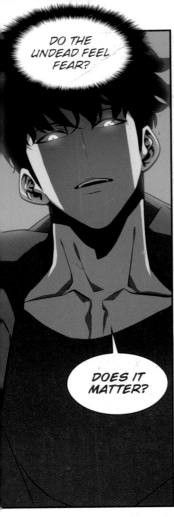

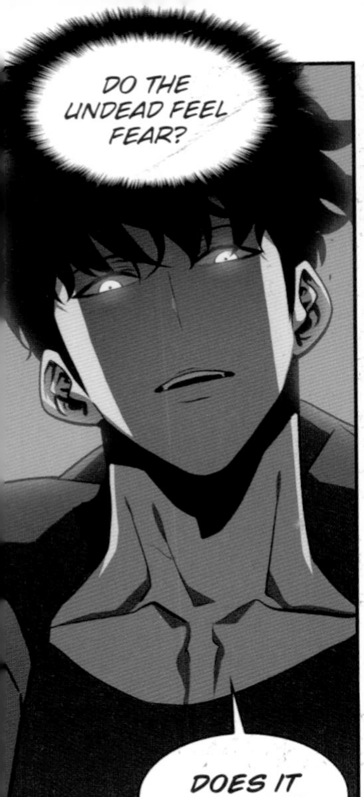
DO THE UNDEAD FEEL FEAR?
DOES IT MATTER?
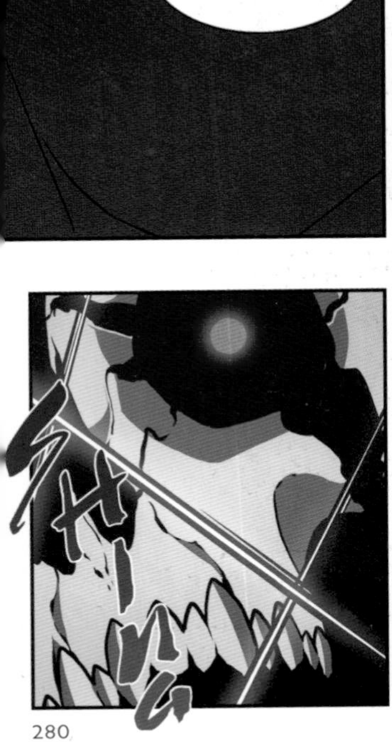
SHING
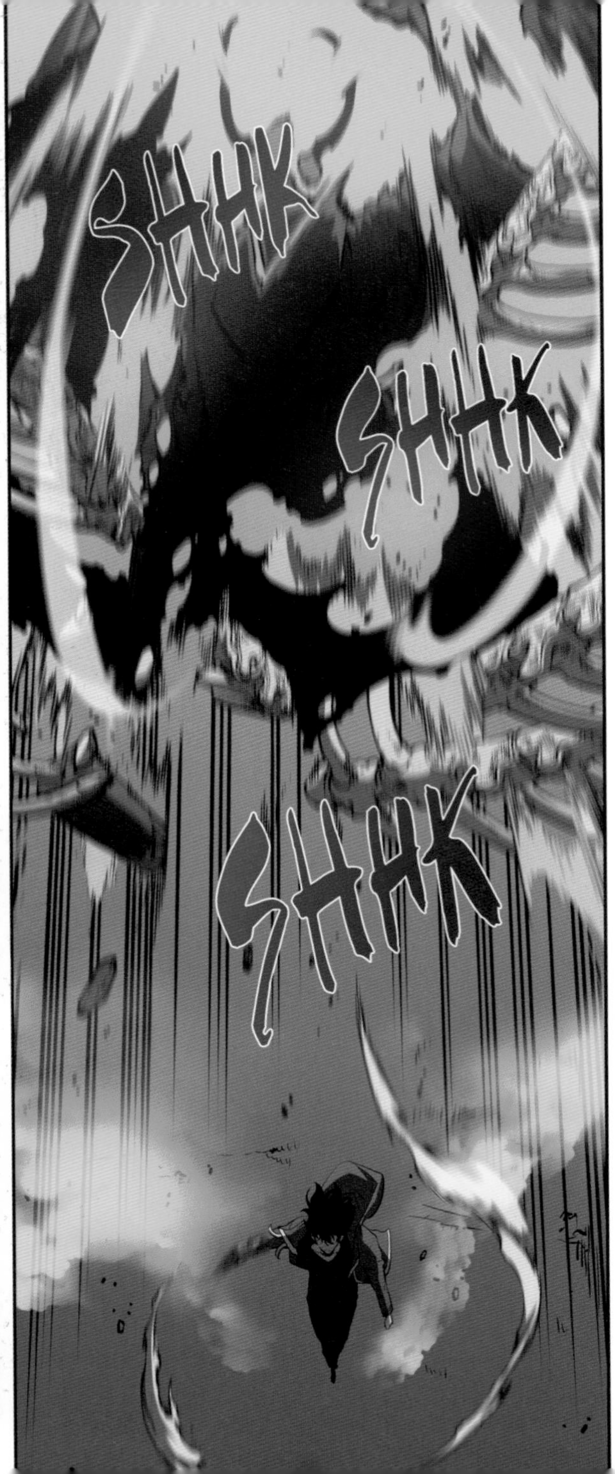
SHHK
SHHK
SHHK

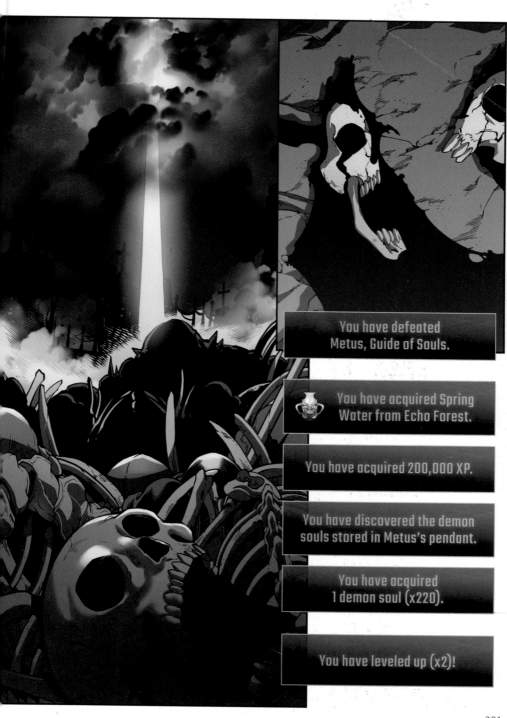

You have defeated
Metus, Guide of Souls.

You have acquired Spring
Water from Echo Forest.

You have acquired 200,000 XP.

You have discovered the demon
souls stored in Metus's pendant.

You have acquired
1 demon soul (x220).

You have leveled up (x2)!

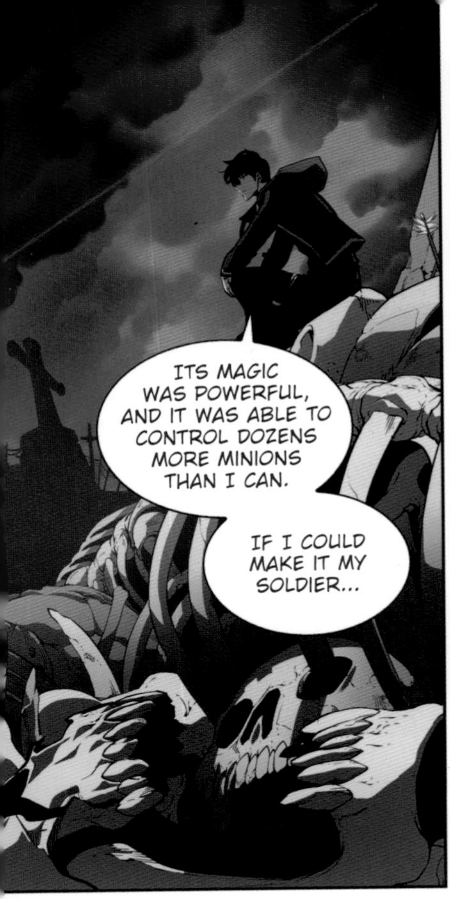
ITS MAGIC WAS POWERFUL, AND IT WAS ABLE TO CONTROL DOZENS MORE MINIONS THAN I CAN.
IF I COULD MAKE IT MY SOLDIER...

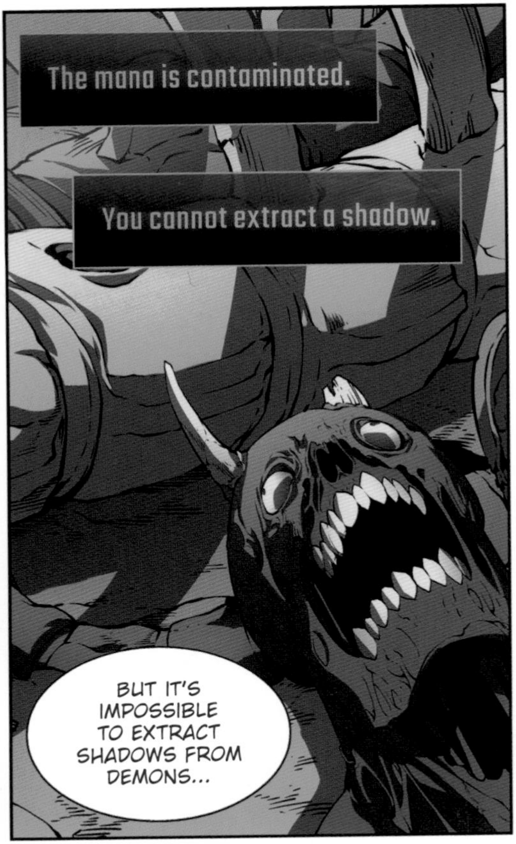
The mana is contaminated.
You cannot extract a shadow.
BUT IT'S IMPOSSIBLE TO EXTRACT SHADOWS FROM DEMONS...

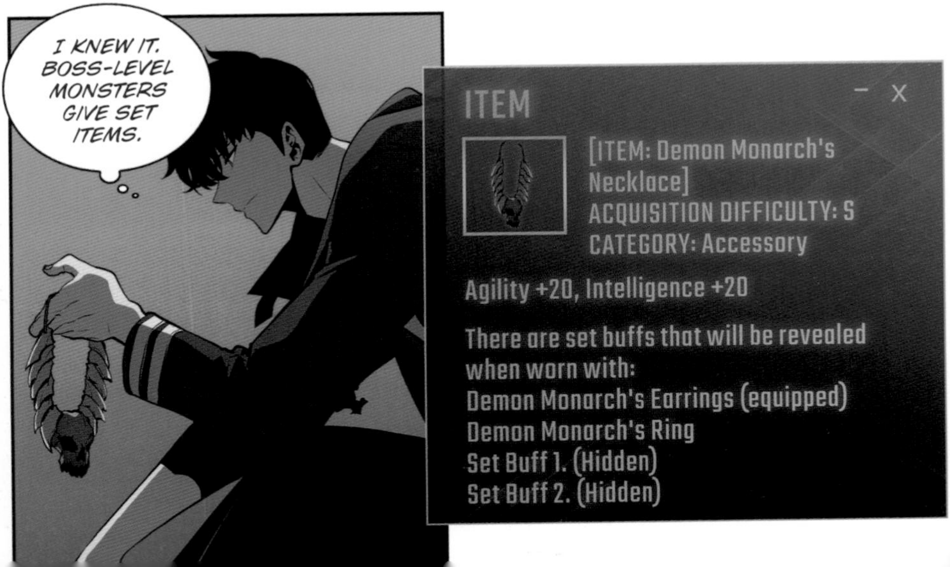
I KNEW IT. BOSS-LEVEL MONSTERS GIVE SET ITEMS.
ITEM
[ITEM: Demon Monarch's Necklace]
ACQUISITION DIFFICULTY: S
CATEGORY: Accessory
Agility +20, Intelligence +20
There are set buffs that will be revealed when worn with:
Demon Monarch's Earrings (equipped)
Demon Monarch's Ring
Set Buff 1. (Hidden)
Set Buff 2. (Hidden)

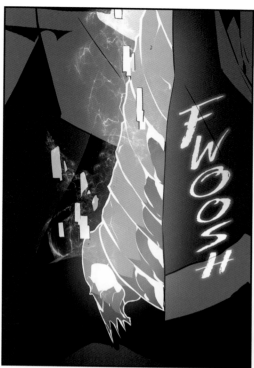

FWOOSH

## SET ITEM EFFECT – ✕

LV.1

THE SET BUFF IS THE SAME AS FIVE LEVEL-UPS!

Set Buff 1. All stats +5
Set Buff 2. (Hidden)

ONLY ONE ITEM LEFT...

THAT MEANS THERE ARE THREE BOSS-LEVEL MONSTERS.

ONLY ONE BASTARD LEFT TO COMPLETE THE SET.

...BUT...

PING!

Demon souls collected: 10,001/10,000

...THE QUEST IS OVER.

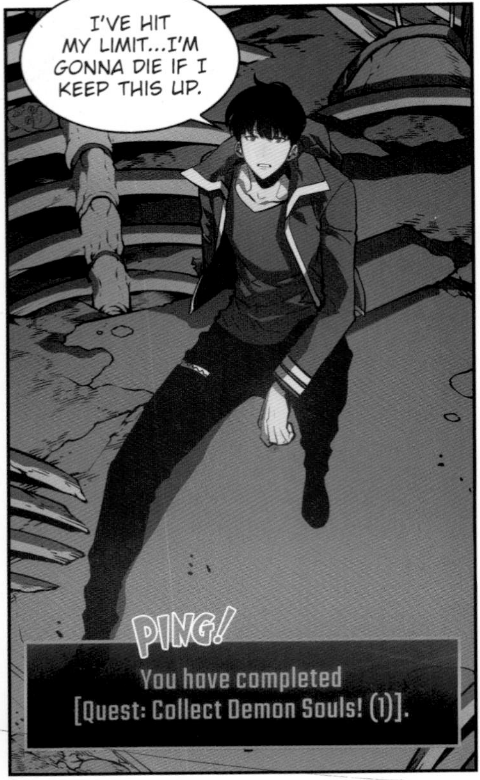
I'VE HIT MY LIMIT...I'M GONNA DIE IF I KEEP THIS UP.
PING!
You have completed
[Quest: Collect Demon Souls! (1)].

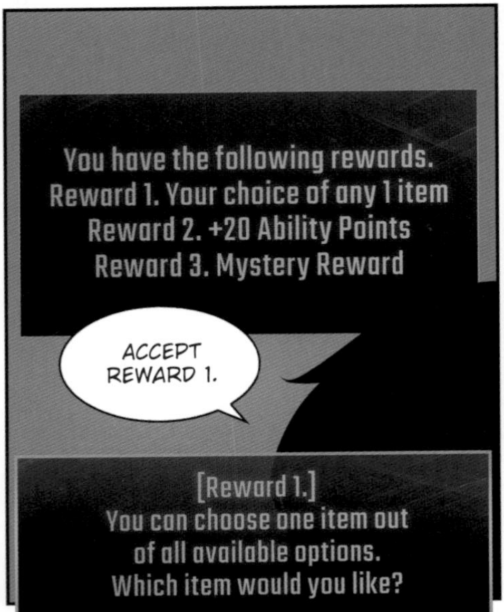
You have the following rewards.
Reward 1. Your choice of any 1 item
Reward 2. +20 Ability Points
Reward 3. Mystery Reward
ACCEPT REWARD 1.
[Reward 1.]
You can choose one item out
of all available options.
Which item would you like?

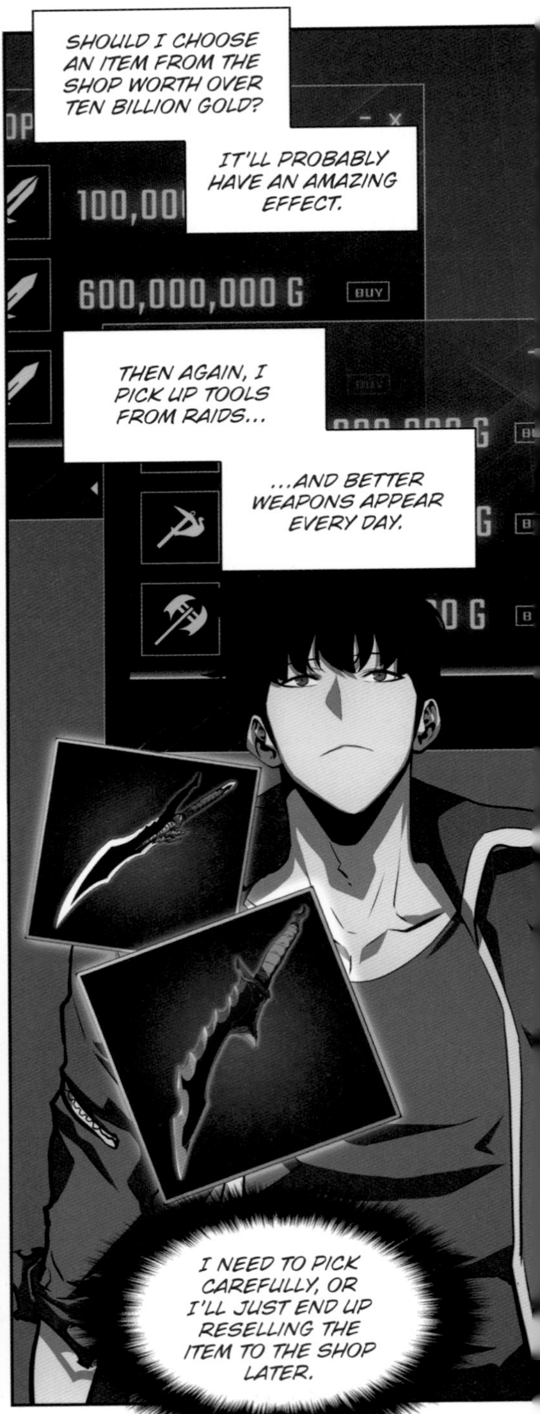
SHOULD I CHOOSE AN ITEM FROM THE SHOP WORTH OVER TEN BILLION GOLD?
IT'LL PROBABLY HAVE AN AMAZING EFFECT.
600,000,000 G
BUY
THEN AGAIN, I PICK UP TOOLS FROM RAIDS...
...AND BETTER WEAPONS APPEAR EVERY DAY.
I NEED TO PICK CAREFULLY, OR I'LL JUST END UP RESELLING THE ITEM TO THE SHOP LATER.

Which item would you like?

CURSED MYSTERY BOX.

FWOOM

You have selected [Item: Cursed Mystery Box].

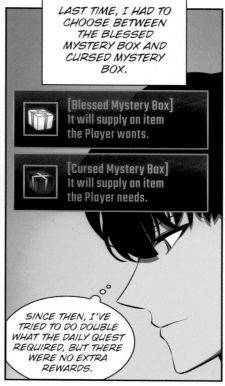

LAST TIME, I HAD TO CHOOSE BETWEEN THE BLESSED MYSTERY BOX AND CURSED MYSTERY BOX.

[Blessed Mystery Box]
It will supply an item the Player wants.

[Cursed Mystery Box]
It will supply an item the Player needs.

SINCE THEN, I'VE TRIED TO DO DOUBLE WHAT THE DAILY QUEST REQUIRED, BUT THERE WERE NO EXTRA REWARDS.

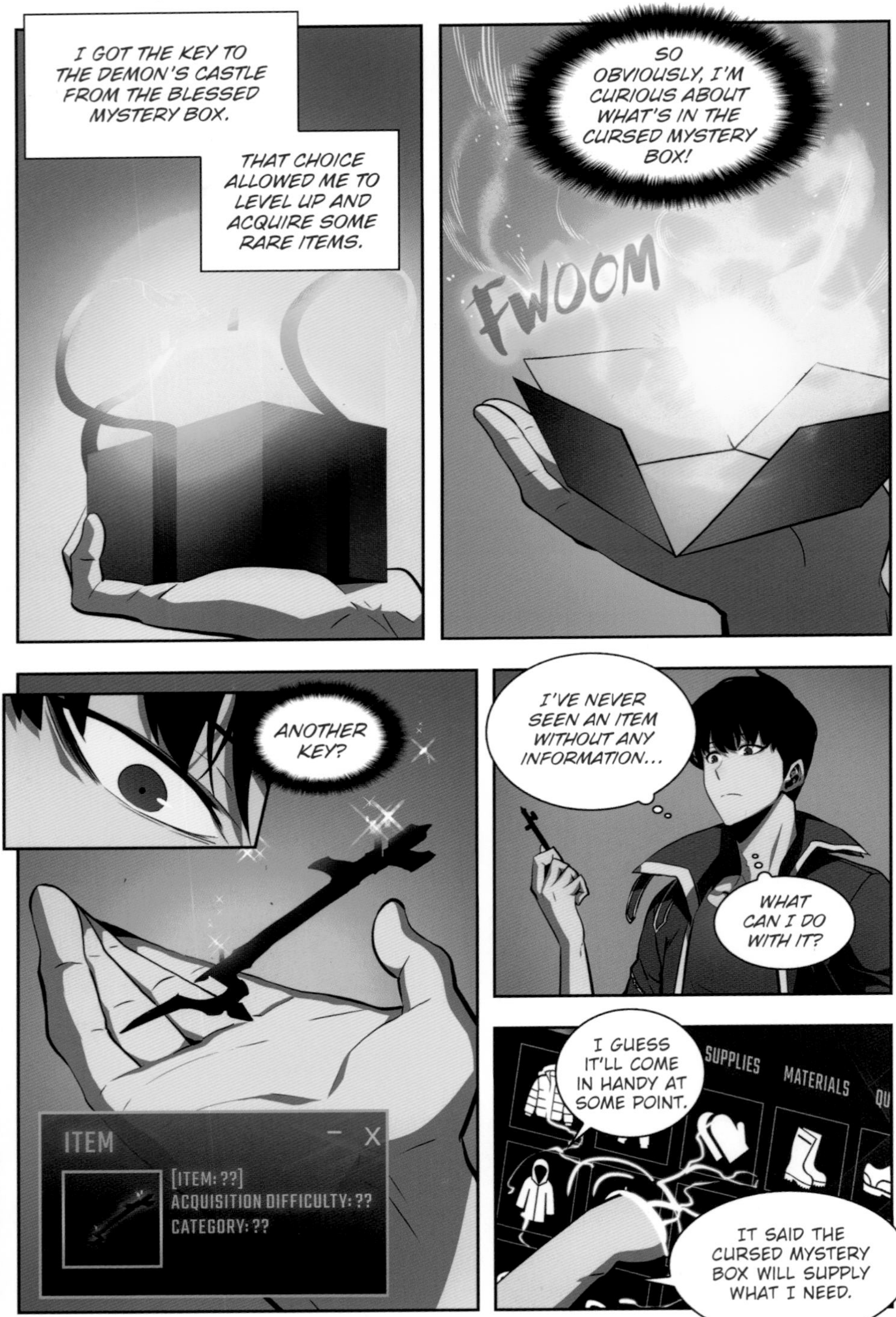
I GOT THE KEY TO THE DEMON'S CASTLE FROM THE BLESSED MYSTERY BOX.
THAT CHOICE ALLOWED ME TO LEVEL UP AND ACQUIRE SOME RARE ITEMS.
SO OBVIOUSLY, I'M CURIOUS ABOUT WHAT'S IN THE CURSED MYSTERY BOX!
FWOOM
ANOTHER KEY?
ITEM
[ITEM: ??]
ACQUISITION DIFFICULTY: ??
CATEGORY: ??
I'VE NEVER SEEN AN ITEM WITHOUT ANY INFORMATION...
WHAT CAN I DO WITH IT?
I GUESS IT'LL COME IN HANDY AT SOME POINT.
SUPPLIES
MATERIALS
IT SAID THE CURSED MYSTERY BOX WILL SUPPLY WHAT I NEED.

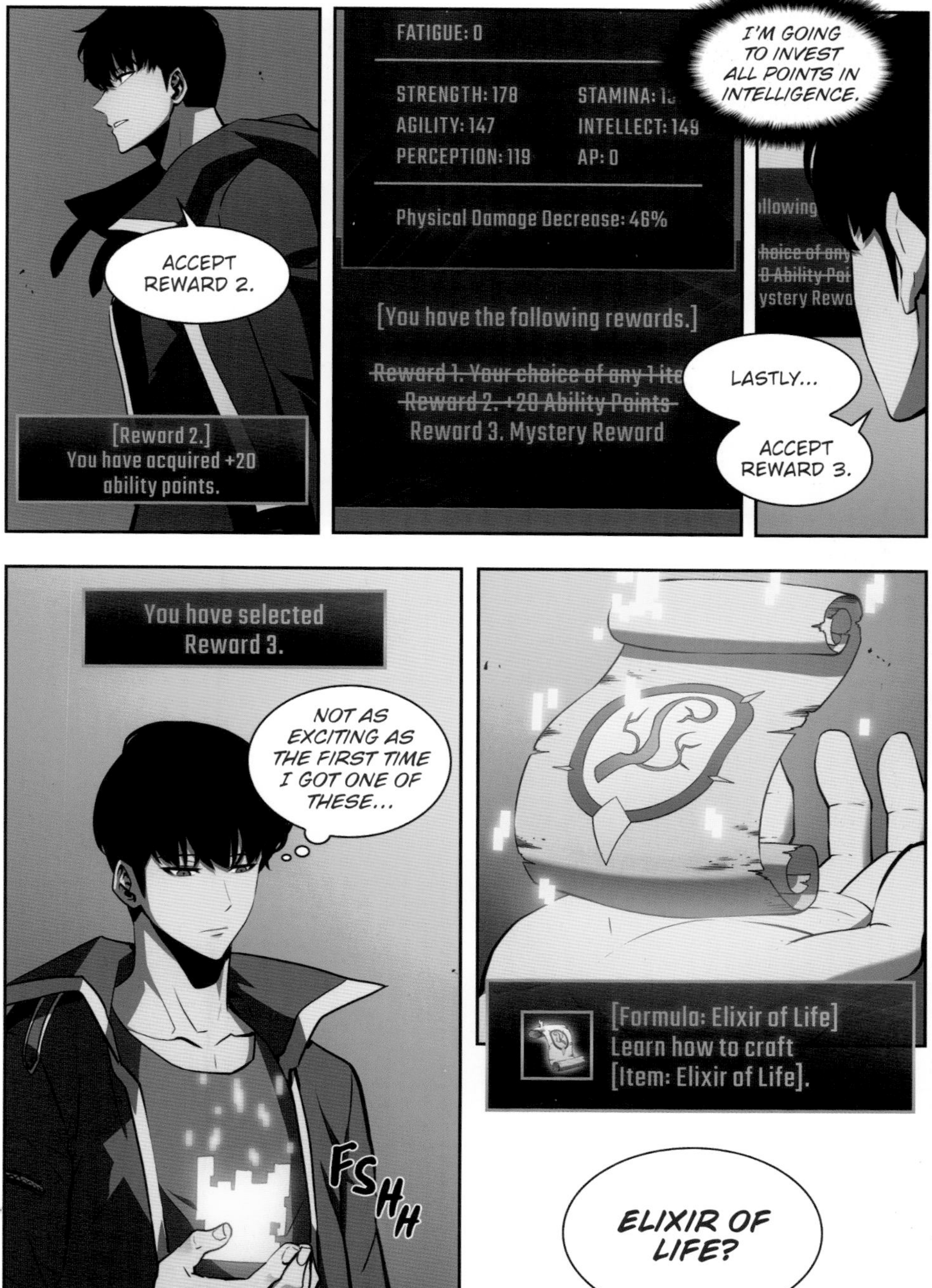
ACCEPT REWARD 2.
[Reward 2.]
You have acquired +20 ability points.
FATIGUE: 0
STRENGTH: 178
STAMINA: 1
AGILITY: 147
INTELLECT: 149
PERCEPTION: 119
AP: 0
Physical Damage Decrease: 46%
[You have the following rewards.]
~~Reward 1. Your choice of any 1 ite~~
~~Reward 2. +20 Ability Points~~
Reward 3. Mystery Reward
I'M GOING TO INVEST ALL POINTS IN INTELLIGENCE.
llowing
hoice of any
0 Ability Poi
ystery Rewa
LASTLY...
ACCEPT REWARD 3.
You have selected Reward 3.
NOT AS EXCITING AS THE FIRST TIME I GOT ONE OF THESE...
FSHH
[Formula: Elixir of Life]
Learn how to craft
[Item: Elixir of Life].
ELIXIR OF LIFE?

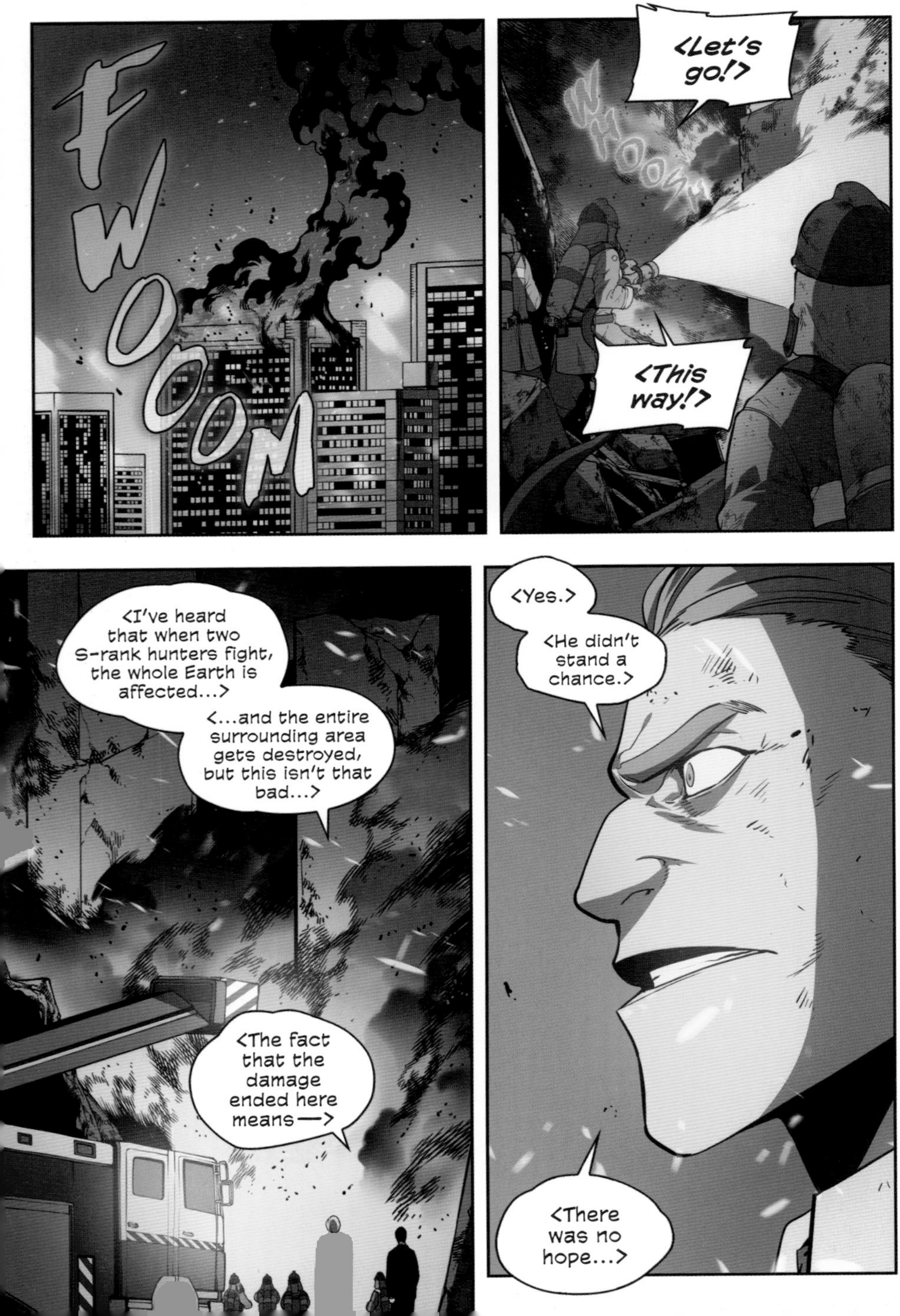
FWOOOOM
<Let's go!>
WHOOM
<This way!>
<I've heard that when two S-rank hunters fight, the whole Earth is affected...>
<...and the entire surrounding area gets destroyed, but this isn't that bad...>
<The fact that the damage ended here means—>
<Yes.>
<He didn't stand a chance.>
<There was no hope...>

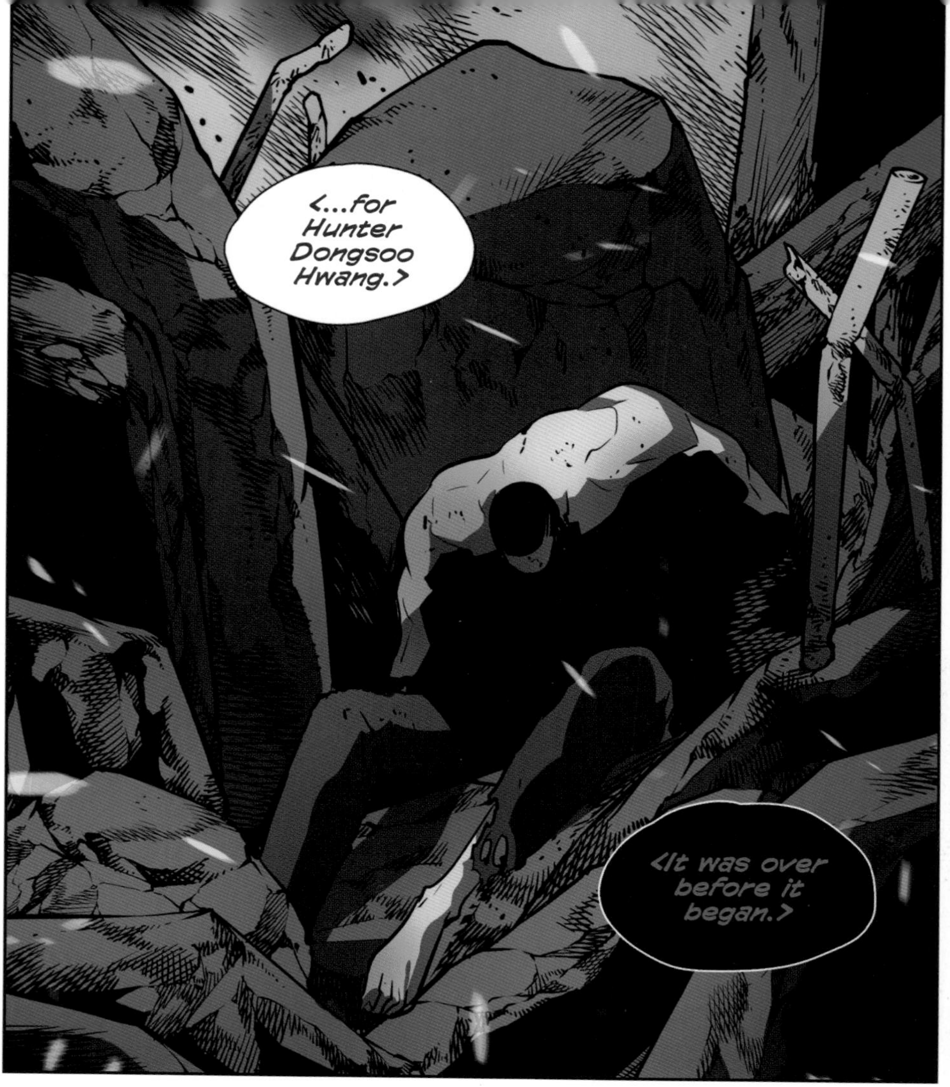
<...for Hunter Dongsoo Hwang.>
<It was over before it began.>
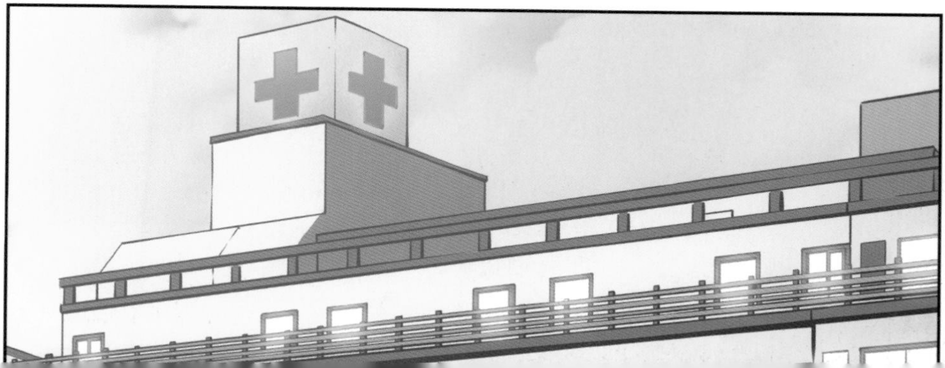

......

...MOM.

SWF

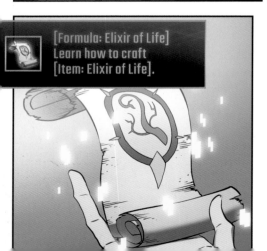

[Formula: Elixir of Life]
Learn how to craft
[Item: Elixir of Life].

ITEM       —   X

[ITEM: Elixir of Life]
AQUISITION DIFFICULTY: S
CATEGORY: Consumable

A mystical potion that cures all diseases using powerful magic. An entire bottle must be consumed for the full effect of the potion.

THE THIRD REWARD—

AN ITEM THAT CAN HEAL ALL...

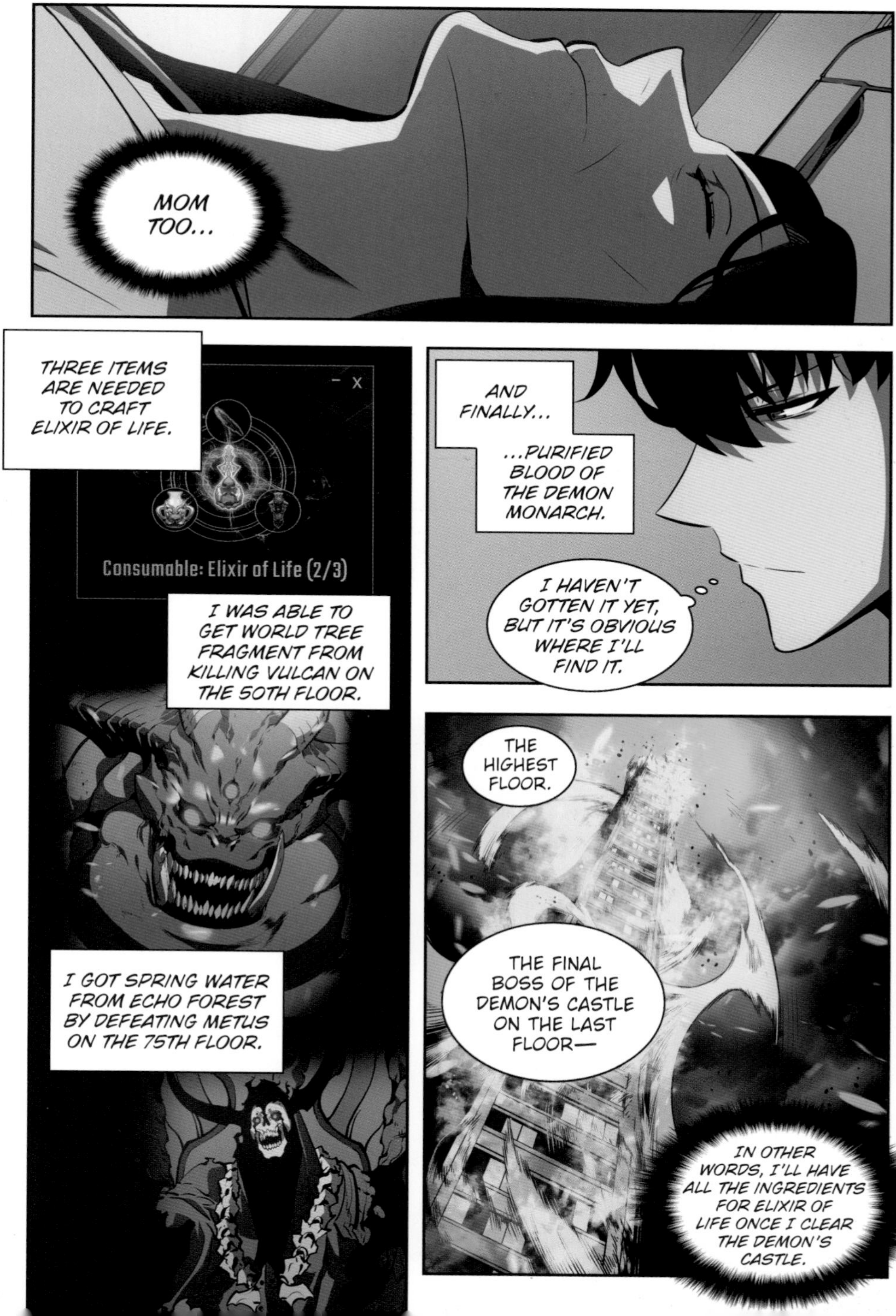
MOM TOO...
THREE ITEMS ARE NEEDED TO CRAFT ELIXIR OF LIFE.
- X
Consumable: Elixir of Life (2/3)
I WAS ABLE TO GET WORLD TREE FRAGMENT FROM KILLING VULCAN ON THE 50TH FLOOR.
I GOT SPRING WATER FROM ECHO FOREST BY DEFEATING METUS ON THE 75TH FLOOR.
AND FINALLY...
...PURIFIED BLOOD OF THE DEMON MONARCH.
I HAVEN'T GOTTEN IT YET, BUT IT'S OBVIOUS WHERE I'LL FIND IT.
THE HIGHEST FLOOR.
THE FINAL BOSS OF THE DEMON'S CASTLE ON THE LAST FLOOR—
IN OTHER WORDS, I'LL HAVE ALL THE INGREDIENTS FOR ELIXIR OF LIFE ONCE I CLEAR THE DEMON'S CASTLE.

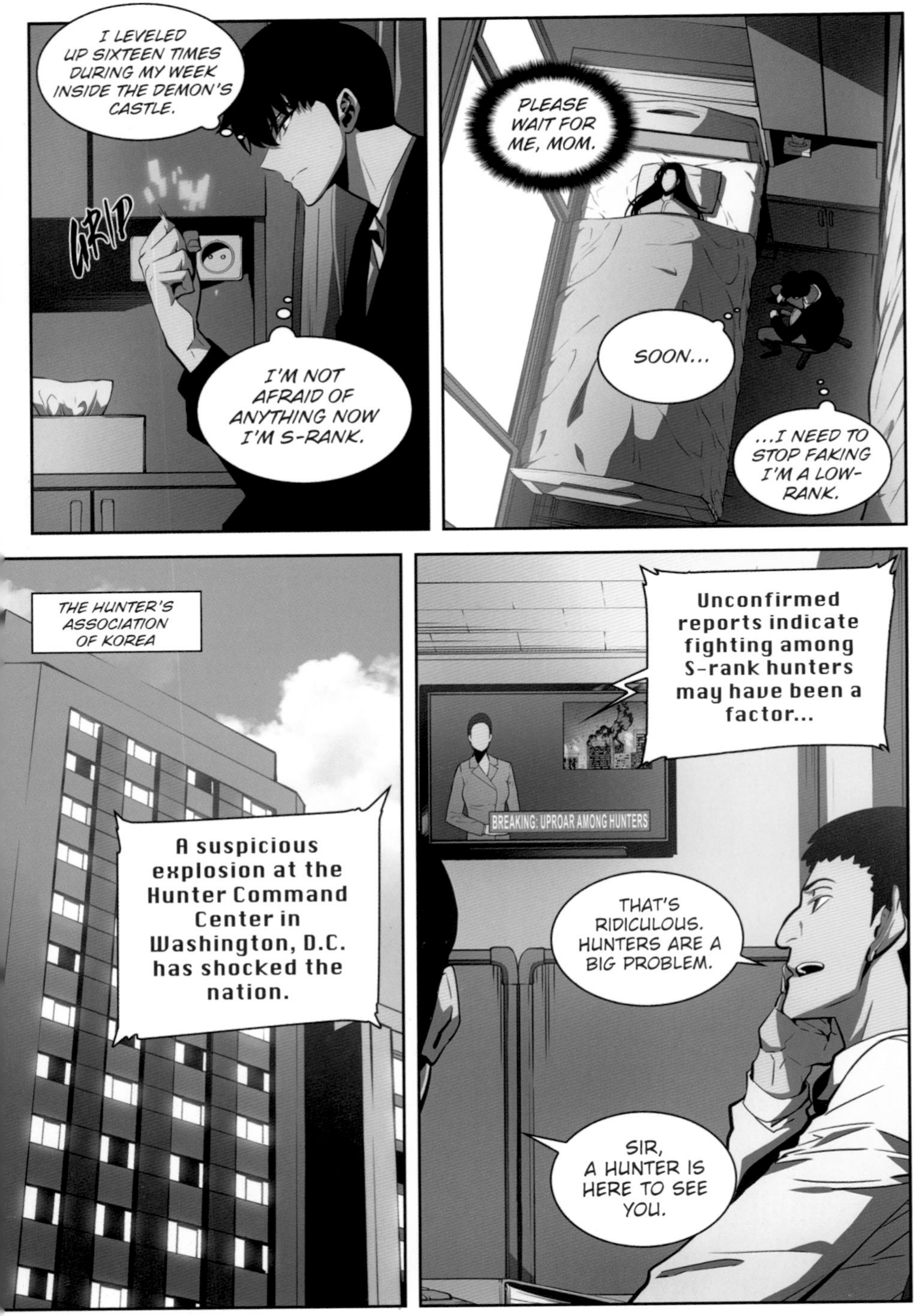
I LEVELED UP SIXTEEN TIMES DURING MY WEEK INSIDE THE DEMON'S CASTLE.
GRIP
I'M NOT AFRAID OF ANYTHING NOW I'M S-RANK.
PLEASE WAIT FOR ME, MOM.
SOON...
...I NEED TO STOP FAKING I'M A LOW-RANK.
THE HUNTER'S ASSOCIATION OF KOREA
A suspicious explosion at the Hunter Command Center in Washington, D.C. has shocked the nation.
Unconfirmed reports indicate fighting among S-rank hunters may have been a factor...
BREAKING: UPROAR AMONG HUNTERS
THAT'S RIDICULOUS. HUNTERS ARE A BIG PROBLEM.
SIR, A HUNTER IS HERE TO SEE YOU.

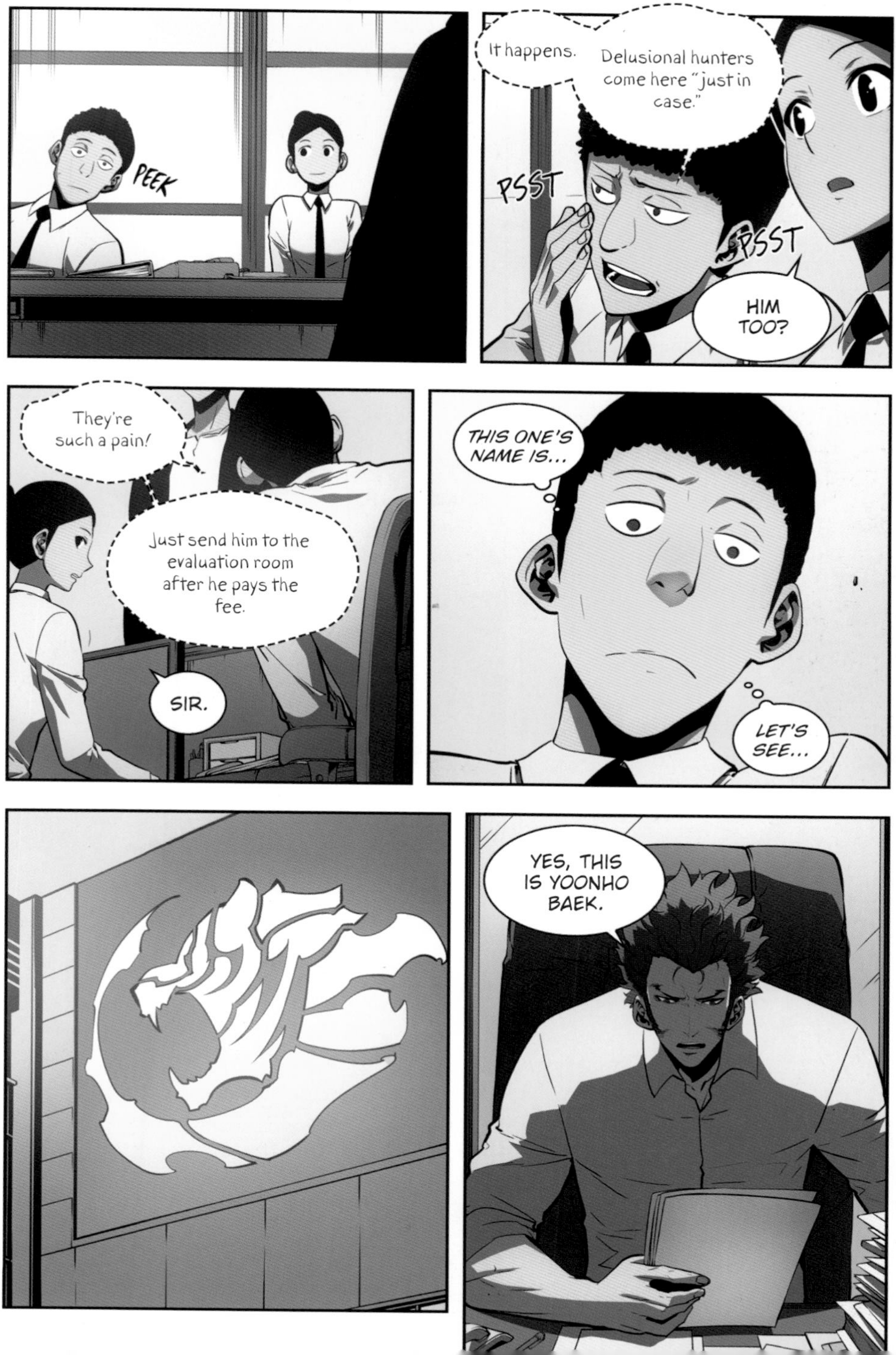
PEEK
It happens.
Delusional hunters come here "just in case."
PSST
PSST
HIM TOO?
They're such a pain!
Just send him to the evaluation room after he pays the fee.
SIR.
THIS ONE'S NAME IS...
LET'S SEE...
YES, THIS IS YOONHO BAEK.

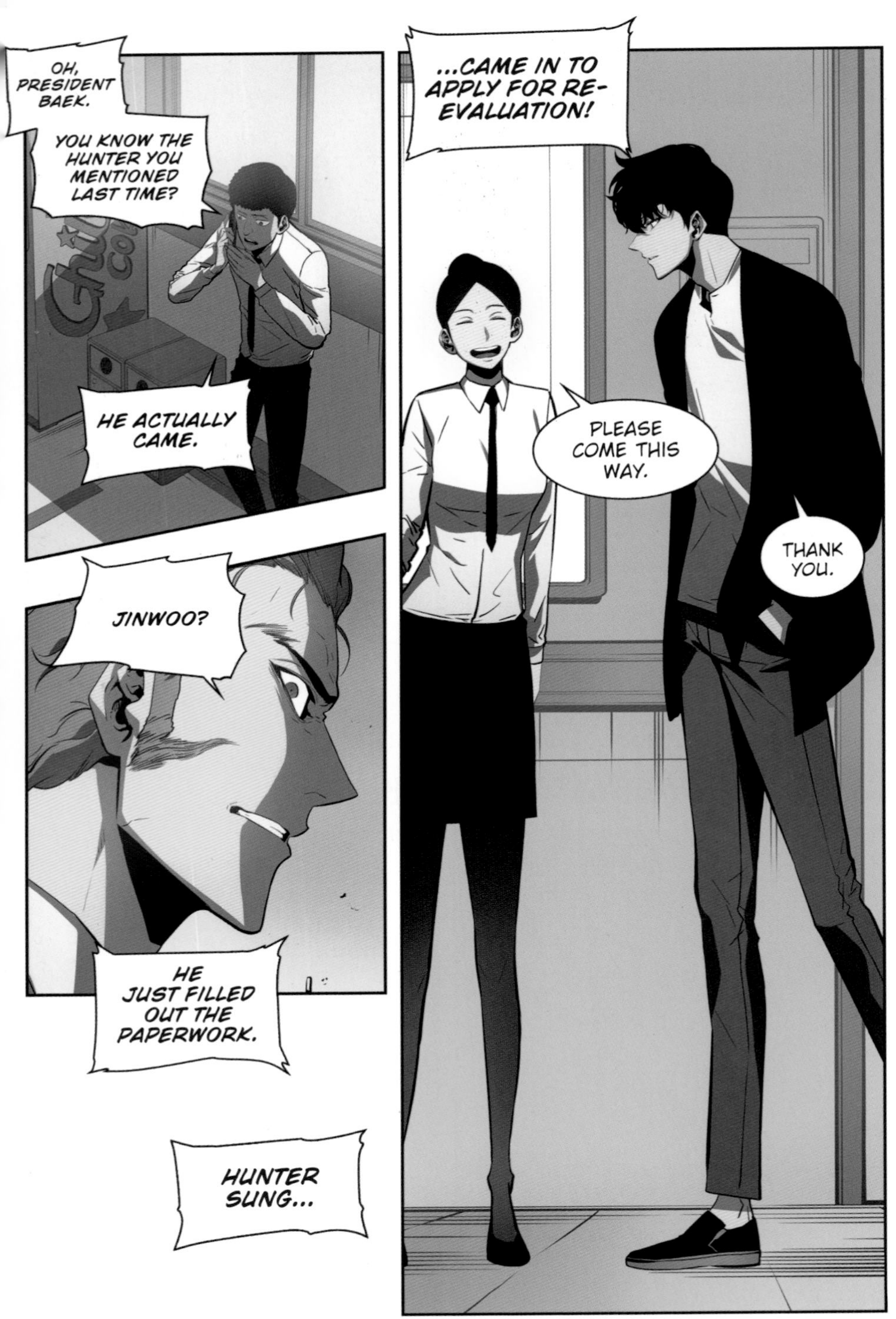
OH, PRESIDENT BAEK.
YOU KNOW THE HUNTER YOU MENTIONED LAST TIME?
HE ACTUALLY CAME.
JINWOO?
HE JUST FILLED OUT THE PAPERWORK.
HUNTER SUNG...
...CAME IN TO APPLY FOR RE-EVALUATION!
PLEASE COME THIS WAY.
THANK YOU.

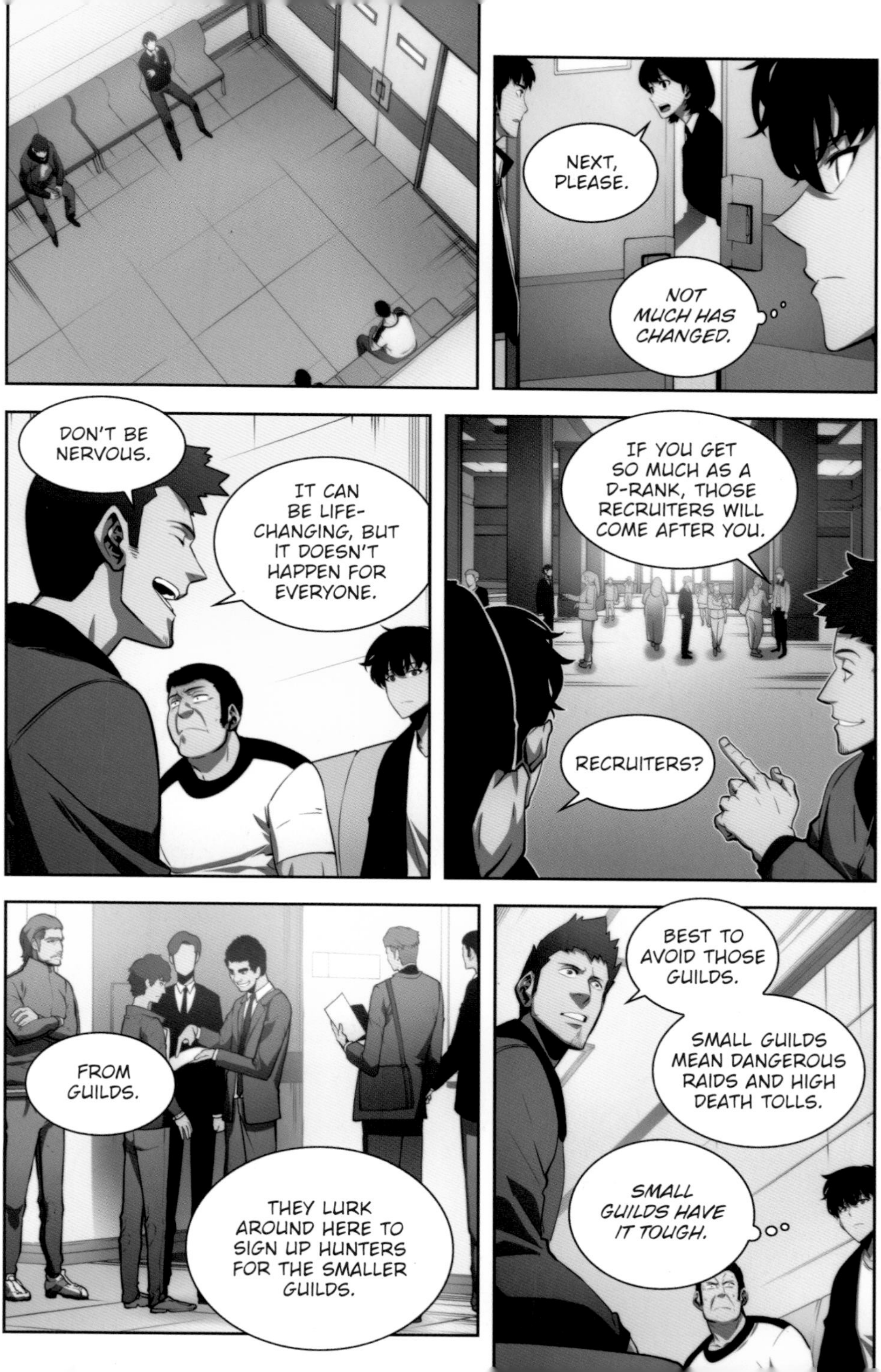
NEXT, PLEASE.
NOT MUCH HAS CHANGED.
DON'T BE NERVOUS.
IT CAN BE LIFE-CHANGING, BUT IT DOESN'T HAPPEN FOR EVERYONE.
IF YOU GET SO MUCH AS A D-RANK, THOSE RECRUITERS WILL COME AFTER YOU.
RECRUITERS?
FROM GUILDS.
THEY LURK AROUND HERE TO SIGN UP HUNTERS FOR THE SMALLER GUILDS.
BEST TO AVOID THOSE GUILDS.
SMALL GUILDS MEAN DANGEROUS RAIDS AND HIGH DEATH TOLLS.
SMALL GUILDS HAVE IT TOUGH.

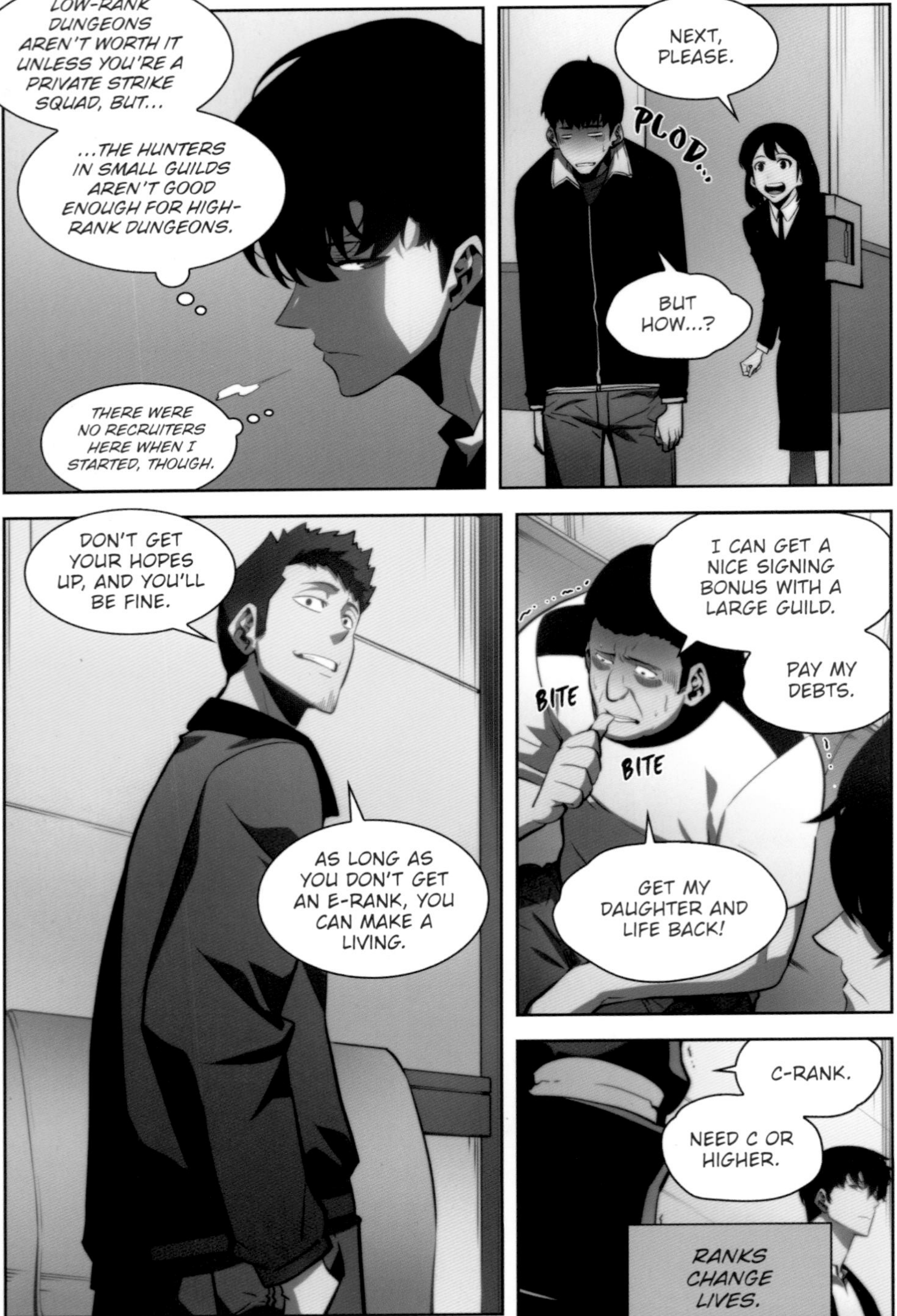
LOW-RANK DUNGEONS AREN'T WORTH IT UNLESS YOU'RE A PRIVATE STRIKE SQUAD, BUT...
...THE HUNTERS IN SMALL GUILDS AREN'T GOOD ENOUGH FOR HIGH-RANK DUNGEONS.
THERE WERE NO RECRUITERS HERE WHEN I STARTED, THOUGH.
NEXT, PLEASE.
PLOD...
BUT HOW...?
DON'T GET YOUR HOPES UP, AND YOU'LL BE FINE.
AS LONG AS YOU DON'T GET AN E-RANK, YOU CAN MAKE A LIVING.
I CAN GET A NICE SIGNING BONUS WITH A LARGE GUILD.
PAY MY DEBTS.
BITE
BITE
GET MY DAUGHTER AND LIFE BACK!
C-RANK.
NEED C OR HIGHER.
RANKS CHANGE LIVES.

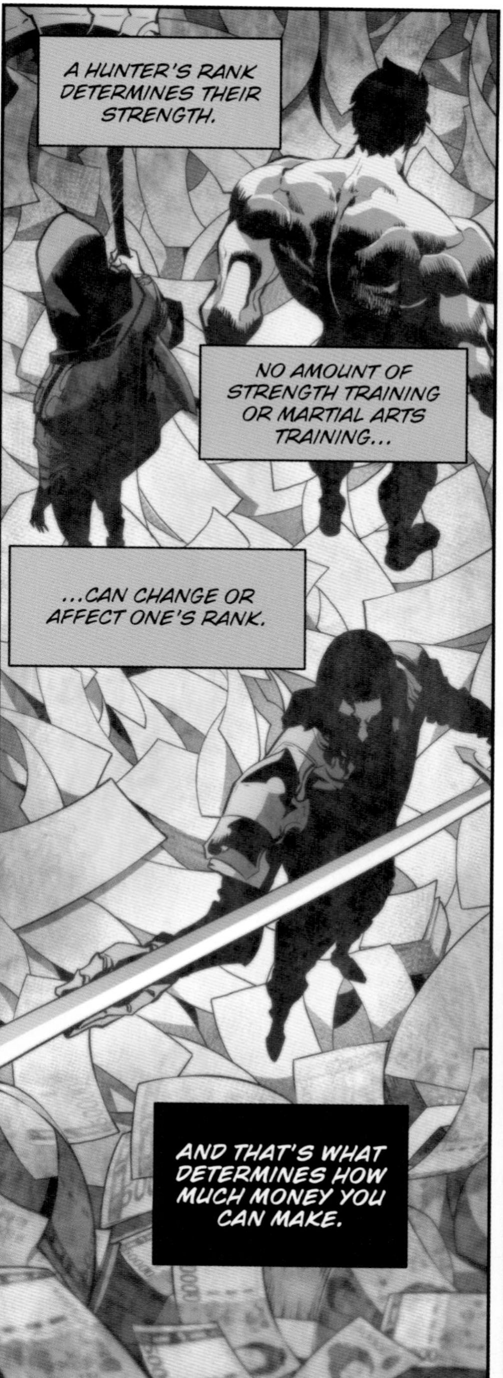
A HUNTER'S RANK DETERMINES THEIR STRENGTH.
NO AMOUNT OF STRENGTH TRAINING OR MARTIAL ARTS TRAINING...
...CAN CHANGE OR AFFECT ONE'S RANK.
AND THAT'S WHAT DETERMINES HOW MUCH MONEY YOU CAN MAKE.

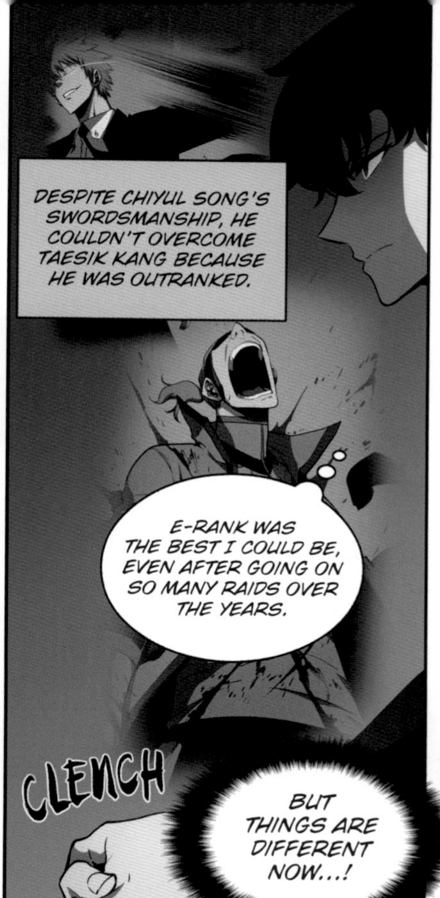
DESPITE CHIYUL SONG'S SWORDSMANSHIP, HE COULDN'T OVERCOME TAESIK KANG BECAUSE HE WAS OUTRANKED.
E-RANK WAS THE BEST I COULD BE, EVEN AFTER GOING ON SO MANY RAIDS OVER THE YEARS.
CLENCH
BUT THINGS ARE DIFFERENT NOW...!

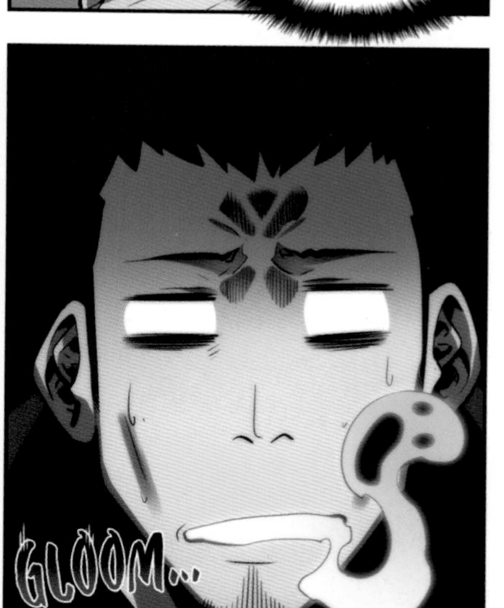
GLOOM...

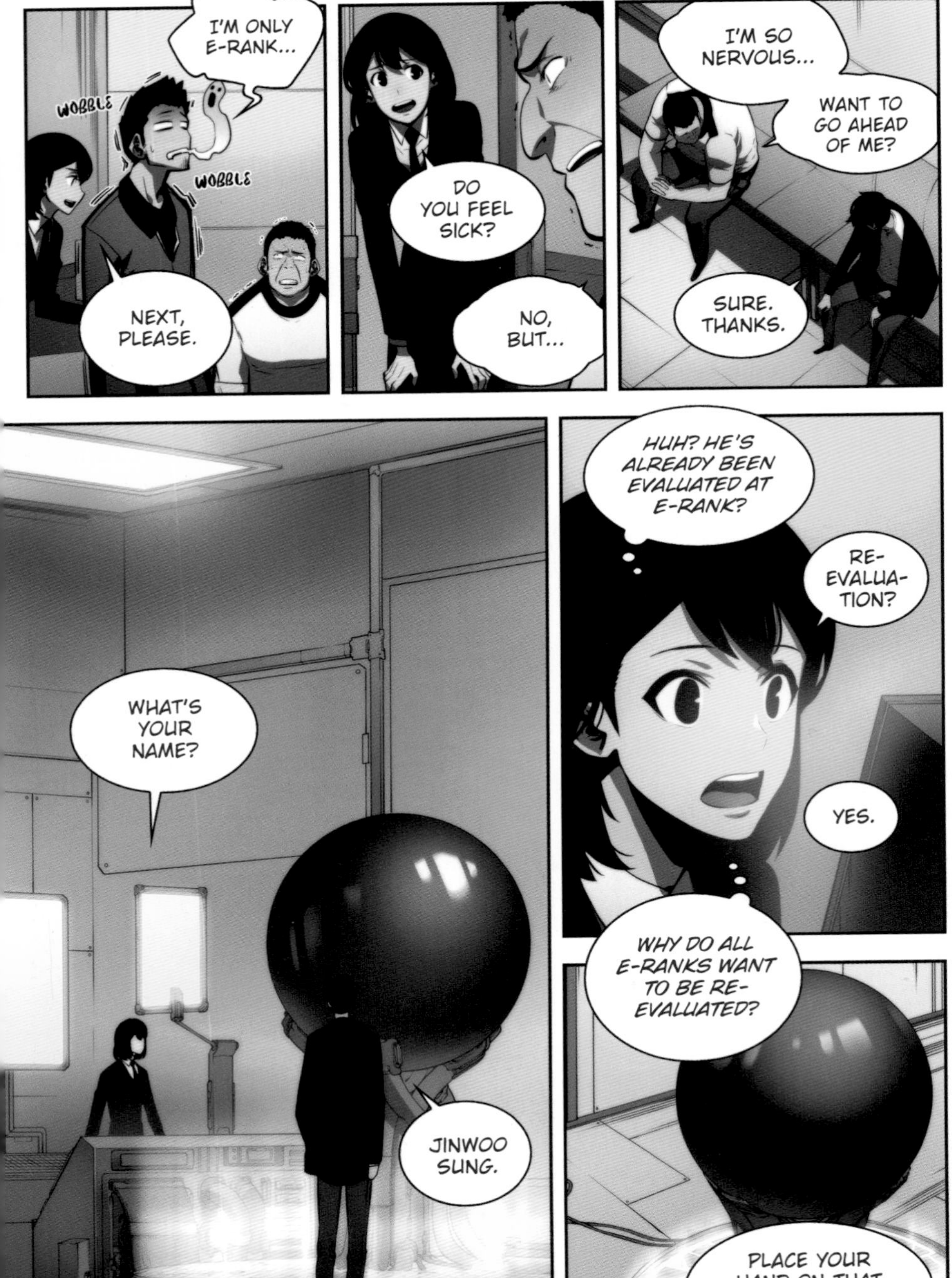
I'M ONLY E-RANK...
WOBBLE
WOBBLE
NEXT, PLEASE.
DO YOU FEEL SICK?
NO, BUT...
I'M SO NERVOUS...
WANT TO GO AHEAD OF ME?
SURE. THANKS.
WHAT'S YOUR NAME?
JINWOO SUNG.
HUH? HE'S ALREADY BEEN EVALUATED AT E-RANK?
RE-EVALUATION?
YES.
WHY DO ALL E-RANKS WANT TO BE RE-EVALUATED?
PLACE YOUR HAND ON THAT BLACK SPHERE AND WAIT.

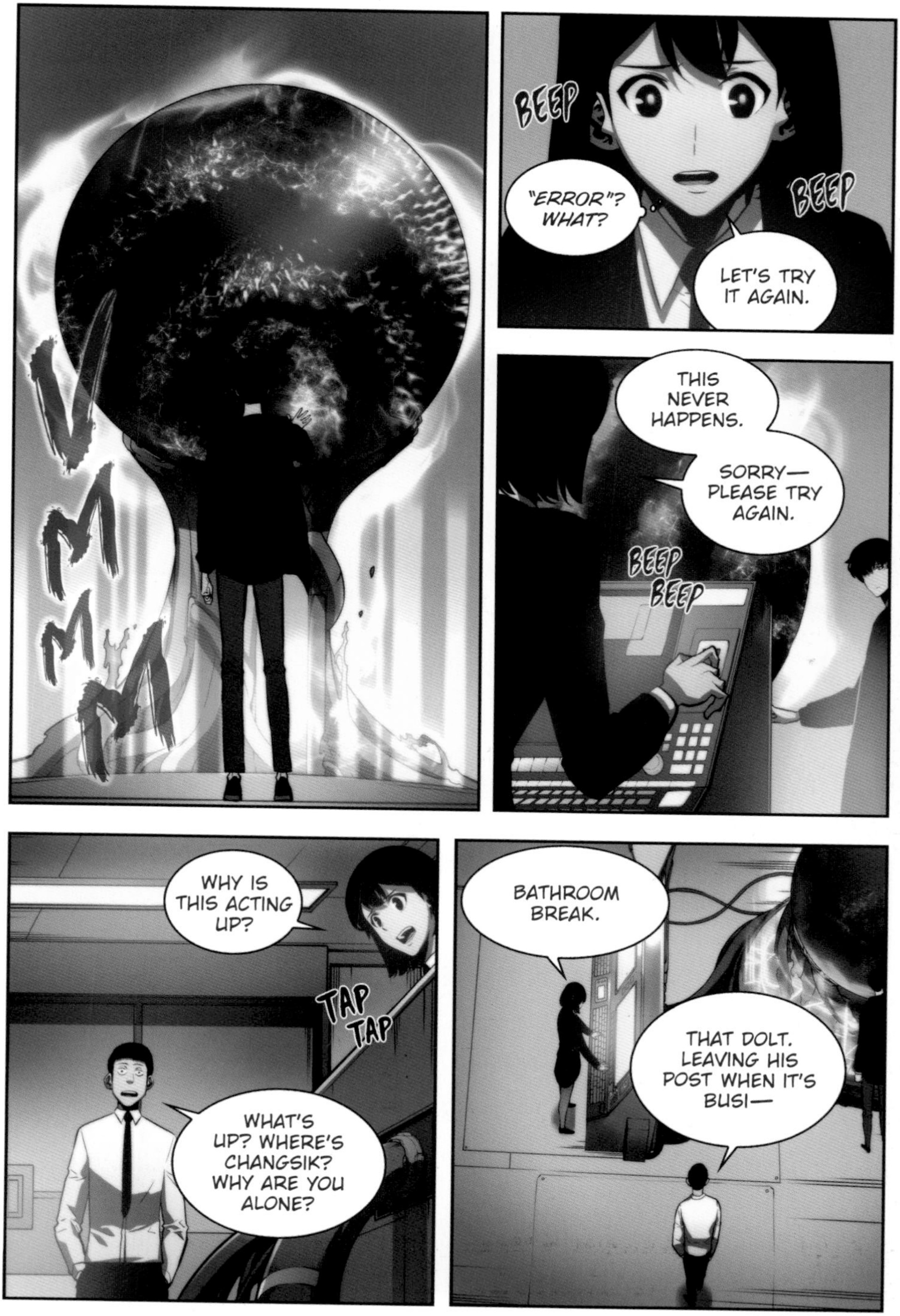
VMMM
BEEP
"ERROR"? WHAT?
BEEP
LET'S TRY IT AGAIN.
THIS NEVER HAPPENS.
SORRY— PLEASE TRY AGAIN.
BEEP BEEP
WHY IS THIS ACTING UP?
TAP TAP
WHAT'S UP? WHERE'S CHANGSIK? WHY ARE YOU ALONE?
BATHROOM BREAK.
THAT DOLT. LEAVING HIS POST WHEN IT'S BUSI—

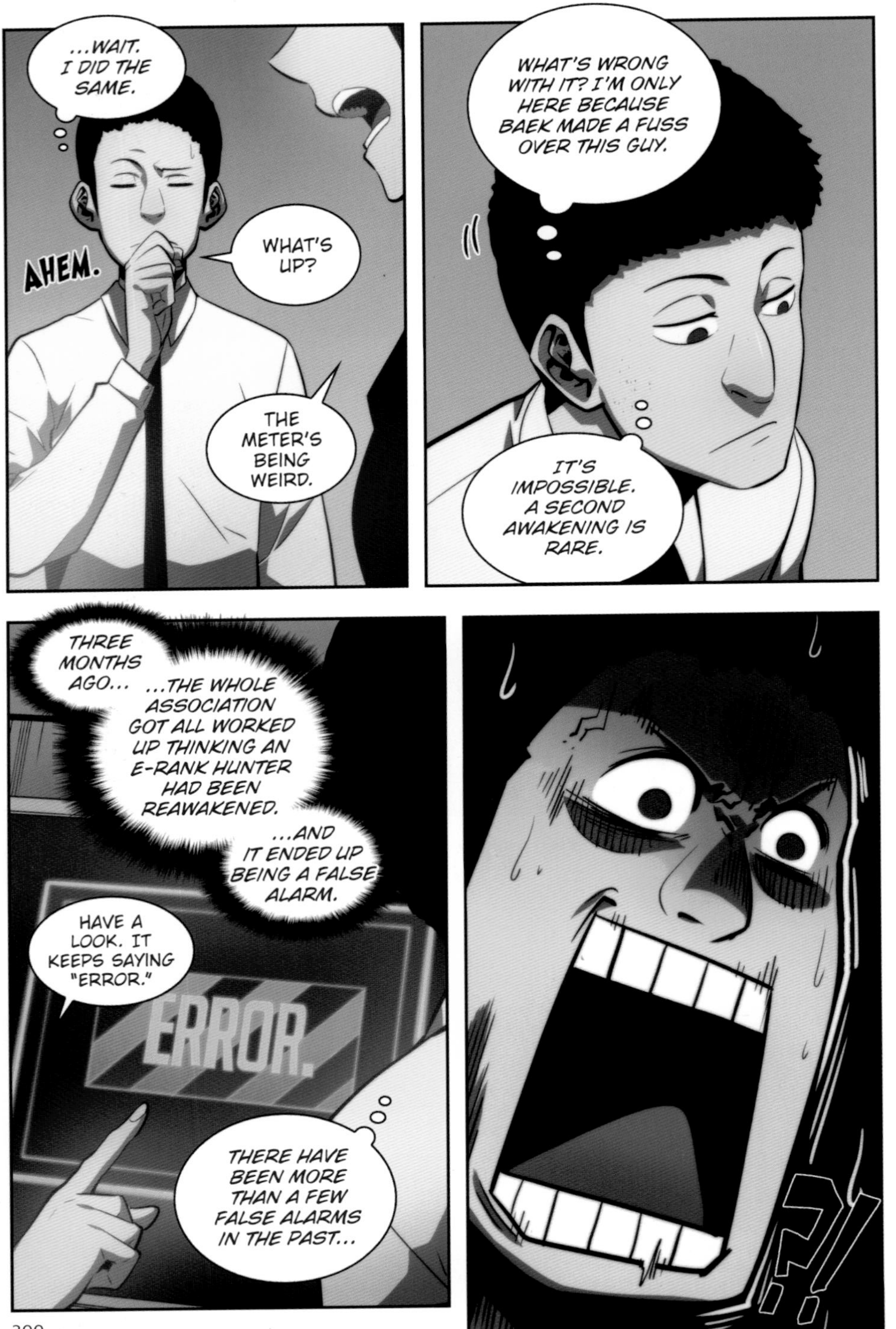
...WAIT. I DID THE SAME.
AHEM.
WHAT'S UP?
THE METER'S BEING WEIRD.
WHAT'S WRONG WITH IT? I'M ONLY HERE BECAUSE BAEK MADE A FUSS OVER THIS GUY.
IT'S IMPOSSIBLE. A SECOND AWAKENING IS RARE.
THREE MONTHS AGO... ...THE WHOLE ASSOCIATION GOT ALL WORKED UP THINKING AN E-RANK HUNTER HAD BEEN REAWAKENED.
...AND IT ENDED UP BEING A FALSE ALARM.
HAVE A LOOK. IT KEEPS SAYING "ERROR."
ERROR.
THERE HAVE BEEN MORE THAN A FEW FALSE ALARMS IN THE PAST...
?!

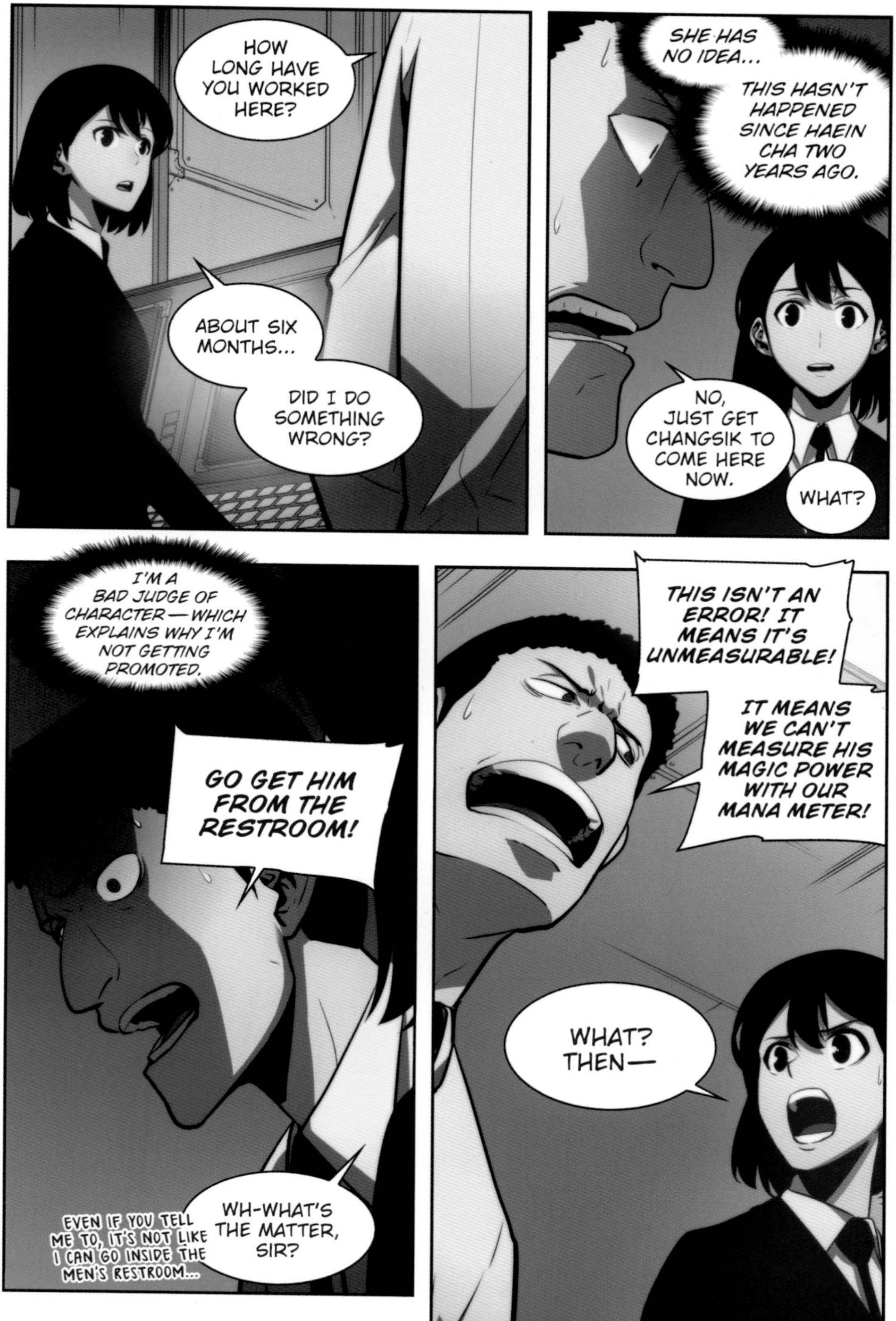
HOW LONG HAVE YOU WORKED HERE?
ABOUT SIX MONTHS...
DID I DO SOMETHING WRONG?
SHE HAS NO IDEA...
THIS HASN'T HAPPENED SINCE HAEIN CHA TWO YEARS AGO.
NO, JUST GET CHANGSIK TO COME HERE NOW.
WHAT?
I'M A BAD JUDGE OF CHARACTER—WHICH EXPLAINS WHY I'M NOT GETTING PROMOTED.
GO GET HIM FROM THE RESTROOM!
EVEN IF YOU TELL ME TO, IT'S NOT LIKE I CAN GO INSIDE THE MEN'S RESTROOM...
WH-WHAT'S THE MATTER, SIR?
THIS ISN'T AN ERROR! IT MEANS IT'S UNMEASURABLE!
IT MEANS WE CAN'T MEASURE HIS MAGIC POWER WITH OUR MANA METER!
WHAT? THEN—

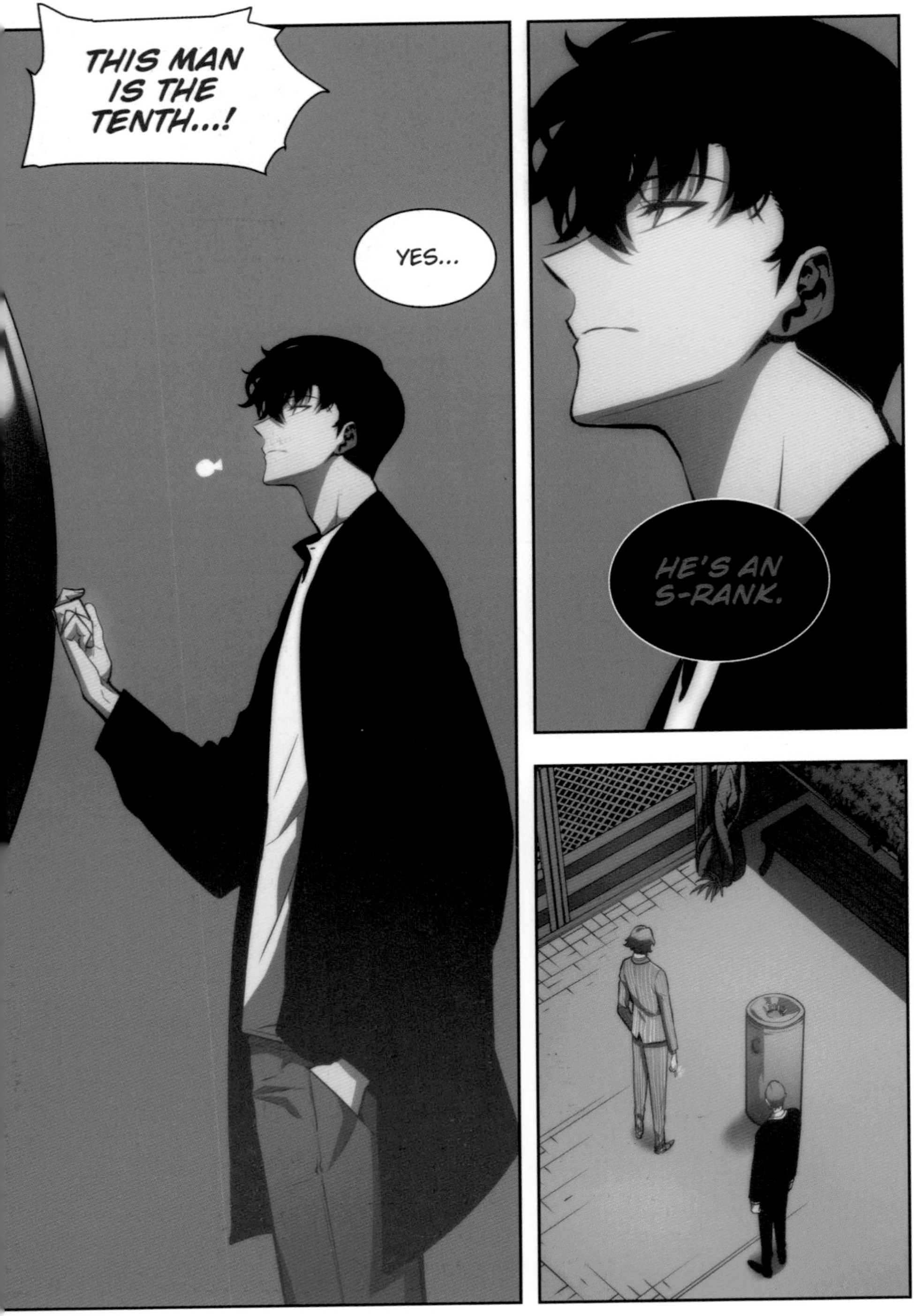
THIS MAN IS THE TENTH...!
YES...
HE'S AN S-RANK.

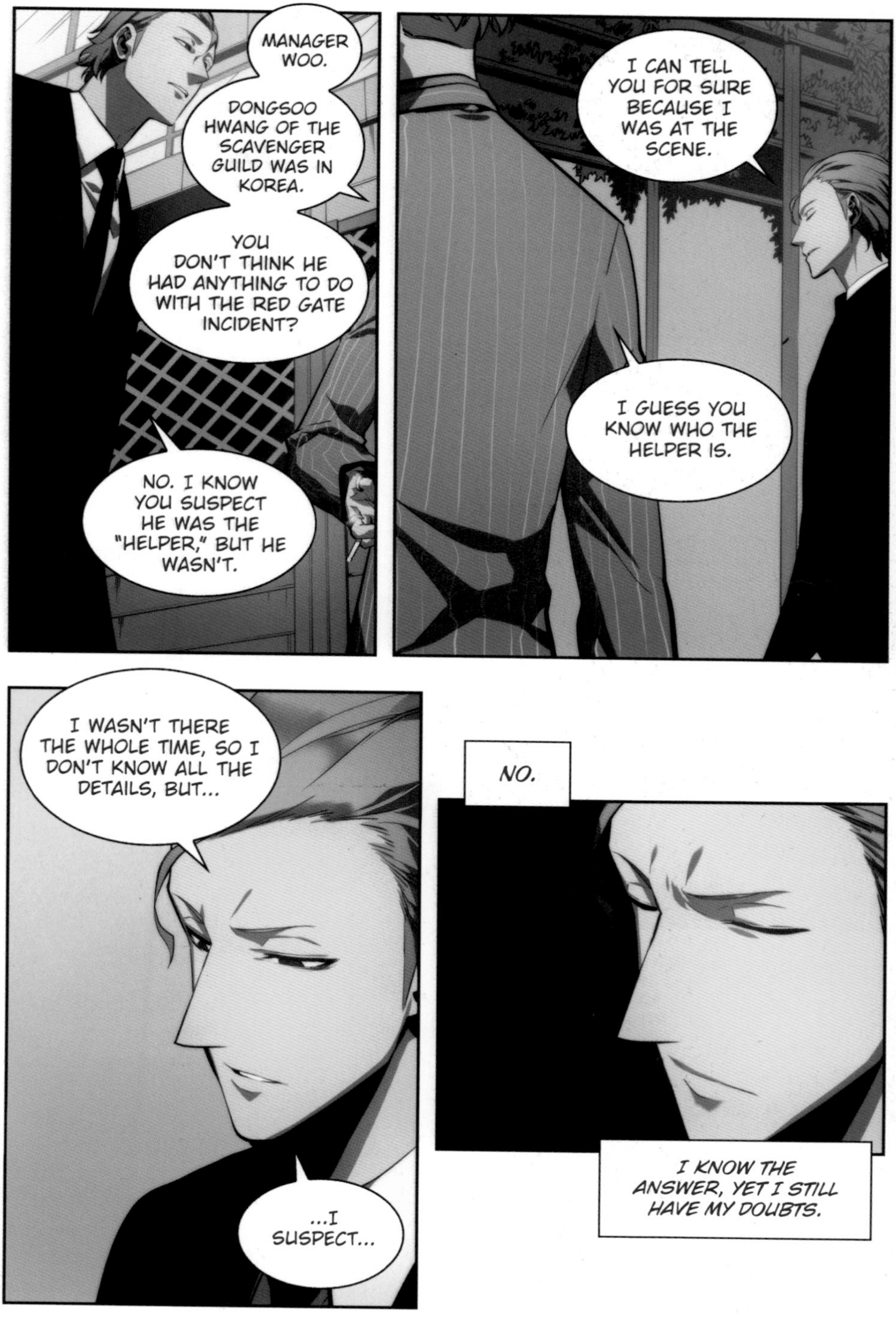
MANAGER WOO.
DONGSOO HWANG OF THE SCAVENGER GUILD WAS IN KOREA.
YOU DON'T THINK HE HAD ANYTHING TO DO WITH THE RED GATE INCIDENT?
NO. I KNOW YOU SUSPECT HE WAS THE "HELPER," BUT HE WASN'T.
I CAN TELL YOU FOR SURE BECAUSE I WAS AT THE SCENE.
I GUESS YOU KNOW WHO THE HELPER IS.
I WASN'T THERE THE WHOLE TIME, SO I DON'T KNOW ALL THE DETAILS, BUT...
...I SUSPECT...
NO.
I KNOW THE ANSWER, YET I STILL HAVE MY DOUBTS.

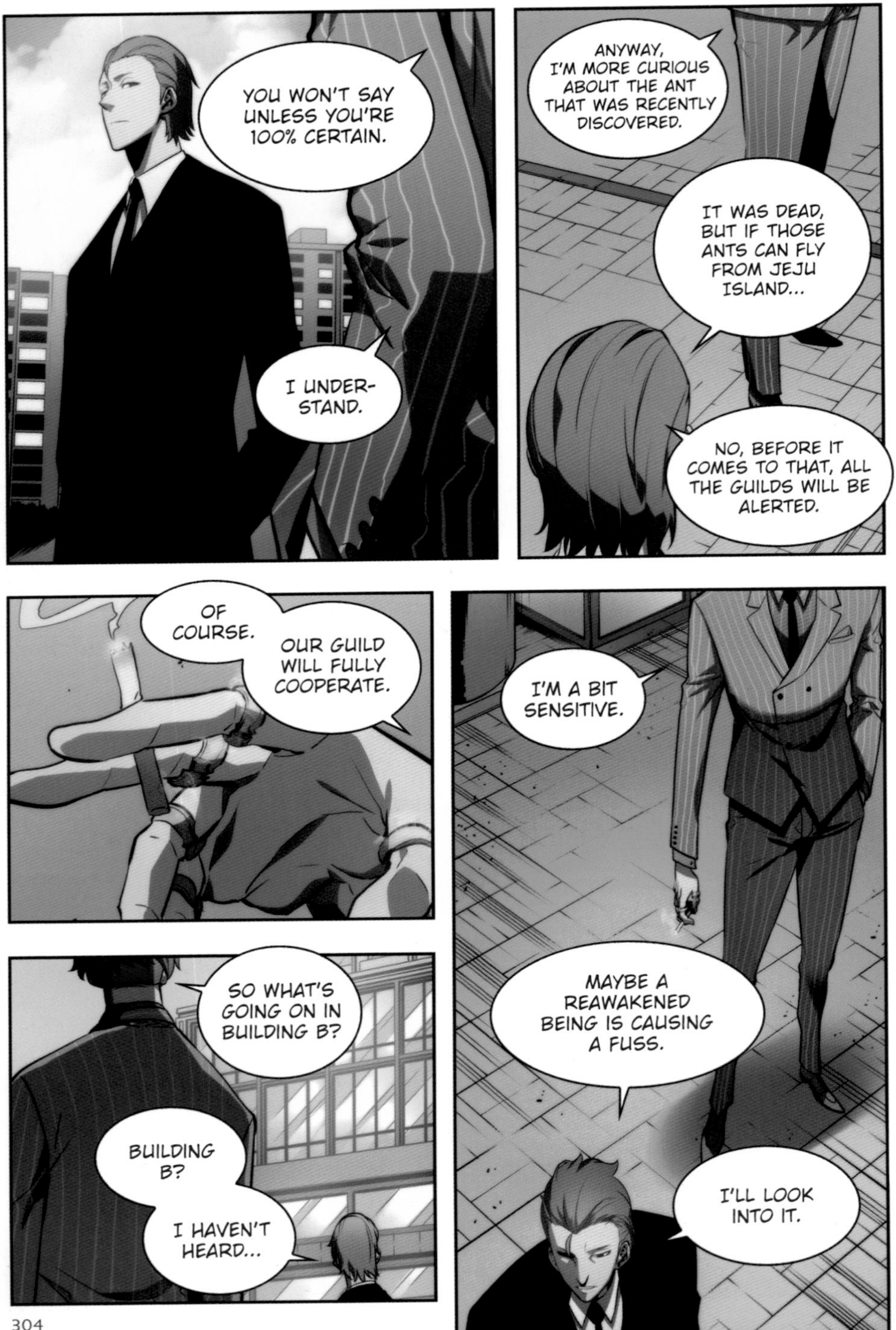
YOU WON'T SAY UNLESS YOU'RE 100% CERTAIN.
I UNDER-STAND.
ANYWAY, I'M MORE CURIOUS ABOUT THE ANT THAT WAS RECENTLY DISCOVERED.
IT WAS DEAD, BUT IF THOSE ANTS CAN FLY FROM JEJU ISLAND...
NO, BEFORE IT COMES TO THAT, ALL THE GUILDS WILL BE ALERTED.
OF COURSE.
OUR GUILD WILL FULLY COOPERATE.
SO WHAT'S GOING ON IN BUILDING B?
BUILDING B?
I HAVEN'T HEARD...
I'M A BIT SENSITIVE.
MAYBE A REAWAKENED BEING IS CAUSING A FUSS.
I'LL LOOK INTO IT.

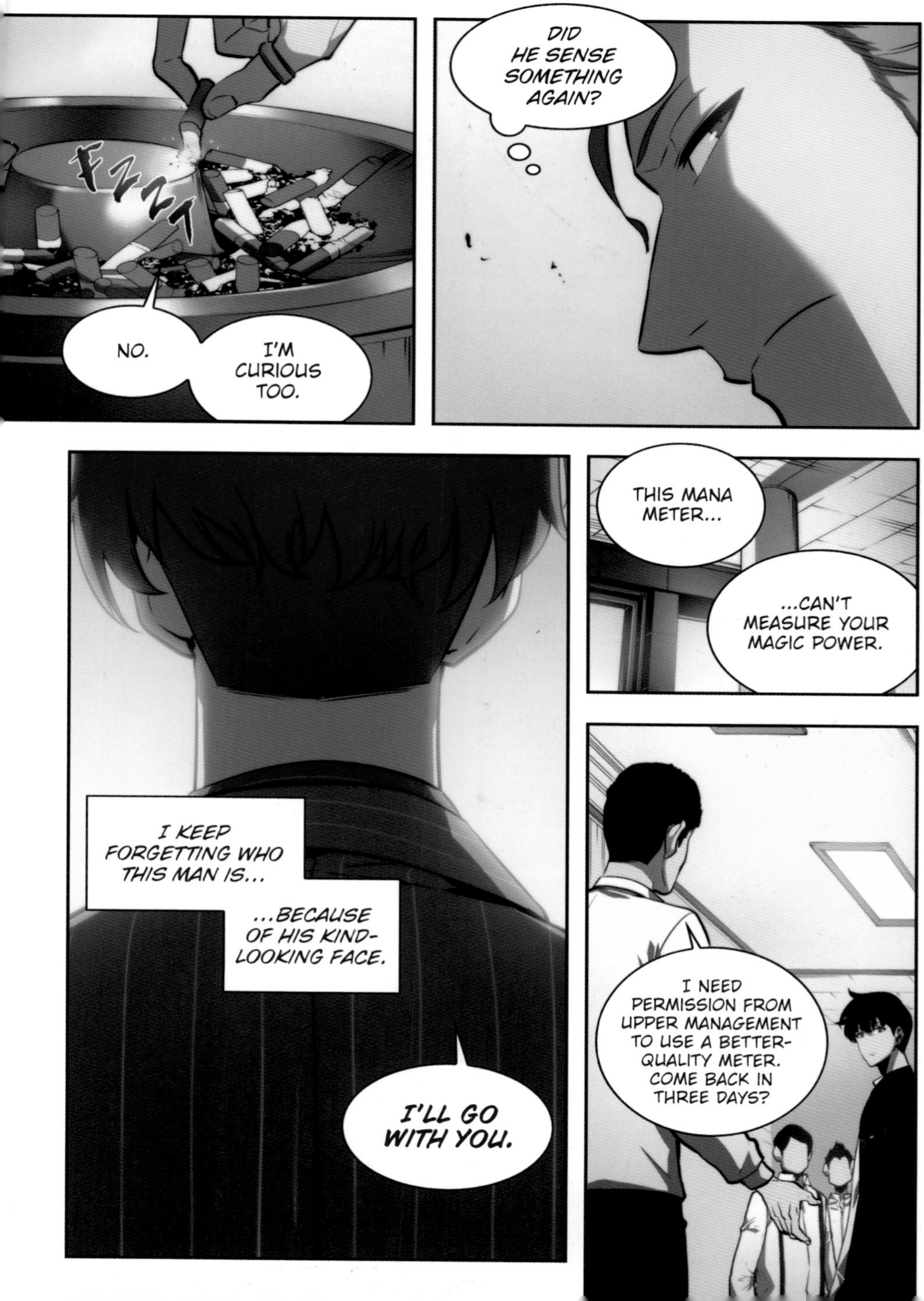
FZZZT
NO.
I'M CURIOUS TOO.
DID HE SENSE SOMETHING AGAIN?
I KEEP FORGETTING WHO THIS MAN IS...
...BECAUSE OF HIS KIND-LOOKING FACE.
I'LL GO WITH YOU.
THIS MANA METER...
...CAN'T MEASURE YOUR MAGIC POWER.
I NEED PERMISSION FROM UPPER MANAGEMENT TO USE A BETTER-QUALITY METER. COME BACK IN THREE DAYS?

THEY STOPPED THE EVALUATION!

HE SAID IT'S UNMEA-SURABLE...

DOESN'T THAT MEAN HE'S AN S-RANK?

I'VE NEVER SEEN THIS HAPPEN IN REAL LIFE...

HE'S THE TENTH S-RANK...!

THESE RECRUITERS CAN'T TOUCH HIM!

DO I HAVE A SHOT?

SHOULD I TAKE A CHANCE AND GO AFTER HIM?

EXCUSE ME...ABOUT MY RANK?

R-RIGHT!

I CAN BE PRETTY PERSUASIVE...

CAN OUR GUILD AFFORD AN S-RANK...?

HUH? OVER THERE...!

OH!

THE HUNTERS—THE NUMBER ONE GUILD IN KOREA!

THE PRESIDENT OF THE HUNTERS?!

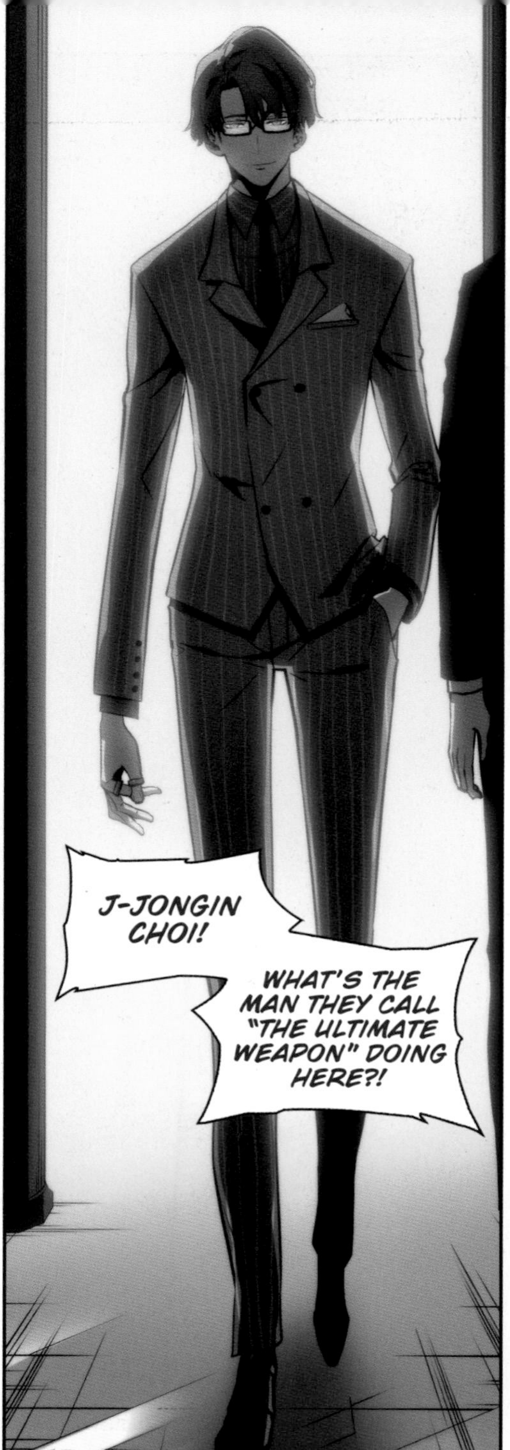
J-JONGIN CHOI!
WHAT'S THE MAN THEY CALL "THE ULTIMATE WEAPON" DOING HERE?!

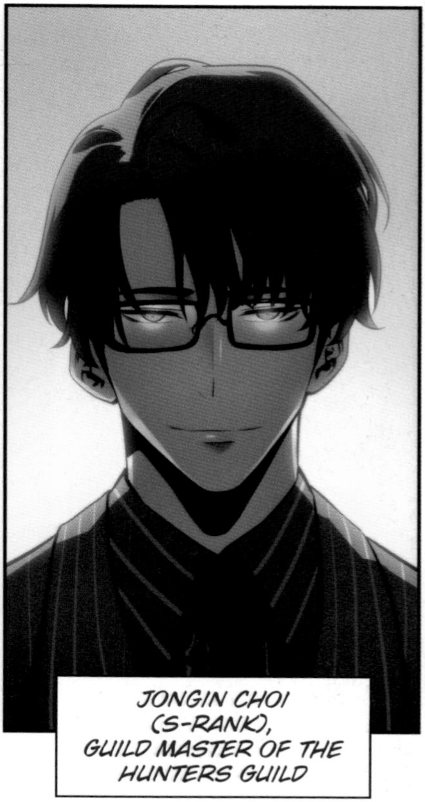
JONGIN CHOI (S-RANK), GUILD MASTER OF THE HUNTERS GUILD

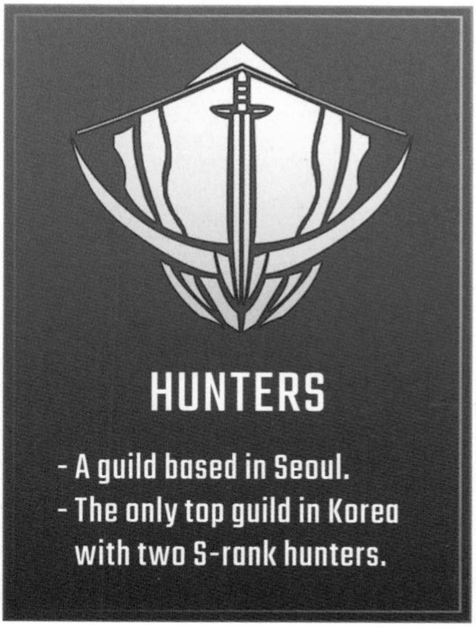
HUNTERS
- A guild based in Seoul.
- The only top guild in Korea with two S-rank hunters.

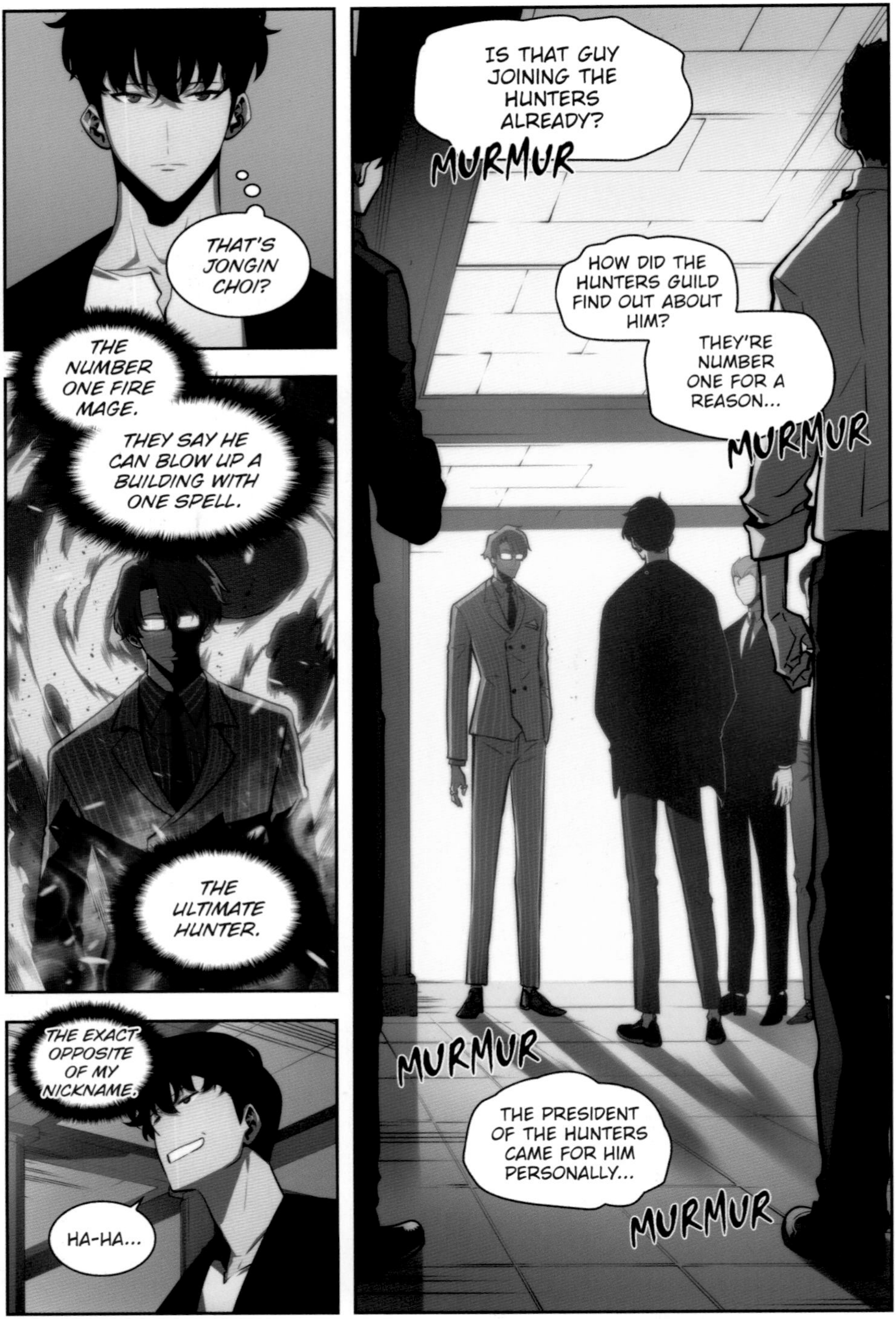
THAT'S JONGIN CHOI?
THE NUMBER ONE FIRE MAGE.
THEY SAY HE CAN BLOW UP A BUILDING WITH ONE SPELL.
THE ULTIMATE HUNTER.
THE EXACT OPPOSITE OF MY NICKNAME.
HA-HA...
IS THAT GUY JOINING THE HUNTERS ALREADY?
MURMUR
HOW DID THE HUNTERS GUILD FIND OUT ABOUT HIM?
THEY'RE NUMBER ONE FOR A REASON...
MURMUR
MURMUR
THE PRESIDENT OF THE HUNTERS CAME FOR HIM PERSONALLY...
MURMUR

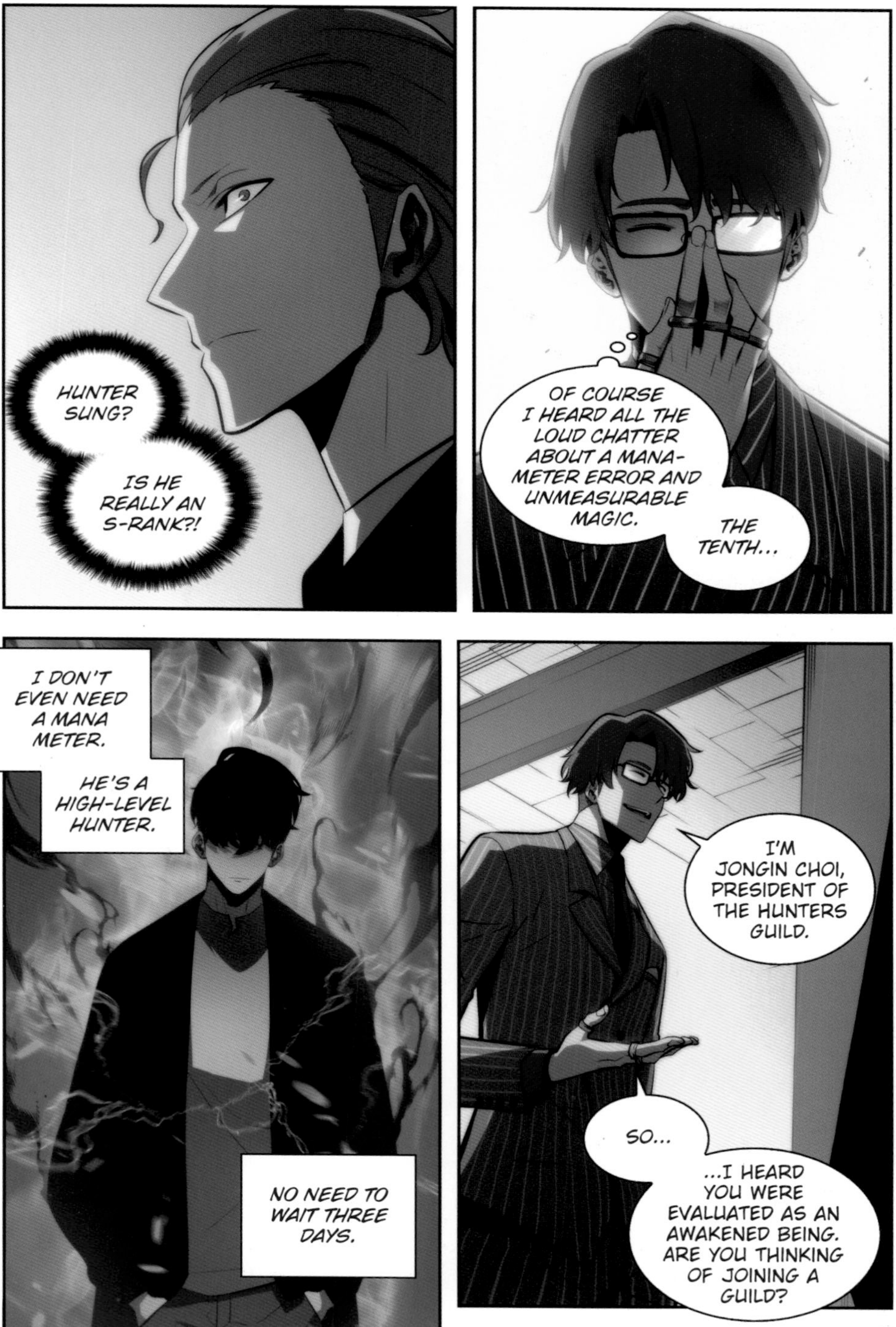
HUNTER SUNG?
IS HE REALLY AN S-RANK?!
OF COURSE I HEARD ALL THE LOUD CHATTER ABOUT A MANA-METER ERROR AND UNMEASURABLE MAGIC.
THE TENTH...
I DON'T EVEN NEED A MANA METER.
HE'S A HIGH-LEVEL HUNTER.
NO NEED TO WAIT THREE DAYS.
I'M JONGIN CHOI, PRESIDENT OF THE HUNTERS GUILD.
SO...
...I HEARD YOU WERE EVALUATED AS AN AWAKENED BEING. ARE YOU THINKING OF JOINING A GUILD?

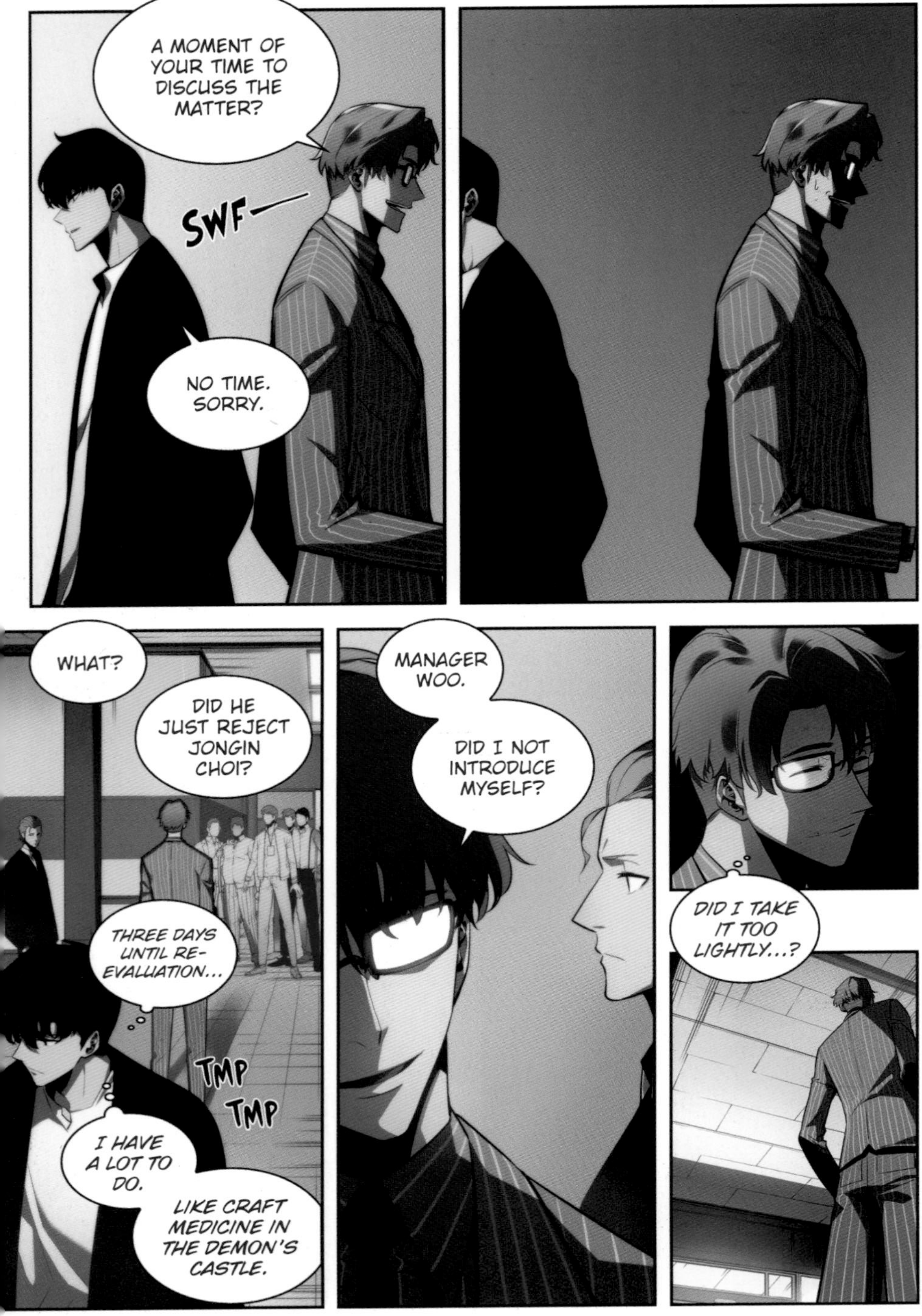
A MOMENT OF YOUR TIME TO DISCUSS THE MATTER?
SWF—
NO TIME. SORRY.
WHAT?
DID HE JUST REJECT JONGIN CHOI?
THREE DAYS UNTIL RE-EVALUATION...
TMP
TMP
I HAVE A LOT TO DO.
LIKE CRAFT MEDICINE IN THE DEMON'S CASTLE.
MANAGER WOO.
DID I NOT INTRODUCE MYSELF?
DID I TAKE IT TOO LIGHTLY...?

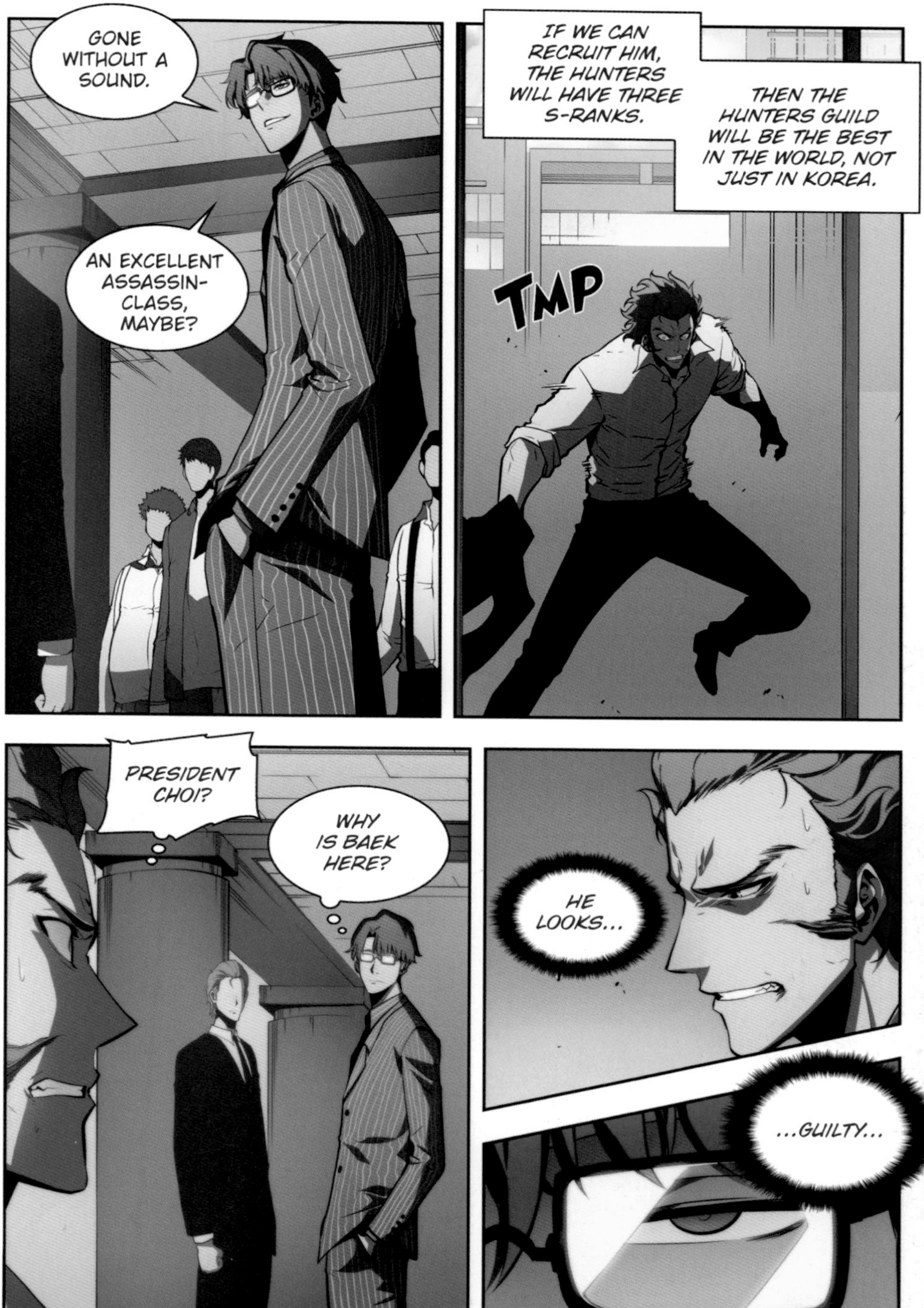
GONE WITHOUT A SOUND.
AN EXCELLENT ASSASSIN-CLASS, MAYBE?
IF WE CAN RECRUIT HIM, THE HUNTERS WILL HAVE THREE S-RANKS.
THEN THE HUNTERS GUILD WILL BE THE BEST IN THE WORLD, NOT JUST IN KOREA.
TMP
PRESIDENT CHOI?
WHY IS BAEK HERE?
HE LOOKS...
...GUILTY...

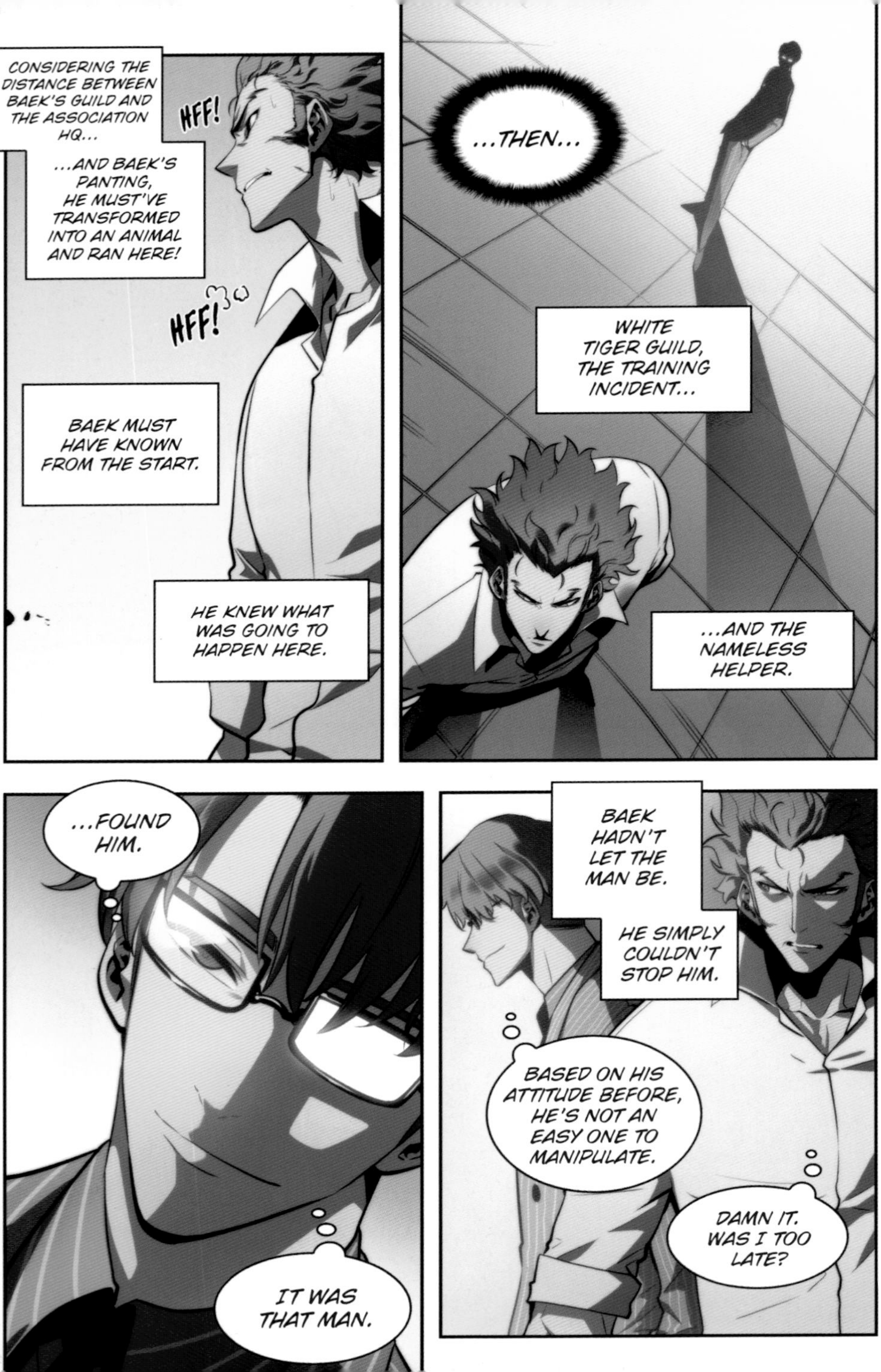
CONSIDERING THE DISTANCE BETWEEN BAEK'S GUILD AND THE ASSOCIATION HQ...
HFF!
...AND BAEK'S PANTING, HE MUST'VE TRANSFORMED INTO AN ANIMAL AND RAN HERE!
HFF!
BAEK MUST HAVE KNOWN FROM THE START.
HE KNEW WHAT WAS GOING TO HAPPEN HERE.
...THEN...
WHITE TIGER GUILD, THE TRAINING INCIDENT...
...AND THE NAMELESS HELPER.
...FOUND HIM.
IT WAS THAT MAN.
BAEK HADN'T LET THE MAN BE.
HE SIMPLY COULDN'T STOP HIM.
BASED ON HIS ATTITUDE BEFORE, HE'S NOT AN EASY ONE TO MANIPULATE.
DAMN IT. WAS I TOO LATE?

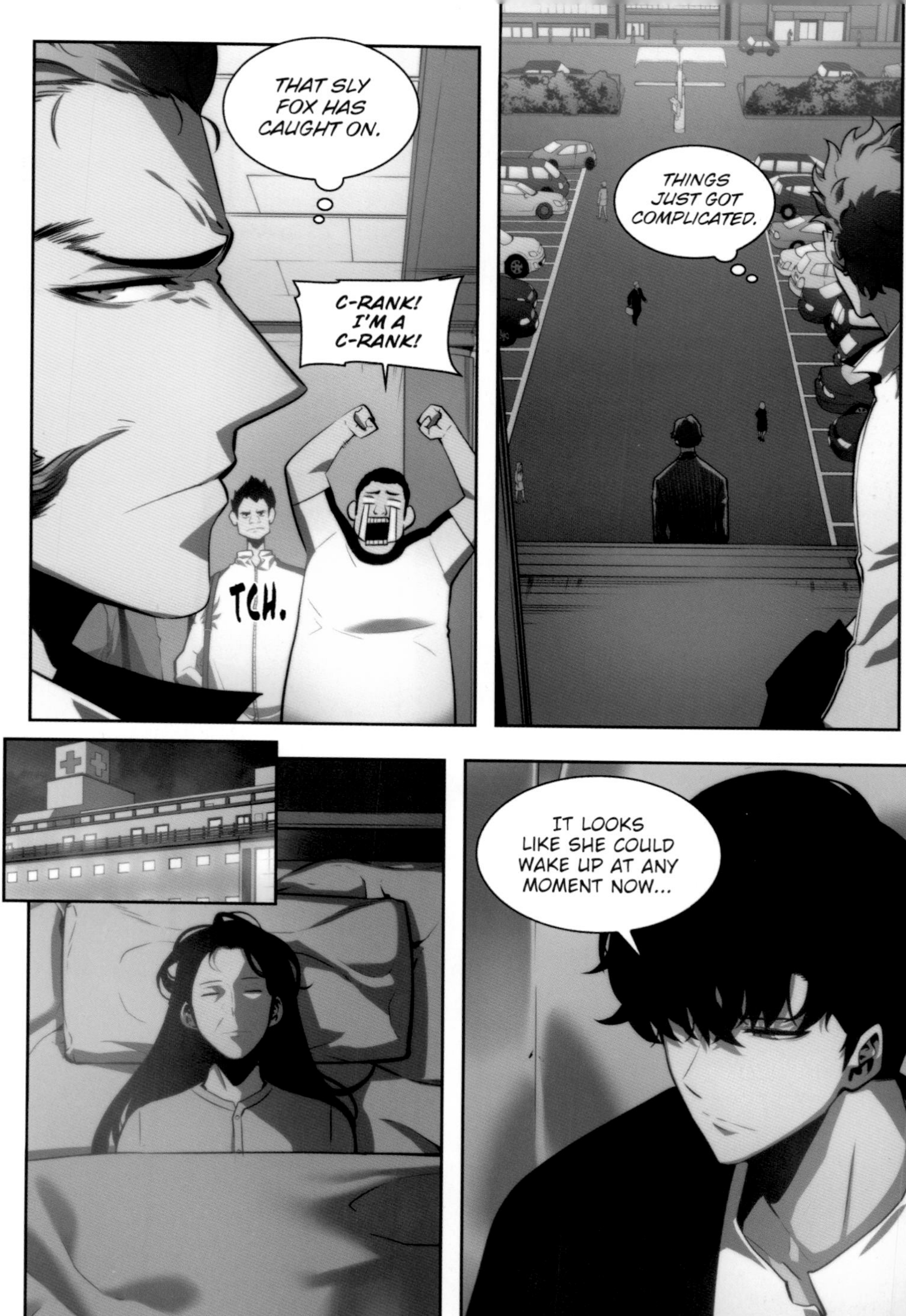
THAT SLY FOX HAS CAUGHT ON.
C-RANK! I'M A C-RANK!
TCH.
THINGS JUST GOT COMPLICATED.
IT LOOKS LIKE SHE COULD WAKE UP AT ANY MOMENT NOW...

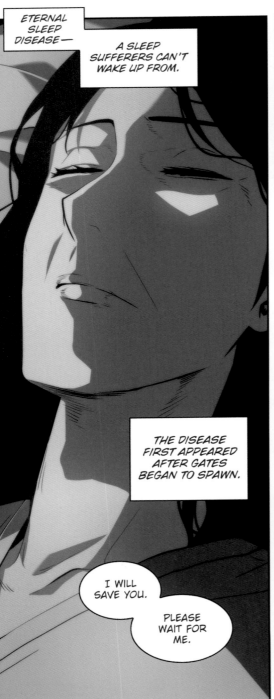

ETERNAL SLEEP DISEASE—

A SLEEP SUFFERERS CAN'T WAKE UP FROM.

THE DISEASE FIRST APPEARED AFTER GATES BEGAN TO SPAWN.

I WILL SAVE YOU.

PLEASE WAIT FOR ME.

I NEED TO GET EVEN STRONGER.

KCHAK

THE MID-LEVEL BOSS WAS HARD ENOUGH THAT I KNOW I CAN'T DEAL WITH THE BIG BOSS YET.

EVEN THOUGH I'LL LEVEL UP AS I CLIMB TO HIGHER FLOORS...

SO...

...YOU KILLED THE MAGIC BEASTS IN THE DOUBLE DUNGEON?

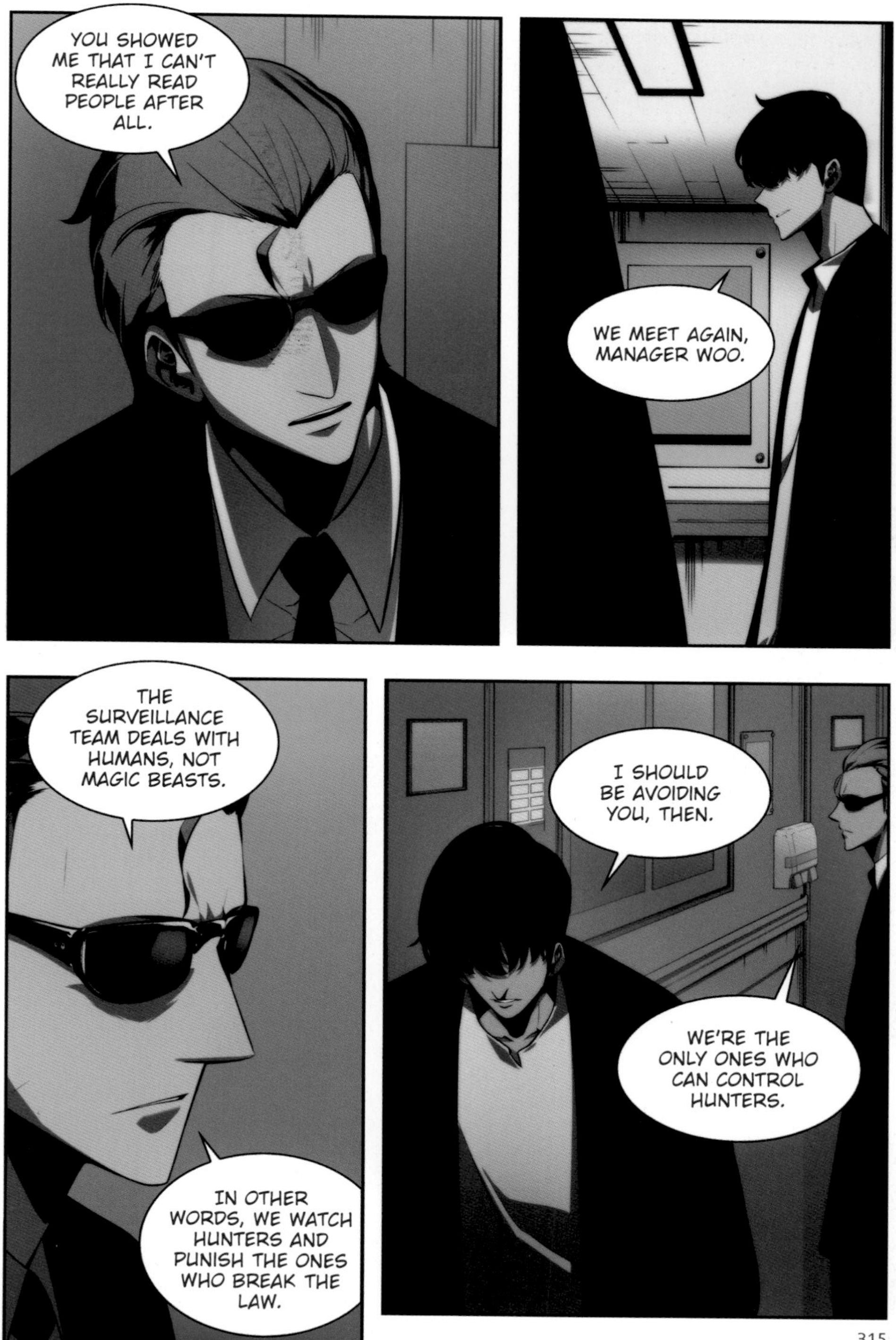
YOU SHOWED ME THAT I CAN'T REALLY READ PEOPLE AFTER ALL.
WE MEET AGAIN, MANAGER WOO.
THE SURVEILLANCE TEAM DEALS WITH HUMANS, NOT MAGIC BEASTS.
IN OTHER WORDS, WE WATCH HUNTERS AND PUNISH THE ONES WHO BREAK THE LAW.
I SHOULD BE AVOIDING YOU, THEN.
WE'RE THE ONLY ONES WHO CAN CONTROL HUNTERS.

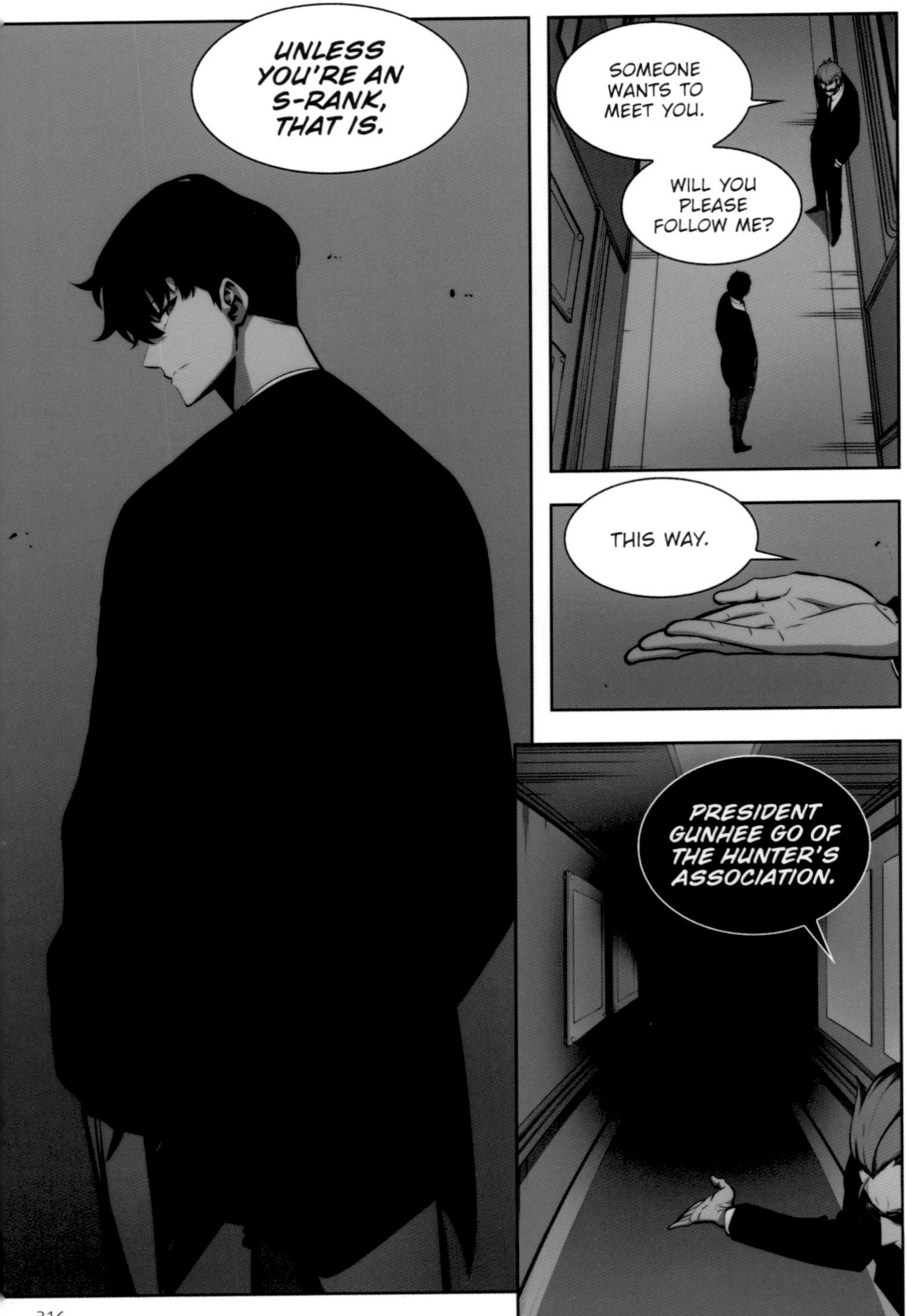
UNLESS YOU'RE AN S-RANK, THAT IS.
SOMEONE WANTS TO MEET YOU.
WILL YOU PLEASE FOLLOW ME?
THIS WAY.
PRESIDENT GUNHEE GO OF THE HUNTER'S ASSOCIATION.

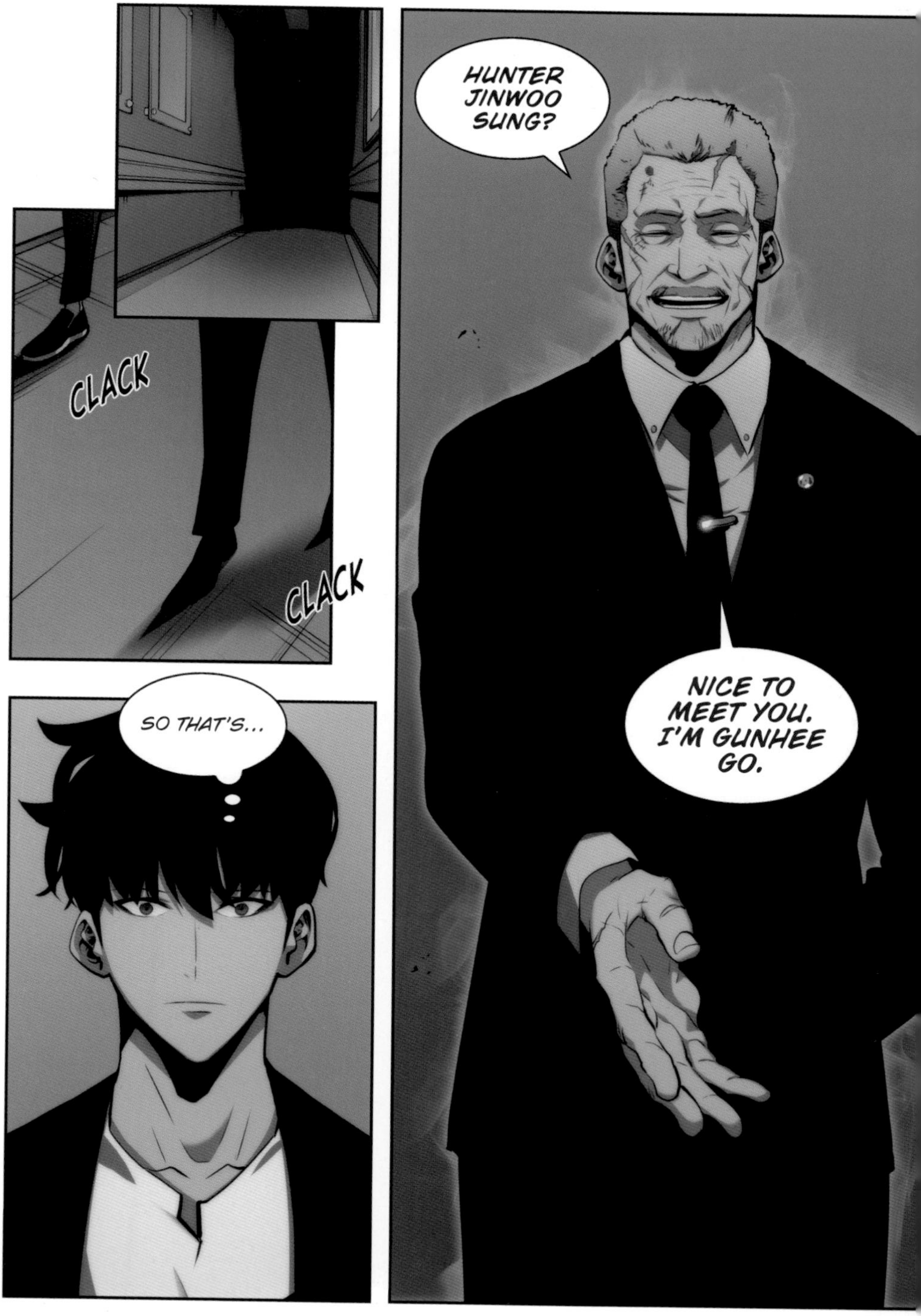
CLACK
CLACK
SO THAT'S...
HUNTER JINWOO SUNG?
NICE TO MEET YOU. I'M GUNHEE GO.

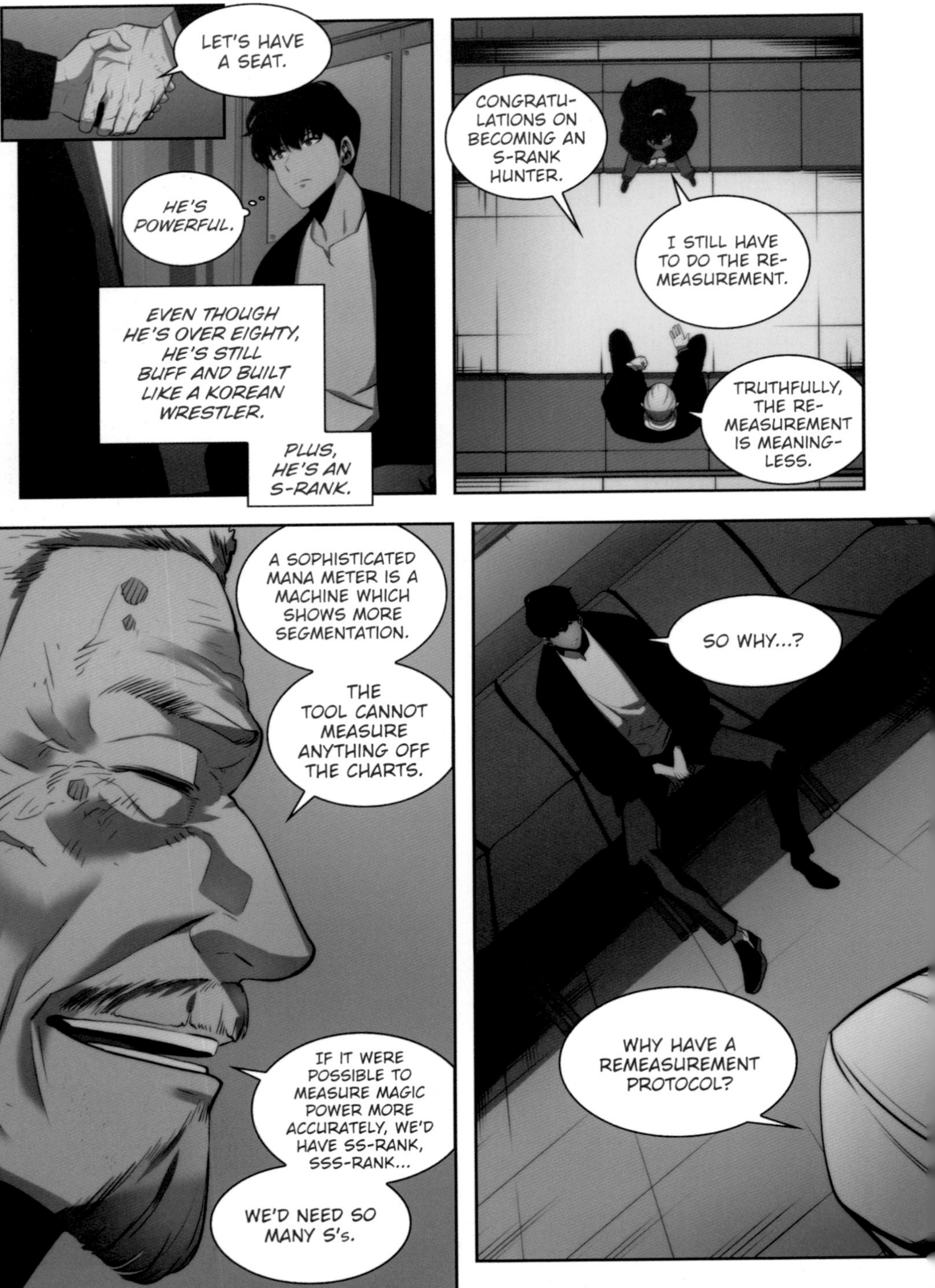
LET'S HAVE A SEAT.
HE'S POWERFUL.
EVEN THOUGH HE'S OVER EIGHTY, HE'S STILL BUFF AND BUILT LIKE A KOREAN WRESTLER.
PLUS, HE'S AN S-RANK.
CONGRATULATIONS ON BECOMING AN S-RANK HUNTER.
I STILL HAVE TO DO THE RE-MEASUREMENT.
TRUTHFULLY, THE RE-MEASUREMENT IS MEANINGLESS.
A SOPHISTICATED MANA METER IS A MACHINE WHICH SHOWS MORE SEGMENTATION.
THE TOOL CANNOT MEASURE ANYTHING OFF THE CHARTS.
IF IT WERE POSSIBLE TO MEASURE MAGIC POWER MORE ACCURATELY, WE'D HAVE SS-RANK, SSS-RANK...
WE'D NEED SO MANY S's.
SO WHY...?
WHY HAVE A REMEASUREMENT PROTOCOL?

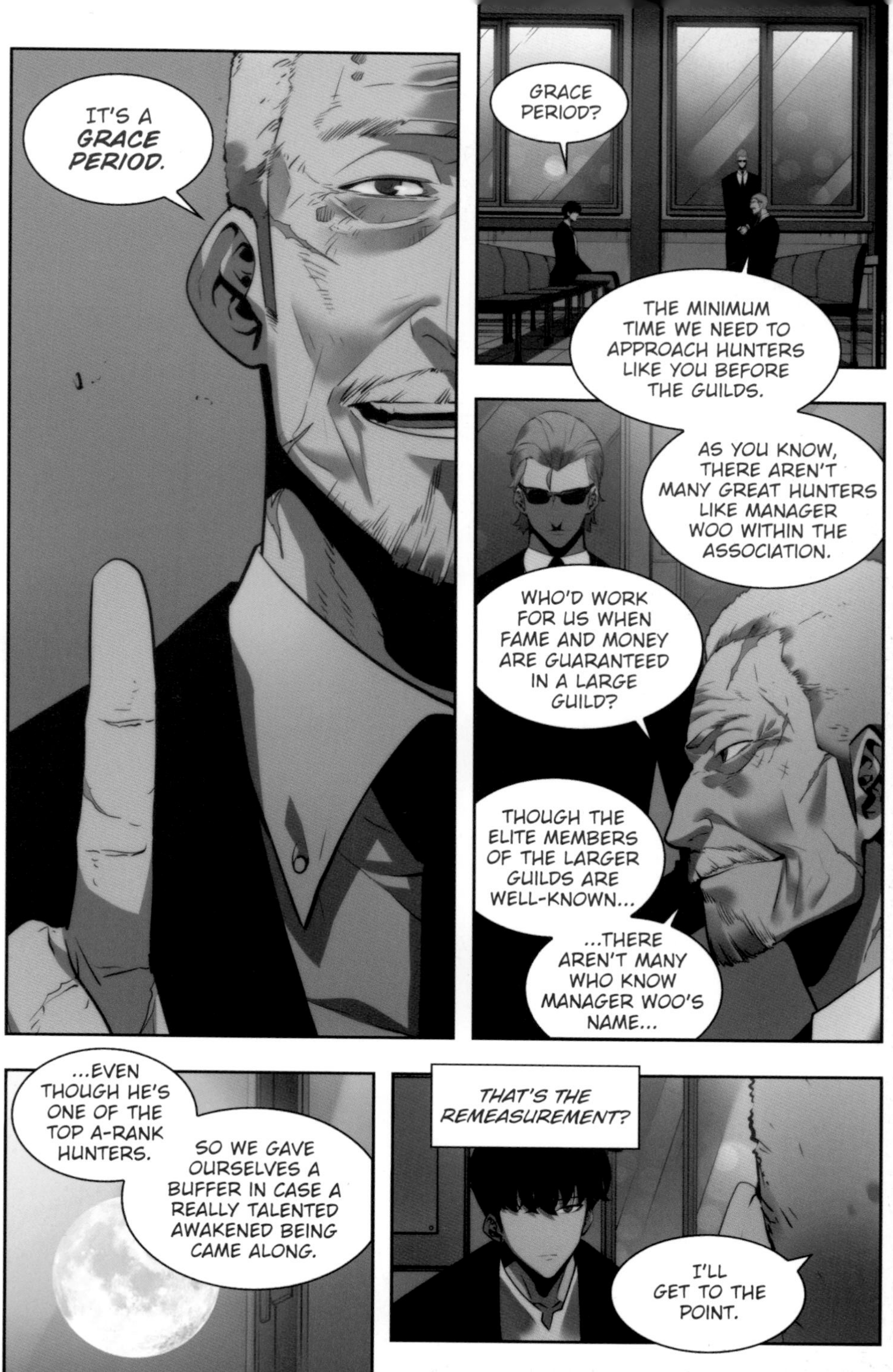
IT'S A *GRACE PERIOD.*
GRACE PERIOD?
THE MINIMUM TIME WE NEED TO APPROACH HUNTERS LIKE YOU BEFORE THE GUILDS.
AS YOU KNOW, THERE AREN'T MANY GREAT HUNTERS LIKE MANAGER WOO WITHIN THE ASSOCIATION.
WHO'D WORK FOR US WHEN FAME AND MONEY ARE GUARANTEED IN A LARGE GUILD?
THOUGH THE ELITE MEMBERS OF THE LARGER GUILDS ARE WELL-KNOWN...
...THERE AREN'T MANY WHO KNOW MANAGER WOO'S NAME...
...EVEN THOUGH HE'S ONE OF THE TOP A-RANK HUNTERS.
SO WE GAVE OURSELVES A BUFFER IN CASE A REALLY TALENTED AWAKENED BEING CAME ALONG.
*THAT'S THE REMEASUREMENT?*
I'LL GET TO THE POINT.

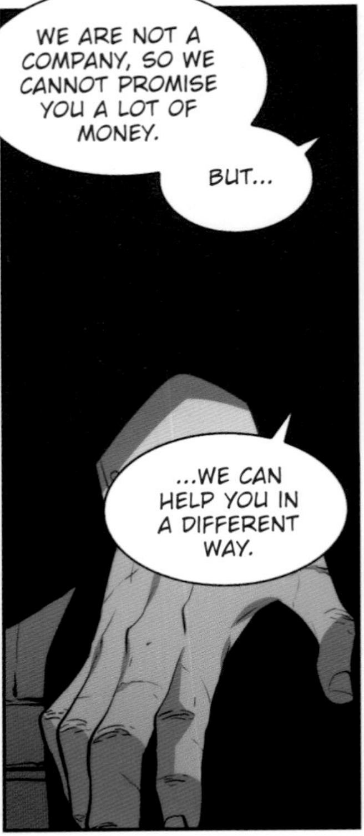
WE ARE NOT A COMPANY, SO WE CANNOT PROMISE YOU A LOT OF MONEY.
BUT...
...WE CAN HELP YOU IN A DIFFERENT WAY.

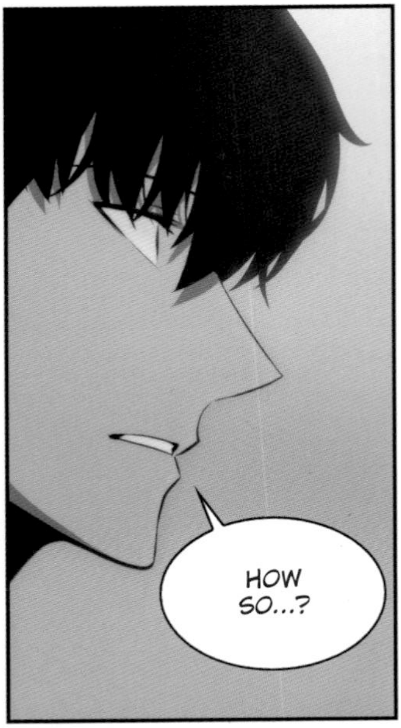
HOW SO...?

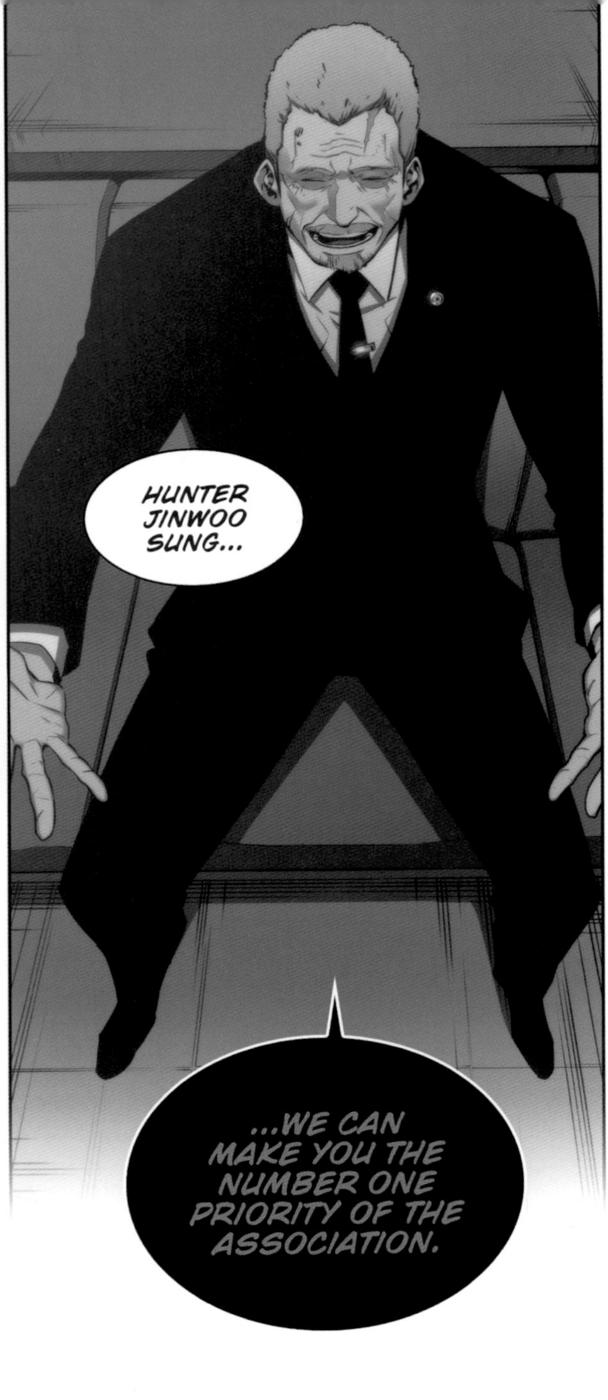
HUNTER JINWOO SUNG...
...WE CAN MAKE YOU THE NUMBER ONE PRIORITY OF THE ASSOCIATION.

TO BE CONTINUED IN VOLUME 5...

## VOLUME 5 PREVIEW

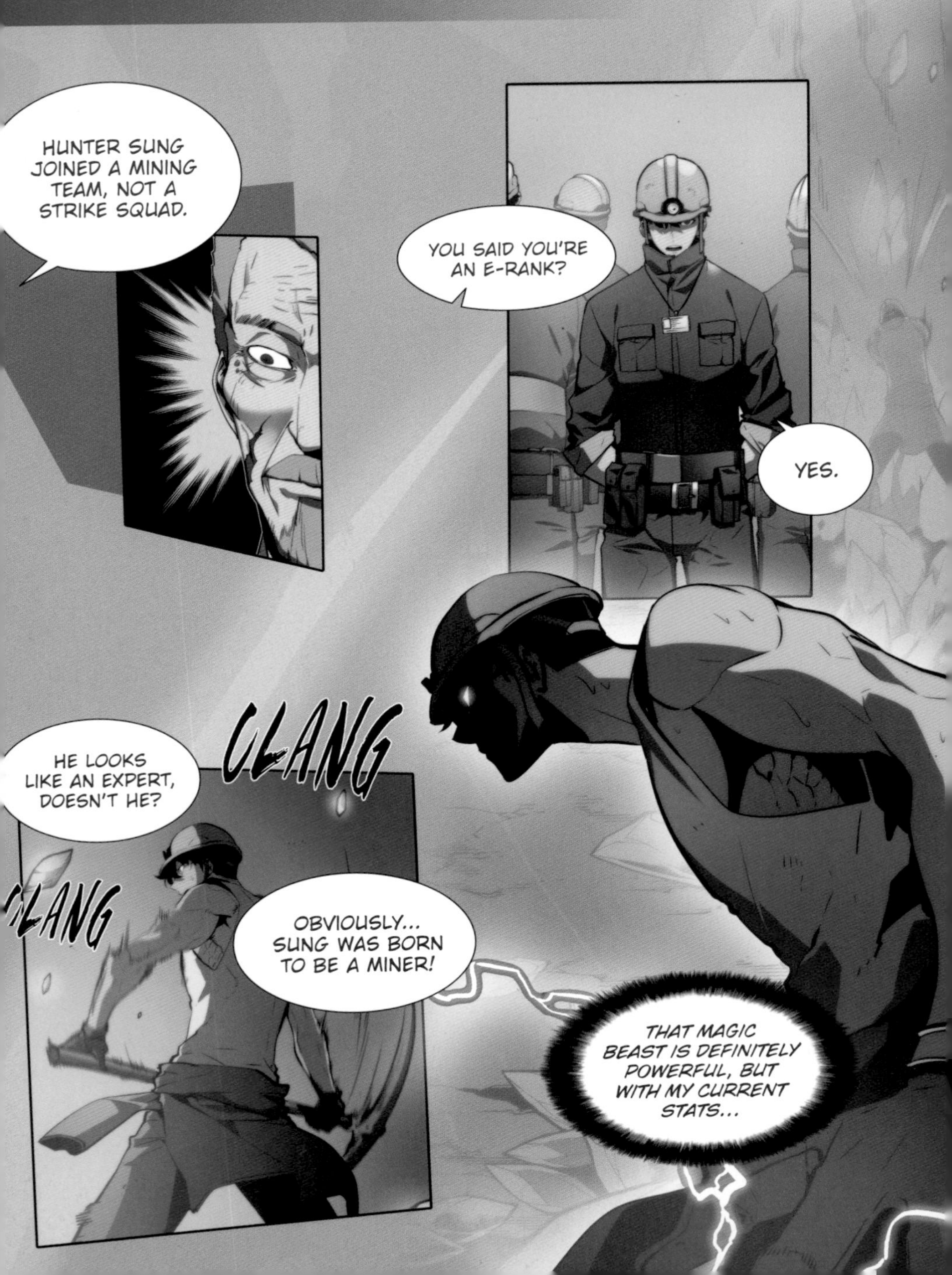
HUNTER SUNG JOINED A MINING TEAM, NOT A STRIKE SQUAD.
YOU SAID YOU'RE AN E-RANK?
YES.
HE LOOKS LIKE AN EXPERT, DOESN'T HE?
CLANG
CLANG
OBVIOUSLY... SUNG WAS BORN TO BE A MINER!
THAT MAGIC BEAST IS DEFINITELY POWERFUL, BUT WITH MY CURRENT STATS...

# JINWOO SUNG JOINS HUNTERS GUILD ON A RAID...

**More danger awaits in the dungeon depths...**
**...as well as some new hunters!**

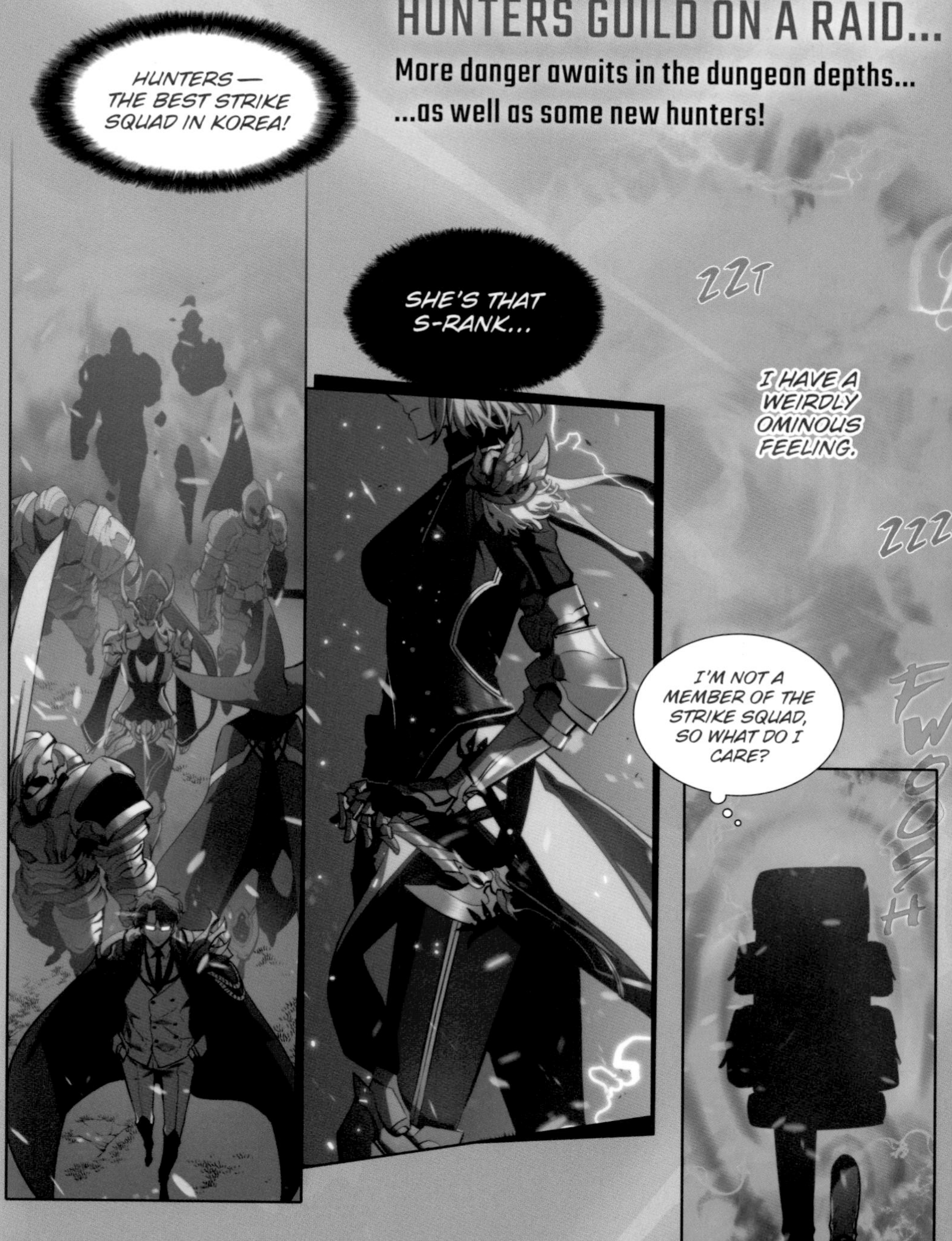
HUNTERS— THE BEST STRIKE SQUAD IN KOREA!
SHE'S THAT S-RANK...
ZZT
I HAVE A WEIRDLY OMINOUS FEELING.
ZZZ
I'M NOT A MEMBER OF THE STRIKE SQUAD, SO WHAT DO I CARE?
FWOOOSH

Solo Leveling

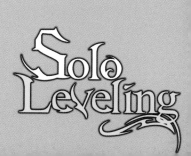

# SOLO LEVELING

### DUBU
#### (REDICE STUDIO)
## 4
### ORIGINAL STORY
## CHUGONG

Translation: Hye Young Im ◆ Rewrite: J. Torres ◆ Lettering: Abigail Blackman

SOLO LEVELING Volume 4
© DUBU(REDICE STUDIO), Chugong 2018 / D&C WEBTOON Biz
All rights reserved.
First published in Korea in 2018 by D&C WEBTOON Biz Co., Ltd.

English translation © 2022 by Yen Press, LLC

Yen Press
150 West 30th Street, 19th Floor
New York, NY 10001

Visit us at yenpress.com
facebook.com/yenpress
twitter.com/yenpress
yenpress.tumblr.com
instagram.com/yenpress

First Yen Press Edition: March 2022

Yen Press is an imprint of Yen Press, LLC.
The Yen Press name and logo are trademarks of Yen Press, LLC.

The publisher is not responsible for websites (or their content) that are not owned by the publisher.

Library of Congress Control Number: 2020950228

ISBNs: 978-1-9753-3724-7 (paperback)
978-1-9753-3725-4 (ebook)

10 9 8 7 6 5 4 3

TPA

Printed in South Korea